THE

BAPTIST

PRAISE BOOK:

PREPARED BY

RICHARD FULLER, E. M. LEVY, S. D. PHELPS, H. C. FISH,
THOMAS ARMITAGE, E. T. WINKLER, W. W. EVERTS,
GEO. C. LORIMER, AND BASIL MANLY, JR.

"*Whoso offereth praise glorifieth me.*"—Ps. 50 : 23.

A. S. BARNES & COMPANY,
NEW YORK AND CHICAGO.
1872.

CONTENTS.

INTRODUCTION .... *Page* v.
A CONFESSION OF FAITH .... vii.
A COVENANT .... viii.
THE LAW OF GOD—SUMMARY .... ix.
SCRIPTURE SENTENCES .... x.
LORD'S PRAYER .... xii.
BENEDICTION .... xii.
WORSHIP .... *Hymns* 1—108
GOD:
The Trinity .... 109—116
Praise to God .... 117—268
Christ's Nativity .... 269—300
" Childhood .... 301—303
" Life and Ministry .... 304—323
" Sufferings and Death .... 324—363
" Resurrection and Glory 364—391
" Second Advent .... 392—408
" Praise to Christ .... 409—492
Holy Spirit .... 493—549
WARNING AND INVITATION .... 550—643
PENITENCE AND CONSECRATION .... 644—728
THE CHURCH:
Baptism .... 729—764
Fellowship .... 765—782
The Lord's Supper .... 783—814
Welfare .... 815—848
THE CHRISTIAN LIFE:
Love and Gratitude... *Hymns* 849— 899
Graces and Duties .... 900— 934
Conflict and Triumph .... 935— 982
Afflictions and Encouragements .... 983—1036
Heaven Anticipated .... 1037—1099
Death and Immortality .... 1100—1148
OCCASIONAL:
The Scriptures .... 1149—1162
The Ministry .... 1163—1179
Dedications .... 1180—1190
Home Missions .... 1191—1196
Home and Foreign Missions. 1197—1246
Benevolence .... 1247—1253
Our Country .... 1254—1270
Seamen .... 1271—1274
Sunday Schools .... 1275—1283
Temperance .... 1284—1288
The Year .... 1289—1311
DOXOLOGIES .... *Pages* 410, 411
CHANTS AND ANTHEMS .... 412—430
INDEX OF SUBJECTS .... 431—433
INDEX OF TEXTS .... 434—436
INDEX OF FIRST LINES .... 437—451

INTRODUCTION.*

PECULIARITIES OF THIS WORK.

THE "BAPTIST PRAISE BOOK" differs from similar publications in most of the following particulars:

1. As its name intimates, it is peculiarly a *praise* book; hymns of praise to the adorable Deity, especially as the glorious Redeemer, being abundant.

2. A primary object in the publication has been to extend and improve Congregational Singing. Hence TUNES, as well as hymns, are given; it being now an accepted conclusion that music must accompany the words in order to secure the best results in the service of song. At the same time, an edition with hymns only (with uniform numbers) has been prepared.

3. It is a BAPTIST publication. When its preparation was commenced, no hymn and tune book for sanctuary use was available, or in prospect, except issued by some other branch of the Christian family and sought to be *adapted* to Baptist Churches; a circumstance for the existence of which at least no good reason could be assigned.

4. This work is the offspring of love. It was voluntarily undertaken with the sole purpose of furnishing the best possible hymn and tune book for the use of the Baptist churches; and with some of the editors it is the product of a life's enthusiasm and painstaking in this special direction.

5. The "Baptist Praise Book" is believed to be richer in the precious gems of hymnology than any other volume extant. Many of the old favorites, and of the most exquisite modern hymns, can be found in no collection except this. As is fitting, the hymns are set in a clear, bold type.

6. The tunes are very largely those which have been tested by use, and pronounced of current value by the universal award of Christian hearts. In some instances these are inserted more than once. The best of new tunes will also here be found.

* Taken from HYMN AND TUNE EDITION.

7. The attempt has here been made, so far as singing goes, to give to the Sabbath service somewhat of the freedom and unction of the social or vestry meetings. It is believed that the soul of the denomination is yearning for more warmth and spirituality in the songs of Zion. Hence revival and other melodies, if they but palpitate with real spiritual utterance, are introduced ; even in some instances where perhaps a cold criticism might have passed the edict of exclusion. Vitality has everywhere been preferred to stiff precision.

8. CHILDREN'S hymns are interspersed, especially adapting the book to Sunday School anniversaries, sermons to the young, and like occasions. These are of rare value. Some are entirely new.

9. The subjects and range of the hymns are broad and comprehensive, making the collection unusually full. They are thoroughly classified, and *each verse* is indexed.

10. *Especial* care has been given to the *adaptation* of hymns and tunes. In this particular no musical author excels Mr. J. P. Holbrook, whose fine taste and varied acquisitions have been admirably displayed in the pages of this book.

11. For such as may desire their use, a collection of Chants and Anthems, with select Scripture Sentences, a very brief Confession of Faith and Church Covenant, the Lord's Prayer and the Commandments are given. The Chants and Anthems are among the grandest that have been composed.

12. Finally; no pains have been spared, either in the carefulness and research of its editors, the expensiveness of copyright tunes, or the skill of mechanical execution, to make the "BAPTIST PRAISE BOOK" an inspiration and a joy with the great brotherhood of the Churches. And may He whose face shines on its every page, accept this labor of love, and cause it to animate the joys of His children until they unite in the chorus of praise with the redeemed in glory.

A CONFESSION OF FAITH.

WE BELIEVE—

In one God, Maker and Ruler of heaven and earth, revealed as the Father, the Son, and the Holy Spirit, equal in every divine perfection;[a]

In the Holy Scriptures as his inspired Word, and the only rule of faith and practice:[b]

In the fall of man and his condemnation as a sinner, and God's sovereign grace and love in redemption and the choice of his people:[c]

In the way of salvation by Jesus Christ, the Son of God incarnate, who obeyed the law, suffered and died for the sins of men, and is risen and exalted a Priest and King:[d]

In the free offer of eternal life to all in the Gospel, and the aggravated guilt of those who reject it:[e]

In the necessity of regeneration by the Holy Spirit, and of repentance toward God and faith in Christ:[f]

In the justification and adoption of the believer, through the blood and righteousness of Jesus:[g]

In the Divine institution of the Christian ministry, and the visible church of professed believers with its initiatory and memorial rites, Baptism * and the Lord's Supper:[h]

In the sacred observance of the Lord's Day, for rest, worship, and religious instruction:[i]

In the final perseverance of all saints, through sanctification of the Spirit and obedience to the truth:[j]

In the present life as man's only day of grace, and the soul's entrance at death into conscious blessedness or woe:[k]

In the resurrection of all the dead at the glorious coming of the Son of Man, and his just adjudgment of the wicked to everlasting punishment and the righteous to life eternal.[l]

[a] Eph. 4 : 6, Is. 37 : 16, Matt. 28 : 19, John 10:30, Acts 5 : 34. [b] 2 Tim. 3 : 16, Prov. 30 : 5, 6, Phil. 3 : 16, 1 Pet. 4 : 11, Is. 8 : 20. [c] Rom. 5 : 12, 18, Gal. 3 : 10; 4 : 4, 5, Eph. 1 : 4, 1 Thess. 1 : 4. [d] Acts 4 : 12, Phil. 2 : 8, 9, 1 Pet. 3 : 18, Heb. 4 : 14; 1 : 8, Ps. 2 : 6. [e] John 3 : 16; 10 : 10, Rev. 22 : 17, Matt. 11 : 24, Heb. 10 : 29. [f] John 3 : 3—8, 16, Mark 16 : 16, Luke 13 : 3; 18 : 13, Acts 20 : 21. [g] Rom. 5 : 1, 9, Acts 13 : 38, 39, Gal. 4 : 4—7, 1 Cor. 1 : 30, 1 Thess. 4 : 3, 1 Thess. 5 : 23, 2 Cor. 7 : 1. [h] Mark 3 : 14, Eph. 4 : 11, 1 Tim. 4 : 14, Matt. 28 : 19, 20. 1 Cor. 1 : 2, Phil. 1 : 1, Acts 2 : 41, 42, Rom. 6 : 4, Luke 22 : 19, 20, 1 Cor. 11 : 26. [i] Acts 20 : 7, Rev. 1 : 10, Ex. 20 : 8, Heb. 10 : 25, Acts 11 : 26. [j] John 10 : 27, 28, 1 John 2 : 19, Phil. 1 : 6, 1 Pet. 1 : 2—5, Rom. 8. [k] Luke 16 : 22—26; 23 : 43, Rev. 22 : 11, Mark 12 : 26, 27. [l] John 5 : 28, 29, Acts 24 : 15, Matt. 25 : 31—46, 2 Cor. 5 : 10.

* Immersion only to show forth in a solemn and beautiful emblem, our faith in the crucified, buried and risen Saviour, and our death to sin and resurrection to a new life. NOTE. By "the visible church" is meant a local congregation, in distinction from the whole body of believers or kingdom of Christ, and from a territorial, national, or hierarchical church. The New Testament churches were evidently organizations of baptized believers, local, and independent, under Christ; their officers being pastors and deacons, bishop and elder being the same as pastor.

A COVENANT.

As we trust we have received, through Divine Grace, the Lord Jesus Christ, and given ourselves wholly to him, and on profession of our faith have been buried with him in baptism and thus united to his church, we do now solemnly and joyfully covenant with each other, and, by the aid of the Holy Spirit, engage—

That we will walk together with brotherly love, exercising a Christian care and watchfulness over each other, participating in each other's joys, and, with tender sympathy, bearing one another's burdens and sorrows:

That we will not forsake the assembling of ourselves together at the Communion and other appointed meetings, but seek and pray for the spirituality, harmony, and prosperity of this church; sustain its worship, ordinances, discipline and doctrines; and give its claims a sacred pre-eminence over all organizations of human origin:

That we will cheerfully contribute of our means, as God has prospered us, for the support of a faithful and evangelical ministry among us; for the relief of the poor; and for spreading the gospel over the earth:

That we will maintain private and family devotions; religiously educate the children committed to our care; and endeavor, in purity of heart and newness of life, and good-will toward all men, to exemplify and commend our holy faith, win souls to the Saviour, and hold fast our profession till he shall come and receive us unto himself.

[*Relying on the grace of God, do you thus covenant and promise?*]

And now the God of peace, who brought again from the dead our Lord Jesus, that Great Shepherd of the sheep, through the blood of the everlasting covenant make us perfect in every good work to do his will, working in us that which is well-pleasing in his sight, through Jesus Christ; to whom be glory for ever and ever. AMEN.

THE LAW OF GOD,

AS WRITTEN IN THE TWENTIETH CHAPTER OF THE BOOK OF EXODUS.

God spake all these words, saying, I am the Lord thy God, which have brought thee out of the land of Egypt, out of the house of bondage.

I.—Thou shalt have no other gods before me.

II.—Thou shalt not make unto thee any graven image, or any likeness of any thing that is in heaven above, or that is in the earth beneath, or that is in the water under the earth: thou shalt not bow down thyself to them, nor serve them: for I the Lord thy God am a jealous God, visiting the iniquity of the fathers upon the children unto the third and fourth generation of them that hate me; and showing mercy unto thousands of them that love me, and keep my commandments.

III.—Thou shalt not take the Name of the Lord thy God in vain; for the Lord will not hold him guiltless that taketh his Name in vain.

IV.—Remember the Sabbath-day to keep it holy. Six days shalt thou labor, and do all thy work: but the seventh day is the Sabbath of the Lord thy God; in it thou shalt not do any work, thou, nor thy son, nor thy daughter, thy man-servant, nor thy maid-servant, nor thy cattle, nor thy stranger that is within thy gates; for in six days the Lord made heaven and earth, the sea, and all that in them is, and rested the seventh day; wherefore the Lord blessed the Sabbath-day, and hallowed it.

V.—Honor thy father and thy mother: that thy days may be long upon the land which the Lord thy God giveth thee.

VI.—Thou shalt not kill.

VII.—Thou shalt not commit adultery.

VIII.—Thou shalt not steal.

IX.—Thou shalt not bear false witness against thy neighbor.

X.—Thou shalt not covet thy neighbor's house, thou shalt not covet thy neighbor's wife, nor his man-servant, nor his maid-servant, nor his ox, nor his ass, nor any thing that is thy neighbor's.

THE SUMMARY OF THE LAW BY OUR LORD JESUS CHRIST.

St. Matthew 22: 37-40.

Thou shalt love the Lord thy God with all thy heart, and with all thy soul, and with all thy mind. This is the first and great commandment. And the second is like unto it, Thou shalt love thy neighbor as thyself. On these two commandments hang all the law and the prophets.

OPENING SENTENCES.

THE Lord is in his holy temple: let all the earth keep silence before him.

Let the words of my mouth and the meditation of my heart be acceptable in thy sight, O Lord, my strength and my Redeemer.

Again I say unto you, that if two of you shall agree on earth as touching any thing they shall ask, it shall be done for them of my Father which is in heaven.

For, where two or three are gathered together in my name, there am I in the midst of them.

Seek ye the Lord while he may be found; call ye upon him while he is near.

Let the wicked forsake his way, and the unrighteous man his thoughts: and let him return unto the Lord, and he will have mercy upon him; and to our God, for he will abundantly pardon.

Thus saith the High and Lofty One that inhabiteth eternity:
Whose Name is holy;
I dwell in the high and holy place;
With him also that is of a contrite and humble spirit,
To revive the spirit of the humble,
And to revive the heart of the contrite ones.

The sacrifices of God are a broken spirit:
A broken and a contrite heart, O God, thou wilt not despise.

Rend your hearts, and not your garments, and turn unto the Lord your God; for he is gracious and merciful, slow to anger, and of great kindness, and repenteth him of the evil.

Wherewith shall I come before the Lord, and bow myself before the high God? shall I come before him with burnt offerings, with calves of a year old? Will the Lord be pleased with thousands of rams, or with ten thousands of rivers of oil? shall I give my first-born for my transgression, the fruit of my body for the sin of my soul? He hath showed thee, O man! what is good; and what doth the Lord require of thee but to do justly, and love mercy, and walk humbly with thy God.

Ask, and it shall be given you; seek, and ye shall find; knock, and it shall be opened unto you.

Give unto the Lord the glory due unto his Name: Bring an offering and come before him: Worship the Lord in the beauty of holiness.

Offer unto God thanksgiving, and pay thy vows unto the Most High.

Let us therefore come boldly unto the throne of grace, that we may obtain mercy, and find grace to help in time of need.

If we say that we have no sin, we deceive ourselves, and the truth is not in us; but, if we confess our sins, God is faithful and just to forgive us our sins, and to cleanse us from all unrighteousness.

I will arise, and go to my father; and will say unto him, Father, I have sinned against heaven and before thee, and am no more worthy to be called thy son.

Blessed are they which do hunger and thirst after righteousness; for they shall be filled.

Even the youth shall faint and be weary, and the young men shall utterly fall: but they that wait on the Lord shall renew their strength; they shall mount up with wings as eagles; they shall run, and not be weary; they shall walk, and not faint.

Serve the Lord with gladness: come before his presence with singing. Know ye that the Lord he is God: it is he that hath made us, and not we ourselves; we are his people, and the sheep of his pasture. Enter into his gates with thanksgiving, and into his courts with praise; be thankful unto him, and bless his name. For the Lord is good: his mercy is everlasting, and his truth endureth to all generations.

Who shall ascend into the hill of the Lord? or who shall stand in his holy place? He that hath clean hands, and a pure heart; who hath not lifted up his soul unto vanity, nor sworn deceitfully. He shall receive the blessing from the Lord, and righteousness from the God of his salvation.

Oh come, let us worship and bow down, and kneel before the Lord our Maker. For he is our God; and we are the people of his pasture, and the sheep of his hand.

O Lord, open thou my lips, and my mouth shall show forth thy praise.

LORD'S PRAYER.

OUR Father which art in heaven:
Hallowed be thy name.
Thy kingdom come.
Thy will be done on earth, as it is in heaven.
Give us this day our daily bread.
And forgive us our debts, as we forgive our debtors.
And lead us not into temptation, but deliver us from evil.
(For thine is the kingdom, and the power, and the glory, forever.) AMEN.

BENEDICTION.

THE Lord bless thee, and keep thee; the Lord make his face to shine upon thee, and be gracious unto thee; the Lord lift up his countenance upon thee, and give thee peace. Amen.—NUMBERS vi. 24—26.

HYMNS.

WORSHIP.

1

7s & 6s.

1 O DAY of rest and gladness,
O day of joy and light,
O balm of care and sadness,
Most beautiful, most bright;
On thee, the high and lowly,
Bending before the throne,
Sing, Holy, Holy, Holy,
To the Great Three in One.

2 On thee, at the creation,
The light first had its birth:
On thee, for our salvation
Christ rose from depths of earth;
On thee, our Lord, victorious,
The Spirit sent from Heaven,
And thus on thee, most glorious,
A triple light was given.

3 To-day on weary nations
The heavenly manna falls;
To holy convocations
The silver trumpet calls,
Where gospel light is glowing
With pure and radiant beams,
And living water flowing
With soul-refreshing streams.

4 New graces ever gaining
From this our day of rest,
We reach the rest remaining
To spirits of the blest:
To Holy Ghost be praises,
To Father and to Son;
The Church her voice upraises
To thee, blest Three in One.

WORDSWORTH.

2

7s. 6 lines.

1 SAFELY through another week
God has brought us on our way;
Let us now a blessing seek,
Waiting in his courts to-day;
Day of all the week the best,
Emblem of eternal rest.

2 While we pray for pardoning grace
Through the dear Redeemer's name,
Show thy reconciléd face,
Take away our sin and shame;
From our worldly cares set free,
May we rest this day in thee.

3 Here we come thy name to praise;
Let us feel thy presence near;

May thy glory meet our eyes
While we in thy house appear:
Here afford us, Lord, a taste
Of our everlasting feast.

4 May thy Gospel's joyful sound
Conquer sinners, comfort saints;
Make the fruits of grace abound;
Bring relief for all complaints:
Thus let all our Sabbaths prove
Till we rest in thee above.

NEWTON.

3

7s. 6 lines.

1 SAVIOUR! who this day didst break
The dark prison of the tomb;
Bid my slumbering soul awake,
Shine through all its sin and gloom:
Let me, from my bonds set free,
Rise from sin, and live to thee.

2 Blesséd Spirit! Comforter!
Sent this day from Christ on high;
Lord, on me thy gifts confer,
Cleanse, illumine, sanctify.
All thine influence shed abroad,
Lead me to the truth of God.

3 Sad and weary were our way,
Fainting oft beneath our load,
But for thee, thou blesséd day,
Resting-place on life's rough road.
Here flow forth the streams of grace,
Strengthened hence we run our race.

4 Soon, too soon, the sweet repose
Of this day of God will cease;
Soon this glimpse of Heaven will close,
Vanish soon the hours of peace;
Soon return the toil, the strife,
All the weariness of life.

JULIA A. ELLIOT.

4

7s.

1 TO thy temple I repair;
Lord, I love to worship there;
When within the veil I meet
Christ before the mercy-seat.

2 While thy glorious praise is sung,
Touch my lips, unloose my tongue,
That my joyful soul may bless
Thee, the Lord my Righteousness!

3 While the prayers of saints ascend,
God of love! to mine attend!
Hear me, for thy Spirit pleads;
Hear, for Jesus intercedes!

4 While I hearken to thy law,
Fill my soul with humble awe;
Till thy Gospel bring to me
Life and immortality.

5 From thy house when I return,
May my heart within me burn;
And at evening let me say,
I have walked with God to-day!

MONTGOMERY.

5

7s.

1 LORD, we come before thee now,
At thy feet we humbly bow;
Oh, do not our suit disdain!
Shall we seek thee, Lord, in vain?

2 Lord, on thee our souls depend,
In compassion now descend;
Fill our hearts with thy rich grace,
Tune our lips to sing thy praise.

3 In thine own appointed way,
Now we seek thee; here we stay;
Lord, we know not how to go,
Till a blessing thou bestow.

4 Send some message from thy word,
That may joy and peace afford;
Let thy Spirit now impart
Full salvation to each heart.

5 Comfort those who weep and mourn,
Let the time of joy return,
Those who are cast down lift up,
Make them strong in faith and hope.

6 Grant that all may seek and find
Thee a God supremely kind;
Heal the sick, the captive free,
Let us all rejoice in thee.

HAMMOND.

6

7s.

1 COME, my soul, thy suit prepare;
Jesus loves to answer prayer;
He himself has bid thee pray;
Therefore will not say thee nay.

2 Thou art coming to a King,
Large petitions with thee bring;
For his grace and power are such,
None can ever ask too much.

3 With my burden I begin;
Lord, remove this load of sin;
Let thy blood, for sinners spilt,
Set my conscience free from guilt.

4 Lord, I come to thee for rest;
Take possession of my breast;
There thy blood-bought right maintain,
And without a rival reign.

NEWTON.

7

7s. Double.

1 PLEASANT are thy courts above,
In the land of light and love;
Pleasant are thy courts below,
In this land of sin and woe.
Oh, my spirit longs and faints
For the converse of thy saints,
For the brightness of thy face,
For thy fullness, God of grace!

2 Happy birds that sing and fly
Round thy altars, O Most High!
Happier souls that find a rest
In their Heavenly Father's breast!
Like the wandering dove that found
No repose on earth around,
They can to their ark repair,
And enjoy it ever there.

3 Happy souls! their praises flow,
Even in this vale of woe
Waters in the desert rise,
Manna feeds them from the skies;
On they go from strength to strength,
Till they reach thy throne at length;
At thy feet adoring fall,
Who hast led them safe through all.

4 Lord, be mine this prize to win,
Guide me through this world of sin;
Keep me by thy saving grace,
Give me at thy side a place;
Sun and Shield alike thou art,
Guide and guard my erring heart;
Grace and glory flow from thee,
Shed, oh, shed them, Lord, on me.

LYTE.

8

7s. Double.

1 LIGHT of life, seraphic fire,
Love divine, thyself impart;
Every fainting soul inspire;
Enter every drooping heart;
Every mournful sinner cheer,
Scatter all our guilty gloom;
Father! in our hearts appear,
To thy human temples come.

2 Come, in this accepted hour,
Bring thy heavenly kingdom in;
Fill us with thy glorious power,
Set us free from all our sin:
Nothing more can we require,
We will covet nothing less;
Be thou all our heart's desire,
All our joy, and all our peace.

C. Wesley.

9 H. M.

1 AWAKE, ye saints, awake,
And hail this sacred day;
In loftiest songs of praise
Your joyful homage pay:
Welcome the day that God hath blest,
The type of heaven's eternal rest.

2 On this auspicious morn
The Lord of life arose;
He burst the bars of death,
And vanquished all our foes;
And now he pleads our cause above,
And reaps the fruits of all his love.

3 All hail, triumphant Lord!
Heaven with hosannas rings,
And earth, in humbler strains,
Thy praise responsive sings:
Worthy the Lamb that once was slain,
Thro' endless years to live and reign.

Cotterill.

10 H. M.

1 WHEN little Samuel woke,
And heard his Maker's voice,
At every word he spoke,
How much did he rejoice!
O blessed, happy child, to find
The God of heaven so near and kind!

2 If God would speak to me,
And say he was my friend,
How happy I should be,
Oh, how would I attend!
The smallest sin I then should fear,
If God Almighty were so near.

3 And does he never speak?
Oh, yes; for, in his word,
He bids me come and seek
The God that Samuel heard:
In almost every page I see
The God of Samuel calls to me.

4 Like Samuel, let me say,
Whene'er I read his word,
"Speak, Lord; I would obey
The voice that I have heard.
And when I in thy house appear,
Speak, for thy servant waits to hear."

11 H. M.

1 NOW to thy sacred house
I come with willing feet;
Where saints, with morning vows,
In full assembly meet:
Thy power divine shall here be shown,
And from thy throne thy mercy shine.

2 Oh send thy light abroad!
Thy truth with heavenly ray
Shall lead my soul to God,
And guide my doubtful way:
I'll hear thy word with faith sincere,
And learn to fear and praise the Lord.

3 Here reach thy bounteous hand,
And all my sorrows heal;
Here health and strength divine,
Oh make my bosom feel!
Like balmy dew, shall Jesus' voice
My bones rejoice, my strength renew.

4 Thus in thy holy hill,
Before thine altar, Lord,
My harp and song shall sound
The glories of thy word:
Henceforth to thee, O God of grace,
A hymn of praise my life shall be.

DWIGHT.

12 H. M.

1 WELCOME, delightful morn,
Thou day of sacred rest;
I hail thy kind return;
Lord, make these moments blest!
From the low train of mortal toys
I soar to reach immortal joys.

2 Now may the King descend
And fill his throne of grace;
Thy sceptre, Lord, extend,
While saints address thy face.
Let sinners feel thy quickening word,
And learn to know and fear the Lord.

3 Descend, celestial Dove,
With all thy quickening powers;
Disclose a Saviour's love,
And bless the sacred hours:
Then shall my soul new life obtain,
Nor Sabbaths be indulged in vain.

HAYWARD.

13 S. P. M.

1 HOW pleased and blest was I
To hear the people cry,
"Come, let us seek our God to-day!"
Yes, with a cheerful zeal
We'll haste to Zion's hill,
And there our vows and honors pay.

2 Zion, thrice happy place,
Adorned with wondrous grace,
And walls of strength embrace thee round:
In thee our tribes appear
To pray, and praise, and hear
The sacred gospel's joyful sound.

3 Here David's greater Son
Has fixed his royal throne;
He sits for grace and judgment here:
He bids the saint be glad,
He makes the sinner sad,
And humble souls rejoice with fear.

4 May peace attend thy gate,
And joy within thee wait
To bless the soul of every guest:
The man who seeks thy peace,
And wishes thine increase—
A thousand blessings on him rest!

5 My tongue repeats her vows,
"Peace to this sacred house!"
For here my friends and kindred dwell;
And since my glorious God
Makes thee his blest abode,
My soul shall ever love thee well.

WATTS.

14 S. P. M.

1 'TIS heaven begun below
To hear Christ's praises flow
In Zion where his name is known:
What will it be above
To sing redeeming love,
And cast our crowns before his throne!

2 Oh, what sweet company
We then shall hear and see!
What harmony will there abound,
When souls unnumbered sing
The praise of Zion's King,
Nor one dissenting voice is found!

3 With everlasting joy,
Such as will never cloy,
We shall be filled, nor wish for more;

Bright as meridian day,
Calm as the evening ray,
Full as a sea without a shore.

4 Till that blest period come,
Zion shall be my home;
And may I never thence remove
Till from the church below
To heaven at once I go,
And there commune in perfect love!

SWAIN.

15 L. M.

1 SWEET is the work, my God, my King,
To praise thy name, give thanks, and sing;
To show thy love by morning light,
And talk of all thy truth at night.

2 Sweet is the day of sacred rest;
No mortal cares shall seize my breast:
O may my heart in tune be found,
Like David's harp of solemn sound!

3 My heart shall triumph in my Lord,
And bless his works, and bless his word;
Thy works of grace how bright they shine!
How deep thy counsels, how divine!

4 Fools never raise their thoughts so high;
Like brutes they live, like brutes they die!
Like grass they flourish, till thy breath
Blasts them in everlasting death.

5 But I shall share a glorious part;
When grace hath well refined my heart;
And fresh supplies of joy are shed,
Like holy oil, to cheer my head.

6 Then shall I see, and hear, and know,
All I desired or wished below;
And every power find sweet employ
In that eternal world of joy.

WATTS.

16 L. M.

1 HOW pleasant, how divinely fair,
O Lord of hosts, thy dwellings are!
With long desire my spirit faints
To meet th' assemblies of thy saints.

2 My flesh would rest in thine abode;
My panting heart cries out for God!
My God, my King, why should I be
So far from all my joys and thee?

3 Blest are the saints who dwell on high,
Around thy throne, above the sky;
Thy brightest glories shine above,
And all their work is praise and love.

4 Blest are the souls who find a place
Within the temple of thy grace;
There they behold thy gentler rays,
And seek thy face, and learn thy praise.

5 Blest are the men whose hearts are set
To find the way to Zion's gate;
God is their strength; and through the road,
They lean upon their helper, God.

WATTS.

17 L. M.

1 HOW sweet to leave the world awhile,
And seek the presence of our Lord!
Dear Saviour, on thy people smile,
According to thy faithful word.

2 From busy scenes we now retreat,
That we may here converse with thee;—
O Lord, behold us at thy feet!
Let this the gate of heaven be.

3 "Chief of ten thousands," now appear,
That we by faith may view thy face;
Oh, speak, that we thy voice may hear,
And let thy presence fill the place!

KELLY.

18 L. M.

1 MY opening eyes with rapture see
The dawn of thy returning day;
My thoughts, O God, ascend to thee,
While thus my early vows I pay.

2 Oh, bid this trifling world retire,
And drive each carnal thought away;
Nor let me feel one vain desire—
One sinful thought through all the day.

3 Then, to thy courts when I repair,
My soul shall rise on joyful wing,
The wonders of thy love declare,
And join the strains which angels sing.

19 L. M.

1 DEAR is the hallowed morn to me,
When Sabbath bells awake the day,
And, by their sacred minstrelsy,
Call me from earthly cares away.

2 And dear to me the wingéd hour
Spent in thy hallowed courts, O Lord!
To feel devotion's soothing power,
And catch the manna of thy word.

3 And dear to me the loud Amen,
Which echoes through the blest abode,
Which swells, and sinks, and swells again,
Dies on the walls, but lives to God.

4 Oft when the world, with iron hands,
Has bound me in its six days' chain,
This bursts them, like the strong man's bands,
And lets my spirit loose again.

5 Go, man of pleasure, strike thy lyre,
Of broken Sabbaths sing the charms;
Ours be the prophet's car of fire
That bears us to a Father's arms.

CUNNINGHAM.

20 L. M.

1 THINE earthly Sabbaths, Lord, we love,
But there's a nobler rest above;
To that our longing souls aspire,
With cheerful hope and strong desire.

2 No more fatigue, no more distress,
Nor sin nor death shall reach the place;
No groans shall mingle with the songs
That warble from immortal tongues.

3 No rude alarms of raging foes,
No cares to break the long repose,
No midnight shade, no clouded sun,
But sacred, high, eternal noon.

4 O long-expected day, begin!
Dawn on these realms of woe and sin;
Fain would we leave this weary road,
And sleep in death to rest with God.

DODDRIDGE.

21

L. M.

1 LORD, how delightful 'tis to see
A whole assembly worship thee!
At once they sing, at once they pray,
They hear of heaven, and learn the way.

2 I have been there, and still would go,
'Tis like a little heaven below;
Not all that careless sinners say,
Shall tempt me to forget this day.

3 Oh, write upon my memory, Lord,
The truths and precepts of thy word!
That I may break thy laws no more,
But love thee better than before.

WATTS.

22

L. M.

1 ANOTHER six days' work is done;
Another Sabbath is begun.
Return, my soul, enjoy the rest;
Improve the day thy God hath blest.

2 Come, bless the Lord, whose love assigns
So sweet a rest to wearied minds;
Provides an antepast of heaven,
And gives this day the food of seven.

3 O that our thoughts and thanks may rise
As grateful incense to the skies;
And draw from heaven that sweet repose
Which none but he that feels it knows.

4 This heavenly calm within the breast
Is the dear pledge of glorious rest
Which for the church of God remains,
The end of cares, the end of pains.

5 In holy duties let the day
In holy pleasures pass away.
How sweet a Sabbath thus to spend,
In hope of one that ne'er shall end!

STENNETT.

23

L. M.

1 SWEET is the light of Sabbath eve,
And soft the sunbeams lingering there;
For these blest hours the world I leave,
Wafted on wings of faith and prayer.

2 Season of rest! the tranquil soul
Feels the sweet calm, and melts to love;
And while these sacred moments roll,
Faith sees the smiling heaven above.

3 Nor will our days of toil be long;
Our pilgrimage will soon be trod;
And we shall join the ceaseless song,
The endless Sabbath of our God.

EDMESTON.

24

L. M.

1 MILLIONS within thy courts have met,
Millions, this day, before thee bowed;
Their faces Zion-ward were set,
Vows with their lips to thee they vowed.

2 Soon as the light of morning broke
O'er island, continent, or deep,
Thy far-spread family awoke,
Sabbath, all round the world, to keep.

3 From east to west the sun surveyed,
From north to south adoring throngs;

And still, when evening stretched her shade,
The stars came out to hear their songs.

4 And not a prayer, a tear, a sigh,
Hath failed this day some suit to gain;
To those in trouble thou wert nigh:
Not one hath sought thy face in vain.

5 Yet one prayer more!—and be it one,
In which both heaven and earth accord.
Fulfill thy promise to thy Son;
Let all that breathe call Jesus LORD!

MONTGOMERY.

25 L. M. 6 lines.

1 SWEET Saviour, bless us ere we go;
Thy word into our minds instill;
And make our lukewarm hearts to glow
With lowly love and fervent will.
Through life's long day, and death's dark night,
O gentle Jesus, be our light.

2 The day is gone, its hours have run,
And thou hast taken count of all,
The scanty triumphs grace hath won,
The broken vow, the frequent fall.
Through life's long day, and death's dark night,
O gentle Jesus, be our light.

3 Grant us, dear Lord, from evil ways
True absolution and release;
And bless us, more than in past days,
With purity and inward peace,
Through life's long day, and death's dark night,
O gentle Jesus, be our light.

4 Do more than pardon, give us joy,
Sweet fear, and sober liberty,
And simple hearts without alloy
That only long to be like thee.
Through life's long day, and death's dark night,
O gentle Jesus, be our light.

FABER.

26 L. M. 6 lines.

1 WHEN, streaming from the eastern skies,
The morning light salutes mine eyes,
O Sun of righteousness divine,
On me with beams of mercy shine!
Oh! chase the clouds of guilt away,
And turn my darkness into day.

2 And when to heaven's all-glorious King
My morning sacrifice I bring,
And, mourning o'er my guilt and shame,
Ask mercy in my Saviour's name;
Then, Jesus, cleanse me with thy blood,
And be my Advocate with God.

3 When each day's scenes and labors close,
And wearied nature seeks repose,
With pardoning mercy richly blest,
Guard me, my Saviour, while I rest;
And, as each morning sun shall rise,
Oh, lead me onward to the skies!

4 And at my life's last setting sun,
My conflicts o'er, my labors done,
Jesus, thy heavenly radiance shed,
To cheer and bless my dying bed;
And from death's gloom my spirit raise,
To see thy face and sing thy praise.

W. SHRUBSOLE.

27 L. M.

1 FROM every stormy wind that blows,
From every swelling tide of woes,
There is a calm, a sure retreat—
'Tis found beneath the mercy-seat.

2 There is a place where Jesus sheds
The oil of gladness on our heads,
A place, than all besides, more sweet—
It is the blood-bought mercy-seat.

3 There is a scene, where spirits blend,
Where friend holds fellowship with friend;
Though sundered far, by faith they meet
Around one common mercy-seat.

4 There, there on eagles' wings we soar,
And sin and sense molest no more,
And heav'n comes down our souls to greet,
And glory crowns the mercy-seat.

5 Oh, let my hand forget her skill,
My tongue be silent, cold and still,
This bounding heart forget to beat,
If I forget thy mercy-seat!

STOWELL.

28 L. M.

1 MY God, is any hour so sweet,
From blush of morn to evening star,
As that which calls me to thy feet,
The calm and holy hour of prayer?

2 Then is my strength by thee renewed;
Then are my sins by thee forgiven;
Then dost thou cheer my solitude,
With clear and beauteous hopes of heaven.

3 No words can tell what sweet relief,
There for my every want I find;
What strength for warfare, balm for grief,
What deep and cheerful peace of mind!

4 Lord, till I reach the blissful shore,
No privilege so dear shall be,
As thus my inmost soul to pour
In faithful, filial prayer to thee!

C. ELLIOT.

29 L. M.

1 WHAT various hindrances we meet
In coming to a mercy-seat!
Yet who that knows the worth of prayer
But wishes to be often there?

2 Prayer makes the darkened clouds withdraw;
Prayer climbs the ladder Jacob saw,
Gives exercise to faith and love,
Brings every blessing from above.

3 Restraining prayer, we cease to fight;
Prayer makes the Christian's armor bright;
And Satan trembles when he sees
The weakest saint upon his knees.

4 Have you no words? ah! think again;
Words flow apace when you complain,
And fill a fellow-creature's ear
With the sad tale of all your care.

5 Were half the breath thus vainly spent
To heaven in supplication sent,
Our cheerful song would oftener be,
"Hear what the Lord hath done for me!"

COWPER.

30 L. M.

1 AWAKE, my soul, and with the sun
Thy daily stage of duty run;
Shake off dull sloth, and joyful rise
To pay thy morning sacrifice.

2 Wake and lift up thyself, my heart,
And with the angels bear thy part,
Who, all night long, unwearied sing
High praise to the eternal King.

3 Glory to thee who safe hast kept,
And hast refreshed me whilst I slept!
Grant, Lord, when I from death shall wake,
I may of endless light partake!

4 Lord, I my vows to thee renew;
Disperse my sins as morning dew;
Guard my first springs of thought and will,
And with thyself my spirit fill.

5 Direct, control, suggest, this day,
All I design, or do, or say;
That all my powers, with all their might,
In thy sole glory may unite.

KEN.

31 L. M.

1 HAST thou within a care so deep,
It chases from thine eyelids sleep?
To thy Redeemer take that care,
And change anxiety to prayer.

2 Hast thou a hope with which thy heart
Would almost feel it death to part?
Entreat thy God that hope to crown,
Or give thee strength to lay it down.

3 Hast thou a friend whose image dear
May prove an idol worshipped here?
Implore the Lord that nought may be
A shadow between heaven and thee.

4 Whate'er the care that breaks thy rest,
Whate'er the wish that swells thy breast,
Spread before God that wish, that care,
And change anxiety to prayer.

32 L. M.

1 GOD of the morning, at whose voice
The cheerful sun makes haste to rise,
And like a giant doth rejoice
To run his journey through the skies.

2 Oh, like the sun may I fulfill
The appointed duties of the day;
With ready mind and active will,
March on and keep my heavenly way.

3 But I shall rove, and lose the race,
If God my Sun should disappear,
And leave me in this world's wide maze,
To follow every wandering star.

4 Give me thy counsel for my guide,
And then receive me to thy bliss;
All my desires and hopes beside
Are faint and cold compared with this.

WATTS.

33 L. M.

1 GLORY to thee, my God, this night,
For all the blessings of the light;
Keep me, O keep me, King of kings,
Beneath thine own Almighty wings.

2 Forgive me, Lord, for thy dear Son,
The ill that I this day have done;

That with the world, myself, and thee,
I, ere I sleep, at peace may be.

3 Teach me to live, that I may dread
The grave as little as my bed;
Teach me to die, that so I may
Rise glorious at the awful day.

4 Oh, may my soul on thee repose;
And may sweet sleep mine eyelids close,
Sleep, that may me more vigorous make
To serve my God when I awake.

5 Praise God from whom all blessings flow;
Praise him, all creatures here below;
Praise him above, ye heavenly host;
Praise Father, Son, and Holy Ghost!

KEN.

34 L. M.

1 THUS far the Lord hath led me on,
Thus far his power prolongs my days;
And every evening shall make known
Some fresh memorial of his grace.

2 Much of my time has run to waste,
And I, perhaps, am near my home;
But he forgives my follies past,
And gives me strength for days to come.

3 I lay my body down to sleep:
Peace is the pillow for my head,
While well-appointed angels keep
Their watchful stations round my bed.

4 Faith in his name forbids my fear;
Oh, may thy presence ne'er depart;
And, in the morning, make me hear
The love and kindness of thy heart.

5 Thus, when the night of death shall come,
My flesh shall rest beneath the ground;
And wait thy voice to rouse my tomb,
With sweet salvation in the sound.

WATTS.

35 L. M.

1 GREAT God, to thee my evening song
With humble gratitude I raise;
Oh, let thy mercy tune my tongue,
And fill my heart with lively praise.

2 My days, unclouded as they pass,
And every gently rolling hour,
Are monuments of wondrous grace,
And witness to thy love and power.

3 And yet this thoughtless, wretched heart,
Too oft regardless of thy love,
Ungrateful, can from thee depart,
And, fond of trifles, vainly rove.

4 Seal my forgiveness in the blood
Of Jesus; his dear name alone
I plead for pardon, gracious God,
And kind acceptance at thy throne.

5 Let this blest hope mine eyelids close;
With sleep refresh my feeble frame;
Safe in thy care may I repose,
And wake with praises to thy name.

ANNE STEELE.

36 L. M.

1 SUN of my soul, thou Saviour dear,
It is not night if thou be near;
Oh, may no earth-born cloud arise
To hide thee from thy servant's eyes.

2 When the soft dews of kindly sleep
My wearied eyelids gently steep,
Be my last thought how sweet to rest
For ever on my Saviour's breast.

3 Abide with me from morn till eve,
For without thee I cannot live;
Abide with me when night is nigh,
For without thee I dare not die.

4 If some poor wandering child of thine
Have spurned to-day the voice divine,
Now, Lord, the gracious work begin;
Let him no more lie down in sin.

5 Watch by the sick; enrich the poor
With blessings from thy boundless store;
Be every mourner's sleep to-night,
Like infant slumbers, pure and light.

6 Come near and bless us when we wake,
Ere through the world our way we take,
Till in the ocean of thy love
We lose ourselves in heaven above.

KEBLE.

37 L. M.

1 O LORD, how joyful 'tis to see
The brethren join in love to thee;
On thee alone their heart relies,
Their only strength thy grace supplies.

2 How sweet, within thy holy place,
With one accord to sing thy grace,
Besieging thine attentive ear
With all the force of fervent prayer.

3 Oh, may we love the house of God,
Of peace and joy the blest abode;
Oh, may no angry strife destroy
That sacred peace, that holy joy.

4 The world without may rage, but we
Will only cling more close to thee,
With hearts to thee more wholly given,
More weaned from earth, more fixed on heaven.

5 Lord, shower upon us from above
The sacred gift of mutual love;
Each other's wants may we supply,
And reign together in the sky.

JOHN CHANDLER.

38 L. M.

1 WHILE now upon this Sabbath eve,
Thy house, Almighty God, we leave,
'Tis sweet, as sinks the setting sun,
To think on all our duties done.

2 Oh! evermore may all our bliss
Be peaceful, pure, divine like this;
And may each Sabbath, as it flies,
Fit us for joys beyond the skies.

39 C. M.

1 AGAIN the Lord of life and light
Awakes the kindling ray,
Dispels the darkness of the night,
And pours increasing day.

2 Oh, what a night was that which wrapt
A guilty world in gloom!
Oh, what a sun which broke this day
Triumphant from the tomb!

3 The powers of darkness leagued in vain
To bind our Lord in death,
He shook their kingdom when he fell,
By his expiring breath.

4 And now his conquering chariot wheels
Ascend the lofty skies;

Broken beneath his powerful cross,
Death's iron sceptre lies.

5 This day be grateful homage paid,
And loud hosannas sung;
Let gladness dwell in every heart,
And praise on every tongue.

6 Ten thousand thousand voices join
To hail this happy morn,
Which scatters blessings from its wings
O'er nations yet unborn.

BARBAULD.

40 C. M.

1 AND now another week begins,
This day we call the Lord's;
This day he rose, who bore our sins—
For so his word records.

2 Hark, how the angels sweetly sing!—
Their voices fill the sky;
They hail their great victorious King,
And welcome him on high.

3 We'll catch the note of lofty praise;
May we their rapture feel;
Our thankful songs with theirs we'll raise,
And emulate their zeal.

4 Come then, ye saints! and grateful sing
Of Christ, our risen Lord—
Of Christ, the everlasting King—
Of Christ, th' incarnate Word.

5 Hail, mighty Saviour! thee we hail:
High on thy throne above;
Till heart and flesh together fail,
We'll sing thy matchless love.

KELLY.

41 C. M.

1 BLEST morning, whose young dawning rays
Beheld our rising God,
That saw him triumph o'er the dust,
And leave his dark abode.

2 In the cold prison of the tomb
The dead Redeemer lay,
Till the revolving skies had brought
The third, th' appointed day.

3 Hell and the grave unite their force
To hold our Lord in vain;
The sleeping Conqueror arose,
And burst their feeble chain.

4 To thy great name, Almighty Lord,
These sacred hours we pay,
And loud hosannas shall proclaim
The triumph of the day.

WATTS.

42 C. M.

1 LORD, in the morning thou shalt hear
My voice ascending high;
To thee will I direct my prayer,
To thee lift up mine eye.

2 Up to the hills where Christ is gone
To plead for all his saints,
Presenting at his Father's throne
Our songs and our complaints.

3 Thou art a God before whose sight
The wicked shall not stand;
Sinners shall ne'er be thy delight,
Nor dwell at thy right hand.

4 But to thy house will I resort,
To taste thy mercies there;

I will frequent thy holy court,
And worship in thy fear.

5 Oh, may the Spirit guide my feet
In ways of righteousness;
Make every path of duty straight
And plain before my face.

WATTS.

43 C. M.

1 WITHIN thy house, O Lord, our God,
In glory now appear;
Make this a place of thine abode,
And shed thy blessings here.

2 When we thine awful seat surround,
Thy Spirit, Lord, impart;
And let thy gospel's joyful sound
With power reach every heart.

3 Here let the blind their sight obtain;
Here give the mourners rest:
Let Jesus here triumphant reign,
Enthroned in every breast.

4 Here let the voice of sacred joy
And humble prayer arise,
Till higher strains our tongues employ,
In realms beyond the skies.

44 C. M.

1 LORD, at thy temple we appear,
As happy Simeon came,
And hope to meet our Saviour here—
Oh make our joys the same.

2 With what divine and vast delight
The good old man was filled,
When fondly in his withered arms
He clasped the holy child!

3 "Thou art the light prepared to shine
Upon the Gentile lands,
Thine Israel's glory, and their hope,
To break their slavish bands."

4 Jesus! the vision of thy face
Hath overpowering charms!
Scarce shall I feel death's cold embrace,
If Christ be in my arms.

WATTS.

45 C. M.

1 HOW did my heart rejoice to hear
My friends devoutly say,
"In Zion let us all appear,
And keep the solemn day!"

2 I love her gates, I love the road;
The Church, adorned with grace,
Stands like a palace, built for God,
To show his milder face.

3 Up to her courts, with joys unknown,
The holy tribes repair;
The Son of David holds his throne,
And sits in judgment there.

4 He hears our praises and complaints;
And, while his awful voice
Divides the sinners from the saints,
We tremble and rejoice.

5 Peace be within this sacred place,
And joy a constant guest!
With holy gifts and heavenly grace
Be her attendants blest!

6 My soul shall pray for Zion still,
While life or breath remains:
There my best friends, my kindred, dwell;
There God, my Saviour reigns.

WATTS.

46 C. M.

1 COME, thou desire of all thy saints!
Our humble strains attend,
While, with our praises and complaints,
Low at thy feet we bend.

2 How should our songs, like those above,
With warm devotion rise!
How should our souls, on wings of love,
Mount upward to the skies!

3 Come, Lord! thy love alone can raise
In us the heavenly flame!
Then shall our lips resound thy praise,
Our hearts adore thy name.

4 Dear Saviour! Let thy glory shine,
And fill thy dwellings here,
Till life, and love, and joy divine
A heaven on earth appear.

5 Then shall our hearts enraptured say,
Come, great Redeemer! come,
And bring the bright, the glorious day,
That calls thy children home.

STEELE.

47 C. M.

1 MY soul, how lovely is the place
To which thy God resorts!
'Tis heaven to see his smiling face,
Though in his earthly courts.

2 There the great Monarch of the skies
His saving power displays;
And light breaks in upon our eyes
With kind and quickening rays.

3 With his rich gifts the heavenly Dove
Descends and fills the place,
While Christ reveals his wondrous love,
And sheds abroad his grace.

4 There, mighty God, thy words declare
The secrets of thy will;
And still we seek thy mercy there,
And sing thy praises still.

WATTS.

48 C. M.

1 EARLY, my God, without delay,
I haste to seek thy face;
My thirsty spirit faints away,
Without thy cheering grace.

2 So pilgrims, on the scorching sand,
Beneath a burning sky,
Long for a cooling stream at hand;
And they must drink, or die.

3 I've seen thy glory, and thy power,
Through all thy temple shine;
My God, repeat that heavenly hour,
That vision so divine.

4 Not all the blessings of a feast
Can please my soul so well,
As when thy richer grace I taste,
And in thy presence dwell.

5 Not life itself, with all its joys,
Can my best passions move,
Or raise so high my cheerful voice,
As thy forgiving love.

6 Thus, till my last, expiring day,
I'll bless my God and King;
Thus will I lift my hands to pray,
And tune my lips to sing.

WATTS.

49 C. M.

1 I LOVE to see the Lord below;
His church displays his grace;
But upper worlds his glory know,
And view him face to face.

2 I love to worship at his feet,
Though sin annoy me there;
But saints, exalted near his seat,
Have no assaults to fear.

3 I love to meet him in his court,
And taste his heavenly love;
But still his visits seem too short,
Or I too soon remove.

4 He shines, and I am all delight;
He hides, and all is pain:
When will he fix me in his sight,
And ne'er depart again?

5 O Lord, I love thy service now;
Thy church displays thy power;
But soon in heaven I hope to bow
And praise thee evermore.

WATTS.

50 C. M.

1 THIS is the day the Lord hath made,
He calls the hours his own;
Let heaven rejoice, let earth be glad,
And praise surround the throne.

2 To-day he rose and left the dead,
And Satan's empire fell;
To-day the saints his triumph spread,
And all his wonders tell.

3 Hosanna to th' anointed King,
To David's holy Son;
Help us, O Lord—descend and bring
Salvation from thy throne.

4 Blest be the Lord who comes to men
With messages of grace;
Who comes in God his Father's name
To save our sinful race.

WATTS.

51 C. M.

1 COME, dearest Lord, and feed thy sheep,
On this sweet day of rest;
Oh, bless this flock, and make this fold
Enjoy a heavenly rest!

2 Welcome and precious to my soul
Are these sweet days of love;
But what a Sabbath shall I keep
When I shall rest above!

3 I come, I wait, I hear, I pray;
Thy footsteps, Lord, I trace;
Here, in thine own appointed way,
I wait to see thy face.

MASON.

52 C. M.

1 AS now the sun's declining rays
At eventide descend;
So life's brief day is sinking down
To its appointed end.

2 Lord, on the cross thine arms were stretched,
To draw thy people nigh;
Oh, grant us then that cross to love,
And in those arms to die.

3 All glory to the Father be,
All glory to the Son,
All glory, Holy Ghost, to thee,
While endless ages run.

53 7s.

1 LORD of hosts, how bright, how fair,
E'en on earth thy temples are!
Here thy waiting people see
Much of heaven and much of thee.

2 From thy gracious presence flows
Bliss that softens all our woes;
While thy Spirit's holy fire
Warms our hearts with pure desire.

3 Here we supplicate thy throne;
Here thou mak'st thy glories known;
Here we learn thy righteous ways,
Taste thy love, and sing thy praise.

4 Thus, with sacred songs of joy,
We our happy lives employ;
Love, and long to love thee more,
Till from earth to heaven we soar.

54 C. M.

1 COME, let us strike our harps afresh,
To great Jehovah's name;
Sweet be the accents of our tongues,
When we his love proclaim.

2 'Twas by his bidding we were called
In pain awhile to part;
'Tis by his care we meet again,
And gladness fills our heart.

3 Blest be the hand that has preserved
Our feet from every snare;
And blest the goodness of the Lord,
Which to this hour we share.

4 O may the Spirit's quickening power
Now sanctify our joy,
And warm our zeal in works of love,
Our talents to employ.

5 Fast, fast our minutes fly away;
Soon shall our wanderings cease;
And with our Father we shall dwell,
A family of peace!

REED.

55 C. M.

1 DEAR Shepherd of thy people, here
Thy presence now display;
As thou hast given a place for prayer,
So give us hearts to pray.

2 Within these walls let holy peace,
And love, and concord dwell;
Here give the troubled conscience ease,
The wounded spirit heal.

3 The feeling heart, the melting eye,
The humble mind bestow;
And shine upon us from on high,
To make our graces grow!

4 May we in faith receive the word,
In faith present our prayers;
And in the presence of our Lord
Unbosom all our cares.

5 And may the gospel's joyful sound,
Enforced by mighty grace,
Awaken many sinners round,
To come and fill the place.

NEWTON.

56 C. M.

1 LORD, thou wilt hear me when I pray;
I am for ever thine;
I fear before thee all the day,
Nor would I dare to sin.

2 And while I rest my weary head,
From cares and business free,
'Tis sweet conversing on my bed
With my own heart and thee.

3 I pay this evening sacrifice;
And when my work is done,

Great God! my faith and hope relies
Upon thy grace alone.

4 Thus, with my thoughts composed to peace,
I give mine eyes to sleep;
Thy hand in safety keeps my days,
And will my slumbers keep.

NEEDHAM.

57 C. M.

1 I LOVE to steal awhile away
From every cumbering care,
And spend the hours of setting day
In humble, grateful prayer.

2 I love, in solitude, to shed
The penitential tear;
And all his promises to plead
Where none but God is near.

3 I love to think on mercies past,
And future good implore;
And all my cares and sorrows cast
On him whom I adore.

4 I love, by faith, to take a view
Of brighter scenes in heaven;
The prospect doth my strength renew,
While here by tempests driven.

5 Thus, when life's toilsome day is o'er,
May its departing ray
Be calm as this impressive hour,
And lead to endless day.

MRS. BROWN.

58 C. M.

1 WHEN the worn spirit wants repose,
And sighs her God to seek,
How sweet to hail the evening's close,
That ends the weary week.

2 How welcome is the early dawn
That opens on the sight,
When first the soul-reviving morn
Sheds forth new rays of light.

3 Blest day! thine hours too soon will cease,
Yet, while they gently roll,
Breathe, heavenly Spirit, source of peace,
A Sabbath o'er my soul.

4 When will my pilgrimage be done,
The world's long week be o'er,
That Sabbath dawn which needs no sun,
That day which fades no more?

EDMESTON.

59 C. M. Double.

1 WHILE thee I seek, protecting Power,
Be my vain wishes stilled;
And may this consecrated hour
With better hopes be filled!
Thy love the power of thought bestowed;
To thee my thoughts would soar;
Thy mercy o'er my life has flowed;
That mercy I adore.

2 In each event of life, how clear
Thy ruling hand I see!
Each blessing to my soul more dear,
Because conferred by thee.
In every joy that crowns my days,
In every pain I bear,
My heart shall find delight in praise,
Or seek relief in prayer.

3 When gladness wings my favored hour,
Thy love my thoughts shall fill;

Resigned, when storms of sorrow lower,
My soul shall meet thy will.
My lifted eye, without a tear,
The gathering storm shall see;
My steadfast heart shall know no fear,
That heart will rest on thee.

WILLIAMS.

60 C. M. Double.

1 ALMIGHTY God, thy word is cast
Like seed into the ground;
Oh may it grow in humble hearts,
And righteous fruits abound.
Let not the foe of Christ and man
This holy seed remove,
But give it root in praying souls
To bring forth fruits of love.

CAWOOD.

61 C. M. Double.

1 IN God's own house pronounce his praise,
His grace he there reveals;
To heaven your joy and wonder raise,
For there his glory dwells.
Let all your secret passions move
While you rehearse his deeds;
But the great work of saving love,
Your highest praise exceeds.

WATTS.

62 C. M.

1 FAR from the world, O Lord, I flee,
From strife and tumult far;
From scenes where Satan wages still
His most successful war.

2 The calm retreat, the silent shade,
With prayer and praise agree;
And seem by thy sweet bounty made
For those who follow thee.

3 There, if thy Spirit touch the soul,
And grace her mean abode,
Oh, with what peace and joy and love
She communes with her God!

4 Author and guardian of my life,
Sweet source of light divine,
And—all harmonious names in one—
My Saviour, thou art mine.

5 What thanks I owe thee, and what love!
A boundless, endless store!
Thy praise shall fill the realms above,
When time shall be no more.

COWPER.

63 C. M.

1 HAIL, tranquil hour of closing day!
Begone, disturbing care!
And look, my soul, from earth away
To him who heareth prayer.

2 How sweet the tear of penitence,
Before his throne of grace,
While to the contrite spirit's sense,
He shows his smiling face.

3 How sweet, through long-remembered years,
His mercies to recall,
And pressed with wants, and griefs, and fears,
To trust his love for all.

4 How sweet to look, in thoughtful hope,
Beyond this fading sky,
And hear him call his children up
To his fair home on high.

5 Calmly the day forsakes our heaven
To dawn beyond the west;
So let my soul in life's last even,
Retire to glorious rest.

BACON.

64

C. M.

1 A THRONE of grace! then let us go
And offer up our prayer;
A gracious God will mercy show
To all that worship there.

2 A throne of grace! oh, at that throne
Our knees have often bent!
And God has showered his blessings down
As often as we went.

3 A throne of grace! rejoice, ye saints;
That throne is open still;
To God unbosom your complaints,
And then inquire his will.

4 A throne of grace we yet shall need
Long as we draw our breath,
A Saviour, too, to intercede,
Till we are changed by death.

CORBIN.

65

C. M.

1 PRAYER is the soul's sincere desire,
Unuttered or expressed;
The motion of a hidden fire
That trembles in the breast.

2 Prayer is the burden of a sigh,
The falling of a tear,
The upward glancing of an eye,
When none but God is near.

3 Prayer is the simplest form of speech
That infant lips can try;
Prayer the sublimest strains that reach
The majesty on high.

4 Prayer is the Christian's vital breath,
The Christian's native air:
His watchword at the gates of death—
He enters heaven with prayer.

5 Prayer is the contrite sinner's voice,
Returning from his ways;
While angels in their songs rejoice,
And cry—"Behold he prays!"

6 O thou, by whom we come to God—
The Life, the Truth, the Way;
The path of prayer thyself hast trod;
Lord! teach us how to pray.

MONTGOMERY.

66

C. M.

1 THERE is an eye that never sleeps
Beneath the wing of night;
There is an ear that never shuts,
When sink the beams of light.

2 There is an arm that never tires,
When human strength gives way;
There is a love that never fails,
When earthly loves decay.

3 That eye is fixed on seraph throngs;
That arm upholds the sky;
That ear is filled with angel songs;
That love is throned on high.

4 But there's a power which man can wield
When mortal aid is vain,
That eye, that arm, that love to reach,
That listening ear to gain.

5 That power is prayer, which soars on high,
Through Jesus, to the throne;
And moves the hand which moves the world,
To bring salvation down!

67 C. M.

1 PRAYER is the breath of God in man,
Returning whence it came;
Love is the sacred fire within,
And prayer the rising flame.

2 It gives the burdened spirit ease,
And soothes the troubled breast;
Yields comfort to the mourning soul,
And to the weary rest.

3 When God inclines the heart to pray,
He hath an ear to hear;
To him there's music in a sigh,
And beauty in a tear.

4 The humble suppliant cannot fail
To have his wants supplied,
Since he for sinners intercedes,
Who once for sinners died.

BEDDOME.

68 S. M.

1 COME, we that love the Lord,
And let our joys be known;
Join in a song with sweet accord,
And thus surround the throne.

2 Let those refuse to sing
Who never knew our God,
But children of the heavenly King
May speak their joys abroad.

3 The men of grace have found
Glory begun below;
Celestial fruits on earthly ground
From faith and hope may grow.

4 The hill of Zion yields
A thousand sacred sweets
Before we reach the heavenly fields,
Or walk the golden streets.

5 Then let our songs abound,
And every tear be dry;
We're marching through Immanuel's ground,
To fairer worlds on high.

WATTS.

69 S. M.

1 SWEET is the work, O Lord,
Thy glorious acts to sing,
To praise thy name, and hear thy word,
And grateful offerings bring.

2 Sweet, at the dawning hour,
Thy boundless love to tell;
And when the night-wind shuts the flower,
Still on the theme to dwell.

3 Sweet, on this day of rest,
To join in heart and voice
With those who love and serve thee best,
And in thy name rejoice.

4 To songs of praise and joy
Be every Sabbath given,
That such may be our blest employ
Eternally in heaven.

LYTE.

70 S. M.

1 WELCOME, sweet day of rest,
That saw the Lord arise!
Welcome to this reviving breast,
And these rejoicing eyes!

2 The King himself comes near,
And feasts his saints to-day;
Here may we sit and see him here,
And love, and praise, and pray.

3 One day amidst the place
Where my dear God hath been,

Is sweeter than ten thousand days
  Of pleasurable sin.

4 My willing soul would stay
  In such a frame as this,
And sit and sing herself away
  To everlasting bliss.

WATTS.

71 S. M.

1 SING to the Lord our might,
  With holy fervor sing;
Let hearts and instruments unite
  To praise the heavenly King.

2 This is his holy house,
  And this his festal day,
When he accepts the humblest vows
  That we sincerely pay.

3 The Sabbath to our sires
  In mercy first was given;
The Church her Sabbaths still requires
  To speed her on to heaven.

LYTE.

72 S. M.

1 HOW charming is the place
  Where my Redeemer, God,
Unveils the beauties of his face,
  And sheds his love abroad!

2 Not the fair palaces,
  To which the great resort,
Are once to be compared with this,
  Where Jesus holds his court.

3 Here, on the mercy-seat,
  With radiant glory crowned,
Our joyful eyes behold him sit,
  And smile on all around.

STENNETT.

73 S. M.

1 HOW sweet to bless the Lord,
  And in his praises join!
With saints his goodness to record,
  And sing his power divine!

2 These seasons of delight
  The dawn of glory seem,
Like rays of pure celestial light,
  Which on our spirits beam.

3 Oh, blest assurance this!
  Bright morn of heavenly day;
Sweet foretaste of eternal bliss,
  That cheers the pilgrim's way.

74

1 JESUS, we look to thee,
  Thy promised presence claim;
Thou in the midst of us wilt be,
  Assembled in thy name.

2 Thy name salvation is,
  Which here we come to prove;
The name is life, and health, and peace,
  And everlasting love.

C. WESLEY.

75 S. M.

1 COME to the house of prayer,
  O thou afflicted, come;
The God of peace shall meet thee there;
  He makes that house his home.

2 Come to the house of praise,
  Ye who are happy now;
In sweet accord your voices raise,
  In kindred homage bow.

3 Ye aged, hither come,
For ye have felt his love;
Soon shall your trembling tongues be dumb,
Your lips forget to move.

4 Ye young, before his throne
Come, bow; your voices raise;
Let not your hearts his praise disown
Who gives the power to praise.

5 Thou, whose benignant eye
In mercy looks on all—
Who seest the tear of misery,
And hear'st the mourner's call—

6 Up to thy dwelling-place
Bear our frail spirits on,
Till they outstrip time's tardy pace,
And heaven on earth be won.

E. Taylor.

76 S. M.

1 COME at the morning hour,
Come, let us kneel and pray;
Prayer is the Christian pilgrim's staff
To walk with God all day.

2 At noon, beneath the Rock
Of Ages, rest and pray;
Sweet is that shelter from the sun,
In the weary heat of day.

3 At evening, in thy home,
Around its altar, pray;
And finding there the house of God,
With heaven then close the day.

4 When midnight vails our eyes,
Oh, it is sweet to say,
I sleep, but my heart waketh, Lord,
With thee to watch and pray.

77 S. M.

1 THIS is the day of light:
Let there be light to-day:
O Day-spring, rise upon our night,
And chase its gloom away.

2 This is the day of rest:
Our failing strength renew!
On weary brain and troubled breast
Shed thou thy freshening dew.

3 This is the day of peace:
Thy peace our spirits fill;
Bid thou the blast of discord cease,
The waves of strife be still.

4 This is the day of prayer:
Let earth to heaven draw near;
Lift up our hearts to seek thee there;
Come down to meet us here.

5 This is the first of days;
Send forth thy quickening breath,
And wake dead souls to love and praise,
O Vanquisher of death!

78 S. M.

1 THE day, O Lord, is spent;
Abide with us, and rest;
Our hearts' desires are fully bent
On making thee our guest.

2 We have not reached that land,
That happy land, as yet,
Where holy angels round thee stand,
Whose sun can never set.

3 Our sun is sinking now;
Our day is almost o'er:
O Sun of Righteousness, do thou
Shine on us evermore!

John Mason Neale.

79

S. M.

1 THE day is past and gone,
The evening shades appear;
O may we all remember well
The night of death draws near.

2 We lay our garments by,
Upon our beds to rest;
So death will soon disrobe us all
Of what we here possess.

3 Lord, keep us safe this night,
Secure from all our fears;
May angels guard us while we sleep,
Till morning light appears.

4 And when we early rise,
And view th' unwearied sun,
May we set out to win the prize,
And after glory run.

5 And when our days are past,
And we from time remove,
O may we in thy bosom rest,
The bosom of thy love.

LELAND.

80

S. M.

1 THE day of praise is done;
The evening shadows fall;
Yet pass not from us with the sun,
True Light that lightenest all.

2 Around thy throne on high,
Where night can never be,
The white-robed harpers of the sky
Bring ceaseless songs to thee.

3 Too faint our anthems here;
Too soon of praise we tire;
But oh, the strains how full and clear
Of that eternal choir!

4 Yet, Lord, to thy dear will,
If thou attune the heart,
We in thine angels' music still
May bear our lower part.

81

S. M.

1 LORD, at this closing hour,
Establish every heart
Upon thy word of truth and power,
To keep us when we part.

2 Peace to our brethren give;
Fill all our hearts with love;
In faith and patience may we live,
And seek our rest above.

E. T. FITCH.

82

7s.

1 SOFTLY fades the twilight ray
Of the holy Sabbath day;
Gently as life's setting sun,
When the Christian's course is run.

2 Night her solemn mantle spreads
O'er the earth, as daylight fades;
All things tell of calm repose
At the holy Sabbath's close.

3 Peace is on the world abroad;
'Tis the holy peace of God—
Symbol of the peace within
When the spirit rests from sin.

4 Still the Spirit lingers near,
Where the evening worshipper
Seeks communion with the skies,
Pressing onward to the prize.

5 Saviour, may our Sabbaths be
Days of peace and joy in thee,
Till in heaven our souls repose,
Where the Sabbath ne'er shall close.

S. F. SMITH.

83

7s.

1 ERE another Sabbath's close,
Ere again we seek repose,
Lord! our song ascends to thee;
At thy feet we bow the knee.

2 For the mercies of the day,
For this rest upon our way,
Thanks to thee alone be given,
Lord of earth, and King of heaven.

3 Cold our services have been;
Mingled every prayer with sin;
But thou canst and wilt forgive;
By thy grace alone we live.

4 Whilst this thorny path we tread,
May thy love our footsteps lead!
When our journey here is past,
May we rest with thee at last.

5 Let these earthly Sabbaths prove
Foretastes of our joys above;
While their steps thy pilgrims bend
To the rest which knows no end.

84

7s.

1 FOR a season called to part,
Let us now ourselves commend
To the gracious eye and heart
Of our ever-present Friend.

2 Jesus, hear our humble prayer:
Tender Shepherd of thy sheep,
Let thy mercy and thy care
All our souls in mercy keep.

3 In thy strength may we be strong;
Sweeten every cross and pain;
And our wasting lives prolong,
Till we meet on earth again.

NEWTON.

85

7s.

1 SOFTLY now the light of day
Fades upon my sight away;
Free from care, from labor free,
Lord, I would commune with thee.

2 Thou, whose all-pervading eye
Naught escapes without, within,
Pardon each infirmity,
Open fault, and secret sin.

3 Thou, who, sinless, yet hast known
All of man's infirmity;
Then from thine eternal throne,
Jesus, look with pitying eye.

4 Soon, for me, the light of day
Shall forever pass away:
Then, from sin and sorrow free,
Take me, Lord, to dwell with thee.

DOANE.

86

8s, 7s & 4s.

1 LORD, dismiss us with thy blessing,
Fill our hearts with joy and peace;
Let us each, thy love possessing,
Triumph in redeeming grace;
Oh, refresh us,
Traveling through the wilderness.

2 Thanks we give and adoration,
For thy gospel's joyful sound;
May the fruits of thy salvation
In our hearts and lives abound;
May thy presence,
With us evermore be found.

3 So, whene'er the signal 's given,
Us from earth to call away,

Borne on angels' wings to heaven,
Glad the summons to obey,
May we ever
Reign with Christ in endless day.

BURDER.

87 8s, 7s & 4s.

1 GOD of our salvation, hear us;
Bless, oh bless us, ere we go;
When we join the world, be near us,
Lest we cold and careless grow:
Saviour, keep us,
Keep us safe from every foe.

2 May we live in view of heaven,
Where we hope to see thy face;
Save us from unhallowed leaven,
All that might obscure thy grace;
Keep us walking
Each in his appointed place.

3 As our steps are drawing nearer
To the place we call our home,
May our view of heaven grow clearer,
Hope more bright of joys to come;
And, when dying,
May thy presence cheer the gloom.

88 8s, 7s & 4s.

1 KEEP us, Lord, oh keep us ever;
Vain our hope, if left by thee;
We are thine, oh leave us never
Till thy glorious face we see:
Then to praise thee
Through a bright eternity.

2 Precious is thy word of promise,
Precious to thy people here;
Never take thy presence from us,
Jesus, Saviour, still be near:
Living, dying,
May thy name our spirits cheer.

89 10s.

1 ABIDE with me! fast falls the eventide,
The darkness deepens; Lord, with me abide;
When other helpers fail, and comforts flee,
Help of the helpless, oh, abide with me.

2 Swift to its close ebbs out life's little day;
Earth's joys grow dim, its glories pass away;
Change and decay on all around I see;
O thou who changest not, abide with me.

3 I need thy presence every passing hour,
What but thy grace can foil the tempter's power?
Who like thyself, my guide and stay can be?
Through cloud and sunshine, Lord, abide with me.

4 I fear no foe, with thee at hand to bless;
Ills have no weight, and tears no bitterness.
Where is death's sting? where, grave, thy victory?
I triumph still, if thou abide with me.

5 Hold thou thy cross before my closing eyes;
Shine through the gloom, and point me to the skies;
Heaven's morning breaks, and earth's vain shadows flee;
In life, in death, O Lord, abide with me.

LYTE.

90

8s & 7s.

1 SILENTLY the shades of evening
Gather round my lowly door;
Silently they bring before me
Faces I shall see no more.

2 Oh, the lost, the unforgotten,
Though the world be oft forgot;
Oh, the shrouded and the lonely,
In our hearts they perish not.

3 Living in the silent hours,
Where our spirits only blend,
They, unlinked with earthly trouble,
We still hoping for its end.

4 How such holy memories cluster,
Like the stars when storms are past,
Pointing up to that fair heaven
We may hope to gain at last.

91

8s & 7s.

1 TARRY with me, O my Saviour,
For the day is passing by;
See! the shades of evening gather,
And the night is drawing nigh.

2 Many friends were gathered round me
In the bright days of the past;
But the grave has closed above them,
And I linger here at last.

3 Deeper, deeper grow the shadows;
Paler now the glowing west;
Swift the night of death advances;
Shall it be the night of rest?

4 Feeble, trembling, fainting, dying,
Lord, I cast myself on thee;
Tarry with me through the darkness!
While I sleep, still watch by me.

5 Tarry with me, O my Saviour!
Lay my head upon thy breast
Till the morning; then awake me—
Morning of eternal rest!

92

8s & 7s.

1 VAINLY through night's weary hours,
Keep we watch lest foes alarm;
Vain our bulwarks and our towers,
But for God's protecting arm.

2 Vain were all our toil and labor
Did not God that labor bless;
Vain, without his grace and favor,
Every talent we possess.

3 Seek we then the Lord's Anointed;
He shall grant us peace and rest:
Ne'er was suppliant disappointed
Who to Christ his prayer addressed.

LYTE.

93

8s & 7s.

1 LO, the day of rest declineth,
Gather fast the shades of night;
May the Sun which ever shineth,
Fill our souls with heavenly light!

2 While thine ear of love addressing,
Thus our parting hymn we sing,
Father, grant thine evening blessing,
Fold us safe beneath thy wing!

ROBBINS.

94

1 FADING, still fading, the last beam is shining,
Father in heaven! the day is declining,
Safety and innocence fly with the light,
Temptation and danger walk forth with the night:

From the fall of the shade till the morning-bells chime,
Shield me from danger, save me from crime.
Father, have mercy, Father, have mercy,
Father, have mercy, through Jesus Christ our Lord.

2 Father in heaven! oh, hear when we call!
Hear, for Christ's sake, who is Saviour of all;
Feeble and fainting we trust in thy might,
In doubting and darkness thy love be our light;
Let us sleep on thy breast while the night taper burns,
Wake in thy arms when morning returns.
Father, have mercy, &c. Amen.

95 L. M.

1 SWEET hour of prayer! sweet hour of prayer!
That calls me from a world of care,
And bids me at my Father's throne
Make all my wants and wishes known.
In seasons of distress and grief,
My soul has often found relief,
And oft escaped the tempter's snare
By thy return, sweet hour of prayer.

2 Sweet hour of prayer! sweet hour of prayer!
Thy wings shall my petition bear,
To him whose truth and faithfulness,
Engage the waiting soul to bless;
And since he bids me seek his face,
Believe his word, and trust his grace,
I'll cast on him my every care,
And wait for thee, sweet hour of prayer!

3 Sweet hour of prayer! sweet hour of prayer!
May I thy consolation share;
Till from Mount Pisgah's lofty height,
I view my home, and take my flight;
This robe of flesh I'll drop, and rise
To seize the everlasting prize;
And shout, while passing through the air,
Farewell, farewell, sweet hour of prayer!

96 S. M.

1 STAND up, and bless the Lord,
Ye people of his choice;
Stand up, and bless the Lord your God
With heart, and soul, and voice.

2 Though high above all praise,
Above all blessing high,
Who would not fear his holy name,
And laud, and magnify?

3 Oh, for the living flame
From his own altar brought,
To touch our lips, our souls inspire,
And wing to heaven our thought!

4 God is our strength and song,
And his salvation ours;
Then be his love in Christ proclaimed
With all our ransomed powers.

5 Stand up, and bless the Lord;
The Lord your God adore;
Stand up, and bless his glorious name,
Henceforth, for evermore!

MONTGOMERY.

97 S. M.

1 LET sinners take their course,
And choose the road to death;
But in the worship of my God
I'll spend my daily breath.

2 My thoughts address his throne,
When morning brings the light;
I seek his blessing every noon,
And pay my vows at night.

3 Thou wilt regard my cries,
O my eternal God,
While sinners perish in surprise,
Beneath thy holy rod.

4 But I, with all my cares,
Will lean upon the Lord;
I'll cast my burdens on his arm,
And rest upon his word.

5 His arm shall well sustain
The children of his love;
The ground on which their safety stands
No earthly power can move.

WATTS.

98 S. M.

1 MY soul, repeat his praise,
Whose mercies are so great,
Whose anger is so slow to rise,
So ready to abate.

2 His power subdues our sins,
And his forgiving love,
Far as the east is from the west,
Doth all our guilt remove.

3 High as the heavens are raised
Above the ground we tread,
So far the riches of his grace
Our highest thoughts exceed.

WATTS.

99 L. M.

1 PRAISE ye the Lord, his servants, raise
Your hearts and voices in his praise;
His presence seek, his name adore;
Oh, praise the Lord for evermore!

2 Above the earth, beyond the sky,
The Lord in glory reigns on high:
The best is vile, the brightest dim,
The loftiest low, compared with him.

3 Yet suppliant misery's fainting groan
Can reach him on his lofty throne;
And all the Godhead from above
Flows down in melting grace and love.

4 Lord, to our feeble cry attend;
Be still the contrite sinner's friend;
Still mark our wants, and hear our plea,
And bear us on to heaven and thee.

100 L. M.

1 O BLESSED God, to thee I raise
My voice in thankful hymns of praise;
And when my voice shall silent be,
My silence shall be praise to thee.

2 For voice and silence both impart
The filial homage of my heart;
And both alike are understood
By thee, thou Parent of all good.

3 Thy grace is all unsearchable,
Thy care for me no tongue can tell:
Thou lov'st my loudest praise to hear,
And lov'st to bless my voiceless prayer.

101 L. M.

1 O JESUS, Lord of heavenly grace,
Thou Brightness of thy Father's face,
Thou Fountain of eternal light,
Whose beams disperse the shades of night!

2 Come, holy Sun of heavenly love,
Send down thy radiance from above;
And to our inmost hearts convey
The Holy Spirit's cloudless ray.

3 Oh, hallowed thus be every day!
Let meekness be our morning ray,
And faithful love our noon-day light,
And hope our sunset, calm and bright.

4 O Christ, with each returning morn,
Thine image to our hearts is borne:
Oh, may we ever clearly see
Our Saviour and our God in thee!

CHANDLER.

102 C. M.

1 HOW sweet, upon this sacred day,
The best of all the seven,
To cast our earthly thoughts away,
And think of God and heaven!

2 How sweet to be allowed to pray
Our sins may be forgiven!
With filial confidence to say,
"Father, who art in heaven!"

3 How sweet the words of peace to hear
From him to whom 'tis given
To wake the penitential tear,
And lead the way to heaven!

4 Then hail, thou sacred, blessèd day,
The best of all the seven,
When hearts unite their vows to pay
Of gratitude to heaven!

MRS. FOLLEN.

103 C. M.

1 THE Lord of glory is my light,
And my salvation, too;
God is my strength, nor will I fear
What all my foes can do.

2 One privilege my heart desires,
Oh, grant me an abode
Among the churches of thy saints,
The temples of my God!

3 There shall I offer my requests,
And see thy beauty still;
Shall hear thy messages of love,
And there inquire thy will.

4 When troubles rise, and storms appear,
There may thy children hide:
God has a strong pavilion, where
He makes my soul abide.

WATTS.

104 C. M.

1 OUR Father, God, who art in heaven,
All hallowed be thy name;
Thy kingdom come; thy will be done
In heaven and earth the same.

2 Give us this day our daily bread;
And as we those forgive
Who sin against us, so may we
Forgiving grace receive.

3 Into temptation lead us not;
From evil set us free;
And thine the kingdom, thine the power,
And glory, ever be.

JUDSON.

105 C. M.

1 NOW that the sun is beaming bright,
Once more to God we pray
That he, the uncreated Light,
May guide our souls this day.

2 No sinful word, nor deed of wrong,
Nor thoughts that idly rove;
But simple truth be on our tongue,
And in our hearts be love.

3 And while the hours in order flow,
O Christ, securely fence
Our gates beleaguer'd by the foe—
The gate of every sense.

AMBROSE.

106

8s & 7s. D.

1 LORD, with glowing heart I'd praise thee,
For the bliss thy love bestows;
For the pardoning grace that saves me,
And the peace that from it flows:
Help, O God, my weak endeavor;
This dull soul to rapture raise;
Thou must light the flame, or never
Can my love be warmed to praise.

2 Praise, my soul, the God that sought thee,
Wretched wanderer, far astray;
Found thee lost and kindly brought thee
From the paths of death away;
Praise, with love's devoutest feeling,
Him who saw thy guilt-born fear,
And, the light of hope revealing,
Bade the blood-stained cross appear.

3 Lord, this bosom's ardent feeling
Vainly would my lips express:
Low before thy footstool kneeling,
Deign thy suppliant's prayer to bless:
Let thy grace, my soul's chief treasure,
Love's pure flame within me raise;
And, since words can never measure,
Let my life show forth thy praise.

KEY.

107

8s & 7s. D.

1 HEAVENLY Shepherd, guide us, feed us,
Through our pilgrimage below,
And beside the waters lead us,
Where thy flock rejoicing go.
Lord, thy guardian presence ever,
Meekly bending, we implore;
We have found thee, and would never,
Never wander from thee more.

108

8s & 7s. D.

1 SAVIOUR! breathe an evening blessing,
Ere repose our eyelids seal;
Sin and want we come confessing;
Thou canst save, and thou canst heal.
Though destruction walk around us,
Though the arrows past us fly,
Angel-guards from thee surround us—
We are safe if thou art nigh.

2 Though the night be dark and dreary,
Darkness can not hide from thee:
Thou art he who, never weary,
Watcheth where thy people be.
Should swift death this night o'ertake us,
And our couch become our tomb,
May the morn in heaven awake us,
Clad in bright and deathless bloom.

EDMESTON.

GOD.

109 L. M.

1 O HOLY, holy, holy Lord!
Bright in thy deeds and in thy name,
Forever be thy name adored,
Thy glories let the world proclaim!

2 O Jesus, Lamb once crucified
To take our load of sins away,
Thine be the hymn that rolls its lay
Along the realms of upper day!

3 O Holy Spirit from above,
In streams of light and glory giv'n,
Thou source of ecstasy and love,
Thy praises ring through earth and heav'n!

4 O God triune, to thee we owe
Our every thought, our every song;
And ever may thy praises flow
From saint and seraph's burning tongue!

J. W. Eastburne.

110 L. M.

1 FATHER of heaven! whose love profound
A ransom for our souls hath found,
Before thy throne we sinners bend:
To us thy pard'ning love extend.

2 Almighty Son! incarnate Word!
Our Prophet, Priest, Redeemer, Lord!
Before thy throne we sinners bend:
To us thy saving grace extend.

3 Eternal Spirit! by whose breath
The soul is raised from sin and death,
Before thy throne we sinners bend:
To us thy quick'ning power extend.

4 Jehovah! Father, Spirit, Son!
Mysterious Godhead! Three in One!
Before thy throne we sinners bend:
Grace, pardon, life, to us extend!

J. Cooper.

111 L. M.

1 THEE we adore, eternal Lord!
We praise thy name with one accord;
Thy saints, who here thy goodness see,
Through all the world do worship thee.

2 To thee aloud all angels cry,
And ceaseless raise their songs on high,
Both cherubim and seraphim,
The heavens and all the powers therein.

3 The apostles join the glorious throng;
The prophets swell the immortal song;
The martyrs' noble army raise
Eternal anthems to thy praise.

4 Thee, holy, holy, holy King;
Thee, O Lord God of hosts, they sing:
Thus earth below, and heaven above,
Resound thy glory and thy love.

Cotterill.

112 H. M.

1 WE give immortal praise
For God the Father's love,
For all our comforts here,
And better hopes above:
He sent his own eternal Son
To die for sins that we had done.

2 To God the Son belongs
Immortal glory too;
Who bought us with his blood
From everlasting woe:
And now he lives and now he reigns,
And sees the fruit of all his pains.

3 To God the Spirit's name
Immortal worship give,
Whose new-creating power
Makes the dead sinner live:
His work completes the great design,
And fills the soul with joy divine.

4 Almighty God, to thee
Be endless honors done,
The undivided Three,
The great and glorious One:
Where reason fails, with all her powers,
There faith prevails and love adores.

WATTS.

113 H. M.

1 TO him that chose us first,
Before the world began;
To him that bore the curse
To save rebellious man;
To him that formed our hearts anew,
Is endless praise and glory due.

2 The Father's love shall run
Through our immortal songs;
We bring to God the Son
Hosannas on our tongues;
Our lips address the Spirit's name
With equal praise and zeal the same.

3 Let every saint above,
And angel round the throne,
Forever bless and love
The sacred Three in One;
Thus heaven shall raise his honors high,
When earth and time grow old and die.

WATTS.

114 6s & 4s.

1 COME, thou Almighty King,
Help us thy name to sing,
Help us to praise:
Father, all glorious,
O'er all victorious,
Come, and reign over us,
Ancient of Days!

2 Come, thou Incarnate Word,
Gird on thy mighty sword;
Our prayer attend!
Come, and thy people bless,
And give thy word success:
Spirit of holiness,
On us descend!

3 Come, Holy Comforter,
Thy sacred witness bear,
In this glad hour!
Thou, who almighty art,
Now rule in every heart,
And ne'er from us depart,
Spirit of power!

4 To the great One in Three,
The highest praises be,
Hence evermore!
His sovereign majesty
May we in glory see,
And to eternity
Love and adore.

C. WESLEY.

115 6s & 4s.

1 THOU, whose almighty word
Chaos and darkness heard,
And took their flight,
Hear us, we humbly pray,
And where the gospel day
Sheds not its glorious ray,
"Let there be light."

2 Thou, who didst come to bring,
On thy redeeming wing,
Healing and sight,
Health to the sick in mind,
Sight to the inly blind,
Oh, now to all mankind
"Let there be light."

3 Spirit of truth and love,
Life-giving, holy Dove,
Speed forth thy flight;
Move on the waters' face,
Bearing the lamp of grace;
And in earth's darkest place
"Let there be light."

MARRIOTT.

116 6s & 4s.

1 FATHER of love and power,
Guard thou our evening hour,
Shield with thy might;
For all thy care this day
Our grateful thanks we pay,
And to our Father pray,
Bless us to-night.

2 Jesus, Immanuel,
Come in thy love to dwell
In hearts contrite;
For many sins we grieve,
But we thy grace receive,
And in thy word believe;
Bless us to-night.

3 Spirit of truth and love,
Life-giving, Holy Dove,
Shed forth thy light;
Heal every sinner's smart,
Still every throbbing heart,
And thine own peace impart;
Bless us to-night.

RAWSON.

117 L. M.

1 BEFORE Jehovah's awful throne,
Ye nations, bow with sacred joy:
Know that the Lord is God alone,
He can create, and he destroy.

2 His sovereign power, without our aid,
Made us of clay, and formed us men;
And when, like wand'ring sheep, we strayed,
He brought us to his fold again.

3 We are his people, we his care—
Our souls, and all our mortal frame:
What lasting honors shall we rear,
Almighty Maker, to thy name?

4 We'll crowd thy gates, with thankful songs,
High as the heaven our voices raise;
And earth, with her ten thousand tongues,
Shall fill thy courts with sounding praise.

5 Wide as the world is thy command;
Vast as eternity thy love;
Firm as a rock thy truth shall stand,
When rolling years shall cease to move.

WATTS.

118 L. M.

1 YE nations round the earth, rejoice
Before the Lord, your sovereign King;
Serve him with cheerful heart and voice;
With all your tongues his glory sing.

2 The Lord is God; 'tis he alone
Doth life, and breath, and being give;
We are his work, and not our own;
The sheep that on his pastures live.

3 Enter his gates with songs of joy,
With praises to his courts repair;
And make it your divine employ
To pay your thanks and honors there.

4 The Lord is good, the Lord is kind,
Great is his grace, his mercy sure;
And the whole race of man shall find
His truth from age to age endure.

WATTS.

119 L. M.

1 WITH deepest reverence at thy throne,
Jehovah, peerless and unknown!
Our feeble spirits strive, in vain,
A glimpse of thee, great God! to gain.

2 Who, by the closest search, can find
The eternal, uncreated mind?
Nor men, nor angels can explore
Thy heights of love, thy depths of power.

3 That power we trace on every side;
Oh! may thy wisdom be our guide!
And while we live, and when we die,
May thine almighty love be nigh.

120 L. M.

1 AWAKE, my tongue, thy tribute bring
To him who gave thee power to sing:
Praise him who is all praise above,
The source of wisdom and of love.

2 How vast his knowledge! how profound!
A depth where all our thoughts are drowned!
The stars he numbers, and their names
He gives to all those heavenly flames.

3 Through each bright world above, behold
Ten thousand thousand charms unfold;
Earth, air, and mighty seas combine
To speak his wisdom all divine.

4 But in redemption, oh, what grace!
Its wonders, oh, what thought can trace!
Here wisdom shines forever bright;
Praise him, my soul, with sweet delight.

NEEDHAM.

121 L. M.

1 BE thou exalted, O my God,
Above the heavens, where angels dwell;
Thy power on earth be known abroad,
And land to land thy wonders tell.

2 My heart is fixed; my song shall raise
Immortal honors to his name;
Awake, my tongue, to sound his praise,
His wondrous goodness to proclaim.

3 High o'er the earth his mercy reigns,
And reaches to the utmost sky;
His truth to endless years remains,
When lower worlds dissolve and die.

WATTS.

122 L. M.

1 THE spacious firmament on high,
With all the blue ethereal sky,
And spangled heavens, a shining frame,
Their great Original proclaim.

2 The unwearied sun, from day to day,
Does his Creator's power display,
And publishes to every land
The work of an Almighty hand.

3 Soon as the evening shades prevail,
The moon takes up the wondrous tale,
And nightly to the listening earth,
Repeats the story of her birth;

4 While all the stars that round her burn,
And all the planets in their turn,
Confirm the tidings as they roll,
And spread the truth from pole to pole.

5 What though in solemn silence, all
Move round this dark terrestrial ball;
What though no real voice nor sound
Amid their radiant orbs be found;

6 In reason's ear they all rejoice,
And utter forth a glorious voice;
For ever singing, as they shine—
"The hand that made us is divine."

ADDISON.

123 L. M.

1 OH, render thanks to God above,
The fountain of eternal love;
Whose mercy firm, through ages past,
Hath stood, and shall forever last.

2 Who can his mighty deeds express,
Not only vast—but numberless?
What mortal eloquence can raise
His tribute of immortal praise.

3 Extend to me that favor, Lord,
Thou to thy chosen dost afford;
When thou return'st to set them free,
Let thy salvation visit me.

4 Oh, render thanks to God above,
The fountain of eternal love:
His mercy firm, through ages past,
Hath stood, and shall forever last.

TATE & BRADY.

124 L. M.

1 COME, O my soul! in sacred lays
Attempt thy great Creator's praise:
But, oh! what tongue can speak his fame?
What mortal verse can reach the theme?

2 Enthroned amid the radiant spheres,
He glory like a garment wears;
To form a robe of light divine,
Ten thousand suns around him shine.

3 In all our Maker's grand designs,
Almighty power with wisdom shines;
His works, through all this wondrous frame,
Declare the glory of his name.

4 Raised on devotion's lofty wing,
Do thou, my soul, his glories sing;
And let his praise employ thy tongue,
Till list'ning worlds shall join the song!

BLACKLOCK.

125 L. M.

1 KINGDOMS and thrones to God belong;
Crown him, ye nations, in your song;
His wondrous names and pow'rs rehearse;
His honors shall enrich your verse.

2 He shakes the heav'ns with loud alarms;
How terrible is God in arms!
In Israel are his mercies known;
Israel is his peculiar throne.

3 Proclaim him King, pronounce him blest;
He's your defence, your joy, your rest;
When terrors rise, and nations faint,
God is the strength of every saint.

WATTS.

126 L. M.

1 O PRAISE the Lord in that blest place
From whence his goodness largely flows;
Praise him in heav'n, where he his face
Unveiled in perfect glory shows.

2 Praise him for all the mighty acts
Which he in our behalf hath done;
His kindness this return exacts,
With which our praise should equal run.

3 Let all, who vital breath enjoy,
The breath he doth to them afford
In just returns of praise employ:
Let every creature praise the Lord.

TATE & BRADY.

127 L. M.

1 OH, come, loud anthems let us sing,
Loud thanks to our Almighty King;
For we our voices high should raise,
When our salvation's Rock we praise.

2 The depths of earth are in his hand,
Her secret wealth at his command;
The strength of hills that threat the skies,
Subjected to his empire lies.

3 The rolling ocean's vast abyss
By the same sovereign right is his;
'Tis moved by his almighty hand,
That formed and fixed the solid land.

4 Oh, let us to his courts repair,
And bow with adoration there:
Down on our knees devoutly all
Before the Lord our Maker fall.

TATE & BRADY.

128 L. M.

1 PRAISE, everlasting praise, be paid
To him who earth's foundation laid;
Praise to the God whose strong decrees
Sway the creation as he please.

2 Firm are the words his prophets give,
Sweet words on which his children live;
Each of them is the voice of God,
Who spoke and spread the skies abroad.

3 Oh, for a strong, a lasting faith,
To credit what th' Almighty saith;
T' embrace the message of his Son,
And call the joys of heaven our own.

4 Then, should the earth's old pillars shake,
And all the wheels of nature break,
Our steady souls shall fear no more
Than solid rocks when billows roar.

WATTS.

129 L. M.

1 LOUD hallelujahs to the Lord,
From distant worlds where creatures dwell!
Let heaven begin the solemn word,
And sound it dreadful down to hell.

2 Mortals, can you refrain your tongue
When nature all around you sings?
Oh for a shout from old and young,
From humble swains and lofty kings!

3 Wide as his vast dominion lies,
Make the Creator's name be known;
Loud as his thunder shout his praise,
And sound it lofty as his throne.

4 Jehovah! 'tis a glorious word!
Oh! may it dwell on every tongue;
But saints who best have known the Lord,
Are bound to raise the noblest song.

5 Speak of the wonders of that love
Which Gabriel plays on every chord:
From all below, and all above,
Loud hallelujahs to the Lord.

WATTS.

130 L. M.

1 BLESS, O my soul, the living God;
Call home thy thoughts that rove abroad:
Let all the pow'rs within me join
In works and worship so divine.

2 Bless, O my soul, the God of grace;
His favors claim thy highest praise:
Why should the wonders he hath wrought
Be lost in silence and forgot?

3 'Tis he, my soul, that sent his Son
To die for crimes which thou hast done;
He owns the ransom, and forgives
The hourly follies of our lives.

4 Let every land his power confess;
Let all the earth adore his grace:
My heart and tongue with rapture join,
In work and worship so divine.

WATTS.

131 L. M.

1 LET Zion in her King rejoice,
Though tyrants rage, and kingdoms rise,
He utters his almighty voice—
The nations melt—the tumult dies.

2 From sea to sea, through all the shores,
He makes the noise of battle cease;
When from on high his thunder roars,
He awes the trembling world to peace.

3 "Be still—and learn that I am God;
I'll be exalted o'er the lands;
I will be known and feared abroad,
But still my throne in Zion stands."

4 O Lord of hosts, Almighty King!
While we so near thy presence dwell,
Our faith shall sit secure, and sing
Defiance to the gates of hell.

WATTS.

132 L. M.

1 THERE is a God!—all nature speaks,
Through earth, and air, and seas, and skies;
See! from the clouds his glory breaks,
When the first beams of morning rise.

2 The rising sun, serenely bright,
O'er the wide world's extended frame,
Inscribes, in characters of light,
His mighty Maker's glorious name.

3 Ye curious minds, who roam abroad,
And trace creation's wonders o'er,
Confess the footsteps of your God,
And bow before him, and adore.

STEELE.

133 L. M.

1 LO, God is here—let us adore,
And own how dreadful is this place;
Let all within us feel his power,
And silent bow before his face.

2 Lo, God is here!—him day and night
United choirs of angels sing;
To him, enthroned above all height,
Let saints their humble worship bring.

3 Lord God of hosts, oh, may our praise
Thy courts with grateful incense fill;
Still may we stand before thy face,
Still hear and do thy sovereign will.

J. WESLEY.

134 L. M.

1 ALMIGHTY God, we praise and own
Thee our Creator, King alone;
All things were made to honor thee,
O Father of eternity.

2 To thee all angels loudly cry;
The heavens and all the powers on high,
Cherubs and seraphim, proclaim,
And cry, Thrice holy to thy name!

3 Lord God of hosts, thy presence bright,
Fills heaven and earth with beauteous light;
The apostles' happy company,
And ancient prophets, all praise thee.

4 The crownèd martyrs' noble host,
The holy church in every coast,
Their Maker for their Father own,
Now reconciled in Christ his Son.

135 L. M.

1 YES, God is good; in earth and sky,
From ocean-depths and spreading wood,
Ten thousand voices seem to cry,
"God made us all, and God is good."

2 The sun that keeps his trackless way,
And downward pours his golden flood,
Night's sparkling hosts, all seem to say,
In accents clear, that God is good.

3 The merry birds prolong the strain,
Their song with every spring renewed;
And balmy air, and falling rain,
Each softly whisper, "God is good."

4 I hear it in the rushing breeze;
The hills that have for ages stood,
The echoing sky and roaring seas,
All swell the chorus, "God is good."

5 Yes, God is good, all Nature says,
By God's own hand with speech endued;
And man, in louder notes of praise,
Should sing for joy that God is good.

6 For all thy gifts we bless thee, Lord;
But chiefly for our heavenly food,
Thy pard'ning grace, thy quick'ning word;
These prompt our song, that God is good.

JOHN H. GURNEY.

136 L. M.

1 PRAISE ye the Lord; my heart shall join
In work so pleasant, so divine;
My days of praise shall ne'er be past,
While life, and thought, and being last.

2 Happy the man whose hopes rely
On Israel's God: he made the sky,
And earth, and seas, with all their train;
And none shall find his promise vain.

3 His truth forever stands secure;
He saves th' oppress'd, he feeds the poor;
He helps the stranger in distress,
The widow and the fatherless.

4 He loves the saints; he knows them well,
But turns the wicked down to hell:
Thy God, O Zion, ever reigns;
Praise him in everlasting strains.

WATTS.

137 L. M.

1 UP to the fields where angels lie,
And living waters gently roll,
Fain would my thoughts leap out and fly,
But sin hangs heavy on my soul.

2 O might I once mount up and see
The glories of th' eternal skies,
What little things these worlds would be!
How despicable to my eyes!

3 Had I a glance of thee, my God,
Kingdoms and men would vanish soon,
Vanish as though I saw them not,
As a dim taper dies at noon.

4 Then they might fight, and rage, and rave,
I should perceive the noise no more
Than we can hear a shaking leaf
When rattling thunders round us roar.

5 Great All in All, Eternal King,
Let me but view thy lovely face,
And all my powers shall bow and sing
Thine endless grandeur and thy grace.

WATTS.

138 L. M.

1 LORD, thou hast searched and seen me through:
Thine eye commands with piercing view
My rising and my resting hours,
My heart and flesh with all their pow'rs.

2 My thoughts, before they are my own,
Are to my God distinctly known;

He knows the words I mean to speak,
Ere from my opening lips they break.

3 Within thy circling power I stand;
On every side I find thy hand:
Awake, asleep, at home, abroad,
I am surrounded still with God.

4 Amazing knowledge, vast and great!
What large extent! what lofty height!
My soul, with all the powers I boast,
Is in the boundless prospect lost.

5 Oh! may these thoughts possess my breast,
Where'er I rove, where'er I rest,
Nor let my weaker passions dare
Consent to sin, for God is there.

WATTS.

139 L. M.

1 GIVE thanks to God, he reigns above;
Kind are his thoughts, his name is love;
His mercy ages past have known,
And ages long to come shall own.

2 Let the redeeméd of the Lord
The wonders of his grace record;
Israel, the nation whom he chose,
And rescued from their mighty foes.

3 He feeds and clothes us all the way,
He guides our footsteps, lest we stray;
He guards us with a powerful hand,
And brings us to the heavenly land.

4 O let us, then, with joy record
The truth and goodness of the Lord;
How great his works—how kind his ways!
Let every tongue pronounce his praise.

WATTS.

140 L. M.

1 MY God, my King, thy various praise
Shall fill the remnant of my days;
Thy grace employ my humble tongue,
Till death and glory raise the song.

2 The wings of every hour shall bear
Some thankful tribute to thine ear;
And every setting sun shall see
New works of duty done for thee.

3 Let distant times and nations raise
The long succession of thy praise;
And unborn ages make my song
The joy and triumph of their tongue.

4 But who can speak thy wondrous deeds?
Thy greatness all our thoughts exceeds:
Vast and unsearchable thy ways!
Vast and immortal be thy praise!

WATTS.

141 L. M.

1 THE Lord is King! lift up thy voice,
O earth, and all ye heavens, rejoice!
From world to world the joy shall ring:
The Lord omnipotent is King!

2 The Lord is King! who then shall dare
Resist his will, distrust his care?
Holy and true are all his ways:
Let every creature speak his praise.

3 The Lord is King! exalt your strains,
Ye saints; your God, your Father reigns;

One Lord, one empire, all secures:
He reigns—and life and death are yours.

4 Oh, when his wisdom can mistake,
His might decay, his love forsake,
Then may his children cease to sing—
The Lord omnipotent is King!

CONDER.

142 L. M.

1 WITH all my powers of heart and tongue,
I'll praise my Maker in my song;
Angels shall hear the notes I raise,
Approve the song, and join the praise.

2 To God I cried when troubles rose;
He heard me, and subdued my foes:
He did my rising fears control,
And strength diffused through all my soul.

3 Amid a thousand snares, I stand
Upheld and guarded by thy hand;
Thy words my fainting soul revive,
And keep my dying faith alive.

WATTS.

143 L. M.

1 GREAT is the Lord! What tongue can frame,
An honor equal to his name?
How awful are his glorious ways!
The Lord is dreadful in his praise!

2 Thy glory, fearless of decline,
Thy glory, Lord, shall ever shine;
Thy praise shall still our breath employ
Till we shall rise to endless joy.

144 L. M.

1 COME, let our voices join to raise
A sacred song of solemn praise:
God is a sovereign King: rehearse
His honor in exalted verse.

2 Come, let our souls address the Lord,
Who framed our natures by his word:
He is our Shepherd: we, the sheep,
His mercy chose, his pastures keep.

3 Come, let us hear his voice to-day,
The counsels of his love obey;
Nor let our hardened hearts renew
The sins and plagues that Israel knew.

4 Come, let us turn, with holy fear,
To him who now invites us near;
Accept the offered grace to-day,
Nor lose the blessing by delay.

5 Come, seize the promise while it waits,
And march to Zion's heavenly gates;
Believe, and take the promised rest;
Obey, and be forever blest.

WATTS.

145 L. M.

1 SING to the Lord that built the skies,
The Lord that reared this stately frame;
Let all the nations sound his praise,
And lands unknown repeat his name.

2 He formed the seas, and formed the hills,
Made every drop and every dust,
Nature and time, with all their wheels,
And pushed them into motion first.

3 Now, from his high, imperial throne,
He looks far down upon the spheres;

He bids the shining orbs roll on,
And round he turns the hasty years.

4 Thus shall this moving engine last,
Till all his saints are gathered in;
Then for the trumpet's dreadful blast
To shake it all to dust again!

5 Yet, when the sound shall tear the skies,
And lightning burn the globe below,
Saints, you may lift your joyful eyes,
There's a new heaven and earth for you.

WATTS.

146 L. M.

1 THY works proclaim thy glory, Lord:
The blooming fields, the singing bird,
The tempests and the sunny hour,
Show forth thy goodness and thy power.

2 And when the setting sun declines,
I view thee in its brilliant lines:
Those tints so beautiful and bright
Teach me the Author of all light.

3 Great God, how should our worship rise
To thee, who formed the earth and skies!
The things that creep and things that fly
Are viewed by thine all-seeing eye.

4 Then will I still adore thy name,
Thou who forever art the same;
But yet thy grace and mercy, Lord,
Shine brightest in thy holy word.

147 L. M.

1 GOD is the refuge of his saints,
When storms of sharp distress invade;
Ere we can offer our complaints,
Behold him present with his aid.

2 Let mountains from their seats be hurl'd
Down to the deep and buried there,
Convulsions shake the solid world—
Our faith shall never yield to fear.

3 Loud may the troubled ocean roar;
In sacred peace our souls abide;
While every nation, every shore,
Trembles and dreads the swelling tide.

4 There is a stream whose gentle flow
Supplies the city of our God,
Life, love, and joy, still gliding through,
And watering our divine abode.

5 That sacred stream, thine holy word,
Our grief allays, our fear controls;
Sweet peace thy promises afford,
And give new strength to fainting souls.

6 Zion enjoys her Monarch's love,
Secure against a threatening hour;
Nor can her firm foundation move,
Built on his truth, and armed with power.

WATTS.

148 L. M.

1 MY God, I love and I adore;
But souls that love would know thee more:
Wilt thou forever hide, and stand
Behind the labors of thy hand?

2 Thy hand, great God, sustains the poles
On which this huge creation rolls;
The starry arch proclaims thy power;
Thy pencil glows in every flower.

3 Across the waves, around the sky,
There's not a spot, or deep or high,
Where the Creator has not trod,
And left the footsteps of a God.

4 Fain would I trace the immortal way
That leads to courts of endless day,
Where the Creator stands confessed,
In his own fairest glories dressed.

149 L. M.

1 THERE'S nothing bright, above, below,
From flowers that bloom to stars that glow,
But in its light my soul can see
Some features of the Deity.

2 There's nothing dark, below, above,
But in its gloom I trace thy love,
And meekly wait the moment when
Thy touch shall make all bright again.

3 The light, the dark, where'er I look,
Shall be one pure and shining book,
Where I may read, in words of flame,
The glories of thy wondrous name.

MOORE.

150 L. M.

1 GREAT God, indulge my humble claim;
Thou art my hope, my joy, my rest;
The glories that compose thy name
Stand all engaged to make me blest.

2 Thou great and good, thou just and wise,
Thou art my Father and my God;
And I am thine, by sacred ties,
Thy son, thy servant, bought with blood.

3 With early feet I love t' appear
Among thy saints, and seek thy face;
Oft have I seen thy glory there,
And felt the power of sovereign grace.

4 I'll lift my hands, I'll raise my voice,
While I have breath to pray or praise;
This work shall make my heart rejoice,
And bless the remnant of my days.

WATTS.

151 L. M.

1 THOU, Lord, who rear'st the mountain's height,
And mak'st the cliffs with sunshine bright,
Oh, grant that we may own thy hand
No less in every grain of sand!

2 With forests huge, of dateless time,
Thy will has hung each peak sublime;
But withered leaves beneath the tree
Have tongues that tell as loud of thee.

3 Teach us that not a leaf can grow
Till life from thee within it flow;
That not a grain of dust can be,
O Fount of being, save by thee!

STERLING.

152 L. M.

1 GREAT Former of this various frame,
Our souls adore thine awful name,
And bow and tremble, while they praise
The Ancient of eternal days.

2 Our days a transient period run
And change with every circling sun;
And, in the firmest state we boast,
Before the moth we sink to dust.

3 But let the creatures fall around;
Let death consign us to the ground;
Let the last general flame arise,
And melt the arches of the skies;—

4 Calm as the summer's ocean, we
Can all the wreck of nature see,
While grace secures us an abode
Unshaken as the throne of God.

DODDRIDGE.

153 L. M.

1 WAIT, O my soul! thy Maker's will;
Tumultuous passions, all be still!
Nor let a murmuring thought arise;
His ways are just, his counsels wise.

2 He in the thickest darkness dwells,
Performs his work, the cause conceals;
But, though his methods are unknown,
Judgment and truth support his throne.

3 In heaven, and earth, and air, and seas,
He executes his firm decrees;
And by his saints it stands confessed,
That what he does is ever best.

BEDDOME.

154 L. M.

1 LORD, from thy unexhausted store,
Thy rain relieves the thirsty ground,
Makes lands that barren were before,
With corn and useful fruits abound.

2 On rising ridges down it pours,
And every furrowed valley fills:
Thou mak'st them soft with gentle showers,
In which a blest increase distils.

3 Thy goodness does the circling year
With fresh returns of plenty crown;
And where thy glorious paths appear,
The fruitful clouds drop fatness down.

4 They drop on barren deserts, changed
By them to pastures fresh and green:
The hills about, in order ranged,
In beauteous robes of joy are seen.

5 Large flocks with fleecy wool adorn
The cheerful downs; the valleys bring
A plenteous crop of full-eared corn,
And seem, for joy, to shout and sing.

155 L. M.

1 PRAISE, Lord, for thee in Zion waits;
Prayer shall besiege thy temple gates;
All flesh shall to thy throne repair,
And find through Christ salvation there.

2 How blest thy saints! how safely led!
How surely kept! how richly fed!

Saviour of all in earth and sea,
How happy they who rest in thee.

3 The year is with thy goodness crowned;
Thy clouds drop wealth the world around;
Through thee the deserts laugh and sing,
And nature smiles and owns her King.

4 Lord, on our souls thy Spirit pour;
The moral waste within restore;
Oh, let thy love our spring-tide be,
And make us all bear fruit to thee!

156 L. M.

1 JUST are thy ways, and true thy word,
Great Rock of my secure abode;
Who is a God, beside the Lord?
Or where's a refuge like our God?

2 'Tis he that girds me with his might,
Gives me his holy sword to wield;
And while with sin and hell I fight,
Spreads his salvation for my shield.

3 He lives, and blessèd be my Rock;
The God of my salvation lives;
The dark designs of hell he broke:
Sweet is the peace my Father gives.

157 L. M

1 WITH glory clad, with strength arrayed,
The Lord, that o'er all nature reigns,
The world's foundation strongly laid,
And the vast fabric still sustains.

2 How sure established is thy throne!
Which shall no change or period see;
For thou, O Lord, and thou alone,
Art God from all eternity.

3 The floods, O Lord, lift up their voice,
And toss the troubled waves on high;
But God above can still their noise,
And make the angry sea comply.

158 L. M.

1 WHAT finite power, with ceaseless toil,
Can fathom the eternal mind?
Or who the Almighty Three in One,
By searching to perfection find?

2 Angels and men in vain may raise,
Harmonious, their adoring songs;
The laboring thought sinks down oppressed,
And praises die upon their tongues.

3 Yet would I lift my trembling voice,
A portion of his ways to sing;
And mingling with his meanest works,
My humble, grateful tribute bring.

E. SCOTT.

159 L. M.

1 O THOU, by long experience tried,
Near whom no grief can long abide;
My Lord, how full of sweet content
My years of pilgrimage are spent.

2 All scenes alike engaging prove,
To souls impressed with sacred love;
Where'er they dwell, they dwell in thee,
In heaven, in earth, or on the sea.

3 To them remains nor place nor time;
Their country is in every clime;

They can be calm and free from care
On any shore, since God is there.

4 While place we seek or place we shun,
The soul finds happiness in none;
But with our God to guide our way,
'Tis equal joy to go or stay.

5 Could I be cast where thou art not,
That were indeed a dreadful lot;
But regions none remote I call,
Secure of finding God in all.

GUION.

160 L. M.

1 NO change of time shall ever shock
My firm affection, Lord, to thee;
For thou hast always been my Rock,
A Fortress and Defence to me.

2 Thou my Deliverer art, O God;
My trust is in thy mighty power,
Thou art my Shield from foes abroad,
At home my Safeguard and my Tower.

3 To thee will I address my prayer,
To whom all praise we justly owe;
So shall I, by thy watchful care,
Be guarded safe from every foe.

TATE & BRADY.

161 L. M.

1 THROUGH every age, eternal God,
Thou art our rest, our safe abode:
High was thy throne ere heaven was made,
Or earth, thy humble footstool, laid.

2 Long hadst thou reign'd ere time began,
Or dust was fashioned into man;
And long thy kingdom shall endure,
When earth and time shall be no more.

3 But man, weak man, is born to die,
Made up of guilt and vanity;
Thy dreadful sentence, Lord, was just:
"Return, ye sinners, to your dust."

4 Death, like an overflowing stream,
Sweeps us away; our life's a dream—
An empty tale—a morning flower,
Cut down and withered in an hour.

5 Teach us, O Lord, how frail is man;
And kindly lengthen out our span,
Till a wise care of piety
Fit us to die and dwell with thee.

WATTS.

162 L. M.

1 GOD of my life, through all my days
My grateful powers shall sound thy praise;
The song shall wake with opening light,
And warble to the silent night.

2 When anxious care would break my rest,
And grief would tear my throbbing breast,
Thy tuneful praises, raised on high,
Shall check the murmur and the sigh.

3 When death o'er nature shall prevail,
And all my powers of language fail,
Joy through my swimming eyes shall break,
And mean the thanks I cannot speak.

4 But, oh, when that last conflict's o'er,
And I am chained to flesh no more,
With what glad accents shall I rise
To join the music of the skies!

5 Soon shall I learn the exalted strains
Which echo o'er the heavenly plains,
And emulate, with joy unknown,
The glowing seraphs round the throne.

DODDRIDGE.

163 L. M.

1 JEHOVAH reigns, his throne is high,
His robes are light and majesty;
His glory shines with beams so bright,
No mortal can sustain the sight.

2 His terrors keep the world in awe,
His justice guards his holy law,
His love reveals a smiling face,
His truth and promise seal the grace.

3 Through all his works what wisdom shines!
He baffles Satan's deep designs;
His power is sovereign to fulfill
The noblest counsels of his will.

4 Thus glorious, will he condescend
To be my Father and my Friend?
Then let my songs with angels join,
Heaven is secure, if God is mine.

WATTS.

164 L. M.

1 LORD, how mysterious are thy ways!
How blind are we! how mean our praise!
Thy steps, can mortal eyes explore?
'Tis ours to wonder and adore.

2 Great God! I would not ask to see
What in my coming life shall be;
Enough for me if love divine,
At length through every cloud shall shine.

3 Are darkness and distress my share?
Then let me trust thy guardian care;
If light and bliss attend my days,
Then let my future hours be praise.

4 Yet this my soul desires to know,
Be this my only wish below,
That Christ be mine;—this great request
Grant, bounteous God, and I am blest!

STEELE.

165 L. M.

1 THE Lord! how wondrous are his ways!
How firm his truth! how large his grace!
He takes his mercy for his throne,
And thence he makes his glories known.

2 Not half so high his power hath spread
The starry heavens above our head,
As his rich love exceeds our praise,
Exceeds the highest hopes we raise.

3 Not half so far has nature placed
The rising morning from the west,
As his forgiving grace removes
The daily guilt of those he loves.

4 How slowly doth his wrath arise!
On swifter wings salvation flies:
Or, if he lets his anger burn,
How soon his frowns to pity turn?

5 His everlasting love is sure
To all his saints, and shall endure;
From age to age his truth shall reign,
Nor children's children hope in vain.

WATTS.

166

L. M.

1 LORD of all being; throned afar,
Thy glory flames from sun and star;
Centre and soul of every sphere,
Yet to each loving heart how near!

2 Sun of our life, thy quickening ray
Sheds on our path the glow of day;
Star of our hope, thy softened light
Cheers the long watches of the night.

3 Our midnight is thy smile withdrawn;
Our noontide is thy gracious dawn;
Our rainbow arch thy mercy's sign;
All, save the clouds of sin, are thine!

4 Lord of all life, below, above,
Whose light is truth, whose warmth is love,
Before thy ever-blazing throne
We ask no lustre of our own.

5 Grant us thy truth to make us free,
And kindling hearts that burn for thee,
Till all thy loving altars claim
One holy light, one heavenly flame!

O. W. HOLMES.

167

L. M.

1 GOD of the world! thy glories shine,
Through earth and heaven, with rays divine:
Thy smile gives beauty to the flower,
Thine anger to the tempest power.

2 God of our lives! the throbbing heart
Doth at thy beck its action start—
Throbs on, obedient to thy will,
Or ceases, at thy fatal chill.

3 God of eternal life! thy love
Doth every stain of sin remove;
The cross, the cross—its hallowed light
Shall drive from earth her cheerless night.

4 God of all goodness! to the skies
Our hearts in grateful anthems rise;
And to thy service shall be given
The rest of life—the whole of heaven.

S. S. CUTTING.

168

L. M.

1 HIGH in the heavens, eternal God!
Thy goodness in full glory shines;
Thy truth shall break through every cloud
That vails and darkens thy designs.

2 Forever firm thy justice stands,
As mountains their foundations keep:
Wise are the wonders of thy hands;
Thy judgments are a mighty deep.

3 My God, how excellent thy grace!
Whence all our hope and comfort springs;
The sons of Adam, in distress,
Fly to the shadow of thy wings.

4 From the provisions of thy house
We shall be fed with sweet repast;
There, mercy like a river flows,
And brings salvation to our taste.

5 Life, like a fountain rich and free,
Springs from the presence of my Lord;
And in thy light our souls shall see
The glories promised in thy word.

WATTS.

169 L. M.

1 LORD God of hosts, by all adored!
Thy name we praise with one accord;
The earth and heavens are full of thee,
Thy light, thy love, thy majesty.

2 Loud hallelujahs to thy name
Angels and seraphim proclaim;
Eternal praise to thee is given
By all the pow'rs and thrones in heav'n.

3 Th' apostles join the glorious throng,
The prophets aid to swell the song,
The noble and triumphant host
Of martyrs make of thee their boast.

4 The holy church in every place
Throughout the world exalts thy praise;
Both heav'n and earth do worship thee,
Thou Father of eternity!

5 From day to day, O Lord, do we
Highly exalt and honor thee;
Thy name we worship and adore,
World without end, forevermore.

170 L. P. M.

1 I'LL praise my Maker with my breath;
And when my voice is lost in death,
Praise shall employ my nobler powers;
My days of praise shall ne'er be past,
While life, and thought, and being last,
Or immortality endures.

2 Happy the man whose hopes rely
On Israel's God; he made the sky
And earth and seas, with all their train;
His truth forever stands secure,
He saves th' opprest, he feeds the poor,
And none shall find his promise vain.

3 He loves his saints, he knows them well;
But turns the wicked down to hell;
Thy God, O Zion! ever reigns;
Let every tongue, let every age,
In this exalted work engage:
Praise him in everlasting strains.

4 I'll praise him while he lends me breath;
And when my voice is lost in death,
Praise shall employ my nobler powers;
My days of praise shall ne'er be past
While life and thought and being last,
Or immortality endures.

WATTS.

171 L. P. M.

1 LET all the earth their voices raise,
To sing the choicest psalm of praise;
To sing and bless Jehovah's name:
His glory let the heathen know;
His wonders to the nations show;
And all his saving works proclaim.

2 He framed the globe, he built the sky,
He made the shining worlds on high,
And reigns complete in glory there.
His beams are majesty and light;
His beauties, how divinely bright!
His temple, how divinely fair!

3 Come the great day, the glorious hour,
When earth shall feel his saving power,
And heathen nations fear his name!
Then shall the race of man confess
The beauty of his holiness,
And in his courts his grace proclaim.

WATTS.

172 C. M.

1 O GOD! our help in ages past,
Our hope for years to come,
Our shelter from the stormy blast,
And our eternal home!

2 Before the hills in order stood,
Or earth received her frame,
From everlasting thou art God,
To endless years the same.

3 A thousand ages in thy sight
Are like an evening gone—
Short as the watch that ends the night
Before the rising sun.

4 Time, like an ever-rolling stream,
Bears all its sons away;
They fly, forgotten, as a dream
Dies at the opening day.

5 O God! our help in ages past,
Our hope for years to come,
Be thou our guide while troubles last,
And our eternal home.

WATTS.

173 C. M.

1 GREAT God, how infinite art thou!
What worthless worms are we!
Let all the race of creatures bow,
And pay their praise to thee.

2 Thy throne eternal ages stood,
Ere seas or stars were made;
Thou art the ever-living God,
Were all the nations dead.

3 Eternity, with all its years,
Stands present in thy view;
To thee there's nothing old appears,
Great God, there's nothing new.

4 Our lives through various scenes are drawn,
And vexed with trifling cares,
While thine eternal thought moves on
Thine undisturbed affairs.

5 Great God, how infinite art thou!
What worthless worms are we!
Let all the race of creatures bow,
And pay their praise to thee.

WATTS.

174 C. M.

1 HOLY and reverend is the name
Of our eternal King;
Thrice holy Lord! the angels cry;
Thrice holy! let us sing.

2 The deepest reverence of the mind,
Pay, O my soul! to God;
Lift with thy hands a holy heart
To his sublime abode.

3 With sacred awe pronounce his name
Whom words nor thoughts can reach;
A broken heart shall please him more
Than the best forms of speech.

4 Thou holy God! preserve our souls
From all pollution free:
The pure in heart are thy delight,
And they thy face shall see.

NEEDHAM.

175 C.M.

1 I SING th' almighty power of God,
That made the mountains rise,
That spread the flowing seas abroad,
And built the lofty skies.

2 I sing the wisdom that ordained
The sun to rule the day;

The moon shines full at his command,
And all the stars obey.

3 I sing the goodness of the Lord,
That filled the earth with food;
He formed the creatures with his word,
And then pronounced them good.

4 Lord! how thy wonders are displayed
Where'er I turn mine eye!
If I survey the ground I tread,
Or gaze upon the sky!

5 There's not a plant or flower below
But makes thy glories known;
And clouds arise, and tempests blow,
By order from thy throne.

6 Creatures that borrow life from thee
Are subject to thy care;
There's not a place where we can flee
But God is present there.

WATTS.

176 C. M.

1 THE Lord our God is Lord of all;
His station who can find?
I hear him in the waterfall;
I hear him in the wind.

2 If in the gloom of night I shroud,
His face I cannot fly;
I see him in the evening cloud,
And in the morning sky.

3 He smiles, we live! he frowns, we die!
We hang upon his word;
He rears his mighty arm on high,
We fall before his sword.

4 He bids his gales the fields deform;
Then, when his thunders cease,
He paints his rainbow on the storm,
And lulls the winds to peace.

H. K. WHITE.

177 C. M.

1 LORD! when my raptured thought surveys
Creation's beauties o'er,
All nature joins to teach thy praise,
And bid my soul adore.

2 Where'er I turn my gazing eyes,
Thy radiant footsteps shine;
Ten thousand pleasing wonders rise,
And speak their source divine.

3 On me thy providence hath shone
With gentle, smiling rays;
Oh! let my lips and life make known
Thy goodness and thy praise.

4 All-bounteous Lord! thy grace impart;
Oh! teach me to improve
Thy gifts, with ever-grateful heart,
And crown them with thy love.

MRS. STEELE.

178 C. M.

1 SOME seraph, lend your heavenly tongue,
Or harp of golden string,
That I may raise a lofty song
To our eternal King.

2 Thy names, how infinite they be!
Great Everlasting One!
Boundless thy might and majesty,
And unconfined thy throne.

3 Thy glory shines immensely bright;
Exhaustless is thy grace;
Immortal day breaks from thine eyes,
And Gabriel veils his face.

4 Thine essence is a vast abyss,
Which angels cannot sound;
An ocean of infinities
Where all our thoughts are drown'd.

WATTS.

179 C. M.

1 FATHER! how wide thy glory shines!
How high thy wonders rise!
Known through the earth by thousand signs—
By thousand through the skies.

2 Those mighty orbs proclaim thy pow'r,
Their motions speak thy skill;
And on the wings of every hour
We read thy patience still.

3 But when we view thy strange design
To save rebellious worms,
Where vengeance and compassion join
In their divinest forms.

4 Here the whole Deity is known;
Nor dares a creature guess
Which of the glories brightest shone,
The justice or the grace.

5 Now the full glories of the Lamb
Adorn the heavenly plains:
Bright seraphs learn Immanuel's name,
And try their choicest strains.

6 Oh! may I bear some humble part,
In that immortal song;
Wonder and joy shall tune my heart,
And love command my tongue.

WATTS.

180 C. M.

THERE'S not a star whose twinkling light
Illumes the distant earth,
And cheers the solemn gloom of night,
But goodness gave it birth.

2 There's not a cloud whose dews distill
Upon the parching clod,
And clothe with verdure vale and hill,
That is not sent by God.

3 There's not a place in earth's vast round,
In ocean deep, or air,
Where skill and wisdom are not found;
For God is everywhere.

4 Around, beneath, below, above,
Wherever space extends,
There Heaven displays its boundless love,
And power with goodness blends.

WALLACE.

181 C. M.

1 IN all my vast concerns with thee,
In vain my soul would try
To shun thy presence, Lord, or flee
The notice of thine eye.

2 Thine all-surrounding sight surveys
My rising and my rest,
My public walks, my private ways,
And secrets of my breast.

3 My thoughts lie open to the Lord,
Before they're formed within;
And ere my lips pronounce the word,
He knows the sense I mean.

4 Oh, wondrous knowledge, deep and high!
Where can a creature hide?
Within thy circling arms I lie,
Enclosed on every side.

5 So let thy grace surround me still,
And like a bulwark prove,
To guard my soul from every ill,
Secured by sovereign love.

WATTS.

182

C. M.

1 JEHOVAH God! thy gracious power
On every hand we see;
Oh, may the blessings of each hour
Lead all our thoughts to thee!

2 If, on the wings of morn, we speed
To earth's remotest bound,
Thy right hand will our footsteps lead,
Thine arm our path surround.

3 Thy power is in the ocean deeps,
And reaches to the skies;
Thine eye of mercy never sleeps,
Thy goodness never dies.

4 From morn till noon, till latest eve,
The hand of God we see;
And all the blessings we receive,
Ceaseless proceed from thee.

5 In all the varying scenes of time,
On thee our hopes depend;
In every age, in every clime,
Our Father and our Friend.

THOMSON.

183

C. M.

1 THY way, O Lord, is in the sea;
Thy paths I cannot trace,
Nor comprehend the mystery
Of thine unbounded grace.

2 As, through a glass, I dimly see
The wonders of thy love;
How little do I know of thee,
Or of the joys above!

3 'Tis but in part I know thy will;
I bless thee for the sight:
When will thy love the rest reveal,
In glory's clearer light?

4 With rapture shall I then survey
Thy providence and grace;
And spend an everlasting day
In wonder, love, and praise.

FAWCETT.

184

C. M.

1 THE Lord, our God, is full of might,
The winds obey his will;
He speaks,—and in his heavenly height,
The rolling sun stands still.

2 Rebel, ye waves, and o'er the land
With threatening aspect roar;
The Lord uplifts his awful hand,
And chains you to the shore.

3 Howl, winds of night, your force combine;
Without his high behest,
Ye shall not, in the mountain pine,
Disturb the sparrow's nest.

4 His voice sublime is heard afar,
In distant peals it dies;
He yokes the whirlwind to his car,
And sweeps the howling skies.

5 Ye nations, bend—in reverence bend;
Ye monarchs, wait his nod,
And bid the choral song ascend,
To celebrate your God.

H. K. WHITE.

185

C. M.

1 THE Lord, how fearful is his name!
How wide is his command!
Nature, with all her moving frame,
Rests on his mighty hand.

2 Immortal glory forms his throne,
And light his awful robe;
While with a smile, or with a frown,
He manages the globe.

3 A word of his almighty breath
Can swell or sink the seas;
Build the vast empires of the earth,
Or break them as he please.

4 On angels, with unveilèd face
His glory beams above;
On men, he looks with softest grace,
And takes his title, Love.

WATTS.

186

C. M.

1 KEEP silence, all created things!
And wait your Maker's nod;
My soul stands trembling, while she sings
The honors of her God.

2 Life, death, and hell, and worlds unknown,
Hang on his firm decree;
He sits on no precarious throne,
Nor borrows leave to be.

3 His providence unfolds the book,
And makes his counsels shine;
Each opening leaf, and every stroke,
Fulfills some deep design.

4 My God! I would not long to see
My fate, with curious eyes—
What gloomy lines are writ for me,
Or what bright scenes may rise.

5 In thy fair book of life and grace,
Oh! may I find my name
Recorded in some humble place,
Beneath my Lord, the Lamb.

WATTS.

187

C. M.

1 ETERNAL Wisdom! thee we praise;
Thee with creation sing;
With thy lov'd name, rocks, hills, and seas,
And heaven's high palace ring.

2 How wide thy hand hath spread the sky!
How glorious to behold!
Tinged with a blue of heavenly dye,
And starred with sparkling gold.

3 Infinite strength, and equal skill,
Shine through the worlds abroad,
Our souls with vast amazement fill,
And speak the builder, God.

4 But still the wonders of thy grace
Our softer passions move;
Pity divine in Jesus' face
We see, adore, and love.

WATTS.

188

C. M.

1 GREAT Ruler of all nature's frame!
We own thy power divine;
We hear thy breath in every storm,
For all the winds are thine.

2 Wide as they sweep their sounding way
They work thy sovereign will;
And, awed by thy majestic voice,
Confusion shall be still.

3 Thy mercy tempers every blast
To them that seek thy face,
And mingles with the tempest's roar
The whispers of thy grace.

4 Those gentle whispers let me hear,
Till all the tumult cease;
And gales of Paradise shall lull
My weary soul to peace.

DODDRIDGE.

189 C. M.

1 THY goodness, Lord, our souls confess,
Thy goodness we adore;
A spring whose blessings never fail,
A sea without a shore!

2 Sun, moon, and stars, thy love attest
In every golden ray;
Love draws the curtains of the night,
And love brings back the day.

3 Thy bounty every season crowns
With all the bliss it yields,
With joyful clusters loads the vines,
With strengthening grain, the fields.

4 But chiefly thy compassion, Lord,
Is in the gospel seen;
There, like a sun, thy mercy shines
Without a cloud between.

5 Pardon, acceptance, peace, and joy,
Through Jesus' name are given;
He on the cross was lifted high
That we might reign in heaven.

GIBBONS.

190 C. M.

1 PRAISE ye the Lord, immortal choir!
In heavenly heights above,
With harp, and voice, and soul of fire,
Burning with perfect love.

2 Shine to his glory, worlds of light!
Ye million suns of space;
Ye moons and glistening stars of night
Running your mystic race.

3 Shout to Jehovah, surging main!
In deep eternal roar;
Let wave to wave resound the strain,
And shore reply to shore.

4 Storm, lightning, thunder, hail, and snow,
Wild winds that keep his word,
With the old mountains far below,
Unite to bless the Lord.

5 And round the wide world let it roll,
Whilst man shall lead it on;
Join, every ransomed human soul,
In glorious unison.

191 C. M.

1 COME, shout aloud the Father's grace,
And sing the Saviour's love;
Soon shall we join the glorious theme,
In loftier strains above.

2 God, the eternal, mighty God,
To dearer names descends;
Calls us his treasure and his joy,
His children and his friends.

3 My Father, God! and may these lips
Pronounce a name so dear?
Not thus could heaven's sweet harmony
Delight my listening ear.

4 Thanks to my God for every gift
His bounteous hands bestow;
And thanks eternal for that love
Whence all those comforts flow.

HIGGINBOTHAM.

192 C. M.

1 WITH songs and honors sounding loud,
Address the Lord on high;
Over the heavens he spreads his cloud,
And waters vail the sky.

2 He sends his showers of blessings down,
To cheer the plains below;
He makes the grass the mountains crown,
And corn in valleys grow.

3 His steady counsels change the face
Of the declining year;
He bids the sun cut short his race,
And wintry days appear.

4 His hoary frost, his fleecy snow,
Descend and clothe the ground;
The liquid streams forbear to flow,
In icy fetters bound.

5 He sends his word and melts the snow,
The fields no longer mourn;
He calls the warmer gales to blow,
And bids the spring return.

WATTS.

193 C. M.

1 GOD moves in a mysterious way
His wonders to perform;
He plants his footsteps in the sea,
And rides upon the storm.

2 Deep in unfathomable mines
Of never-failing skill,
He treasures up his vast designs,
And works his sovereign will.

3 Ye fearful saints, fresh courage take;
The clouds ye so much dread
Are big with mercy, and will break
In blessings on your head.

4 Judge not the Lord by feeble sense,
But trust him for his grace;
Behind a frowning providence
He hides a smiling face.

5 His purposes will ripen fast,
Unfolding every hour;
The bud may have a bitter taste,
But sweet will be the flower.

6 Blind unbelief is sure to err,
And scan his work in vain;
God is his own interpreter,
And he will make it plain.

COWPER.

194 C. M.

1 GOD is a Spirit, just and wise;
He sees our inmost mind;
In vain to heaven we raise our cries
And leave our hearts behind.

2 Nothing but truth before his throne
With honor can appear;
The painted hypocrites are known,
Whate'er the guise they wear.

3 Their lifted eyes salute the skies,
Their bending knees the ground;
But God abhors the sacrifice
Where not the heart is found.

4 Lord, search my thoughts, and try my ways,
And make my soul sincere;
Then shall I stand before thy face,
And find acceptance there.

WATTS.

195 C. M.

1 THROUGH endless years thou art the same,
O thou eternal God;
Each future age shall know thy name,
And tell thy works abroad.

2 The strong foundations of the earth
Of old by thee were laid;
By thee the beauteous arch of heaven
With matchless skill was made.

3 Soon shall this goodly frame of things,
Created by thy hand,
Be, like a vesture, laid aside,
And changed at thy command.

4 But thy perfections, all divine,
Eternal as thy days,
Through everlasting ages shine,
With undiminished rays.

196 C. M.

1 BEGIN, my tongue, some heavenly theme,
And speak some boundless thing;
The mighty works, or mightier name,
Of our eternal King.

2 Tell of his wondrous faithfulness,
And sound his power abroad;
Sing the sweet promise of his grace,
And the performing God.

3 His every word of grace is strong,
As that which built the skies;
The voice that rolls the stars along,
Speaks all the promises.

4 Oh, might I hear thy heavenly tongue
But whisper, "Thou art mine!"
Those gentle words should raise my song,
To notes almost divine.

WATTS.

197 C. M.

1 HOW dread are thine eternal years,
O everlasting Lord!
By prostrate spirits day and night
Incessantly adored!

2 Yet I may love thee too, O Lord!
Almighty as thou art,
For thou hast stooped to ask of me,
The love of my poor heart.

3 No earthly father loves like thee,
No mother half so mild
Bears and forbears as thou hast done
With me, thy sinful child.

4 Only to sit and think of God—
Oh, what a joy it is!
To think the thought, to breathe the name,
Earth has no higher bliss!

5 Father of Jesus! love's reward!
What rapture will it be,
Prostrate before thy throne to lie,
And gaze and gaze on thee!

LYRA CATH.

198 C. M.

1 O GOD of Bethel! by whose hand
Thy people still are fed;
Who through this weary pilgrimage
Hast all our fathers led;—

2 Our vows, our prayers, we now present
Before thy throne of grace;
God of our fathers! be the God
Of their succeeding race.

3 Through each perplexing path of life
Our wandering footsteps guide:
Give us each day our daily bread,
And raiment fit provide.

4 Oh spread thy covering wings around,
Till all our wanderings cease,
And, at our Father's loved abode,
Our souls arrive in peace.

5 Such blessings from thy gracious hand
Our humble prayers implore;
And thou shalt be our chosen God
And portion evermore.

LOGAN.

199 C. M.

1 TO thee, my righteous King and Lord,
My grateful soul I'll raise;
From day to day thy works record,
And ever sing thy praise.

2 Thy greatness human thought exceeds;
Thy glory knows no end;
The lasting record of thy deeds
Through ages shall descend.

3 Thy wondrous acts, thy power, and might,
My constant theme shall be;
That song shall be my soul's delight,
Which breathes in praise to thee.

4 The Lord is bountiful and kind,
His anger slow to move:
His tender mercies all shall find,
And all his goodness prove.

5 From all thy works, O Lord, shall spring
The sound of joy and praise;
Thy saints shall of thy glory sing,
And show the world thy ways.

6 Throughout all ages shall endure
Thine everlasting reign;
And thy dominion, firm and sure,
Forever shall remain.

WRANGHAM.

200 C. M.

1 SWEET is the memory of thy grace,
My God, my heavenly King;
Let age to age thy righteousness
In songs of glory sing.

2 God reigns on high, but ne'er confines
His goodness to the skies;
Through the whole earth his bounty shines,
And every want supplies.

3 With longing eyes thy creatures wait
On thee for daily food,
Thy lib'ral hand provides their meat,
And fills their mouth with good.

4 Creatures with all their endless race,
Thy power and praise proclaim;
But saints that taste thy richer grace
Delight to bless thy name.

WATTS.

201 C. M.

1 ALMIGHTY Father of mankind!
On thee my hopes remain;
And when the day of trouble comes,
I shall not trust in vain.

2 In early years, thou wast my guide,
And of my youth, the friend;
And, as my days began with thee,
With thee my days shall end.

3 Therefore, in life I'll trust in thee;
In death I will adore;
And after death will sing thy praise,
When time shall be no more.

202 C. M.

1 THROUGH all the changing scenes of life,
In trouble and in joy,
The praises of my God shall still
My heart and tongue employ.

2 The hosts of God encamp around
The dwellings of the just;
Deliverance he affords to all
Who on his succor trust.

3 Oh, make but trial of his love!
Experience will decide
How blest are they, and only they,
Who in his truth confide.

4 Fear him, ye saints, and you will then
Have nothing else to fear;
Make you his service your delight;
He'll make your wants his care.

TATE & BRADY.

203 C. M.

1 WHAT shall I render to my God
For all his kindness shown?
My feet shall visit thine abode,
My songs address thy throne.

2 Among the saints that fill thy house,
My offerings shall be paid;
There shall my zeal perform the vows
My soul in anguish made.

3 How much is mercy thy delight,
Thou ever-blessèd God!
How dear thy servants in thy sight!
How precious is their blood!

4 How happy all thy servants are!
How great thy grace to me!
My life, which thou hast made thy care,
Lord, I devote to thee.

5 Now I am thine, forever thine,
Nor shall my purpose move;
Thy hand hath loosed my bonds of pain,
And bound me with thy love.

6 Here in thy courts I leave my vow,
And thy rich grace record;
Witness, ye saints, who hear me now,
If I forsake the Lord.

WATTS.

204 C. M.

1 TO heaven I lift my waiting eyes;
There all my hopes are laid;
The Lord that built the earth and skies
Is my perpetual aid.

2 Their steadfast feet shall never fall
Whom he designs to keep;
His ear attends the softest call,
His eyes can never sleep.

3 Israel, rejoice, and rest secure;
Thy keeper is the Lord;
His wakeful eyes employ his power
For thine eternal guard.

4 He guards thy soul, he keeps thy breath,
Where thickest dangers come;
Go and return, secure from death,
Till God commands thee home.

WATTS.

205 C. M.

1 WHEN all thy mercies, O my God,
My rising soul surveys,
Transported with the view, I'm lost
In wonder, love, and praise.

2 Unnumbered comforts on my soul
Thy tender care bestowed,
Before my infant heart conceived
From whom those comforts flowed.

3 When in the slippery path of youth
With heedless steps I ran,
Thine arm, unseen, conveyed me safe,
And led me up to man.

4 Ten thousand thousand precious gifts
My daily thanks employ;
Nor is the least a cheerful heart,
That tastes those gifts with joy.

5 Through every period of my life,
Thy goodness I'll pursue;
And after death, in distant worlds,
The glorious theme renew.

6 Through all eternity, to thee
A joyful song I'll raise:
But oh! eternity's too short
To utter all thy praise!

ADDISON.

206 C. M.

1 LONG as I live I'll bless thy name,
My King! my God of love!
My work and joy shall be the same
In the bright world above.

2 Great is the Lord, his pow'r unknown,
And let his praise be great;
I'll sing the honors of thy throne,
Thy works of grace repeat.

3 Thy grace shall dwell upon my tongue,
And, while my lips rejoice,
The men who hear my sacred song
Shall join their cheerful voice.

4 Fathers to sons shall teach thy name,
And children learn thy ways;
Ages to come thy truth proclaim,
And nations sound thy praise.

WATTS.

207 C. M.

1 GOD, in the high and holy place,
Looks down upon the spheres;
Yet in his providence and grace,
To every eye appears.

2 He bows the heavens; the mountains stand
A highway for our God,
He walks amid the desert land;
'Tis Eden where he trod.

3 The forests in his strength rejoice;
Hark! on the evening breeze,
As once of old, Jehovah's voice
Is heard among the trees.

4 If God hath made this world so fair,
Where sin and death abound;
How beautiful, beyond compare,
Will Paradise be found!

MONTGOMERY.

208 C. M.

1 COME, ye that know and fear the Lord,
And raise your souls above;
Let every heart and voice accord
To sing that—God is love.

2 This precious truth his word declares,
And all his mercies prove;
While Christ, th' atoning Lamb, appears,
To show that—God is love.

3 Behold his loving-kindness waits
For those who from him rove,
And calls for mercy reach their hearts,
To teach them—God is love.

4 The work begun is carried on,
By power from heaven above;
And every step, from first to last,
Proclaims that—God is love.

5 Oh! may we all, while here below,
This best of blessings prove;
Till warmer hearts, in brighter worlds,
Shall shout that—God is love.

G. BURDER.

209 C. M.

1 SOVEREIGN of all the worlds on high,
Allow my humble claim;
Nor, while a worm would raise its head,
Disdain a Father's name.

2 My Father God! how sweet the sound!
How tender and how dear!
Not all the melody of heaven,
Could so delight the ear.

3 Come, sacred Spirit, seal the name
On my expanding heart;
And show, that in Jehovah's grace
I share a filial part.

4 Cheer'd by a signal so divine,
Unwavering I believe;
And Abba, Father, humbly cry,
Nor can the sign deceive.

DODDRIDGE.

210 C. M.

1 SING to the Lord Jehovah's name,
And in his strength rejoice;
When his salvation is our theme,
Exalted be our voice.

2 With thanks approach his awful sight,
And psalms of honor sing:
The Lord 's a God of boundless might,
The whole creation's King.

3 Earth, with its caverns dark and deep,
Lies in his spacious hand;
He fixed the sea what bounds to keep,
And where the hills must stand.

4 Come, and with humble souls adore,
Come, kneel before his face;
Oh, may the creatures of his power
Be children of his grace!

5 Now is the time—he bends his ear,
And waits for your request;
Come, lest he rouse his wrath and swear
"Ye shall not see my rest."

WATTS.

211 C. M.

1 SINCE all the varying scenes of time
God's watchful eye surveys,
Oh, who so wise to choose our lot,
Or to appoint our ways?

2 Good when he gives, supremely good,
Nor less when he denies;
E'en crosses, from his sovereign hand,
Are blessings in disguise.

3 Why should we doubt a Father's love,
So constant and so kind?

To his unerring, gracious will
Be every wish resigned.

4 In thy fair book of life divine,
My God, inscribe my name;
There let it fill some humble place.
Beneath my Lord, the Lamb.

HERVEY.

212 C. M.

1 GOD, my supporter and my hope,
My help for ever near,
Thine arm of mercy held me up,
When sinking in despair.

2 Thy counsels, Lord, shall guide my feet
Through this dark wilderness:
Thy hand conduct me near thy seat,
To dwell before thy face.

3 Were I in heaven without my God,
'T would be no heav'n to me;
And while this earth is my abode,
I long for none but thee.

4 What if the springs of life were broke,
And flesh and heart should faint?
God is my soul's eternal rock,
The strength of every saint.

5 But to draw near to thee, my God,
Shall be my sweet employ:
My tongue shall sound thy works abroad
And tell the world my joy.

WATTS.

213 C. M.

1 YES, I will bless thee, O my God!
Through all my earthly days;
And to eternity prolong
Thy vast, thy boundless praise.

2 In every smiling, happy hour,
Be this my sweet employ:
Thy praise refines my earthly bliss,
And doubles all my joy.

3 When gloomy care, and keen distress
Afflict my throbbing breast,
Thy praise shall mingle with my tears,
And lull each pain to rest.

4 Nor shall my tongue alone proclaim
The honors of my God:
My life, with all its active powers,
Shall spread thy praise abroad.

5 Nor death itself shall stop my song,
Though it will close my eyes:
My thoughts shall then to nobler heights
And sweeter raptures rise.

HEGINBOTHAM.

214 C. M.

1 YE humble souls, approach your God
With songs of sacred praise;
For he is good, supremely good,
And kind are all his ways.

2 All nature owns his guardian care,
In him we live and move;
But nobler benefits declare
The wonders of his love.

3 He gave his Son, his only Son,
To ransom rebel worms;
'Tis here he makes his goodness known
In its diviner forms.

4 To this dear refuge, Lord, we come,
'Tis here our hope relies;
A safe defence, a peaceful home,
When storms of trouble rise.

5 Thine eye beholds, with kind regard,
The souls who trust in thee;
Their humble hope thou wilt reward
With bliss divinely free.

6 Great God, to thy almighty love,
What honors shall we raise;
Not all th' angelic songs above
Can render equal praise.

STEELE.

215 C. M.

1 LET children hear the mighty deeds
Which God performed of old,
Which in our younger years we saw,
And which our fathers told.

2 He bids us make his glories known,
His works of power and grace;
And we'll convey his wonders down
Through every rising race.

3 Our lips shall tell them to our sons,
And they again to theirs,
That generations yet unborn
May teach them to their heirs.

4 Thus shall they learn, in God alone
Their hope securely stands,
That they may ne'er forget his works,
But practice his commands.

WATTS.

216 C. M.

1 FAITHFUL, O Lord, thy mercies are,
A rock that cannot move;
A thousand promises declare
Thy constancy of love.

2 Thou waitest to be gracious still;
Thou dost with sinners bear,
That, saved, we may thy goodness feel,
And all thy grace declare.

5

3 Its streams the whole creation reach,
So plenteous is the store;
Enough for all, enough for each,
Enough forevermore.

4 Throughout the universe it reigns;
It stands for ever sure;
And while thy truth, O God, remains,
Thy goodness shall endure.

C. WESLEY.

217 C. M.

1 THERE is a little lonely fold,
Whose flock One Shepherd keeps,
Through summer's heat and winter's cold,
With eye that never sleeps.

2 By evil beast, or burning sky,
Or damp of midnight air,
Not one in all that flock shall die
Beneath that Shepherd's care.

3 For if, unheeding or beguiled,
In danger's path they roam,
His pity follows through the wild,
And guards them safely home.

4 Oh, gentle Shepherd, still behold
Thy helpless charge in me!
And take a wanderer to thy fold,
That trembling turns to thee.

LITCHFIELD'S COLL.

218 C. M.

1 MY Shepherd will supply my need;
Jehovah is his name;
In pastures fresh he makes me feed,
Beside the living stream.

2 He brings my wandering spirit back
When I forsake his ways,

And leads me, for his mercy's sake,
In paths of truth and grace.

3 When I walk through the shades of death,
Thy presence is my stay;
A word of thy supporting breath
Drives all my fears away.

4 Thy hand, in sight of all my foes,
Doth still my table spread;
My cup with blessings overflows;
Thine oil anoints my head.

5 The sure provisions of my God
Attend me all my days;
Oh, may thine house be mine abode,
And all my works be praise!

6 There would I find a settled rest,
While others go and come—
No more a stranger or a guest,
But like a child at home.

WATTS.

219 C. M.

1 LORD, 'tis an infinite delight
To see thy lovely face,
To dwell whole ages in thy sight,
And feel thy vital rays.

2 While the bright nation sounds thy praise
From each eternal hill,
Sweet odors of exhaling grace
The happy region fill.

3 Thy love a sea without a shore,
Spreads life and joy abroad—
Oh, 'tis a heaven worth dying for,
To see a smiling God!

4 Show me thy face, and I'll away
From all inferior things;
Speak, Lord, and here I quit my clay,
And stretch my airy wings.

WATTS.

220 C. M.

1 MY God, my portion, and my love,
My everlasting all,
I've none but thee in heaven above,
Or on this earthly ball.

2 In vain the bright, the burning sun
Scatters his feeble light;
'Tis thy sweet beams create my noon—
If thou withdraw, 'tis night.

3 And while upon my restless bed
Through midnight hours I roll,
If my Redeemer shows his head,
'Tis morning with my soul.

4 To thee I owe my wealth and friends,
My health and safe abode;
Thanks to thy name for meaner things,
But they are not my God.

5 Were I possessor of the earth,
And called the stars my own,
Without thy graces and thyself,
I were a wretch undone.

6 Let others stretch their arms like seas,
And grasp in all the shore,
Grant me the visits of thy face,
And I desire no more.

WATTS.

221 C. M.

1 MY God! the spring of all my joys,
The life of my delights,
The glory of my brightest days,
And comfort of my nights.

2 In darkest shades if he appear,
My dawning is begun!
He is my soul's sweet morning star,
And he my rising sun.

3 The opening heavens around me shine
With beams of sacred bliss,
While Jesus shows his heart is mine,
And whispers, I am his!

4 My soul would leave this heavy clay
At that transporting word,
Run up with joy the shining way,
T' embrace my dearest Lord.

5 Fearless of hell, and ghastly death,
I'd break through every foe;
The wings of love, and arms of faith,
Should bear me conqueror through.

WATTS.

222. C. M.

1 THE mercies of my God and King
My tongue shall still pursue:
Oh, happy they who, while they sing
Those mercies, share them too!

2 As bright and lasting as the sun,
As lofty as the sky,
From age to age thy word shall run,
And chance and change defy.

3 The covenant of the King of kings
Shall stand forever sure;
Beneath the shadow of thy wings
Thy saints repose secure.

LYTE.

223 C. M.

1 AS pants the hart for cooling streams,
When heated in the chase,
So longs my soul, O God, for thee,
And thy refreshing grace.

2 For thee, my God, the living God,
My thirsty soul doth pine;
Oh, when shall I behold thy face,
Thou Majesty Divine?

3 Why restless, why cast down, my soul?
Trust God, and he'll employ
His aid for thee, and change these sighs
To thankful hymns of joy.

4 God of my strength, how long shall I,
Like one forgotten, mourn;
Forlorn, forsaken, and exposed
To my oppressor's scorn?

5 My heart is pierced, as with a sword,
While thus my foes upbraid:
"Vain boaster, where is now thy God?
And where his promised aid?"

6 Why restless, why cast down, my soul?
Hope still, and thou shalt sing
The praise of him who is thy God,
Thy health's eternal Spring.

TATE & BRADY.

224 C. M.

1 WITH earnest longings of the mind,
My God, to thee I look;
So pants the hunted hart to find
And taste the cooling brook.

2 'Tis with a mournful pleasure now
I think on ancient days;
Then to thy house did numbers go,
And all our work was praise.

3 But why, my soul, sunk down so far
Beneath this heavy load?
Why do my thoughts indulge despair,
And sin against my God?

4 Hope in the Lord, whose mighty hand
Can all thy woes remove;
For I shall yet before him stand,
And sing restoring love.

WATTS.

225 C. M.

1 HOW long, sometimes, a day appears!
And weeks, how long are they!
Months move on slow, as if the years
Would never pass away.

2 But even years are passing by,
And soon must all be gone;
For day by day, as minutes fly,
Eternity comes on.

3 Days, months, and years must have an end,
Eternity has none;
'Twill always have as long to spend
As when it first begun.

4 Great God! a creature cannot tell
How such a thing can be,
I only pray that I may dwell
Eternally with thee.

TAYLOR.

226 C. M.

1 THE Lord himself, the mighty Lord,
Vouchsafes to be my guide;
The shepherd, by whose constant care
My wants are all supplied.

2 In tender grass he makes me feed,
And gently there repose;
Then leads to cooling shades, and where
Refreshing water flows.

3 He does my wandering soul reclaim,
And, to his endless praise,
Instruct with humble zeal to walk
In his most righteous ways.

4 I pass the gloomy vale of death,
From fear and danger free;
For there his aiding rod and staff
Defend and comfort me.

5 Since God doth thus his wondrous love
Through all my life extend,
That life to him I will devote,
And in his service spend.

227 C. M.

1 WHEN morning's first and hallowed ray
Breaks, with its trembling light,
To chase the pearly dews away,
Bright tear-drops of the night—

2 My heart, O Lord, forgets to rove,
But rises gladly free,
On wings of everlasting love,
And finds its home in thee.

3 When evening's silent shades descend,
And nature sinks to rest,
Still, to my Father and my Friend,
My wishes are addressed.

4 Though tears may dim my hours of joy,
And bid my pleasures flee,
Thou reign'st where grief cannot annoy;
I will be glad in thee.

5 And e'en when midnight's solemn gloom
Above, around is spread,
Sweet dreams of everlasting bloom,
Are hovering o'er my head.

6 I dream of that fair land, O Lord!
Where all thy saints shall be;
I wake to lean upon thy word,
And still delight in thee.

228 C. M.

1 THERE is a safe and secret place
  Beneath the wings divine,
Reserved for all the heirs of grace:
  Oh, be that refuge mine!

2 The least and feeblest there may bide,
  Uninjured and unawed;
While thousands fall on every side,
  He rests secure in God.

3 He feeds in pastures large and fair,
  Of love and truth divine;
O child of God, O glory's heir,
  How rich a lot is thine!

4 A hand almighty to defend,
  An ear for every call,
An honored life, a peaceful end,
  And heaven to crown it all!

LYTE.

229 S. M.

1 COME, sound his praise abroad,
  And hymns of glory sing;
Jehovah is the sov'reign God,
  The universal King.

2 He form'd the deeps unknown,
  He gave the seas their bound;
The watery worlds are all his own,
  And all the solid ground.

3 Come, worship at his throne,
  Come, bow before the Lord;
We are his works and not our own,
  He form'd us by his word.

4 To-day attend his voice,
  Nor dare provoke his rod;
Come, like the people of his choice,
  And own your gracious God.

WATTS.

Occasional Chorus.

Praise ye the Lord, Hallelujah!
  Praise ye the Lord, Hallelujah,
Hallelujah, Hallelujah,
  Hallelujah, Praise ye the Lord.

230 S. M.

1 O LORD, our heavenly King,
  Thy name is all divine;
Thy glories round the earth are spread,
  And o'er the heavens they shine.

2 When I survey the stars,
  And all their shining forms,
Lord, what is man, that feeble thing,
  Akin to dust and worms?

3 Lord, what is worthless man,
  That thou shouldst love him so?
Next to thine angels is he placed,
  And lord of all below.

4 How rich thy bounties are!
  How wondrous are thy ways!
Of dust and worms thy power can frame
  A monument of praise.

5 O Lord, our heavenly King,
  Thy name is all divine;
Thy glories round the earth are spread,
  And o'er the heavens they shine.

WATTS.

231 S. M.

1 OH, bless the Lord, my soul!
  Let all within me join,
And aid my tongue to bless his name,
  Whose favors are divine.

2 Oh, bless the Lord, my soul!
  Nor let his mercies lie

Forgotten in unthankfulness,
And without praises die.

3 'Tis he forgives thy sins;
'Tis he relieves thy pain;
'Tis he that heals thy sicknesses,
And gives thee strength again.

4 He crowns thy life with love,
When ransomed from the grave;
He, who redeemed my soul from hell,
Hath sovereign power to save.

5 He fills the poor with good;
He gives the sufferers rest;
The Lord hath judgments for the proud,
And justice for th' oppressed.

WATTS.

232 S. M.

1 THE Lord Jehovah reigns;
Let all the nations fear;
Let sinners tremble at his throne,
And saints be humble there.

2 Jesus the Saviour reigns;
Let earth adore its Lord;
Bright cherubs his attendants stand,
And swift fulfill his word.

3 In Zion is his throne;
His honors are divine;
His church shall make his wonders known,
For there his glories shine.

4 How holy is his name!
How terrible his praise!
Justice, and truth, and judgment join,
In all his works of grace.

WATTS.

233 S. M.

1 ALMIGHTY Maker, God!
How wondrous is thy name!
Thy glories how diffused abroad
Through the creation's frame!

2 The lark mounts up the sky
With unambitious song,
And bears her Maker's praise on high
Upon her artless tongue.

3 My soul would rise and sing
To her Creator, too:
Fain would my tongue adore my King,
And pay the worship due.

4 And yet the songs I frame
Are faithless to thy cause,
And steal the honors of thy name
To build their own applause.

5 Create my soul anew,
Else all my worship's vain;
This wretched heart will ne'er be true
Until 'tis formed again.

WATTS.

234 S. M.

1 TO God the only wise,
Our Saviour and our King,
Let all the saints below the skies
Their humble praises bring.

2 'Tis his almighty love,
His counsel and his care,
Preserve us safe from sin and death,
And every hurtful snare.

3 He will present our souls,
Unblemished and complete,
Before the glory of his face,
With joys divinely great.

4 Then all the chosen seed
Shall meet around the throne,
Shall bless the conduct of his grace,
And make his wonders known.

5 To our Redeemer God
Wisdom and power belong,
Immortal crowns of majesty,
And everlasting song. WATTS.

235 S. M.

1 WHEN man grows bold in sin,
My heart within me cries,
"He hath no faith of God within,
Nor fear before his eyes."

2 But there's a dreadful God,
Though men renounce his fear;
His justice, hid behind the cloud,
Shall one great day appear.

3 His truth transcends the sky;
In heaven his mercies dwell;
Deep as the sea his judgments lie;
His anger burns to hell.

4 How excellent his love,
Whence all our safety springs!
Oh, never let my soul remove
From underneath his wings. WATTS.

236 S. M.

1 MY God, my Life, my Love,
To thee, to thee I call;
I cannot live, if thou remove,
For thou art all in all.

2 Thy shining grace can cheer
This dungeon where I dwell;
'Tis paradise when thou art here;
If thou depart, 'tis hell.

3 To thee, and thee alone,
The angels owe their bliss;
They sit around thy gracious throne,
And dwell where Jesus is.

4 Not all the harps above
Can make a heavenly place,
If God his residence remove,
Or but conceal his face.

5 Nor earth, nor all the sky,
Can one delight afford,
No, not a drop of real joy,
Without thy presence, Lord.

6 Thou art the sea of love,
Where all my pleasures roll;
The circle where my passions move,
And centre of my soul. WATTS.

237 S. M.

1 THE Lord my Shepherd is;
I shall be well supplied:
Since he is mine, and I am his,
What can I want beside?

2 He leads me to the place
Where heavenly pasture grows,
Where living waters gently pass,
And full salvation flows.

3 If e'er I go astray,
He doth my soul reclaim;
And guides me in his own right way,
For his most holy name.

4 While he affords his aid,
I cannot yield to fear;
Though I should walk through death's
dark shade,
My Shepherd 's with me there.

5 In spite of all my foes,
Thou dost my table spread;
My cup with blessings overflows,
And joy exalts my head.

6 The bounties of thy love
Shall crown my future days;
Nor from thy house will I remove,
Nor cease to speak thy praise.

WATTS.

238. S. M.

1 HOW gentle God's commands!
How kind his precepts are!
Come, cast your burdens on the Lord,
And trust his constant care.

2 Beneath his watchful eye
His saints securely dwell;
That hand which bears all nature up
Shall guard his children well.

3 Why should this anxious load
Press down your weary mind?
Haste to your heavenly Father's throne,
And sweet refreshment find.

4 His goodness stands approved,
Unchanged from day to day:
I'll drop my burden at his feet,
And bear a song away.

DODDRIDGE.

239 S. M.

1 THE pity of the Lord
To those that fear his name,
Is such as tender parents feel;
He knows our feeble frame.

2 He knows we are but dust
Scattered with every breath;
His anger, like a rising wind,
Can send us swift to death.

3 Our days are as the grass,
Or like the morning flower;
If one sharp blast sweep o'er the field,
It withers in an hour.

4 But thy compassions, Lord,
To endless years endure;
And children's children ever find
Thy words of promise sure.

WATTS.

240 7s.

1 SING, my soul, his wondrous love,
Who, from yon bright throne above,
Ever watchful o'er our race,
Still to man extends his grace.

2 Heaven and earth by him were made,
All is by his sceptre swayed;
What are we that he should show
So much love to us below!

3 God, the merciful and good,
Bought us with the Saviour's blood;
And, to make our safety sure,
Guides us by his Spirit pure.

4 Sing, my soul, adore his name;
Let his glory be thy theme;
Praise him till he calls thee home,
Trust his love for all to come.

241 7s.

1 PRAISE the Lord, his glories show,
Saints within his courts below,
Angels round his throne above,
All that see and share his love.

2 Earth to heaven, and heaven to earth,
Tell his wonders, sing his worth;
Age to age, and shore to shore,
Praise him, praise him, evermore!

3 Praise the Lord, his mercies trace;
Praise his providence and grace,
All that he for man hath done,
All he sends us through his Son.

4 Strings and voices, hands and hearts,
In the concert bear your parts;
All that breathe, your Lord adore,
Praise him, praise him, evermore!

LYTE.

242

7s.

1 PRAISE the Lord—his power confess;
Praise him in his holiness;
Praise him as the theme inspires—
Praise him as his fame requires.

2 Let the trumpet's lofty sound
Spread its loudest notes around;
Let the harp unite, in praise,
With the sacred minstrel's lays.

3 Let the organ join to bless
God, the Lord of righteousness;
Tune your voice to spread the fame
Of the great Jehovah's name.

4 All who dwell beneath his light,
In his praise your hearts unite;
While the stream of song is poured,
Praise and magnify the Lord.

WRANGHAM.

243

7s.

1 SONGS of praise the angels sang,
Heaven with hallelujahs rang,
When Jehovah's work begun,
When he spake, and it was done.

2 Songs of praise awoke the morn,
When the Prince of Peace was born;
Songs of praise arose, when he
Captive led captivity.

3 Heaven and earth must pass away,
Songs of praise shall crown that day;
God will make new heavens and earth,
Songs of praise shall hail their birth.

4 And shall man alone be dumb
Till that glorious kingdom come?
No, the Church delights to raise
Psalms and hymns and songs of praise.

5 Saints below, with heart and voice,
Still in songs of praise rejoice;
Learning here, by faith and love,
Songs of praise to sing above.

6 Borne upon their latest breath,
Songs of praise shall conquer death;
Then, amid eternal joy,
Songs of praise their powers employ.

MONTGOMERY.

244

7s.

1 ALL ye nations, praise the Lord,
All ye lands, your voices raise;
Heaven and earth with loud accord,
Praise the Lord, forever praise.

2 For his truth and mercy stand,
Past and present and to be,
Like the years of his right hand,
Like his own eternity.

3 Praise him, ye who know his love,
Praise him from the depths beneath;
Praise him in the heights above;
Praise your Maker all that breathe.

MONTGOMERY.

245

7s.

1 HERALDS of creation! cry—
Praise the Lord, the Lord most high;
Heaven and earth, obey the call,
Praise the Lord, the Lord of all.

2 For he spake, and forth from night
Sprang the universe to light;
He commanded,—nature heard,
And stood fast upon his word.

3 Praise him, all ye hosts above;
Spirits perfected in love;
Sun and moon, your voices raise;
Sing, ye stars, your Maker's praise.

4 Earth, from all thy depths below,
Ocean's hallelujahs flow;
Lightning, vapor, wind, and storm,
Hail and snow, his will perform.

5 Birds, on wings of rapture soar,
Warble at his temple door;
Joyful sounds from herds and flocks,
Echo back, ye caves and rocks.

6 High above all height, his throne;
Excellent his name alone;
Him let all his works confess,
Him let all his children bless.

MONTGOMERY.

246

7s.

1 MAGNIFY Jehovah's name;
For his mercies ever sure,
From eternity the same,
To eternity endure.

2 Let his ransomed flock rejoice,
Gathered out of every land,
As the people of his choice,
Plucked from the destroyer's hand.

3 In the wilderness astray,
In the lonely waste they roam,
Hungry, fainting by the way,
Far from refuge, shelter, home:—

4 To the Lord their God they cry;
He inclines a gracious ear,
Sends deliverance from on high,
Rescues them from all their fear:

5 Them to pleasant lands he brings,
Where the vine and olive grow;
Where, from verdant hills, the sprin
Through luxuriant valleys flow.

6 Oh that men would praise the Lord
For his goodness to their race;
For the wonders of his word,
And the riches of his grace!

247

7s.

1 HARK, my soul, how every thing
Strives to serve our bounteous King;
Each a double tribute pays,
Sings its part, and then obeys.

2 Nature's chief and sweetest choir
Him with cheerful notes admire;
Chanting every day their lauds,
While the grove their song applauds.

3 Though their voices lower be,
Streams have too their melody;
Night and day they warbling run,
Never pause, but still sing on.

4 All the flowers that gild the spring
Hither their still music bring;
If heaven bless them, thankful they
Smell more sweet, and look more gay.

5 Only man can scarce afford
This short office to his Lord;
Man, on whom his bounty flows,
All things gives, and nothing owes.

6 Wake, for shame, my sluggish heart,
Wake, and gladly sing thy part;

Learn of birds, and springs, and flowers,
How to use thy nobler powers.

7 Call whole nature to thy aid,
Since 't was he whole nature made;
Join in one eternal song,
Who to one God all belong.

JOHN AUSTIN. 1668.

248 7s. D.

1 LORD of earth! thy forming hand
Well this beauteous frame hath planned;
Woods that wave, and hills that tower,
Ocean rolling in his power:
Yet, amid this scene so fair,
Should I cease thy smile to share,
What were all its joys to me?
Whom have I on earth but thee?

2 Lord of heaven! beyond our sight
Shines a world of purer light;
There in love's unclouded reign
Parted hands shall meet again;
Oh, that world is passing fair!
Yet, if thou wert absent there,
What were all its joys to me?
Whom have I in heaven but thee?

3 Lord of earth and heaven! my breast
Seeks in thee its only rest:
I was lost; thy accents mild
Homeward lured thy wandering child:
Oh! should once thy smile divine
Cease upon my soul to shine,
What were earth or heaven to me?
Whom have I in each but thee?

GRANT.

249 7s. D.

1 PRAISE to God, immortal praise,
For the love that crowns our days;
Bounteous source of every joy!
Let thy praise our tongues employ.
Flocks that whiten all the plain,
Yellow sheaves of ripened grain;
Clouds that drop their fattening dews,
Suns that temperate warmth diffuse:—

2 All that spring with bounteous hand
Scatters o'er the smiling land;
All that liberal autumn pours
From her rich o'erflowing stores;—
Lord, for these our souls shall raise
Grateful vows, and solemn praise;
And, when every blessing 's flown,
Love thee for thyself alone.

BARBAULD.

250 8s & 7s.

1 PRAISE the Lord! ye heavens adore him,
Praise him, angels in the height;
Sun and moon, rejoice before him;
Praise him, all ye stars of light!

2 Praise the Lord, for he hath spoken;
Worlds his mighty voice obeyed;
Laws which never shall be broken,
For their guidance he hath made.

3 Praise the Lord—for he is glorious;
Never shall his promise fail;
God hath made his saints victorious,
Sin and death shall not prevail.

4 Praise the God of our salvation,
Hosts on high his power proclaim;
Heaven and earth, and all creation,
Laud and magnify his name.

251 8s & 7s.

1 PRAISE to thee, thou great Creator!
Praise to thee from every tongue;
Join, my soul, with every creature,
Join the universal song.

2 Father, source of all compassion!
Pure, unbounded grace is thine:
Hail the God of our salvation,
Praise him for his love divine!

3 For ten thousand blessings given,
For the hope of future joy,
Sound his praise through earth and heaven,
Sound Jehovah's praise on high!

4 Praise to God, the great Creator,
Father, Son, and Holy Ghost;
Praise him, every living creature,
Earth and heaven's united host.

5 Joyfully on earth adore him,
Till in heaven our song we raise:
Then enraptured fall before him,
Lost in wonder, love, and praise!

FAWCETT.

252 8s & 7s.

1 GOD is love; his mercy brightens
All the path in which we rove;
Bliss he wakes, and woe he lightens;
God is wisdom, God is love.

2 Time and change are busy ever;
Man decays, and ages move;
But his mercy waneth never;
God is wisdom, God is love.

3 E'en the hour that darkest seemeth
Will his changeless goodness prove;
From the gloom his brightness streameth,
God is wisdom, God is love.

4 He with earthly cares entwineth
Hope and comfort from above;
Everywhere his glory shineth;
God is wisdom, God is love.

BOWRING.

253 H. M.

1 SING to the Lord most high;
Let every land adore;
With grateful voice make known
His goodness and his power;
With cheerful songs declare his ways,
And let his praise inspire your tongues.

2 Enter his courts with joy;
With fear address the Lord;
He formed us with his hand,
And quickened by his word;
With wide command he spreads his sway,
O'er every sea and every land.

3 His hands provide our food,
And every blessing give;
We feed upon his care,
And in his pastures live:
With cheerful songs declare his ways,
And let his praise inspire your tongues.

4 Good is the Lord our God,
His truth and mercy sure;
While earth and heaven shall last,
His promises endure:
With wide command he spreads his sway,
O'er every sea and every land.

DWIGHT.

254 H. M.

1 COME, let us gladly sing
To God, our Saviour-King;
With thanks his presence seek,
In psalms his praises speak;
He's God most high; let all draw nigh,
And crown him—Lord of earth and sky.

2 He gave the mountains birth,
He made the spacious earth;
His are the sea and land—
They rose at his command:
With reverence all before him fall,
And on his name devoutly call.

3 Come, kneel before his throne,
For he is God alone;
We are the flock he leads—
The sheep his bounty feeds:
To-day—to-day—his voice obey;
Grieve not the Holy Ghost away.

HATFIELD.

255 11s & 8s.

1 BE joyful in God, all ye lands of the earth,
Oh, serve him with gladness and fear;
Exult in his presence with music and mirth,
With love and devotion draw near.

2 For Jehovah is God, and Jehovah alone,
Creator and Ruler o'er all;
And we are his people, his sceptre we own;
His sheep, and we follow his call.

3 Oh enter his gates with thanksgiving and song,
Your vows in his temple proclaim!
His praise with melodious accordance prolong,
And bless his adorable name.

4 For good is the Lord, inexpressibly good,
And we are the work of his hand;
His mercy and truth from eternity stood,
And shall to eternity stand.

MONTGOMERY.

256 11s & 8s.

1 THE Lord is great! ye hosts of heaven adore him,
And ye who tread this earthly ball;
In holy songs rejoice aloud before him,
And shout his praise who made you all.

2 The Lord is great; his majesty how glorious!
Resound his praise from shore to shore;
O'er sin, and death, and hell, now made victorious,
He rules and reigns forevermore.

3 The Lord is great; his mercy how abounding!
Ye angels, strike your golden chords;
Oh, praise our God, with voice and harp resounding,
The King of kings and Lord of lords!

257 10s & 11s.

1 OH, worship the King, all glorious above,
Oh, gratefully sing his wonderful love!
Our Shield and Defender, the Ancient of days,
Pavilioned in splendor, and girded with praise.

2 Oh tell of his might, oh sing of his grace,
Whose robe is the light, whose canopy space!
His chariot of wrath deep thunder-clouds form,
And dark is his path on the wings of the storm.

3 Thy bountiful care what tongue can recite?
It breathes in the air, it shines in the light,
It streams from the hills, it descends to the plain,
And sweetly distills in the dew and the rain.

4 Frail children of dust, and feeble as frail,
In thee do we trust, nor find thee to fail:
Thy mercies how tender, how firm to the end,
Our Maker, Defender, Redeemer, and Friend!

5 O measureless Might, ineffable Love!
While angels delight to hymn thee above,
The humbler creation, though feeble their lays,
With true adoration shall lisp to thy praise.

GRANT.

258 10s & 11s.

1 OUR Father in heaven, we hallow thy Name:
May thy kingdom holy on earth be the same:
Oh give to us daily our portion of bread:
It is from thy bounty that all must be fed.

2 Forgive our transgressions, and teach us to know
That humble compassion which pardons each foe;
Keep us from temptation, from evil and sin,
And thine be the glory, forever! Amen!

259 10s & 11s.

1 O PRAISE ye the Lord! prepare your glad voice,
His praise in the great assembly to sing,
In their great Creator let all men rejoice,
And heirs of salvation be glad in their King.

2 Let them his great name devoutly adore;
In loud-swelling strains his praises express,
Who graciously opens his bountiful store,
Their wants to relieve, and his children to bless.

3 With glory adorned, his people shall sing
To God, who defence and plenty supplies;
Their loud acclamations to him, their great King,
Through earth shall be sounded, and reach to the skies.

4 Ye angels above, his glories who 've sung,
In loftiest notes, now publish his praise:
We mortals, delighted, would borrow your tongue—
Would join in your numbers, and chant to your lays.

TATE, VARIED.

260 10s & 11s.

1 YE servants of God, your Master proclaim,
And publish abroad his wonderful name;
The name all-victorious of Jesus extol;
His kingdom is glorious; he rules over all.

2 God ruleth on high, almighty to save;
And still he is nigh: his presence we have;
The great congregation his triumph shall sing,
Ascribing salvation to Jesus, our King.

3 "Salvation to God, who sits on the throne,"
Let all cry aloud, and honor the Son;
The praises of Jesus the angels proclaim,
Fall down on their faces, and worship the Lamb.

4 Then let us adore, and give him his right—
All glory and power, and wisdom and might;
All honor and blessing, with angels above,
And thanks never ceasing, for infinite love.

C. WESLEY.

261 H. M.

1 YE boundless realms of joy,
Exalt your Maker's fame;
His praise your song employ,
Above the starry frame:
Your voices raise, ye Cherubim
And Seraphim, to sing his praise.

2 Thou moon, that rul'st the night,
And sun that guid'st the day,
Ye glittering stars of light,
To him your homage pay:
His praise declare, ye heavens above,
And clouds that move in liquid air.

3 Let them adore the Lord,
And praise his holy name,
By whose almighty word
They all from nothing came:
And all shall last from changes free;
His firm decree stands ever fast.

4 Let all of richest birth
With those of humbler name
And judges of the earth,
His matchless praise proclaim.
In this design, let youths with maids,
And hoary heads with children, join.

5 United zeal be shown
His wondrous fame to raise,
Whose glorious name alone
Deserves our endless praise;
Earth's utmost ends his power obey;
His glorious sway the sky transcends.

TATE & BRADY.

262 H. M.

1 THE Lord Jehovah reigns,
His throne is built on high;
The garments he assumes
Are light and majesty;
His glories shine with beams so bright,
No mortal eye can bear the sight.

2 The thunders of his hand
Keep the wide world in awe;
His wrath and justice stand,
To guard his holy law;
And where his love resolves to bless,
His truth confirms and seals the grace.

3 Through all his perfect work,
Surprising wisdom shines;
Confounds the powers of hell,
And breaks their curst designs;
Strong is the arm—and shall fulfill
His great decrees, his sovereign will.

4 And can this mighty King
Of glory condescend—
And will he write his name,
My Father and my Friend?
I love his name, I love his word;
Join, all my powers, and praise the Lord!

WATTS.

263 C. P. M.

1 BEGIN, my soul, th' exalted lay;
Let each enraptured thought obey,
And praise th' Almighty's name;
Let heaven and earth, and seas and skies,
In one melodious concert rise,
To swell th' inspiring theme.

2 Ye angels, catch the thrilling sound,
While all the adoring thrones around
His boundless mercy sing;
Let every listening saint above
Wake all the tuneful soul of love,
And touch the sweetest string.

3 Whate'er this living world contains,
That wings the air or treads the plains,
United praise bestow;
Ye tenants of the ocean wide,
Proclaim him through the mighty tide,
And in the deeps below.

4 Wake, all ye soaring throngs, and sing;
Ye feathered warblers of the spring,
Harmonious anthems raise
To him who shaped your finer mold,
Who tipped your glittering wings with gold,
And tuned your voice to praise.

5 Let man, by nobler passions swayed,
Let man, in God's own image made,
His breath in praise employ;
Spread wide his Maker's name around,
While heaven's broad arch rings back the sound,
The song of holy joy!

OGILVIE.

264 C. P. M.

1 YE fields of light, celestial plains,
Where pure, serene effulgence reigns,
Ye scenes divinely fair,
Your Maker's wondrous power proclaim,
Tell how he formed your shining frame,
And breathed the fluid air.

2 Join all ye stars, the vocal choir;
Thou dazzling orb of liquid fire,
The mighty chorus aid;
And, soon as evening vails the plain,
Thou moon, prolong the hallowed strain,
And praise him in the shade.

3 Thou heaven of heavens, his vast abode,
Proclaim the glories of thy God;
Ye worlds declare his might;
He spake the word, and ye were made,
Darkness and dismal chaos fled,
And nature sprung to light.

4 Let every element rejoice;
Ye thunders, burst with awful voice
To him who bids you roll;
His praise in softer notes declare,
Each whispering breeze of yielding air,
And breathe it to the soul. OGILVIE.

265 C. P. M.

1 MY God, thy boundless love I praise;
How bright on high its glories blaze!
How sweetly bloom below!
It streams from thy eternal throne;
Through heaven its joys forever run,
And o'er the earth they flow.

2 'Tis love that paints the purple morn,
And bids the clouds, in air upborne,
Their genial drops distil;
In every vernal beam it glows,
It breathes in every gale that blows,
And glides in every rill.

3 It robes in cheerful green the ground,
And pours its flowery beauties round,
Whose sweets perfume the gale;
Its bounties richly spread the plain,
The blushing fruit, the golden grain,
And smile in every vale.

4 But in thy word, I see it shine
With grace and glories more divine,
Proclaiming sin forgiven;
There Faith, bright cherub, points the way
To realms of everlasting day,
And opens all her heaven.

5 Then let the love that makes me blest
With cheerful praise inspire my breast,
And ardent gratitude;
And all my thoughts and passions tend
To thee, my Father and my Friend,
My soul's eternal good!

266 C. P. M.

1 ALTHOUGH the vine its fruit deny,
The budding fig-tree droop and die,
No oil the olive yield,
Yet will I trust still in my God,
Yea, bend rejoicing to his rod,
And by his grace be healed.

2 Though fields, in verdure once arrayed,
By whirlwinds desolate be laid,
Or parched by scorching beam;
Still in the Lord shall be my trust,
My joy; for, though his frown is just,
His mercy is supreme.

3 Though from the fold the flock decay,
Though herds lie famished o'er the lea,
And round the empty stall;
My soul above the wreck shall rise,
Its better joys are in the skies,
There God is all in all.

4 In God my strength, howe'er distrest,
I yet will hope and calmly rest,
Nay, triumph in his love;
My lingering soul, my tardy feet,
Free as the hind he makes, and fleet,
To speed my course above.

H. U. ONDERDONK.

267 P. M.

1 HOLY, holy, holy is the Lord!
Sing, O ye people, gladly adore him;
Let the mountains tremble at his word;
Let the hills be joyful before him;
Mighty in wisdom, boundless in mercy,
Great is Jehovah, King over all.

2 Praise him, praise him! shout aloud for joy,
Watchman of Zion, herald the story;
Sin and death his kingdom shall destroy;
All the earth shall sing of his glory;
Praise him, ye angels, ye who behold him
Robed in his splendor matchless divine.

3 King eternal, blesséd be his name!
So may his children gladly adore him,
When in heaven we join the happy strain,
When we cast our bright crowns before him;
There in his likeness, joyful awaking,
There we shall see him, there we shall sing.

Occasional Chorus.

Holy, holy, holy is the Lord,
Let the hills be joyful before him.

268 8s & 7s.

1 PRAISE the Lord, oh! praise him, praise him,
Praise the Lord who reigns above!
Now with cheerful voices raise him
Songs of gratitude and love.

2 Praise the Lord of life and glory,
Praise the Lord of truth and grace;
Tell to all his wond'rous story:
Bid them early seek his face.

3 Praise the Lord with loud hosannas,
Praise him with the mighty throng:
Write his name upon your banners,
Be his praise your battle song!

4 Praise the Giver of Salvation,
Praise him every clime and tongue:
Heav'n and earth, and all creation
Shout aloud in joyful song.

CAMERON.

Occasional Chorus.

Praise him, all ye great creation;
Praise him, every clime and nation;
Praise the Giver of Salvation;
Praise the Lord for evermore.

269 8s & 7s.

1 HARK! what mean those holy voices,
Sweetly sounding through the skies?
Lo! th' angelic host rejoices;
Heavenly hallelujahs rise.

2 Hear them tell the wondrous story,
Hear them chant in hymns of joy,
"Glory in the highest—glory!
Glory be to God most high!

3 "Peace on earth, good-will from heaven,
Reaching far as man is found;

Souls redeemed, and sins forgiven!"—
Loud our golden harps shall sound.

4 "Christ is born, the great Anointed;
Heaven and earth his praises sing!
Oh receive whom God appointed,
For your Prophet, Priest, and King!

5 "Haste, ye mortals, to adore him;
Learn his name, and taste his joy;
Till in heaven ye sing before him—
'Glory be to God most high!'"

CAWOOD.

270

8s & 7s.

1 SHEPHERDS! hail the wondrous stranger;
Now to Bethle'm speed your way;
Lo! in yonder humble manger,
Christ, the Lord, is born to-day!

2 Christ, by prophets long-predicted,
Joy of Israel's chosen race;
Light to Gentiles long-afflicted,
Lost in error's darkest maze.

3 Bright the star of your salvation,
Pointing to his rude abode!
Rapturous news for every nation:
Mortals! now behold your God!

4 Glad, we trace th' amazing story,
Angels leave their bliss to tell;
Theme sublime, replete with glory—
Sinners saved from death and hell.

5 Love eternal moved the Saviour
Thus to lay his radiance by;
Blessings on the Lamb forever—
Glory be to God on high!

271

8s & 7s.

1 ANGELS, from the realms of glory,
Wing your flight o'er all the earth,
Ye who sang creation's story,
Now proclaim Messiah's birth;
Come and worship,
Worship Christ the new-born King.

2 Shepherds, in the field abiding,
Watching o'er your flocks by night,
God with man is now residing;
Yonder shines the infant Light;
Come and worship,
Worship Christ the new-born King.

3 Sages, leave your contemplations,
Brighter visions beam afar;
Seek the great Desire of nations;
Ye have seen his natal star;
Come and worship,
Worship Christ the new-born King.

4 Saints, before the altar bending,
Watching long in hope and fear,
Suddenly the Lord, descending,
In his temple shall appear;
Come and worship,
Worship Christ the new-born King.

5 Sinners, wrung with true repentance,
Doomed for guilt to endless pains,
Justice now revokes the sentence;
Mercy calls you; break your chains;
Come and worship,
Worship Christ the new-born King.

MONTGOMERY.

272

7s. D.

1 HARK! the herald angels sing,
"Glory to the new-born King!
Peace on earth, and mercy mild,
God and sinners reconciled."
Joyful, all ye nations, rise,
Join the triumph of the skies;
With th' angelic host proclaim,
"Christ is born in Bethlehem."

2 Christ, by highest heaven adored;
Christ the everlasting Lord;
Late in time behold him come,
Offspring of the favored one.
Veil'd in flesh, the Godhead see;
Hail the incarnate Deity:
Pleased, as man, with men to dwell,
Jesus, our Immanuel!

3 Hail! the heaven-born Prince of peace!
Hail! the Sun of Righteousness!
Light and life to all he brings,
Risen with healing in his wings.
Mild he lays his glory by,
Born that man no more may die:
Born to raise the sons of earth,
Born to give them second birth.

WESLEY.

Occasional Chorus.

Hark! the herald angels sing,
"Glory to the new-born King!"

273

7s.

1 HARK! the herald angels sing,
"Glory to the new-born King!
Peace on earth, and mercy mild,
God and sinners reconciled."

2 Joyful, all ye nations, rise;
Join the triumphs of the skies;
With the angelic hosts proclaim,
"Christ is born in Bethlehem."

3 Mild he lays his glory by;
Born that man no more may die;
Born to raise the sons of earth;
Born to give them second birth.

4 Veiled in flesh, the Godhead see:
Hail, the incarnate Deity,
Pleased, as man, with men to appear,
Jesus, our Immanuel, here.

5 Let us then with angels sing,
"Glory to the new-born King!—
Peace on earth and mercy mild,
God and sinners reconciled!"

C. WESLEY.

274

7s.

1 HE has come, the Christ of God!
Left for us his glad abode;
Stooping from his throne of bliss,
To this darksome wilderness!

2 He has come, the Prince of peace!
Come to bid our sorrows cease;
Come to scatter, with his light,
All the shadows of our night.

3 He, the mighty King, has come!
Making this poor earth his home;
Come to bear our sin's sad load,
Son of David, Son of God!

4 He has come, whose name of grace
Speaks deliverance to our race;
Left for us his glad abode,
Son of Mary, Son of God!

275 7s.

1 GOD with us! oh, wondrous name!
Manifest in flesh he came,
Hiding in a form like mine
All his attributes divine.

2 Equal with the Father, still
He obeys the Father's will,
Lays his rightful glories by,
Comes, as man, for man to die.

3 While as man on earth he dwelt,
As true God his power was felt;
At his voice diseases fled,
Opening graves restored their dead.

4 As a man he groans and dies,
Prisoned in the tomb he lies;
Soon he rises from the grave,
Man to die, but God to save.

B. MANLY, JR.

276 8s & 7s.

1 HAIL! thou long-expected Jesus,
Born to set thy people free:
From our sins and fears release us,
Let us find our rest in thee.

2 Israel's strength and consolation,
Hope of all the saints, thou art;
Long desired of every nation,
Joy of every waiting heart.

3 Born thy people to deliver,
Born a child, yet God our King,
Born to reign in us forever,
Now thy gracious kingdom bring.

4 By thine own eternal Spirit,
Rule in all our hearts alone;
By thine all-sufficient merit,
Raise us to thy glorious throne.

C. WESLEY.

277 8s & 7s.

1 HARK! a thrilling voice is sounding;
"Christ is nigh," it seems to say;
"Cast away the dreams of darkness,
O ye children of the day!"

2 Wakened by the solemn warning,
Let the earth-bound soul arise;
Christ, her Sun, all ill dispelling,
Shines upon the morning skies.

3 Lo! the Lamb, so long-expected,
Comes with pardon down from heaven;
Let us haste, with tears of sorrow,
One and all to be forgiven.

4 That when next he comes with glory
And the world is wrapped in fear,
With his mercy he may shield us,
And with words of love draw near.

5 Honor, glory, might, and blessing,
To the Father, and the Son,
With the everlasting Spirit,
While eternal ages run.

278 8s & 7s.

1 COME ye lofty, come ye lowly,
Let your songs of gladness ring;
In a stable lies the Holy,
In a manger rests the King.

2 Come ye poor, no pomp of station
Robes the child your hearts adore:
He, the Lord of your salvation,
Shares your want, is weak and poor.

3 Oxen, round about behold them!
All is naked, cold and bare!

See the shepherds, God has told them
That the Prince of Life lies there.

4 Let us bring our poor oblations,
Thanks and love and faith and praise,
Come ye people, come ye nations,
One and all on him to gaze.

5 Hark, the heaven of heavens is ringing,
Christ the Lord to man is born!
Are not all our hearts, too, singing,
Welcome, welcome, happy morn!

279

SHOUT the glad tidings, exultingly sing;
Jerusalem triumphs, Messiah is King!

1 Zion, the marvellous story be telling,
The Son of the Highest, how lowly his birth!
The brightest archangel in glory excelling,
He stoops to redeem thee, he reigns upon earth!
Shout the glad tidings, exultingly sing;
Jerusalem triumphs, Messiah is King!

2 Tell how he cometh; from nation to nation,
The heart-cheering news let the earth echo round;
How free to the faithful he offers salvation,
How his people with joy everlasting are crown'd.
Shout the glad tidings, exultingly sing;
Jerusalem triumphs, Messiah is King!

3 Mortals, your homage be gratefully bringing,
And sweet let the gladsome hosanna arise;
Ye angels, the full hallelujah be singing;
One chorus resound through the earth and the skies.
Shout the glad tidings, exultingly sing;
Jerusalem triumphs, Messiah is King!

MUHLENBURG.

280

8s & 7s.

1 SAW you never in the twilight,
When the sun has left the skies,
Up in heaven the clear stars shining
Through the gloom like silver eyes?
So of old the wise men, watching,
Saw a little stranger star:
And they knew the King was given;
And they followed it from far.

2 Heard you never of the story
How they crossed the desert wild,
Journeyed on by plain and mountain,
Till they found the holy Child—
How they opened all their treasure,
Kneeling to that infant King,
Gave the gold and fragrant incense,
Gave the myrrh in offering?

3 Know you not that lowly infant
Was the bright and Morning Star,
He who came to light the Gentiles
And the darkened isles afar?
And we too may seek his cradle,
There our hearts' best treasure bring:
Love and faith and true devotion,
For our Saviour, God, and King.

281 C. M.

1 JOY to the world, the Lord is come!
Let earth receive her King!
Let every heart prepare him room,
And heaven and nature sing.

2 Joy to the world, the Saviour reigns;
Let men their songs employ;
While fields and floods, rocks, hills, and plains
Repeat the sounding joy.

3 No more let sin and sorrow grow,
Nor thorns infest the ground;
He comes to make his blessings flow
Far as the curse is found.

4 He rules the world with truth and grace,
And makes the nations prove
The glories of his righteousness,
And wonders of his love.

WATTS.

282 C. M.

1 SING to the Lord, ye distant lands,
Ye tribes of every tongue;
His new-discovered grace demands
A new and nobler song.

2 Say to the nations Jesus reigns,
God's own almighty Son;
His power the sinking world sustains,
And grace surrounds his throne.

3 Let heaven proclaim the joyful day;
Joy through the earth be seen;
Let cities shine in bright array,
And fields in cheerful green.

4 Let an unusual joy surprise
The islands of the sea;
Ye mountains, sink; ye valleys, rise;
Prepare the Lord his way.

5 Behold, he comes; he comes to bless
The nations, as their God,
To show the world his righteousness,
And send his truth abroad.

6 But when his voice shall raise the dead,
And bid the world draw near,
How will the guilty nations dread
To see their Judge appear!

WATTS.

283 C. M.

1 MORTALS, awake, with angels join,
And chant the solemn lay;
Joy, love, and gratitude, combine
To hail th' auspicious day.

2 In heaven the rapturous song began,
And sweet seraphic fire
Through all the shining legions ran,
And strung and tuned the lyre.

3 Swift through the vast expanse it flew,
And loud the echo rolled;
The theme, the song, the joy, was new,
'Twas more than heaven could hold.

4 Down through the portals of the sky
Th' impetuous torrent ran;
And angels flew, with eager joy,
To bear the news to man.

5 Hail! Prince of life! forever hail,
Redeemer, brother, friend!
Though earth, and time, and life should fail,
Thy praise shall never end.

MEDLEY.

284 C. M.

1 HARK! the glad sound! the Saviour comes,
The Saviour promised long!
Let every heart prepare a throne,
And every voice a song.

2 He comes, the prisoner to release,
In Satan's bondage held;
The gates of brass before him burst,
The iron fetters yield.

3 He comes, from thickest films of vice
To clear the mental ray,
And on the eyeballs of the blind
To pour celestial day.

4 He comes, the broken heart to bind,
The bleeding soul to cure,
And with the treasures of his grace
To enrich the humble poor.

5 Our glad hosannas, Prince of Peace,
The welcome shall proclaim,
And heaven's eternal arches ring
With thy beloved name. DODDRIDGE.

285 C. M.

1 ANGELS rejoiced and sweetly sung
At our Redeemer's birth;
Mortals! awake; let every tongue
Proclaim his matchless worth.

2 Glory to God, who dwells on high,
And sent his only Son
To take a servant's form, and die,
For evils we had done!

3 Good-will to men; ye fallen race!
Arise, and shout for joy;
He comes, with rich, abounding grace,
To save, and not destroy.

4 Lord! send the gracious tidings forth,
And fill the world with light,
That Jew and Gentile, through the earth,
May know thy saving might.
HURN.

286 C. M. D.

1 WHILE angels thus, O Lord, rejoice,
Shall men no anthem raise?
Oh, may we lose these useless tongues,
When we forget to praise.
Then let us swell responsive notes,
And join the heavenly throng;
For angels no such love have known,
As we, to wake their song.

2 Good-will to sinful dust is shown,
And peace on earth is given;
For lo! th' incarnate Saviour comes,
With news of joy from heaven.
Mercy and truth with sweet accord,
His rising beams adorn;
Let heaven and earth in concert sing,
"The promised child is born!"

287 C. M. D.

1 IT came upon the midnight clear,
That glorious song of old,
From angels bending near the earth
To touch their harps of gold:
"Peace to the earth, good-will to man,
From heaven's all-gracious King:"
The earth in solemn stillness lay,
To hear the angels sing.

2 Still through the cloven skies they come,
With peaceful wings unfurled;

And still celestial music floats
O'er all the weary world;
Above its sad and lowly plains
They bend on heavenly wing,
And ever o'er its Babel sounds,
The blessèd angels sing.

3 Oh ye, beneath life's crushing load,
Whose forms are bending low,
Who toil along the climbing way,
With painful steps and slow,
Look up! for glad and golden hours
Come swiftly on the wing:
Oh rest beside the weary road,
And hear the angels sing!

4 For lo, the days are hastening on,
By prophet-bards foretold,
When with the ever-circling years
Comes round the age of gold!
When peace shall over all the earth
Its final splendors fling,
And the whole world send back the song
Which now the angels sing! SEARS.

288 C. M.

1 WHILE shepherds watch'd their flocks by night,
All seated on the ground,
The angel of the Lord came down,
And glory shone around.

2 "Fear not," said he,—for mighty dread
Had seized their troubled mind,—
"Glad tidings of great joy I bring,
To you and all mankind.

3 "To you, in David's town, this day,
Is born of David's line,
The Saviour, who is Christ, the Lord,
And this shall be the sign:—

4 "The heavenly babe you there shall find
To human view displayed,
All meanly wrapped in swathing bands,
And in a manger laid."

5 Thus spake the seraph—and forthwith
Appeared a shining throng
Of angels, praising God, who thus
Addressed their joyful song:—

6 "All glory be to God on high,
And to the earth be peace;
Good-will henceforth from heaven to men
Begin, and never cease!" TATE.

289 C. M.

1 MESSIAH! at thy glad approach
The howling winds are still;
Thy praises fill the lonely waste,
And breathe from every hill.

2 Renewed, the earth a robe of light,
A robe of beauty wears;
And in new heavens a brighter sun
Leads on the promised years.

3 Let Israel to the Prince of Peace
The loud hosanna sing;
With hallelujahs, and with hymns,
O Zion, hail thy King! LOGAN.

290 C. M.

1 AWAKE, awake the sacred song
To our incarnate Lord!
Let every heart and every tongue
Adore th' eternal Word.

2 That awful Word, that sovereign Power
By whom the worlds were made—

Oh, happy morn! illustrious hour!—
Was once in flesh arrayed!

3 Then shone almighty power and love,
In all their glorious forms,
When Jesus left his throne above,
To dwell with sinful worms.

4 Adoring angels tuned their songs
To hail the joyful day:
With rapture then let mortal tongues
Their grateful worship pay.

5 What glory, Lord, to thee is due!
With wonder we adore;
But could we sing as angels do,
Our highest praise were poor.

STEELE.

291 L. M.

1 WHEN marshall'd on the nightly plain,
The glittering host bestud the sky,
One star alone, of all the train,
Can fix the sinner's wandering eye.

2 Hark! hark! to God the chorus breaks,
From ev'ry host, from ev'ry gem;
But one alone the Saviour speaks—
It is the Star of Bethlehem.

3 Once on the raging seas I rode,
The storm was loud, the night was dark;
The ocean yawned, and rudely blowed
The wind that tossed my foundering bark.

4 Deep horror then my vitals froze,
Death-struck, I ceased the tide to stem;
When suddenly a Star arose—
It was the Star of Bethlehem.

5 It was my guide, my light, my all;
It bade my dark forebodings cease;
And through the storm, and danger's thrall,
It led me to the port of peace.

6 Now safely moored—my perils o'er,
I'll sing, first in night's diadem,
Forever and forevermore,
The Star—the Star of Bethlehem!

H. KIRKE WHITE.

292 L. M.

1 WHEN Jordan hushed his waters still,
And silence slept on Zion's hill,
When Bethlehem's shepherds, through the night,
Watched o'er their flocks by starry light—

2 Hark! from the midnight hills around,
A voice of more than mortal sound,
In distant hallelujahs stole,
Wild murmuring o'er the raptured soul.

3 On wheels of light, on wings of flame,
The glorious hosts of Zion came;
High heaven with songs of triumph rung,
While thus they struck their harps and sung:

4 "O Zion, lift thy raptured eye;
The long-expected hour is nigh;
The joys of nature rise again;
The Prince of Salem comes to reign.

5 "See, Mercy, from her golden urn,
Pours a rich stream to them that mourn;
Behold, she binds, with tender care,
The bleeding bosom of despair.

6 "He comes to cheer the trembling heart;
Bids Satan and his host depart;
Again the day-star gilds the gloom,
Again the bowers of Eden bloom.

T. CAMPBELL.

293 L. M.

1 WAKE, O my soul, and hail the morn,
For unto us a Saviour 's born;
See, how the angels wing their way,
To usher in the glorious day!

2 Hark! what sweet music, what a song,
Sounds from the bright, celestial throng!
Sweet song, whose melting sounds impart
Joy to each raptured, listening heart.

294 7s & 6s.

1 HAIL to the Lord's Anointed,
Great David's greater Son;
Hail, in the time appointed,
His reign on earth begun!
He comes to break oppression,
To set the captive free,
To take away transgression,
And rule in equity.

2 He comes with succor speedy,
To those who suffer wrong;
To help the poor and needy,
And bid the weak be strong;
To give them songs for sighing,
Their darkness turn to light,
Whose souls, condemned and dying,
Were precious in his sight.

3 He shall descend like showers
Upon the fruitful earth;
And love and joy, like flowers,
Spring in his path to birth:
Before him, on the mountains,
Shall peace, the herald, go;
And righteousness, in fountains,
From hill to valley flow.

4 Arabia's desert-ranger
To him shall bow the knee,
The Ethiopian stranger
His glory come to see;
With offerings of devotion,
Ships from the Isles shall meet,
To pour the wealth of ocean
In tribute at his feet.

5 Kings shall fall down before him,
And gold and incense bring,
All nations shall adore him,
His praise all people sing:
For he shall have dominion
O'er river, sea, and shore,
Far as the eagle's pinion
Or dove's light wing can soar.

6 To him shall prayer unceasing,
And daily vows ascend;
His kingdom, still increasing,
A kingdom without end:
The tide of time shall never
His covenant remove;
His name shall stand forever;
That name to us is Love.

MONTGOMERY.

295 7s & 6s.

1 WHEN his salvation bringing,
To Zion Jesus came,
The children all stood singing
Hosanna to his name.

2 Nor did their zeal offend him,
But as he rode along,
He bade them still attend him,
And smiled to hear their song.

3 Then since the Lord retaineth
His love for children still—
Though now as King he reigneth
On Zion's heavenly hill—

4 We'll flock around his banner,
Who sits upon the throne,
And sing aloud, Hosanna!
To David's royal Son.

296 H. M.

1 HARK! what celestial sounds,
What music fills the air!
Soft warbling to the morn,
It strikes the ravished ear;
Now all is still; now wild it floats
In tuneful notes, loud, sweet, and shrill.

2 The angelic hosts descend
With harmony divine;
See how from heaven they bend,
And in full chorus join.
"Fear not," say they; "great joy we bring:
Jesus, your King, is born to-day.

3 "He comes, your souls to save
From death's eternal gloom;
To realms of bliss and light
He lifts you from the tomb:
Your voices raise; with sons of light
Your songs unite of endless praise.

4 "Glory to God on high!
Ye mortals, spread the sound,
And let your raptures fly,
To earth's remotest bound;
For peace on earth, from God in heaven
To man is given, at Jesus' birth."

297 H. M.

1 HARK! hark! the notes of joy
Roll o'er the heavenly plains,
And seraphs find employ
For their sublimest strains;
Some new delight in heaven is known;
Loud sound the harps around the throne.

2 Hark! hark!—the sounds draw nigh,
The joyful hosts descend;
Jesus forsakes the sky,
To earth his footsteps bend;
He comes to bless our fallen race;
He comes with messages of grace.

3 Bear, bear the tidings round;
Let every mortal know
What love in God is found,
What pity he can show;
Ye winds that blow, ye waves that roll,
Bear the glad news from pole to pole.

4 Strike, strike the harps again,
To great Immanuel's name;
Arise, ye sons of men,
And all his grace proclaim;
Angels and men, wake every string,
'Tis God the Saviour's praise we sing!

298 11s.

1 BRIGHTEST and best of the sons of the morning!
Dawn on our darkness, and lend us thine aid!
Star of the East, the horizon adorning,
Guide where our infant Redeemer is laid.

2 Cold on his cradle the dew-drops are shining;
Low lies his head with the beasts of the stall:
Angels adore him in slumber reclining,
Maker, and Monarch, and Saviour of all.

3 Say, shall we yield him, in costly devotion,
Odors of Edom, and offerings divine,
Gems of the mountain, and pearls of the ocean,
Myrrh from the forest, and gold from the mine?

4 Vainly we offer each ample oblation,
Vainly with gifts would his favor secure;
Richer, by far, is the heart's adoration,
Dearer to God are the prayers of the poor.

5 Brightest and best of the sons of the morning!
Dawn on our darkness, and lend us thine aid!
Star of the East, the horizon adorning,
Guide where our infant Redeemer is laid.

HEBER.

299 C. M.

1 BRIGHT was the guiding star that led
With mild, benignant ray,
The Gentiles to the lowly shed,
Where the Redeemer lay.

2 But lo! a brighter, clearer light,
Now points to his abode;
It shines through sin and sorrow's night,
To guide us to our God.

3 Oh, haste to follow where it leads!
The gracious call obey;
Be rugged wilds, or flowery meads,
The Christian's destined way.

4 Oh, gladly tread the narrow path
While light and grace are given!
Who meekly follow Christ on earth
Shall reign with him in heaven.

LYTE.

300 C. M.

1 TO us a Child of hope is born,
To us a Son is given;
Him shall the tribes of earth obey,
Him all the hosts of heaven.

2 His name shall be the Prince of Peace,
Forevermore adored,
The Wonderful, the Counsellor,
The great and mighty Lord.

3 His power increasing still shall spread,
His reign no end shall know:
Justice shall guard his throne above,
And peace abound below.

JOHN MORRISON.

301 C. M.

1 IN stature grows the heavenly Child,
With death before his eyes;
A Lamb unblemished, meek and mild,
Prepared for sacrifice.

2 The Son of God his glory hides
With parents mean and poor;
And he who made the heavens abides
In dwelling-place obscure.

3 Those mighty hands that stay the sky,
No earthly toil refuse;
And he who set the stars on high,
A humble trade pursues.

4 He before whom the angels stand,
At whose behest they fly,
Now yields himself to man's command,
And lays his glory by.

5 The Father's name we loudly raise,
The Son we all adore,
The Holy Ghost, One God, we praise,
Both now and evermore.

302 L. M.

1 THE Word, with God the Father One,
Before the heav'ns and earth were made,
Is now the Virgin's new-born Son,
Upon her lowly bosom laid.

2 Already on his sinless head
The streams of wrath begin to flow;
Already on his infant bed
The pangs of grief he deigns to know.

3 The lowliest poverty he bears
That we may be with wealth supplied,
He weeps: O precious grief and tears!
Through him the world is purified.

4 Jesus, who camest from on high
To be the Lamb for sinners slain,
Leave not thy ransomed flock to die,
Nor let thy toil be spent in vain.

303 L. M.

1 JESUS a child his course begun:
How radiant dawned his heavenly day!
And those who such a race would run,
As early should be on their way.

2 His Father's business was his care;
Yet in man's favor still he grew:
Oh, might we learn by thought and prayer,
Like him a work of love to do!

3 For all mankind he came, nor yet
An infant's visit would deny;
Nor friend nor mother did forget
In his last hour of agony.

4 O children, ask him to impart
That spirit clear, that temper mild,
Which made the mother in her heart
Keep all the sayings of her Child.

5 Bless him who said, of such as you
His Father's kingdom is, and still,
His yoke to bear, his work to do,
Study his life to learn his will.

Ossoli.

304 L. M.

1 "SEE how he loved!" exclaimed the Jews,
As tender tears from Jesus fell;
My grateful heart the thought pursues,
And on the theme delights to dwell.

2 See how he loved, who traveled on,
Teaching the doctrine from the skies!
Who bade disease and pain begone,
And called the sleeping dead to rise.

3 See how he loved, who never shrank
From toil or danger, pain or death!
Who all the cup of sorrow drank,
And meekly yielded up his breath.

4 Such love can we, unmoved, survey?
Oh, may our breasts with ardor glow,
To tread his steps, his laws obey,
And thus our warm affections show!

305 11s & 8s.

1 I THINK, when I read that sweet story of old,
When Jesus was here among men,
How he called little children as lambs to his fold,
I should like to have been with them then.

2 I wish that his hands had been placed on my head,
That his arms had been thrown around me,
And that I might have seen his kind look, when he said,
"Let the little ones come unto me."

3 Yet still to his footstool in prayer I may go,
And ask for a share in his love;
And if I thus earnestly seek him below,
I shall see him and hear him above—

4 In that beautiful place he has gone to prepare,
For all who are washed and forgiv'n;
And many dear children are gathering there,
"For of such is the kingdom of heav'n."

5 I long for the joys of that glorious time,
The sweetest, and brightest, and best,
When the dear little children of every clime,
Shall crowd to his arms and be blest.

JEMIMA LUKE.

306 C. M.

1 SEE the kind Shepherd, Jesus, stands
With all-engaging charms;
Hark! how he calls the tender lambs,
And folds them in his arms.

2 Permit them to approach, he cries,
Nor scorn their humble name;
For 'twas to bless such souls as these
The Lord of angels came.

3 He'll lead us to the heavenly streams
Where living waters flow:
And guide us to the fruitful fields
Where trees of knowledge grow.

4 The feeblest lamb amidst the flock
Shall be its Shepherd's care:
While folded in the Saviour's arms
We're safe from every snare.

DODDRIDGE.

307 L. M.

1 WHAT are those soul-reviving strains,
Which echo thus from Salem's plains?
What anthems loud, and louder still,
So sweetly sound from Zion's hill?

Glory, glory let us sing,
While heaven and earth with glory ring;
Hosanna! hosanna!
Hosanna to the Lamb of God.

2 Lo! 'tis an infant chorus sings
Hosanna to the King of kings:
The Saviour comes!—and babes proclaim
Salvation, sent in Jesus' name.
Glory, glory let us sing, &c.

3 Nor these alone their voice shall raise,
For we will join this song of praise;
Still Israel's children forward press
To hail the Lord their Righteousness.
Glory, glory let us sing, &c.

4 Messiah's name shall joy impart
Alike to Jew and Gentile heart:
He bled for us, he bled for you,
And we will sing hosanna too.
Glory, glory let us sing, &c.

5 Proclaim hosannas loud and clear;
See David's Son and Lord appear!
All praise on earth to him be given,
And glory shout through highest heaven.
Glory, glory let us sing, &c.

308 L. M.

1 TO thee be glory, honor, praise,
Jesus, Redeemer, Saviour, King!
Inspired with joy at thine approach,
Thy children loud hosannas sing.

2 Hail, Israel's King! hail, David's Son!
Hail, thou that in Jehovah's name
Didst come thy people to redeem,
And comest now thy crown to claim!

3 Then, in thy way to Salem's courts,
They met thee with triumphal palms;
Now, for thy glad return we watch
With longing prayers, and vows, and psalms.

309 8s & 7s.

1 FIERCELY came the tempest sweeping,
Down the lake of Galilee;
But the ship where Christ lay sleeping
Might not sink in that wild sea.
When he rose, the tempest chiding,
When he bade the waters rest;
Calm the little ship went gliding
On the blue lake's quiet breast.

2 And the white waves rushing past her,
Round her keel lay smooth and still;
For the wild waves knew their Master,
And the waves obeyed his will.
Thou who heard'st those seamen pleading,
Waking at their anguish cry—
Sleep not now, when comfort needing,
Saviour, unto thee we fly.

3 When at night our homes are shaken,
And the howling winds we hear—
As in terror we awaken,
Keep us safe from harm and fear.
When the waves of pride, or anger,
Rise to vex our hearts within;
Keep us from a greater danger,
From the passion storms of sin.

310 8s & 7s.

1 ONCE upon the heaving ocean
Rode a bark at evening tide,
While the waves, in wild commotion,
Dashed against the vessel's side.
Jesus, sleeping on a pillow,
Heeded not the raging billow;
While the winds were all abroad,
Calmly slept the Son of God.

2 In that dark and stormy hour
Fearful hearts awaked their Lord;
Jesus, by his sovereign power,
Calmed the tempest with a word.
On life's dark and restless ocean,
Mid the billows' wild commotion,
Trembling soul, your Lord is there;
He will make you still his care.

MRS. DANA.

311 L. M.

1 HOW sweetly flowed the gospel sound
From lips of gentleness and grace,
When listening thousands gathered round,
The voice of Jesus filled the place.

2 From heaven he came, of heaven he spoke,
To heaven he led his followers way;
Dark clouds of gloomy night he broke,
Unveiling an immortal day.

3 "Come, wanderers, to my Father's home;
Come, all ye weary ones, and rest:"
Yes, sacred Teacher, we will come,
Obey thee, love thee, and be blest.

4 Decay, then, tenements of dust;
Pillars of earthly pride, decay:
A nobler mansion waits the just,
And Jesus has prepared the way.

BOWRING.

312 L. M.

1 AT even ere the sun was set,
The sick, O Lord, around thee lay;
Oh, in what divers pains they met!
Oh, with what joy they went away!

2 Once more 'tis eventide, and we
Oppressed with various ills draw near:
What if thy form we cannot see?
We know and feel that thou art here.

3 O Saviour Christ, our woes dispel;
For some are sick, and some are sad,
And some have never loved thee well,
And some have lost the love they had.

4 And some have found the world is vain,
Yet from the world they break not free;
And some have friends who give them pain,
Yet have not sought a friend in thee.

5 O Saviour Christ, thou too art Man;
Thou hast been troubled, tempted, tried;
Thy kind but searching glance can scan
The very wounds that shame would hide.

6 The touch has still its ancient power;
No word from thee can fruitless fall;
Hear in this solemn evening hour,
And in thy mercy heal us all.

313 L. M.

1 WHEN power divine, in mortal form,
Hushed with a word the raging storm,
In soothing accents Jesus said—
Lo! it is I; be not afraid."

2 Blest be the voice that breathes from heaven,
To every heart in sunder riven,
When love, and joy, and hope are fled—
"Lo! it is I; be not afraid."

3 And when the last dread hour is come,
While shuddering nature wails her doom,
This voice shall call the pious dead—
"Lo! it is I; be not afraid."

J. E. SMITH.

314 L. M.

1 MY dear Redeemer, and my Lord,
I read my duty in thy word;
But in thy life the law appears,
Drawn out in living characters.

2 Such was thy truth, and such thy zeal,
Such deference to thy Father's will,
Such love, and meekness so divine,
I would transcribe and make them mine.

3 Cold mountains and the midnight air
Witnessed the fervor of thy prayer;
The desert thy temptations knew,
Thy conflict and thy victory too.

4 Be thou my pattern; make me bear
More of thy gracious image here;
Then God, the Judge, shall own my name
Among the followers of the Lamb.

WATTS.

315 L. M.

1 HOW beauteous were the marks divine,
That in thy meekness used to shine,
That lit thy lonely pathway, trod
In wondrous love, O Son of God!

2 Oh, who like thee, so calm, so bright,
So pure, so made to live in light?
Oh, who like thee did ever go
So patient through a world of woe?

3 Oh, who like thee, so humbly bore
The scorn, the scoffs of men, before?
So meek, forgiving, godlike, high,
So glorious in humility?

4 The bending angels stooped to see
The lisping infant clasp thy knee,
And smile as in a father's eye,
Upon thy mild divinity.

5 And death, which sets the prisoner free,
Was pang, and scoff, and scorn to thee;
Yet love through all thy torture glowed,
And mercy with thy life-blood flowed.

6 Oh, in thy light be mine to go,
Illuming all my way of woe;
And give me ever on the road
To trace thy footsteps, Son of God!

A. C. COXE.

316 L. M.

1 WHEN like a stranger on our sphere,
The lowly Jesus wandered here,
Where'er he went, affliction fled,
And sickness reared her fainting head.

2 The eye that rolled in irksome night,
Beheld his face,—for God is light;
The opening ear, the loosened tongue,
His precepts heard, his praises sung.

3 With bounding steps, the halt and lame
To hail their great Deliverer came;
O'er the cold grave he bowed his head,
He spake the word, and raised the dead.

4 Despairing madness, dark and wild,
In his inspiring presence smiled;
The storm of horror ceased to roll,
And reason lightened through the soul.

MONTGOMERY

317 C. M.

1 WHAT grace, O Lord, and beauty shone
Around thy steps below;
What patient love was seen in all
Thy life and death of woe.

2 For, ever on thy burdened heart
A weight of sorrow hung;
Yet no ungentle, murmuring word
Escaped thy silent tongue.

3 Thy foes might hate, despise, revile,
Thy friends unfaithful prove;
Unwearied in forgiveness still,
Thy heart could only love.

4 Oh, give us hearts to love like thee!
Like thee, O Lord, to grieve
Far more for others' sin than all
The wrongs that we receive.

5 One with thyself, may every eye,
In us, thy brethren, see
The gentleness and grace that spring
From union, Lord, with thee.

318 C. M.

1 INCARNATE Word! by every grief,
By each temptation tried,
Who lived to yield our ills relief,
And to redeem us died!

2 If gaily clothed, and proudly fed,
In dangerous wealth we dwell,
Remind us of thy manger bed,
And lowly cottage cell.

3 If press'd by poverty severe,
In envious want we pine,
Oh may the Spirit whisper near,
How poor a lot was thine!

4 Through fickle fortune's various scene
From sin preserve us free;
Like us thou hast a mourner been,
May we rejoice with thee!

319 C. M.

1 THOU art the Way: to thee alone
From sin and death we flee;
And he who would the Father seek,
Must seek him, Lord, by thee.

2 Thou art the Truth: thy word alone
True wisdom can impart;
Thou only canst instruct the mind,
And purify the heart.

3 Thou art the Life: the rending tomb
Proclaims thy conquering arm;
And those who put their trust in thee
Nor death nor hell shall harm.

4 Thou art the Way, the Truth, the Life:
Grant us to know that Way;
That Truth to keep, that Life to win,
Which leads to endless day. DOANE.

320 8s & 7s.

1 JESUS wept! those tears are over,
But his heart is still the same;
Kinsman, Friend, and Elder Brother,
Is his everlasting name.
Saviour, who can love like thee,
Gracious One of Bethany?

2 When the pangs of trial seize us,
When the waves of sorrow roll,
I will lay my head on Jesus,
Pillow of the troubled soul.
Surely, none can feel like thee,
Weeping One of Bethany.

3 Jesus wept! and still in glory,
He can mark each mourner's tear;
Living to retrace the story
Of the hearts he solaced here.
Lord, when I am called to die,
Let me think of Bethany.

4 Jesus wept! that tear of sorrow
Is a legacy of love;
Yesterday, to-day, to-morrow,
He the same doth ever prove.
Thou art all in all to me,
Living One of Bethany!

321 L. M.

1 RIDE on, ride on in majesty!
In lowly pomp ride on to die:
O Christ, thy triumphs now begin
O'er captive death and conquered sin.

2 Ride on, ride on in majesty!
Hark! all the tribes hosanna cry!
Thy humble beast pursues his road,
With palms and scattered garments strowed.

3 Ride on, ride on in majesty!
The wingéd squadrons of the sky
Look down, with sad and wondering eyes
To see th' approaching sacrifice.

4 Ride on, ride on in majesty!
Thy last and fiercest strife is nigh:
The Father, on his sapphire throne,
Expects his own anointed Son.

5 Ride on, ride on in majesty!
In lowly pomp ride on to die:
Bow thy meek head to mortal pain;
Then take, O God, thy power, and reign!

MILMAN.

322 L. M.

1 O WONDROUS type, O vision fair,
Of glory that the Church shall share,
Which Christ upon the mountain shows,
Where brighter than the sun he glows!

2 With shining face and bright array,
Christ deigns to manifest to-day
What glory shall be theirs above,
Who joy in God with perfect love.

3 And faithful hearts are raised on high
By this great vision's mystery;
For which in joyful strains we raise
The voice of prayer, the hymn of praise.

4 O Father, with the Eternal Son,
And Holy Spirit, ever One,
Vouchsafe to bring us by thy grace
To see thy glory face to face.

323 L. M.

1 FLOW fast, my tears! the cause is great;
This tribute, claims an injured Friend:
One whom I long pursued with hate,
And yet he loved me to the end.

2 Fast flow my tears; yet faster flow,
Stream copious as yon purple tide;
'Twas I that dealt the deadly blow,
I urged the hand that pierced his side.

3 Fast, and yet faster flow my tears,
Love breaks the heart and drowns the eyes,

His visage marred, towards heaven he rears,
And, pleading for his murderers, dies!

4 My grief no measure knows, nor end,
Till he appears the sinner's Friend!
And gives me in a happy hour,
To feel the risen Saviour's power.

324 L. M.

1 'TIS midnight; and on Olive's brow
The star is dimmed that lately shone:
'Tis midnight; in the garden, now,
The suffering Saviour prays alone.

2 'Tis midnight; and from all removed,
The Saviour wrestles lone with fears;
Ev'n that disciple whom he loved
Heeds not his Master's grief and tears.

3 'Tis midnight; and for others' guilt
The Man of Sorrows weeps in blood;
Yet he that hath in anguish knelt
Is not forsaken by his God.

4 'Tis midnight; and from ether-plains
Is borne the song that angels know;
Unheard by mortals are the strains
That sweetly soothe the Saviour's woe.

TAPPAN.

325 L. M.

1 LORD! in thy garden agony,
No light seemed on thy soul to break,
No form of seraph lingered nigh,
Nor yet the voice of comfort spake—

2 Till, by thine own triumphant word,
The victory over ill was won;
Till the sweet, mournful cry was heard,
"Thy will, O God, not mine, be done!"

3 Lord, bring these precious moments back,
When, fainting, against sin we strain;
Or in thy counsels fail to track
Aught but the present grief and pain.

4 In weakness, help us to contend;
In darkness, yield to God our will;
And true hearts, faithful to the end,
Cheer by thine holy angels still!

326 L. M.

1 FROM Calvary a cry was heard—
A bitter and heart-rending cry;
My Saviour! every mournful word
Bespoke thy soul's deep agony.

2 A horror of great darkness fell
On thee, thou spotless, holy One!
And all the eager hosts of hell
Conspired to tempt God's only Son.

3 The scourge, the thorns, the deep disgrace—
Those thou could'st bear, nor once repine;
But when Jehovah vailed his face,
Unutterable pangs were thine.

4 Let the dumb world its silence break;
Let pealing anthems rend the sky;
Awake, my sluggish soul, awake!
He died, that we might never die.

CUNNINGHAM.

327 L. M.

1 THE morning dawns upon the place
Where Jesus spent the night in prayer;
Through yielding glooms behold his face!
Nor form, nor comeliness is there.

2 Brought forth to judgment, now he stands
Arraigned, condemned, at Pilate's bar;
Here, spurned by fierce prætorian bands,
There, mocked by Herod's men of war.

3 He bears their buffeting and scorn—
Mock-homage of the lip, the knee—
The purple robe, the crown of thorn—
The scourge, the nail, th'accursed tree.

4 No guile within his mouth is found;
He neither threatens nor complains;
Meek as a lamb for slaughter bound,
Dumb, 'mid his murderers, he remains.

5 But hark! he prays: 'tis for his foes:
And speaks: 'tis comfort to his friends;
Answers: and paradise bestows;
He bows his head: the conflict ends.

MONTGOMERY.

328 L. M.

1 SOFT be the gently breathing notes,
That sing the Saviour's dying love;—
Soft as the evening zephyr floats;
Soft as the tuneful lyres above:

2 Soft as the morning dews descend,
While the sweet lark exulting soars;
So soft, to your Almighty Friend,
Be every sigh your bosom pours:

3 Pure as the sun's enlivening ray,
That scatters life and joy abroad;
Pure as the lucid car of day,
That wide proclaims its Maker, God;

4 Pure as the breath of vernal skies;—
So pure let our contrition be;
So purely let our love arise
To him who bled upon the tree.

COLLIER.

329 L. M.

1 O CHRIST! our King, Creator, Lord!
Saviour of all who trust thy word!
To them who seek thee ever near,
Now to our praises bend an ear.

2 In thy dear cross a balm is found,
It flows from every streaming wound,
Whose power our inbred sin controls,
Breaks the firm bond, and frees our souls.

3 Thou didst create the stars of night;
Yet thou hast vailed in flesh thy light,
Hast deigned a mortal form to wear,
A mortal's painful lot to bear.

4 When thou didst hang upon the tree,
The quaking earth acknowledged thee:
When thou didst there yield up thy breath,
The world grew dark as shades of death.

GREGORY.

330 L. M.

1 WHEN I survey the wondrous cross
On which the Prince of Glory died,
My richest gain I count but loss,
And pour contempt on all my pride.

2 Forbid it, Lord, that I should boast
Save in the death of Christ, my God;
All the vain things that charm me most,
I sacrifice them to his blood.

3 See, from his head, his hands, his feet,
Sorrow and love flow mingled down;
Did e'er such love and sorrow meet,
Or thorns compose so rich a crown?

4 Were the whole realm of nature mine,
That were a present far too small;
Love so amazing, so divine,
Demands my soul, my life, my all.

WATTS.

Occasional Chorus.

The cross, the cross, the precious cross,
The wondrous cross of Jesus;
From all our sin, its guilt and power,
And every stain it frees us.

Then I'm clinging, clinging, clinging,
Oh, I'm clinging to the cross;
Yes, I'm clinging, clinging, clinging,
Clinging to the cross.

331 L. M.

1 STRETCHED on the cross, the Saviour dies;
Hark! his expiring groans arise;
See, from his hands, his feet, his side,
Descends the sacred, crimson tide.

2 And didst thou bleed?—for sinners bleed?
And could the sun behold the deed?
No; he withdrew his cheering ray,
And darkness veiled the mourning day.

3 Can I survey this scene of woe,
Where mingling grief and mercy flow,
And yet my heart so hard remain,
Unmoved by either love or pain?

4 Come, dearest Lord, thy grace impart,
To warm this cold, this stupid heart,
Till all its powers and passions move
In melting grief and ardent love.

STEELE.

332 L. M.

1 YE that pass by, behold the Man!
The Man of Grief, condemned for you,
The Lamb of God for sinners slain,
Weeping to Calvary pursue.

2 His sacred limbs they stretch, they tear,
With nails they fasten to the wood;
His sacred limbs! exposed and bare,
Or only covered with his blood.

3 Behold his temples crowned with thorn,
His bleeding hands extended wide,
His streaming feet transfixed and torn,
The fountain gushing from his side.

4 Oh thou dear suffering Son of God,
How doth thy heart to sinners move?
Sprinkle on us thy precious blood,
And melt us with thy dying love!

C. WESLEY.

333 L. M.

1 "'TIS finished!"—so the Saviour cried,
And meekly bowed his head and died:
"'Tis finished!"—yes, the race is run,
The battle fought, the victory won.

2 "'Tis finished!"—this his dying groan
Shall sins of deepest hue atone,
And millions be redeemed from death
By Jesus' last, expiring breath.

3 "'Tis finished!"—Heaven is reconciled,
And all the powers of darkness spoiled;
Peace, love, and happiness again
Return, and dwell with sinful men.

4 "'Tis finished!"—let the joyful sound
Be heard through all the nations round:
"'Tis finished!"—let the triumph rise,
And swell the chorus of the skies.

STENNETT.

334 L. M.

1 NATURE with open volume stands
To spread her Maker's praise abroad;
And every labor of his hands
Shows something worthy of a God.

2 But in the grace that rescued man
His brightest form of glory shines;
Here on the cross 'tis fairest drawn
In precious blood and crimson lines.

3 Oh the sweet wonders of that cross,
Where God the Saviour loved and died;
Her noblest life my spirit draws
From his dear wounds and bleeding side.

4 I would forever speak his name
In sounds to mortal ears unknown;
With angels join to praise the Lamb,
And worship at his Father's throne.

WATTS.

335 L. M.

1 HE dies!—the Friend of sinners dies;
Lo! Salem's daughters weep around;
A solemn darkness veils the skies;
A sudden trembling shakes the ground.

2 Ye saints approach! the anguish view
Of him who groans beneath your load;
He gives his precious life for you,
For you he sheds his precious blood.

3 Here's love and grief beyond degree,
The Lord of Glory dies for men;
But lo! what sudden joys we see,
Jesus, the dead, revives again.

4 Break off your tears, ye saints, and tell
How high our great Deliverer reigns;
Sing how he spoiled the hosts of hell,
And led the tyrant death in chains.

5 Say, "Live forever, glorious King,
Born to redeem, and strong to save!"
Then ask,—"O death, where is thy sting?
And where thy victory, O grave?"

WATTS.

336 L. M.

1 OH come and mourn with me awhile!
Oh come ye to the Saviour's side!
Oh come, together let us mourn!
Jesus, our Lord, is crucified.

2 Have we no tears to shed for him,
While soldiers scoff and Jews deride?
Ah! look how patiently he hangs:
Jesus, our Lord, is crucified.

3 How fast his hands and feet are nailed:
His throat with parching thirst is dried:
His fainting eyes are dimmed with blood!
Jesus, our Lord, is crucified.

4 Come, let us stand beneath the cross;
So may the blood from out his side
Fall gently on us—drop by drop;
Jesus, our Lord, is crucified.

5 A broken heart, a fount of tears
Ask, and they will not be denied:
Lord Jesus, may we love and weep,
Since thou for us art crucified.

337 L. M.

1 SAVIOUR, I think upon that hour,
When thou, the Shepherd of the flock,
The Prince of peace, the Lord of power,
Wert the priests' scorn, the soldiers' mock.

2 And bleeding from the Roman rod,
And scoffed at by the heartless Jew,
I hear thee plead for them to God,—
"Father, they know not what they do!"

3 And then I lift my trembling eyes
To that bright seat, where, placed on high,
The great, the atoning sacrifice,
For me, for all, is ever nigh.

4 Be thou my guard on peril's brink;
Be thou my guide through weal or woe;
And teach me of thy cup to drink;
And make me in thy path to go.

338 L. M.

1 OUR spirits join t' adore the Lamb;
Oh, that our feeble lips could move
In strains immortal as his name,
And melting as his dying love.

2 Was ever equal pity found?
The Prince of heaven resigns his breath,
And pours his life out on the ground
To ransom guilty worms from death.

3 In vain our mortal voices strive
To speak compassion so divine;
Had we a thousand lives to give,
A thousand lives should all be thine.

339 L. M.

1 LORD Jesus, when we stand afar,
And gaze upon thy holy cross,
In love of thee and scorn of self,
Oh! may we count the world as loss.

2 When we behold thy bleeding wounds,
And the rough way that thou hast trod,
Make us to hate the load of sin
That lay so heavy on our God.

3 O holy Lord! uplifted high
With outstretched arms, in mortal woe,
Embracing in thy wondrous love
The sinful world that lies below!

4 Give us an ever-living faith
To gaze beyond the things we see;
And in the mystery of thy death
Draw us and all men unto thee.

WM. WALSHAM HOW.

340 L. M.

1 BENEATH thy cross I lay me down,
And mourn to see thy bloody crown;
Love drops in blood from every vein;
Love is the spring of all thy pain.

2 Here, Jesus, I shall ever stay,
And spend my longing hours away,
Think on thy bleeding wounds and pain,
And contemplate thy woes again.

3 The rage of Satan and of sin,
Of foes without, and fears within,
Shall ne'er my conquering soul remove,
Or from thy cross, or from thy love.

4 Secured from harm beneath thy shade,
Here death and hell shall ne'er invade;
Nor Sinai, with its thundering noise,
Shall e'er disturb my happier joys.

5 O unmolested, happy rest!
Where inward fears are all suppress;
Here I shall love, and live secure,
And patiently my cross endure.

WILLIAMS.

341 C. M.

1 THE Saviour, what a noble flame
Was kindled in his breast,
When, hasting to Jerusalem,
He marched before the rest!

2 Good-will to men, and zeal for God,
His every thought engross;
He longs to be baptized in blood,
He pants to reach the cross.

3 With all his sufferings full in view,
And woes to us unknown,
Forth to the task his spirit flew;
'Twas love that urged him on.

4 Lord, we return thee what we can;
Our hearts shall sound abroad,
Salvation to the dying man,
And to the rising God!

5 And while thy bleeding glories here
Engage our wondering eyes,
We learn our lighter cross to bear,
And hasten to the skies.

COWPER.

342 C. M.

1 BEHOLD, where, in a mortal form
Appears each grace divine;
The virtues, all in Jesus met,
With mildest radiance shine.

2 To spread the rays of heavenly light,
To give the mourner joy,

To preach glad tidings to the poor,
Was his divine employ.

3 'Midst keen reproach, and cruel scorn,
Patient and meek he stood;
His foes, ungrateful, sought his life;
He labored for their good.

4 In the last hour of deep distress,
Before his Father's throne,
With soul resigned, he bowed, and said,
"Thy will, not mine, be done!"

5 Be Christ our pattern and our guide;
His image may we bear;
Oh, may we tread his holy steps,
His joy and glory share.

ENFIELD.

343 C. M.

1 HOW wondrous was the burning zeal
Which filled the Master's breast,
When, all his suff'rings full in view,
To Salem's towers he pressed!

2 Dear Lord! no tongue can duly tell
Thy love's prevailing might;
No thought can comprehend its length
And breadth and depth and height!

3 Yet grant that we may follow thee
Through all thine hours of scorn;
And learn with thee to watch and pray—
With thee to weep and mourn.

4 And still, O blessèd Nazarene!
The more thy cross we see,
The more may each exclaim with joy,
The Saviour died for me!

344 C. M.

1 FROM whence these direful omens round,
Which heaven and earth amaze?
And why do earthquakes cleave the ground?
Why hides the sun his rays?

2 Well may the earth astonished shake,
And nature sympathize;
The sun as darkest night be black:
Their Maker, Jesus, dies!

3 Behold, fast streaming from the tree,
His all-atoning blood!
Is this the Infinite? 'tis he,
My Saviour and my God!

4 For me these pangs his soul assail,
For me this death is borne;
My sins gave sharpness to the nail,
And pointed every thorn.

5 Let sin no more my soul enslave,
Break, Lord, its tyrant chain;
Oh save me, whom thou cam'st to save,
Nor bleed, nor die in vain.

S. WESLEY, Jr.

345 C. M.

1 A PILGRIM through this lonely world,
The blessèd Saviour passed;
A mourner all his life was he,
A dying Lamb at last.

2 That tender heart that felt for all,
For all its life-blood gave;
It found on earth no resting-place,
Save only in the grave.

3 Such was our Lord; and shall we fear
The cross, with all its scorn?
Or love a faithless evil world,
That wreathed his brow with thorn?

4 No! facing all its frowns or smiles,
Like him, obedient still,
We homeward press through storm or calm,
To Zion's blessèd hill.

BONAR.

346 C. M.

1 BEHOLD the Saviour of mankind,
Nailed to the shameful tree!
How vast the love that him inclined
To bleed and die for me!

2 Hark! how he groans, while nature shakes,
And earth's strong pillars bend!
The temple's vail asunder breaks,
The solid marbles rend.

3 'Tis finished! now the ransom 's paid.
"Receive my soul!" he cries:
See—how he bows his sacred head!
He bows his head and dies!

4 But soon he'll break death's iron chain,
And in full glory shine;
O Lamb of God! was ever pain—
Was ever love like thine!

S. WESLEY, SR.

347 C. M.

1 ALAS! and did my Saviour bleed?
And did my Sovereign die?
Would he devote that sacred head
For such a worm as I?

2 Was it for crimes that I had done
He groaned upon the tree?
Amazing pity! grace unknown!
And love beyond degree!

3 Well might the sun in darkness hide,
And shut his glories in,
When God, the mighty Maker, died,
For man the creature's sin.

4 Thus might I hide my blushing face
While his dear cross appears,
Dissolve my heart in thankfulness,
And melt mine eyes to tears.

5 But drops of grief can ne'er repay
The debt of love I owe:
Here, Lord, I give myself away;
'Tis all that I can do.

WATTS.

348 C. M.

1 DARK was the night, and cold the ground
On which the Lord was laid;
His sweat like drops of blood ran down;
In agony he prayed—

2 "Father, remove this bitter cup,
If such thy sacred will;
If not, content to drink it up,
Thy pleasure I fulfill."

3 Go to the Garden, sinner; see
Those precious drops that flow;
The heavy load he bore for thee;
For thee he lies so low.

4 Then learn of him the cross to bear;
Thy Father's will obey;
And, when temptations press thee near,
Awake to watch and pray.

HAWEIS.

349 C. M.

1 AND did the Holy and the Just,
The Sovereign of the skies,
Stoop down to wretchedness and dust,
That guilty man might rise?

2 He took the dying sinner's place,
And suffered in his stead;
For man, oh miracle of grace!
For man the Saviour bled.

3 Dear Lord, what heavenly wonders dwell
In thine atoning blood!
By this are sinners saved from hell,
And rebels brought to God.

STEELE.

350 C. M.

1 HOW condescending and how kind
Was God's eternal Son!
Our misery reached his heavenly mind,
And pity brought him down.

2 He sunk beneath our heavy woes,
To raise us to his throne;
There's ne'er a gift his hand bestows,
But cost his heart a groan.

3 This was compassion, like a God,
That when the Saviour knew
The price of pardon was his blood,
His pity ne'er withdrew.

WATTS.

351 S. M.

1 BEHOLD th' amazing sight,
The Saviour lifted high;
Behold the Son of God's delight
Expire in agony.

2 For whom, for whom, my heart,
Were all these sorrows borne?
Why did he feel that painful smart,
And meet that various scorn?

3 For us he hung and bled,
For us in torture died;
'Twas love that bowed his fainting head,
And oped his gushing side.

4 I see, and I adore
In sympathy of love;
I feel the strong, attractive power
To lift my soul above.

5 Drawn by such cords as these,
Let all the earth combine,
With cheerful ardor, to confess
The energy divine.

DODDRIDGE.

352 S. M.

1 O'ERWHELMED in depths of woe,
Upon the tree of scorn
Hangs the Redeemer of mankind,
With racking anguish torn.

2 See how the nails those hands
And feet so tender rend;
See down his face, and neck, and breast
His sacred blood descend.

3 Oh, hear that awful cry
Which pierced his mother's heart,
As into God the Father's hands
He bade his soul depart.

4 Earth hears, and trembling quakes
Around that tree of pain;

The rocks are rent; the graves are burst;
The veil is rent in twain.

5 The sun withdraws his light;
The mid-day heavens grow pale;
The moon, the stars, the universe
Their Maker's death bewail.

6 Shall man alone be mute?
Have we no griefs, or fears?
Come, old and young, come all mankind,
And bathe those feet in tears.

7 Come, fall before his cross,
Who shed for us his blood;
Who died, the victim of pure love,
To make us sons of God.

353 S. M.

1 LIKE sheep we went astray,
And broke the fold of God,
Each wand'ring in a different way,
But all the downward road.

2 How dreadful was the hour,
When God our wand'rings laid,
And did at once his vengeance pour
Upon the Shepherd's head!

3 How glorious was the grace,
When Christ sustained the stroke!
His life and blood the Shepherd pays,
A ransom for his flock! WATTS.

354 7s & 6s.

1 O SACRED Head, now wounded,
With grief and shame weigh'd down,
Now scornfully surrounded
With thorns, thine only crown;
O sacred Head, what glory,
What bliss, till now, was thine!
Yet, though despis'd and gory,
I joy to call thee mine.

2 What thou, my Lord, hast suffered
Was all for sinners' gain;
Mine, mine was the transgression,
But thine the deadly pain:
Lo, here I fall, my Saviour!
'Tis I deserve thy place;
Look on me with thy favor,
Vouchsafe to me thy grace.

3 What language shall I borrow
To thank thee, dearest Friend,
For this thy dying sorrow,
Thy pity without end?
Oh make me thine forever;
And should I fainting be,
Lord, let me never, never,
Outlive my love to thee!

4 Be near me when I'm dying,
Oh show thy cross to me!
And for my succor flying,
Come, Lord, and set me free!
These eyes, new faith receiving,
From Jesus shall not move;
For he who dies believing,
Dies safely, through thy love.

BERNARD, 1153.

355 6s.

1 BLOOD is the price of heaven;
All sin that price exceeds;
Oh, come to be forgiven;
He bleeds, my Saviour bleeds!

2 Under the olive boughs,
Falling like ruby beads,

The blood drops from his brows ;
He bleeds, my Saviour bleeds !

3 While the fierce scourges fall
The precious blood still pleads ;
In front of Pilate's hall
He bleeds, my Saviour bleeds !

4 Beneath the thorny crown
The crimson fountain speeds ;
See how it trickles down ;
He bleeds, my Saviour bleeds !

5 Bearing the fatal wood,
His band of saints he leads,
Marking the way with blood ;
He bleeds, my Saviour bleeds !

6 He hangs upon the tree,
Hangs there for my misdeeds ;
He sheds his blood for me ;
He bleeds, my Saviour bleeds !

FABER.

356 7s, 6s, & 8s.

1 BEHOLD ! behold ! the Lamb of God,
On the cross, on the cross !
For you he shed his precious blood,
On the cross, on the cross !
Now hear his all-important cry,
"Eloi lama sabacthani ;"
Draw near, and see your Saviour die,
On the cross, on the cross !

2 Where'er I go I'll tell the story
Of the cross, of the cross !
In nothing else my soul shall glory,
Save the cross, save the cross !
Yes, this my constant theme shall be,
Through time and in eternity,
That Jesus suffered death for me,
On the cross, on the cross !

3 Let every mourner come and cling
To the cross, to the cross !
Let every Christian come and sing,
Round the cross, round the cross !
Here let the preacher take his stand,
And with the Bible in his hand,
Proclaim the triumphs of the Lamb
On the cross, on the cross !

357 7s. D.

1 BOUND upon th' accursèd tree,
Faint and bleeding, who is he ?
By the eyes so pale and dim,
Streaming blood and writhing limb,
By the flesh with scourges torn,
By the crown of twisted thorn,
By the drooping, death-dew'd brow,
Son of Man, 'tis thou ! 'tis thou !

2 Bound upon th' accursèd tree,
Dread and awful, who is he ?
By the sun at noonday pale,
Shivering rocks and rending veil,
By earth that trembles at his doom,
By yonder saints that burst their tomb,
Trembling nature knows thee now ;
Son of God, 'tis thou ! 'tis thou !

3 Bound upon th' accursèd tree,
Faint and bleeding, who is he ?
By the prayer for them that slew,
"Lord ! they know not what they do !"
By Eden, promised ere he died
To the felon at his side,
Lord, our suppliant knees we bow,
Son of God, 'tis thou ! 'tis thou !

4 Bound upon th' accursèd tree,
Sad and dying, who is he ?
By the last and bitter cry
The life given up in agony ;

By the baffled burning thirst,
By the side so deeply pierced,
Crucified! we know thee now;
Son of Man, 'tis thou! 'tis thou!

5 Bound upon th' accursèd tree,
Cold and lifeless, who is he?
By the lifeless body laid
In the chamber of the dead:
By the mourners come to weep
Where the bones of Jesus sleep;
By the linen round thy brow,
Son of Man, 'tis thou! 'tis thou!

6 Bound upon th' accursèd tree,
Dread and awful, who is he?
By the spoiled and empty grave,
By the souls he died to save,
By the conquests he hath won,
By the saints before his throne,
By the rainbow round his brow;
Son of God, 'tis thou! 'tis thou!

MILMAN.

358 8s, 7s, & 4s.

1 HARK! the voice of love and mercy
Sounds aloud from Calvary;
See, it rends the rocks asunder,
Shakes the earth, and veils the sky:
"It is finished!"
Hear the dying Saviour cry.

2 It is finished,—oh, what pleasure
Do these precious words afford!
Heavenly blessings, without measure,
Flow to us from Christ the Lord.
"It is finished!"
Saints, the dying words record.

3 Finished all the types and shadows
Of the ceremonial law,—
Finished—all that God hath promised,
Death and hell no more shall awe:
"It is finished!"
Saints, from hence your comfort draw.

4 Tune your harps anew, ye seraphs,
Join to sing the pleasing theme;
All on earth and all in heaven
Join to praise Immanuel's name:
Hallelujah!
Glory to the bleeding Lamb!

EVANS.

359 8s, 7s, & 4s.

1 WHO is this that comes from Edom,
All his raiment stained with blood,
To the captive speaking freedom,
Bringing and bestowing good;
Glorious in the garb he wears,
Glorious in the spoil he bears?

2 'Tis the Saviour, now victorious,
Traveling onward in his might;
'Tis the Saviour; oh, how glorious
To his people is the sight!
Satan conquered, and the grave;
Jesus now is strong to save.

3 Why that blood his raiment staining?
'Tis the blood of many slain;
Of his foes there's none remaining,
None, the contest to maintain;
Fallen now, no more to rise,
All their glory prostrate lies.

4 Mighty Victor, reign forever,
Wear the crown so dearly won;
Never shall thy people, never,
Cease to sing what thou hast done.
Thou hast slain thy people's foes;
Thou hast healed thy people's woes.

360

7s. D.

1 MARY to the Saviour's tomb
Hasted at the early dawn;
Spice she brought, and sweet perfume,
But the Lord she loved was gone.
For awhile she lingering stood,
Filled with sorrow and surprise;
Trembling, while a crystal flood
Issued from her weeping eyes.

2 Jesus, who is always near,
Though too often unperceived,
Came his drooping child to cheer,
Kindly asking why she grieved:
Though at first she knew him not,
When he callèd her by name
Then her griefs were all forgot,
For she found he was the same.

3 Grief and sighing quickly fled
As she heard his welcome voice;
Just before, she thought him dead,
Now, he bids her heart rejoice.
What a change his word can make,
Turning darkness into day!
You who weep for Jesus' sake,
He will wipe your tears away.

4 He who came to comfort her,
When she thought her all was lost,
Will for your relief appear,
Though you now are tempest-tost.
On his word your burden cast,
On his love your thoughts employ;
Weeping for awhile may last,
But the morning brings the joy.

NEWTON.

361

7s. D.

1 RESTING from his work to-day,
In the tomb the Saviour lay;
Still he slept; from head to feet
Shrouded in the winding sheet,—
Lying in the rock alone,
Hidden by the sealèd stone.

2 Late at even there was seen
Watching long the Magdalene;
Early, ere the break of day,
Sorrowful she took her way
To the holy garden glade,
Where her buried Lord was laid.

3 So with thee till life shall end
I would solemn vigil spend;
Let me hew thee, Lord, a shrine
In this rocky heart of mine,
Where in pure embalmèd cell
None but thee may ever dwell.

4 Myrrh and spices will I bring,
True affection's offering;
Close the door from sight and sound
Of the busy world around;
And in patient watch remain
Till my Lord appear again.

WHYTEHEAD.

362

7s. 6 lines.

1 GO to dark Gethsemane,
Ye that feel the tempter's power;
Your Redeemer's conflict see:
Watch with him one bitter hour:
Turn not from his griefs away;
Learn of Jesus Christ to pray.

2 Follow to the judgment-hall;
View the Lord of life arraigned.

Oh the wormwood and the gall!
Oh the pangs his soul sustained!
Shun not suffering, shame, or loss:
Learn of him to bear the cross.

3 Calvary's mournful mountain climb;
There, adoring at his feet,
Mark that miracle of time,
God's own sacrifice complete.
"It is finished!" hear him cry;
Learn of Jesus Christ to die.

4 Early hasten to the tomb,
Where they laid his breathless clay;
All is solitude and gloom:
Who hath taken him away?
Christ is risen, he seeks the skies;
Saviour, teach us so to rise.

MONTGOMERY.

363 7s. 6 lines.

1 WOULDST thou learn the depth of sin,
All its bitterness and pain?
What it cost thy God to win
Sinners to himself again?
Come, poor sinner, come with me;
Visit sad Gethsemane.

2 Wouldst thou know God's wondrous love?
Seek it not beside the throne;
List not angels' praise above;
Come and hear the heavy groan
By the Godhead heaved for thee,
Sinner, in Gethsemane.

3 When his tears and bloody sweat,
When his passion and his prayer,
When his pangs on Olivet
Wake within thee thoughts of care,
Think, O sinner, 'twas for thee
He suffered in Gethsemane.

4 Hate the sin that cost so dear;
Love the God that loved thee so;
Weep thou must, but likewise fear
Lest that fountain freshly flow,
That once freely gushed for thee
In sorrowful Gethsemane. MONSELL.

364 7s.

1 CHRIST the Lord is risen to-day,
Sons of men and angels say;
Raise your joys and triumphs high,
Sing, ye heavens, and earth reply.

2 Love's redeeming work is done,
Fought the fight, the battle won:
Lo! our Sun's eclipse is o'er;
Lo! he sets in blood no more.

3 Vain the stone, the watch, the seal;
Christ hath burst the gates of hell!
Death in vain forbids his rise;
Christ hath opened Paradise!

4 Lives again our glorious King:
Where, O Death, is now thy sting?
Once he died, our souls to save:
Where thy victory, O Grave?

5 Soar we now where Christ has led,
Following our exalted head;
Made like him, like him we rise;
Ours the cross, the grave, the skies.

C. WESLEY.

365 7s.

1 ANGELS! roll the rock away;
Death! yield up thy mighty prey;
See! the Saviour leaves the tomb,
Glowing with immortal bloom.

2 Now, ye saints, lift up your eyes,
See him high in glory rise!
Hosts of angels, on the road,
Hail him—the incarnate God.

3 Heaven unfolds its portals wide;
See the Conqueror through them ride!
King of glory! mount thy throne—
Boundless empire is thine own.

4 Praise him, ye celestial choirs!
Tune, and sweep your golden lyres;
Raise, O earth! your noblest songs,
From ten thousand thousand tongues.

5 Every note with wonder swell,
Sin o'erthrown, and captive hell!
Where, O Death, is now thy sting?
Where thy terrors, vanquished king?

GIBBONS.

366

7s.

1 MORNING breaks upon the tomb,
Jesus scatters all its gloom;
Day of triumph through the skies—
See the glorious Saviour rise!

2 Ye, who are of death afraid,
Triumph in the scattered shade;
Drive your anxious cares away;
See the place where Jesus lay!

3 Christian, dry your flowing tears,
Chase your unbelieving fears;
Look on his deserted grave;
Doubt no more his power to save!

COLLIER.

367

7s.

1 CHRIST the Lord is risen again,
Christ hath broken every chain;
Hark! angelic voices cry,
Singing evermore on high,
Hallelujah! Praise the Lord!

2 He who gave for us his life,
Who for us endured the strife,
Is our paschal Lamb to-day!
We, too, sing for joy, and say,
Hallelujah! Praise the Lord!

3 He who bore all pain and loss,
Comfortless, upon the cross,
Lives in glory now on high,
Pleads for us and hears our cry;
Hallelujah! Praise the Lord!

4 Now he bids us tell abroad
How the lost may be restored,
How the penitent forgiven,
How we, too, may enter heaven!
Hallelujah! Praise the Lord!

BOHEMIAN HYMN.

368

7s.

1 HAIL to thee, our risen King!
Joyfully thy praise we sing;
For, the mighty conflict o'er,
Now thou livest evermore.

2 Thou within the tomb hast slept,
Angel guards thy vigil kept;
'Twas their word to Mary brought
Tidings of the Lord she sought.

3 "Seek him not among the dead,
He is risen as he said:"
Gladdened by the angelic word,
Turning, she beheld her Lord.

4 Fain like Mary, Lord, would we
In thy glorious presence be,
Hear thy voice and see thy face,
Praise thee for thy wondrous grace.

369 7s.

1 HAIL the day that sees him rise,
Glorious, to his native skies!
Christ, awhile to mortals given,
Enters now the gates of heaven.

2 There the glorious triumph waits:
Lift your heads, eternal gates!
Christ hath vanquished death and sin;
Take the King of glory in.

3 Still for us he intercedes,
His prevailing death he pleads;
Near himself prepares our place,
Great Forerunner of our race.

4 Master, will we ever say,
Taken from our head to-day,
See thy faithful servants, see,
Ever gazing up to thee?

5 Grant, though parted from our sight,
High above yon azure height,
Grant, our hearts may thither rise,
Following thee beyond the skies!

C. Wesley.

370 H. M.

1 YES, the Redeemer rose,
The Saviour left the dead,
And o'er our hellish foes
High raised his conquering head;
In wild dismay the guards around
Fall to the ground and sink away.

2 Lo, the angelic bands
In full assembly meet
To wait his high commands,
And worship at his feet:
Joyful they come, and wing their way
From realms of day to Jesus' tomb.

3 Then back to heaven they fly,
And the glad tidings bear;
Hark! as they soar on high,
What music fills the air!
Their anthems say, "Jesus who bled
Hath left the dead; he rose to-day."

4 Ye mortals, catch the sound,
Redeemed by him from hell,
And send the echo round
The globe on which you dwell;
Transported cry, "Jesus who bled
Hath left the dead, no more to die."

Doddridge.

371 H. M.

1 YE saints! your music bring,
And swell the rapturous sound;
Strike every trembling string,
Till earth and heaven resound:
The triumphs of the cross we sing—
Awake, ye saints! each joyful string.

2 The cross—the cross alone—
Subdued the powers of hell;
Like lightning from his throne,
The prince of darkness fell;
The triumphs of the cross we sing—
Awake, ye saints! each joyful string.

3 The cross hath power to save,
From all the foes that rise;
The cross hath made the grave
A passage to the skies;
The triumphs of the cross we sing—
Awake, ye saints! each joyful string.

Reed.

372 L. M. D.

1 OUR Lord is risen from the dead,
Our Jesus is gone up on high;
The powers of hell are captive led,
Dragged to the portals of the sky.

There his triumphal chariot waits,
And angels chant the solemn lay:
"Lift up your heads, ye heav'nly gates,
Ye everlasting doors, give way."

2 Loose all your bars of massy light
And wide unfold the radiant scene;
He claims those mansions as his right;
Receive the King of Glory in.
"Who is the King of Glory, who?"
The Lord that all his foes o'ercame,
The world, sin, death, and hell o'erthrew;
And Jesus is the conqueror's name.

C. WESLEY.

373 L. M. D.

1 NOW for a tune of lofty praise,
To great Jehovah's equal Son!
Awake, my voice, in heavenly lays,
Tell the loud wonders he hath done.
Sing, how he left the worlds of light,
And the bright robes he wore above;
How swift and joyful was the flight,
On wings of everlasting love.

2 Deep in the shades of gloomy death,
Th' almighty Captive Prisoner lay;
Th' almighty Captive left the earth,
And rose to everlasting day.
Amongst a thousand harps and songs,
Jesus the God exalted reigns;
His sacred name fills all their tongues,
And echoes through the heavenly plains.

WATTS.

374 L. M. D.

1 HAIL! morning known among the blest,—
Morning of hope, and joy, and love,—
Of heavenly peace, and holy rest,
Pledge of the endless rest above.
Blest be the Father of our Lord,
Who from the dead hath brought his Son,
Hope to the lost was then restored,
And everlasting glory won.

2 Scarce morning twilight had begun
To chase the shades of night away,
When Christ arose—unsetting Sun—
The dawn of joy's eternal day.
Mercy looked down with smiling eye,
When our Immanuel left the dead;
Faith marked his bright ascent on high,
And hope, with gladness, raised her head.

WARDLAW.

375 L. M.

1 WHERE high the heavenly temple stands,
The house of God not made with hands,
A great High-Priest our nature wears,
The guardian of mankind appears.

2 Though now ascended up on high,
He bends to earth a brother's eye;
Partaker of the human name,
He knows the frailty of our frame.

3 Our fellow-sufferer yet retains
A fellow-feeling for our pains;
And still remembers, in the skies,
His tears, his agonies, and cries.

4 In every pang that rends the heart,
The Man of Sorrows had a part;
He sympathizes in our grief,
And to the sufferer sends relief.

5 With boldness, therefore, at the throne,
Let us make all our sorrows known,
And ask the aids of heavenly power,
To help us in the evil hour.
LOGAN.

376 L. M.

1 WHEN I the holy grave survey,
Where once my Saviour deigned to lie,
I see fulfilled what prophets say,
And all the power of death defy.

2 This empty tomb shall now proclaim,
How weak the bands of conquered death:
Sweet pledge that all who trust his name
Shall rise, and draw immortal breath.

3 Jesus, once numbered with the dead,
Unseals his eyes to sleep no more,
And ever lives their cause to plead,
For whom the pains of death he bore.

4 Thy risen Lord, my soul, behold!
See the rich diadem he wears!
Thou too shalt bear a harp of gold—
A crown of joy, when he appears.

5 Though in the dust I lay my head,
Yet, gracious God, thou wilt not leave
My flesh forever with the dead,
Nor lose thy children in the grave.
WALLIN.

377 L. M.

1 HE lives, the great Redeemer lives;
What joy the blest assurance gives!
And now, before his Father God,
Pleads the full merit of his blood.

2 Repeated crimes awake our fears,
And justice, armed with frowns, appears;
But in the Saviour's lovely face
Sweet mercy smiles, and all is peace!

3 Hence, then, ye black, despairing thoughts;
Above our fears, above our faults,
His powerful intercessions rise,
And guilt recedes, and terror dies.

4 In every dark, distressful hour,
When sin and Satan join their power,
Let this dear hope repel the dart,
That Jesus bears us on his heart.

5 Great Advocate, almighty Friend!
On him our humble hopes depend;
Our cause can never, never fail,
For Jesus pleads, and must prevail.

378 C. M.

1 I KNOW that my Redeemer lives;
What comfort this sweet sentence gives;
He lives, he lives, who once was dead,
He lives, my ever-living Head!

2 He lives triumphant from the grave;
He lives eternally to save;
He lives all-glorious in the sky;
He lives exalted there on high.

3 He lives to bless me with his love;
He lives to plead for me above;
He lives my hungry soul to feed;
He lives to help in time of need.

4 He lives to grant me rich supply;
He lives to guide me with his eye;
He lives to comfort me when faint;
He lives to hear my soul's complaint.

5 He lives to silence all my fears;
He lives to stoop and wipe my tears;
He lives to calm my troubled heart;
He lives all blessings to impart.

2 He lives, and grants me daily breath;
He lives, and I shall conquer death;
He lives my mansion to prepare;
He lives to bring me safely there.

3 He lives, all glory to his name!
He lives, my Jesus, still the same;
Oh, the sweet joy this sentence gives,
"I know that my Redeemer lives!"

MEDLEY.

379 C. M.

1 THE morning kindles all the sky,
The heavens resound with anthems high,
The shining angels as they speed,
Proclaim, "The Lord is risen indeed!"

2 Vainly with rocks his tomb was barred,
While Roman guards kept watch and ward;
Majestic from the spoilèd tomb,
In pomp of triumph he has come!

3 When the amazed disciples heard,
Their hearts with speechless joy were stirred;
Their Lord's belovèd face to see,
Eager they haste to Galilee.

4 His piercèd hands to them he shows,
His face with love's own radiance glows;
They with the angels' message speed,
And shout, "The Lord is risen indeed!"

5 O Christ, thou King compassionate!
Our hearts possess; on thee we wait;
Help us to render praises due
To thee the endless ages through.

380 C. M.

1 HE lives, my kind, wise, heavenly Friend;
He lives and loves me to the end;
He lives, and while he lives I'll sing;
He lives, my Prophet, Priest, and King.

MEDLEY.

381 C. M.

1 HOSANNA to the Prince of Light,
Who clothed himself in clay,
Entered the iron gates of death,
And tore the bars away.

2 See how the Conqueror mounts aloft,
And to his Father flies,
With scars of honor in his flesh,
And triumph in his eyes.

3 There our exalted Saviour reigns,
And scatters blessings down;
Our Jesus fills the middle seat
Of the celestial throne.

4 Raise your devotion, mortal tongues,
To reach his blest abode;
Sweet be the accents of your songs,
To our incarnate God.

5 Bright angels, strike your loudest strings,
Your sweetest voices raise;
Let heaven, and all created things,
Sound our Immanuel's praise.

WATTS.

382 C. M.

1 JESUS, our Lord, ascend thy throne,
And near thy Father sit:
In Zion shall thy power be known,
And make thy foes submit.

2 What wonders shall thy Gospel do!
Thy converts shall surpass
The numerous drops of morning dew,
And own thy sovereign grace.

3 God hath pronounced a firm decree,
Nor changes what he swore:—
"Eternal shall thy priesthood be,
When Aaron is no more."

4 Jesus, our Priest, forever lives,
To plead for us above;
Jesus, our King, forever gives
The blessings of his love.

5 God will exalt his glorious head,
His lofty throne maintain,
And strike the powers and princes dead,
Who dare oppose his reign.

WATTS.

383 C. M.

1 ARISE, ye people, and adore,
Exulting strike the chord!
Let all the earth, from shore to shore,
Confess the Almighty Lord!

2 Glad shouts aloud, wide echoing round,
The ascending God proclaim;
The angelic choir respond the sound,
And shake creation's frame.

3 They sing of death and hell o'erthrown,
In that triumphant hour;
And God exalts his conquering Son
To his right hand of power.

4 Oh shout, ye people, and adore;
Exulting strike the chord!
Let all the earth, from shore to shore,
Confess the Almighty Lord.

LYTE.

384 C. M.

1 YE humble souls that seek the Lord,
Chase all your fears away;
And bow with reverence down, to see
The place where Jesus lay.

2 Thus low the Lord of life was brought,
Such wonders love can do!
Thus cold in death that bosom lay,
Which throbbed and bled for you.

3 If ye have wept at yonder cross,
And still your sorrows rise,
Stoop down and view the vanquished grave,
Then wipe your weeping eyes.

4 Yes, dry your tears, and tune your songs,
The Saviour lives again;
Not all the bolts and bars of death
The Conqueror could detain.

5 High o'er th' angelic band he rears
His once dishonored head;
And through unnumbered years he reigns,
Who dwelt among the dead.

DODDRIDGE.

385 C. M.

1 NOW let our cheerful eyes survey
Our great High Priest above,
And celebrate his constant care,
And sympathetic love.

2 Though raised to a superior throne,
Where angels bow around,
And high o'er all the shining train,
With matchless honors crowned;—

3 The names of all his saints he bears
Deep graven on his heart;
Nor shall a name once treasured there
E'er from his care depart.

4 Those characters shall fair abide,
Our everlasting trust,
When gems, and monuments, and crowns,
Are moldered into dust.

5 So, gracious Saviour, on my breast
May thy dear name be worn,
A sacred ornament and guard,
To endless ages borne.

DODDRIDGE.

386 C. M.

1 WITH joy we meditate the grace
Of our High Priest above:
His heart is made of tenderness,
His bosom glows with love.

2 Touched with a sympathy within,
He knows our feeble frame;
He knows what sore temptations mean,
For he hath felt the same.

3 He in the days of feeble flesh
Poured out his cries and tears;
And in his measure feels afresh
What every member bears.

4 Then let our humble faith address
His mercy and his power;
We shall obtain delivering grace
In the distressing hour.

WATTS.

387 C. M.

1 I SAY to all men, far and near,
That he is risen again;
That he is with us now and here,
And ever shall remain.

2 And what I say, let each this morn
Go tell it to his friend,
That soon in every place shall dawn
His kingdom without end.

3 Now first to souls who thus awake,
Seems earth a fatherland;
A new and endless life they take
With rapture from his hand.

4 The fears of death and of the grave
Are whelmed beneath the sea;
And every heart, now light and brave,
May face the things to be.

5 Now let the mourner grieve no more,
Though his belovéd sleep;
A happier meeting shall restore
Their light to eyes that weep.

NOVALIS.

388 C. M.

1 THE morning purples all the sky,
The air with praises rings,
Defeated hell stands sullen by,
The world exulting sings:

2 While he, the King all strong to save,
Rends the dark doors away,
And through the breaches of the grave
Strides forth into the day.

3 Death's captive, in his gloomy prison
Fast fettered he has lain;
But he has mastered death, is risen,
And now death wears the chain.

4 The shining angels cry, "Away
With grief; no spices bring;
Not tears, but songs, this joyful day,
Should greet the rising King!"

5 Glory to God! our glad lips cry;
All praise and worship be
On earth, in heaven, to God Most high,
For Christ's great victory!

A. R. THOMPSON.

389 C. M.

1 OH! for a shout of sacred joy
To God, the sovereign King;
Let all the lands their tongues employ,
And hymns of triumph sing.

2 Jesus, our God, ascends on high;
His heavenly guards around
Attend him rising through the sky,
With trumpets' joyful sound.

3 While angels shout and praise their King,
Let mortals learn their strains;
Let all the earth his honor sing;—
O'er all the earth he reigns.

4 Rehearse his praise, with awe profound;
Let knowledge lead the song;
Nor mock him with a solemn sound
Upon a thoughtless tongue.

WATTS.

390 C. M.

1 THE head that once was crowned with thorns
Is crowned with glory now;
A royal diadem adorns,
The mighty Victor's brow.

2 The highest place that heaven affords
Is his by sovereign right:
The King of kings, and Lord of lords,
He reigns in glory bright;—

3 The joy of all who dwell above,
The joy of all below,
To whom he manifests his love,
And grants his name to know.

4 To them, the cross, with all its shame,
With all its grace is given;
Their name, an everlasting name,
Their joy—the joy of heaven.

5 To them the cross is life and health,
Though shame and death to him;
His people's hope, his people's wealth,
Their everlasting theme.

KELLY.

391 C. M.

1 WELCOME thou Victor in the strife,
Welcome from out the cave!
To-day we triumph in thy life
Around thine empty grave.

2 Our enemy is put to shame,
His short-lived triumph o'er;
Our God is with us, we exclaim,
We fear our foe no more.

3 Oh share with us the spoils, we pray,
Thou diedst to achieve;
We meet within thy house to-day,
Our portion to receive.

4 And let thy conquering banner wave
O'er hearts thou makest free,
And point the path that from the grave
Leads heavenward up to thee.

5 We die with thee: oh, let us live
Henceforth to thee aright!
The blessings thou hast died to give
Be daily in our sight.

6 Fearless we lay us in the tomb,
And sleep the night away,
If thou art there to break the gloom,
And call us back to day.

SCHMOLKE.

392 8s & 7s.

1 HARK! ten thousand harps and voices
Sound the note of praise above;
Jesus reigns, and heaven rejoices;
Jesus reigns, the God of love;
See, he sits on yonder throne!
Jesus rules the world alone.

2 Jesus, hail! whose glory brightens
All above, and gives it worth;
Lord of life, thy smile enlightens,
Cheers and charms thy saints on earth:
When we think of love like thine,
Lord, we own it love divine.

3 King of glory, reign forever!
Thine an everlasting crown;
Nothing from thy love shall sever
Those whom thou hast made thine own:
Happy objects of thy grace,
Chosen to behold thy face.

4 Saviour, hasten thine appearing!
Bring, oh bring the glorious day,
When, the awful summons hearing,
Heaven and earth shall pass away!
Then with golden harps we'll sing,
"Glory, glory, to our King!"
Hallelujah, Amen!

KELLY.

393 8s & 7s.

1 HAIL, thou once despisèd Jesus:
Crowned in mockery a king!
Thou didst suffer to release us;
Thou didst free salvation bring.
Hail, thou agonizing Saviour,
Bearer of our sin and shame!
By thy merits we find favor;
Life is given through thy name.

2 Jesus, hail! enthroned in glory,
There forever to abide;
All the heavenly host adore thee,
Seated at thy Father's side:
There for sinners thou art pleading;
There thou dost our place prepare:
Ever for us interceding,
Till in glory we appear.

3 Worship, honor, power, and blessing
Thou art worthy to receive:
Loudest praises, without ceasing,
Meet it is for us to give.
Help, ye bright angelic spirits;
Bring your sweetest, noblest lays;
Help to sing our Saviour's merits;
Help to chant Immanuel's praise.

BAKEWELL.

394 8s, 7s, & 4s.

1 LOOK, ye saints; — the sight is glorious;—
See the Man of Sorrows now;
From the fight returned victorious,
Every knee to him shall bow;
Crown him, crown him;
Crowns become the Victor's brow.

2 Crown the Saviour, angels, crown him;
Rich the trophies Jesus brings;

In the seat of power enthrone him,
While the heavenly concert rings;
Crown him, crown him;
Crown the Saviour King of kings.

3 Sinners in derision crowned him,
Mocking thus the Saviour's claim;
Saints and angels crowd around him,
Own his title, praise his name:
Crown him, crown him;
Spread abroad the Victor's fame.

4 Hark! those bursts of acclamation!
Hark! those loud, triumphant chords!
Jesus takes the highest station;
Oh, what joy the sight affords!
Crown him, crown him,
King of kings, and Lord of lords.

KELLY.

395 8s, 7s, & 4s.

1 HAIL, thou happy morn, so glorious!
Come, ye saints, your griefs give o'er;
Sing how Jesus rose victorious,
By his own almighty power:
Hallelujah!
To the glorious Son of God.

2 Countless bands of angels glorious,
Cloth'd in bright ethereal blue;
Straight the sound of Christ victorious
From their silver trumpets flew:
Christ triumphant,
Rises, Conqueror o'er the tomb.

3 Is this he who died on Calvary,
Who was pierc'd with many a spear?
Clad with countless suns of glory,
See, he rises through the air:
Hallelujah!
Zion's mourner, now rejoice.

4 Tremble, ye who him rejected,
Lo! he breaks through yonder cloud;
Rise, ye saints, and shout triumphant,
Victory! through Jesus' blood:
Hark! the trumpet
Sounds the resurrection morn.

396 8s, 7s, & 4s.

1 LO! he comes, with clouds descending,
Once for favored sinners slain;
Thousand thousand saints, attending,
Swell the triumph of his train:
Hallelujah!
Jesus shall forever reign.

2 Every eye shall now behold him,
Robed in dreadful majesty:
Those who set at nought and sold him,
Pierced, and nailed him to the tree,
Deeply wailing,
Shall the true Messiah see.

3 When the solemn trump has sounded,
Heaven and earth shall flee away;
All who hate him must, confounded,
Hear the summons of that day—
"Come to judgment!—
Come to judgment!—come away!"

4 Now the Saviour, long expected,
See, in solemn pomp, appear;

All his saints, by man rejected,
Now shall meet him in the air:
Hallelujah!
See the day of God appear.

WESLEY & CENNICK.

397 8s, 7s, & 4s.

1 CHRIST is coming! let creation
Bid her groans and travail cease;
Let the glorious proclamation
Hope restore and faith increase—
Christ is coming!
Come, thou blessèd Prince of peace.

2 Earth can now but tell the story
Of thy bitter cross and pain;
She shall yet behold thy glory
When thou comest back to reign—
Christ is coming!
Let each heart repeat the strain.

3 Though once cradled in a manger,
Oft no pillow but the sod;
Here an alien and a stranger,
Mocked of men, disowned of God—
All creation
Yet shall own that kingly rod.

4 Long thy exiles have been pining,
Far from rest and home and thee;
But, in heavenly vesture shining,
Soon they shall thy glory see—
Christ is coming!
Haste the joyous jubilee.

5 With that "blessèd hope" before us,
Let no harp remain unstrung;
Let the mighty advent chorus
Onward roll from tongue to tongue—
Christ is coming!
Come, Lord Jesus, quickly come.

MACDUFF.

398 8s, 7s, & 4s.

1 LO, he cometh! countless trumpets
Blow to raise the sleeping dead;
'Mid ten thousand saints and angels,
See their great exalted Head!
Hallelujah!
Welcome, welcome, Son of God!

2 Now his merit, by the harpers,
Through the eternal deep resounds;
Now resplendent shine his nail-prints,
Every eye shall see his wounds;
They who pierced him
Shall at his appearance wail.

3 Full of joyful expectation,
Saints behold the Judge appear;
Truth and justice go before him;
Now the royal sentence hear:
Hallelujah!
Welcome, welcome, Judge divine.

4 "Come, ye blessèd of my Father,
Enter into life and joy;
Banish all your fears and sorrows;
Endless praise be your employ:"
Hallelujah!
Welcome, welcome to the skies.

CENNICK.

399 8s, 7s, & 4s.

1 LO! he comes, with clouds descending!
Hark! the trump of God is blown,
And th' Archangel's voice attending
Makes the high procession known:
Sons of Adam
Rise, and stand before your God!

2 Crowns and sceptres fall before him,
Kings and conquerors own his sway;

Haughtiest monarchs now adore him,
While they see his lightnings play:
How triumphant
Is the world's Redeemer now!

3 Hear his voice, as mighty thunder
Sounding in eternal roar,
While its echo rends in sunder
Rocks and mountains, sea and shore;
Hark! his accents
Through th' unfathomed deep resound!

4 "Come, Lord Jesus! oh! come quickly!"
Oft has prayed the mourning bride:
"Lo!" he answers, "I come quickly!"
Who thy coming may abide?
All who loved him,
All who longed to see his day.

5 "Come," he saith, "ye heirs of glory;
Come, ye purchase of my blood;
Claim the kingdom now before you,
Rise, and fill the mount of God,
Fixed forever
Where the Lamb on Zion stands."

OLIVERS.

400 8s, 7s, & 4s.

1 O'ER the distant mountains breaking,
Comes the reddening dawn of day;
Rise, my soul, from sleep awaking,
Rise, and sing, and watch, and pray:
'Tis thy Saviour,
On his bright, returning way.

2 O thou long-expected, weary
Waits my anxious soul for thee;
Life is dark, and earth is dreary,
Where thy light I do not see:
O my Saviour,
When wilt thou return to me!

3 Nearer is my soul's salvation,
Spent the night, the day at hand;
Keep me in my lowly station,
Watching for thee, till I stand,
O my Saviour,
In thy bright and promised land!

4 With my lamp well-trimmed and burning,
Swift to hear, and slow to roam,
Watching for thy glad returning,
To restore me to my home,
Come, my Saviour!
O my Saviour, quickly come!

MONSELL.

401 8s, 7s, & 4s.

1 JESUS comes to souls rejoicing,
Bringing news of sin forgivén;
Jesus comes in sounds of gladness,
Lifting up our souls to heavén;
Hallelujah!
Now the gate of death is rivén.

2 Jesus comes in joy and sorrow,
Shares alike our hopes and fears;
"Jesus comes" whate'er befalls us,
Cheers our hearts and dries our tears,
Hallelujah!
Cheering e'en our falling years.

3 Jesus comes on clouds, triumphant,
When the heavens shall pass away;
Jesus comes again in glory;
Let us then our homage pay:
Hallelujah!
Sing we till the break of day.

402 L. M.

1 WHEN Christ came down on earth of old,
He took our nature poor and low;
He wore no form of angel mould,
But shared our weakness and our woe.

2 But when he cometh back once more,
Then shall be set the great white throne;
And earth and heaven shall flee before
The face of him that sits thereon.

3 O Son of God! in glory crown'd,
The Judge ordain'd of quick and dead;
And Son of man! so pitying found
For all the tears thy people shed;

4 Be with us in that awful hour,
And by thy crown, and by thy grave,
And all thy love and all thy power,
In that great day of judgment save!

403 L. M.

1 O SAVIOUR, is thy promise fled,
Nor longer might thy grace endure
To hear the sick, and raise the dead,
And preach thy gospel to the poor?

2 Come, Jesus, come! return again;
With brighter beam thy servants bless,
Who long to feel thy perfect reign,
And share thy kingdom's happiness!

3 Come, Jesus, come! and, as of yore,
The prophet went to clear thy way,
A harbinger thy feet before,
A dawning to thy brighter day;

4 So now may grace with heavenly shower
Our stony hearts for truth prepare;
Sow in our souls the seed of power,
Then come and reap thy harvest there.

HEBER.

404 L. M.

1 THE Lord will come! the earth shall quake;
The hills their fixèd seat forsake;
And, withering, from the vault of night
The stars withdraw their feeble light.

2 The Lord will come! but not the same
As once in lowly form he came,
A silent Lamb to slaughter led,
The bruised, the suffering, and the dead.

3 The Lord will come! a dreadful form,
With wreath of flame, and robe of storm,
On cherub wings, and wings of wind,
Anointed Judge of human kind.

4 Can this be he who wont to stray
A pilgrim on the world's highway,
By power oppress'd, and mock'd by pride,
The Nazarene, the Crucified?

5 Go, tyrants! to the rocks complain;
Go, seek the mountain's cleft in vain!
But faith, victorious o'er the tomb,
Shall sing for joy—the Lord is come!

HEBER.

405 7s & 6s.

1 REJOICE, all ye believers,
And let your lights appear;
The evening is advancing,
And darker night is near;
The Bridegroom is arising,
And soon he draweth nigh:
Up! pray, and watch, and wrestle!
At midnight comes the cry.

2 The watchers on the mountain
Proclaim the Bridegroom near;
Go meet him as he cometh,
With hallelujahs clear:
The marriage-feast is waiting,
The gates wide-open stand;
Up, up, ye heirs of glory!
The Bridegroom is at hand.

3 Our hope and expectation,
O Jesus, now appear;
Arise, thou Sun so longed for,
O'er this benighted sphere!
With heart and hands uplifted,
We plead, O Lord, to see
The day of earth's redemption,
That brings us unto thee.

LAURENTI.

406 7s & 6s.

1 THE world is very evil;
The times are waxing late:
Be sober and keep vigil,
The Judge is at the gate;
The Judge who comes in mercy,
The Judge who comes in might,
To terminate the evil,
And vindicate the right.

2 Prepare we then to meet him;
Let right to wrong succeed;
Let penitential sorrow
To heavenly gladness lead:
So may we sound his praises,
Who from destruction saved,
Bore with us in defilement,
And from defilement laved.

3 Far, far, as we have wandered,
And deep as is our fall,
His mercies never fail us,
Who freely pardons all;
Who bids his grace abounding
Love's mightiness display,
And David's royal fountain,
Purge every sin away.

BERNARD.

407 S. M.

1 COME, Lord, and tarry not,
Bring the long-looked-for day;
Oh, why these years of waiting here,
These ages of delay?

2 Come! for the good are few,
They lift the voice in vain;
Faith waxes fainter on the earth,
And love is on the wane.

3 Come! for love waxes cold,
Its steps are faint and slow;
Faith now is lost in unbelief;
Hope's lamp burns dim and low.

4 Come! for creation groans,
Impatient of thy stay,
Worn out with these long years of ill,
These ages of delay.

5 Come! and make all things new;
Build up this ruined earth,
Restore our faded Paradise,
Creation's second birth!

6 Come, and begin thy reign
Of everlasting peace;
Come, take the kingdom to thyself,
Great King of Righteousness!

BONAR.

408

S. M.

1 THE Church has waited long
Her absent Lord to see;
And still in loneliness she waits,
A friendless stranger she.

2 Age after age has gone,
Sun after sun has set,
And still, in weeds of widowhood,
She weeps a mourner yet.

3 Saint after saint on earth
Has lived, and loved, and died;
And as they left us one by one,
We laid them side by side:

4 We laid them down to sleep,
But not in hope forlorn;
We laid them but to ripen there
Till the last glorious morn.

5 The whole creation groans,
And waits to hear that voice
That shall restore her comeliness,
And make her wastes rejoice.

6 Come, Lord, and wipe away
The curse, the sin, the stain,
And make this blighted world of ours
Thine own fair world again.

BONAR.

409

8s & 5s.

1 SING of Jesus, sing forever
Of the love that changes never!
Who, or what, from him can sever
Those he makes his own?

2 With his blood the Lord hath bought them,
When they knew him not, he sought them,
And from all their wanderings brought them;
His the praise alone.

3 Through the desert Jesus leads them,
With the bread of heaven he feeds them,
And through all their way he speeds them
To their home above.

4 There they see the Lord who bought them,
Him who came from heaven and sought them,
Him who by his Spirit taught them,
Him they serve and love.

KELLY.

410

8s & 5s.

1 SAINTS in glory! we together
Know the song that ceases never;
Song of songs thou art, O Saviour,
All that endless day.

2 Theme of Adam when forgiven,
Theme of Abraham, David, Stephen;
Souls, ye chant it entering heaven,
Now, henceforth, alway.

3 O the God-man! O Immanuel!
Cloud by day! Jehovah-Angel!
Fire by night! he led his Israel,
So he leads us home.

4 Come, ye angels, round us gather,
While to Jesus we draw nearer;
In his throne he'll seat forever,
Those for whom he died.

5 Underneath his throne, a river
Clear as crystal flows forever,
Like his fulness, failing never:
Hail, enthronèd Lamb!

6 Oh, th' unsearchable Redeemer!
Shoreless Ocean, sounded never!
Yesterday, to-day, forever,
Jesus Christ, the same.

MAHMIED.

411 6s & 4s.

1 LET us awake our joys,
Strike up with cheerful voice,
Each creature sing--
Angels, begin the song,
Mortals, the strain prolong,
In accents sweet and strong,
"Jesus is King."

2 Proclaim abroad his name,
Tell of his matchless fame:
What wonders done!
Shout through hell's dark profound,
Let all the earth resound,
Till heaven's high arch rebound,
"Victory is won."

3 All hail the glorious day,
When through the heavenly way
Lo, he shall come!
While they who pierced him wail,
His promise shall not fail;
Saints, see your King prevail:
Great Saviour, come.

RUGBURY.

412 6s & 4s.

1 RISE, glorious Conqueror, rise;
Into thy native skies,—
Assume thy right:
And where in many a fold
The clouds are backward rolled—
Pass through those gates of gold,
And reign in light!

2 Victor o'er death and hell!
Cherubic legions swell
Thy radiant train:
Praises all heaven inspire;
Each angel sweeps his lyre,
And waves his wings of fire,—
Thou Lamb once slain!

3 Enter, incarnate God!—
No feet but thine, have trod
The serpent down;
Blow the full trumpets, blow!
Wider yon portals throw!
Saviour triumphant—go,
And take thy crown!

4 Lion of Judah—hail!
And let thy name prevail
From age to age;
Lord of the rolling years;—
Claim for thine own the spheres,
For thou hast bought with tears
Thy heritage!

BRYDGES.

413 6s & 4s.

1 SOUND, sound the truth abroad!
Bear ye the word of God
Through the wide world;
Tell what our Lord has done,
Tell how the day is won,
And from his lofty throne
Satan is hurled.

2 Ye, who forsaking all,
At your loved Master's call,
Comforts resign;

Soon will your work be done;
Soon will the prize be won;
Brighter than yonder sun
  Then shall ye shine.

KELLY.

414 6s & 4s.

1 GLORY to God on high!
  Let heaven and earth reply,
  "Praise ye his name!"
His love and grace adore,
Who all our sorrows bore;
Sing loud forevermore,
  "Worthy the Lamb!"

2 While they around the throne
Cheerfully join in one,
  Praising his name,—
Ye who have felt his blood
Sealing your peace with God,
Sound his dear name abroad,
  "Worthy the Lamb!"

3 Join, all ye ransomed race,
Our Lord and God to bless:
  Praise ye his name!
In him we will rejoice,
And make a joyful noise,
Shouting with heart and voice,
  "Worthy the Lamb!"

4 Soon must we change our place,
Yet will we never cease
  Praising his name:
To him our songs we bring;
Hail him our gracious King;
And through all ages sing,
  "Worthy the Lamb!"

JAMES ALLEN.

415 6s & 4s.

1 SING, sing his lofty praise,
  Whom angels cannot raise,
  But whom they sing;
Jesus, who reigns above,
Object of angels' love,
Jesus, whose grace we prove,
  Jesus, our King.

2 Rich is the grace we sing,
Poor is the praise we bring,
  Not as we ought;
But when we see his face,
In yonder glorious place,
Then shall we sing his grace,
  Sing without fault.

416 6s & 4s.

1 COME, all ye saints of God,
  Wide through the earth abroad,
  Spread Jesus' fame:
Tell what his love hath done;
Trust in his name alone;
Shout to his lofty throne,
  "Worthy the Lamb!"

2 Hence, gloomy doubts and fears!
Dry up your mournful tears;
  Swell the glad theme:
To Christ, our gracious King,
Strike each melodious string;
Join heart and voice to sing,
  "Worthy the Lamb!"

3 Hark! how the choirs above,
Filled with the Saviour's love,
  Dwell on his name!
There, too, may we be found,
With light and glory crowned,
While all the heavens resound,
  "Worthy the Lamb!"

JAMES BODEN.

417

6s.

1 WHEN morning gilds the skies,
My heart awaking cries,
May Jesus Christ be praised:
Alike at work and prayer,
To Jesus I repair;
May Jesus Christ be praised.

2 Whene'er the sweet church bell
Peals over hill and dell,
May Jesus Christ be praised:
Oh, hark to what it sings,
As joyously it rings,
May Jesus Christ be praised.

3 My tongue shall never tire,
Of chanting with the choir,
May Jesus Christ be praised:
This song of sacred joy,
It never seems to cloy;
May Jesus Christ be praised.

4 When sleep her balm denies,
My silent spirit sighs
May Jesus Christ be praised:
When evil thoughts molest
With this I shield my breast,
May Jesus Christ be praised.

5 Does sadness fill my mind?
A solace here I find,
May Jesus Christ be praised:
Or fades my earthly bliss?
My comfort still is this,
May Jesus Christ be praised.

6 The night becomes as day,
When from the heart we say,
May Jesus Christ be praised:
The powers of darkness fear,
When this sweet chant they hear,
May Jesus Christ be praised.

7 In heaven's eternal bliss
The loveliest strain is this,
May Jesus Christ be praised:
Let earth, and sea, and sky,
From depth to height reply,
May Jesus Christ be praised.

8 Be this, while life is mine,
My canticle divine,
May Jesus Christ be praised:
Be this th' eternal song,
Through all the ages on,
May Jesus Christ be praised.

418

7s.

1 ASK ye what great thing I know
That delights and stirs me so?
What the high reward I win?
Whose the name I glory in?
Jesus Christ, the Crucified.

2 What is faith's foundation strong?
What awakes my lips to song?
He who bore my sinful load,
Purchased for me peace with God,
Jesus Christ, the Crucified.

3 Who defeats my fiercest foes?
Who consoles my saddest woes?
Who revives my fainting heart,
Healing all its hidden smart?
Jesus Christ, the Crucified.

4 Who is life in life to me?
Who the death of death will be?
Who will place me on his right
With the countless hosts of light?
Jesus Christ, the Crucified.

5 This is that great thing I know;
This delights and stirs me so;
Faith in him who died to save,
Him who triumphed o'er the grave,
Jesus Christ, the Crucified.

MONSELL.

419 7s.

1 EARTH has nothing sweet or fair,
Lovely forms or beauties rare,
But before my eyes they bring
Christ, of beauty source and spring.

2 When the morning paints the skies,
When the golden sunbeams rise,
Then my Saviour's form I find
Brightly imaged on my mind.

3 When the day-beams pierce the night,
Oft I think on Jesus' light,
Think how bright that light will be,
Shining through eternity.

4 When, as moonlight softly steals,
Heaven its thousand eyes reveals,
Then I think: Who made their light
Is a thousand times more bright.

5 When I see in spring-tide gay,
Fields their varied tints display,
Wakes the thrilling thought in me,
What must their Creator be?

6 Lord of all that's fair to see,
Come, reveal thyself to me!
Let me, 'mid thy radiant light,
See thine unveiled glories bright.

SILESIUS.

420 8s & 7s.

1 MIGHTY God! while angels bless thee,
May a mortal lisp thy name?
Lord of men, as well as angels!
Thou art every creature's theme;
Lord of every land and nation!
Ancient of eternal days!
Sounded through the wide creation
Be thy just and awful praise.

2 For the grandeur of thy nature,—
Grand, beyond a seraph's thought;
For the wonders of creation,
Works with skill and kindness wrought;
For thy providence, that governs
Through thine empire's wide domain,
Wings an angel, guides a sparrow;
Blessèd be thy gentle reign.

3 For thy rich, thy free redemption,
Bright, though vailed in darkness long,
Thought is poor, and poor expression;
Who can sing that wondrous song?
Brightness of the Father's glory!
Shall thy praise unuttered lie?
Break, my tongue! such guilty silence,
Sing the Lord who came to die:—

4 From the highest throne of glory,
To the cross of deepest woe,
Came to ransom guilty captives!—
Flow, my praise! forever flow:
Re-ascend, immortal Saviour!
Leave thy footstool, take thy throne;
Thence return and reign forever;—
Be the kingdom all thine own!

ROBINSON.

421 8s & 7s.

1 CROWN his head with endless blessing,
Who, in God the Father's name,
With compassions never ceasing,
Comes salvation to proclaim.

Hail, ye saints, who know his favor,
Who within his gates are found;
Hail, ye saints, the exalted Saviour,
Let his courts with praise resound.

2 Lo, Jehovah, we adore thee;
Thee our Saviour! thee our God!
From his throne his beams of glory
Shine through all the world abroad.
In his word his light arises,
Brightest beams of truth and grace;
Bind, oh, bind your sacrifices,
In his courts your offerings place.

3 Jesus, thee our Saviour hailing,
Thee our God in praise we own;
Highest honors, never failing,
Rise eternal round thy throne;
Now, ye saints, his power confessing,
In your grateful strains adore;
For his mercy, never ceasing,
Freely flows forevermore.

William Soode.

422 8s & 7s.

1 ONE there is, above all others,
Well deserves the name of Friend;
His is love beyond a brother's,
Costly, free, and knows no end.

2 Which of all our friends, to save us,
Could or would have shed his blood?
But our Jesus died to have us
Reconciled in him to God.

3 When he lived on earth abasèd,
Friend of sinners was his name;
Now, above all glory raisèd,
He rejoices in the same.

4 Could we bear from one another
What he daily bears from us?
Yet this glorious Friend and Brother
Loves us though we treat him thus.

5 Oh for grace our hearts to soften!
Teach us, Lord, at length to love!
We, alas! forget too often
What a Friend we have above.

Newton.

423 8s & 7s.

1 CHRIST, above all glory seated!
King eternal, strong to save!
To thee, Death, by death defeated,
Triumph high and glory gave.

2 Thou art gone, where now is given,
What no mortal might could gain:
On the eternal throne of heaven,
In thy Father's power to reign.

3 There thy kingdoms all adore thee,
Heaven above, and earth below,
While the depths of hell before thee,
Trembling and defeated bow.

4 We, O Lord, with hearts adoring,
Follow thee above the sky:
Hear our prayers thy grace imploring,
Lift our souls to thee on high.

5 So when thou again in glory
On the clouds of heaven shalt shine,
We thy flock shall stand before thee,
Owned forevermore as thine.

424 8s & 7s.

1 JESUS comes, his conflict over,
Comes to claim his great reward;
Angels round the victor hover,
Crowding to behold their Lord.

2 Yonder throne for him erected,
Now becomes the victor's seat;
Lo, the man on earth rejected!
Angels worship at his feet.

3 Day and night they cry before him,—
"Holy, holy, holy Lord!"
All the powers of heaven adore him;
All obey his sovereign word.

KELLY.

425 C. P. M.

1 OH, could I speak the matchless worth,
Oh, could I sound the glories forth,
Which in my Saviour shine,
I'd soar and touch the heavenly strings,
And vie with Gabriel while he sings
In notes almost divine.

2 I'd sing the precious blood he spilt,
My ransom from the dreadful guilt
Of sin, and wrath divine:
I'd sing his glorious righteousness,
In which all-perfect heavenly dress
My soul shall ever shine.

3 I'd sing the characters he bears,
And all the forms of love he wears,
Exalted on his throne:
In loftiest songs of sweetest praise,
I would to everlasting days
Make all his glories known.

4 Well, the delightful day will come
And my dear Lord will bring me home,
When I shall see his face:
Then with my Saviour, Brother, Friend,
A blest eternity I'll spend,
Triumphant in his grace.

MEDLEY.

426 C. P. M.

1 COME join, ye saints, with heart and voice,
Alone in Jesus to rejoice,
And worship at his feet;
Come, take his praises on your tongues,
And raise to him your thankful songs,
"In him ye are complete!"

2 In him, who all our praise excels,
The fullness of the Godhead dwells,
And all perfections meet:
The head of all celestial powers,
Divinely theirs, divinely ours;
"In him ye are complete!"

3 Still onward urge your heavenly way,
Dependent on him day by day,
His presence still entreat;
His precious name forever bless,
Your glory, strength, and righteousness,
"In him ye are complete!"

4 Nor fear to pass the vale of death;
In his dear arms resign your breath,
He'll make the passage sweet;
The gloom and fears of death shall flee,
And your departing soul shall see
"In him ye are complete!"

427 H. M.

1 ARISE, my soul, arise!
Shake off thy guilty fears;
The bleeding Sacrifice
In my behalf appears.
Before the throne my Surety stands,
My name is written on his hands.

2 Five bleeding wounds he bears,
Received on Calvary;
They pour effectual prayers,
They strongly plead for me:
Forgive him, oh forgive, they cry,
Nor let that ransomed sinner die!

3 The Father hears him pray,—
His dear anointed One;
He cannot turn away
The presence of his Son;
His Spirit answers to the blood,
And tells me I am born of God.

4 My God is reconciled;
His pardoning voice I hear;
He owns me for his child;
I can no longer fear:
With confidence I now draw nigh,
And Father, Abba, Father, cry.

C. WESLEY.

428 H. M.

1 COME, every pious heart,
That loves the Saviour's name,
Your noblest powers exert
To celebrate his fame:
Tell all above, and all below,
The debt of love to him you owe.

2 He left his starry crown,
And laid his robes aside;
On wings of love came down,
And wept, and bled, and died:
What he endured, no tongue can tell,
To save our souls from death and hell.

3 From the dark grave he rose—
The mansion of the dead;
And thence his mighty foes
In glorious triumph led;
Up through the sky the Conqueror rode,
And reigns on high, the Saviour God.

4 From thence he'll quickly come—
His chariot will not stay—
And bear our spirits home
To realms of endless day:
There shall we see his lovely face,
And ever rest in his embrace.

STENNETT.

429 H. M.

1 JOIN all the glorious names
Of wisdom, love, and power
That ever mortals knew,
That angels ever bore,
All are too mean to speak his worth,
Too mean to set my Saviour forth.

2 Great Prophet of my God,
My tongue would bless thy name;
By thee the joyful news
Of our salvation came:
The joyful news of sin forgivèn,
Of hell subdued, and peace with heavèn.

3 Jesus, my Great High-Priest,
Offered his blood and died;
My guilty conscience seeks
No sacrifice beside:
His powerful blood did once atone,
And now it pleads before the throne.

4 My dear almighty Lord!
My Conqueror and my King!
Thy sceptre and thy sword,
Thy reigning grace I sing:
Thine is the power; behold, I sit,
In willing bonds, beneath thy feet.

5 Now let my soul arise,
And tread the tempter down;

My Captain leads me forth
To conquest and a crown;
A feeble saint shall win the day,
Though death and hell obstruct the way.

WATTS.

430 H. M.

1 PRAISE to the Lord on high,
Who spreads his triumphs wide;
While Jesus' fragrant name
Is breathed from every side:
Balmy and rich the odors rise,
And fill the earth and reach the skies.

2 Ten thousand dying souls
Its influence feel, and live;
Sweeter than vital air
The incense they receive:
They breathe anew, and rise and sing
Jesus, the Lord, their conquering King.

3 But sinners scorn the grace
That brings salvation nigh;
They turn their face away,
And faint, and fall, and die:
So sad a doom, ye saints deplore;
For oh, they fall to rise no more!

431 L. M.

1 WHAT equal honors shall we bring
To thee, O Lord our God, the Lamb,
When all the notes that angels sing
Are far inferior to thy name?

2 Worthy is he that once was slain,
The Prince of Life, that groaned and died,
Worthy to rise, and live and reign
At his almighty Father's side.

3 Honor immortal must be paid,
Instead of scandal and of scorn;
While glory shines around his head,
He wears a crown without a thorn.

4 Blessings forever on the Lamb,
Who bore the curse for wretched men!
Let angels sound his sacred name,
And every creature say, "Amen!"

WATTS.

432 L. M.

1 COME, let us sing the song of songs—
The saints in heaven began the strain—
The homage which to Christ belongs:
"Worthy the Lamb, for he was slain!"

2 Slain to redeem us by his blood,
To cleanse from every sinful stain,
And make us kings and priests to God:
"Worthy the Lamb, for he was slain!"

3 To him who suffered on the tree,
Our souls, at his soul's price, to gain,
Blessing, and praise, and glory be:
"Worthy the Lamb, for he was slain!"

4 To him, enthroned by filial right,
All power in heaven and earth proclaim,
Honor, and majesty, and might:
"Worthy the Lamb, for he was slain!"

5 Long as we live, and when we die,
And while in heaven with him we reign,
This song, our song of songs shall be:
"Worthy the Lamb, for he was slain!"

MONTGOMERY.

433 L. M.

1 NOW to the Lord, who makes us know
The wonders of his dying love,
Be humble honors paid below,
And strains of nobler praise above.

2 'Twas he who cleansed our foulest sins,
And washed us in his precious blood;
'Tis he who makes us priests and kings,
And brings us rebels near to God.

3 To Jesus, our atoning Priest,
To Jesus, our eternal King,
Be everlasting power confessed:
Let every tongue his glory sing.

4 Behold! on flying clouds he comes,
And every eye shall see him move;
Though with our sins we pierced him once,
He now displays his pardoning love.

5 The unbelieving world shall wail,
While we rejoice to see the day;
Come, Lord! nor let thy promise fail,
Nor let thy chariot long delay.

WATTS.

434 L. M.

1 NOW to the Lord a noble song;
Awake, my soul, awake, my tongue;
Hosanna to th' eternal name,
And all his boundless love proclaim.

2 See where it shines in Jesus' face,
The brightest image of his grace;
God, in the person of his Son,
Has all his mightiest works outdone.

3 The spacious earth and spreading flood
Proclaim the wise, the powerful God,
And thy rich glories from afar
Sparkle in every rolling star.

4 But in his look a glory stands,
The noblest labor of thine hands:
The pleasing lustre of his eyes
Outshines the wonders of the skies.

5 Grace, 'tis a sweet, a charming theme;
My thoughts rejoice at Jesus' name;
Ye angels, dwell upon the sound;
Ye heavens, reflect it to the ground.

6 Oh, may I reach the happy place
Where he unveils his lovely face,
His beauties there may I behold,
And sing his name to harps of gold.

WATTS.

435 L. M.

1 JESUS, thou everlasting King!
Accept the tribute which we bring;
Accept the well-deserved renown,
And wear our praises as thy crown.

2 Let every act of worship be
Like our espousals, Lord, to thee:
Like the dear hour, when from above
We first received thy pledge of love.

3 The gladness of that happy day!
Our hearts would wish it long to stay;
Nor let our faith forsake its hold,
Nor comfort sink, nor love grow cold.

4 Each following minute, as it flies,
Increase thy praise, improve our joys,
Till we are raised to sing thy name,
At the great supper of the Lamb.

WATTS.

436 L. M.

1 THERE is none other name than thine,
Jehovah-Jesus! Name divine!—
On which to rest for sins forgiven—
For peace with God, for hope of heaven.

2 There is none other name than thine,
When cares, and fears, and griefs are mine,
That, with a gracious power, can heal
The care, and fear, and grief I feel.

3 There is none other name than thine,
When called my spirit to resign,
To bear me through that latest strife,
And e'en in death to be my life.

4 Name above every name! thy praise
Shall fill the remnant of my days:
Jehovah-Jesus! Name divine!
Rock of salvation! thou art mine.

437 L. M.

1 ALL-GLORIOUS God, what hymns of praise
Shall our transported voices raise!
What ardent love and zeal are due,
While heaven stands open to our view.

2 Once we were fallen, oh, how low!
Just on the brink of endless woe:
When Jesus, from the realms above,
Came on the wings of boundless love:

3 Scattered the shades of death and night,
And spread around his heavenly light.
By him what wondrous grace is shown
To souls impoverished and undone!

4 He shows, beyond these mortal shores,
A bright inheritance as ours;
Where saints in light our coming wait
To share their holy, happy state.

438 L. M.

1 AROUND the Saviour's lofty throne,
Ten thousand times ten thousand sing;
They worship him as God alone,
And crown him everlasting King.

2 Approach, ye saints! this God is yours!
'Tis Jesus fills the throne above:
Ye cannot want, while God endures;
Ye cannot fail, while God is love.

3 Jesus, thou everlasting King!
To thee the praise of heaven belongs;
Yet smile on us, who fain would bring
The tribute of our humble songs.

4 Though sin defile our worship here,
We hope ere long thy face to view;
And, when our souls in heaven appear,
We'll praise thy name as angels do.

KELLY.

439 L. M.

1 HAIL to the Prince of life and peace,
Who holds the keys of death and hell!

The spacious world unseen is his,
And sovereign power becomes him well.

2 In shame and anguish once he died;
But now he lives forevermore:
Bow down, ye saints, around his seat,
And all ye angel-bands adore.

3 So live forever, glorious Lord,
To crush thy foes, and guard thy friends;
While all thy chosen tribes rejoice,
That thy dominion never ends.

4 Worthy thy hand to hold the keys,
Guided by wisdom and by love;
Worthy to rule o'er mortal life,
O'er worlds below, and worlds above.

5 Forever reign, victorious King,
Wide through the earth thy name be known;
And call my longing soul to sing
Sublimer anthems near thy throne.

DODDRIDGE.

440 L. M.

1 NOW be my heart inspired to sing
The glories of my Saviour King,—
Jesus, the Lord; how heavenly fair
His form! how bright his beauties are!

2 O'er all the sons of human race
He shines with a superior grace;
Love from his lips divinely flows,
And blessings all his state compose.

3 Thy throne, O God, forever stands;
Grace is the sceptre in thy hands
Thy laws and works are just and right;
Justice and grace are thy delight.

4 God! thine own God has richly shed
His oil of gladness on thy head;
And with his sacred Spirit blessed
His first-born Son above the rest.

WATTS.

441 L. M.

1 IN Christ I've all my soul's desire;
His Spirit does my heart inspire
With boundless wishes large and high;
And Christ will all my wants supply.

2 Christ is my Hope, my Strength, and Guide;
For me he bled, and groaned, and died;
He is my Sun, to give me light;
He is my soul's supreme Delight.

3 Christ is the Source of all my bliss;
My Wisdom and my Righteousness,
My Saviour, Brother, and my Friend;
On him alone I now depend.

4 Christ is my King, to rule and bless,
And all my troubles to redress;
He's my Salvation and my All,
Whate'er on earth shall me befall.

5 Christ is my Strength and Portion too;
My soul in him can all things do;
Through him I'll triumph o'er the grave,
And death and every foe outbrave.

DOBEL'S COLLECTION.

442 L. M.

1 WE sing the praise of him who died,
Of him who died upon the cross;
The sinner's hope let men deride,
For this we count the world but loss.

2 Inscribed upon the cross we see,
In shining letters, God is love;
He bears our sins upon the tree,
He brings us mercy from above.

3 The cross! it takes our guilt away;
It holds the fainting spirit up;
It cheers with hope the gloomy day,
And sweetens every bitter cup.

4 It makes the timid spirit brave,
And nerves the feeble arm for fight;
It takes the terror from the grave,
And gilds the bed of death with light.

5 The balm of life, the cure of woe,
The measure and the pledge of love,
The sinner's refuge here below,
The angels' theme in heaven above.

KELLY.

443 C. M.

1 COME, let us lift our joyful eyes,
Up to the courts above,
And smile to see our Father there,
Upon a throne of love.

2 Now we may bow before his feet,
And venture near the Lord;
No fiery cherubs guard his seat,
Nor double-flaming sword.

3 The peaceful gates of heavenly bliss
Are opened by the Son;
High let us raise our notes of praise,
And reach the almighty throne.

4 To thee, ten thousand thanks we bring,
Great Advocate on high,
And glory to the eternal King,
Who lays his anger by.

WATTS.

444 C. M.

1 MY Saviour! my almighty Friend!
When I begin thy praise,
Where will the growing numbers end—
The numbers of thy grace?

2 Thou art my everlasting trust;
Thy goodness I adore:
And since I knew thy graces first
I speak thy glories more.

3 My feet shall travel all the length
Of the celestial road;
And march, with courage, in thy strength,
To see my Father God.

4 When I am filled with sore distress
For some surprising sin,
I'll plead thy perfect righteousness,
And mention none but thine.

5 How will my lips rejoice to tell
The vict'ries of my King!
My soul, redeemed from sin and hell,
Shall thy salvation sing.

6 Awake, awake, my tuneful powers!
With this delightful song
I'll entertain the darkest hours,
Nor think the season long.

WATTS.

445 C. M.

1 HOSANNA be our cheerful song,
To Christ our Saviour King;
His praise, to whom we all belong,
Let all unite to sing.

2 Hosanna here in joyful bands,
Let old and young proclaim;
And hail, with voices, hearts, and hands,
The Son of David's name.

3 Hosanna sound from hill to hill,
And spread from plain to plain;
While louder, sweeter, clearer still
Woods echo to the strain.

4 Hosanna on the wings of light,
O'er earth and ocean fly;
Till morn to eve, and noon to night,
And heaven to earth, reply.

446 C. M.

1 ALL hail the pow'r of Jesus' name!
Let angels prostrate fall!
Bring forth the royal diadem,
And crown him Lord of all.

2 Ye chosen seed of Israel's race,
Ye ransomed from the fall;
Hail him, who saves you by his grace,
And crown him Lord of all.

3 Sinners, whose love can ne'er forget
The wormwood and the gall;
Go, spread your trophies at his feet,
And crown him Lord of all.

4 Let every kindred, every tribe,
On this terrestrial ball,
To him all majesty ascribe,
And crown him Lord of all.

5 Oh! that with yonder sacred throng,
We at his feet may fall;
We'll join the everlasting song,
And crown him Lord of all.

PERRENET.

447 C. M.

1 BEHOLD the glories of the Lamb,
Amid his Father's throne;
Prepare new honors for his name,
And songs before unknown.

2 Let elders worship at his feet,
The church adore around,
With vials full of odors sweet,
And harps of sweeter sound.

3 Those are the prayers of all the saints,
And these the hymns they raise:
Jesus is kind to our complaints;
He loves to hear our praise.

4 Now to the Lamb that once was slain,
Be endless blessings paid!
Salvation, glory, joy remain
Forever on thy head!

5 Thou hast redeemed our souls with blood,
Hast set the prisoners free,
Hast made us kings and priests to God,
And we shall reign with thee.

WATTS.

448 C. M.

1 SING we the song of those who stand
Around the eternal throne,
Of every kindred, clime, and land,
A multitude unknown.

2 Life's poor distinctions vanish here;
To-day the young, the old,
Our Saviour and his flock appear,
One Shepherd and one fold.

3 Toil, trial, suffering, still await
On earth the pilgrims' throng;
Yet learn we in our low estate
The Church Triumphant's song.

4 "Worthy the Lamb for sinners slain,"
Cry the redeemed above,
"Blessing and honor to obtain,
And everlasting love!"

5 "Worthy the Lamb," on earth we sing,
"Who died our souls to save!
Henceforth, O Death! where is thy sting?
Thy victory, O Grave!"

MONTGOMERY.

449 C. M. 5 l.

1 GO, tune thy voice to sacred song,
Exert thy noblest powers,
Go, mingle with the choral throng,
The Saviour's praises to prolong,
Amid life's fleeting hours.

2 Oh! hast thou felt a Saviour's love,
That flame of heavenly birth?
Then let thy strains melodious prove,
With raptures soaring far above
The trifling toys of earth.

3 Hast found the pearl of price unknown,
That cost a Saviour's blood?
Heir of a bright celestial crown,
That sparkles near th' eternal throne,
Oh sing the praise of God!

4 Sing of the Lamb that once was slain,
That man might be forgiven;
Sing how he broke death's bars in twain,
Ascending high in bliss to reign,
The God of earth and heaven.

HASTINGS.

450 C. M.

1 JESUS—the name high over all,
In hell, or earth, or sky—
Angels and men before it fall,
And devils fear and fly.

2 Jesus—the name to sinners dear,
The name to sinners given—
It scatters all their guilt and fear;
It turns their hell to heaven.

3 Oh that a dying world might know
The glory of his name;
My voice shall his salvation show,
And cry—"Behold the Lamb!"

4 Happy, if with my latest breath
I may but lisp his name,—
Proclaim his love, and say in death—
"Behold, behold the Lamb!"

C. WESLEY.

451 C. M.

1 COME, ye that love the Saviour's name,
And joy to make it known,
The Sovereign of your hearts proclaim,
And bow before his throne.

2 Behold your King, your Saviour crowned
With glories all divine;
And tell the wondering nations round,
How bright those glories shine.

3 When in his earthly courts we view
The beauties of our King,
We long to love as angels do,
And with their voice to sing.

4 And shall we long and wish in vain?
Lord, teach our songs to rise:
Thy love can raise our humble strain,
And bid it reach the skies.

5 Oh for the day, the glorious day!
When heaven and earth shall raise,
With all their powers, the raptured lay,
To celebrate thy praise.

STEELE.

452 C. M.

1 OH, for a thousand tongues to sing
My great Redeemer's praise,
The glories of my God and King,
The triumphs of his grace!

2 My gracious Master and my God,
Assist me to proclaim,
To spread, through all the earth abroad,
The honors of thy name.

3 Jesus, the name that calms our fears,
That bids our sorrows cease;
'Tis music in the sinner's ears,
'Tis life, and health, and peace!

4 He speaks, and, listening to his voice,
New life the dead receive:
The mournful, broken hearts rejoice,
The humble poor believe.

5 Hear him, ye deaf; his praise, ye dumb,
Your loosened tongues employ:
Ye blind, behold your Saviour come,
And leap, ye lame, for joy!

C. WESLEY.

453 C. M.

1 COME, let us join our cheerful songs
With angels round the throne;
Ten thousand thousand are their tongues,
But all their joys are one.

2 "Worthy the Lamb that died," they cry,
"To be exalted thus!"
"Worthy the Lamb!" our lips reply,
"For he was slain for us."

3 Jesus is worthy to receive
Honor and power divine;
And blessings, more than we can give,
Be, Lord, forever thine!

4 Let all that dwell above the sky,
And air, and earth, and seas,
Conspire to lift thy glories high,
And speak thine endless praise.

5 The whole creation join in one,
To bless the sacred name
Of him who sits upon the throne,
And to adore the Lamb!

WATTS.

454 C. M.

1 TO our Redeemer's glorious name
Awake the sacred song!
Oh, may his love—immortal flame—
Tune every heart and tongue.

2 His love what mortal thought can reach!
What mortal tongue display!
Imagination's utmost stretch
In wonder dies away.

3 Dear Lord, while we, adoring, pay
Our humble thanks to thee,
May every heart with rapture say,
"The Saviour died for me."

4 Oh, may the sweet, the blissful theme
Fill every heart and tongue,
Till strangers love thy charming name,
And join the sacred song.

STEELE.

455 C. M.

1 OH, sing to him who loved and bled,
Ye heaven-born sinners, sing;
'Twas Jesus suffered in your stead;
Own him your God and King.

2 He washed us, in his precious blood,
From every guilty stain;
He made us kings and priests to God,
And we shall with him reign.

3 Sing of his everlasting love,
From whence salvation flows;
Sing to him here, then sing above,
Of all that he bestows.

4 To him that loved us when depraved,
When guilty, blind, and poor;
To him that loved, and died, and saved,
Be glory evermore.

456 C. M.

1 THE Saviour! oh, what endless charms
Dwell in that blissful sound!
Its influence every fear disarms,
And spreads delight around.

2 Here pardon, life, and joy divine,
In rich profusion flow,
For guilty rebels, lost in sin,
And doomed to endless woe.

3 The mighty Former of the skies
Descends to our abode,
While angels view with wondering eyes,
And hail th' incarnate God.

4 How rich the depths of love divine!
Of bliss, a boundless store!
Dear Saviour, let me call thee mine;
I cannot wish for more.

STEELE.

457 C. M.

1 FROM thee, my God, my joys shall rise,
And run eternal rounds,
Beyond the limits of the skies,
And all created bounds.

2 The holy triumphs of my soul
Shall death itself outbrave,
Leave dull mortality behind,
And fly beyond the grave.

3 There, where my blessèd Jesus reigns,
In heaven's unmeasured space,
I'll spend a long eternity
In pleasure and in praise.

4 Millions of years my wondering eyes
Shall o'er thy beauties rove,
And endless ages I'll adore
The glories of thy love.

5 My Saviour, every smile of thine
Shall fresh endearments bring,
And thousand tastes of new delight
From all thy graces spring.

6 Haste, my Belovéd, fetch my soul
Up to thy blest abode;
Fly, for my spirit longs to see
My Saviour and my God.
WATTS.

458 C. M.

1 I KNOW that my Redeemer lives,
And ever prays for me:
A token of his love he gives,
A pledge of liberty.

2 I find him lifting up my head;
He brings salvation near:
His presence makes me free indeed,
And he will soon appear.

3 He wills that I should holy be:
What can withstand his will?
The counsel of his grace in me,
He surely shall fulfill.

4 Jesus, I hang upon thy word:
I steadfastly believe
Thou wilt return, and claim me, Lord,
And to thyself receive.
C. WESLEY.

459 C. M.

1 JESUS! delightful, charming name!
It spreads a fragrance round:
Justice and mercy, truth and peace,
In union here are found.

2 He is our life, our joy, our strength,
In him all glories meet;
He is a shade above our heads,
A light to guide our feet.

3 The thickest clouds are soon dispersed,
If Jesus shows his face:
To weary, heavy-laden souls,
He is the resting-place.

4 When storms arise and tempests blow,
He speaks the stilling word;
The threatening billows cease to flow,
The winds obey their Lord.

5 Through every age he's still the same;
But we ungrateful prove,
Forget the savor of his name,
The sweetness of his love.
BEDDOME.

460 C. M.

1 COME, let us join our songs of praise
To our ascended Priest;
He entered heaven with all our names
Engraven on his breast.

2 Below he washed our guilt away,
By his atoning blood;
Now he appears before the throne,
And pleads our cause with God.

3 Clothed with our nature still, he knows
The weakness of our frame,
And how to shield us from the foes
Whom he himself o'ercame.

4 Nor time, nor distance, e'er shall quench
The fervor of his love;
For us he died in kindness here,
For us he lives above.

5 Oh! may we ne'er forget his grace,
Nor blush to bear his name;
Still may our hearts hold fast his faith,
Our lips his praise proclaim.

461 C. M.

1 I KNOW that my Redeemer lives;
He lives who once was dead;
To me in grief he comfort gives;
With peace he crowns my head.

2 He lives, triumphant o'er the grave,
At God's right hand on high,
My ransomed soul to keep and save,
To bless and glorify.

3 He lives to fill my breast with love,
With joy my heart to feed;
He lives to plead for me above,
To succor me in need.

4 He lives that I may also live,
And now his grace proclaim;
He lives that I may honor give
To his most holy name.

5 Let strains of heavenly music rise,
While all their anthem sing
To Christ, my precious sacrifice,
And ever-living King.

462 C. M.

1 THERE is a name I love to hear,
I love to speak its worth:
It sounds like music in mine ear,
The sweetest name on earth.

2 It tells me of a Saviour's love,
Who died to set me free;
It tells me of his precious blood,
The sinner's perfect plea.

3 Jesus! the name I love so well,
The name I love to hear!
No saint on earth its worth can tell,
No heart conceive how dear.

4 This name shall shed its fragrance still
Along life's thorny road,
Shall sweetly smooth the rugged hill
That leads me up to God.

5 And there, with all the blood-bought throng,
From sin and sorrow free,
I'll sing the new eternal song
Of Jesus' love for me.

463 C. M.

1 THOU dear Redeemer, dying Lamb,
We love to hear of thee;
No music 's like thy charming name,
Nor half so sweet can be.

2 Oh may we ever hear thy voice
In mercy to us speak;
And in our Priest we will rejoice,
Thou great Melchisedec.

3 Our Saviour shall be still our theme,
While in this world we stay;
We'll sing our Jesus' lovely name,
When all things else decay.

4 When we appear in yonder cloud,
With all the favored throng,
Then will we sing more sweet, more loud,
And Christ shall be our song.

MADAN'S COLL.

464 C. M.

1 O JESUS, when I think of thee,
Thy manger, cross, and throne,
My spirit trusts exultingly
In thee, and thee alone.

2 I see thee in thy weakness first;
Then, glorious from thy shame
I see thee death's strong fetters burst,
And reach heaven's mightiest name.

3 In all, a brother's love I trace
By power divine exprest;
One in thy Father's dear embrace,
And on thy mother's breast.

4 For me thou didst become a man,
For me didst weep and die;
For me achieve thy wondrous plan,
For me ascend on high.

5 Oh let me share thy holy birth,
Thy faith, thy death to sin!
And, strong amidst the toils of earth,
My heavenly life begin.

BETHUNE.

465 C. M.

1 JESUS! I love thy charming name,
'Tis music to mine ear;
Fain would I sound it out so loud,
That earth and heaven should hear.

2 Yes!—thou art precious to my soul,
My transport and my trust;
Jewels, to thee, are gaudy toys,
And gold is sordid dust.

3 All my capacious powers can wish,
In thee doth richly meet;
Nor to mine eyes is light so dear,
Nor friendship half so sweet.

4 Thy grace still dwells upon my heart,
And sheds its fragrance there;—
The noblest balm of all its wounds,
The cordial of its care.

5 I'll speak the honors of thy name,
With my last laboring breath;
Then, speechless, clasp thee in mine arms,
The Conqueror of death.

DODDRIDGE.

466 C. M.

1 O JESUS, thou the beauty art
Of angel-worlds above;
Thy name is music to the heart,
Enchanting it with love.

2 O Jesus, Saviour, hear the sighs
Which unto thee I send;
To thee my inmost spirit cries,
My being's hope and end.

3 Stay with us, Lord, and with thy light
Illume the soul's abyss;
Scatter the darkness of our night,
And fill the world with bliss.

4 O Jesus, King of earth and heaven,
Our life and joy, to thee
Be honor, thanks, and blessing given
Through all eternity!

BERNARD.

467 C. M.

1 PLUNGED in a gulf of dark despair,
We wretched sinners lay,
Without one cheerful beam of hope,
Or spark of glimmering day.

2 With pitying eyes the Prince of grace
Beheld our helpless grief;
He saw, and, oh amazing love!
He ran to our relief.

3 Down from the shining seats above
With joyful haste he fled,
Entered the grave in mortal flesh,
And dwelt among the dead.

4 He spoiled the powers of darkness thus,
And brake our iron chains;

Jesus has freed our captive souls
From everlasting pains.

5 Oh! for this love let rocks and hills
Their lasting silence break;
And all harmonious human tongues
The Saviour's praises speak.

WATTS.

468 C. M.

1 JESUS, the very thought of thee
With sweetness fills my breast:
But sweeter far thy face to see,
And in thy presence rest.

2 Nor voice can sing, nor heart can frame,
Nor can the memory find
A sweeter sound than thy blest name,
O Saviour of mankind!

3 O Hope of every contrite heart!
O Joy of all the meek!
To those who fall, how kind thou art!
How good to those who seek!

4 But what to those who find? Ah! this,
Nor tongue nor pen can show;
The love of Jesus, what it is,
None but his loved ones know.

5 Jesus, our only joy be thou,
As thou our prize wilt be;
Jesus, be thou our glory now,
And through eternity.

BERNARD.

469 C. M.

1 MY soul doth magnify the Lord,
My spirit doth rejoice
In him, my Saviour and my God;
I hear his joyful voice.

2 I need not go abroad for joy,
Who have a feast at home;
My sighs are turned to happy songs;
The Comforter is come.

3 Down from on high, the blessèd Dove
Is come into my breast,
To witness God's eternal love:
This is my heavenly feast.

4 Glory to God the Father be,
Glory to God the Son,
Glory to God the Holy Ghost,
Glory to God alone.

470 C. M.

1 HOW sweet the name of Jesus sounds
In a believer's ear!
It soothes his sorrows, heals his wounds,
And drives away his fear.

2 It makes the wounded spirit whole,
And calms the troubled breast;
'Tis manna to the hungry soul,
And to the weary rest.

3 Jesus, my Shepherd, Guardian, Friend,
My Prophet, Priest, and King,—
My Lord, my Life, my Way, my End,
Accept the praise I bring.

4 Weak is the effort of my heart,
And cold my warmest thought;
But, when I see thee as thou art,
I'll praise thee as I ought.

5 Till then I would thy love proclaim
With every fleeting breath;
And may the music of thy name
Refresh my soul in death.

NEWTON.

471 C. M.

1 DEAREST of all the names above,
My Jesus and my God,
Who can resist thy heavenly love,
Or trifle with thy blood?

2 'Tis by the merits of thy death
The Father smiles again;
'Tis by thine interceding breath
The Spirit dwells with men.

3 Till God in human flesh I see,
My thoughts no comfort find;
The holy, just, and sacred Three
Are terrors to my mind.

4 But if Immanuel's face appear,
My hope, my joy begins;
His name forbids my slavish fear,
His grace removes my sins.

5 While Jews on their own law rely,
And Greeks of wisdom boast,
I love the Incarnate Mystery,
And there I fix my trust.

WATTS.

472 C. M.

1 TO thee, my Shepherd and my Lord,
A grateful song I'll raise;
Oh, let the humblest of thy flock
Attempt to speak thy praise.

2 My life, my joy, my hope, I owe
To thine amazing love;
Ten thousand thousand comforts here,
And nobler bliss above.

3 To thee my trembling spirit flies,
With sin and grief oppress'd;
Thy gentle voice dispels my fears,
And lulls my cares to rest.

4 Lead on, dear Shepherd!—led by thee,
No evil shall I fear;
Soon shall I reach thy fold above,
And praise thee better there.

HIGGINBOTHAM.

473 C. M.

1 THERE is a fountain filled with blood,
Drawn from Immanuel's veins;
And sinners, plunged beneath that flood,
Lose all their guilty stains.

2 The dying thief rejoiced to see
That fountain in his day;
And there have I, as vile as he,
Wash'd all my sins away.

3 Dear dying Lamb! thy precious blood
Shall never lose its power,
Till all the ransom'd Church of God
Are saved, to sin no more.

4 E'er since, by faith, I saw the stream
Thy flowing wounds supply,
Redeeming love has been my theme,
And shall be till I die.

5 And when this feeble, stam'ring tongue
Lies silent in the grave,
Then, in a nobler, sweeter song,
I'll sing thy power to save.

COWPER.

474 C. M.

1 MAJESTIC sweetness sits enthroned
Upon the Saviour's brow;
His head with radiant glories crowned,
His lips with grace o'erflow.

2 No mortal can with him compare,
Among the sons of men;
Fairer is he than all the fair
That fill the heavenly train.

3 He saw me plunged in deep distress,
And flew to my relief;
For me he bore the shameful cross,
And carried all my grief.

4 To him I owe my life and breath,
And all the joys I have;
He makes me triumph over death,
And saves me from the grave.

5 To heaven, the place of his abode,
He brings my weary feet,
Shows me the glories of my God,
And makes my joys complete.

6 Since from his bounty I receive
Such proofs of love divine,
Had I a thousand hearts to give,
Lord, they should all be thine.

STENNETT.

475 C. M.

1 I'VE found the pearl of greatest price!
My heart doth sing for joy;
And sing I must, for Christ is mine!
Christ shall my song employ.

2 Christ is my Prophet, Priest, and King;
My Prophet full of light,
My great High-Priest before the throne,
My King of heavenly might.

3 Christ is my Peace; he died for me,
For me he gave his blood;
And as my wondrous Sacrifice,
Offered himself to God.

4 Christ Jesus is my All in All,—
My Comfort and my Love;
My Life below, and he shall be
My Joy and Crown above.

476 C. M.

1 I LOVE thee, O my God, and still
I ever will love thee,
Solely because my God thou art
Who first hast lovèd me.

2 For me, to lowest depths of woe
Thou didst thyself abase;
For me didst bear the cross, the shame,
And manifold disgrace:

3 For me didst suffer pains unknown,
Blood-sweat and agony,
Yea, death itself,—all, all for me,
For me, thine enemy.

4 Then shall I not, O Saviour mine,
Shall I not love thee well?
Not with the hope of winning heaven,
Nor of escaping hell:

5 Not with the hope of gaining aught,
Nor seeking a reward;
But as thyself hast lovèd me,
O everlasting Lord!

XAVIER.

477 S. M.

1 GRACE, 'tis a charming sound,
Harmonious to the ear!
Heaven with the echo shall resound,
And all the earth shall hear.

2 Grace first contrived the way
To save rebellious man;
And all the steps that grace display
Which drew the wondrous plan.

3 Grace led my roving feet
  To tread the heavenly road ;
And new supplies, each hour, I meet,
  While pressing on to God.

4 Grace all the work shall crown,
  Through everlasting days ;
It lays in heaven the topmost stone,
  And well deserves the praise.

DODDRIDGE.

478 S. M.

1 RAISE your triumphant songs
  To an immortal tune ;
Wide let the earth resound the deeds
  Celestial grace has done.

2 Sing how eternal love
  Its chief Belovèd chose,
And bade him raise our wretched race
  From their abyss of woes.

3 His hand no thunder bears,
  No terror clothes his brow,
No bolts to drive our guilty souls
  To fiercer flames below.

4 'Twas mercy filled the throne,
  And wrath stood silent by,
When Christ was sent with pardons down
  To rebels doomed to die.

WATTS.

479 S. M.

1 NOT all the blood of beasts
  On Jewish altars slain,
Could give the guilty conscience peace,
  Or wash away the stain.

2 But Christ, the heavenly Lamb,
  Takes all our sins away ;
A sacrifice of nobler name,
  And richer blood, than they.

3 My faith would lay her hand
  On that dear head of thine,
While like a penitent I stand,
  And there confess my sin.

4 My soul looks back to see
  The burdens thou didst bear,
When hanging on the cursèd tree,
  And hopes her guilt was there.

5 Believing, we rejoice
  To see the curse remove ;
We bless the Lamb with cheerful voice,
  And sing his bleeding love.

WATTS.

480 S. M.

1 TO praise our Shepherd's care,
  His wisdom, love, and might,
Your loudest, loftiest songs prepare,
  And bid the world unite.

2 Supremely good and great,
  He tends his blood-bought fold ;
He stoops, though thron'd in highest state,
  The feeblest to uphold.

3 He hears their softest plaint ;
  He sees them when they roam ;
And if his meanest lamb should faint,
  His bosom bears it home.

4 Kind Shepherd of the sheep,
  A weakly flock are we ;
And snares and foes are nigh ; but keep
  The lambs who look to thee.

HAVERGAL.

481 C. M.

1 SALVATION ! oh, the joyful sound !
  'Tis pleasure to our ears !
A sovereign balm for every wound,
  A cordial for our fears.

2 Buried in sorrow and in sin,
At hell's dark door we lay;
But we arise, by grace divine,
To see a heavenly day.

3 Salvation! let the echo fly
The spacious earth around,
While all the armies of the sky
Conspire to raise the sound!

4 Salvation! O thou bleeding Lamb,
To thee the praise belongs:
Our hearts shall kindle at thy Name,
Thy Name inspire our songs.

Chorus.

Glory, honor, praise, and power,
Be unto the Lamb forever!
Jesus Christ is our Redeemer,
Hallelujah! praise the Lord!

482 C. M.

1 HOSANNA! raise the pealing hymn
To David's Son and Lord;
With cherubim and seraphim
Exalt the Incarnate Word.

2 Hosanna! Master, lo, we bring
Our offerings to thy throne;
Nor gold, nor myrrh, nor mortal thing,
But hearts to be thine own.

3 Hosanna! once thy gracious ear
Approved a lisping throng;
Be gracious still, and deign to hear
Our poor but grateful song.

4 O Saviour, if redeemed by thee,
Thy temple we behold,
Hosannas through eternity
We'll sing to harps of gold.

483 S. M.

1 AWAKE, and sing the song
Of Moses and the Lamb!
Wake, every heart, and every tongue,
To praise the Saviour's name!

2 Sing of his dying love;
Sing of his rising power:
Sing how he intercedes above,
For those whose sins he bore.

3 Sing, till we feel our hearts
Ascending with our tongues;
Sing, till the love of sin departs,
And grace inspires our songs.

4 Sing on your heavenly way,
Ye ransomed sinners, sing!
Sing on, rejoicing every day
In Christ, th' exalted King.

5 Soon shall we hear him say,
"Ye blesséd children, come!"
Soon will he call us hence away
To our eternal home.

HAMMOND.

484 S. M.

1 ENTHRONED is Jesus now
Upon his heavenly seat;
The kingly crown is on his brow,
The saints are at his feet.

2 In shining white they stand,—
A great and countless throng;
A palmy sceptre in each hand,
On every lip a song.

3 They sing the Lamb of God,
Once slain on earth for them;
The Lamb, through whose atoning blood,
Each wears his diadem.

4 Thy grace, O Holy Ghost,
Thy blessèd help supply,
That we may join that radiant host,
Triumphant in the sky.

JUDKIN.

485 S. M.

1 O CHRIST, what gracious words,
Are ever, ever thine!
Thy voice is music to the soul,
And life, and peace divine.

2 Grace, everlasting grace,
Glad tidings, full of joy,
Flow from thy lips, the lips of truth,
And flow without alloy.

3 The broken heart, the poor,
The bruised, the deaf, the blind,
The dumb, the dead, the captive wretch,
In thee compassion find.

4 Lord Jesus, speed the day,
The promised day of grace,
To all the poor, the dumb, the deaf,
The dead, of Adam's race.

486 8s & 7s.

1 IN the cross of Christ I glory,
Towering o'er the wrecks of time;
All the light of sacred story
Gathers round its head sublime.

2 When the woes of life o'ertake me,
Hopes deceive, and fears annoy,
Never shall the cross forsake me:
Lo! it glows with peace and joy.

3 When the sun of bliss is beaming
Light and love upon my way,
From the cross the radiance streaming
Adds new lustre to the day.

4 Bane and blessing, pain and pleasure,
By the cross are sanctified;
Peace is there, that knows no measure,
Joys that through all time abide.

5 In the cross of Christ I glory,
Tow'ring o'er the wrecks of time;
All the light of sacred story
Gathers round its head sublime.

BOWRING

487 8s & 7s.

1 SWEET the moments, rich in blessing,
Which before the cross I spend;
Life, and health, and peace possessing,
From the sinner's dying Friend.

2 Here I'll sit, forever viewing
Mercy streaming in his blood;
Precious drops! my soul bedewing,
Plead and claim my peace with God.

3 Truly blessèd is my station,
Low before his cross to lie;
While I see divine compassion
Floating in his languid eye.

4 Here it is I find my heaven
While upon the cross I gaze;
Love I much? I've much forgiven,
I'm a miracle of grace.

5 Love and grief my heart dividing,
With my tears his feet I'll bathe;
Constant still in faith abiding,
Life deriving from his death.

ALLEN.

488 8s & 7s.

1 HARK, the sound of holy voices
Chanting at the crystal sea,
Hallelujah, hallelujah,
Hallelujah! Lord, to thee.

2 Multitudes which none can number,
Like the stars in glory, stand
Clothed in white apparel, holding
Victor-palms in every hand.

3 They have come from tribulation,
And have washed their robes in blood,
Washed them in the blood of Jesus;
Tried they were, and firm they stood.

4 Now they reign in heavenly glory,
Now they walk in golden light;
Now they drink, as from a river,
Holy bliss and infinite.

WORDSWORTH.

489

1 THERE is no name so sweet on earth,
No name so sweet in heaven,—
The name before his wondrous birth
To Christ, the Saviour, given.

2 And when he hung upon the tree,
They wrote this name above him,
That all might see the reason we
Forevermore must love him.

3 So now, upon his Father's throne,
Almighty to release us
From sin and pains, he ever reigns,
The Prince and Saviour Jesus.

4 O Jesus, by that matchless name,
Thy grace shall fail us never;
To-day as yesterday the same,
Thou art the same forever.
Then let us sing, around our King,
The faithful, precious Jesus, etc.

Chorus.

We love to sing around our King,
And hail him blessèd Jesus:
For there's no word ear ever heard
So dear, so sweet as Jesus.

490 7s & 6s.

1 COME, let us sing of Jesus,
While hearts and accents blend;
Come, let us sing of Jesus,
The sinner's only Friend;
His holy soul rejoices,
Amid the choirs above,
To hear our youthful voices
Exulting in his love.

2 We love to sing of Jesus,
Who wept our path along;
We love to sing of Jesus,
The tempted and the strong;
None who besought his healing,
He passed unheeded by:
And still retains his feeling
For us above the sky.

3 We love to sing of Jesus,
Who died our souls to save;
We love to sing of Jesus,
Triumphant o'er the grave;
And in our hour of danger,
We'll trust his love alone,
Who once slept in a manger,
And now sits on the throne.

4 Then let us sing of Jesus,
While yet on earth we stay,
And hope to sing of Jesus
Throughout eternal day;

For those who here confess him,
He will in heaven confess;
And faithful hearts that bless him,
He will forever bless.

491 8s & 7s.

1 WHO shall sing, if not the children?
Did not Jesus die for them?
May they not, with other jewels,
Sparkle in his diadem?
Why to them were voices given,
Bird-like voices, sweet and clear?
Why, unless the song of heaven
They begin to practice here?

2 There's a choir of infant songsters,
White-robed, round the Saviour's throne;
Angels cease, and, waiting, listen:
Oh, 'tis sweeter than their own!
Faith can hear the rapturous choral,
When her ear is upward turn'd:
Is not this the same, perfected,
Which upon the earth they learn'd?

3 Jesus, when on earth sojourning,
Loved them with a wondrous love:
And will he, to heaven returning,
Faithless to his blessing prove?
Oh, they cannot sing too early:
Fathers, stand not in their way!
Birds do sing while day is breaking:
Tell me, then, why should not they?

492 7s & 3s.

1 WORTHY, worthy is the Lamb,
Worthy, worthy is the Lamb,
Worthy, worthy is the Lamb,
That was slain.

2 Sons of Morning sing his praise,
In the noblest strains you raise,
Man's redemption claims your lays,
Praise the Lamb.

3 Christ has come in very deed,
Born to bruise the serpent's head;
Sinner, he's the Friend you need,
Praise the Lamb.

4 See, in sad Gethsemane,
See, on tragic Calvary,
Sinner, see his love to thee,
Praise the Lamb.

5 Penitents, dry up your tears,
God hath heard believing prayers,
He forgives you when he hears
His dear Lamb.

6 Thus may we each moment feel,
Love him, serve him, praise him still,
Till we all on Zion's hill
See the Lamb.

493 C. M.

1 HE'S come, let every knee be bent,
All hearts new joy resume;
Sing, ye redeemed, with one consent,
"The Comforter is come."

2 What greater gift, what greater love,
Could God on man bestow?
Angels for this rejoice above,
Let man rejoice below.

3 Hail, blessèd Spirit! may each soul
Thy sacred influence feel;
Do thou each sinful thought control,
And fix our wavering zeal.

4 Thou to the conscience dost convey
Those checks which we should know;
Thy motions point to us the way;
Thou giv'st us strength to go.

494 C. M.

1 GREAT Spirit, by whose mighty power
All creatures live and move,
On us thy benediction shower;
Inspire our souls with love.

2 Hail, Source of light! arise and shine;
All gloom and doubt dispel;
Give peace and joy, for we are thine;
In us forever dwell.

3 From death to life our spirits raise;
Complete redemption bring;
New tongues impart to speak the praise
Of Christ, our God and King.

4 Thine inward witness bear, unknown
To all the world beside;
Exulting, then, we feel and own
Our Saviour glorified.

495 C. M.

1 NO track is on the sunny sky,
No footprints on the air;
Jesus hath gone; the face of earth
Is desolate and bare.

2 That Upper Room is heaven on earth;
Within its precincts lie
All that earth has of faith, or hope,
Or heaven-born charity.

3 One moment—and the silentness
Was breathless as the grave:
The fluttered earth forgot to quake,
The troubled trees to wave.

4 He comes! he comes! that mighty Breath
From heaven's eternal shores;
His uncreated freshness fills
His Bride, as she adores.

5 Earth quakes before that rushing blast,
Heaven echoes back the sound,
And mightily the tempest wheels
That Upper Room around.

6 One moment—and the Spirit hung
O'er all with dread desire:
Then broke upon the heads of all
In cloven tongues of fire.

FABER.

496 L. M.

1 ETERNAL Spirit, we confess
And sing the wonders of thy grace;
Thy pow'r conveys our blessings down
From God the Father and the Son.

2 Enlightened by the heavenly ray,
Our shades and darkness turn to day;
Thine inward teachings make us know
Our danger, and our refuge too.

3 Thy power and glory work within,
And break the chains of reigning sin;
All our imperious lusts subdue,
And form our wretched hearts anew.

4 The troubled conscience knows thy voice;
Thy cheering words awake our joys;
Thy words allay the stormy wind,
And calm the surges of the mind.

WATTS.

497 L. M.

1 COME, O Creator Spirit blest!
And in our souls take up thy rest;
Come, with thy grace and heavenly aid,
To fill the hearts which thou hast made.

2 Great Comforter! to thee we cry;
O highest Gift of God most high!
O fount of life! O fire of love!
Send sweet anointing from above!

3 Kindle our senses from above,
And make our hearts o'erflow with love;
With patience firm, and virtue high,
The weakness of our flesh supply.

4 Far from us drive the foe we dread,
And grant us thy true peace instead;
So shall we not, with thee for guide,
Turn from the path of life aside.

LYRA CATH.

498 L. M.

1 THE Spirit, like a peaceful dove,
Flies from the realms of noise and strife:
Why should we vex and grieve his love,
Who seals our souls to heavenly life!

2 Tender and kind be all our thoughts;
Through all our lives let mercy run;
So God forgives our numerous faults,
Through grace abounding in the Son.

WATTS.

499 L. M.

1 COME, blessèd Spirit! source of light!
Whose power and grace are unconfined,
Dispel the gloomy shades of night,—
The thicker darkness of the mind.

2 To mine illumined eyes display
The glorious truth thy word reveals;
Cause me to run the heavenly way,
Thy book unfold, and loose the seals.

3 While through this dubious maze I stray,
Spread, like the sun, thy beams abroad,
To show the dangers of the way,
And guide my feeble steps to God.

BEDDOME.

500 L. M.

1 SURE the blest Comforter is nigh,
'Tis he sustains my fainting heart;
Else would my hopes forever die,
And every cheering ray depart.

2 Whene'er, to call the Saviour mine,
With ardent wish my heart aspires,—
Can it be less than power divine,
That animates these strong desires?

3 And, when my cheerful hope can say,—
I love my God and taste his grace,—
Lord! is it not thy blissful ray,
That brings this dawn of sacred peace?

4 Let thy good Spirit in my heart
Forever dwell, O God of love!
And light and heavenly peace impart,—
Sweet earnest of the joys above.

STEELE.

501 L. M.

1 COME, gracious Spirit, heavenly Dove,
With light and comfort from above:
Be thou our guardian, thou our guide!
O'er every thought and step preside.

2 To us the light of truth display,
And make us know and choose thy way;
Plant holy fear in every heart,
That we from God may ne'er depart.

3 Lead us to holiness—the road
That we must take to dwell with God;
Lead us to Christ, the living way,
Nor let us from his precepts stray.

4 Lead us to God, our final rest,
To be with him forever blest;
Lead us to heaven, its bliss to share—
Fullness of joy forever there!

BROWNE.

502 L. M.

1 COME, Holy Spirit, calm my mind,
And fit me to approach my God;
Remove each vain, each worldly thought,
And lead me to thy blest abode.

2 Hast thou imparted to my soul
A living spark of holy fire?
Oh kindle now the sacred flame,
Make me to burn with pure desire!

3 A brighter faith and hope impart,
And let me now my Saviour see;
Oh soothe and cheer my burden'd heart,
And bid my spirit rest in thee!

BURDER COLL.

503 L. M.

1 AS when in silence, vernal showers
Descend, and cheer the fainting flowers,
So, in the secrecy of love,
Falls the sweet Spirit from above.

2 That heavenly Spirit let me find
In holy silence of the mind,
While every grace maintains its bloom,
Diffusing wide its rich perfume.

3 Nor let these blessings be confined
To me, but poured on all mankind,
Till earth's wild wastes in verdure rise,
And a young Eden bless our eyes.

504 L. M.

1 AT anchor laid, remote from home,
Toiling I cry, "Sweet Spirit, come!
Celestial breeze, no longer stay,
But swell my sails, and speed my way."

2 "Fain would I mount, fain would I glow,
And loose my cable from below;
But I can only spread my sail;
Thou, thou must breathe the auspicious gale."

505 L. M.

1 COME, dearest Lord, descend and dwell
By faith and love in every breast;
Then shall we know, and taste, and feel
The joys that cannot be expressed.

2 Come, fill our hearts with inward strength,
Make our enlargéd souls possess,
And learn the height, and breadth, and length
Of thine immeasurable grace.

3 Now to the God, whose power can do
More than our thoughts or wishes know,
Be everlasting honors done
By all the church, through Christ his Son.

WATTS.

506 L. M.

1 SPIRIT of mercy, truth, and love,
Oh shed thine influence from above:
And still from age to age convey
The blessings of this sacred day.

2 In every clime, by every tongue,
Be God's redeeming mercy sung;
Let all the listening earth be taught
The wonders by the Saviour wrought.

3 Unfailing Comfort! heavenly Guide!
Still o'er thy ransomed church preside!
Let every heart thy blessing prove,
Spirit of mercy, truth, and love.

507 L. M.

1 COME, sacred Spirit, from above,
And fill the coldest heart with love:
Oh! turn to flesh the flinty stone,
And let thy sovereign power be known.

2 Speak thou, and from the haughtiest eyes
Shall floods of contrite sorrow rise;
While all their glowing souls are borne
To seek that grace which now they scorn.

3 Oh! let a holy flock await,
In crowds around thy temple-gate!
Each pressing on with zeal to be
A living sacrifice to thee.

4 In answer to our fervent cries,
Give us to see thy church arise;
Or, if that blessing seem too great,
Give us to mourn its low estate.

DODDRIDGE.

508 L. M.

1 STAY, thou insulted Spirit, stay,
Though I have done thee such despite;
Cast not a sinner quite away,
Nor take thine everlasting flight.

2 Though I have most unfaithful been
Of all who e'er thy grace received,—
Ten thousand times thy goodness seen,
Ten thousand times thy goodness grieved.

3 Yet, oh, the chief of sinners spare,
In honor of my great High Priest;
Nor, in thy righteous anger, swear
I shall not see thy people's rest.

4 Now, Lord, my weary soul release,
Upraise me with thy powerful hand;
Oh, guide me into perfect peace,
And bring me to the promised land!

C. WESLEY.

509 L. M.

1 O LORD, and shall our fainting souls
Thy just displeasure ever mourn?
Thy Spirit grieved, and long withdrawn,
Will he no more to us return?

2 Great Source of light and peace! return
Nor let us mourn and sigh in vain;
Come, repossess these longing hearts
With all the graces of thy train.

3 This temple, hallowed by thine hand,
Once more be with thy presence blest;
Here be thy grace anew displayed,
Be this thine everlasting rest!

THOMAS SCOTT.

510 L. M.

1 COME, thou celestial Spirit, come,
And call my roving passions home;
To mine enlightened eyes display
The heritage of heavenly day.

2 My God, that heritage is thine:
How rich, how glorious, how divine!
How far above all mortal things,
The little pride of courts and kings.

3 Of endless joy th' unbounded store;
Why is its lustre known no more?
Away, ye mists of envious night,
That veil salvation from my sight!

11

511 L. M.

1 COME, thou eternal Spirit, come
From heaven thy glorious dwelling-place;
Oh, make my sinful heart thy home,
And consecrate it by thy grace.

2 There fix, O Lord, thy blest abode,
And drive thy foes forever thence;
There shed a Saviour's love abroad,
And light, and life, and joy dispense.

3 My wants supply; my fears suppress;
Direct my way, and hold me up;
Teach me, in times of deep distress,
To pray in faith, and wait in hope.

BEDDOME.

512 L. M.

1 COME, Holy Ghost, who ever one
Art with the Father and the Son;
Come, Holy Ghost, our souls possess
With thy full flood of holiness.

2 In word and deed, by heart and tongue,
With all our powers, thy praise be sung;
May love enwrap our mortal frame,
And others catch the living flame.

513 8s & 7s. D.

1 LOVE divine, all love excelling,
Joy of heaven, to earth come down;
Fix in us thy humble dwelling;
All thy faithful mercies crown.
Jesus, thou art all compassion,—
Pure, unbounded love thou art;
Visit us with thy salvation;
Enter every trembling heart.

2 Breathe, oh breathe thy loving Spirit
Into every troubled breast;
Let us all in thee inherit;
Let us find thy promised rest;
Take away our bent to sinning:
Alpha and Omega be;
End of faith, as its beginning,
Set our hearts at liberty.

3 Come, almighty to deliver,
Let us all thy life receive;
Suddenly return, and never,
Never more thy temples leave:
Thee we would be always blessing,
Serve thee as thy hosts above;
Pray, and praise thee without ceasing,
Glory in thy perfect love.

4 Finish then thy new creation;
Pure and spotless let us be;
Let us see thy great salvation,
Perfectly restored in thee:
Changed from glory into glory
Till in heaven we take our place,—
Till we cast our crowns before thee,
Lost in wonder, love, and praise.

C. Wesley.

514 8s. & 7s. D.

1 HOLY Ghost! dispel our sadness;
Pierce the clouds of nature's night;
Come, thou Source of joy and gladness,
Breathe thy life, and spread thy light.
Hear, oh hear our supplication,
Blessed Spirit! God of peace!
Rest upon the congregation
With the fullness of thy grace.

2 Author of our new creation,
May we all thine influence prove;
Make our souls the habitation,—
Shed abroad the Saviour's love.
Source of sweetest consolation,
Breathe thy peace on all below;
Bless, oh bless this congregation;
On each soul thy grace bestow!

Jay.

515 C. M.

1 COME, Holy Ghost, Creator, come,
Inspire these souls of thine;
Till every heart which thou hast made
Be filled with grace divine.

2 Thou art the Comforter, the gift
Of God, and fire of love;
The everlasting spring of joy,
And unction from above.

3 Enlighten our dark souls, till they
Thy sacred love embrace;
Assist our minds, by nature frail,
With thy celestial grace.

516 C. M.

1 WHEN God of old came down from heaven,
In power and wrath he came;
Before his feet the clouds were riven,
Half darkness and half flame:

2 But when he came the second time,
He came in power and love;
Softer than gale at morning prime
Hovered his holy dove.

3 The fires, that rushed on Sinai down
In sudden torrents dread,
Now gently light, a glorious crown,
On every sainted head.

4 And as on Israel's awe-struck ear
The voice exceeding loud,
The trump, that angels quake to hear,
Thrill'd from the deep, dark cloud:

5 So, when the Spirit of our God
Came down his flock to find,
A voice from heaven was heard abroad,
A rushing, mighty wind.

6 He fills the church of God: he fills
The sinful world around;
Only in stubborn hearts and wills
No place for him is found.

7 Come, Lord, come Wisdom, Love, and Power,
Open our ears to hear;
Let us not miss th' accepted hour,
Save, Lord, by love or fear.

KEBLE.

517 C. M.

1 ETERNAL Spirit, God of truth,
Our contrite hearts inspire;
Revive the flame of heavenly love,
And feed the pure desire.

2 'Tis thine to soothe the sorrowing mind,
With guilt and fear oppressed;
'Tis thine to bid the dying live,
And give the weary rest.

3 Subdue the power of every sin,
Whate'er that sin may be,
That we, with humble, holy heart,
May worship only thee.

4 Then with our spirits witness bear
That we are sons of God,
Redeemed from sin, from death and hell,
Through Christ's atoning blood.

518 C. M.

1 SPIRIT of Truth! on this thy day
To thee for help we cry,
To guide us through the dreary way
Of dark mortality.

2 We ask not, Lord, the cloven flame
Or tongues of various tone;
But long thy praises to proclaim,
With fervor in our own.

3 We mourn not that prophetic skill
Is found on earth no more;
Enough for us to trace thy will
In Scripture's sacred lore.

4 Though tongues shall cease and power decay,
And knowledge empty prove,
Do thou thy trembling servants stay
With faith, with hope, with love.

HEBER.

519 C. M.

1 SPIRIT Divine! attend our prayer,
And make our hearts thy home;
Descend with all thy gracious power:
Come, Holy Spirit, come!

2 Come as the light: to us reveal
Our sinfulness and woe;
And lead us in those paths of life
Where all the righteous go.

3 Come as the fire, and purge our hearts
Like sacrificial flame:
Let our whole soul an offering be
To our Redeemer's name.

4 Come as the dew, and sweetly bless
This consecrated hour;
Shed richly on my fruitless soul
Thy fertilizing power.

5 Come as the wind, with rushing sound,
With Pentecostal grace;
And make the great salvation known
Wide as the human race.

6 Spirit Divine, attend our prayer,
And make our hearts thy home;
Descend with all thy gracious power,
Come, Holy Spirit, come! REED.

520 C. M.

1 THE blessèd Spirit, like the wind,
Blows when and where he please:
How happy are the men who feel
The soul-enlivening breeze!

2 He moulds the carnal mind afresh,
Subdues the power of sin,
Transforms the heart of stone to flesh,
And plants his grace within.

3 He sheds abroad the Father's love,
Applies redeeming blood,
Bids both our guilt and fear remove,
And brings us home to God.

4 Lord, fill each dead, benighted soul
With light, and life, and joy:
None can thy mighty power control,
Or shall thy work destroy. BEDDOME.

521 C. M.

1 COME, Holy Spirit, heavenly Dove,
With all thy quickening powers,
Come, shed abroad a Saviour's love
In these cold hearts of ours.

2 Look! how we grovel here below,
Fond of these trifling toys!
Our souls can neither fly nor go,
To reach eternal joys.

3 In vain we tune our formal songs;
In vain we strive to rise;
Hosannas languish on our tongues,
And our devotion dies.

4 Dear Lord, and shall we ever live
At this poor, dying rate,—
Our love so faint, so cold to thee,
And thine to us so great?

5 Come, Holy Spirit, heavenly Dove,
With all thy quickening powers,
Come, shed abroad a Saviour's love,
And that shall kindle ours.

WATTS.

522 C. M.

1 GREAT Father of our feeble race,
Behold, thy servants wait;
With longing eyes and lifted hands,
We flock around thy gate.

2 Oh, shed abroad that royal gift,
That Spirit from above,
To bless our eyes with sacred light,
And fire our hearts with love!

3 With speedy flight may he descend,
And solid comfort bring,
And o'er our languid souls extend
His all-reviving wing.

4 Blest earnest of eternal joy,
Declare our sins forgiven,
And bear, with energy divine,
Our raptured thoughts to heaven.

5 Diffuse, O God, refreshing showers,
That earth its fruit may yield,
And change this barren wilderness
To Carmel's flowery field.

DODDRIDGE.

523 C. M.

1 SPIRIT of holiness, look down,
Our fainting hearts to cheer;
And, when we tremble at thy frown,
Oh, bring thy comforts near!

2 The fear which thy convictions wrought,
Oh, let thy grace remove!
And may the souls which thou hast taught
To weep, now learn to love.

3 Now let thy saving mercy heal
The wounds it made before;
Now on our hearts impress thy seal,
That we may doubt no more.

4 Complete the work thou hast begun,
And make our darkness light,
That we a glorious race may run,
Till faith be lost in sight.

BATHURST.

524 C. M

1 SPIRIT of holiness, descend;
Thy people wait for thee;
Thine ear, in kind compassion, lend;
Let us thy mercy see.

2 Behold, thy weary churches wait,
With wishful, longing eyes;
Let us no more lie desolate;
Oh, bid thy light arise!

3 Thy light, that on our souls hath shone,
Leads us in hope to thee;
Let us not feel its rays alone—
Alone thy people be.

4 Oh, bring our dearest friends to God;
Remember those we love;
Fit them, on earth, for thine abode;
Fit them for joys above.

5 Spirit of holiness, 'tis thine
To hear our feeble prayer;
Come,—for we wait thy power divine,—
Let us thy mercy share.

S. F. SMITH.

525 C. M.

1 O HOLY Ghost, the Comforter,
How is thy love despised,
While the heart longs for sympathy
And friends are idolized.

2 O Spirit of the living God,
Brooding with dove-like wings
Over the helpless and the weak
Among created things!

3 Where should our feebleness find strength,
Our helplessness a stay,
Didst thou not bring us strength, and help,
And comfort, day by day?

4 Great are thy consolations, Lord,
And mighty is thy power,
In sickness and in solitude,
In sorrow's darkest hour.

5 Oh, if the souls that now despise
And grieve thee, heavenly Dove,
Would seek thee, and would welcome thee,
How would they prize thy love!

526 C. M.

1 LET songs of praises fill the sky!
Christ, our ascended Lord,
Sends down his Spirit from on high,
According to his word.

2 The Spirit, by his heavenly breath,
New life creates within;
He quickens sinners from their death
Of trespasses and sin.

3 The things of Christ the Spirit takes,
And to our hearts reveals;
Our bodies he his temple makes,
And our redemption seals.

4 Come, Holy Spirit, from above,
With thy celestial fire;
Come, and with flames of zeal and love
Our hearts and tongues inspire!

COTTERILL.

527 C. M.

1 WHY should the children of a King
Go mourning all their days?
Great Comforter! descend, and bring
Some tokens of thy grace.

2 Dost thou not dwell in all the saints,
And seal the heirs of heaven?
When wilt thou banish my complaints,
And show my sins forgiven?

3 Assure my conscience of her part
In the Redeemer's blood;
And bear thy witness with my heart
That I am born of God.

4 Thou art the earnest of his love,
The pledge of joys to come;
And thy soft wings, celestial Dove,
Wilt safe convey me home.

WATTS.

528 C. M.

1 ENTHRONED on high, Almighty Lord!
The Holy Ghost send down;
Fulfill in us thy faithful word,
And all thy mercies crown.

2 Though on our heads no tongues of fire
Their wondrous powers impart,
Grant, Saviour, what we more desire,
Thy Spirit in our heart.

3 Spirit of life, and light, and love,
Thy heavenly influence give;
Quicken our souls, our guilt remove,
That we in Christ may live.

4 To our benighted minds reveal
The glories of his grace,
And bring us where no clouds conceal
The brightness of his face.

5 His love within us shed abroad,
Life's ever-springing well;
Till God in us, and we in God,
In love eternal dwell.

529 C. M.

1 SPIRIT of power and might, behold
A world by sin destroyed!
Creator Spirit, as of old,
Move on the formless void.

2 Give thou the word: that healing sound
Shall quell the deadly strife,
And earth again, like Eden crowned,
Produce the tree of life.

3 If sang the morning stars for joy
When nature rose to view,
What strains will angel harps employ
When thou shalt all renew!

4 And if the sons of God rejoice
To hear a Saviour's name,
How will the ransomed raise their voice,
To whom that Saviour came!

5 Lo! every kindred, tongue, and tribe,
Assembling round the throne,
The new creation shall ascribe
To sovereign love alone.
MONTGOMERY.

530 C. M.

1 THE God of grace will never leave
Or cast away his own;
And yet, when we his Spirit grieve,
His comforts are withdrawn.

2 If noisy war, or strife, abound,
We grieve the peaceful Dove;
His gracious aid is ever found
In paths of truth and love.

3 Should we indulge one secret sin,
Or disregard his laws,
His succors and support, within,
The Spirit, vexed, withdraws.

4 Forbid it, gracious Lord, that we,
Who, from thy hand, receive
The Spirit's power to make us free,
Should e'er that Spirit grieve.

531 C. M.

1 NOT all the outward forms on earth,
Nor rites that God has given,
Nor will of man, nor blood, nor birth,
Can raise a soul to heaven.

2 The sovereign will of God alone
Creates us heirs of grace,
Born in the image of his Son,
A new, peculiar race.

3 The Spirit, like some heavenly wind,
Breathes on the sons of flesh,
Creates anew the carnal mind,
And forms the man afresh.

4 Our quickened souls awake and rise
From their long sleep of death;
On heavenly things we fix our eyes,
And praise employs our breath.
WATTS.

532 C. M.

1 O HOLY SPIRIT, Fount of Love,
Blest Source of gifts divine,
Kindle, we pray thee, from above,
The inmost souls of thine.

2 Bond of the sacred Trinity,
Knit thou our hearts in one,
To know the blessèd unity
Of Father and of Son!

3 Shed in each faithful heart abroad
Love that doth all excel;
That God in us and we in God
For evermore may dwell.

533 C. M.

1 HOW helpless guilty nature lies,
Unconscious of its load!
The heart, unchanged, can never rise,
To happiness and God.

2 Can aught, beneath a power divine,
The stubborn will subdue?
'Tis thine, almighty Spirit! thine,
To form the heart anew.

3 'Tis thine, the passions to recall,
And upward bid them rise;
To make the scales of error fall,
From reason's darkened eyes;—

4 To chase the shades of death away,
And bid the sinner live;
A beam of heaven, a vital ray,
'Tis thine alone to give.
STEELE.

534 S. M.

1 LORD God the Holy Ghost,
In this accepted hour,
As on the day of Pentecost,
Descend in all thy power!

2 We meet with one accord
In our appointed place,
And wait the promise of our Lord,
The Spirit of all grace.

3 Like mighty rushing wind
Upon the waves beneath,
Move with one impulse every mind,
One soul, one feeling breathe.

4 The young, the old, inspire
With wisdom from above,
And give us hearts and tongues of fire
To pray, and praise, and love.

5 Spirit of Truth, be thou
In life and death our Guide!
O Spirit of adoption, now
May we be sanctified.

MONTGOMERY.

535 S. M.

1 DESCEND, immortal Dove,
Spread thy kind wings abroad;
And wrapt in flames of holy love
Bear all my soul to God.

2 Jesus, my Lord, reveal
In charms of grace divine,
And be thyself the sacred seal
That pearl of price is mine.

3 Behold, my heart expands
To catch the heavenly fire,
It longs to feel the gentle bands,
And groans with strong desire.

4 Thy love, my God, appears,
And brings salvation down,
My cordial through this vale of tears,
In Paradise my crown.

DODDRIDGE.

536 S. M.

1 THE Holy Ghost is here,
Where saints in prayer agree;
As Jesus' parting gift, he's near
Each pleading company.

2 Not far away is he,
To be by prayer brought nigh;
But here in present majesty,
As in his courts on high.

3 He dwells within our soul,
An ever-welcome Guest;
He reigns with absolute control
As Monarch in the breast.

4 Our bodies are his shrine,
And he th' indwelling Lord:
All hail, thou Comforter divine!
Be evermore adored.

5 Obedient to thy will,
We wait to feel thy power;
O Lord of life, our hopes fulfill,
And bless this hallowed hour.

SPURGEON.

537 S. M.

1 SPIRIT of faith come down,
Reveal the things of God,
And make to us the Godhead known,
And witness with the blood.

2 No man can truly say
That Jesus is the Lord,
Unless thou take the veil away,
And breathe the living word.

3 Then, only then, we feel
Our interest in his blood,
And cry, with joy unspeakable,
"Thou art my Lord, my God!"

4 Oh that the world might know
The all-atoning Lamb!
Spirit of faith, descend, and show
The virtue of his name.

538 S. M.

1 COME, Holy Spirit, come,
Let thy bright beams arise,
Dispel the sorrow from our minds,
The darkness from our eyes.

2 Revive our drooping faith,
Our doubts and fears remove,
And kindle in our breasts the flame
Of never-dying love.

3 Convince us of our sin,
Then lead to Jesus' blood,
And to our wondering view reveal
The secret love of God.

4 Show us that loving One
Who rules the courts of bliss,
The Lord of Hosts, the Mighty God,
The Eternal Prince of Peace.

5 'Tis thine to cleanse the heart,
To sanctify the soul,
To pour fresh life in every part,
And new-create the whole.

6 Dwell, Spirit, in our hearts,
Our minds from bondage free;
Then we shall know, and praise, and love
The Father, Son, and Thee!

HART.

539 S. M.

1 BLEST Comforter Divine,
Let rays of heavenly love
Amid our gloom and darkness shine,
And guide our souls above.

2 Draw us with still small voice,
From every sinful way,
And bid the mourning saint rejoice,
Though earthly joys decay.

3 By thine inspiring breath
Make every cloud of care,
And e'en the gloomy vale of death,
A smile of glory wear.

4 Oh fill thou every heart
With love to all our race!
Great Comforter, to us impart
These blessings of thy grace.

540 S. M.

1 'TIS God, the Spirit, leads
In paths before unknown;
The work to be performed is ours,
The strength is all his own.

2 Supported by his grace,
We still pursue our way;
And hope at last to reach the prize,
Secure in endless day.

3 'Tis he that works to will,
'Tis he that works to do;
His is the power by which we act,
His be the glory too.

BEDDOME.

541 S. M.

1 THE Comforter has come,
We feel his presence here,
Our hearts would now no longer roam,
But bow in filial fear.

2 This tenderness of love,
This hush of solemn power,—
'Tis heaven descending from above,
To fill this favored hour.

3 Earth's darkness all has fled,
Heaven's light serenely shines,
And every heart, divinely led,
To holy thought inclines.

4 No more let sin deceive,
Nor earthly cares betray,
Oh, let us never, never grieve
The Comforter away!

542 S. M.

1 COME, Spirit, source of light,
Thy grace is unconfined;
Dispel the gloomy shades of night,
The darkness of the mind.

2 Now to our eyes display
The truth thy words reveal;
Cause us to run the heavenly way,
Delighting in thy will.

3 Thy teachings make us know
The mysteries of thy love,
The vanity of things below,
The joy of things above.

4 While through this maze we stray,
Oh, spread thy beams abroad!
Disclose the dangers of the way,
And guide our steps to God.

543 S. M.

1 COME, Holy Spirit, come,
With energy divine;
And on this poor benighted soul
With beams of mercy shine.

2 Oh! melt this frozen heart;
This stubborn will subdue;
Each evil passion overcome,
And form me all anew.

3 Mine will the profit be,
But thine shall be the praise;
And unto thee will I devote
The remnant of my days.

BEDDOME.

544 7s.

1 GRACIOUS Spirit, Love divine!
Let thy light within me shine;
All my guilty fears remove,
Fill me full of heaven and love.

2 Speak thy pardoning grace to me,
Set the burdened sinner free;
Lead me to the Lamb of God,
Wash me in his precious blood.

3 Life and peace to me impart,
Seal salvation on my heart;
Breathe thyself into my breast,—
Earnest of immortal rest.

4 Let me never from thee stray,
Keep me in the narrow way;
Fill my soul with love divine,
Keep me, Lord, forever thine.

STOCKER.

545 7s.

1 HOLY Spirit! Lord of light!
From thy clear celestial height,
Come, thou Light of all that live!
Thy pure beaming radiance give!

2 Come, thou hope of all the poor!
Come with treasures which endure;
Thou, of all consolers best,
Visiting the troubled breast.

3 Thou in toil art comfort sweet;
Pleasant coolness in the heat;
Solace in the midst of woe;
Dost refreshing peace bestow.

4 Light immortal! light divine!
Visit thou these hearts of thine;
If thou take thy grace away,
Nothing pure in man will stay.

5 Heal our wounds—our strength renew;
On our dryness pour thy dew;
Wash the stains of guilt away;
Guide the steps that go astray.

6 Give us comfort when we die;
Give us life with thee on high;
In thy gracious gifts descend;
Give us joys which never end.

546

7s.

1 HOLY Ghost! with light divine,
Shine upon this heart of mine;
Chase the shades of night away,
Turn my darkness into day.

2 Holy Ghost! with power divine,
Cleanse this guilty heart of mine;
Long hath sin, without control,
Held dominion o'er my soul.

3 Holy Ghost! with joy divine,
Cheer this saddened heart of mine;
Bid my many woes depart,
Heal my wounded, bleeding heart.

4 Holy Spirit! all divine,
Dwell within this heart of mine;
Cast down every idol-throne,
Reign supreme—and reign alone.

REED.

547

7s.

1 HOLY Spirit! in my breast,
Grant that lively faith may rest,
And subdue each rebel thought
To believe what thou hast taught.

2 When around my sinking soul
Gathering waves of sorrow roll,
Spirit blest, the tempest still,
And with hope my bosom fill.

3 Holy Spirit, from my mind
Thought and wish and will unkind,
Deed and word unkind remove,
And my bosom fill with love.

4 Faith, and Hope, and Charity,
Comforter, descend from thee;
Thou the Anointing Spirit art,
These thy gifts to us impart.

5 Till our faith be lost in sight,
Hope be swallowed in delight,
And love return to dwell with thee,
In the threefold Deity!

RICHARD MANT.

548

7s.

1 HOLY Spirit, from on high,
Bend o'er us a pitying eye;
Now refresh the drooping heart;
Bid the power of sin depart.

2 Light up every dark recess
Of our heart's ungodliness;
Show us every devious way
Where our steps have gone astray.

3 Teach us, with repentant grief,
Humbly to implore relief;
Then the Saviour's blood reveal,
And our broken spirits heal.

4 May we daily grow in grace,
And pursue the heavenly race,
Trained in wisdom, led by love,
Till we reach our rest above.

BATHURST.

549 7s.

1 HOLY Spirit, source of light,
We invoke thy kindling ray:
Dawn upon our spirit's night,
Turn our darkness into day.

2 To the anxious soul impart
Hope, all other hopes above;
Stir the dull and hardened heart
With a longing and a love.

3 Give the struggling peace for strife,
Give the doubting light for gloom;
Speed the living into life,
Warn the dying of their doom.

4 Work in all, in all renew,
Day by day, the life divine;
All our wills to thee subdue,
All our hearts to thee incline.

WARNING AND INVITATION.

550 L. M.

1 WHY will ye waste on trifling cares
That life which God's compassion spares,
While, in the various range of thought,
The one thing needful is forgot?

2 Shall God invite you from above?
Shall Jesus urge his dying love?
Shall troubled conscience give you pain?
And all these pleas unite in vain?

3 Not so your eyes will always view
Those objects which you now pursue;
Not so will heaven and hell appear,
When death's decisive hour is near.

4 Almighty God, thy grace impart;
Fix deep conviction on each heart;
Nor let us waste on trifling cares
That life which thy compassion spares.

DODDRIDGE.

551 L. M.

1 MAN has a soul of vast desires;
He burns within with restless fires;
Tossed to and fro, his passions fly
From vanity to vanity.

2 In vain on earth we hope to find
Some solid good to fill the mind;
We try new pleasures, but we feel
The inward thirst and torment still.

3 Great God, subdue this vicious thirst,
This love to vanity and dust;
Cure the wild fever of the mind,
And feed our souls with joys refined.

WATTS.

552 L. M.

1 NOT to condemn the sons of men,
Did Christ, the Son of God, appear:
No weapons in his hands are seen,
No flaming sword nor thunder there.

2 Such was the pity of our God,
He loved the race of man so well,
He sent his Son to bear our load
Of sins, and save our souls from hell.

3 Sinners, believe the Saviour's word;
Trust in his mighty name, and live;
A thousand joys his lips afford,
His hands a thousand blessings give.

WATTS.

553 L. M.

1 COME, weary souls, with sins distressed,
Come, and accept the promised rest;
The Saviour's gracious call obey,
And cast your gloomy fears away.

2 Oppressed with guilt—a painful load—
Oh, come and bow before your God!
Divine compassion, mighty love,
Will all that painful load remove.

3 Here mercy's boundless ocean flows,
To cleanse your guilt and heal your woes;
Pardon, and life, and endless peace—
How rich the gift, how free the grace!

STEELE.

554 L. M.

1 LIFE is the time to serve the Lord,
The time t' insure the great reward;
And while the lamp holds out to burn,
The vilest sinner may return.

2 The living know that they must die;
But all the dead forgotten lie;
Their memory and their sense are gone,
Alike unknowing and unknown.

3 Then what my thoughts design to do;
My hands, with all your might pursue,
Since no device, nor work, is found,
Nor faith, nor hope, beneath the ground.

4 There are no acts of pardon passed
In the cold grave to which we haste;
But darkness, death, and long despair
Reign in eternal silence there.

WATTS.

555 L. M.

1 GOD of eternity, from thee
Did infant Time its being draw;
Moments, and days, and months, and years,
Revolve, by thine unvaried law.

2 Silent and slow, they glide away;
Steady and strong the current flows,
Lost in eternity's wide sea—
The boundless gulf from whence it rose.

3 With it the thoughtless sons of men
Before the rapid stream are borne.
On to that everlasting home,
Whence not one soul can e'er return.

4 Great Source of wisdom, teach my heart
To know the price of every hour,
That time may bear me on to joys
Beyond its measure and its power.

DODDRIDGE.

556 L. M.

1 BROAD is the road that leads to death,
And thousands walk together there;
But wisdom shows a narrow path,
With here and there a traveler.

2 "Deny thyself and take thy cross,"—
Is the Redeemer's great command:
Nature must count her gold but dross,
If she would gain this heavenly land.

3 The fearful soul that tires and faints,
And walks the ways of God no more,
Is but esteemed almost a saint,
And makes his own destruction sure.

4 Lord! let not all my hopes be vain:
Create my heart entirely new:
Which hypocrites could ne'er attain,
Which false apostates never knew.

WATTS.

557 L. M.

1 ETERNITY is just at hand!
And shall I waste my ebbing sand,
And careless view departing day,
And throw my inch of time away?

2 Eternity!—tremendous sound!
To guilty souls a dreadful wound;
But oh, if Christ and heaven be mine,
How sweet the accents! how divine!

3 What countless millions of mankind
Have left this fleeting world behind!
They're gone! but where?—ah, pause and see!
Gone to a long eternity.

4 Sinner! canst thou forever dwell
In all the fiery deeps of hell?
Has death no warning sound for thee?
Oh! turn, and to the Saviour flee.

558 L. M.

1 AWAKE, awake, each drowsy soul!
Awake and view the setting sun!
See how the shades of death advance,
Ere half the task of life is done.

2 Soon will he close all drowsy eyes,
Nor shall we hear these warnings more;
Soon will the mighty Judge approach;
E'en now he stands before the door.

3 To-day, attend his gracious voice!
This is the summons which he sends—
"Awake! for on this passing hour
Thy long eternity depends."

HIGGINBOTHAM.

559 L. M.

1 ETERNITY! Eternity!
How long art thou, Eternity!
As in a ball's concentric round
Nor starting-point nor end is found;

2 So thou, Eternity, so vast,
No entrance and no exit hast;
Mark well, O man, Eternity!
Eternity! Eternity!

COXE, FROM THE GERMAN

560 L. M.

1 BEHOLD the path that mortals tread
Down to the regions of the dead!
Nor will the fleeting moments stay,
Nor can we measure back our way.

Our kindred and our friends are gone;
Know, O my soul, this doom thine own:
Feeble as theirs, my mortal frame,
The same my way, my house the same.

561 L. M.

1 WHILE life prolongs its precious light,
Mercy is found, and peace is given;
But soon, ah! soon, approaching night
Shall blot out every hope of heaven.

2 While God invites, how blest the day!
How sweet the gospel's charming sound!
Come, sinners, haste, oh, haste away,
While yet a pardoning God he's found.

3 Soon, borne on time's most rapid wing,
Shall death command you to the grave,
Before his bar your spirits bring,
And none be found to hear or save.

4 In that lone land of deep despair
No Sabbath's heavenly light shall rise;
No God regard your bitter prayer,
Nor Saviour call you to the skies.

5 Now God invites—how blest the day!
How sweet the gospel's charming sound!
Come, sinners, haste, oh, haste away,
While yet a pardoning God is found.

DWIGHT.

562 L. M.

1 THAT day of wrath, that dreadful day,
When heaven and earth shall pass away,
What power shall be the sinner's stay?
How shall he meet that dreadful day?

2 When, shriveling like a parched scroll,
The flaming heavens together roll;
When, louder yet, and yet more dread,
Swells the high trump that wakes the dead;

3 Oh, on that day, that dreadful day,
When man to judgment wakes from clay,
Be thou, O Christ, the sinner's stay,
Though heaven and earth shall pass away.

SIR WALTER SCOTT.

563 L. M.

1 RETURN, O wanderer, return,
And seek thine injured Father's face;
Those new desires that in thee burn,
Were kindled by reclaiming grace.

2 Return, O wanderer, return,
And seek a Father's melting heart;
His pitying eyes thy grief discern,
His heavenly balm shall heal thy smart.

3 Return, O wanderer, return,
Thy dying Saviour bids thee live;
Go, view his bleeding side, and learn
How freely Jesus can forgive.

COLLYER.

564 L. M.

1 SINNER, oh, why so thoughtless grown!
Why in such dreadful haste to die!
Daring to leap to worlds unknown,
Heedless against thy God to fly?

2 Wilt thou despise eternal fate,
Urged on by sin's fantastic dreams?
Madly attempt th' infernal gate
And force thy passage to the flames?

3 Stay, sinner! on the Gospel plains,
Behold the God of love unfold
The glories of his dying pains,
Forever telling, yet untold.

565. L. M.

1 OH, do not let the word depart,
And close thine eyes against the light;
Poor sinner, harden not thy heart:
Thou wouldst be saved; why not to-night?

2 To-morrow's sun may never rise
To bless thy long-deluded sight;
This is the time; oh, then be wise!
Thou wouldst be saved; why not to-night?

3 Our God in pity lingers still;
And wilt thou thus his love requite?
Renounce at length thy stubborn will:
Thou wouldst be saved; why not to-night?

4 The world has nothing left to give—
It has no new, no pure delight;
Oh! try the life which Christians live;
Thou wouldst be saved; why not to-night?

5 Our blessèd Lord refuses none
Who would to him their souls unite;
Then be the work of grace begun!
Thou wouldst be saved; why not to-night?

566 L. M.

1 IF thou dost truly seek to live
With all the joys that life can give;
If thy young feet would gladly press
The ways of peace and happiness;

2 Go thou, with fresh and fervent love,
To him who dwells in light above,
Who sees ten thousand sons obey
Yet listens when the lowly pray.

3 Cling thou to Jesus faithfully,
As vines embrace their guardian tree;
Nor fail in this thy day of youth
To find the Way, the Life, the Truth;

4 And thou shalt breathe in this low world,
An eagle chained, with wings unfurled,
Prepared, when once thy bonds are riven,
To soar away, and flee to heaven.

LYONS.

567 L. M.

1 NOW, in the heat of youthful blood,
Remember your Creator, God;
Behold! the months come hastening on,
When you shall say, "My joys are gone."

2 Behold! the aged sinner goes,
Laden with guilt and heavy woes,
Down to the regions of the dead,
With endless curses on his head.

3 Eternal King! I fear thy name;
Teach me to know how frail I am;
And when my soul must hence remove,
Give me a mansion in thy love.

WATTS.

568 L. M.

1 SAY, sinner, hath a voice within
Oft whispered to thy secret soul,
Urged thee to leave the ways of sin,
And yield thy heart to God's control?

2 Hath something met thee in the path
Of worldliness and vanity,
And pointed to the coming wrath,
And warned thee from that wrath to flee?

3 Sinner, it was a heavenly voice,
It was the Spirit's gracious call;
It bade thee make the better choice,
And haste to seek in Christ thine all.

4 Spurn not the call to life and light;
Regard in time the warning kind;
That call thou mayest not always slight,
And yet the gate of mercy find.

5 God's Spirit will not always strive
With hardened, self-destroying man;
Ye who persist his love to grieve,
May never hear his voice again.

Sinner, perhaps this very day
Thy last accepted time may be;
Oh, shouldst thou grieve him now away,
Then hope may never beam on thee.

HYDE.

569 L. M.

1 "COME, take my yoke," the Saviour said,
"To follow me be not afraid;
For I in heart am lowly, meek,
And offer you the rest you seek.

2 "The yoke of pleasure may allure,
And promise bliss that will endure;
But when it has thy youth despoiled,
'Twill cast thee off as garment soiled.

3 "Take not on thee the yoke of wealth;
'Twill eat thy soul, destroy thy health,
And make thee feel how cheap the cost
If worlds could buy the peace it lost!

4 "Ambition, too, its yoke displays,
And hangs out its perennial bays;
Be not, poor soul, by it misled;
I offer thee a crown instead.

5 "Then take my yoke: 'tis soft and light,
'Twill ne'er disturb thy rest at night,
But bring thee to that world above,
Where no restraint is known but love."

570 L. M.

1 I HEAR a voice that comes from far;
From Calvary it sounds abroad;
It soothes my soul, and calms my fear;
It speaks of pardon bought with blood.

2 And is it true, that many fly
The sound that bids my soul rejoice;
And rather choose in sin to die,
Than turn an ear to mercy's voice!

3 Alas, for those!—the day is near,
When mercy will be heard no more;
Then will they ask in vain to hear
The voice they would not heed before.

KELLY.

571 L. M.

1 BEHOLD a Stranger at the door!
He gently knocks, has knock'd before;
Has waited long—is waiting still:
You treat no other friend so ill.

2 Oh, lovely attitude, he stands
With melting heart and loaded hands!
Oh, matchless kindness! and he shows
This matchless kindness to his foes;

3 But will he prove a friend indeed?
He will; the very friend you need:
The friend of sinners—yes, 'tis he,
With garments dyed on Calvary.

4 Rise, touch'd with gratitude divine;
Turn out his enemy and thine,
That soul-destroying monster, sin,
And let the heavenly Stranger in.

5 Admit him, ere his anger burn—
His feet departed, ne'er return:
Admit him, or the hour 's at hand
You 'll at his door rejected stand.

GREGG.

572 L. M.

1 COME hither, all ye weary souls!
Ye heavy-laden sinners, come!
I'll give you rest from all your toils,
And raise you to my heavenly home.

2 They shall find rest who learn of me,—
I'm of a meek and lowly mind;
But passion rages like the sea,
And pride is restless as the wind.

3 Blessed is the man, whose shoulders take
My yoke, and bear it with delight;
My yoke is easy to his neck,
My grace shall make the burden light.

4 Jesus! we come at thy command;
With faith, and hope, and humble zeal,
Resign our spirits to thy hand,
To mould and guide us at thy will.

WATTS.

573 L. M.

1 GOD calling yet! shall I not hear?
Earth's pleasures shall I still hold dear?
Shall life's swift passing years all fly,
And still my soul in slumbers lie!

2 God calling yet! shall I not rise?
Can I his loving voice despise,
And basely his kind care repay?
He calls me still; can I delay?

3 God calling yet! and shall he knock,
And I my heart the closer lock?
He still is waiting to receive,
And shall I dare his Spirit grieve?

4 God calling yet! and shall I give
No heed, but still in bondage live?
I wait, but he does not forsake;
He calls me still; my heart, awake!

5 God calling yet! I cannot stay;
My heart I yield without delay:
Vain world, farewell! from thee part;
The voice of God hath reached m heart.

TERSTEEGI

574 C. M.

1 OH! what amazing words of grace
Are in the gospel found,
Suited to every sinner's case
Who hears the joyful sound!

2 Come, then, with all your wants and wounds,
Your every burden bring;
Here love, unchanging love, abounds,
A deep, celestial spring.

3 This spring with living water flows,
And heavenly joy imparts;
Come, thirsty souls! your wants disclose,
And drink, with thankful hearts.

4 Millions of sinners, vile as you,
Have here found life and peace;
Come, then, and prove its virtues too,
And drink, adore, and bless.

MEDLEY.

575 C. M.

1 THE King of heaven his table spreads,
And dainties crown the board:
Not Paradise, with all its joys,
Could such delight afford.

2 Ye hungry poor, that long have strayed
In sin's dark mazes, come;
Come from your most obscure retreats,
And grace shall find you room.

3 Millions of souls, in glory now,
Were fed and feasted here;
And millions more, still on the way,
Around the board appear.

4 Yet are his house and heart so large,
That millions more may come;
Nor could the whole assembled world
O'erfill the spacious room.

5 All things are ready; come away,
Nor weak excuses frame:
Come, taste the dainties of the feast,
And bless the Master's name.

DODDRIDGE.

576 C. M.

1 LET every mortal ear attend,
And every heart rejoice;
The trumpet of the gospel sounds,
With an inviting voice.

2 Ho! all ye hungry, starving souls,
That feed upon the wind,
And vainly strive with earthly toys
To fill th' immortal mind,—

3 Eternal wisdom has prepared
A soul-reviving feast,
And bids your longing appetites
The rich provision taste.

4 Ho! ye that pant for living streams,
And pine away and die—
Here you may quench your raging thirst
With springs that never dry.

5 The happy gates of gospel grace
Stand open night and day;—
Lord, we are come to seek supplies,
And drive our wants away.

WATTS.

577 C. M.

1 THE Saviour calls; let every ear
Attend the heavenly sound;
Ye doubting souls, dismiss your fear;
Hope smiles reviving round.

2 For every thirsty, longing heart,
Here streams of bounty flow,
And life, and health, and bliss impart,
To banish mortal woe.

3 Ye sinners, come ; 'tis mercy's voice ;
That gracious voice obey ;
'Tis Jesus calls to heavenly joys ;
And can you yet delay?

4 Dear Saviour, draw reluctant hearts ;
To thee let sinners fly,
And take the bliss thy love imparts,
And drink, and never die.

STEELE.

578 C. M.

1 AMAZING sight! the Saviour stands
And knocks at every door!
Ten thousand blessings in his hands,
To satisfy the poor.

2 "Behold," he saith, "I bleed and die
To bring you to my rest:
Hear, sinners, while I'm passing by,
And be forever blest.

3 "Will you despise my bleeding love,
And choose the way to hell?
Or in the glorious realms above,
With me, forever dwell?

4 "Say, will you hear my gracious voice,
And have your sins forgiven?
Or will you make that wretched choice,
And bar yourselves from heaven?"

579 C. M.

1 AND will the Lord thus condescend
To visit sinful worms?
Thus at the door shall Mercy stand,
In all her winning forms?

2 Surprising grace!—and shall my heart
Unmoved and cold remain?
Has it no soft, no tender part?
Must Mercy plead in vain?

3 Shall Jesus for admission sue,
His charming voice unheard?
And shall my heart, his rightful due,
Remain forever barred?

4 O Lord, exert thy conquering grace ;
Thy mighty power display :
One beam of glory from thy face
Can melt my sin away.

STEELE.

580 C. M.

1 INQUIRE, ye pilgrims! for the way
That leads to Zion's hill,
And thither set your steady face,
With a determined will.

2 Oh! come, and to his temple haste,
And seek his favor there ;
Before his footstool humbly bow,
And pour your fervent prayer.

3 Oh! come and join your souls to God
In everlasting bands ;
Accept the blessings he bestows,
With thankful hearts and hands.

DODDRIDGE.

581 C. M.

1 SEE, in the vineyard of the Lord,
A barren fig-tree stands ;
It yields no fruit, no blossom bears,
Though planted by his hands.

2 From year to year the tree he views,
And still no fruit is found ;

Then "cut it down," the Lord commands,
"Why cumbers it the ground?"

3 But lo! the gracious Saviour pleads:
"The barren fig-tree spare,
Another year in mercy wait,
It yet may bloom and bear."

582 C. M.

1 COME, sinner, to the gospel feast;
Oh, come without delay!
For there is room in Jesus' breast
For all who will obey.

2 There's room in God's eternal love
To save thy precious soul;
Room in the Spirit's grace above
To heal and make thee whole.

3 There's room within the church, redeemed
With blood of Christ divine;
Room in the white-robed throng, convened
For that dear soul of thine.

4 There's room in heaven among the choir,
And harps and crowns of gold,
And glorious palms of victory there,
And joys that ne'er were told.

HUNTINGDON.

583 C. M.

1 YE hearts with joyful vigor warm,
In smiling crowds draw near,
And turn from every mortal charm,
A Saviour's voice to hear.

2 He, Lord of all the worlds on high,
Stoops to converse with you;
And lays his radiant glories by,
Your friendship to pursue.

3 "The soul that longs to see my face,
Is sure my love to gain;
And those that early seek my grace,
Shall never seek in vain."

DODDRIDGE.

584 C. M.

1 "REPENT!" the voice celestial cries;
No longer dare delay:
The soul that scorns the mandate dies,
And meets a fiery day.

2 No more the sovereign eye of God
O'erlooks the crimes of men;
His heralds now are sent abroad
To warn the world of sin.

3 O sinners, in his presence bow,
And all your guilt confess;
Accept the offered Saviour now,
Nor trifle with his grace.

4 Soon will the awful trumpet sound,
And call you to his bar;
His mercy knows th' appointed bound,
And yields to justice there.

DODDRIDGE.

585 C. M.

1 BY cool Siloam's shady rill,
How fair the lily grows!
How sweet the breath, beneath the hill,
Of Sharon's dewy rose!

2 Lo! such the youth, whose early feet
The paths of peace have trod—
Whose secret heart, with influence sweet,
Is upward drawn to God.

3 By cool Siloam's shady rill,
The lily must decay;

The rose, that blooms beneath the hill,
Must shortly fade away.

4 And soon, too soon, the wintry hour,
Of man's maturer age,
May shake the soul with sorrow's power,
And stormy passion's rage.

5 O thou, whose infancy was found
With heavenly rays to shine,—
Whose years, with changeless virtue crowned,
Were all alike divine,—

6 Dependent on thy bounteous breath,
We seek thy grace alone,
In childhood, manhood, and in death,
To keep us still thine own. HEBER.

586 C. M.

1 REMEMBER thy Creator now,
In these thy youthful days;
He will accept thine earliest vow,
And listen to thy praise.

2 Remember thy Creator now,
Seek him while he is near;
For evil days will come, when thou
Shalt find no comfort here.

3 Remember thy Creator now;
His willing servant be:
Then, when thy head in death shall bow,
He will remember thee.

587 C. M.

1 IN the bright morn of life, when youth
With vital ardor glows,
And shines in all the fairest charms
That beauty can disclose,

2 Deep in thy soul, before its powers
Are yet by vice enslaved,
Be thy Creator's glorious name
And character engraved:

3 Ere yet the shades of sorrow cloud
The sunshine of thy days;
And cares, and toils, in endless round
Encompass all thy ways:

4 Ere yet thy heart the woes of age
With vain regret deplore,
And sadly muse on former joys,
That now return no more.

5 True wisdom, early sought and gained,
In age will give thee rest;
Oh then, improve the morn of life,
To make its evening blest!

588 C. M.

1 THAT awful day will surely come,
Th' appointed hour makes haste—
When I must stand before my Judge,
And pass the solemn test.

2 Thou lovely Chief of all my joys,
Thou Sovereign of my heart,
How could I bear to hear thy voice
Pronounce the sound "Depart!"

3 The thunder of that dismal word
Would so distress my ear,
'Twould tear my soul asunder, Lord,
With most tormenting fear.

4 Oh, wretched state of deep despair,
To see my God remove—
And fix my doleful station where
I must not taste his love!

5 Jesus, I throw my arms around,
And hang upon thy breast,

Without a gracious smile from thee,
My spirit cannot rest.

6 Oh! tell me that my worthless name
Is graven on thy hands;
Show me some promise in thy book,
Where my salvation stands.

WATTS.

589 C. M.

1 THE day approacheth, O my soul,
The great decisive day,
Which from the verge of mortal life,
Shall bear thee far away.

2 Another day, more awful, dawns;
And lo, the Judge appears;
Ye heavens, retire before his face,
And sink, ye darkened stars.

3 Yet does one short, preparing hour,
One precious hour remain;
Rouse thee, my soul, with all thy power,
Nor let it pass in vain.

4 For this, thy temple, Lord, we throng,
For this, thy board surround;
Here may our service be approved,
And in thy presence crowned.

DODDRIDGE.

590 C. M.

1 COME to the ark, come to the ark;
To Jesus come away:
The pestilence walks forth by night,
The arrow flies by day.

2 Come to the ark: the waters rise,
The seas their billows rear;
While darkness gathers o'er the skies,
Behold a refuge near!

3 Come to the ark, all, all that weep
Beneath the sense of sin:
Without, deep calleth unto deep,
But all is peace within.

4 Come to the ark, ere yet the flood
Your lingering steps oppose;
Come, for the door which open stood
Is now about to close.

591 C. M.

1 VAIN man, thy fond pursuits forbear,
Repent, thy end is nigh!
Death, at the farthest, can't be far—
Oh, think before thou die!

2 Reflect—thou hast a soul to save:
Thy sins, how high they mount!
What are thy hopes beyond the grave?
How stands that dread account?

3 Death enters, and there's no defence;
His time, there's none can tell:
He'll in a moment call thee hence,
To heaven, or to hell!

4 To-day the gospel call obey:
Oh, hear; it speaks to you!
This moment, then, forsake your way,
And mercy will ensue.

HART.

592 C. M.

1 SINNER, the voice of God regard;
His mercy pleads to-day;
He calls you, by his sovereign word,
From sin's destructive way.

2 Like the rough sea, that cannot rest,
You live devoid of peace;
A thousand stings within your breast
Deprive your soul of ease.

3 Why will you in the crooked ways
Of sin and folly go?
In pain you travel all your days,
To reap immortal woe.

4 But he who turns to God shall live,
Through his abounding grace;
His mercy will the guilt forgive
Of those who seek his face.

5 Bow to the sceptre of his word,
Renouncing every sin;
Submit to him, your sovereign Lord,
And learn his will divine.

6 His love exceeds your highest thoughts,
He pardons like a God;
He will forgive your numerous faults
Through our Redeemer's blood.

FAWCETT.

593 C. M.

1 HOW short and hasty is our life!
How vast our soul's affairs!
Yet senseless mortals vainly strive
To lavish out their years.

2 Our days run thoughtlessly along,
Without a moment's stay;
Just like a story, or a song,
We pass our lives away.

3 God from on high invites us home,
But we march heedless on,
And, ever hastening to the tomb,
Stoop downward as we run.

4 How we deserve the deepest hell,
Who slight the joys above!
What chains of vengeance should we feel,
Who break such cords of love!

5 Draw us, O God! with sovereign grace,
And lift our thoughts on high,
That we may end this mortal race,
And see salvation nigh.

WATTS.

594 C. M.

1 RETURN, O wand'rer, to thy home,
Thy Father calls for thee;
No longer now an exile roam
In guilt and misery.
Return, return!

2 Return, O wand'rer, to thy home,
'Tis Jesus calls for thee;
The Spirit and the Bride say—come;
Oh! now for refuge flee;
Return, return!

3 Return, O wand'rer, to thy home,
'Tis madness to delay;
There are no pardons in the tomb,
And brief is mercy's day:
Return, return!

T. HASTINGS.

595 L. M.

1 TO-DAY, if you will hear his voice,
Now is the time to make your choice;
Say, will you to Mount Zion go?
Say, will you have this Christ, or no?

2 Ye wandering souls, who find no rest,
Say, will you be forever blest?
Will you be saved from sin and hell?
Will you with Christ in glory dwell?

3 Come now, dear youth, for ruin bound,
Obey the Gospel's joyful sound:
Come, go with us, and you shall prove
The joy of Christ's redeeming love.

4 Once more we ask you, in his name,
For yet his love remains the same,
Say, will you to Mount Zion go?
Say, will you have this Christ, or no?

Chorus. MILLER.

We are passing away,
We are passing away,
We are passing away,
To the great Judgment-day.

596 S. M.

1 THE Spirit, in our hearts,
Is whispering, "Sinner, come!"
The bride, the church of Christ, proclaims,
To all his children, "Come!"

2 Let him that heareth say
To all about him, "Come!"
Let him that thirsts for righteousness,
To Christ, the fountain, come!

3 Yes, whosoever will,
Oh let him freely come,
And freely drink the stream of life;
'Tis Jesus bids him come.

4 Lo! Jesus, who invites,
Declares, "I quickly come;"
Lord, even so! we wait thine hour;
O blest Redeemer, come!

H. U. ONDERDONK.

597 S. M.

1 YE trembling captives! hear;
The gospel-trumpet sounds;
No music more can charm the ear,
Or heal your heart-felt wounds.

2 'Tis not the trump of war,
Nor Sinai's awful roar;
Salvation's news it spreads afar,
And vengeance is no more.

3 Forgiveness, love, and peace,
Glad heaven aloud proclaims;
And earth, the jubilee's release,
With eager rapture claims.

4 Far, far to distant lands
The saving news shall spread;
And Jesus all his willing bands,
In glorious triumph lead.

PRATT'S COLL.

598 S. M.

1 COME to the land of peace,
From shadows come away,
Where all the sounds of weeping cease,
And storms no more have sway.

2 Fear hath no dwelling here;
But pure repose and love
Breathe through the bright, celestial air,
The spirit of the dove.

3 Come to the bright and blest,
Gathered from every land;
For here thy soul shall find its rest,
Amidst the shining band.

BRIGGS' COLL.

599 S. M.

1 NOW is th' accepted time;
Now is the day of grace;
Now, sinners, come, without delay,
And seek the Saviour's face.

2 Now is th' accepted time;
The Saviour calls to-day;
To-morrow it may be too late;
Then why should you delay?

3 Now is th' accepted time;
The gospel bids you come,
And every promise in his word
Declares there yet is room.

4 Lord, draw reluctant souls,
And feast them with thy love;
Then will the angels swiftly fly
To bear the news above. DOBELL.

600 S. M.

1 BEHOLD, the day is come;
The righteous Judge is near;
And sinners, trembling at their doom,
Shall soon their sentence hear.

2 Angels, in bright attire,
Conduct him through the skies;
Darkness and tempest, smoke and fire
Attend him as he flies.

3 How awful is the sight!
How loud the thunders roar!
The sun forbears to give his light,
And stars are seen no more.

4 The whole creation groans;
But saints arise and sing:
They are the ransomed of the Lord,
And he their God and King.
BEDDOME.

601 S. M.

1 AND canst thou, sinner, slight
The call of love divine?
Shall God with tenderness invite,
And gain no thought of thine?

2 Wilt thou not cease to grieve
The Spirit from thy breast,
Till he thy wretched soul shall leave
With all thy sins opprest?

3 To-day, a pardoning God
Will hear the suppliant pray;
To-day, a Saviour's cleansing blood
Will wash thy guilt away.

4 But grace, so dearly bought,
If yet thou wilt despise,
Thy fearful doom, with vengeance fraught,
Will fill thee with surprise. HYDE.

602 S. M.

1 YE sinners, fear the Lord,
While yet 'tis called to-day;
Soon will the awful voice of death
Command your souls away.

2 Soon will the harvest close,
The summer soon be o'er;
O sinners, then your injured God
Will heed your cries no more.

3 Then, while 'tis called to-day,
Oh, hear the gospel's sound;
Come, sinners, haste, oh, haste away,
While pardon may be found.
DWIGHT.

603 S. M.

1 AND will the Judge descend,
And must the dead arise,
And not a single soul escape
His all-discerning eyes?

2 How will my heart endure
The terrors of that day,
When earth and heaven before his face
Astonished shrink away?

3 But, ere the trumpet shakes
The mansions of the dead,
Hark! from the Gospel's cheering sound
What joyful tidings spread!

4 Ye sinners! seek his grace
Whose wrath ye cannot bear;
Fly to the shelter of his cross,
And find salvation there. DODDRIDGE.

604 S. M.

1 THE swift-declining day,
How fast its moments fly,
While evening's broad and gloomy shade
Gains on the western sky!

2 Ye mortals, mark its pace,
And use the hours of light;
For know, its Maker can command
An instant, endless night.

3 Give glory to the Lord,
Who rules the rolling sphere;
Submissive, at its footstool bow,
And seek salvation there.

4 Then shall new lustre break
Through all the heavy gloom,
And lead you to unchanging light,
In your celestial home.

DODDRIDGE.

605 S. M.

1 OH, where shall rest be found—
Rest for the weary soul?
'Twere vain the ocean depths to sound,
Or pierce to either pole.

2 The world can never give
The bliss for which we sigh:
'Tis not the whole of life to live,
Nor all of death to die.

3 Beyond this vale of tears
There is a life above,
Unmeasured by the flight of years;
And all that life is love.

4 There is a death whose pang
Outlasts the fleeting breath:
Oh, what eternal horrors hang
Around the second death!

5 Lord God of truth and grace,
Teach us that death to shun,
Lest we be banished from thy face,
And evermore undone.

MONTGOMERY.

606 S. M.

1 I SAW, beyond the tomb,
The awful Judge appear,
Prepar'd to scan, with strict account,
My blessings wasted here.

2 His wrath, like flaming fire,
Burn'd to the lowest hell—
And in that hopeless world of woe
He bade my spirit dwell.

3 Ye sinners, fear the Lord,
While yet 'tis called to-day;
Soon will the awful voice of death
Command your souls away.

4 Soon will the harvest close—
The summer soon be o'er—
And soon your injur'd, angry God
Will hear your prayers no more.

DWIGHT.

607 7s. D.

1 PILGRIM, burdened with thy sin,
Come the way to Zion's gate;
There, till mercy speaks within,
Knock, and weep, and watch, and wait;
Knock—he knows the sinner's cry;
Weep—he loves the mourner's tears;
Watch, for saving grace is nigh;
Wait, till heavenly grace appears.

2 Hark! it is the Saviour's voice—
"Welcome, pilgrim, to thy rest!"

Now within the gate rejoice,
Safe, and owned, and bought, and blest:
Safe, from all the lures of vice;
Owned, by joys the contrite know;
Bought by love, and life the price;
Blest, the mighty debt to owe.

3 Weary pilgrim! what for thee
In a world like this remains?
From thy guarded breast shall flee
Fear, and shame, and doubts, and pains:
Fear, the hope of heaven shall fly,
Shame, from glory's view retire;
Doubt, in full belief, shall die,
Pain, in endless bliss, expire.

CRABBE.

608

7s.

1 WHEN thy mortal life is fled,
When the death-shades o'er thee spread,
When is finished thy career,
Sinner, where wilt thou appear?

2 When the world has passed away,
When draws near the judgment day,
When the awful trump shall sound,
Say, oh, where wilt thou be found?

3 When the Judge descends in light,
Clothed in majesty and might,
When the wicked quail with fear,
Where, oh, where wilt thou appear?

4 What shall soothe thy bursting heart,
When the saints and thou must part?
When the good with joy are crowned,
Sinner, where wilt thou be found?

5 While the Holy Ghost is nigh,
Quickly to the Saviour fly;
Then shall peace thy spirit cheer;
Then in heaven shalt thou appear.

S. F. SMITH.

609

7s. D.

1 SINNER, what has earth to show
Like the joys believers know?
Is thy path, of fading flowers,
Half so bright, so sweet, as ours?
Doth a skilful, healing friend
On thy daily path attend,
And, where thorns and stings abound,
Shed a balm on every wound?

2 When the tempest rolls on high,
Hast thou still a refuge nigh?
Can, oh, can thy dying breath
Summon one more strong than death?
Canst thou, in that awful day,
Fearless tread the gloomy way,
Plead a glorious ransom given,
Burst from earth, and soar to heaven?

610

7s.

1 HASTEN, sinner, to be wise;
Stay not for the morrow's sun:
Wisdom, if you still despise,
Harder is it to be won.

2 Hasten mercy to implore;
Stay not for the morrow's sun;
Lest thy season should be o'er,
Ere this evening's stage be run.

3 Hasten, sinner, to return;
Stay not for the morrow's sun;
Lest thy lamp should cease to burn,
Ere salvation's work is done.

4 Hasten, sinner, to be blest;
Stay not for the morrow's sun;
Lest perdition thee arrest,
Ere the morrow is begun.

T. SCOTT.

611 7s.

1 SINNERS, turn; why will ye die?
God, your Maker, asks you why;
God, who did your being give,
Made you with himself to live.

2 Sinners, turn; why will ye die?
God, your Saviour asks you why;
Will ye not in him believe?
He has died that ye might live.

3 Will ye let him die in vain?
Crucify your Lord again?
Why, ye ransomed sinners, why
Will ye slight his grace, and die?

4 Sinners, turn; why will ye die?
God, the Spirit, asks you why—
He, who all your lives hath strove,
Wooed you to embrace his love.

5 Will ye not his grace receive?
Will ye still refuse to live?
Oh, ye dying sinners, why,
Why will ye forever die?

C. WESLEY.

612 7s.

1 SINNER, rouse thee from thy sleep;
Wake, and o'er thy folly weep;
Raise thy spirit, dark and dead;
Jesus waits his light to shed.

2 Wake from sleep; arise from death;
See the bright and living path;
Watchful, tread that path; be wise;
Leave thy folly, seek the skies.

3 Leave thy folly, cease from crime;
From this hour redeem thy time;
Life secure without delay;
Evil is thy mortal day.

4 Oh, then, rouse thee from thy sleep!
Wake, and o'er thy folly weep;
Jesus calls from death and night;
Jesus waits to shed his light.

EPIS. COLL.

613 7s. 6 lines.

1 FROM the cross, uplifted high,
Where the Saviour deigns to die,—
What melodious sounds we hear,
Bursting on the ravished ear!—
"Love's redeeming work is done;
Come and welcome, sinner, come.

2 "Sprinkled now with blood the throne,
Why beneath thy burdens groan?
On my piercèd body laid,
Justice owns the ransom paid;
Bow the knee, and kiss the Son—
Come and welcome, sinner, come.

3 "Spread for thee, the festal board
See with richest dainties stored;
To thy Father's bosom pressed,
Yet again a child confessed,
Never from his house to roam,
Come and welcome, sinner, come.

4 "Soon the days of life shall end;
Lo, I come, your Saviour, Friend,
Safe your spirits to convey
To the realms of endless day,
Up to my eternal home;
Come and welcome, sinner, come."

HAWEIS.

614 7s.

1 COME, said Jesus' sacred voice,
Come, and make my paths your choice:
I will guide you to your home:
Weary wanderer, hither come.

2 Thou, who, homeless and forlorn,
Long hast borne the proud world's scorn,
Long hast roamed the barren waste,
Weary wanderer, hither haste.

3 Hither come, for here is found
Balm that flows for every wound!
Peace, that ever shall endure,
Rest eternal, sacred, sure.

BARBAULD.

615 8s, 7s & 4s.

1 DAY of judgment, day of wonders!
Hark! the trumpet's awful sound,
Louder than a thousand thunders,
Shakes the vast creation round:
How the summons
Will the sinner's heart confound!

2 See the Judge, our nature wearing,
Clothed in majesty divine:
You who long for his appearing,
Then shall say, "This God is mine:"
Glorious Saviour!
Own me in that day for thine.

3 At his call the dead awaken,
Rise to life from earth and sea;
All the powers of nature, shaken
By his voice, prepare to flee:
Careless sinner,
What will then become of thee?

4 But to those who have confessèd,
Loved and served the Lord below,
He will say, "Come near, ye blessèd;
See the kingdom I bestow:
You forever
Shall my love and glory know."

NEWTON.

616 8s, 7s & 4s.

1 TO the ark away! or perish;
Sinners, to the ark away!
Vain the hope, that thousands cherish,
Of deliverance in that day,
When destruction
Cometh, that no arm can stay.

2 Careless ones, be warned, and haste ye
To the ark that open lies;
Why, oh, why, in folly waste ye
Precious time that quickly flies?
Soon your laughter
Will be turned to bitter cries.

3 Hear the Lord himself invite you
To his arms—a refuge sure;
Oh, believe him, lest he smite you
With a curse that none can cure!
When he thunders,
Who his anger can endure?

4 They are safe, and none besides them
Who the Saviour's word obey;
They are safe, for he will hide them,
In the dark and dreadful day;
They shall triumph,
When the world has passed away.

KELLY.

617 8s, 7s & 4s.

1 SINNER, hear the melting story
Of the Lamb that once was slain;

'Tis the Lord of life and glory:
Shall he plead with you in vain?
Oh, receive him,
And salvation now obtain!

2 All your sins to him confessing
Who is ready to forgive,
Seek the Saviour's richest blessing;
On his precious name believe:
He is waiting;
Will you not his grace receive?

618 8s, 7s & 4s.

1 SEE th' eternal Judge descending!
View him seated on his throne!
Now, poor sinner, now lamenting,
Stand, and hear thine awful doom:
Trumpets call thee,
Stand, and hear thine awful doom!

2 Hear the cries he now is venting,
Fill'd with dread of fiercer pain;
While in anguish thus lamenting
That he ne'er was born again—
Greatly mourning
That he ne'er was born again:

3 "Yonder sits my slighted Saviour,
With the marks of dying love;
Oh that I had sought his favor,
When I felt his Spirit move—
Golden moments,
When I felt his Spirit move!"

4 Now, despisers, look and wonder!
Hope and sinners here must part;
Louder than a peal of thunder,
Hear the dreadful sound, "Depart!"
Lost for ever,
Hear the dreadful sound, "Depart!"

619 8s, 7s & 4s.

1 HEAR, O sinner! mercy hails you;
Now with sweetest voice she calls;
Bids you haste to seek the Saviour,
Ere the hand of justice falls:
Hear, O sinner!
'Tis the voice of mercy calls.

2 See! the storm of vengeance gathering
O'er the path you dare to tread!
Hark! the awful thunder rolling
Loud and louder o'er your head!
Turn, O sinner!
Lest the lightning strike you dead.

3 Haste, O sinner! to the Saviour;
Seek his mercy while you may;
Soon the day of grace is over;—
Soon your life will pass away;
Haste, O sinner!
You must perish if you stay. REED

620 8s, 7s & 4s.

1 HEAR the heralds of the Gospel
News from Zion's King proclaim:—
"To each rebel sinner pardon;
Free forgiveness in his name:"
Oh, what mercy!
"Free forgiveness in his name."

2 Sinners, will you scorn the message
Sent in mercy from above?
Every sentence, oh, how tender!
Every line is full of love:
Listen to it;
Every line is full of love.

3 Oh, ye angels, hovering round us,
Waiting spirits, speed your way;
Hasten to the court of heaven;
Tidings bear without delay;
Rebel sinners
Glad the message will obey. ALLEN.

621 C. P. M.

1 WHEN thou, my righteous Judge, shalt come
To take thy ransomed people home,
Shall I among them stand?
Shall such a worthless worm as I,
Who sometimes am afraid to die,
Be found at thy right hand?

2 I love to meet thy people now,
Before thy feet with them to bow,
The vilest of them all;
But, can I bear the piercing thought,
What if my name should be left out,
When thou for them shalt call?

3 O Lord, prevent it by thy grace,
Be thou my only hiding-place,
In this the accepted day;
Thy pardoning voice, oh, let me hear,
To still my unbelieving fear,
Nor let me fall, I pray.

4 Among thy saints let me be found,
Whene'er the archangel's trump shall sound,
To see thy smiling face;
Then loudest of the throng I'll sing,
While heaven's resounding mansions ring
With shouts of sovereign grace.
COUNTESS OF HUNTINGDON.

622 C. P. M.

1 LO! on a narrow neck of land,
'Twixt two unbounded seas I stand,
Secure! insensible!
A point of time, a moment's space,
Removes me to that heavenly place,
Or shuts me up in hell.

2 O God! my inmost soul convert,
And deeply on my thoughtful heart
Eternal things impress;
Give me to feel their solemn weight,
And tremble on the brink of fate,
And wake to righteousness.

3 Before me place, in dread array,
The pomp of that tremendous day,
When thou with clouds shalt come
To judge the nations at thy bar;
And tell me, Lord! shall I be there
To meet a joyful doom?

4 Be this my one great business here,—
With holy trembling, holy fear,
To make my calling sure!
Thine utmost counsel to fulfill,
And suffer all thy righteous will,
And to the end endure!

5 Then, Saviour, then my soul receive,
Transported from this earth, to live
And reign with thee above;
Where faith is sweetly lost in sight,
And hope, in full, supreme delight,
And everlasting love. C. WESLEY.

623 H. M.

1 FAIR shines the morning star;
The silver trumpets sound,
Their notes re-echoing far,
While dawns the day around:

Joy to the slave: the slave is free;
It is the year of Jubilee.

2 Prisoners of hope, in gloom
And silence left to die,
With Christ's unfolding tomb,
Your portals open fly;
Rise with your Lord;—he sets you free;
It is the year of Jubilee.

3 Ye, who yourselves have sold
For debts to Justice due,
Ransom'd, but not with gold,
He gave himself for you!
The blood of Christ hath made you free;
It is the year of Jubilee.

4 Captives of sin and shame,
O'er earth and ocean, hear
An angel's voice proclaim
The Lord's accepted year:
Let Jacob rise, be Israel free;
It is the year of Jubilee.

MONTGOMERY.

624 H. M.

1 YE dying sons of men,—
Immerged in sin and woe,
The gospel's voice attend,
While Jesus sends to you:
Ye perishing and guilty, come,
In Jesus' arms there yet is room.

2 No longer now delay,
Nor vain excuses frame:
He bids you come to-day,
Though poor, and blind, and lame:
All things are ready; sinners, come,
For every trembling soul there's room.

3 Compelled by bleeding love,
Ye wandering sheep, draw near;
Christ calls you from above;
His charming accents hear;
Let whosoever will now come:
In mercy's breast there still is room.

BODEN.

625 H. M.

1 BLOW ye the trumpet, blow;
The gladly-solemn sound!
Let all the nations know,
To earth's remotest bound,
The year of jubilee is come;
Return, ye ransomed sinners, home.

2 Jesus, our great High Priest,
Hath full atonement made:
Ye weary spirits, rest;
Ye mournful souls, be glad;
The year of jubilee is come;
Return, ye ransomed sinners, home.

3 Extol the Lamb of God,
The sin-atoning Lamb;
Redemption by his blood
Throughout the world proclaim:
The year of jubilee is come;
Return, ye ransomed sinners, home.

4 Ye slaves of sin and hell,
Your liberty receive,
And safe in Jesus dwell,
And blest in Jesus live:
The year of jubilee is come;
Return, ye ransomed sinners, home.

5 Ye who have sold for naught
Your heritage above,
Receive it back unbought,
The gift of Jesus' love:
The year of jubilee is come;
Return, ye ransomed sinners, home.

6 The Gospel trumpet hear,
The news of heavenly grace;

And, saved from earth, appear
Before your Saviour's face:
The year of jubilee is come;
Return, ye ransomed sinners, home.

WESLEY.

626

8s & 7s.

1 COME, ye sinners, poor and needy,
Weak and wounded, sick and sore:
Jesus ready stands to save you,
Full of pity, love, and power.

2 Now, ye needy, come and welcome,
God's free bounty glorify;
True belief and true repentance,
Every grace that brings you nigh.

3 Let not conscience make you linger,
Nor of fitness fondly dream;
All the fitness he requireth,
Is to feel your need of him.

4 Come, ye weary, heavy laden,
Bruised and mangled by the fall,
If you tarry till you 're better,
You will never come at all.

5 Agonizing in the garden,
Lo! your Maker prostrate lies!
On the bloody tree behold him—
There he groans, and bleeds, and dies.

6 Lo! th' Incarnate God ascending
Pleads the merit of his blood;
Venture on him—venture wholly,
Let no other trust intrude.

HART.

Chorus.

Turn to the Lord, and seek salvation,
Sound the praise of his dear name;
Glory, honor, and salvation,
Christ the Lord is come to reign.

627

8s & 7s.

1 COME, ye sinners, heavy laden,
Bruised and mangled by the fall,
If you tarry till you 're better,
You will never come at all;
Not the righteous,
Sinners Jesus came to call.

2 Let no sense of guilt prevent you,
Nor of fitness fondly dream;
All the fitness he requireth,
Is to feel your need of him;
This he gives you—
'Tis the Spirit's rising beam.

3 Agonizing in the garden,
Lo, your Maker prostrate lies;
On the bloody tree behold him;
Hear him cry before he dies,
"It is finished!"
Sinners, will not this suffice?

4 Lo! th' Incarnate God ascended
Pleads the merit of his blood;
Venture on him, venture wholly;
Let no other trust intrude;
None but Jesus
Can do helpless sinners good.

HART.

628

11s.

1 OH, turn ye, oh, turn ye, for why will ye die,
When God, in great mercy, is coming so nigh?
Now Jesus invites you, the Spirit says, Come,
And angels are waiting to welcome you home.

2 How vain the delusion, that while you delay,
Your hearts may grow better; your chains melt away!
Come guilty, come wretched, come just as you are;
All helpless and dying, to Jesus repair.

3 Come, give us your hand, and the Saviour your heart;
In him once united, we never shall part;
Oh, how can we leave you? why will you not come?
We'll journey together, and soon be at home.

629 11s.

1 DELAY not, delay not, O sinner, draw near,
The waters of life are now flowing for thee;
No price is demanded, the Saviour is here;
Redemption is purchased, salvation is free.

2 Delay not, delay not, why longer abuse
The love and compassion of Jesus thy God?
A fountain is open, how canst thou refuse
To wash and be cleansed in his pardoning blood?

3 Delay not, delay not, the Spirit of grace
Long grieved and resisted may take his sad flight,
And leave thee in darkness to finish thy race,
To sink in the gloom of eternity's night.

4 Delay not, delay not, the hour is at hand,
The earth shall dissolve, and the heavens shall fade;
The dead, small and great, in the judgment shall stand;
What power then, O sinner, will lend thee its aid!

HASTINGS.

630 11s & 10s.

1 COME, ye disconsolate, where'er ye languish:
Come to the mercy-seat, fervently kneel;
Here bring your wounded hearts, here tell your anguish;
Earth has no sorrow that heaven cannot heal.

2 Joy of the desolate, light of the straying,
Hope when all others die, fadeless and pure;
Here speaks the Comforter, tenderly saying—
"Earth has no sorrow that heaven cannot cure."

3 Here see the Bread of Life; see waters flowing,
Forth from the throne of God, pure from above;
Come to the feast of love—come, ever knowing
"Earth has no sorrow but heaven can remove."

4 Go ask the infidel what boon he brings us,
What charm for aching hearts he can reveal,

Sweet as that heavenly promise hope brings us—
"Earth has no sorrow that heaven cannot heal."
MOORE.

631 6s & 4s.

1 TO-DAY the Saviour calls!
Ye wand'rers, come;
Oh, ye benighted souls,
Why longer roam?

2 To-day the Saviour calls;
Oh, hear him now!
Within these sacred walls
To Jesus bow.

3 To-day the Saviour calls;
For refuge fly;
The storm of justice falls,
And death is nigh.

4 The Spirit calls to-day:
Yield to his power;
Oh, grieve him not away,
'Tis mercy's hour.

632 P. M.

1 A BEAUTIFUL land by faith I see—
A land of rest from sorrow free;
The home of the ransomed, bright and fair,
And beautiful angels, too, are there.

2 That beautiful land, the City of Light,
It ne'er has known the shades of night;
The glory of God, the light of day,
Hath driven the darkness far away.

3 In vision I see its streets of gold;
Its beautiful gates I too behold,
The river of life, the crystal sea,
The ambrosial fruit of life's fair tree.

4 The heavenly throng arrayed in white,
In rapture range the plains of light;
And in one harmonious choir they praise
Their glorious Saviour's matchless grace.

Chorus.

Will you go? Will you go?
Go to that beautiful land with me?
Will you go? Will you go?
Go to that beautiful land?

633 12s & 8s.

1 WHEN the harvest is past, and the summer is gone,
And sermons and prayers shall be o'er,
When the beams cease to break of the blest Sabbath morn,
And Jesus invites thee no more.

2 When the rich gales of mercy no longer shall blow,
The gospel no message declare,—
Sinner, how canst thou bear the deep wailing of woe,
How suffer the night of despair?

3 When the holy have gone to the regions of peace,
To dwell in the mansions above;
When their harmony wakes, in the fullness of bliss,
Their song to the Saviour of love,—

4 Say, O sinner, now living at rest and secure,
And fearing no trouble to come,
Can thy spirit the swellings of sorrow endure,
Or bear the impenitent's doom?

S. F. SMITH.

634 L. M.

1 HASTE, traveler, haste! the night comes on,
And many a shining hour is gone;
The storm is gathering in the west,
And thou art far from home and rest.

2 The rising tempest sweeps the sky;
The rains descend, the winds are high;
The waters swell, and death and fear
Beset thy path, nor refuge near;

3 Then linger not in all the plain,
Flee for thy life, the mountain gain;
Look not behind, make no delay,
Oh speed thee, speed thee on thy way!

COLLYER.

635 P. M.

1 NOTHING, either great or small,
Nothing, sinner, no;
Jesus died, and paid it all,
Long, long ago.

2 When he from his lofty throne
Stooped to do and die,
Everything was fully done—
"'Tis finished," was his cry.

3 Weary, working, plodding one,
Wherefore toil you so?
Cease your doing; all was done
Long, long ago.

4 Till to Jesus' work you cling,
By a simple faith,
"Doing is a deadly thing,
Doing ends in death."

5 Cast your deadly doing down,
Down at Jesus' feet;
Stand in him, in him alone,
Glorious and complete.

Chorus.

Jesus paid it all,
All the debt I owe,
And nothing, either great or small,
Remains for me to do.

636 L. M. 6 lines.

1 PEACE, troubled soul, whose plaintive moan,
Hath taught each scene the notes of woe;
Cease thy complaint, suppress thy groan,
And let thy tears forget to flow;
Behold, the precious balm is found,
To lull thy pain, to heal thy wound.

2 Come, freely come, by sin oppressed;
On Jesus cast thy weighty load;
In him thy refuge find, thy rest,
Safe in the mercy of thy God:
Thy God's thy Saviour—glorious word!
Forever love and praise the Lord.

SHERLEY.

637 L. M. 6 lines.

1 TO weary hearts, to mourning homes,
God's meekest angel gently comes;
No power hath he to banish pain,
Or give us back our lost again,
And yet, in tenderest love, our dear
And Heavenly Father sends him here.

2 Angel of patience! sent to calm
Our feverish brows with cooling balm,
To lay with hope the storms of fear,
And reconcile life's smile and tear,
The throbs of wounded pride to still,
And make our own our Father's will!

3 O thou, who mournest on thy way,
With longings for the close of day,
He walks with thee, that angel kind,
And gently whispers, "Be resign'd!
Bear up, bear on, the end shall tell,
The dear Lord ordereth all things well."

GERMAN, *Tr.* WHITTIER.

638 P. M.

1 COME to Jesus, come to Jesus,
Come to Jesus, just now,
Just now come to Jesus,
Come to Jesus, just now.

2 He will save you.
3 Oh, believe him.
4 He is able.
5 He is willing.
6 He'll receive you.
7 Call upon him.
8 He will hear you.
9 Look unto him.
10 He'll forgive you.
11 Flee to Jesus.
12 He will cleanse you.
13 He will clothe you.
14 Jesus loves you.
15 Don't reject him.
16 Only trust him.
17 Hallelujah, Amen.

639 8s & 3s.

1 WE'RE traveling home to heaven above,
Will you go?
To sing the Saviour's dying love,
Will you go?
Millions have reached that blest abode,
Anointed kings and priests to God,
And millions more are on the road,
Will you go?

2 We're going to see the bleeding Lamb,
Will you go?
In rapturous strains to praise his name,
Will you go?
The crown of life we there shall wear,
The Conqueror's palms our hands shall bear,
And all the joys of heaven we'll share,
Will you go?

3 We're going to join the heavenly choir,
Will you go?
To raise our voice and tune the lyre,
Will you go?
There saints and angels gladly sing
Hosanna to their God and King,
And make the heavenly arches ring,
Will you go?

640 7s & 6s.

1 GO thou in life's fair morning,
Go, in thy bloom of youth;
And seek, for thine adorning,
The precious pearl of truth:
Secure the heavenly treasure,
And bind it on thy heart;
And let no earthly pleasure,
E'er cause it to depart.

2 Go, while the day-star shineth,
Go, while thy heart is light,
Go, ere thy strength declineth,
While every sense is bright:
Sell all thou hast and buy it;
'Tis worth all earthly things,—

Rubies, and gold, and diamonds,
Sceptres and crowns of kings!

3 Go, ere the cloud of sorrow
Steals o'er thy bloom of youth;
Defer not till to-morrow;
Go now, and buy the truth.
Go, seek thy great Creator;
Learn early to be wise;
Go, place upon the altar
A morning sacrifice.

641 7s & 6s.

1 O JESUS, thou art standing
Outside the fast-closed door,
In lowly patience waiting
To pass the threshold o'er:
Shame on us, guilty mortals,
Who can his favor share,
Oh, shame, thrice shame upon us,
To keep him standing there!

2 O Jesus, thou art knocking:
And lo! that hand is scarred,
And thorns thy brow encircle,
And tears thy face have marred:
Oh, love that passeth knowledge
So patiently to wait!
Oh, sin that hath no equal
So fast to bar the gate!

3 O Jesus, thou art pleading
In accents meek and low,
"I died for you, poor sinners,
And will ye treat me so?"
O Lord, with shame and sorrow
We open now the door:
Dear Saviour, enter, enter,
And leave us never more.

Hymns Ancient and Modern.

642 12s.

1 THE voice of free grace cries,
Escape to the mountain,
For Adam's lost race Christ hath opened a fountain;
For sin and uncleanness, and every transgression,
His blood flows most freely in streams of salvation.
Hallelujah to the Lamb, who hath purchased our pardon,
We'll praise him again when we pass over Jordan.

2 Ye souls that are wounded! oh, flee to the Saviour!
He calls you in mercy, 'tis infinite favor;
Your sins are increasing, escape to the mountain—
His blood can remove them, it flows from the fountain.
Hallelujah to the Lamb, etc.

3 O Jesus! ride onward, triumphantly glorious!
O'er sin, death, and hell, thou art more than victorious;
Thy name is the theme of the great congregation,
While angels and men raise the shout of salvation.
Hallelujah to the Lamb, etc.

4 With joy shall we stand, when escaped to the shore;
With harps in our hands, we'll praise him the more;

We'll range the sweet plains on, the banks of the river,
And sing of salvation forever and ever!
Hallelujah to the Lamb, etc.

THORNBY.

643 P. M.

1 LATE, late, so late! and dark the night, and chill!
Late, late, so late! But we can enter still.—
Too late, too late! ye cannot enter now.

2 No light had we;—for that we do repent,
And learning this, the Bridegroom will relent.—
Too late, too late, ye cannot enter now.

3 No light! so late! and dark and chill the night—
Oh, let us in, that we may find the light.
Too late! too late, ye cannot enter now!

4 Have we not heard the Bridegroom is so sweet!
Oh, let us in, that we may kiss his feet;
Oh, let us in, though late, to kiss his feet,
No! no! too late; ye cannot enter now!

TENNYSON.

PENITENCE AND CONSECRATION.

644 L. M.

1 SHOW pity, Lord! O Lord, forgive;
Let a repenting rebel live;
Are not thy mercies large and free?
May not a sinner trust in thee?

2 My crimes are great, but ne'er surpass
The power and glory of thy grace:
Great God, thy nature hath no bound,
So let thy pardoning love be found.

3 Oh, wash my soul from every sin,
And make my guilty conscience clean!
Here on my heart the burden lies,
And past offences pain mine eyes.

4 My lips with shame my sins confess,
Against thy law, against thy grace;
Lord, should thy judgment grow severe,
I am condemned, but thou art clear.

5 Should sudden vengeance seize my breath,
I must pronounce thee just in death;
And if my soul were sent to hell,
Thy righteous law approves it well.

6 Yet save a trembling sinner, Lord!
Whose hope, still hovering round thy word,
Would light on some sweet promise there,
Some sure support against despair.

WATTS.

645 L. M.

1 WEARY of wandering from my God,
And now made willing to return,
I hear, and bow me to the rod;
For him, not without hope, I mourn.

2 O Jesus, full of pardoning grace,
More full of grace than I of sin;
Yet once again I seek thy face,
Open thine arms and take me in.

3 Thou know'st the way to bring me back,
My fallen spirit to restore;
Oh, for thy truth and mercy's sake,
Forgive, and bid me sin no more!

4 Give to mine eyes refreshing tears,
And kindle my relentings now;
Fill all my soul with filial fears,
To thy sweet yoke my spirit bow.

C. WESLEY.

646 L. M.

1 A BROKEN heart, my God, my King,
Is all the sacrifice I bring:
The God of grace will ne'er despise
A broken heart for sacrifice.

2 My soul lies humbled in the dust,
And owns thy dreadful sentence just:
Look down, O Lord, with pitying eye,
And save the soul condemned to die.

3 Then will I teach the world thy ways;
Sinners shall learn thy sovereign grace:
I'll lead them to my Saviour's blood,
And they shall praise a pardoning God.

WATTS.

647 L. M.

1 WITH broken heart and contrite sigh,
A trembling sinner, Lord, I cry;
Thy pardoning grace is rich and free:
O God, be merciful to me!

2 I smite upon my troubled breast,
With deep and conscious guilt oppressed;
Christ and his cross my only plea:
O God, be merciful to me!

3 Far off I stand with tearful eyes,
Nor dare uplift them to the skies;
But thou dost all my anguish see:
O God, be merciful to me!

4 Nor alms, nor deeds that I have done,
Can for a single sin atone;
To Calvary alone I flee:
O God, be merciful to me!

5 And when redeemed from sin and hell,
With all the ransomed throng I dwell,
My raptured song shall ever be,
God has been merciful to me!

C. ELVEN.

648 L. M.

1 MY sufferings all to thee are known,
Tempted in every point like me;
Regard my grief, regard thine own:
Jesus, remember Calvary!

2 For whom didst thou the cross endure?
Who nailed thy body to the tree?

Did not thy death my life procure?
Oh! let thy mercy answer me.

3 Art thou not touched with human woe?
Hath pity left the Son of Man?
Dost thou not all my sorrows know,
And claim a share in all my pain?

4 Thou wilt not break a bruisèd reed,
Nor quench the smallest spark of grace,
Till through the soul thy power is spread,
Thy all-victorious righteousness.

5 The day of small and feeble things,
I know thou never wilt despise;
I know, with healing in his wings,
The Sun of Righteousness shall rise.

C. WESLEY.

649 L. M.

1 I LEFT the God of truth and light;
I left the God who gave me breath,
To wander in the wilds of night,
And perish in the snares of death!

2 Sweet was his service, and his yoke
Was light and easy to be borne:
Through all his bonds of love I broke;
I cast away his gifts with scorn!

3 Heart-broken, friendless, poor, cast down,
Where shall the chief of sinners fly,
Almighty Vengeance! from thy frown,
Eternal Justice! from thine eye?

4 Lo! through the gloom of guilty fears,
My faith discerns a dawn of grace:
The Sun of Righteousness appears
In Jesus' reconciling face!

MONTGOMERY.

650 L. M.

1 WHEN at thy footstool, Lord, I bend,
And plead with thee for mercy there,
Think of the sinner's dying Friend,
And for his sake receive my prayer.

2 Oh think not of my shame and guilt,
My thousand stains of deepest dye;
Think of the blood which Jesus spilt,
And let that blood my pardon buy.

3 Oh think upon thy holy word,
And every plighted promise there;
How prayer should evermore be heard,
And how thy glory is to spare.

4 Oh think not of my doubts and fears,
My strivings with thy grace divine;
Think upon Jesus' woes and tears,
And let his merits stand for mine.

5 Thine eye, thine ear, they are not dull;
Thine arm can never shortened be;
Behold me here; my heart is full;
Behold, and spare, and succor me!

LYTE.

651 L. M.

1 OH! that my load of sin were gone!
Oh! that I could at last submit
At Jesus' feet to lay it down—
To lay my soul at Jesus' feet!

2 Rest for my soul I long to find:
Saviour of all, if mine thou art,
Give me thy meek and lowly mind,
And stamp thine image on my heart.

3 Break off the yoke of inbred sin,
And fully set my spirit free:

I cannot rest till pure within—
Till I am wholly lost in thee.

4 Fain would I learn of thee, my God;
Thy light and easy burden prove;—
The cross all stained with hallowed blood,
The labor of thy dying love.

5 I would—but thou must give the power;
My heart from every sin release;
Bring near, bring near the joyful hour,
And fill me with thy perfect peace!

C. WESLEY.

652 L. M.

1 OH! where is now that glowing love
That marked our union with the Lord?
Our hearts were fixed on things above,
Nor could the world a joy afford.

2 Where is the zeal that led us then
To make our Saviour's glory known?
That freed us from the fear of men,
And kept our eye on him alone?

3 Where are the happy seasons spent
In fellowship with him we loved?
The sacred joy, the sweet content,
The blessedness that then we proved?

4 Behold, again we turn to thee;
Oh! cast us not away, though vile;
No peace we have, no joy we see,
O Lord our God, but in thy smile.

KELLY.

653 L. M.

1 THE Saviour smiles! upon my soul
New tides of hope tumultuous roll—
His voice proclaims my pardon found,
Seraphic transport wings the sound.

2 Earth has a joy unknown in heaven,
The new-born peace of sin forgiven!
Tears of such pure and deep delight,
Ye angels, never dimmed your sight.

3 Ye saw of old, on chaos rise
The beauteous pillars of the skies:
Ye know where morn exulting springs,
And evening folds her drooping wings.

4 Bright heralds of th' eternal will,
Abroad his errands ye fulfill;
Or, throned in floods of beamy day,
Symphonious, in his presence play.

5 But I amid your choirs shall shine,
And all your knowledge will be mine:
Ye on your harps must learn to hear
A secret chord that mine will bear.

HILLHOUSE.

654 L. M.

1 I THIRST, thou wounded Lamb of God,
To wash me in thy cleansing blood;
To dwell within thy wounds: then pain
Is sweet, and life or death is gain.

2 Take my poor heart, and let it be
Forever closed to all but thee;
Seal thou my breast, and let me wear
That pledge of love forever there.

3 How blest are they who still abide
Close shelter'd in thy bleeding side!

Who thence their life and strength derive,
And by thee move, and in thee live.

4 What are our works but sin and death,
Till thou thy quick'ning Spirit breathe?
Thou giv'st the power thy grace to move;
O wondrous grace! O boundless love!

ZINZENDORF, *tr. by* J. WESLEY.

655 L. M.

1 LORD, I am thine, entirely thine,
Purchased and saved by blood divine,
With full consent thine I would be,
And own thy sov'reign right in me.

2 Grant one poor sinner more a place
Among the children of thy grace;
A wretched sinner, lost to God,
But ransom'd by Immanuel's blood.

3 Thine would I live—thine would I die;
Be thine through all eternity;
The vow is past beyond repeal,
And now I set the solemn seal.

4 Here, at that cross where flows the blood
That bought my guilty soul to God,—
Thee, my new Master, now I call,
And consecrate to thee my all.

DAVIES.

656 L. M.

1 JUST as I am, without one plea
But that thy blood was shed for me,
And that thou bid'st me come to thee,
O Lamb of God, I come! I come!

2 Just as I am, and waiting not
To rid my soul of one dark blot,
To thee whose blood can cleanse each spot,
O Lamb of God, I come! I come!

3 Just as I am, though tossed about
With many a conflict, many a doubt,
Fightings within, and fears without,
O Lamb of God, I come! I come!

4 Just as I am—poor, wretched, blind;
Sight, riches, healing of the mind,
Yea, all I need, in thee to find,
O Lamb of God, I come! I come!

5 Just as I am—thou wilt receive,
Wilt welcome, pardon, cleanse, relieve;
Because thy promise I believe,
O Lamb of God, I come! I come!

6 Just as I am—thy love unknown
Hath broken every barrier down;
Now, to be thine, yea, thine alone,
O Lamb of God, I come! I come!

CHARLOTTE ELLIOT.

657 L. M.

1 JESUS, the sinner's Friend, to thee,
Lost and undone, for aid I flee;
Weary of earth, myself, and sin,
Open thine arms and take me in.

2 Pity and save my ruined soul;
'Tis thou alone canst make me whole;
Dark, till in me thine image shine,
And lost I am, till thou art mine.

3 At last I own it cannot be
That I should fit myself for thee:
Here, then, to thee I all resign;
Thine is the work, and only thine.

4 What can I say thy grace to move?
Lord, I am sin—but thou art love:
I give up every plea beside,
Lord, I am lost,—but thou hast died!

C. WESLEY.

658 L. M.

1 OH, for a glance of heavenly day,
To take this stubborn heart away;
And thaw, with beams of love divine,
This heart, this frozen heart of mine.

2 The rocks can rend; the earth can quake;
The seas can roar; the mountains shake:
Of feeling, all things show some sign,
But this unfeeling heart of mine.

3 To hear the sorrows thou hast felt,
O Lord, an adamant would melt:
But I can read each moving line,
And nothing moves this heart of mine.

4 But Power Divine can do the deed;
And, Lord, that power I greatly need:
Thy Spirit can from dross refine,
And melt and change this heart of mine.

HART.

659 C. M.

1 LORD, when we bow before thy throne,
And our confessions pour,
Oh, may we feel the sins we own,
And hate what we deplore.

2 Our contrite spirits, pitying, see;
True penitence impart;
And let a healing ray from thee
Beam hope on every heart.

3 When we disclose our wants in prayer,
Oh, let our wills resign,
And not a thought our bosom share
Which is not wholly thine.

4 Let faith each meek petition fill,
And waft it to the skies,
And teach our hearts 'tis goodness, still,
That grants it, or denies.

660 C. M.

1 JESUS, and didst thou condescend,
When vailed in human clay,
To heal the sick, the lame, the blind,
And drive disease away?

2 Didst thou regard the beggar's cry,
And give the blind to see?
Jesus, thou Son of David, hear—
Have mercy, too, on me.

3 And didst thou pity mortal woe,
And sight and health restore?
Then pity, Lord, and save my soul,
Which needs thy mercy more.

4 Didst thou regard thy servant's cry,
When sinking in the wave?
I perish, Lord—oh, save my soul,
For thou alone canst save.

BRADLEY.

661 C. M.

1 O THOU, whose tender mercy hears
Contrition's humble sigh;
Whose hand, indulgent, wipes the tears
From sorrow's weeping eye.

2 See, low before thy throne of grace,
A wretched wanderer mourn;
Hast thou not bid me seek thy face?
Hast thou not said—"Return?"

3 And shall my guilty fears prevail
To drive me from thy feet?
Oh, let not this dear refuge fail,
This only safe retreat!

STEELE.

662 C. M.

1 DEAR Saviour, when my thoughts recall
The wonders of thy grace,
Low at thy feet, ashamed, I fall
And hide this wretched face.

2 Shall love like thine be thus repaid?
Ah, vile, ungrateful heart!
By earth's low cares so oft betrayed
From Jesus to depart.

3 Oh, while I breathe to thee, my Lord,
The deep, repentant sigh,
Confirm the kind, forgiving word,
With pity in thine eye!

STEELE.

663 C. M.

1 APPROACH, my soul! the mercy-seat,
Where Jesus answers prayer;
There humbly fall before his feet,
For none can perish there.

2 Thy promise is my only plea,
With this I venture nigh:
Thou callest burdened souls to thee,
And such, O Lord! am I.

3 Bowed down beneath a load of sin,
By Satan sorely pressed;
By wars without, and fears within,
I come to thee for rest.

4 Be thou my shield and hiding-place,
That, sheltered near thy side,
I may my fierce accuser face,
And tell him—thou hast died.

5 Oh! wondrous Love—to bleed and die,
To bear the cross and shame,
That guilty sinners, such as I,
Might plead thy gracious name!

NEWTON.

664 C. M.

1 JESUS! thou art the sinner's Friend;
As such I look to thee;
Now in the fullness of thy love,
O Lord! remember me.

2 Remember thy pure word of grace—
Remember Calvary;
Remember all thy dying groans,
And then remember me.

3 Thou wondrous Advocate with God!
I yield myself to thee;
While thou art sitting on thy throne,
Dear Lord! remember me.

4 Lord! I am guilty—I am vile,
But thy salvation 's free;
Then, in thine all-abounding grace,
Dear Lord! remember me.

5 And, when I close my eyes in death,
When creature-helps all flee,
Then, O my dear Redeemer-God!
I pray, remember me.

R. BURNHAM.

665 C. M.

1 WHEN wounded sore the stricken soul
Lies bleeding and unbound,
One only hand, a piercéd hand,
Can salve the sinner's wound.

2 When sorrow swells the laden breast,
And tears of anguish flow,
One only heart, a broken heart,
Can feel the sinner's woe.

3 When penitence has wept in vain
Over some foul dark spot,
One only stream, a stream of blood,
Can wash away the blot.

4 'Tis Jesus' blood that washes white,
His hand that brings relief,
His heart that's touched with all our joys
And feeleth for our grief.

5 Lift up thy bleeding hand, O Lord;
Unseal that cleansing tide;
We have no shelter from our sin,
But in that wounded side.

CECIL FRANCES ALEXANDER.

666 C. M.

1 SWEET was the time when first I felt
The Saviour's pardoning blood
Applied to cleanse my soul from guilt,
And bring me home to God.

2 Soon as the morn the light revealed,
His praises tuned my tongue;
And when the evening shades prevailed
His love was all my song.

3 In prayer my soul drew near the Lord,
And saw his glory shine;
And when I read his holy word,
I called each promise mine.

4 But now, when evening shade prevails,
My soul in darkness mourns?
And when the morn the light reveals,
No light to me returns.

5 Rise, Lord, and help me to prevail;
Oh, make my soul thy care!
I know thy mercy cannot fail;
Let me that mercy share.

NEWTON.

667 C. M.

1 OH, that I knew the secret place,
Where I might find my God!
I'd spread my wants before his face,
And pour my woes abroad.

2 I'd tell him how my sins arise,
What sorrows I sustain;
How grace decays, and comfort dies,
And leaves my heart in pain.

3 He knows what arguments I'd take
To wrestle with my God:
I'd plead for his own mercy's sake—
I'd plead my Saviour's blood.

WATTS.

668 C. M.

1 PROSTRATE, dear Jesus, at thy feet
A guilty rebel lies;
And upward to thy mercy-seat
Presumes to lift his eyes.

2 If tears of sorrow would suffice
To pay the debt I owe,
Tears should from both my weeping eyes
In ceaseless torrents flow.

3 But no such sacrifice I plead
To expiate my guilt;
No tears, but those which thou hast shed,
No blood, but thou hast spilt.

STENNETT.

669 C. M.

1 OH, could I lose myself in thee,
Thou depth of mercy prove,—
Thou vast, unfathomable sea
Of unexhausted love.

2 My humbled soul, when thou art near,
In dust and ashes lies:
How shall a sinful worm appear,
Or meet thy purer eyes?

3 I loathe myself when God I see,
And into nothing fall;
Content if thou exalted be,
And Christ be all in all.

C. WESLEY.

670 C. M.

1 COME, trembling sinner, in whose breast
A thousand thoughts revolve—
Come, with your guilt and fear oppressed,
And make this last resolve:

2 "I'll go to Jesus, though my sin
Hath like a mountain rose;
I know his courts, I'll enter in,
Whatever may oppose.

3 "Prostrate I'll lie before his throne,
And there my guilt confess;
I'll tell him I'm a wretch undone,
Without his sovereign grace.

4 "Perhaps he will admit my plea,
Perhaps will hear my prayer;
But if I perish, I will pray,
And perish only there.

5 "I can but perish if I go;
I am resolved to try;
For if I stay away, I know
I must forever die.

6 "But if I die with mercy sought,
When I the King have tried,
This were to die (delightful thought!)
As sinner never died."

JONES.

671 C. M.

1 AND are we wretches yet alive?
And do we yet rebel?
'Tis boundless, 'tis amazing love,
That bears us up from hell.

2 Almighty goodness cries, "Forbear!"
And straight the thunder stays:
And dare we now provoke his wrath
And weary out his grace?

3 Lord, we have long abused thy love,
Too long indulged our sin,
Our aching hearts now bleed to see
What rebels we have been.

WATTS.

672 C. M.

1 I SEE the crowd in Pilate's hall,
And mark their wrathful mien;
Their shouts of "Crucify!" appall,
With blasphemies between.

2 I see the scourges tear his back,
I see the piercing crown;
And of that crowd who smite and mock,
I feel that I am one.

3 Around yon Cross a throng I see,
Mocking the Sufferer's groan;
Yet still my voice it seems to be,
As if I mocked alone.

4 'Twas I that shed the Saviour's blood,
I nailed him to the tree,
I crucified the Son of God,
I joined the mockery.

5 Yet not the less that blood avails
To wash away my sin;
And not the less that Cross prevails
To give me peace within.

BONAR.

673 C. M.

1 HOW sad our state by nature is!
Our sin, how deep it stains!
And Satan binds our captive minds
Fast in his slavish chains.

2 But, hark! a voice of sovereign love!
'Tis Christ's inviting word—
"Ho! ye despairing sinners, come,
And trust upon the Lord."

3 To the dear fountain of thy blood,
Incarnate God, I fly;
Here let me wash my spotted soul
From stains of deepest dye.

4 A guilty, weak, and helpless worm,
On thy kind arms I fall;
Be thou my strength and righteousness,
My Saviour and my all.

WATTS.

674 C. M.

1 IN evil long I took delight,
Unawed by shame or fear,
Till a new object struck my sight,
And stopped my wild career.

2 I saw One hanging on a tree,
In agonies and blood,
Who fixed his languid eyes on me,
As near his cross I stood.

3 Sure never till my latest breath
Can I forget that look:
It seemed to charge me with his death,
Though not a word he spoke

4 My conscience felt and owned the guilt,
And plunged me in despair;
I saw my sins his blood had spilt,
And helped to nail him there.

5 Alas! I knew not what I did!
But now my tears are vain:
Where shall my trembling soul be hid?
For I the Lord have slain!

6 A second look he gave, which said,
"I freely all forgive;
This blood is for thy ransom paid;
I die that thou may'st live."

7 Thus, while his death my sin displays
In all its blackest hue,
Such is the mystery of grace,
It seals my pardon too.

NEWTON.

675 C. M.

1 FOREVER here my rest shall be,
Close to thy bleeding side;
This all my hope, and all my plea,
For me the Saviour died!

2 My dying Saviour and my God,
Fountain for guilt and sin,
Sprinkle me ever with thy blood,
And cleanse and keep me clean!

3 Wash me, and make me thus thine own,
Wash me, and mine thou art!
Wash me, but not my feet alone:
My hands, my head, my heart?

C. WESLEY.

676 C. P. M.

1 O THOU that hear'st the prayer of faith,
Wilt thou not save a soul from death,
That casts itself on thee:

I have no refuge of my own,
But fly to what my God hath done,
And suffered once for me.

2 Slain in the guilty sinner's stead,
His spotless righteousness I plead,
And his availing blood;
That righteousness my robe shall be,
That merit shall atone for me,
And bring me near to God.

3 Then save me from eternal death,
The spirit of adoption breathe,
His consolations send;
By him some word of life impart,
And sweetly whisper to my heart—
"Thy Maker is thy Friend."

4 The king of terrors then would be
A welcome messenger to me,
To bid me come away:
Unclogged by earth, or earthly things,
I'd mount, I'd fly, with eager wings,
To everlasting day.

TOPLADY.

677 C. P. M.

1 NO room for mirth or trifling here,
For worldly hope, or worldly fear,
If life so soon is gone:
If now the Judge is at the door,
And all mankind must stand before
The inexorable throne!

2 No matter which my thoughts employ,
A moment's misery or joy;
But oh! when both shall end,
Where shall I find my destined place?
Shall I my everlasting days
With fiends or angels spend?

3 Nothing is worth a thought beneath,
But how I may escape the death
That never, never dies!
How make mine own election sure
And when I fail on earth, secure
A mansion in the skies.

C. WESLEY.

678 C. P. M.

1 THE mind was formed, to mount sublime
Beyond the narrow bounds of time,
To everlasting things;
But earthly vapors dim her sight,
And hang, with cold oppressive weight,
Upon her drooping wings.

2 Bright scenes of bliss, unclouded skies
Invite my soul;—oh! could I rise,
Nor leave a thought below,
I'd bid farewell to anxious care,
And say to every tempting snare,—
Heaven calls and I must go!

STEELE.

679 S. M.

1 IS this the kind return?
Are these the thanks we owe?
Thus to abuse eternal love,
Whence all our blessings flow.

2 To what a stubborn frame
Has sin reduced our mind!
What strange, rebellious wretches we,
And God as strangely kind!

3 Turn, turn us, mighty God,
And mould our souls afresh;
Break, sovereign grace, these hearts of stone,
And give us hearts of flesh.

4 Let past ingratitude
Provoke our weeping eyes,
And hourly, as new mercies fall,
Let hourly thanks arise.

WATTS.

680

7s.

1 I AM coming to the cross;
I am poor, and weak, and blind;
I am counting all but dross;
I shall thy salvation find.

2 Long my heart has sighed for thee;
Long has evil reigned within;
Jesus sweetly speaks to me,
I will cleanse you from all sin.

3 Here I give my all to thee—
Friends, and time, and earthly store;
Soul and body thine to be—
Wholly thine—forevermore.

4 In the promises I trust;
Now I feel the blood applied
I am prostrate in the dust;
I with Christ am crucified.

Chorus.

I am trusting, Lord, in thee,
Dear Lamb of Calvary;
Humbly at the cross I bow;
Save me, Jesus, save me now.

W. McDONALD.

681

S. M.

1 DID Christ o'er sinners weep,
And shall our cheeks be dry?
Let floods of penitential grief
Burst forth from every eye.

2 The Son of God in tears
The wondering angels see;
Be thou astonished, O my soul;
He shed those tears for thee.

3 He wept that we might weep;
Each sin demands a tear:
In heaven alone no sin is found,
And there's no weeping there.

BEDDOME.

682

S. M.

1 AND can I yet delay
My little all to give?—
To tear my soul from earth away,
And Jesus to receive?

2 Nay, but I yield, I yield!
I can hold out no more:
I sink, by dying love compelled,
And own thee Conqueror.

3 Though late, I all forsake;
My friends, my all, resign;
Gracious Redeemer, take, oh, take,
And seal me ever thine.

4 Come, and possess me whole,
Nor hence again remove:
Settle and fix my wavering soul
With all thy weight of love.

C. WESLEY.

683

S. M.

1 UNTO thine altar, Lord,
A broken heart I bring;
And wilt thou graciously accept
Of such a worthless thing?

2 To Christ, the bleeding Lamb,
My faith directs her eyes;
Thou may'st reject that worthless thing,
But not his sacrifice.

3 When he gave up his life,
The law was satisfied;
And now to its most rigorous claims
I answer, "Jesus died."

684 S. M.

1 DID Jesus weep for me?
And sigh o'er sinners here?
My soul that weeping Saviour see,
And shed thyself a tear.

2 Did Jesus pray for me?
For such a wand'rer care?
My heart subdued and broken be,
And drawn to him in prayer.

3 Did Jesus die for me?
Oh, depth of love divine!
I die to sin—I'll live to thee;
O Saviour, make me thine!

S. D. PHELPS.

685 7s. D.

1 JESUS, lover of my soul,
Let me to thy bosom fly,
While the billows near me roll,
While the tempest still is high;
Hide me, O my Saviour, hide,
Till the storm of life is past;
Safe into the haven guide,
Oh, receive my soul at last.

2 Other refuge have I none;
Hangs my helpless soul on thee:
Leave, ah! leave me not alone,
Still support and comfort me:
All my trust on thee is stayed,
All my help from thee I bring;
Cover my defenceless head
With the shadow of thy wing.

3 Thou, O Christ, art all I want,
More than all in thee I find:
Raise the fallen, cheer the faint,
Heal the sick, and lead the blind:
Just and holy is thy name;
I am all unrighteousness:
False and full of sin I am;
Thou art full of truth and grace.

4 Plenteous grace with thee is found,
Grace to cover all my sin;
Let the healing streams abound,
Make and keep me pure within:
Thou of life the fountain art,
Freely let me take of thee;
Spring thou up within my heart;
Rise to all eternity.

C. WESLEY.

686 8s, 7s & 3s.

1 LORD, I hear of show'rs of blessing,
Thou art scatt'ring, full and free—
Show'rs, the thirsty land refreshing;
Let some droppings fall on me,—
Even me, even me,
Let some droppings fall on me.

2 Pass me not, O God, our Father!
Sinful though my heart may be;
Thou might'st leave me, but the rather
Let thy mercy light on me!—
Even me.

3 Pass me not, O gracious Saviour!
Let me live and cling to thee;
For I'm longing for thy favor;
Whilst thou art calling, oh! call me—
Even me.

4 Pass me not, O mighty Spirit!
Thou canst make the blind to see;
Witnesser of Jesus' merit!
Speak some word of power to me—
Even me.

5 Have I long in sin been sleeping—
Long been slighting, grieving thee?
Has the world my heart been keeping?
Oh! forgive, and rescue me!—
Even me.

6 Love of God—so pure and changeless;
Blood of Christ—so rich, so free;
Grace of God—so strong and boundless,
Magnify it all in me!—
Even me.

687 C. M.

1 FATHER, I stretch my hands to thee;
No other help I know;
If thou withdraw thyself from me,
Ah, whither shall I go?

2 What did thine only Son endure
Before I drew my breath!
What pain, what labor, to secure
My soul from endless death!

3 Author of faith, to thee I lift
My weary, longing eyes;
Oh, may I now receive that gift;
My soul, without it, dies.

Chorus. C. WESLEY.

I do believe, I now believe
That Jesus died for me;
And through his blood, his precious blood,
I shall from sin be free.

688 7s. D.

1 SAVIOUR, when in dust, to thee
Low we bow th' adoring knee;
When, repentant, to the skies
Scarce we lift our streaming eyes:
Oh! by all thy pain and woe,
Suffered once for man below,
Bending from thy throne on high,
Hear thy people while they cry!

2 By thy birth and early years,
By thy human griefs and fears,
By thy fasting and distress
In the lonely wilderness:
By thy victory in the hour
Of the subtle tempter's power;
Jesus, look with pitying eye;
Hear thy people while they cry.

3 By thine hour of dark despair,
By thine agony of prayer,
By thy purple robe of scorn,
By thy wounds—thy crown of thorn;
By thy cross—thy pangs and cries;
By thy perfect sacrifice;
Jesus, look with pitying eye;
Hear thy people while they cry.

689 P. M

1 JESUS, I come—I come to-night;
Restore to me my blinded sight;
And in my soul, "let there be light!"
Jesus, to thee I come!

2 Jesus, I come—I cannot stay
From thee another precious day;
I would thy word this night obey—
Jesus, to thee I come!

3 Jesus, I come—"just as I am,"
To thee, the holy, spotless Lamb;
Thou wilt receive me as I am—
Jesus, to thee I come!

690 7s. 6 lines.

1 PITY, Lord, the child of clay,
Who can only weep and pray,
Only on thy love depend,
Thou who art the sinner's Friend,

Thou, the sinner's only plea,
Jesus, Saviour, pity me!

2 From thy flock a straying lamb,
Tender Shepherd, though I am,
Now upon the mountain cold,
Lost, I long to gain the fold,
And within thine arms to be;
Jesus, Saviour, pity me!

3 Oh, where stillest streams are poured,
In green pastures, lead me, Lord!
Bring me back, where angels sound
Joy to the poor wanderer found;
Evermore my Shepherd be;
Jesus, Saviour, pity me!

691 7s. 6 lines.

1 HEART of stone, relent, relent!
Break, by Jesus' cross subdued!
See his body mangled, rent,
Covered with a gore of blood;
Sinful soul, what hast thou done?
Crucified the Incarnate Son!

2 Yes, thy sins have done the deed,
Driven the nails that fixed him there,
Crowned with thorns his sacred head,
Pierced him with the cruel spear,
Made his soul a sacrifice,
While for sinful man he dies!

3 Wilt thou let him bleed in vain?
Still to death thy Lord pursue?
Open all his wounds again,
And the shameful cross renew?
No; with all my sins I'll part;
Break, oh break, my bleeding heart!

C. WESLEY.

692 7s. 6 lines.

1 ROCK of Ages, cleft for me,
Let me hide myself in thee;
Let the water and the blood,
From thy riven side which flowed,
Be of sin the double cure;
Cleanse me from its guilt and power.

2 Not the labors of my hands
Can fulfill thy laws' demands;
Could my zeal no respite know,
Could my tears forever flow,
All for sin could not atone;
Thou must save, and thou alone.

3 Nothing in my hand I bring;
Simply to the cross I cling;
Naked, come to thee for dress;
Helpless, look to thee for grace;
Foul, I to the Fountain fly;
Wash me, Saviour, or I die!

4 While I draw this fleeting breath,
When my eyelids close in death,
When I soar to worlds unknown,
See thee on the judgment-throne,
Rock of Ages, cleft for me,
Let me hide myself in thee.

TOPLADY.

693 7s. 6 lines.

1 WEEPING soul, no longer mourn;
Jesus all thy griefs hath borne;
View him bleeding on the tree,
Pouring out his life for thee;
There thy every sin he bore,
Weeping soul, lament no more.

2 All thy crimes on him were laid;
See upon his blameless head

Wrath its utmost vengeance pours,
Due to my offence and yours;
Weary sinner, keep thine eyes
On the atoning sacrifice.

3 Cast thy guilty soul on him,
Find him mighty to redeem;
At his feet thy burden lay,
Look thy doubts and fears away;
Now by faith the Son embrace,
Plead his promise, trust his grace.

4 Lord, thy arm must be revealed,
Ere I can by faith be healed;
Since I scarce can look to thee,
Cast a gracious eye on me;
At thy feet myself I lay,
Shine, oh, shine my sins away.

TOPLADY.

694

7s.

1 GOD of mercy! God of love!
Hear our sad, repentant song;
Sorrow dwells on every face,
Penitence on every tongue.

2 Deep regret for follies past,
Talents wasted, time misspent;
Hearts debased by worldly cares,
Thankless for the blessings lent;

3 Foolish fears and fond desires,
Vain regrets for things as vain;
Lips too seldom taught to praise,
Oft to murmur and complain;

4 These, and every secret fault,
Filled with grief and shame we own;
Humbled at thy feet we lie,
Seeking pardon from thy throne.

5 God of mercy! God of grace!
Hear our sad, repentant songs;
Oh, restore thy suppliant race,
Thou to whom all praise belongs!

J. TAYLOR.

695

7s.

1 DOES the Gospel word proclaim
Rest for those that weary be?
Then, my soul, put in thy claim—
Sure that promise speaks to thee!

2 Marks of grace I cannot show,
All polluted is my best;
But I weary am, I know,
And the weary long for rest.

3 Burdened with a load of sin,
Harassed with tormenting doubt,
Hourly conflicts from within,
Hourly crosses from without;—

4 All my little strength is gone,
Sink I must without supply;
Sure upon the earth is none
Can more weary be than I.

5 In the ark the weary dove
Found a welcome resting-place;
Thus my spirit longs to prove
Rest in Christ, the Ark of grace.

6 Tempest-tossed I long have been,
And the flood increases fast;
Open, Lord, and take me in,
Till the storm be overpast!

NEWTON.

696

7s.

1 GENTLY, gently, lay the rod
On my sinful head, O God!
Stay thy wrath, in mercy stay,
Lest I sink beneath its sway.

2 Heal me, for my flesh is weak;
Heal me, for thy grace I seek;
This my only plea I make,—
Heal me for thy mercy's sake.

3 Who, within the silent grave,
Shall proclaim thy power to save?
Lord, my sinking soul reprieve;
Speak, and I shall rise and live.

4 Lo! he comes—he heeds my plea;
Lo! he comes—the shadows flee;
Glory round me dawns once more;
Rise, my spirit! and adore.

LYTE.

697 7s, 6s & 8s.

1 JESUS, let thy pitying eye
Call back a wandering sheep;
False to thee, like Peter, I
Would fain like Peter weep!
Turn, and look upon me, Lord!
And break my heart of stone,
Let me be by grace restored,
On me be all long-suffering shown.

2 Saviour, Prince, enthroned above,
Repentance to impart,
Give me, through thy dying love,
The humble, contrite heart:
Give what I have long implored,
A portion of thy grief unknown;
Turn, and look upon me, Lord!
And break my heart of stone.

3 For thine own compassion's sake,
The gracious wonder show;
Cast my sins behind thy back,
And wash me white as snow:
If thy mercies now are stirred,
If now I do myself bemoan,
Turn, and look upon me, Lord!
And break my heart of stone.

C. WESLEY.

698 7s, 6s & 8s.

1 VAIN, delusive world, adieu,
With all of creature good!
Only Jesus I pursue,
Who bought me with his blood:
All thy pleasures I forego;
I trample on thy wealth and pride;
Only Jesus will I know,
And Jesus crucified.

2 Other knowledge I disdain;
'Tis all but vanity:
Christ, the Lamb of God, was slain,—
He tasted death for me.
Me to save from endless woe
The sin-atoning Victim died:
Only Jesus will I know,
And Jesus crucified.

3 Him to know is life and peace,
And pleasure without end;
This is all my happiness,
On Jesus to depend;
Daily in his grace to grow,
And ever in his faith abide;
Only Jesus will I know,
And Jesus crucified.

C. WSLEY.

699 8s & 7s.

1 LORD, I know thy grace is nighme,
Though thyself I cannot see;
Jesus, Master, pass not by me;
Son of David, pity me.

2 While I sit in weary blindness,
Longing for the blessèd light,
Many taste thy loving-kindness;
"Lord, I would receive my sight."

3 I would see thee and adore thee,
And thy word the power can give;
Hear the sightless soul implore thee;
Let me see thy face and live.

4 Ah! what touch is this that thrills me?
What this burst of strange delight?
Lo, the rapturous vision fills me!
This is Jesus! this is sight!

5 Room, ye saints that throng behind him!
Let me follow in the way;
I will teach the blind to find him
Who can turn their night to day.

GANSE.

700 7s.

1 DEPTH of mercy! can there be
Mercy still reserved for me?
Can my God his wrath forbear?
Me, the chief of sinners, spare?

2 I have long withstood his grace;
Long provoked him to his face;
Would not hearken to his calls;
Grieved him by a thousand falls.

3 Now incline me to repent;
Let me now my sins lament;
Now my foul revolt deplore,
Weep, believe, and sin no more.

4 Kindled his relentings are;
Me he now delights to spare;
Cries, "How shall I give thee up?"
Lets the lifted thunder drop.

5 There for me the Saviour stands,
Shows his wounds, and spreads his hands;
God is love! I know, I feel;
Jesus weeps, and loves me still.

C. WESLEY.

Chorus.

God is love! I know, I feel;
Jesus weeps, and loves me still;
Jesus weeps; he weeps, and loves me still.

701 P. M.

1 NOTHING but leaves! the spirit grieves
Over a wasted life;
O'er sins indulged while conscience slept,
O'er vows and promises unkept,
And reap from years of strife—
Nothing but leaves.

2 Nothing but leaves! no gathered sheaves
Of life's fair ripening grain;
We sow our seeds, lo! tares and weeds,
Words, idle words for earnest deeds,
We reap with toil and pain—
Nothing but leaves.

3 Nothing but leaves! sad memory weaves
No veil to hide the past;
And as we trace our weary way,
Counting each lost and misspent day,
Sadly we find at last—
Nothing but leaves.

4 Ah! who shall thus the Master meet,
Bearing but withered leaves?
Ah! who shall at the Saviour's feet,
Before the awful judgment-seat,
Lay down, for golden sheaves,
Nothing but leaves?

702 10s.

1 GO, and tell Jesus, weary, sin-sick soul,
He'll ease thee of thy burden, make thee whole;
Look up to him, he only can forgive,
Believe on him, and thou shalt surely live.

2 Go, and tell Jesus, when your sins arise
Like mountains of deep guilt before your eyes:
His blood was spilt, his precious life he gave,
That mercy, peace and pardon you might have.

3 Go, and tell Jesus, he'll dispel thy fears,
Will calm thy doubts, and wipe away thy tears;
He'll take thee in his arm, and on his breast
Thou may'st be happy, and forever rest.

Chorus.

Go, and tell Jesus, he only can forgive;
Go, and tell Jesus, oh, turn to him and live.
Go, and tell Jesus; go, and tell Jesus;
Go, and tell Jesus, he only can forgive.

703 C. P. M.

1 AWAKED by Sinai's awful sound,
My soul in bonds of guilt I found,
And knew not where to go;
One solemn truth increased my pain,
The sinner "must be born again,"
Or sink to endless woe.

2 I heard the law its thunders roll,
While guilt lay heavy on my soul—
A vast oppressive load;
All creature-aid I saw was vain;
The sinner "must be born again,"
Or drink the wrath of God.

3 The saints I heard with rapture tell—
How Jesus conquered death and hell
To bring salvation near;
Yet still I found this truth remain—
The sinner "must be born again,"
Or sink in deep despair.

4 But while I thus in anguish lay,
The bleeding Saviour passed that way,
My bondage to remove;
The sinner, once by justice slain,
Now by his grace is born again,
And sings redeeming love.

OCKUM.

704 C. P. M.

1 LORD, thou hast won—at length I yield,
My heart, by mighty grace compelled,
Surrenders all to thee:
Against thy terrors long I strove,
But who can stand against thy love?—
Love conquers even me.

2 Yes, since thou hast thy love revealed,
And shown my soul a pardon sealed,
I can resist no more;
Couldst thou for such a sinner bleed?
Canst thou for such a rebel plead?
I wonder and adore!

3 If thou hadst bid thy thunders roll,
And lightnings flash to blast my soul,
I still had stubborn been;
But mercy has my heart subdued,
A bleeding Saviour I have viewed,
And now, I hate my sin.

4 Now, Lord, I would be thine alone—
Come, take possession of thine own,
For thou hast set me free;
Released from Satan's hard command,
See all my powers in waiting stand,
To be employed by thee.

NEWTON.

705 8s & 7s.

1 JESUS, I my cross have taken,
All to leave, and follow thee;
Naked, poor, despised, forsaken,
Thou, from hence, my all shalt be!
Perish, every fond ambition,
All I've sought, or hoped, or known,
Yet how rich is my condition,
God and heaven are still my own!

2 Let the world despise and leave me,
They have left my Saviour, too;
Human hearts and looks deceive me—
Thou art not, like them, untrue;
Oh! while thou dost smile upon me,
God of wisdom, love, and might,
Foes may hate, and friends disown me,
Show thy face, and all is bright.

3 Man may trouble and distress me,
'Twill but drive me to thy breast,
Life with trials hard may press me,
Heaven will bring me sweeter rest!
Oh! 'tis not in grief to harm me,
While thy love is left to me;
Oh! 'twere not in joy to charm me,
Were that joy unmixed with thee.

4 Go then, earthly fame and treasure!
Come disaster, scorn, and pain!
In thy service pain is pleasure,
With thy favor, loss is gain.
I have called thee, Abba, Father!
I have stayed my heart on thee!
Storms may howl, and clouds may gather,
All must work for good to me.

5 Soul, then know thy full salvation,
Rise o'er sin, and fear, and care;
Joy to find in every station
Something still to do or bear.
Think what Spirit dwells within thee;
Think what Father's smiles are thine;
Think that Jesus died to win thee;
Child of heaven, canst thou repine?

6 Haste thee on from grace to glory,
Armed by faith, and winged by prayer!
Heaven's eternal day's before thee;
God's own hand shall guide thee there:
Soon shall close thy earthly mission,
Soon shall pass thy pilgrim days,
Hope shall change to glad fruition,
Faith to sight, and prayer to praise.

LYTE.

706 L. M.

1 I SEND the joys of earth away;
Away! ye tempters of the mind,
False as the smooth, deceitful sea,
And empty as the whistling wind!

2 Your streams were floating me along,
Down to the gulf of black despair;
And while I listened to your song,
Your streams had e'en conveyed me there.

3 Lord! I adore thy matchless grace,
Which warned me of that dark abyss,
Which drew me from those treacherous seas,
And bade me seek superior bliss.

4 Now to the shining realms above
I stretch my hands and glance my eyes;
Oh for the pinions of a dove,
To bear me to the upper skies!

WATTS.

707 L. M.

1 NO more, my God, I boast no more
Of all the duties I have done;
I quit the hopes I held before,
To trust the merits of thy Son.

2 Now, for the love I bear his name,
What was my gain I count my loss;
My former pride I call my shame,
And nail my glory to his cross.

3 Yes, and I must and will esteem
All things but loss for Jesus' sake;
Oh, may my soul be found in him,
And of his righteousness partake.

WATTS.

708 L. M.

1 JESUS, my all, to heaven is gone—
He, whom I fix my hopes upon;
His track I see, and I'll pursue
The narrow way, till him I view.

2 The way the holy prophets went,—
The road that leads from banishment,
The King's highway of holiness,
I'll go, for all his paths are peace.

3 This is the way I long had sought,
And mourned because I found it not;
My grief, my burden, long have been
Because I could not cease from sin.

4 The more I strove against their power,
I sinned and stumbled but the more;
Till late I heard my Saviour say,
"Come hither, soul, for I'm the Way!"

5 Lo! glad I come, and thou, blest Lamb,
Shalt take me to thee, as I am:
Nothing but sin I thee can give;
Nothing but love shall I receive.

6 I'll tell to all poor sinners round
What a dear Saviour I have found;
I'll point to thy redeeming blood,
And say, "Behold the way to God!"

CENNICK.

709 7s & 6s.

1 OH, who'll stand up for Jesus,
The lowly Nazarene?
And raise the blood-stained banner,
Amid the hosts of sin?

2 Oh, who will follow Jesus,
Amid reproach and shame?
Where others shrink and falter,
Who'll glory in his name?

3 My all to Christ I've given,
My talents, time, and voice,
Myself, my reputation,
The lone way is my choice.

4 O Jesus, precious Saviour,
My all-sufficient Friend!
Come, fold me to thy bosom,
E'en to the journey's end.

HARTSOUGH.

Chorus.

The Cross for Christ I'll cherish,
Its crucifixion bear;
All hail! reproach or sorrow,
If Jesus leads me there.

710 — 7s & 6s.

1 ASHAMED to be a Christian,
Afraid the world should know
I'm on the way to Zion,
Where joys eternal flow!
Forbid it, blessèd Saviour,
That I should ever be
Afraid the cross to cherish,
Or blush to follow thee.

2 Ashamed to be a Christian,
To love my God and King!
The fire of zeal is burning,
My soul is on the wing.
I want a faith made perfect,
That all the world may see,
I stand a living witness,
Of mercy, rich and free.

711 — 7s & 6s.

1 O LORD, thy heavenly grace impart,
And fix my frail, inconstant heart;
Henceforth my chief desire shall be,
To dedicate myself to thee.

2 Whate'er pursuits my time employ,
One thought shall fill my soul with joy;
That silent, secret thought shall be,
That all my hopes are fixed on thee.

3 Renouncing every worldly thing,
And safe beneath thy spreading wing,
My sweetest thought henceforth shall be,
That all I want I find in thee.

J. F. OBERLIN.

712 — L. M.

1 JESUS! and shall it ever be,
A mortal man ashamed of thee!
Ashamed of thee, whom angels praise,
Whose glories shine through endless days!

2 Asham'd of Jesus! sooner far
Let evening blush to own a star:
He sheds the beams of light divine
O'er this benighted soul of mine.

3 Asham'd of Jesus!—just as soon
Let midnight be asham'd of noon:
'Tis midnight with my soul, till he,
Bright morning Star, bid darkness flee.

4 Asham'd of Jesus!—that dear Friend
On whom my hopes of heav'n depend?
No! when I blush, be this my shame,
That I no more revere his name.

5 Asham'd of Jesus!—yes, I may,
When I've no guilt to wash away;
No tear to wipe; no good to crave;
No fear to quell—no soul to save.

6 Till then—nor is my boasting vain—
Till then I boast a Saviour slain!
And oh, may this my glory be,
That Christ is not asham'd of me!

GREGG.

713 L. M.

1 HAIL, sov'reign love, that form'd the plan
To save rebellious, ruin'd man,
Hail, matchless, free, eternal grace,
That gave my soul a hiding-place.

2 Against the God that rules the sky
I fought, with weapons lifted high;
I madly ran the sinful race,
Regardless of a hiding-place.

3 Yet when God's justice rose in view,
To Sinai's burning mount I flew;
Keen were the pangs of my distress,—
The mountain was no hiding-place.

4 But a celestial voice I heard,
A bleeding Saviour then appear'd,
Led by the Spirit of his grace,—
I found in him a hiding-place.

BREWER.

714 L. M.

1 THE wondering world inquires to know,
Why I should love my Jesus so:
"What are his charms," say they, "above
The objects of a mortal love?"

2 All human beauties, all divine,
In my belovéd meet and shine,
The fairest of ten thousand fairs,
A sun amongst ten thousand stars.

3 All over glorious is my Lord,
He is beloved and yet adored;
His worth, if all the nations knew,
Sure, the whole earth would love him too.

WATTS.

715 L. M.

1 OH, happy day that fixed my choice
On thee, my Saviour and my God!
Well may this glowing heart rejoice,
And tell its raptures all abroad.

2 Oh, happy bond, that seals my vows
To him who merits all my love!
Let cheerful anthems fill his house,
While to that sacred shrine I move.

3 'Tis done; the great transaction 's done;
I am my Lord's, and he is mine;
He drew me, and I followed on,
Charmed to confess the voice divine.

4 Now rest, my long-divided heart!
Fixed on this blissful centre, rest;
Here have I found a nobler part,
Here heavenly pleasures fill my breast.

DODDRIDGE.

Chorus.

Happy day, happy day,
When Jesus wash'd my sins away!
He taught me how to watch and pray,
And live rejoicing every day.

716 C. M.

1 YE valiant soldiers of the cross,
Ye happy, praying band,
Though in this world ye suffer loss,
You'll reach fair Canaan's land.

2 All earthly pleasures we'll forsake,
When heaven appears in view,
In Jesus' strength we'll undertake
To fight our passage through.

3 Oh, what a glorious shout there'll be,
When we arrive at home!
Our friends and Jesus we shall see,
And God shall say "Well done."

Chorus.

Let us never mind the scoffs nor the frowns of the world,
For we all have the cross to bear;
It will only make the crown the brighter to shine,
When we have the crown to wear.

717 C. M.

1 MUST Jesus bear the cross alone,
And all the world go free?
No, there's a cross for every one,
And there's a cross for me.

2 The consecrated cross I'll bear,
Till death shall set me free;
And then go home my crown to wear,
For there's a crown for me.

3 How happy are the saints above,
Who once went sorrowing here!
But now they taste unmingled love,
And joy without a tear.

4 Upon the crystal pavement, down
At Jesus' piercèd feet,
Joyful I'll cast my golden crown,
And his dear name repeat.

5 And palms shall wave, and harps shall ring,
Beneath heaven's arches high;
The Lord that lives, the ransomed sing,
That lives, no more to die.

6 Oh, precious cross! oh, glorious crown!
Oh, resurrection day!
Ye angels, from the stars flash down,
And bear my soul away.

ALLEN.

718 C. M.

1 THE Saviour, by whose name I'm called,
Will grant me strength within,
To own his name before the world,
And fight the fight with sin.

2 So will I sing, oh blessèd be
The Lord who is my Strength!
The weakest child who calls on thee,
Shall overcome at length.

3 The swift may stumble in the race,
The strong in battle fail;
But they who ever seek thy face,
Shall in thy might prevail.

4 And oh, when on each brow shall shine
Thy gift, a fadeless crown,
What joy to own the glory thine,
And lowly cast it down.

719 C. M.

1 MY God, accept my heart this day,
And make it always thine;
That I from thee no more may stray,
No more from thee decline.

2 Before the cross of him who died,
Behold, I prostrate fall;
Let every sin be crucified,
Let Christ be all in all.

3 May the dear blood, once shed for me,
My blest atonement prove;
That I, from first to last, may be
The purchase of thy love.

4 Let every thought and work and word
To thee be ever given;
Then life shall be thy service, Lord,
And death the gate of heaven!

LYRA CATH.

720 C. M.

1 AM I a soldier of the cross,
A follower of the Lamb?
And shall I fear to own his cause,
Or blush to speak his name?

2 Must I be carried to the skies
On flowery beds of ease,
While others fought to win the prize,
And sailed through bloody seas?

3 Are there no foes for me to face?
Must I not stem the flood?
Is this vile world a friend to grace,
To help me on to God?

4 Sure I must fight, if I would reign;
Increase my courage, Lord:
I'll bear the toil, endure the pain,
Supported by thy word.

5 Thy saints in all this glorious war
Shall conquer, though they die;
They see the triumph from afar,
And seize it with their eye.

6 When that illustrious day shall rise,
And all thy armies shine
In robes of victory through the skies,
The glory shall be thine.

WATTS.

721 C. M.

1 WITNESS, ye men and angels now,
Before the Lord we speak;
To him we make our solemn vow,
A vow we dare not break:

2 That, long as life itself shall last,
Ourselves to Christ we yield;
Nor from this cause will we depart,
Or ever quit the field.

3 We trust not in our native strength,
But on his grace rely,
That, with returning wants, the Lord
Will all our need supply.

4 Oh, guide our doubtful feet aright,
And keep us in thy ways;
And while we turn our vows to prayers,
Turn thou our prayers to praise.

BEDDOME.

722 C. M.

1 I'M not ashamed to own my Lord,
Or to defend his cause;
Maintain the honor of his word,
The glory of his cross.

2 Jesus, my God!—I know his name—
His name is all my trust;
Nor will he put my soul to shame,
Nor let my hope be lost.

3 Firm as his throne, his promise stands,
And he can well secure
What I've committed to his hands,
Till the decisive hour.

4 Then will he own my worthless name,
Before his Father's face,
And in the new Jerusalem
Appoint my soul a place. WATTS.

723 S. M. D.

1 I WAS a wandering sheep,
I did not love the fold,
I did not love my Shepherd's voice,
I would not be controlled:
I was a wayward child,
I did not love my home,
I did not love my Father's voice,
I loved afar to roam.

2 The Shepherd sought his sheep,
The Father sought his child;
He followed me o'er vale and hill,
O'er deserts waste and wild:
He found me nigh to death,
Famished, and faint, and lone;
He bound me with the bands of love,
He saved the wandering one.

3 Jesus my Shepherd is;
'Twas he that loved my soul,
'Twas he that washed me in his blood,
'Twas he that made me whole:
'Twas he that sought the lost,
That found the wandering sheep;
'Twas he that brought me to the fold,
'Tis he that still doth keep.

4 No more a wandering sheep,
I love to be controlled,
I love my tender Shepherd's voice,
I love the peaceful fold:
No more a wayward child,
I seek no more to roam;
I love my heavenly Father's voice,
I love, I love his home! BONAR.

724 S. M. D.

1 I WAS a foe to God,
I fought in Satan's host,
I trifled all his grace away,
Alas! my soul was lost:
Yet God forgets my sin;
His heart, with pity moved,
He gives me, Son of God, to thee;
Lo, thus our God hath loved!

2 Once, blind with sin and self,
Along the treacherous way
That ends in ruin at the last,
I hastened far astray:
Then God sent down his Son;
For with a love most deep,
Most undeserved, his heart still yearned
O'er me, poor wandering sheep!

3 God with his life of love
To me was far and strange;
My heart clung only to the world
Of sight, and sense, and change:
In thee, Immanuel,
Are God and man made one;
In thee my heart hath peace with God,
And union in the Son.

725 8s & 7s.

1 "MERCY, O thou Son of David!"
Thus blind Bartimeus prayed;
"Others by thy word are saved,
Now to me afford thine aid."

2 Many for his crying chid him,
But he called the louder still;
Till the gracious Saviour bade him,
"Come, and ask me what you will."

3 Money was not what he wanted,
Though by begging used to live;
But he ask'd, and Jesus granted
Alms which none but he could give.

4 "Lord, remove this grievous blindness,
Let my eyes behold the day!"
Straight he saw, and won by kindness,
Follow'd Jesus in the way.

5 Now, methinks I hear him praising,
Publishing to all around:
"Friends, is not my case amazing?
What a Saviour I have found!

6 "Oh, that all the blind but knew him,
And would be advised by me!
Surely they would hasten to him,
He would cause them all to see."

NEWTON.

726

8s, 7s & 4s.

1 WELCOME, welcome, dear Redeemer,
Welcome to this heart of mine;
Lord, I make a full surrender,
Every power and thought be thine;
Thine entirely,
Through eternal ages, thine.

2 Known to all to be thy mansion,
Earth and hell will disappear;
Or in vain attempt possession,
When they find the Lord is near—
Shout, O Zion!
Shout, ye saints, the Lord is here!

727

7s. D.

1 PEOPLE of the living God,
I have sought the world around,
Paths of sin and sorrow trod,
Peace and comfort nowhere found.
Now to you my spirit turns,
Turns, a fugitive unblest;
Brethren, where your altar burns,
Oh receive me into rest!

2 Lonely I no longer roam,
Like the cloud, the wind, the wave;
Where you dwell shall be my home,
Where you die shall be my grave;
Mine the God whom you adore,
Your Redeemer shall be mine
Earth can fill my heart no more,
Every idol I resign.

3 Tell me not of gain or loss,
Ease, enjoyment, pomp, and power;
Welcome poverty and cross,
Shame, reproach, affliction's hour:
"Follow me!"—I know the voice;
Jesus, Lord, thy steps I see;
Now I take thy yoke by choice,
Light thy burden now to me.

MONTGOMERY.

728

7s. D.

1 HARK! my soul! it is the Lord;
'Tis thy Saviour—hear his word;
Jesus speaks, and speaks to thee
"Say, poor sinner, lovest thou me?
I delivered thee when bound,
And when bleeding, healed thy wound:
Sought thee wandering, set thee right,
Turned thy darkness into light.

2 "Can a woman's tender care
Cease toward the child she bare?
Yes, she may forgetful be,
Yet will I remember thee.

Mine is an unchanging love,
Higher than the heights above;
Deeper than the depths beneath—
Free and faithful—strong as death.

3 "Thou shalt see my glory soon,
When the work of grace is done;
Partner of my throne shalt be!
Say, poor sinner! lovest thou me?"
Lord! it is my chief complaint,
That my love is weak and faint;
Yet I love thee, and adore;—
Oh! for grace to love thee more.

COWPER.

THE CHURCH.

729 11s.

1 O THOU who in Jordan didst bow thy meek head,
And whelmed in our sorrow, didst sink to the dead,
Then rose from the darkness to glory above,
And claimed for thy chosen the kingdom of love.

2 Thy footsteps we follow, to bow in the tide,
And are buried with thee in the death thou hast died,
Then wake with thy likeness to walk in the way
That brightens and brightens to shadowless day.

3 O Jesus, our Saviour, O Jesus, our Lord!
By the life of thy passion, the grace of thy word,
Accept us, redeem us, dwell ever within,
To keep, by thy Spirit, our spirits from sin.

4 Till crowned with thy glory, and waving the palm,
Our garments all white from the blood of the Lamb,
We join the bright millions of saints gone before,
And bless thee, and wonder, and praise evermore.

GEO. W. BETHUNE.

730 7s & 6s.

1 AROUND thy grave, Lord Jesus,
Thine empty grave we stand,
With hearts all full of praises,
To keep thy blest command.
By faith our souls rejoicing,
To trace thy path of love,
Thro' death's dark, angry billows,
Up to the Throne above.

2 Lord Jesus, we remember
The travail of thy soul,
When, in thy love's deep pity,
The waves did o'er thee roll.
Baptized in death's cold waters,
For us thy blood was shed;
For us the Lord of Glory
Was numbered with the dead.

3 O Lord, thou now art risen,
Thy travail all is o'er,
For sin thou once hast suffered,
Thou liv'st to die no more;
Sin, death and hell are vanquished
By thee, thy church's Head;
And lo! we share thy triumph,
Thou First Born from the dead!

J. G. Deck.

731 H. M.

1 DESCEND, celestial Dove,
And make thy presence known;
Reveal our Saviour's love,
And seal us for thine own:
Unblest by thee, our works are vain;
Nor can we e'er acceptance gain.

2 When our incarnate God,
The sovereign Prince of light,
In Jordan's swelling flood
Received the holy rite,
In open view thy form came down,
And, dove-like, flew the King to crown.

3 Continue still to shine,
And fill us with thy fire:
This ordinance is thine;
Do thou our souls inspire:
Thou wilt attend on all thy sons:
"Till time shall end," thy promise runs.

Fellows.

732 7s. D.

1 CHRIST, who came my soul to save,
Entered Jordan's yielding wave,
Rose from out the crystal flood,
Owned and sealed the Son of God,
By the Father's voice of love,
By the heaven-descending Dove;
Saviour, Pattern, Guide for me,
I, like him, baptized would be.

2 In the Garden, o'er his soul
Sorrow's whelming waves did roll;
Ah! on Calvary's cruel tree,
Jesus bowed in death for me.
I with him am crucified:
All my hope is—he hath died:
At his feet my place I take,
Bear the cross for his dear sake.

3 In the new-made tomb he lay,
Taking all its dread away;
Burst he through its rock-bound door,
Glorious now, and evermore.
I with Christ would buried be
In this rite required of me—
Rising from the mystic flood,
Living hence anew to God.

S. D. Phelps.

733 8s, 7s & 4s.

1 THOU hast said, exalted Jesus,
"Take thy cross, and follow me;"
Shall the word with terror seize us?
Shall we from the burden flee?
Lord, I'll take it,
And, rejoicing, follow thee.

2 While this liquid tomb surveying,
Emblem of my Saviour's grave,
Shall I shun its brink, betraying
Feelings worthy of a slave?
No! I'll enter:
Jesus entered Jordan's wave.

3 Sweet the sign that thus reminds me,
Saviour, of thy love for me;
Sweeter still the love that binds me
In its deathless bonds to thee:
Oh, what pleasure,
Buried with my Lord to be!

4 Should it rend some fond connection,
Should I suffer shame or loss,
Yet the fragrant, blest reflection,
I have been where Jesus was,
Will revive me
When I faint beneath the cross.

5 Fellowship with him possessing,
Let me die to all around,
So I rise to enjoy the blessing,
Kept for those in Jesus found,
When the archangel
Wakes the sleepers under ground.

6 Then, baptized in love and glory,
Lamb of God, thy praise I'll sing;
Loudly, with the immortal story,
All the harps of heaven shall ring:
Saints and seraphs
Sound it loud from every string.

JOHN E. GILES.

734 8s, 7s & 4s.

1 JESUS, mighty King in Zion,
Thou alone our Guide shall be;
Thy commission we rely on;
We would follow none but thee.

2 As an emblem of thy passion,
And thy victory o'er the grave,
We, who know thy great salvation,
Are baptized beneath the wave.

3 Fearless of the world's despising,
We the ancient path pursue,
Buried with our Lord, and rising
To a life divinely new.

JOHN FELLOWS.

735 8s, 7s & 4s.

1 LORD, in humble, sweet submission,
Here we meet to follow thee:
Trusting in thy great salvation,
Which alone can make us free.

2 Nought have we to claim as merit;
All the duties we can do
Can no crown of life inherit:
All the praise to thee is due.

3 Yet we come in Christian duty,
Down beneath the wave to go;
Oh the bliss! the heavenly beauty!
Christ the Lord was buried so.

ROBERT T. DANIEL.

736 L. M.

1 COME, happy souls, adore the Lamb,
Who loved our race ere time began!
Who veiled his Godhead in our clay,
And in an humble manger lay.

2 To Jordan's stream the Spirit led,
To mark the path his saints should tread;
Joyful they trace the sacred way,
To see the place where Jesus lay.

3 Immersed by John in Jordan's wave,
The Saviour left his watery grave;
Heaven owned the deed, approved the way,
And blessed the place where Jesus lay.

4 Come, all who love his precious name,
Come, tread his steps and learn of him:
Happy beyond expression they,
Who find the place where Jesus lay.

BALDWIN.

737 L. M.

1 COME, Holy Spirit, Dove divine,
On these baptismal waters shine,
And teach our hearts, in highest strain,
To praise the Lamb, for sinners slain.

2 We love thy name, we love thy laws,
And joyfully embrace thy cause;
We love thy cross, the shame, the pain,
O Lamb of God, for sinners slain.

3 We sink beneath thy mystic flood;
Oh, bathe us in thy cleansing blood!
We die to sin, and seek a grave,
With thee, beneath the yielding wave.

4 And as we rise, with thee to live,
Oh, let the Holy Spirit give
The sealing unction from above,
The breath of life, the fire of love!

JUDSON.

738 L. M.

1 GREAT God, we in thy courts appear,
With humble joy and holy fear,
Thy wise injunctions to obey;
Let saints and angels hail the day!

2 Great things, O everlasting Son,
Great things for us thy grace hath done;
Constrain'd by thy almighty love,
Our willing feet to meet thee move.

3 In thy assembly here we stand,
Obedient to thy great command;
The sacred flood is full in view,
And thy sweet voice invites us through.

4 The Word, the Spirit, and the Bride,
Must not invite and be denied;
Was not the Lord, who came to save,
Interr'd in such a liquid grave?

5 Thus we, dear Saviour, own thy name,
Receive us rising from the stream;
Then to thy table let us come,
And dwell in Zion as our home.

FELLOWS.

739 L. M.

1 OUR Saviour bowed beneath the wave,
And meekly sought a watery grave;
Come, see the sacred path he trod—
A path well-pleasing to our God.

2 His voice we hear, his footsteps trace,
And hither come to seek his face,
To do his will, to feel his love,
And join our songs with those above.

3 Hosanna to the Lamb divine!
Let endless glories round him shine;
High o'er the heavens forever reign,
O Lamb of God, for sinners slain.

JUDSON.

740 L. M.

1 O FATHER, Lord of earth and heaven,
O Son incarnate, Christ our King,
O Spirit for our guidance given,
Hear and accept the vow we bring!

2 Thy gospel now we would obey;
We follow, and thy hand shall guide;
We seek through Jordan's wave the way
That leads thy loved ones to thy side.

3 With faith upon thy name we come,
The Spirit's cleansing power confess:
Bend, Saviour, from thy heavenly home,
And seal the covenant of thy grace!

4 Thy bright example marks our way
To thy immersion—wondrous sign!
We come, O Lord, and humbly pray,
That we may be forever thine.

J. W. Willmarth.

741 L. M.

1 BLEST Saviour, we thy will obey:
Not of constraint, but with delight,
Thy servants hither come to-day,
To honor thine appointed rite.

2 Descend, descend, celestial Dove,
On these dear followers of the Lord;
Exalted Head of all the church,
Thy promised aid to them afford.

3 Let faith, assisted now by signs,
The wonders of thy love explore;
And, washed in thy redeeming blood,
Let them depart, and sin no more.

Beddome.

742 L. M.

HOW blest the hour when first we gave
Our guilty souls to thee, O God;
A cheerful sacrifice of love,
Bought with the Saviour's precious blood.

2 How blest the vow we here record!
How blest the grace we now receive!
Buried in baptism with our Lord,
New lives of holiness to live.

3 How blest the solemn rite that seals
Our death to sin, our guilt forgiven;—
How blest the emblem that reveals
God reconciled, and peace with heaven.

4 Thus through the emblematic grave
The glorious, suffering Saviour trod;
Thou art our pattern, through the wave
We follow thee, blest Son of God.

S. F. Smith.

743 C. M.

1 IN all my Lord's appointed ways
My journey I'll pursue;
"Hinder me not," ye much-loved saints,
For I must go with you.

2 Through floods and flames, if Jesus lead,
I'll follow where he goes;
"Hinder me not," shall be my cry,
Though earth and hell oppose.

3 Through duties, and through trials too,
I'll go at his command;
"Hinder me not;" for I am bound
To my Immanuel's land.

4 And, when my Saviour calls me home,
Still this my cry shall be,—
"Hinder me not," come, welcome, death;
I'll gladly go with thee.

J. Ryland.

744 C. M.

1 BURIED beneath the yielding wave
The great Redeemer lies;
Faith views him in the watery grave,
And thence beholds him rise.

2 Thus do his willing saints, to-day,
Their ardent zeal express,
And, in the Lord's appointed way,
Fulfill all righteousness.

3 With joy we in his footsteps tread,
And would his cause maintain,—
Like him be numbered with the dead,
And with him rise and reign.

BEDDOME.

745 C. M.

1 WHILE in this sacred rite of thine,
We yield our spirits now,
Shine o'er the waters, Dove divine,
And seal the cheerful vow.

2 All glory be to him whose life
For ours was freely given,
Who aids us in the spirit's strife,
And makes us meet for heaven.

3 To thee we gladly now resign
Our life and all our powers;
Accept us in this rite divine,
And bless these hallowed hours.

4 Oh, may we die to earth and sin,
Beneath the mystic flood!
And when we rise, may we begin
To live anew for God.

S. F. SMITH.

746 C. M.

1 DEAR Lord, and will thy pardoning love
Embrace a wretch so vile?
Wilt thou my load of guilt remove,
And bless me with thy smile?

2 Hast thou the cross for me endured,
And all its shame despised?
And shall I be ashamed, O Lord,
With thee to be baptized?

3 Didst thou the great example lead,
In Jordan's swelling flood?
And shall my pride disdain the deed
That's worthy of my God?

4 O Lord, the ardor of thy love
Reproves my cold delays;
And now my willing footsteps move
In thy delightful ways.

FELLOWS.

747 C. M.

1 TO Jordan's stream the Saviour goes,
To do his Father's will;
His breast with sacred ardor glows,
Each precept to fulfill.

2 Behold him buried in the flood,
The emblem of his grave,
Who, from the bosom of his God,
Came down a world to save.

3 As from the water he ascends,
What miracles appear!
God, with a voice, his Son commends!
Let all the nations hear.

4 Hear it, ye Christians, and rejoice;
Let this your courage raise;
What God approves, be this your choice,
And glory in his ways.

748 C. M.

1 'TIS God the Father we adore
In this baptismal sign;
'Tis he whose voice on Jordan's shore
Proclaimed the Son divine.

2 The Father owned him; let our breath
In answering praise ascend,
As in the image of his death
We own our heavenly Friend.

3 We seek the consecrated grave
Along the path he trod:
Receive us in the hallowed wave,
Thou holy Son of God.

4 Let earth and heaven our zeal record,
And future witness bear
That we to Zion's mighty Lord
Our full allegiance swear.

SAFFERY.

749 C. M.

1 O LORD, we in thy footsteps tread,
With joy thy cause maintain;
Like Jesus numbered with the dead,
Like him we rise and reign.

2 Down to the hallowed grave we go,
Obedient to thy word;
'Tis thus the world around shall know
We're buried with the Lord.

3 'Tis thus we bid its pomps adieu,
And boldly venture in:
Oh, may we rise to live anew,
And only die to sin!

ENG. BAP. COLL.

750 C. M.

1 HOW calmly wakes the hallowed morn!
How tranquil earth's repose!—
Meet emblem of the Sabbath morn,
When, early, Jesus rose.

2 How fair, along the rippling wave,
The radiant light is cast!—
A symbol of the mystic grave
Through which the Saviour passed.

3 Around this scene of sacred love
The peace of heaven is shed:
So came the Spirit, like a dove,
To rest on Jesus' head.

4 Lord, meet us in this path of thine;
We come thy rite to seal;
Move o'er the waters, Dove divine,
And all thy grace reveal.

S. F. SMITH.

751 C. M.

1 MEEKLY in Jordan's holy stream
The great Redeemer bowed;
Bright was the glory's sacred beam
That hushed the wondering crowd.

2 Thus God descended to approve
The deed that Christ had done;
Thus came the emblematic Dove,
And hovered o'er the Son.

3 So, blessèd Spirit, come to-day
To our baptismal scene;
Let thoughts of earth be far away,
And every mind serene.

4 This day we give to holy joy;
This day to heaven belongs;
Raised to new life, we will employ
In melody our tongues.

S. F. SMITH.

752 C. M.

1 ALMIGHTY Saviour, here we stand,
Ranged by the water side;
Hither we come at thy command,
To wait upon thy bride.

2 Thy footsteps marked this humble way
For all that love thy cause;
Lord, thy example we obey,
And glory in the cross.

3 Our dearest Lord, we'll follow thee,
Where'er thou lead'st the way,
Through floods, through flames, through death's dark vale,
To realms of endless day.

753 C. M.

1 CONSTRAINED by love, we follow where
Our Saviour leads the way;
His blest example is our law,—
That law we love t' obey.

2 He as our pattern bowed his head
In Jordan's yielding wave,
We, in his footsteps, joyful tread,
We seek his liquid grave.

3 Come, Holy Spirit, Dove divine,
Thy grace to us be given:
To a new life our souls incline,
A life for God, and heaven.

S. F. SMITH.

754 C. M.

1 WITH Christ we share a mystic grave;
With Christ we buried lie;
But 'tis not in the darksome cave
By mournful Calvary.

2 The pure and bright baptismal flood—
The type of cleansing plain;
New creatures, from the yielding wave
With Christ we rise again.

3 Thrice blest, if, through this world of sin,
And lust, and selfish care,
Our resurrection-mantle white
And undefiled we wear.

4 Thrice blest, if, through the gate of death,
Glorious at last and free,
We to our joyful rising pass,
O Risen Lord, with thee.

J. M. NEALE.

755 C. M.

1 WE long to move and breathe in thee,
Inspired with thine own breath,
To live thy life, O Lord, and be
Baptized into thy death.

2 Thy death to sin we die below,
But we shall rise in love;
We here are planted in thy woe,
But we shall bloom above.

3 Above we shall thy glory share,
As we thy cross have borne;
E'en we shall crowns of honor wear,
When we the thorns have worn.

4 Thy crown of thorns is all our boast,
While now we fall before
The Father, Son, and Holy Ghost,
And tremble, love, adore.

756 C. M.

1 LORD, I am thine, and in thy aid
I place my firmest trust:
How large the price thy love has paid
For vile, polluted dust!

2 In thine assembly now I stand;
My vows to thee I bring,
Obedient to thy great command,
My Saviour and my King.

3 I stand before the sacred flood;
Thy gracious words invite:
How poor an offering, O my God,
I make thee in this rite!

4 Thine ordinance, great Saviour, bless;
Support me all my days;
May I each gospel truth confess,
And walk in all thy ways.

757 C. M.

1 WELCOME, O Saviour! to my heart;
Possess thine humble throne;
Bid every rival hence depart,
And claim me for thine own.

2 The world and Satan I forsake—
To thee, I all resign;
My longing heart, O Jesus! take,
And fill with love divine.

3 Oh! may I never turn aside,
Nor from thy bosom flee;
Let nothing here my heart divide—
I give it all to thee.

758 S. M.

1 OH what, if we are Christ's,
Is earthly shame or loss?
Bright shall the crown of glory be,
When we have borne the cross.

2 Keen was the trial once,
Bitter the cup of woe,
When martyred saints, baptized in blood,
Christ's sufferings shared below.

3 Bright is their glory now,
Boundless their joy above,
Where, on the bosom of their God,
They rest in perfect love.

4 Lord! may that grace be ours;
Like them in faith to bear
All that of sorrow, grief, or pain
May be our portion here!

5 Enough, if thou at last
The word of blessing give,
And let us rest beneath thy feet,
Where saints and angels live!

6 All glory, Lord, to thee,
Whom heaven and earth adore;
To Father, Son, and Holy Ghost,
One God forevermore.

HENRY W. BAKER.

759 S. M.

1 TO sit at Jesus' feet
And listen all the day
To words of truth and grace, is sweet,
But sweeter to obey.

2 'Tis excellent to know,
But oh! diviner still,
To do what God enjoins, and so
All righteousness fulfill.

3 The least of his commands
In any wise to break,
Is like the attempts of impious hands
His very throne to shake.

4 Without defect or flaw,
Fit, holy, just, and good,
We may not change in aught his law,
Nor would we if we could.

5 The time this rite was done
To speak the Father seized;—
"Lo! this is my Beloved Son
In whom I am well pleased."

6 The buried Christ arose:
So here, in figure plain,
O'er our dead selves the waters close;
We die, but live again.

A. Coles.

760 S. M.

1 WITH willing hearts we tread
The path the Saviour trod;
We love th' example of our Head,
The glorious Lamb of God.

2 On thee, on thee alone,
Our hope and faith rely,
O thou who didst for sin atone,
Who didst for sinners die.

3 We trust thy sacrifice;
To thy dear cross we flee:
Oh, may we die to sin, and rise
To life and bliss in thee.

761 S. M.

1 DOWN to the sacred wave
The Lord of life was led:
And he who came our souls to save
In Jordan bowed his head.

2 He taught the solemn way;
He fixed the holy rite;
He bade his ransomed ones obey,
And keep the path of light.

3 Blest Saviour, we will tread
In thy appointed way;
Let glory o'er these scenes be shed,
And smile on us to-day.

S. F. Smith.

762 S. M.

1 CHOOSE ye his cross to bear,
Who bowed to Jordan's wave?—
Clad in his armor will ye dare
In faith, a watery grave?

2 All hail! ye blessèd band,
Shrink not to do his will;
In deep humility, this work
Of righteousness fulfill;—

3 Tread in his steps,—with prayer,
Invoke his Spirit free,
And as he burst the gates of death,
So may your rising be.

L. H. Sigourney.

763 S. M.

1 HERE, Saviour, we do come,
In thine appointed way;
Obedient to thy high commands,
Our solemn vows we pay.

2 Oh, bless this sacred rite,
To bring us near to thee!
And may we find that as our day
Our strength shall also be.

Eng. Bap. Coll.

764 S. M.

1 SAVIOUR, thy law we love,
Thy pure example bless,
And, with a firm, unwavering zeal,
Would in thy footsteps press.

2 Not to the fiery pains
By which the martyrs bled;

Not to the scourge, the thorn, the cross,
Our favored feet are led:

3 But, at this peaceful tide,
Assembled in thy fear,
The homage of obedient hearts
We humbly offer here.

L. H. SIGOURNEY.

765 L. M.

1 HOW blest the sacred tie that binds
In union sweet, according minds!
How swift the heavenly course they run,
Whose hearts, whose faith, whose hopes are one.

2 To each, the soul of each how dear!
What watchful love, what holy fear!
How doth the gen'rous flame within
Refine from earth, and cleanse from sin!

3 Their streaming eyes together flow
For human guilt and mortal woe;
Their ardent prayers together rise,
Like mingling flames in sacrifice.

4 Nor shall the glowing flame expire
'Midst nature's drooping, sick'ning fire:
Soon shall they meet in realms above,
A heaven of joy, a heaven of love.

MRS. BARBAULD.

766 L. M.

1 COME in, thou blessèd of our God,
In Jesus' name we bid thee come;
No more thy feet shall roam abroad,
Henceforth a brother,—welcome home.

2 Those joys which earth can not afford,
We'll seek in fellowship to prove,
Joined in one spirit to our Lord,
Together bound by mutual love.

3 And while we pass this vale of tears,
We'll make our joys and sorrows known;
We'll share each other's hopes and fears,
And count a brother's cares our own.

4 Once more our welcome we repeat;
Receive assurance of our love;
Oh may we all together meet
Around the throne of God above!

KELLY.

767 L. M.

1 KINDRED in Christ! for his dear sake
A hearty welcome here receive;
May we together now partake
The joys which only he can give.

2 May he, by whose kind care we meet,
Send his good Spirit from above;
Make our communications sweet,
And cause our hearts to burn with love.

3 Forgotten be each worldly theme,
When Christians meet together thus;
We only wish to speak of him,
Who lived, and died, and reigns, for us.

4 We'll talk of all he did and said,
And suffered for us here below;—
The path he marked for us to tread,
And what he's doing for us now.

5 Thus,—as the moments pass away,—
We'll love, and wonder, and adore,
And hasten to the glorious day
When we shall meet to part no more.

NEWTON.

768 C. M.

1 OUR souls, by love together knit,
Cemented, mixed in one;
One hope, one heart, one mind, one voice,
'Tis heaven on earth begun.

2 Our hearts have often burned within,
And glowed with sacred fire,
While Jesus spoke, and fed, and blessed,
And filled the enlarged desire.

3 The little cloud increases still,
The heavens are big with rain;
We haste to catch the teeming shower,
And all its moisture drain.

4 A rill, a stream, a torrent flows!
But pour a mighty flood;
Oh sweep the nations, shake the earth,
Till all proclaim thee, God!

5 And when thou mak'st thy jewels up,
And sett'st thy starry crown;
When all thy sparkling gems shall shine,
Proclaimed by thee thine own:

6 May we, a little band of love,
We, sinners saved by grace,
From glory unto glory changed,
Behold thee face to face!

MILLER.

769 C. M.

1 COME, let us join our friends above,
Who have obtained the prize,
And on the eagle wings of love
To joy celestial rise.

2 Let saints below in concert sing
With those to glory gone;
For all the servants of our King
In heaven and earth are one.

3 One family, we dwell in him;
One church above, beneath;
Though now divided by the stream—
The narrow stream—of death.

4 One army of the living God,
To his command we bow;
Part of the host have crossed the flood,
And part are crossing now.

5 Ten thousand to their endless home
This solemn moment fly:
And we are to the margin come,
And we expect to die.

6 E'en now, by faith, we join our hands
With those that went before,
And greet the blood-besprinkled bands
On the eternal shore.

7 Oh! that we now might grasp our Guide,
Oh! that the word were given!
Come, Lord of hosts, the waves divide,
And land us all in heaven.

C. WESLEY.

770 C. M.

1 HOW sweet, how heavenly is the sight,
When those who love the Lord
In one another's peace delight,
And so fulfil his word:

2 When each can feel his brother's sigh,
And with him bear a part;
When sorrow flows from eye to eye,
And joy from heart to heart.

3 When, free from envy, scorn and pride,
Our wishes all above,
Each can his brother's failings hide,
And show a brother's love!

4 Let love in one delightful stream
Through every bosom flow,
And union sweet, and dear esteem,
In every action glow.

5 Love is the golden chain that binds
The happy souls above;
And he's an heir of heaven who finds
His bosom glow with love.

SWAIN.

771 C. M.

1 HAPPY the souls to Jesus joined,
And saved by grace alone:
Walking in all his ways, they find
Their heaven on earth begun.

2 The church triumphant in thy love,—
Their mighty joys we know:
They sing the Lamb in hymns above,
And we in hymns below.

3 Thee, in thy glorious realm, they praise,
And bow before thy throne:
We in the kingdom of thy grace;—
The kingdoms are but one.

4 The holy to the holiest leads;
From thence our spirits rise:
And he that in thy statutes treads
Shall meet thee in the skies.

C. WESLEY.

772 C. M.

1 HAIL, sweetest, dearest tie, that binds
Our glowing hearts in one;
Hail, sacred hope, that tunes our minds
To harmony divine.

2 What though the northern wint'ry blast
Shall howl around our cot;
What though beneath an eastern sun
Be cast our distant lot:

3 No lingering look, no parting sigh,
Our future meeting knows;
There friendship beams from every eye,
And love immortal glows.

4 O sacred hope! O blissful hope!
Which Jesus' grace has given—
The hope, when days and years are past,
We all shall meet in heaven.

SUTTON.

773 C. M.

1 COME in, thou blessèd of the Lord,
Stranger nor foe art thou:
We welcome thee with warm accord,
Our friend, our brother, now.

2 The hand of fellowship, the heart
Of love, we offer thee:
Leaving the world, thou dost but part
From lies and vanity.

3 Come with us,—we will do thee good,
As God to us hath done;
Stand but in him, as those have stood
Whose faith the victory won.

4 And when, by turns, we pass away,
As star by star grows dim,
May each, translated into day,
Be lost and found in him.

MONTGOMERY.

774 C. M.

1 LORD, thou on earth didst love thine own,
Didst love them to the end;
Oh, still from thy celestial throne,
Let gifts of love descend!

2 The love the Father bears to thee,
His own eternal Son,
Fill all thy saints, till all shall be
In pure affection one.

3 One blessèd fellowship of love,
Thy living church should stand,
Till, faultless, she at last above
Shall shine at thy right hand.

4 Oh, glorious day, when she, the Bride,
With her dear Lord appears!
Then, robed in beauty at his side,
She shall forget her tears.

RAY PALMER.

775 C. M.

1 BLESS'D be the dear, uniting love,
That will not let us part;
Our bodies may far off remove—
We still are one in heart.

2 Joined in one Spirit to our Head,
Where he appoints, we go;
And still in Jesus' footsteps tread,
And show his praise below.

3 Partakers of the Saviour's grace,
The same in mind and heart—
Nor joy, nor grief, nor time, nor place,
Nor life, nor death, can part.

4 But let us hasten to the day
Which shall our flesh restore,
When death shall all be done away,
And we shall part no more.

C. WESLEY.

776 C. M.

1 BENEATH the shadow of the Cross,
As earthly hopes remove,
His new commandment Jesus gives,
His blessèd word of Love.

2 Oh, bond of union strong and deep!
Oh, bond of perfect peace!
Not e'en the lifted cross can harm,
If we but hold to this.

3 Then, Jesus, be thy Spirit ours!
And swift our feet shall move
To deeds of pure self-sacrifice,
And the sweet tasks of love.

LONGFELLOW.

777 8s.

1 FROM whence doth this union arise,
That hatred is conquered by love?
That fastens our souls in such ties
As nature and time can't remove?

2 It cannot in Eden be found,
Nor yet in a paradise lost;
It grows on Immanuel's ground,
And Jesus' rich blood it did cost.

3 My friends are so dear unto me,
Our hearts are united in love:
Where Jesus is gone we shall be,
In yonder blest mansions above.

4 Then why so unwilling to part,
Since there we shall all meet again?
Engraved on Immanuel's heart,
At distance we cannot remain.

5 Oh, when shall we see that bright day,
And join with the angels above,
Set free from these prisons of clay,
United with Jesus in love!

6 With Jesus we ever shall reign,
And all his bright glories shall see!
And sing, Hallelujah! amen!
Amen! even so let it be.

DR. T. BALDWIN.

778 8s.

1 SAY, brothers, will you meet us,
Say, brothers, will you meet us,
Say, brothers, will you meet us,
On Canaan's happy shore?

2 By the grace of God we'll meet you,
By the grace of God we'll meet you,
By the grace of God we'll meet you,
Where parting is no more.

3 Jesus lives and reigns for ever,
Jesus lives and reigns for ever,
Jesus lives and reigns for ever,
On Canaan's happy shore.

Chorus.

Glory, glory, hallelujah,
Glory, glory, hallelujah,
Glory, glory, hallelujah,
For ever, evermore.

779 S. M.

1 BLEST be the tie that binds
Our hearts in Christian love:
The fellowship of kindred minds
Is like to that above.

2 Before our Father's throne
We pour our ardent prayers;
Our fears, our hopes, our aims are one,
Our comforts and our cares.

3 We share our mutual woes,
Our mutual burdens bear;
And often for each other flows
The sympathizing tear.

4 When we asunder part,
It gives us inward pain;
But we shall still be joined in heart,
And hope to meet again.

5 This glorious hope revives
Our courage by the way;
While each in expectation lives,
And longs to see the day.

6 From sorrow, toil, and pain,
And sin, we shall be free,
And perfect love and friendship reign
Through all eternity.

FAWCETT.

780 S. M.

1 AND are we yet alive
To see each other's face?
Glory and praise to Jesus give,
For his redeeming grace.

2 What troubles have we seen!
What conflicts have we past!
Fightings without, and fears within,
Since we assembled last!

3 But out of all, the Lord
Hath brought us by his love ;
And still he doth his help afford,
And hides our life above.

4 Then let us make our boast
Of his redeeming power,
Which saves us to the uttermost,
Till we can sin no more.

5 Let us take up the cross,
Till we the crown obtain ;
And gladly reckon all things loss,
So we may Jesus gain.

C. Wesley.

781 S. M.

1 ONCE more before we part,
Oh, bless the Saviour's name!
Let every tongue and every heart
Adore and praise the same.

2 Lord, in thy grace we came,
That blessing still impart ;
We meet in Jesus' sacred name,
In Jesus' name we part.

3 Still on thy holy word
We'll live, and feed, and grow,
And still go on to know the Lord,
And practice what we know.

4 Now, Lord, before we part,
Help us to bless thy name ;
Let every tongue and every heart
Adore and praise the same.

Hart.

782 P. M.

1 WHEN shall we meet again,
Meet ne'er to sever?
When will peace wreathe her chain
Round us forever?
Our hearts will ne'er repose,
Safe from each blast that blows,
In this dark vale of woes,
Never—no, never!

2 When shall love freely flow
Pure as life's river?
When shall sweet friendship glow
Changeless forever?
Where the joys celestial thrill,
Where bliss each heart shall fill,
And fears of parting chill
Never—no, never!

3 Up to that world of light
Take us, dear Saviour ;
May we all there unite,
Happy forever ;
Where kindred spirits dwell,
There may our music swell,
And time our joys dispel
Never—no, never!

4 Soon shall we meet again,
Meet ne'er to sever ;
Soon shall peace wreathe her chain
Round us forever ;
Our hearts will then repose
Secure from worldly woes ;
Our songs of praise shall close
Never—no, never!

783 L. M.

1 'TWAS on that dark, that doleful night,
When powers of earth and hell arose
Against the Son of God's delight,
And friends betrayed him to his foes.

2 Before the mournful scene began,
He took the bread, and blessed, and brake ;

What love through all his actions ran!
What wondrous words of grace he spake!

3 "This is my body, broke for sin;
Receive and eat the living food;"
Then took the cup, and blessed the wine;
"'Tis the new covenant in my blood."

4 "Do this," he cried, "till time shall end,
In memory of your dying Friend;
Meet at my table, and record
The love of your departed Lord."

5 Jesus, thy feast we celebrate;
We show thy death, we sing thy name,
Till thou return, and we shall eat
The marriage supper of the Lamb.

WATTS.

784 7s.

1 BREAD of heaven, on thee we feed,
For thy flesh is meat indeed;
Ever let our souls be fed
With this true and living bread!

2 Vine of heaven, thy blood supplies
This blest cup of sacrifice;
Lord, thy wounds our healing give,
To thy cross we look and live.

3 Day by day, with strength supplied
Through the life of him who died,
Lord of life, oh, let us be
Rooted, grafted, built in thee!

CONDER.

785 L. M.

1 O JESUS, bruis'd and wounded more
Than bursted grape, or bread of wheat,
The Life of life within our souls,
The cup of our salvation sweet!

2 We come to show thy dying hour,
Thy streaming vein, thy broken flesh;
And still that blood is warm to save,
And still thy fragrant wounds are fresh.

3 O Heart, that with a double tide
Of blood and water, maketh pure!
O Flesh, once offered on the cross,
The gift that makes our pardon sure!

4 Let nevermore our sinful souls
The anguish of thy cross renew;
Nor forge again the cruel nails
That pierced thy victim body through!

5 Come, Bread of heav'n, to feed our souls!
O blessèd Jesus, enter in!
Come, Wine of God! and as we drink
Thy precious blood, wash out our sin!

786 L. M.

1 AT thy command, our dearest Lord,
Here we attend thy dying feast;
Thy blood, like wine, adorns thy board,
And thine own flesh feeds every guest.

2 Our faith adores thy bleeding love,
And trusts for life in One that died;

We hope for heavenly crowns above
From a Redeemer crucified.

3 Let the vain world pronounce it shame,
And fling their scandals on the cause;
We come to boast our Saviour's name,
And make our triumphs in his cross.

4 With joy we tell the scoffing age,
He that was dead has left his tomb;
He lives above their utmost rage,
And we are waiting till he come.

WATTS.

787 L. M.

1 JESUS is gone above the skies,
Where our weak senses reach him not;
And carnal objects court our eyes,
To thrust our Saviour from our thought.

2 He knows what wandering hearts we have,
Apt to forget his lovely face;
And, to refresh our minds, he gave
These kind memorials of his grace.

3 Let sinful joys be all forgot,
And earth grow less in our esteem,
Christ and his love fill every thought,
And faith and hope be fixed on him.

4 While he is absent from our sight,
'Tis to prepare our souls a place,
That we may dwell in heavenly light,
And live forever near his face.

WATTS.

788 L. M.

1 O THOU, my soul, forget no more
The Friend who all thy sorrows bore;
Let every idol be forgot;
But, O my soul, forget him not.

2 Renounce thy works and ways, with grief,
And fly to this divine relief;
Nor him forget, who left his throne,
And for thy life gave up his own.

3 Eternal truth and mercy shine
In him, and he himself is thine:
And canst thou then, with sin beset,
Such charms, such matchless charms, forget?

4 Oh, no; till life itself depart,
His name shall cheer and warm my heart;
And, lisping this, from earth I'll rise,
And join the chorus of the skies.

KRISHNA PAL.

789 L. M.

1 DRAW near, O Holy Dove, draw near,
With peace and gladness on thy wing;
Reveal the Saviour's presence here,
And light, and life, and comfort bring.

2 "Eat, O my friends—drink, O beloved!"
We hear the Master's voice exclaim:
Our hearts with new desire are moved,
And kindled with a heavenly flame.

3 No room for doubt, no room for dread,
Nor tears, nor groans, nor anxious sighs;
We do not mourn a Saviour dead,
But hail him living in the skies!

A. R. W.

790 L. M.

1 AMIDST us our Belovèd stands,
And bids us view his piercèd hands;
Points to the wounded feet and side,
Blest emblems of the crucified.

2 What food luxurious loads the board,
When at his table sits the Lord!
The wine how rich, the bread how sweet,
When Jesus deigns the guests to meet.

3 If now, with eyes defiled and dim,
We see the signs, but see not him,
Oh may his love the scales displace,
And bid us see him face to face.

SPURGEON.

791 L. M.

1 MY God, and is thy table spread,
And doth thy cup with love o'erflow!
Thither be all thy children led,
And let them all thy sweetness know.

2 Hail, sacred feast, which Jesus makes,
Rich banquet of his Flesh and Blood!
Thrice happy he who here partakes
That sacred stream, that heavenly food.

3 Oh let thy table honored be,
And furnished well with joyful guests;
And may each soul salvation see,
That here its sacred pledges tastes.

DODDRIDGE.

792 L. M.

1 I FEED by faith on Christ; my bread,
His body broken on the tree;
I live in him, my living Head,
Who died, and rose again for me.

2 This be my joy and comfort here,
This pledge of future glory mine:
Jesus, in spirit now appear,
And break the bread, and pour the wine.

3 From thy dear hand, may I receive
The tokens of thy dying love,
And while I feast on earth, believe
That I shall feast with thee above.

MONTGOMERY.

793 L. M.

1 STILL one in life and one in death,
One in our hope of rest above,
One in our joy, our trust, our faith,
One in each other's faithful love;

2 Yet must we part, and parting weep;
What else has earth for us in store?
Our farewell pangs, how sharp and deep!
Our farewell words, how sad and sore!

3 Yet shall we meet again in peace,
To sing the song of festal joy,
Where none shall bid our gladness cease,
And none our fellowship destroy:

4 Where none shall beckon us away,
Nor bid our festival be done;

Our meeting-time the eternal day,
Our meeting-place the eternal throne.

5 There, hand in hand, firm-linked at last,
And heart to heart enfolded all,
We'll smile upon the troubled past,
And wonder why we wept at all.

BONAR.

794 C. M.

1 O GOD, unseen, yet ever near,
Thy presence may we feel;
And thus, inspired with holy fear,
Before thine altar kneel.

2 Here may thy faithful people know
The blessings of thy love;
The streams that through the desert flow,
The manna from above.

3 We come, obedient to thy word,
To feast on heavenly food;
Our meat, the body of the Lord,
Our drink, his precious blood.

OSLER.

795 C. M.

1 AROUND thy table, holy Lord,
In fellowship we meet;
Obedient to thy blest command,
This feast of love to eat.

2 By faith we take the bread of life,
With which our souls are fed;
And cup, in token of thy blood
That was for sinners shed.

3 Under thy banner thus we sing
The wonders of thy love,
While we anticipate by faith,
The heavenly feast above. COTTERILL.

796 C. M.

1 HOW sweet and awful is the place,
With Christ within the doors,
While everlasting love displays
The choicest of her stores!

2 While all our hearts, and all our songs,
Join to admire the feast,
Each of us cries, with thankful tongue,
"Lord, why was I a guest?"

3 "Why was I made to hear thy voice,
And enter while there's room,
When thousands make a wretched choice,
And rather starve than come?"

4 'Twas the same love that spread the feast,
That sweetly forced us in;
Else we had still refused to taste,
And perished in our sin.

5 Pity the nations, O our God!
Constrain the earth to come;
Send thy victorious word abroad,
And bring the strangers home.

WATTS.

797 C. M.

1 OPPREST with noon-day's scorching heat,
To yonder cross I flee;
Beneath its shelter take my seat:
No shade like this for me!

2 Beneath that cross clear waters burst—
A fountain sparkling free;
And there I quench my desert thirst:
No spring like this for me!

3 A stranger here, I pitch my tent
Beneath this spreading tree;

Here shall my pilgrim life be spent:
No home like this for me!

4 For burdened ones a resting-place,
Beside that cross I see;
I here cast off my weariness:
No rest like this for me!

BONAR.

798 C. M.

1 LORD, may the spirit of this feast—
The earnest of thy love—
Maintain a dwelling in our breast,
Until we meet above.

2 And if no more with kindred dear
The broken bread we share,
Nor at the banquet-board appear
To breathe the grateful prayer;—

3 Forget us not,—when on the bed
Of dire disease we waste,
Or to the chambers of the dead,
And bar of judgment haste.

4 Forget not,—thou who bore the woe
Of Calvary's fatal tree,—
Those who within these courts below
Have thus remembered thee.

SIGOURNEY.

799 C. M.

1 JESUS! thy love shall we forget,
And never bring to mind
The grace that paid our hopeless debt,
And bade us pardon find?

2 Shall we thy life of grief forget,
Thy fasting and thy prayer;
Thy locks with mountain vapors wet,
To save us from despair?

3 Gethsemane, can we forget—
Thy struggling agony—
When night lay dark on Olivet,
And none to watch with thee?

4 Can we the crown of thorns forget,
The buffeting and shame;
When hell thy sinking soul beset,
And earth reviled thy name?

5 The nails, the spear, can we forget;
The agonizing cry—
"My God! my Father! wilt thou let
Thy Son forsaken die?"

6 Life's brightest joys we may forget—
Our kindred cease to love;
But he who paid our hopeless debt,
Our constancy shall prove.

7 Our sorrows and our sins were laid
On thee—alone on thee:
Thy precious blood our ransom paid—
Thine all the glory be.

800 C. M.

1 IF human kindness meets return,
And owns the grateful tie;
If tender thoughts within us burn
To feel a friend is nigh:

2 Oh, shall not warmer accents tell
The gratitude we owe
To him who died our fears to quell,
Our more than orphan's woe!

3 While yet his anguished soul surveyed
Those pangs he would not flee,
What love his latest words displayed,
"Meet and remember me!"

4 Remember thee! thy death, thy shame,
Our sinful hearts to share!
O memory, leave no other name,
But his recorded there!

NOEL.

801 C. M.

1 HERE at thy table, Lord, we meet,
To feed on food divine:
Thy body is the bread we eat,
Thy precious blood the wine.

2 Here peace and pardon sweetly flow:
Oh, what delightful food!
We eat the bread, and drink the wine,
But think on nobler good.

3 Deep was the suffering he endured
Upon th' accursed tree;
"For me," each welcome guest may say,
"'Twas all endured for me."

4 Sure there was never love so free—
Dear Saviour—so divine:
Well thou may'st claim that heart of me,
Which owes so much to thine.

STENNETT.

802 C. M.

1 WITH humble faith, and thankful heart,
Lord, I accept thy love:
'Tis a rich banquet I have had,
What will it be above!

2 Ye saints below, and hosts of heaven,
Join all your raptured powers;
No theme is like redeeming love,
No Saviour is like ours.

3 Had I ten thousand hearts, dear Lord,
I'd give them all to thee;
Had I ten thousand tongues, they all
Should join the harmony.

STENNETT.

803 C. M.

1 LORD, at thy table we behold
The wonders of thy grace,
But most of all admire that we
Should find a welcome place;—

2 We, who were all defiled with sin,
And rebels to our God;
We, who have crucified thy Son,
And trampled on his blood.

3 What strange, surprising grace is this,
That we, so lost, have room!
Jesus our weary souls invites,
And freely bids us come.

804 C. M.

1 LET vain pursuits and vain desires
Be banished from the heart,
The Saviour's love fill every breast,
And life and light impart.

2 He knows how frail our nature is,
Our souls how apt to stray;
How much we need his gracious help
To keep us in the way!

3 These faithful pledges of his love
His mercy did ordain,
To bring refreshment to our souls,
And faith and hope sustain.

4 Since such his condescending grace,
Let us, with hearts sincere,
Obedient to his holy will,
His table now draw near.

805 S. M.

1 BLEST feast of love divine!
'Tis grace that makes us free
To feed upon this bread and wine,
In memory, Lord, of thee!

2 That blood which flowed for sin,
In symbol here we see,
And feel the blessèd pledge within,
That we are loved of thee.

3 Oh, if this glimpse of love
Be so divinely sweet,
What will it be, my Lord, above,
Thy gladdening smile to meet!

4 To see thee face to face,
Thy perfect likeness wear,
And all thy ways of wondrous grace
Through endless years declare!

806

S. M.

1 JESUS invites his saints
To meet around his board;
Here pardoned rebels sit and hold
Communion with their Lord.

2 Thus do the bread and wine
Revive our fainting breath,
By union with our living Lord,
And interest in his death.

3 Our heavenly Father calls
Christ and his members one;
We, the young children of his love,
And he, the First-born Son.

4 Let all our powers be joined
His glorious Name to raise;
Pleasure and love fill every mind,
And every voice be praise.

WATTS.

807

S. M.

1 JESUS, we thus obey
Thy last and kindest word,
And in thine own appointed way,
We come to meet our Lord.

2 Thus we remember thee,
And take this bread and wine
As thine own dying legacy,
And our redemption's sign.

3 Thy presence makes the feast;
Now let our spirits feel
The glory not to be expressed,
The joy unspeakable.

4 With high and heavenly bliss
Thou dost our spirits cheer;
Thy house of banqueting is this,
And thou hast brought us here.

5 Now let our souls be fed
With manna from above,
And over us thy banner spread
Of everlasting love.

808

S. M.

1 BEHOLD! what wondrous grace
The Father has bestowed
On sinners of a mortal race,
To call them sons of God.

2 'Tis no surprising thing
That we should be unknown;
The Jewish world knew not their King,
God's everlasting Son.

3 Nor doth it yet appear
How great we must be made;
But when we see our Saviour here,
We shall be like our Head.

4 A hope so much divine
May trials well endure;
May purge our souls from sense and sin,
As Christ, the Lord, is pure.

5 If in my Father's love
I share a filial part,
Send down thy Spirit like a dove,
To rest upon my heart.

6 We would no longer lie,
Like slaves, beneath the throne;
Our faith shall "Abba, Father!" cry,
And thou the kindred own.

WATTS.

809 S. M.

1 A PARTING hymn we sing,
Around thy table, Lord,
Again our grateful tribute bring,
Our solemn vows record.

2 Here have we seen thy face,
And felt thy presence here,
So may the savor of thy grace
In word and life appear.

3 The purchase of thy blood—
By sin no longer led—
The path our dear Redeemer trod
May we rejoicing tread.

4 In self-forgetful love
Be our communion shown,
Until we join the church above,
And know as we are known.

810 S. M.

1 DEAR Saviour! we are thine,
By everlasting bands;
Our hearts, our souls, we would resign
Entirely to thy hands.

2 To thee we still would cleave
With ever-growing zeal;
If millions tempt us Christ to leave,
Oh, let them ne'er prevail!

3 The Spirit shall unite
Our souls to thee, our Head;
Shall form in us thine image bright,
And teach thy paths to tread.

4 Death may our souls divide
From these abodes of clay;
But love shall keep us near thy side,
Through all the gloomy way.

5 Since Christ and we are one,
Why should we doubt or fear?
If he in heaven has fixed his throne,
He'll fix his members there.

DODDRIDGE.

811 7s. 6 lines.

1 "TILL he come!" oh, let the words
Linger on the trembling chords;
Let the little while between,
In their golden light be seen;
Let us think how heaven and home
Lie beyond that "Till he come."

2 When the weary ones we love
Enter on their rest above,
Seems the earth so poor and vast,
All our life-joy overcast?
Hush! be every murmur dumb;
It is only "Till he come."

3 Clouds and conflicts round us press;
Would we have one sorrow less?
All the sharpness of the cross,
All that tells the world is loss,
Death and darkness and the tomb
Only whisper, "Till he come."

4 See, the feast of love is spread;
Drink the wine and break the bread;
Sweet memorials,—till the Lord
Call us round his heavenly board;
Some from earth, from glory some,—
Severed only "till he come."

E. W. Bickersteth.

812 7s.

1 WHEN on Sinai's top I see
God descend, in majesty,
To proclaim his holy law,
All my spirit sinks with awe.

2 When, in ecstacy sublime,
Tabor's glorious steep I climb,
At the too transporting light
Darkness rushes o'er my sight.

3 When on Calvary I rest,
God, in flesh made manifest,
Shines in my Redeemer's face,
Full of beauty, truth, and grace.

4 Here I would forever stay,
Weep and gaze my soul away;
Thou art heaven on earth to me,
Lovely, mournful Calvary!

Montgomery.

813 9s & 8s.

1 BREAD of the world in mercy broken,
Wine of the soul in mercy shed,
By whom the words of life were spoken,
And in whose death our sins are dead:

2 Look on the heart by sorrow broken,
Look on the tears by sinners shed,
And be thy feast to us the token
That by thy grace our souls are fed.

Heber.

814 8s & 7s.

1 COME, O my soul, to Calvary,
And see the Man who died for thee
Upon th' accursed tree.

2 Behold the Saviour's agony—
While groaning in Gethsemane,
Beneath the sins of men.

3 With purple robe, and thorny crown,
And mocking soldiers—bowing down,
The Saviour bears my shame.

4 Behold, they shed his precious blood,
Oh! hear him cry, "My God, my God,
Hast thou forsaken me?"

5 He died; the earth was rob'd in gloom,
They laid him then in Joseph's tomb,
While soldiers watched around.

6 But in the light of dawning day,
Bright angels rolled the rock away,
And Christ the conqueror rose.

7 Soon he who once was scourged and bound,
Shall come again with glory crowned,
And reign forevermore.

8 His saints shall crown him Lord of all;
Before him every foe shall fall,
And every knee shall bow.

Chorus.

How can I forget thee?
How can I forget my Lord?
How can I forget thee?
Dear Lord, remember me.

Hastings.

815
8s & 7s.

1 GLORIOUS things of thee are spoken,
Zion, city of our God;
He whose word cannot be broken,
Formed thee for his own abode:
On the Rock of Ages founded,
What can shake thy sure repose?
With salvation's walls surrounded,
Thou may'st smile at all thy foes.

2 See, the streams of living waters,
Springing from eternal love,
Well supply thy sons and daughters,
And all fear of want remove:
Who can faint, while such a river
Ever flows their thirst t'assuage?
Grace which, like the Lord the Giver,
Never fails from age to age.

3 Round each habitation hovering,
See the cloud and fire appear
For a glory and a covering,
Showing that the Lord is near:
Thus deriving from their banner
Light by night and shade by day,
Safe they feed upon the manna
Which he gives them when they pray.

4 Saviour, if of Zion's city
I, through grace, a member am,
Let the world deride or pity,
I will glory in thy Name:
Fading is the worldling's pleasure,
All his boasted pomp and show;
Solid joys and lasting treasure
None but Zion's children know.

NEWTON.

816
8s & 7s.

1 LO! he comes! let all adore him!
'Tis the God of grace and truth!
Go! prepare the way before him,
Make the rugged places smooth!
Lo! he comes, the mighty Lord!
Great his work, and his reward.

2 Let the valleys all be raiséd;
Go, and make the crooked straight;
Let the mountains be abaséd;
Let all nature change its state;
Through the desert mark a road,
Make a highway for our God.

3 Through the desert God is going,
Through the desert waste and wild,
Where no goodly plant is growing,
Where no verdure ever smiled:
But the desert shall be glad,
And with verdure soon be clad.

KELLY.

817
C. M.

1 PLANTED in Christ, the living Vine,
This day, with one accord,
Ourselves, with humble faith and joy,
We yield to thee, O Lord.

2 Joined in one body may we be;
One inward life partake;
One be our heart; one heavenly hope
In every bosom wake.

3 In prayer, in efforts, tears, and toils,
One wisdom be our guide;
Taught by one Spirit from above,
In thee may we abide.

4 Complete in us, whom grace hath called,
Thy glorious work begun,
O thou, in whom the church on earth
And church in heaven are one.

5 Around this feeble, trusting band
Thy sheltering pinions spread,
Nor let the storms of trial beat
Too fiercely on our head.

6 Then, when, among the saints in light,
Our joyful spirits shine,
Shall anthems of immortal praise,
O Lamb of God, be thine.

S. F. SMITH.

818

C. M.

1 BEHOLD the sure foundation-stone,
Which God in Zion lays,
To build our heavenly hopes upon,
And his eternal praise.

2 Chosen of God, to sinners dear,
Let saints adore the name;
They trust their whole salvation here,
Nor shall they suffer shame.

3 The foolish builders, scribe and priest,
Reject it with disdain;
Yet on this rock the church shall rest,
And envy rage in vain.

4 What though the gates of hell withstood,
Yet must this building rise:
'Tis thine own work, Almighty God,
And wondrous in our eyes.

WATTS.

819

C. M.

1 COME, Lord, in mercy come again,
With thy converting power;
The fields of Zion thirst for rain,
O send a gracious shower!

2 Our hearts are filled with sore distress,
While sinners all around
Are pressing on to endless death,
And no relief is found.

3 Dear Saviour, come with quickening power,
Thy mourning people cry;
Salvation bring in mercy's hour,
Nor let the sinner die.

4 Once more let converts throng thy house,
And shouts of victory raise;
Then shall our griefs be turned to joy,
And sighs to songs of praise.

COLVER.

820

C. M.

1 OH, where are kings and empires now
Of old that went and came?
But, Lord, thy church is praying yet,
A thousand years the same.

2 We mark her goodly battlements,
And her foundations strong;
We hear within the solemn voice
Of her unending song.

3 For not like kingdoms of the world
Thy holy church, O God!

Though earthquake shocks are threatening her,
And tempests are abroad.

4 Unshaken as eternal hills,
Immovable she stands,
A mountain that shall fill the earth,
A house not made by hands.

A. C. Coxe.

821 C. M.

1 Oh, how the hearts of those revive,
Who fear and love the Lord,
When sinners dead are made alive,
By his all-quickening word.

2 The parent views, with joyful eyes,
His now returning son,
And, lost in grateful rapture, cries,
What hath the Saviour done!

3 The ministers of Christ rejoice,
When souls the word receive;
When sinners hear the Saviour's voice,
And in his name believe.

4 The church of God their praises join,
And of salvation sing;
They glorify the grace divine,
Of their victorious King.

Hoskins.

822 C. M.

1 Church of the ever-living God,
The Father's gracious choice,
Amid the voices of this earth
How feeble is thy voice!

2 A little flock!—so calls he thee
Who bought thee with his blood;
A little flock, disowned of men,
But owned and loved of God.

3 Not many rich or noble called,
Not many great or wise;
They whom God makes his kings and priests
Are poor in human eyes.

4 But the chief Shepherd comes at length;
Their feeble days are o'er,
No more a handful in the earth,
A little flock no more.

5 No more a lily among thorns,
Weary and faint and few;
But countless as the stars of heaven,
Or as the early dew.

6 Then entering th' eternal halls,
In robes of victory,
That mighty multitude shall keep
The joyous jubilee.

Bonar.

823 C. M.

1 Daughter of Zion, from the dust
Exalt thy fallen head;
Again in thy Redeemer trust;
He calls thee from the dead.

2 Awake, awake, put on thy strength,
Thy beautiful array;
The day of freedom dawns at length,
The Lord's appointed day.

3 Rebuild thy walls, thy bounds enlarge,
And send thy heralds forth;
Say to the south, "Give up thy charge,
And keep not back, O north!"

4 They come, they come;—thine exiled bands,
Where'er they rest or roam,

Have heard thy voice in distant lands,
And hasten to their home.

5 Thus, though the universe shall burn,
And God his works destroy,
With songs thy ransomed shall return,
And everlasting joy.

MONTGOMERY.

824 C. M.

1 BEHOLD, the mountain of the Lord,
In latter days, shall rise
On mountain tops, above the hills,
And draw the wond'ring eyes.

2 To this the joyful nations round,
All tribes and tongues, shall flow;
"Up to the hill of God," they say,
"And to his house we'll go."

3 The beams that shine on Zion's hill
Shall lighten every land;
The King who reigns in Salem's towers
Shall all the world command.

4 No longer hosts encountering hosts,
Their millions slain deplore;
They hang the trumpet in the hall,
And study war no more.

LOGAN.

825 C. M.

1 LET Zion and her sons rejoice—
Behold the promised hour!
Her God hath heard her mourning voice,
And comes to exalt his power.

2 Her dust and ruins that remain
Are precious in our eyes;
Those ruins shall be built again,
And all that dust shall rise.

3 The Lord will raise Jerusalem,
And stand in glory there;
Nations shall bow before his name,
And kings attend with fear.

4 He frees the soul condemned to death,
Nor, when his saints complain,
Shall it be said that praying breath
Was ever spent in vain.

5 This shall be known when we are dead,
And left on long record,
That nations yet unborn may read,
And trust and praise the Lord.

WATTS.

826 C. M.

1 NOT to the terrors of the Lord,
The tempest, fire, and smoke;
Not to the thunder of that word
Which God on Sinai spoke;—

2 But we are come to Zion's hill,
The city of our God,
Where milder words declare his will,
And spread his love abroad.

3 Behold the great, the glorious host
Of angels clothed in light;
Behold the spirits of the just,
Whose faith is turned to sight.

4 Behold the blest assembly there,
Whose names are writ in heaven,
And God, the Judge, who doth declare
Their vilest sins forgiven.

5 The saints on earth, and all the dead,
But one communion make;

All join in Christ, their living Head,
And of his grace partake.

6 In such society as this
Our weary souls would rest;
The man who dwells where Jesus is
Must be forever blest.

WATTS.

827 C. M.

1 A MOTHER may forgetful be,
For human love is frail;
But thy Creator's love to thee,
O Zion, cannot fail.

2 No, thy dear name engraven stands,
In characters of love,
On thy almighty Father's hands;
And never shall remove.

3 Before his ever-watchful eye
Thy mournful state appears,
And every groan, and every sigh,
Divine compassion hears.

4 O Zion, learn to doubt no more,
Be every fear suppressed;
Unchanging truth, and love, and power,
Dwell in thy Saviour's breast.

STEELE.

828 C. M.

1 ARISE, O King of grace, arise,
And enter to thy rest;
Behold, thy church, with longing eyes
Waits to be owned and blest.

2 Enter, with all thy glorious train,
Thy Spirit and thy Word;
All that the ark did once contain
Could no such grace afford.

3 Here, mighty God, accept our vows;
Here let thy praise be spread;
Bless the provisions of thy house,
And fill thy poor with bread.

4 Here let the Son of David reign,
Let God's Anointed shine;
Justice and truth his court maintain,
With love and power divine.

WATTS.

829 L. M.

1 TRIUMPHANT Zion! lift thy head
From dust, and darkness, and the dead;
Though humbled long, awake at length,
And gird thee with thy Saviour's strength.

2 Put all thy beauteous garments on,
And let thy excellence be known;
Decked in the robes of righteousness,
The world thy glories shall confess.

3 No more shall foes unclean invade,
And fill thy hallowed walls with dread;
No more shall hell's insulting host
Their victory and thy sorrows boast.

4 God, from on high, has heard thy prayer;
His hand thy ruins shall repair;
Nor will thy watchful Monarch cease
To guard thee in eternal peace.

DODDRIDGE.

830 L. M.

1 WHILE to its grief my soul gave way,
To see the work of God decline,
Methought I heard the Saviour say—
"Dismiss thy fears, the ark is mine.

2 "Though for a time I hide my face,
Rely upon my love and power;
Still wrestle at the throne of grace,
And wait for a reviving hour.

3 "Take down thy long-neglected harp,
I've seen thy tears, and heard thy prayer;
The winter season has been sharp,
But spring shall all its wastes repair."

4 Lord! I obey, my hopes revive;
Come, join with me, ye saints, and sing:
Our foes in vain against us strive,
For God will help and triumph bring.

NEWTON.

831 L. M.

1 WHEN God descends with men to dwell,
And all creation wakes anew,
What tongue can half the wonders tell?
What eye the dazzling glory view?

2 Zion, the desolate, again
Shall see her lands with roses bloom;
And Carmel's mount, and Sharon's plain,
Shall yield their spices and perfume:

3 Celestial streams shall gently flow;
The wilderness shall joyful be;
Lilies on parchéd ground shall grow;
And gladness spring on every tree:

4 The weak be strong, the fearful bold,
The deaf shall hear, the dumb shall sing,
The lame shall walk, the blind behold,
And joy through all the earth shall ring:

5 Monarchs and slaves shall meet in love;
Old pride shall die, and meekness reign,
When God descends from worlds above,
To dwell with men on earth again.

BALLOU.

832 S. M.

1 I LOVE thy kingdom, Lord,—
The house of thine abode,
The church our blest Redeemer saved
With his own precious blood.

2 I love thy Church, O God!
Her walls before thee stand,
Dear as the apple of thine eye,
And graven on thy hand.

3 For her my tears shall fall;
For her my prayers ascend;
To her my cares and toils be given,
Till toils and cares shall end.

4 Beyond my highest joy
I prize her heavenly ways,
Her sweet communion, solemn vows,
Her hymns of love and praise.

5 Jesus, thou Friend divine,
Our Saviour and our King,
Thy hand from every snare and foe
Shall great deliverance bring.

6 Sure as thy truth shall last,
To Zion shall be given
The brightest glories earth can yield,
And brighter bliss of heaven.

DWIGHT.

833 S. M.

1 FAR as thy name is known,
The world declares thy praise;
The saints, O Lord, before thy throne,
Their songs of honor raise.

2 With joy thy people stand
On Zion's chosen hill,
Proclaim the wonders of thy hand,
And counsels of thy will.

3 Let strangers walk around
The city where we dwell,
Survey with care thine holy ground,
And mark the building well,—

4 The order of thy house,
The worship of thy court,
The cheerful songs, the solemn vows,
And make a fair report.

5 How decent, and how wise!
How glorious to behold!
Beyond the pomp that charms the eyes,
And rites adorned with gold.

6 The God we worship now
Will guide us till we die—
Will be our God while here below,
And ours above the sky.

WATTS.

834 S. M.

1 WHO can forbear to sing,
Who can refuse to praise,
When Zion's high, celestial King
His saving power displays?

2 When sinners at his feet,
By mercy conquered, fall?
When grace, and truth, and justice meet,
And peace unites them all?

3 Who can forbear to praise
Our high, celestial King,
When sovereign, rich, redeeming grace
Invites our tongues to sing?

SWAIN.

835 S. M.

1 O LORD, thy work revive,
In Zion's gloomy hour,
And make her dying graces live
By thy restoring power.

2 Awake thy chosen few
To fervent, earnest prayer;
Again may they their vows renew,
Thy blessèd presence share.

3 Thy Spirit then will speak
Through lips of feeble clay,
And hearts of adamant will break,
And rebels will obey.

4 Lord, lend thy gracious ear;
Oh, listen to our cry!
Oh, come and bring salvation here!
Our hopes on thee rely.

HASTINGS.

836 S. M.

1 GREAT is the Lord our God,
And let his praise be great;
He makes his churches his abode,
His most delightful seat.

2 These temples of his grace,
How beautiful they stand!
The honors of our native place,
And bulwarks of our land.

3 In Zion God is known,
A refuge in distress:
How bright has his salvation shone,
Through all her palaces!

4 When kings against her joined,
And saw the Lord was there,
In wild confusion of the mind,
They fled with hasty fear.

5 Oft have our fathers told,
Our eyes have often seen,
How well our God secures the fold
Where his own sheep have been.

6 In every new distress
We'll to his house repair;
We'll call to mind his wondrous grace,
And seek deliverance there.

WATTS.

837 S. M.

1 OH, for the happy hour
When God will hear our cry,
And send, with a reviving power,
His Spirit from on high.

2 We meet, we sing, we pray,
We listen to the word,
In vain;—we see no cheering ray,
No cheering voice is heard.

3 While many crowd thy house,
How few, around thy board,
Meet to recount their solemn vows,
And bless thee as their Lord!

4 Thou, thou alone canst give
Thy gospel sure success;
Canst bid the dying sinner live
Anew in holiness.

5 Come, then, with power divine,
Spirit of life and love!
Then shall this people all be thine,
This church like that above.

BETHUNE.

838 8s, 7s & 4s.

1 SAVIOUR, visit thy plantation,
Grant us, Lord, a gracious rain;
All will come to desolation,
Unless thou return again.
Lord, revive us;
All our help must come from thee.

2 Keep no longer at a distance,
Shine upon us from on high,
Lest for want of thine assistance,
Every plant should droop and die.
Lord, revive us;
All our help must come from thee.

3 Let our mutual love be fervent,
Make us prevalent in prayers;
Let each one esteemed thy servant,
Shun the world's bewitching snares.
Lord, revive us;
All our help must come from thee.

4 Break the tempter's fatal power
Turn the stony heart to flesh;
And begin, from this good hour,
To revive thy work afresh.
Lord, revive us;
All our help must come from thee.

NEWTON.

839 8s & 7s.

1 ONCE, O Lord, thy garden flourished,
Every part looked gay and green;
Then thy word our spirits nourished,
Happy seasons we have seen!

2 But a drought has since succeeded,
And a sad decline we see;
Lord, thy help is greatly needed,
Help can only come from thee.

3 Some, in whom we once delighted,
We shall meet no more below;
Some, alas! we fear are blighted,—
Scarce a single leaf they show.

4 Dearest Saviour, hasten hither,
Thou canst make them bloom again;
Oh, permit them not to wither,
Let not all our hopes be vain!

NEWTON.

840 8s & 7s.

1 ZION, dreary and in anguish,
'Mid the desert hast thou strayed!
Oh, thou weary, cease to languish;
Jesus shall lift up thy head.

2 Still lamenting and bemoaning,
'Mid thy follies and thy woes!
Soon repenting and returning,
All thy solitude shall close.

3 Though benighted and forsaken,
Though afflicted and distressed;
His almighty arm shall waken;
Zion's King shall give thee rest.

HASTINGS.

841 8s, 7s & 4s.

1 ON the mountain's top appearing,
Lo! the sacred herald stands,
Welcome news to Zion bearing—
Zion, long in hostile lands:
Mourning captive!
God himself shall loose thy bands.

2 Has thy night been long and mournful?
Have thy friends unfaithful proved?
Have thy foes been proud and scornful?
By thy sighs and tears unmoved?
Cease thy mourning;
Zion still is well beloved.

3 God, thy God, will now restore thee;
He himself appears thy Friend;
All thy foes shall flee before thee;
Here their boasts and triumphs end:
Great deliverance
Zion's King will surely send.

4 Peace and joy shall now attend thee;
All thy warfare now is past;
God thy Saviour will defend thee;
Victory is thine at last:
All thy conflicts
End in everlasting rest.

KELLY.

842 8s, 7s & 4s.

1 ZION stands with hills surrounded—
Zion, kept by power divine;
All her foes shall be confounded,
Though the world in arms combine;
Happy Zion,
What a favored lot is thine!

2 Every human tie may perish;
Friend to friend unfaithful prove;
Mothers cease their own to cherish;
Heaven and earth at last remove:
But no changes
Can attend Jehovah's love.

3 In the furnace God may prove thee,
Thence to bring thee forth more bright,
But can never cease to love thee;
Thou art precious in his sight;
God is with thee—
God, thine everlasting light.

KELLY.

843 8s, 7s & 4s.

1 SEE, from Zion's sacred mountain,
Streams of living water flow;
God has opened there a fountain
That supplies the world below;
They are blessèd
Who its sovereign virtues know.

2 Through ten thousand channels flowing
Streams of mercy find their way:

Life, and health, and joy bestowing
Waking beauty from decay.
Oh, ye nations,
Hail the long-expected day!

3 Gladdened by the flowing treasure,
All-enriching as it goes,
Lo! the desert smiles with pleasure,
Buds and blossoms as the rose;
Lo! the desert
Sings for joy where'er it flows.

KELLY.

844 H. M.

1 O ZION! tune thy voice,
And raise thy hands on high;
Tell all the earth thy joys,
And boast salvation nigh;
Cheerful in God, arise and shine,
While rays divine stream all abroad.

2 He gilds thy mourning face
With beams that cannot fade;
His all-resplendent grace
He pours around thy head;
The nations round, thy form shall view,
With lustre new divinely crowned.

3 In honor to his name,
Reflect that sacred light;
And loud that grace proclaim,
Which makes thy darkness bright;
Pursue his praise, till sovereign love,
In worlds above, the glory raise.

4 There, on his holy hill,
A brighter sun shall rise,
And, with his radiance, fill
Those fairer, purer skies;
While, round his throne, ten thousand stars,
In nobler spheres, his influence own.

DODDRIDGE.

845 H. M.

1 CHRIST is our Corner-stone;
On him alone we build;
With his true saints alone
The courts of heaven are filled:
On his great love our hopes we place,
Of present grace and joys above.

2 Oh, then, with hymns of praise
Our hallowed courts shall ring!
Our voices we will raise,
The Three in One to sing;
And thus proclaim in joyful song,
Both loud and long, that glorious Name.

3 Here, gracious God, do thou
Forevermore draw nigh;
Accept each faithful vow,
And mark each suppliant sigh:
In copious shower, on all who pray,
Each holy day, thy blessings pour.

4 Here may we gain from heaven
The grace which we implore,
And may that grace, once given,
Be with us evermore,—
Until that day when all the blest
To endless rest are called away.

CHANDLER.

846 11s & 10s.

1 HAIL to the brightness of Zion's glad morning!
Joy to the lands that in darkness have lain;
Hushed be the accents of sorrow and mourning,
Zion in triumph begins her mild reign.

2 Hail to the brightness of Zion's glad morning,
Long by the prophets of Israel foretold;
Hail to the millions from bondage returning,
Gentiles and Jews the blest vision behold.

3 Lo! in the desert, rich flowers are springing,
Streams ever copious are gliding along;
Loud from the mountain-tops echoes are ringing,
Wastes rise in verdure, and mingle in song.

4 See, from all lands—from the isles of the ocean,
Praise to Jehovah ascending on high;
Fallen are the engines of war and commotion,
Shouts of salvation are rending the sky.

HASTINGS.

847 7s & 6s.

1 THE Church's one foundation
Is Jesus Christ her Lord;
She is his new creation
By water and the Word:
From heaven he came and sought her,
To be his holy Bride,
With his own blood he bought her,
And for her life he died.

2 Though with a scornful wonder
Men see her sore opprest,
By schisms rent asunder,
By heresies distrest,
Yet saints their watch are keeping,
Their cry goes up, "How long?"
And soon the night of weeping
Shall be the morn of song.

3 'Mid toil, and tribulation,
And tumult of her war,
She waits the consummation
Of peace forevermore;
Till with the vision glorious
Her longing eyes are blest,
And the great Church victorious
Shall be the Church at rest.

848 C. P. M.

1 THE Lord into his garden comes;
The spices yield a rich perfume;
The lilies grow and thrive;
Refreshing showers of grace divine,
From Jesus flow to every vine,
Which makes the dead revive.

2 Oh that this dry and barren ground
In springs of water may abound,
A fruitful soil become!
The desert blossoms as the rose,
When Jesus conquers all his foes,
And makes his people one.

3 The glorious time is rolling on,
The gracious work is now begun,
My soul a witness is!
"Oh, taste and see the pardon free,
For all mankind as well as me!
Oh, come to Christ and live!"

4 Amen, amen, my soul replies,
I'm bound to meet you in the skies,
And claim my mansion there!
Now here's my heart, and here's my hand,
To meet you in that heavenly land,
Where we shall part no more.

THE CHRISTIAN LIFE.

849 8s & 7s.

1 COME, thou Fount of every blessing!
Tune my heart to sing thy grace;
Streams of mercy, never ceasing,
Call for songs of loudest praise.

2 Teach me some melodious sonnet
Sung by flaming tongues above;
Praise the mount—I'm fix'd upon it!—
Mount of thy redeeming love.

3 Here I'll raise mine Ebenezer;
Hither by thy help I'm come;
And I hope, by thy good pleasure,
Safely to arrive at home.

4 Jesus sought me when a stranger,
Wandering from the fold of God;
He, to rescue me from danger,
Interposed his precious blood.

5 Oh, to grace how great a debtor
Daily I'm constrained to be!
Let thy grace, Lord, like a fetter,
Bind my wandering heart to thee.

6 Prone to wander, Lord, I feel it;
Prone to leave the God I love;
Here's my heart; oh, take and seal it!
Seal it from thy courts above.

ROBINSON.

Chorus.

I love Jesus, Hallelujah!
I love Jesus, yes, I do;
I do love Jesus, he's my Saviour;
Jesus smiles, and loves me too.

850 L. M.

1 AWAKE, my soul, in joyful lays,
And sing thy great Redeemer's praise;
He justly claims a song from me:
His loving-kindness, oh, how free!

2 He saw me ruined in the fall,
Yet loved me notwithstanding all;
He saved me from my lost estate:
His loving-kindness, oh, how great!

3 Though numerous hosts of mighty foes,
Though earth and hell my way oppose,
He safely leads my soul along:
His loving-kindness, oh, how strong!

4 When trouble, like a gloomy cloud,
Has gathered thick and thundered loud,
He near my soul has always stood:
His loving-kindness, oh, how good!

5 Often I feel my sinful heart
Prone from my Jesus to depart;
But though I have him oft forgot,
His loving-kindness changes not.

6 Soon shall I pass the gloomy vale;
Soon all my mortal powers must fail:
Oh, may my last expiring breath
His loving-kindness sing in death!

7 Then, let me mount and soar away
To the bright world of endless day,
And sing with rapture and surprise,
His loving-kindness in the skies!

MEDLEY.

851 11s & 9s.

1 OH! how happy are they
Who their Saviour obey,
And have laid up their treasure above!
Tongue can never express
The sweet comfort and peace
Of a soul in its earliest love.

2 That sweet comfort was mine
When the favor divine
I had found in the blood of the Lamb.
When at first I believed,
What true joy I received!
What a heaven in Jesus' sweet name!

3 'Twas a heaven below
My Redeemer to know;
And the angels could do nothing more
Than to fall at his feet,
And the story repeat,
And the Lover of sinners adore.

4 Jesus, all the day long,
Was my joy and my song:
Oh, that all his salvation might see!
"He hath loved me," I cried,
"He hath suffered and died
To redeem such a rebel as me!"

C. WESLEY.

852 11s & 9s.

1 O THOU, in whose presence
My soul takes delight,
On whom in affliction I call,
My comfort by day,
And my song in the night,
My hope, my salvation, my all.

2 Where dost thou, dear Shepherd,
Resort with thy sheep,
To feed them in pastures of love;
Say, why in the valley
Of death should I weep,
Or alone in this wilderness rove.

3 Ye daughters of Zion,
Declare, have you seen
The star that on Israel shone?
Say, if in your tents
My Beloved has been,
And where with his flocks he is gone?

4 Love sits in his eyelids,
And scatters delight
Through all the bright mansions on high!
Their faces the cherubim
Veil in his sight,
And tremble with fulness of joy.

5 He looks! and ten thousands
Of angels rejoice,
And myriads wait for his word;
He speaks! and eternity,
Filled with his voice,
Re-echoes the praise of the Lord.

6 Dear Shepherd! I hear, and
Will follow thy call;
I know the sweet sound of thy voice;
Restore and defend me,
For thou art my all,
And in thee I will ever rejoice.

SWAIN.

853 6s

1 THY works, not mine, O Christ!
Speak gladness to this heart;
They tell me all is done;
They bid my fear depart:

2 Thy tears, not mine, O Christ,
Have wept my guilt away;
And turned this night of mine
Into a blessèd day:

3 Thy wounds, not mine, O Christ,
Can heal my bruiséd soul;
Thy stripes, not mine, contain
The balm that makes me whole:

4 Thy cross, not mine, O Christ,
Has borne the awful load
Of sins that none could bear
But the incarnate God:

5 Thy death, not mine, O Christ,
Has paid the ransom due;
Ten thousand deaths like mine
Would have been all too few:

6 Thy righteousness alone
Can clothe and beautify;
I wrap it round my soul,
In this I'll live and die.

BONAR. *Arr.*

Chorus.

Jesus paid it all;
All to him I owe;
Sin had left a crimson stain:
He washed it white as snow.

854

6s.

1 I BRING my sins to thee,
The sins I cannot count,
That all may cleanséd be
In thy once-opened fount.

2 My heart to thee I bring,
The heart I cannot read,
A faithless, wandering thing,
An evil heart indeed.

3 To thee I bring my care,
The care I cannot flee;
Thou wilt not only share,
But take it all for me.

4 I bring my grief to thee,
The grief I cannot tell;
No words shall needed be,
Thou knowest all so well.

5 My joys to thee I bring,
The joys thy love has given,
That each may be a wing
To lift me nearer heaven.

6 My life I bring to thee,
I would not be my own;
O Saviour, let me be
Thine ever, thine alone!

SUNDAY MAG. *Altered.*

855

7s & 6s.

1 I LAY my sins on Jesus,
The spotless Lamb of God;
He bears them all, and frees us
From the accurséd load:
I bring my guilt to Jesus,
To wash my crimson stains,
White in his blood most precious,
Till not a stain remains.

2 I lay my wants on Jesus;
All fullness dwells in him;
He healeth my diseases,
He doth my soul redeem:
I lay my griefs on Jesus,
My burdens and my cares;
He from them all releases,
He all my sorrow shares.

3 I rest my soul on Jesus,
This weary soul of mine;
His right hand me embraces,
I on his breast recline:
I love the name of Jesus,
Immanuel, Christ, the Lord;

Like fragrance on the breezes,
His name abroad is poured.

4 I long to be like Jesus,
Meek, loving, lowly, mild;
I long to be like Jesus,
The Father's holy child:
I long to be with Jesus
Amid the heavenly throng,
To sing with saints his praises,
And learn the angels' song.

BONAR.

856

7s & 6s.

1 O BLESSED feet of Jesus,
Weary with seeking me!
Stand at God's bar of judgment
And intercede for me.
O knees which bent in anguish
In dark Gethsemane!
Kneel at the throne of glory
And intercede for me.

2 O hands that were extended
Upon the awful tree!
Hold up those precious nail prints
Which intercede for me.
O head so deeply pierced
With thorns which sharpest be!
Bend low before thy Father,
And intercede for me.

3 O body scarred and wounded,
My sacrifice to be!
Present thy perfect offering
And intercede for me.
O loving risen Saviour,
From death and sorrow free!
Though throned in endless glory,
Still intercede for me.

TRANS. FROM THE ITALIAN.

857

7s. 6 l.

1 BLESSED are the sons of God;
They are bought with Jesus' blood;
They are ransomed from the grave—
Life eternal they shall have:
With them numbered may we be,
Here, and in eternity.

2 They are justified by grace,
They enjoy the Saviour's peace;
All their sins are washed away;
They shall stand in God's great day:
With them numbered may we be,
Here, and in eternity.

3 They produce the fruits of grace,
In the works of righteousness;
They are harmless, meek, and mild,
Holy, blameless, undefiled:
With them numbered may we be,
Here, and in eternity.

4 They are lights upon the earth,
Children of a heavenly birth;
One with God, with Jesus one;
Glory is in them begun:
With them numbered may we be,
Here, and in eternity.

HUMPHREYS.

858

7s. 6 l.

1 NOW, O God, thine own I am!
Now I give thee back thine own:
Freedom, friends, and health, and fame,
Consecrate to thee alone:
Thine I live, thrice happy I!
Happier still if thine I die.

2 Take me, Lord, and all my powers;
Take my mind, and heart, and will;
All my goods, and all my hours,
All I know, and all I feel,
All I think, or speak, or do—
Take my soul and make it new!

C. WESLEY.

859 7s. 6 lines.

1 WHEN this passing world is done,—
When has sunk yon glorious sun;
When, from off the mount of God,
We review the path we've trod;
Then, Lord, shall I fully know—
Not till then—how much I owe!

2 When I hear the wicked call
On the rocks and hills to fall;
When I see them start and shrink,
On the fiery deluge brink;
Then, Lord, shall I fully know—
Not till then—how much I owe!

3 When I stand before the throne,
Clothed in beauty not my own;
When I see thee as thou art,
Love thee with unsinning heart;
Then, Lord, shall I fully know—
Not till then—how much I owe!

4 When the praise of heaven I hear,
Loud as thunders to the ear,
Loud as many waters' noise,
Sweet as harps' melodious voice,
Then, Lord, shall I fully know—
Not till then—how much I owe!

McCHEYNE.

860 7s. 6 lines.

1 CHOSEN not for good in me,
Wakened up from wrath to flee,
Hidden in the Saviour's side,
By the Spirit sanctified—
Teach me, Lord, on earth to show,
By my love, how much I owe.

2 Oft I walk beneath the cloud,
Dark as midnight's gloomy shroud;
But, when fear is at the height,
Jesus comes, and all is light;
Blessèd Jesus! bid me show,
Doubting saints how much I owe.

3 Oft the nights of sorrow reign—
Weeping, sickness, sighing, pain;
But a night thine anger burns—
Morning comes, and joy returns:
God of comforts! bid me show
To thy poor how much I owe.

4 When in flowery paths I tread,
Oft by sin I'm captive led;
Oft I fall, but still arise—
Jesus comes—the tempter flies:
Blessèd Jesus! bid me show
Weary sinners all I owe.

McCHEYNE.

861 6s & 4s.

1 NOW I have found a Friend,
Jesus is mine;
His love shall never end,
Jesus is mine.
Though earthly joys decrease,
Though human friendships cease,
Now I have lasting peace;
Jesus is mine.

2 Though I grow poor and old,
  Jesus is mine;
He will my faith uphold,
  Jesus is mine;
He shall my wants supply,
His precious blood is nigh,
Nought can my hope destroy,
  Jesus is mine.

3 When earth shall pass away,
  Jesus is mine!
In the great Judgment day,
  Jesus is mine!
Oh! what a glorious thing,
Then to behold my King,
On tuneful harp to sing,
  Jesus is mine.

4 Farewell mortality!
  Jesus is mine.
Welcome eternity!
  Jesus is mine.
He my Redemption is,
Wisdom and Righteousness,
Life, Light, and Holiness,
  Jesus is mine.

5 Father! thy name I bless,
  Jesus is mine;
Thine was the sovereign grace,
  Jesus is mine.
Spirit of holiness,
Sealing the Father's grace
Thou mad'st my soul embrace,
  Jesus as mine.

RYLE.

862

6s & 4s.

1 FADE, fade, each earthly joy;
  Jesus is mine!
Break, every tender tie;
  Jesus is mine.
Dark is the wilderness;
Earth has no resting-place;
Jesus alone can bless;
  Jesus is mine.

2 Tempt not my soul away;
  Jesus is mine:
Here would I ever stay;
  Jesus is mine:
Perishing things of clay
Born but for one brief day,
Pass from my heart away;
  Jesus is mine.

3 Farewell, ye dreams of night,
  Jesus is mine:
Lost in this dawning bright,
  Jesus is mine:
All that my soul has tried
Left but a dismal void
Jesus has satisfied;
  Jesus is mine.

4 Farewell mortality;
  Jesus is mine:
Welcome, eternity;
  Jesus is mine:
Welcome, O loved and blest!
Welcome, sweet scenes of rest;
Welcome, my Saviour's breast;
  Jesus is mine!

BONAR.

863

7s & 6s.

1 I LOVE to tell the story
  Of unseen things above,
Of Jesus and his glory,
  Of Jesus and his love.
I love to tell the story,
  Because I know it's true;
It satisfies my longings,
  As nothing else would do.

2 I love to tell the story:
More wonderful it seems
Than all the golden fancies
Of all our golden dreams.
I love to tell the story:
It did so much for me!
And that is just the reason
I tell it now to thee.

3 I love to tell the story:
'Tis pleasant to repeat
What seems, each time I tell it,
More wonderfully sweet.
I love to tell the story:
For some have never heard
The message of salvation
From God's own holy word.

4 I love to tell the story;
For those who know it best
Seem hungering and thirsting
To hear it like the rest.
And when, in scenes of glory,
I sing the New, New Song,
'Twill be—the Old, Old Story
That I have loved so long!

Chorus.

I love to tell the story,
'Twill be my theme in glory,
To tell the old, old story
Of Jesus and his love.

864 L. M.

1 I THIRST, but not as once I did
The vain delights of earth to share;
Thy wounds, Immanuel, all forbid
That I should seek my pleasure there.

2 It was the sight of thy dear cross,
First weaned my soul from earthly things,
And taught me to esteem as dross
The mirth of fools and pomp of kings.

3 I want that grace that springs from thee,
That quickens all things where it flows,
And makes a wretched thorn like me
Bloom as the myrtle or the rose.

4 For sure, of all the plants that share
The notice of my Father's eye,
None proves less grateful to his care,
Or yields him meaner fruit than I.

COWPER.

865 L. M.

1 JESUS, thy boundless love to me
No thought can reach, no tongue declare;
Unite my thankful heart to thee,
And reign without a rival there.

2 Thy love, how cheering is its ray!
All pain before its presence flies;
Care, anguish, sorrow, melt away
Where'er its healing beams arise.

3 Oh, let thy love my soul inflame,
And to thy service sweetly bind;
Transfuse it through my inmost frame,
And mould me wholly to thy mind.

4 Thy love, in sufferings, be my peace;
Thy love, in weakness, make me strong,
And, when the storms of life shall cease,
Thy love shall be in heaven my song.

C. WESLEY.

866 L. M.

1 'TIS not the skill of human art,
Which gives me power my God to know;
The sacred lessons of the heart
Come not from instruments below.

2 Love is my teacher; he can tell
The wonders that he learnt above:
No other Master knows so well;
'Tis Love alone can tell of Love.

MADAME GUION.

867 L. M.

1 O LOVE! who gav'st thy life for me,
And won an everlasting good
Through thy sore anguish on the tree,
I ever think upon thy blood.

2 I ever thank thy sacred wounds,
Thou wounded Love, thou Holiest!
But most when life is near its bounds,
And in thy bosom safe I rest.

3 O Love! who unto death has grieved
For this cold heart, unworthy thine,
Whom the cold grave and death received,
I thank thee for that grief divine.

868 8s & 7s.

1 I WOULD love thee, God and Father,
My Redeemer, and my King;
I would love thee; for, without thee,
Life is but a bitter thing.

2 I would love thee; every blessing
Flows to me from out thy throne:
I would love thee; he who loves thee
Never feels himself alone.

3 I would love thee; look upon me,
Ever guide me with thine eye:
I would love thee; if not nourished
By thy love, my soul would die.

4 I would love thee; I have vowed it,
On thy love my heart is set:
While I love thee, I will never
My Redeemer's blood forget.

869 8s & 7s. D.

1 HAIL, my ever-blessèd Jesus!
Only thee I wish to sing;
To my soul thy name is precious,
Thou my Prophet, Priest, and King;
Oh, what mercy flows from heaven!
Oh, what joy and happiness!
Love I much? I've much forgiven,—
I'm a miracle of grace.

2 Once with Adam's race in ruin,
Unconcerned in sin I lay;
Swift destruction still pursuing,
Till my Saviour passed that way;
Witness, all ye hosts of heaven,
My Redeemer's tenderness:
Love I much? I've much forgiven,—
I'm a miracle of grace!

3 Shout, ye bright angelic choir!
Praise the Lamb enthroned above!
While, astonished, I admire
God's free grace and boundless love:
That blest moment I received him
Filled my soul with joy and peace:
Love I much? I've much forgiven,—
I'm a miracle of grace!

WINGROVE.

870 C. M.

1 I HEARD the voice of Jesus say,
"Come unto me, and rest;
Lay down, thou weary one, lay down
Thy head upon my breast."
I came to Jesus as I was,
Weary, and worn, and sad;
I found in him a resting-place,
And he has made me glad.

2 I heard the voice of Jesus say,
"Behold, I freely give
The living water; thirsty one,
Stoop down, and drink, and live."
I came to Jesus, and I drank
Of that life-giving stream:
My thirst was quenched, my soul revived,
And now I live in him.

3 I heard the voice of Jesus say,
"I am this dark world's Light;
Look unto me, thy morn shall rise,
And all thy day be bright."
I looked to Jesus, and I found
In him my Star, my Sun;
And in that Light of life I'll walk
Till all my journey's done.

BONAR.

871 C. M.

1 HOW happy every child of grace,
Who knows his sins forgiven!
This earth, he cries, is not my place,
I seek my place in heaven:
A country far from mortal sight,
Yet oh, by faith I see
The land of rest, the saints' delight,
The heaven prepared for me.

2 Oh what a blessèd hope is ours!
While here on earth we stay,
We more than taste the heavenly powers,
And antedate that day:
We feel the resurrection near—
Our life in Christ concealed—
And with his glorious presence here
Our earthen vessels filled.

3 Oh, would he more of heaven bestow,
And let the vessels break,
And let our ransomed spirits go
To grasp the God we seek;
In rapturous awe on him to gaze,
Who bought the sight for me,
And shout and wonder at his grace
To all eternity.

C. WESLEY.

872 C. M.

1 OH, gift of gifts! oh, grace of faith!
My God! how can it be
That thou, who hast discerning love,
Shouldst give that gift to me?

2 How many hearts thou mightst have had
More innocent than mine!
How many souls more worthy far
Of that sweet touch of thine!

3 Ah, grace! into unlikeliest hearts
It is thy boast to come,
The glory of thy light to find
In darkest spots a home.

4 The crowd of cares, the weightiest cross,
Seem trifles less than light—

Earth looks so little and so low
When faith shines full and bright.

5 Oh, happy, happy that I am!
If thou canst be, O faith,
The treasure that thou art in life,
What wilt thou be in death!

LYRA CATH.

873 C. M.

1 ALL that I was, my sin and guilt,
My death was all my own,—
All that I am, I owe to thee,
My gracious God, alone.

2 The evil of my former state
Was mine, and only mine;
The good in which I now rejoice,
Is thine, and only thine.

3 The darkness of my former state,
The bondage, all was mine;
The light of life, in which I walk,
The liberty, is thine.

4 That grace first made me feel my sin,
It taught me to believe;
Then, in believing, peace I found,
And now I live—I live!

5 All that I am, e'en here on earth;
All that I hope to be,
When Jesus comes, and glory dawns,
I owe it, Lord, to thee.

BONAR.

874 C. M.

1 O DEAREST Lamb, take thou my heart!
Where can such sweetness be,
As I have tasted in thy love,
As I have found in thee?

2 If there's a fervor in my soul,
And fervor sure there is,
Now it shall be at thy control,
And but to serve thee rise.

3 If love, that mildest flame, can rest
In hearts so hard as mine,
Come, gentle Saviour, to my breast,
Its love shall all be thine.

4 Now the gay world with treacherous art
Shall tempt my heart in vain,
I have conveyed away that heart,
Ne'er to return again.

MORAVIAN.

875 C. M.

1 DO not I love thee, O my Lord?
Behold my heart and see;
And turn the dearest idol out
That dares to rival thee.

2 Do not I love thee from my soul?
Then let me nothing love:
Dead be my heart to every joy
When Jesus cannot move.

3 Is not thy name melodious still
To mine attentive ear?
Doth not each pulse with pleasure bound,
My Saviour's voice to hear?

4 Hast thou a lamb in all thy flock
I would disdain to feed?
Hast thou a foe before whose face
I fear thy cause to plead?

5 Thou know'st I love thee, dearest Lord,
But oh, I long to soar
Far from the sphere of mortal joys,
And learn to love thee more.

DODDRIDGE.

876 C. M.

1 MY God, what silken cords are thine,
How soft, and yet how strong;
While power and truth, and love combine
To draw our souls along.

2 Thou saw'st us crushed beneath the yoke
Of Satan and of sin;
Thy hand the iron bondage broke,
Our worthless hearts to win.

3 The guilt of twice ten thousand sins
One offering takes away;
And grace, when first the war begins,
Secures the crowning day.

4 Comfort through all this vale of tears
In rich profusion flows,
And glory of unnumbered years
Eternity bestows.

5 Drawn by such cords we onward move,
Till round thy throne we meet;
And, captives in the chains of love,
Embrace our Conq'ror's feet.

DODDRIDGE.

877 C. M.

1 HOW can I sink with such a prop
As my eternal God,
Who bears the earth's huge pillars up
And spreads the heavens abroad?

2 How can I die while Jesus lives,
Who rose and left the dead?
Pardon and grace my soul receives
From mine exalted Head.

18

3 All that I am, and all I have,
Shall be forever thine;
Whate'er my duty bids me give,
My cheerful hands resign.

4 Yet if I might make some reserve,
And duty did not call,
I love my God with zeal so great,
That I would give him all.

WATTS.

878 L. M.

1 NOT all the nobles of the earth,
Who boast the honors of their birth,
So high a dignity can claim,
As those who bear the Christian name.

2 To them the privilege is given
To be the sons and heirs of heaven;
Sons of the God who reigns on high,
And heirs of joy beyond the sky.

3 His will he makes them early know,
And teaches their young feet to go;
Whispers instruction to their minds,
And on their hearts his precepts binds.

4 Their daily wants his hands supply,
Their steps he guards with watchful eye:
Leads them from earth to heaven above,
And crowns them with eternal love.

STENNETT.

879 L. M.

1 COMPLETE in thee! no work of mine
May take, dear Lord, the place of thine;
Thy blood has pardon bought for me,
And I am now complete in thee.

2 Complete in thee—no more shall sin
Thy grace has conquered, reign within;
Thy voice will bid the tempter flee,
And I shall stand complete in thee.

3 Complete in thee—each want supplied,
And no good thing to me denied,
Since thou my portion, Lord, wilt be,
I ask no more—complete in thee.

4 Dear Saviour! when, before thy bar,
All tribes and tongues assembled are,
Among thy chosen may I be
At thy right hand—complete in thee.

A. R. W.

880 L. M.

1 LORD, how secure and blest are they
Who feel the joys of pardoned sin!
Should storms of wrath shake earth and sea,
Their minds have heaven and peace within.

2 The day glides swiftly o'er their heads,
Made up of innocence and love;
And soft and silent as the shades,
Their nightly minutes gently move.

3 Quick as their thoughts their joys come on,
But fly not half so swift away;
Their souls are ever bright as noon,
And calm as summer evenings be.

4 How oft they look to heavenly hills,
Where streams of living pleasures flow,
And longing hopes and cheerful smiles
Sit undisturbed upon their brow!

5 They scorn to seek earth's golden toys,
But spend the day, and share the night,
In numbering o'er the richer joys
That heaven prepares for their delight.

WATTS.

881 L. M.

1 JESUS! thy robe of righteousness
My beauty is, my glorious dress;
'Mid flaming worlds, in this arrayed,
With joy shall I lift up my head.

2 When from the dust of death I rise,
To claim my mansion in the skies,
E'en then shall this be all my plea—
"Jesus hath lived and died for me."

3 This spotless robe the same appears,
When ruined nature sinks in years;
No age can change its lovely hue;
Its glory is forever new.

4 O let the dead now hear thy voice;
Now bid thy banished ones rejoice;
Their beauty this, their glorious dress,
Jesus, the Lord, our righteousness.

882 L. M.

1 HOW vast the treasure we possess,
How rich thy bounty, King of grace!
This world is ours, and worlds to come;
Earth is our lodge, and heaven our home.

2 All things are ours, the gifts of God,
The purchase of a Saviour's blood;
While the good Spirit shows us how
To use and to improve them too.

3 If peace and plenty crown my days,
They help me, Lord, to speak thy praise;
If bread of sorrows be my food,
Those sorrows work my lasting good.

4 I would not change my blest estate
For all the world calls good or great;
And, while my faith can keep her hold,
I envy not the sinner's gold.

883 L. M.

1 NO more, ye wise! your wisdom boast;
No more, ye strong! your valor trust;
No more, ye rich! survey your store,
Elate with heaps of shining ore.

2 Glory, ye saints, in this alone,—
That God, your God, to you is known;
That you have owned his sovereign sway,
That you have felt his cheering ray.

3 All else, which we our treasure call,
May in one fatal moment fall;
But what their happiness can move,
Whom God, the blesséd, deigns to love?

DODDRIDGE.

884 L. M.

1 MY precious Lord, for thy dear Name
I bear the cross, despise the shame;
Nor do I faint while thou art near;
I lean on thee; how can I fear?

2 No other name but thine is given
To cheer my soul, in earth or heaven;
No other wealth will I require;
No other friend can I desire.

3 Yea, into nothing would I fall
For thee alone, my All in All;
To feel thy love, my only joy,
To tell thy love, my sole employ.

885 L. M.

1 THOU, whom my soul admires above
All earthly joy and earthly love—
Tell me, dear Shepherd, let me know,
Where do thy sweetest pastures grow?

2 Where is the shadow of that rock,
That from the sun defends thy flock?
Fain would I feed among thy sheep,
Among them rest, among them sleep.

3 Why should thy bride appear like one
That turns aside to paths unknown?
My constant feet would never rove,
Would never seek another love.

4 The footsteps of thy flock I see;
The sweetest pastures here they be;
A wondrous feast thy love prepares,
Bought with thy wounds, and groans, and tears.

5 His dearest flesh he makes my food,
And bids me drink his richest blood;
Here to these hills, my soul would come,
Till my Belovéd leads me home.

WATTS.

886 L. M.

1 OF all the joys we mortals know,
Jesus, thy love exceeds the rest;
Love the best blessing here below,
The nearest image of the blest.

2 While we are held in thine embrace,
There's not a thought attempts to rove;
Each smile upon thy beauteous face
Fixes, and charms, and fires our love.

3 While of thy absence we complain,
And long, or weep in all we do,
There's a strange pleasure in the pain,
And tears have their own sweetness too.

4 When round thy courts by day we rove,
Or ask the watchman of the night
For some kind tidings of our love,
Thy very name creates delight.

5 Jesus, our God, yet rather come,—
Our eyes would dwell upon thy face:
'Tis best to see our Lord at home,
And feel the presence of his grace.

WATTS.

887

L. M.

1 I LOVE, I love thee, Lord most high!
Because thou first hast lovèd me;
I seek no other liberty
But that of being bound to thee.

2 May memory no thought suggest,
But shall to thy pure glory tend:
My understanding find no rest,
Except in thee, its only end.

3 All mine is thine; say but the word,
Whate'er thou willest shall be done;
I know thy love, all-gracious Lord;
I know it seeks my good alone.

4 Apart from thee all things are naught;
Then grant, O my supremest Bliss,—
Grant me to love thee as I ought;
Thou givest all in giving this.

XAVIER.

888

1 THE Shadow of the Rock!
Stay, pilgrim, stay!
Night treads upon the heels of day;
There is no other resting-place this way.
The Rock is near,
The well is clear.
Rest in the Shadow of the Rock!

2 The Shadow of the Rock!
All come alone;
All, ever since the sun hath shone,
Who traveled by this road, have com[e] alone.
Be of good cheer—
A home is here—
Rest in the Shadow of the Rock!

3 The Shadow of the Rock!
To weary feet,
That have been diligent and fleet,
The sleep is deeper, and the shad[e] more sweet.
O weary, rest!
Thou art sore pressed—
Rest in the Shadow of the Rock!

4 The Shadow of the Rock!
One day of pain,
Thou scarce wilt hope the Rock [to] gain,
Yet there wilt sleep thy last sleep [on] the plain.
And only wake
In heaven's daybreak—
Rest in the Shadow of the Rock!

FA[BER.]

889

8s & 6s.

1 THE cross! the cross! the blood-stained cross!
The hallowed cross I see!
Reminding me of precious blood
That once was shed for me.

2 The cross! the cross! that heavy cross,
My Saviour bore for me;
It bowed him to the earth with grief
On sad Mount Calvary.

3 The wounds! the wounds! those painful wounds;
Oh! they were made for me!
His hands and feet, his holy head,
All pierced and torn I see.

4 The death! the death! the awful death
That Jesus died for me!
I heard his groans, his prayer, "Forgive,"
His bleeding side I see.

5 The love! the love! the matchless love,
That bled upon the tree!
It melts my heart, it wins my love,
It brings me, Lord, to thee.

Chorus.

Oh, the blood! the precious blood!
That Jesus shed for me;
Upon the cross, in crimson flood,
Just now by faith I see.

890

6s & 4s.

1 JESUS, thy name I love,
All other names above,
Jesus, my Lord!
Oh, thou art all to me!
Nothing to please I see,
Nothing apart from thee,
Jesus, my Lord!

2 Thou, blessèd Son of God,
Hast bought me with thy blood,
Jesus, my Lord!
Oh! how great is thy love,
All other loves above,
Love that I daily prove,
Jesus, my Lord!

3 When unto thee I flee,
Thou wilt my refuge be,
Jesus, my Lord!
What need I now to fear?
What earthly grief or care,
Since thou art ever near?
Jesus, my Lord!

4 Soon thou wilt come again!
I shall be happy then,
Jesus, my Lord!
Then thine own face I'll see,
Then I shall like thee be,
Then evermore with thee,
Jesus, my Lord!

891

C. M.

1 AMAZING grace! how sweet the sound
That saved a wretch like me!
I once was lost, but now am found—
Was blind, but now I see.

2 'Twas grace that taught my heart to fear,
And grace my fears relieved;
How precious did that grace appear,
The hour I first believed!

3 Through many dangers, toils and snares,
I have already come;
'Tis grace hath brought me safe thus far,
And grace will lead me home.

4 Yes—when this flesh and heart shall fail,
And mortal life shall cease,
I shall possess, within the vail,
A life of joy and peace.

NEWTON.

Chorus.

Oh, how I love Jesus;
Oh, how I love Jesus;
Oh, how I love Jesus;
Because he first loved me.

892 C. M.

1 WHEN God revealed his gracious name,
And changed my mournful state,
My rapture seemed a pleasing dream,
The grace appeared so great.

2 The world beheld the glorious change,
And did thy hand confess;
My tongue broke out in unknown strains,
And sung surprising grace.

3 "Great is the work," my neighbors cried,
And owned thy power divine;
"Great is the work," my heart replied,
"And be the glory thine."

4 The Lord can clear the darkest skies,
Can give us day for night;
Make drops of sacred sorrow rise
To rivers of delight.

5 Let those that sow in sadness wait
Till the fair harvest come;
They shall confess their sheaves are great,
And shout the blessings home.

WATTS.

893 L. M.

1 JESUS, engrave it on my heart,
That thou the one thing needful art;
I could from all things parted be,
But never, never, Lord, from thee.

2 Needful is thy most precious blood,
To reconcile my soul to God;
Needful is thy indulgent care;
Needful thy all-prevailing prayer.

3 Needful thy presence, dearest Lord,
True peace and comfort to afford;
Needful thy promise, to impart
Fresh life and vigor to my heart.

4 Needful art thou, my guide, my stay,
Through all life's dark and weary way;
Nor less in death thou 'lt needful be,
To bring my spirit home to thee.

5 Then needful still, my God, my King,
Thy name eternally I'll sing!
Glory and praise be ever his,—
The one thing needful Jesus is!

MEDLEY.

894 L. M.

1 THOU only Sovereign of my heart,
My Refuge, my Almighty Friend,
And can my soul from thee depart,
On whom alone my hopes depend?

2 Whither, ah! whither shall I go,
A wretched wanderer from my Lord?
Can this dark world of sin and woe
One glimpse of happiness afford?

3 Eternal life thy words impart;
On these my fainting spirit lives;
Here sweeter comforts cheer my heart
Than all the round of nature gives.

4 Thy name my inmost powers adore;
Thou art my Life, my Joy, my Care;
Depart from thee! 'tis death, 'tis more;
'Tis endless ruin, deep despair!

5 Low at thy feet my soul would lie;
Here safety dwells, and peace divine;
Still let me live beneath thine eye,
For life, eternal life, is thine.

STEELE.

895 L. M.

1 MY God, permit me not to be
A stranger to myself and thee;
Amid a thousand thoughts I rove,
Forgetful of my highest love.

2 Why should my passions mix with earth,
And thus debase my heavenly birth?
Why should I cleave to things below,
And let my God, my Saviour, go?

3 Call me away from flesh and sense;
One sovereign word can draw me thence;
I would obey the voice divine,
And all inferior joys resign.

4 Be earth, with all her scenes, withdrawn;
Let noise and vanity be gone:
In secret silence of the mind
My heaven, and there my God, I find.

WATTS.

896 L. M.

1 WHITHER, oh, whither should I fly
But to my loving Saviour's breast?
Secure within thine arms to lie,
And safe beneath thy wings to rest!

2 I have no skill the snare to shun,
But thou, O Christ, my Wisdom art;
I ever into ruin run,
But thou art greater than my heart.

3 I have no might t' oppose the foe,
But everlasting strength is thine;
Show me the way that I should go,
Show me the path I should decline.

4 Foolish, and impotent, and blind,
Lead me a way I have not known;
Bring me where I my heaven may find,
The heaven of loving thee alone.

WESLEY.

897 L. M.

1 AND dost thou say, "Ask what thou wilt?"
Lord, I would seize the golden hour:
I pray to be released from guilt,
And freed from sin and Satan's power.

2 More of thy presence, Lord, impart;
More of thine image let me bear:
Erect thy throne within my heart,
And reign without a rival there.

3 Give me to read my pardon sealed,
And from thy joy to draw my strength;
Oh, be thy boundless love revealed
And all its height and breadth and length.

4 Grant these requests—I ask no more,
But to thy care the rest resign:
Sick, or in health, or rich, or poor,
All shall be well, if thou art mine.

898 L. M.

1 OH, not my own these verdant hills,
And fruits, and flowers, and stream, and wood;
But his who all with glory fills,
Who bought me with his precious blood.

2 Oh, not my own this wondrous frame,
Its curious work, its living soul;
But his who for my ransom came;
Slain for my sake, he claims the whole.

3 Oh, not my own the grace that keeps
My feet from fierce temptations free;
Oh, not my own the thought that leaps,
Adoring, blessèd Lord, to thee.

4 Oh, not my own; I'll soar and sing,
When life, with all its toils, is o'er,
And thou thy trembling lamb shalt bring
Safe home, to wander nevermore.

S. F. SMITH.

899 L. M.

1 DENY thee? what! deny the way
That leads to heaven's eternal day?
Deny the Shepherd who will keep
Within the fold his wandering sheep?

2 Deny thee, Lord! then who will bear
My grief, my burden, and my care?
Thou, thou alone canst calm my breast,
And bid its weary throbbings rest.

900 L. M.

1 'TIS by the faith of joys to come
We walk through deserts dark as night;
Till we arrive at heaven, our home,
Faith is our guide, and faith our light.

2 The want of sight she well supplies;
She makes the pearly gates appear;
Far into distant worlds she pries,
And brings eternal glories near.

3 Cheerful we tread the desert through,
While faith inspires a heavenly ray,
Though lions roar, and tempests blow,
And rocks and dangers fill the way.

WATTS.

901 L. M.

1 GO, labor thou, while it is day;
The world's dark night is hastening on:
Speed, speed thy work,—cast sloth away!
It is not thus that souls are won.

2 Men die in darkness at your side,
Without a hope to cheer the tomb:
Take up the torch and wave it wide—
The torch that lights time's thickest gloom.

3 Toil on—faint not; keep watch and pray!
Be wise the erring soul to win;

Go forth into the world's highway;
Compel the wanderer to come in.

4 Go, labor on; your hands are weak;
Your knees are faint, your soul cast down;
But falter not, the prize you seek
Is near,—a kingdom and a crown!

BONAR.

902 L. M.

1 HAD I the tongues of Greeks and Jews,
And nobler speech than angels use,
If love be absent, I am found
Like tinkling brass, an empty sound.

2 Should I distribute all my store
To feed the hungry, clothe the poor;
Or give my body to the flame,
To gain a martyr's glorious name:

3 If love to God and love to men
Be absent, all my hopes are vain;
Nor tongues, nor gifts, nor fiery zeal,
The work of love can e'er fulfill.

WATTS.

903 L. M.

1 SO let our lips and lives express
The holy gospel we profess;
So let our works and virtues shine,
To prove the doctrine all divine.

2 Thus shall we best proclaim abroad
The honors of our Saviour God,
When his salvation reigns within,
And grace subdues the power of sin.

3 Our flesh and sense must be denied,
Ambition, envy, lust, and pride;
While justice, temperance, truth, and love,
Our inward piety approve.

4 Religion bears our spirits up,
While we expect that blessèd hope,
The bright appearance of the Lord,
And faith stands leaning on his word.

WATTS.

904 L. M.

1 MY gracious Lord, I own thy right
To every service I can pay;
And call it my supreme delight
To hear thy dictates and obey.

2 What is my being but for thee,
Its sure support, its noblest end,—
Thine ever-smiling face to see,
And serve the cause of such a Friend!

3 I would not breathe for worldly joy,
Or to increase my worldly good;
Nor future days nor powers employ
To spread a sounding name abroad.

4 'Tis to my Saviour I would live,
To him who for my ransom died;
Nor could the bowers of Eden give
Such bliss as blossoms at his side.

5 His work my hoary age shall bless,
When youthful vigor is no more;
And my last hour of life confess
His dying love, his saving power.

DODDRIDGE.

905 L. M.

1 WHEN Jesus dwelt in mortal clay,
What were his works from day to day,
But miracles of power and grace,
That spread salvation through our race?

2 Teach us, O Lord, to keep in view
Thy pattern, and thy steps pursue;
Let alms bestowed, let kindness done,
Be witnessed by each rolling sun.

3 That man may last, but never lives,
Who much receives, but nothing gives;
Whom none can love, whom none can thank,
Creation's blot, creation's blank!

4 But he who marks, from day to day,
In generous acts his radiant way,
Treads the same path his Saviour trod,
The path to glory and to God.

GIBBONS.

906 L. M.

1 GO, labor on; spend and be spent;
Thy joy to do the Father's will;
It is the way the Master went,
Should not the servant tread it still?

2 Go, labor on; 'tis not for nought;
Thine earthly loss is heavenly gain,
Men heed thee, love thee, praise thee not;
The Master praises,—what are men!

3 Go, labor on; enough while here
If he shall praise thee; if he deign
Thy willing heart to mark and cheer;
No toil for him shall be in vain.

4 Toil on, and in thy toil rejoice;
For toil comes rest, for exile home;
Soon shalt thou hear the Bridegroom's voice,
The midnight peal: "Behold, I come!"

BONAR.

907 C. M.

1 HAPPY the heart where graces reign,
Where love inspires the breast;
Love is the brightest of the train,
And strengthens all the rest.

2 Knowledge, alas! 'tis all in vain,
And all in vain our fear;
Our stubborn sins will fight and reign,
If love be absent there.

3 This is the grace that lives and sings,
When faith and hope shall cease;
'Tis this shall strike our joyful strings,
In the sweet realms of bliss.

WATTS.

908 C. M.

1 LORD, as to thy dear Cross we flee,
And plead to be forgiven,
So let thy life our pattern be,
And form our souls for heaven.

2 Help us, through good report and ill,
Our daily cross to bear;
Like thee, to do our Father's will,
Our brethren's griefs to share.

3 Let grace our selfishness expel,
Our earthliness refine;
And kindness in our bosoms dwell,
As free and true as thine.

4 Should friends misjudge, or foes defame,
Or brethren faithless prove,
Then, like thine own, be all our aim
To conquer them by love.

5 Kept peaceful in the midst of strife,
Forgiving and forgiven,
Oh, may we lead the pilgrim's life,
And follow thee to heaven!

909 C. M.

1 SCORN not the slightest word or deed,
Nor deem it void of power;
There's fruit in each wind-wafted seed,
That waits its natal hour.

2 A whispered word may touch the heart,
And call it back to life;
A look of love bid sin depart,
And still unholy strife.

3 No act falls fruitless; none can tell
How vast its power may be,
Nor what results infolded dwell
Within it silently.

4 Work on, despair not, bring thy mite,
Nor care how small it be;
God is with all that serve the right,
The holy, true, and free.

910 C. M.

1 RICH are the joys which cannot die,
With God laid up in store;
Treasures beyond the changing sky,
Brighter than golden ore.

2 The seeds which piety and love
Have scattered here below,
In the fair fertile fields above
To ample harvests grow.

3 The mite my willing hands can give
At Jesus' feet I lay;
Grace shall the humble gift receive,
Abounding grace repay.

911 C. M.

1 OH, for a heart to praise my God,
A heart from sin set free;
A heart that always feels thy blood,
So freely shed for me!

2 A heart resigned, submissive, meek,
My dear Redeemer's throne;
Where only Christ is heard to speak,
Where Jesus reigns alone!

3 An humble, lowly, contrite heart,
Believing, true, and clean!
Which neither life nor death can part
From him that dwells within.

4 A heart in every thought renewed
And filled with love divine;
Perfect, and right, and pure, and good;
A copy, Lord, of thine.

5 Thy nature, gracious Lord, impart;
Come quickly from above;
Write thy new name upon my heart,—
Thy new, best name of love.

C. WESLEY.

912 C. M.

1 FAITH adds new charms to earthly bliss,
And saves us from its snares;
It yields support in all our toils,
And softens all our cares.

2 The wounded conscience knows its power
The healing balm to give;
That balm the saddest heart can cheer,
And make the dying live.

3 Unveiling wide the heavenly world,
Where endless pleasures reign,

It bids us seek our portion there,
Nor bids us seek in vain.

4 Faith shows the promise fully sealed
With our Redeemer's blood;
It helps our feeble hope to rest
Upon a faithful God.

5 There, still unshaken, would we rest,
Till this frail body dies,
And then, on faith's triumphant wing,
To endless glory rise.

WATTS.

913 C. M.

1 BLEST is the man whose softening heart
Feels all another's pain;
To whom the supplicating eye
Was never raised in vain:—

2 Whose breast expands with generous warmth,
A stranger's woes to feel;
And bleeds in pity o'er the wound
He wants the power to heal.

3 He spreads his kind, supporting arms,
To every child of grief;
His secret bounty largely flows,
And brings unasked relief.

4 To gentle offices of love
His feet are never slow:
He views, through mercy's melting eye,
A brother in a foe.

BARBAULD.

914 C. M.

1 I WORSHIP thee, sweet Will of God!
And all thy ways adore;
And every day I live, I seem
To love thee more and more.

2 I love to kiss each print where thou
Hast set thine unseen feet;
I cannot fear thee, blessèd will,
Thine empire is so sweet.

3 I have no cares, O blessèd will,
For all my cares are thine;
I live in triumph, Lord, for thou
Hast made thy triumphs mine.

4 He always wins who sides with God,
To him no chance is lost;
God's will is sweetest to him when
It triumphs at his cost.

5 Ill, that God blesses, is our good,
And unblest good is ill;
And all is right that seems most wrong,
If it be his dear will!

6 When obstacles and trials seem
Like prison-walls to be,
I do the little I can do,
And leave the rest to thee.

FABER.

915 C. M.

1 OH, it is hard to work for God,
To rise and take his part
Upon this battle-field of earth,
And not sometimes lose heart!

2 He hides himself so wondrously,
As though there was no God;
He is least seen when all the powers
Of ill are most abroad;

3 Or he deserts us in the hour
The fight is all but lost;
And seems to leave us to ourselves
Just when we need him most.

4 It is not so, but so it looks;
And we lose courage then;
And doubts will come if God hath kept
His promises to men.

5 But right is right, since God is God;
And right the day must win;
To doubt would be disloyalty,
To falter would be sin!

FABER.

916

C. M.

1 GOD'S glory is a wondrous thing,
Most strange in all its ways,
And, of all things on earth, least like
What men agree to praise.

2 Oh, blessed is he to whom is given
The instinct that can tell
That God is on the field, when he
Is most invisible!

3 Workman of God! oh lose not heart,
But learn what God is like;
And in the darkest battle-field
Thou shalt know where to strike.

4 Oh, learn to scorn the praise of men!
Oh, learn to lose with God!
For Jesus won the world through shame,
And beckons thee his road.

FABER.

917

C. M.

1 OH, for a faith that will not shrink,
Though pressed by every foe,
That will not tremble on the brink
Of any earthly woe!

2 That will not murmur nor complain
Beneath the chastening rod,
But, in the hour of grief or pain,
Will lean upon its God;—

3 A faith that shines more bright and clear
When tempests rage without;
That when in danger knows no fear,
In darkness knows no doubt;—

4 That bears, unmoved, the world's dread frown,
Nor heeds its scornful smile:
That seas of trouble cannot drown,
Nor Satan's arts beguile;—

5 A faith that keeps the narrow way
Till life's last hour is fled,
And with a pure and heavenly ray
Lights up a dying bed.

6 Lord, give us such a faith as this,
And then, whate'er may come,
We'll taste, e'en here, the hallowed bliss
Of an eternal home.

BATH COLL.

918

C. M.

1 WE bless thee for thy peace, O God!
Deep as the soundless sea,
Which falls like sunshine on the road
Of those who trust in thee.

2 We ask not, Father, for repose
Which comes from outward rest,
If we may have through all life's woes
Thy peace within our breast;—

3 That peace which suffers and is strong,
Trusts where it cannot see,

Deems not the trial way too long,
But leaves the end with thee ;—

4 That peace which flows serene and deep—
A river in the soul,
Whose banks a living verdure keep,—
God's sunshine o'er the whole !

919 C. M.

1 CALM me, my God, and keep me calm ;
Let thine outstretchèd wing
Be like the shades of Elim's palm,
Beside her desert spring.

2 Yes, keep me calm, though loud and rude
The sounds my ear that greet,—
Calm in the closet's solitude,
Calm in the bustling street ;—

3 Calm in the hour of buoyant health,
Calm in the hour of pain,
Calm in my poverty or wealth,
Calm in my loss or gain ;—

4 Calm in the suffering of wrong,
Like him who bore my shame,
Calm 'mid the threatening, taunting throng,
Who hate thy holy name.

5 Calm me, my God, and keep me calm,
Soft resting on thy breast ;
Soothe me with holy hymn and psalm,
And bid my spirit rest. BONAR.

920 C. M.

1 SPEAK gently—it is better far
To rule by love than fear ;
Speak gently—let no harsh word mar
The good we may do here.

2 Speak gently to the little child !
Its love be sure to gain ;
Teach it in accents soft and mild—
It may not long remain.

3 Speak gently to the young—for they
Will have enough to bear ;
Pass through this life as best they may,
'Tis full of anxious care.

4 Speak gently to the aged one,
Grieve not the careworn heart ;
The sands of life are nearly run,
Let them in peace depart.

5 Speak gently, kindly, to the poor ;
Let no harsh tone be heard ;
They have enough they must endure,
Without an unkind word !

6 Speak gently to the erring ones—
They must have toiled in vain ;
Perchance unkindness made them so ;
Oh, win them back again !

7 Speak gently—'tis a little thing,
Dropped in the heart's deep well ;
The good, the joy, that it may bring,
Eternity shall tell. BATES.

921 C. M.

1 WHO is thy neighbor ? he whom thou
Hast power to aid or bless ;
Whose aching heart or burning brow
Thy soothing hand may press.

2 Thy neighbor ? 'tis the fainting poor,
Whose eye with want is dim ;
Oh enter thou his humble door,
With aid and peace for him.

3 Thy neighbor? he who drinks the cup
When sorrow drowns the brim;
With words of high sustaining hope,
Go thou and comfort him.

4 Thy neighbor? pass no mourner by;
Perhaps thou canst redeem
A breaking heart from misery;
Go, share thy lot with him.

PEABODY.

922 C. M.

1 MAKE channels for the streams of love,
Where they may broadly run;
And love has overflowing streams,
To fill them every one.

2 But if at any time we cease
Such channels to provide,
The very founts of love for us
Will soon be parched and dried.

3 For we must share, if we would keep
That blessing from above;
Ceasing to give, we cease to have;—
Such is the law of love.

TRENCH.

923 S. M.

1 SOW in the morn thy seed,
At eve hold not thine hand;
To doubt and fear give thou no heed,
Broadcast it o'er the land.

2 Beside all waters sow,
The highway furrows stock,
Drop it where thorns and thistles grow,
Scatter it on the rock.

3 Thou knowest not which may thrive,
The late or early sown;
Grace keeps the precious germ alive,
When and wherever strown.

4 And duly shall appear,
In verdure, beauty, strength,
The tender blade, the stalk, the ear,
And the full corn at length.

5 Thou canst not toil in vain;
Cold, heat, and moist and dry,
Shall foster and mature the grain
For garners in the sky.

6 Thence when the glorious end,
The day of God shall come,
The angel-reapers shall descend,
And heaven cry, "Harvest home!"

MONTGOMERY.

924 S. M.

1 LABORERS of Christ, arise,
And gird you for the toil;
The dew of promise from the skies
Already cheers the soil.

2 Go where the sick recline,
Where mourning hearts deplore;
And where the sons of sorrow pine,
Dispense your hallowed lore.

3 Urge, with a tender zeal,
The erring child along
Where peaceful congregations kneel,
And pious teachers throng.

4 Be faith, which looks above,
With prayer, your constant guest,
And wrap the Saviour's changeless love
A mantle round your breast.

5 So shall you share the wealth
That earth may ne'er despoil,
And the blest gospel's saving health
Repay your arduous toil.

MRS. SIGOURNEY.

925 S. M.

1 LOVE is the fountain whence
All true obedience flows;
The Christian serves the God he loves,
And loves the God he knows.

2 He treads the heavenly road,
And neither faints nor tires;
That generous love which warms his breast,
With fortitude inspires.

3 No burden seems so great,
No task so hard appears,
But this he cheerfully performs,
And that he meekly bears.

4 May love,—that shining grace,
O'er all my powers preside;
Direct my thoughts, suggest my words,
And every action guide!

BEDDOME.

926 S. M.

1 A CHARGE to keep I have,
A God to glorify,
A never-dying soul to save,
And fit it for the sky.

2 To serve the present age,
My calling to fulfill;
Oh, may it all my powers engage
To do my Master's will.

3 Arm me with jealous care,
As in thy sight to live;
And oh, thy servant, Lord, prepare
A strict account to give.

4 Help me to watch and pray,
And on thyself rely,
Assured, if I my trust betray,
I shall forever die.

C. WESLEY.

927 S. M.

1 YE servants of the Lord,
Each in his office wait;
With joy obey his heavenly word
And watch before his gate.

2 Let all your lamps be bright,
And trim the golden flame;
Gird up your loins, as in his sight,
For awful is his name.

3 Watch!—'tis your Lord's command;
And while we speak, he's near;
Mark every signal of his hand,
And ready all appear.

4 Oh, happy servant he,
In such a posture found!
He shall his Lord with rapture see,
And be with honor crowned.

DODDRIDGE.

928 S. M.

1 FAITH is a precious grace,
Where'er it is bestowed;
It boasts a high, celestial birth,
And is the gift of God.

2 Jesus it owns as King,
And all-atoning Priest;
It claims no merit of its own,
But looks for all in Christ.

3 To him it leads the soul,
When filled with deep distress,
Flies to the fountain of his blood,
And trusts his righteousness.

BEDDOME.

929 S. M.

1 WE give thee but thine own,
Whate'er the gift may be:
All that we have is thine alone,
A trust, O Lord, from thee.

2 Oh! hearts are bruised and dead,
And homes are bare and cold,
And lambs, for whom the Shepherd bled,
Are straying from the fold.

3 To comfort and to bless,
To find a balm for woe,
To tend the lone and fatherless,
Is now our work below.

4 The captive to release,
To God the lost to bring,
To teach the way of life and peace,
It is a Christ-like thing.

930 8s & 7s.

1 ALWAYS with us, always with us—
Words of cheer, and words of love;
Thus the risen Saviour whispers,
From his dwelling-place above.

2 With us when we toil in sadness,
Sowing much and reaping none;
Telling us that in the future
Golden harvests shall be won.

3 With us when the storm is sweeping
O'er our pathway dark and drear;
Waking hope within our bosoms,
Stilling every anxious fear.

4 With us in the lonely valley,
When we cross the chilling stream,
Lighting up the steps to glory
With salvation's radiant beam.

NEVIN.

931 8s & 7s.

1 BLESSED angels, high in heaven
O'er the penitent rejoice:
Hast thou for thy brother striven
With an importuning voice?

2 Art thou not thy brother's keeper,
Canst thou not his soul obtain?
He that wakes his brother sleeper
Double life himself shall gain.

3 Think how words in season spoken,
In the sinful heart sink deep,
And the first link may have broken
Of the chains that round him creep.

4 Think of that day when each brother
To his brother shall be known:
If thy prayers have saved another,
God will then thy service own.

5 Then, when ends this life's short fever,
They, who many turn to God,
Like the stars shall shine forever,
In th' eternal brotherhood!

932 8s & 7s.

1 HE that goeth forth with weeping,
Bearing precious seed in love,
Never tiring, never sleeping,
Findeth mercy from above.

2 Soft descend the dews of heaven,
Bright the rays celestial shine;
Precious fruits will thus be given,
Through an influence all divine.

3 Sow thy seed, be never weary,
Let no fears thy soul annoy;
Be the prospect ne'er so dreary,
Thou shalt reap the fruits of joy.

4 Lo, the scene of verdure brightening!
See the rising grain appear;
Look again! the fields are whitening,
For the harvest time is near.

HASTINGS.

933 7s & 6s.

1 WORK, for the night is coming,
Work thro' the morning hours;
Work, while the dew is sparkling,
Work 'mid springing flowers;
Work, when the day grows brighter,
Work in the glowing sun;
Work, for the night is coming,
When man's work is done.

2 Work, for the night is coming,
Work through the sunny noon;
Fill brightest hours with labor,
Rest comes sure and soon.
Give every flying minute,
Something to keep in store:
Work, for the night is coming,
When man works no more.

3 Work, for the night is coming,
Under the sunset skies;
While their bright tints are glowing,
Work, for daylight flies.
Work till the last beam fadeth,
Fadeth to shine no more;
Work while the night is dark'ning,
When man's work is o'er.

934

1 WHEN faint and weary, toiling,
The sweat-drops on my brow,
I long to rest from labor,
To drop the burden now—
There comes a gentle chiding
To quell each mourning sigh:
"Work, while the day is shining,
There's resting by and by."

2 This life to toil is given,
And he improves it best
Who seeks by patient labor
To enter into rest;
Then pilgrim, worn and weary,
Press on, the goal is nigh;
The prize is straight before thee,
There's resting by and by.

3 Nor ask, when overburdened,
You long for friendly aid,
"Why idle stands my brother,
No yoke upon him laid?"
Perhaps he's told to tarry;
Nor stop to ask him why:
"Go labor in my vineyard,"
There's resting by and by.

4 Wan reaper in the harvest,
Let this thy strength sustain,—
Each sheaf that fills the garner
Brings you eternal gain.
Then bear the cross with patience,
To fields of duty hie;
'Tis sweet to work for Jesus—
There's resting by and by.

SIDNEY DYER.

Chorus.

Resting by and by,
There's resting by and by;
We shall not always labor,
We shall not always cry;
The end is drawing nearer,
The end for which we sigh;
We'll lay our heavy burdens down,
There's resting by and by.

935 C. M.

1 LORD, shall we part with gold for dross,
With solid good for show?
Outlive our bliss, and mourn our loss
In everlasting woe?

2 Let us not lose the living God,
For one short dream of joy:
With fond embrace cling to a clod,
And fling all heaven away.

3 Vain world, thy weak attempts forbear,
We all thy charms defy;
And rate our precious souls too dear,
For all thy wealth to buy.

936 C. M.

1 OH not to fill the mouth of fame
My longing soul is stirred;
Oh give me a diviner name,—
Call me thy servant, Lord.

2 Sweet title that delighteth me,
Rank earnestly implored;
Oh what can reach the dignity
Of thy true servants, Lord?

3 No longer would my soul be known
As self-sustained and free;
Oh, not mine own, oh, not mine own,
Lord, I belong to thee.

4 In life, in death, on earth, in heaven,
No other name for me;
The same sweet style and title given
Through all eternity.

THOMAS H. GILL.

937 C. M.

1 ONE thing alone, dear Lord! I dread—
To have a secret spot
That separates my soul from thee,
And yet to know it not.

2 But if this weariness hath come
A present from on high,
Teach me to find the hidden wealth
That in its depths may lie.

3 If this drear change be thine, O Lord!
If it be thy sweet will,
Spare not, but to the very brim
The bitter chalice fill.

4 But if it hath been sin of mine,
Oh, show that sin to me!
Not to get back the sweetness lost,
But to make peace with thee.

5 So in this darkness I can learn
To tremble and adore,
To sound my own vile nothingness,
And thus to love thee more.

6 Oh, blessèd be this darkness then,
This deep in which I lie,
And blessèd be all things that teach
God's dread Supremacy!

FABER.

938 8s. D.

1 HOW tedious and tasteless the hours
When Jesus no longer I see!
Sweet prospects, sweet birds and sweet flow'rs
Have lost all their sweetness with me:
The midsummer sun shines but dim,
The fields strive in vain to look gay,
But when I am happy in him,
December's as pleasant as May.

2 His name yields the richest perfume,
And sweeter than music his voice;
His presence disperses my gloom,
And makes all within me rejoice:
I should, were he always so nigh,
Have nothing to wish or to fear;
No mortal so happy as I;
My summer would last all the year.

3 Content with beholding his face,
My all to his pleasure resigned,
No changes of season or place
Would make any change in my mind:
While blest with a sense of his love,
A palace a toy would appear;
And prisons would palaces prove,
If Jesus would dwell with me there.

4 Dear Lord, if indeed I am thine,
If thou art my sun and my song,
Say, why do I languish and pine?
And why are my winters so long?
Oh, drive these dark clouds from my sky;
Thy soul-cheering presence restore;
Or take me to thee up on high,
Where winter and clouds are no more.

NEWTON.

939 C. M.

1 OH, could I find, from day to day
A nearness to my God,
Then would my hours glide sweet away,
While leaning on his word.

2 Lord, I desire with thee to live
Anew from day to day,
In joys the world can never give,
Nor ever take away.

3 Blest Jesus, come, and rule my heart,
And make me wholly thine,
That I may never more depart,
Nor grieve thy love divine.

4 Thus, till my last, expiring breath,
Thy goodness I'll adore;
And when my frame dissolves in death,
My soul shall love thee more.

B. CLEAVLAND.

940 C. M.

1 LONG have I sat beneath the sound
Of thy salvation, Lord;
But still how weak my faith is found,
And knowledge of thy word!

2 Oft I frequent thy holy place,
And hear almost in vain;
How small a portion of thy grace
My memory can retain!

3 How cold and feeble is my love,
How negligent my fear,
How low my hope of joys above,
How few affections there!

4 Great God, thy sovereign power impart
To give thy word success;
Write thy salvation in my heart,
And make me learn thy grace.

5 Show my forgetful feet the way
That leads to joys on high:
There knowledge grows without decay,
And love shall never die.

WATTS.

941 C. M.

1 THE bird let loose in eastern skies,
When hastening fondly home,
Ne'er stoops to earth her wing, nor flies
Where idle warblers roam.

2 But high she shoots through air and light,
Above all low delay,
Where nothing earthly bounds her flight,
Nor shadow dims her way.

3 So grant me, Lord, from every snare
And stain of passion free,
Aloft through faith's serener air
To hold my course to thee.

4 No sin to cloud, no lure to stay
My soul, as home she springs;
Thy sunshine on her joyful way,
Thy freedom in her wings.

MOORE.

942 C. M.

1 OH, for a closer walk with God!
A calm and heavenly frame!
A light to shine upon the road
That leads me to the Lamb!

2 Where is the blessedness I knew
When first I saw the Lord?
Where is the soul-refreshing view
Of Jesus and his word?

3 What peaceful hours I once enjoyed!
How sweet their memory still!
But they have left an aching void
The world can never fill.

4 Return, O holy Dove, return
Sweet messenger of rest;
I hate the sins that made thee mourn,
And drove thee from my breast.

5 The dearest idol I have known,
Whate'er that idol be,
Help me to tear it from thy throne,
And worship only thee.

6 So shall my walk be close with God,
Calm and serene my frame;
So purer light shall mark the road
That leads me to the Lamb.

COWPER.

943 L. M.

1 MY only Saviour! when I feel
O'erwhelmed in spirit, faint, oppressed,
'Tis sweet to tell thee, while I kneel
Low at thy feet, thou art my rest.

2 I'm weary of the strife within;
Strong powers against my soul contest;
Oh, let me turn from self and sin
To thy dear cross, for there is rest!

3 Oh! sweet will be the welcome day,
When, from its toils and woes released,
My parting soul in death shall say,
"Now, Lord, I come to thee for rest!"

944 L. M.

1 O LOVE Divine! that stooped to share
Our sharpest pang, our bitterest tear,
On thee we cast each earth-born care,
We smile at pain while thou art near.

2 Though long the weary way we tread,
And sorrow crown each lingering year,
No path we shun, no darkness dread,
Our hearts still whispering, Thou art near.

3 When drooping pleasure turns to grief,
And trembling faith is changed to fear,
The murmuring wind, the quivering leaf,
Shall softly tell us thou art near.

4 On thee we fling our burdening woe,
O Love Divine, forever dear;
Content to suffer while we know,
Living or dying, thou art near!

O. W. Holmes.

945 L. M.

1 FATHER! beneath thy shelt'ring wing
In sweet security we rest,
And fear no evil earth can bring,
In life, in death, supremely blest.

2 For life is good whose tidal flow
The motions of thy will obeys;
And death is good, that makes us know
The Life Divine that all things sways.

3 And good it is to bear the cross,
And so thy perfect peace to win:
And nought is ill, nor brings us loss,
Nor works us harm, save only sin.

4 Redeemed from this, we ask no more,
But trust the love that saves to guide:
The grace that yields so rich a store,
Will grant us all we need beside.

W. H. Burleigh.

946 6s & 4s.

1 NEARER, my God, to thee,
Nearer to thee!
E'en though it be a cross
That raiseth me,
Still all my song shall be,
Nearer, my God, to thee,
Nearer to thee!

2 Though like the wanderer,
The sun gone down,
Darkness be over me,
My rest a stone;
Yet in my dreams I'd be
Nearer, my God, to thee,
Nearer to thee!

3 There let the way appear
Steps unto heaven;
All that thou sendest me,
In mercy given;
Angels to beckon me
Nearer, my God, to thee,
Nearer to thee!

4 Then with my waking thoughts
Bright with thy praise,
Out of my stony griefs
Bethel I'll raise;
So by my woes to be
Nearer, my God, to thee,
Nearer to thee!

5 Or if on joyful wing,
Cleaving the sky,
Sun, moon, and stars forgot,
Upward I fly,
Still all my song shall be,
Nearer, my God, to thee,
Nearer to thee.

Sarah F. Adams.

947 6s & 4s.

1 SAVIOUR! thy gentle voice
Gladly we hear;
Author of all our joys,
Ever be near;

Our souls would cling to thee,
Let us thy fullness see,
Our life to cheer.

2 Fountain of life divine!
Thee we adore;
We would be wholly thine
Forevermore;
Freely forgive our sin,
Grant heavenly peace within,
Thy light restore.

3 Though to our faith unseen,
While darkness reigns,
On thee alone we lean
While life remains;
By thy free grace restored,
Our souls shall bless the Lord
In joyful strains!

HASTINGS.

948 L. M.

1 STAND up, my soul, shake off thy fears,
And gird the gospel armor on;
March to the gates of endless joy,
Where Jesus, thy great Captain's gone.

2 Hell and thy sins resist thy course;
But hell and sin are vanquished foes;
Thy Saviour nailed them to the cross,
And sung the triumph when he rose.

3 Then let my soul march boldly on,—
Press forward to the heavenly gate;
There peace and joy eternal reign,
And glittering robes for conquerors wait.

4 There shall I wear a starry crown,
And triumph in almighty grace,
While all the armies of the skies
Join in my glorious Leader's praise.

WATTS.

949 L. M.

1 LET me but hear my Saviour say,
"Strength shall be equal to thy day;"
Then I rejoice in deep distress,
Upheld by all-sufficient grace.

2 I can do all things—or can bear
All suffering, if my Lord be there;
Sweet pleasures mingle with the pains,
While he my sinking head sustains.

3 I glory in infirmity,
That Christ's own power may rest on me;
When I am weak, then am I strong;
Grace is my shield, and Christ my song.

WATTS.

950 L. M.

1 JESUS, while this rough desert soil
I tread, be thou my guide and stay:
Nerve me for conflict and for toil;
Uphold me on my stranger-way!

2 Jesus, in heaviness and fear,
'Mid cloud, and shade, and gloom I stray,
For earth's last night is drawing near;
Oh, cheer me on my stranger-way!

3 Jesus, in solitude and grief,
When sun and stars withhold their ray,

Make haste, make haste to my relief!
Oh, light me on my stranger-way!

4 Jesus, in weakness of this flesh,
When Satan grasps me for his prey,
Oh, give me victory afresh,
And speed me on my stranger-way!

BONAR.

951 L. M.

1 BESET with snares on every hand,
In life's uncertain path I stand;
Saviour Divine! diffuse thy light,
To guide my doubtful footsteps right.

2 Engage this roving treacherous heart,
Great God! to choose the better part;
To scorn the trifles of a day
For joys that none can take away.

3 If thou, my Saviour, still art nigh,
Cheerful I live, and joyful die:
Secure, when mortal comforts flee,
To find eternal joys in thee.

952 L. M.

1 AWAKE, my soul! away, our fears!
Let every trembling thought be gone;
Awake, and run the heavenly race,
And put a cheerful courage on!

2 True, 'tis a strait and thorny road,
And mortal spirits tire and faint;
But they forget the mighty God,
Who feeds the strength of every saint.

3 The mighty God, whose matchless power
Is ever new and ever young,
And firm endures, while endless years
Their everlasting circles run.

4 From thee, the overflowing spring,
Our souls shall drink a fresh supply;
While such as trust their native strength
Shall melt away, and droop, and die.

5 Swift as an eagle cuts the air,
We'll mount aloft to thine abode;
On wings of love our souls shall fly,
Nor tire amid the heavenly road!

WATTS.

953 L. M.

1 AWAKE, my soul! lift up thine eyes;
See where thy foes against thee rise,
In long array, a numerous host;
Awake, my soul! or thou art lost.

2 See where rebellious passions rage,
And fierce desires and lusts engage;
The meanest foe of all the train
Has thousands and ten thousands slain.

3 Thou treadest on enchanted ground;
Perils and snares beset thee round;
Beware of all, guard every part—
But most the traitor in thy heart.

4 The terror and the charm repel,
The powers of earth, and powers of hell;
The Man of Calv'ry triumphed here:
Why should his faithful followers fear?

5 Come, then, my soul! now learn to wield
The weight of thine immortal shield;
Put on the armor, from above,
Of heavenly truth, and heavenly love.

BARBAULD.

954 L. M.

1 MY soul, what hast thou done for God?
Look o'er thy misspent years and see,
Sum up what thou hast done for God,
And then what God hath done for thee.

2 He made thee when he might have made
A soul that would have loved him more;
He rescued thee from nothingness,
And set thee on life's happy shore.

3 What hast thou done for God, my soul?
Look o'er thy misspent years and see;
Cry from thy worse than nothingness—
Cry for his mercy upon thee!

955 C. M.

1 AWAKE, my soul, stretch every nerve,
And press with vigor on:
A heavenly race demands thy zeal,
And an immortal crown.

2 A cloud of witnesses around
Hold thee in full survey;
Forget the steps already trod,
And onward urge thy way.

3 'Tis God's all-animating voice
That calls thee from on high;
'Tis his own hand presents the prize
To thine aspiring eye.

4 That prize with peerless glories bright,
Which shall new lustre boast,
When victor's wreaths and monarch's gems
Shall blend in common dust.

5 Blest Saviour, introduced by thee,
Have I my race begun;
And, crowned with victory, at thy feet
I'll lay my honors down. DODDRIDGE.

956 L. M.

1 O ISRAEL, to thy tents repair:
Why thus secure on hostile ground?
Thy King commands thee to beware,
For many foes thy camp surround.

2 The trumpet gives a martial strain:
O Israel, gird thee for the fight!
Arise, the combat to maintain,
And put thine enemies to flight!

3 Thou shouldst not sleep, as others do;
Awake; be vigilant; be brave!
The coward, and the sluggard too,
Must wear the fetters of the slave.

4 A nobler lot is cast for thee;
A kingdom waits thee in the skies:
With such a hope, shall Israel flee,
Or yield, through weariness, the prize?

5 No! let a careless world repose
And slumber on through life's short day,
While Israel to the conflict goes,
And bears the glorious prize away!
KELLY.

957 C. M.

1 MY drowsy powers, why sleep ye so?
Awake, my sluggish soul!
Nothing has half thy work to do,
Yet nothing's half so dull.

2 The little ants, for one poor grain,
Labor, and tug, and strive;
Yet we, who have a heaven t' obtain,
How negligent we live!

3 We, for whose sake all nature stands,
And stars their courses move;
We, for whose guard the angel bands
Come flying from above;—

4 We, for whom God the Son came down,
And labored for our good,
How careless to secure that crown
He purchased with his blood!

WATTS.

958 S. M.

1 MY soul, be on thy guard,
Ten thousand foes arise;
And hosts of sin are pressing hard
To draw thee from the skies.

2 Oh, watch, and fight, and pray;
The battle ne'er give o'er;
Renew it boldly every day,
And help divine implore.

3 Ne'er think the victory won,
Nor lay thine armor down:
Thy arduous work will not be done
Till thou obtain thy crown.

4 Fight on, my soul, till death
Shall bring thee to thy God;
He'll take thee, at thy parting breath,
To his divine abode.

HEATH.

959 S. M.

1 MY soul, it is thy God
Who calls thee by his grace;
Now loose thee from each cumbering load,
And bend thee to the race.

2 Make thy salvation sure;
All sloth and slumber shun;
Nor a moment rest secure,
Till thou the goal hast won.

3 Thy crown of life hold fast;
Thy heart with courage stay;
Nor let one trembling glance be cast
Along the backward way.

4 Thy path ascends the skies,
With conq'ring footsteps bright;
And thou shalt win and wear the prize
In everlasting light.

960 S. M.

1 THE people of the Lord
Are on their way to heaven;
There they obtain their great reward;
The prize will there be given.

2 'Tis conflict here below;
'Tis triumph there, and peace:
On earth we wrestle with the foe;
In heaven our conflicts cease.

3 'Tis gloom and darkness here;
'Tis light and joy above;
There all is pure, and all is clear;
There all is peace and love.

4 There rest shall follow toil,
And ease succeed to care:
The victors there divide the spoil;
They sing and triumph there.

5 Then let us joyful sing;
The conflict is not long:
We hope in heaven to praise our King
In one eternal song.

961 S. M.

1 THE harvest dawn is near,
The year delays not long;
And he who sows with many a tear,
Shall reap with many a song.

2 Sad to his toil he goes,
His seed with weeping leaves;
But he shall come, at twilight's close,
And bring his golden sheaves.

BURGESS.

962 S. M.

1 SOLDIERS of Christ, arise,
And gird your armor on,
Strong in the strength which God supplies,
Through his eternal Son:

2 Strong in the Lord of hosts,
And in his mighty power,
Who in the strength of Jesus trusts,
Is more than conqueror.

3 Leave no unguarded place,
No weakness of the soul;
Take every virtue, every grace,
And fortify the whole.

4 Stand, then, in his great might,
With all his strength endued,
And take, to arm you for the fight,
The panoply of God:

5 That, having all things done,
And all your conflicts past,
You may o'ercome thro' Christ alone,
And stand complete at last.

6 From strength to strength go on;
Wrestle, and fight, and pray;
Tread all the powers of darkness down,
And win the well-fought day.

C. WESLEY.

963 S. M.

1 WHAT cheering words are these;
Their sweetness who can tell?
In time and to eternal days,
"'Tis with the righteous well."

2 In every state secure,
Kept as Jehovah's eye,
'Tis well with them while life endures,
And well when called to die.

3 Well when they see his face,
Or sink amidst the flood;
Well in affliction's thorny maze,
Or on the mount with God.

4 'Tis well when joys arise,
'Tis well when sorrows flow,
'Tis well when darkness vails the skies,
And strong temptations grow.

5 'Tis well when Jesus calls,
"From earth and sin arise,
To join the hosts of ransomed souls,
Made to salvation wise!"

KENT.

964 S. M.

1 MY soul, weigh not thy life
Against thy heavenly crown;
Nor suffer Satan's deadliest strife
To beat thy courage down.

2 With prayer and crying strong,
Hold on the fearful fight,
And let the breaking day prolong
The wrestling of the night.

3 The battle soon will yield
If thou thy part fulfil;
For strong as is the hostile shield,
Thy sword is stronger still.

4 Thine armor is divine,
  Thy feet with victory shod;
And on thy head shall quickly shine
  The diadem of God.

965

7s & 6s.

1 STAND up, stand up for Jesus,
  Ye soldiers of the cross!
Lift high his royal banner,
  It must not suffer loss:
From victory unto victory
  His army shall he lead,
Till every foe is vanquished,
  And Christ is Lord indeed.

2 Stand up, stand up for Jesus!
  The trumpet call obey;
Forth to the mighty conflict,
  In this his glorious day:
"Ye that are men, now serve him"
  Against unnumbered foes;
Your courage rise with danger,
  And strength to strength oppose.

3 Stand up, stand up for Jesus!
  Stand in his strength alone;
The arm of flesh will fail you,
  Ye dare not trust your own:
Put on the gospel armor,
  And, watching unto prayer,
Where duty calls, or danger,
  Be never wanting there.

4 Stand up, stand up for Jesus!
  The strife will not be long;
This day the noise of battle,
  The next the victor's song:
To him that overcometh,
  A crown of life shall be;
He with the King of Glory
  Shall reign eternally.

DUFFIELD.

966

7s & 6s.

1 I NEED thee, Precious Jesus,
  For I am very poor;
A stranger and a pilgrim,
  I have no earthly store;
I need the love of Jesus
  To cheer me on my way,
To guide my doubting footsteps,
  To be my strength and stay.

2 I need thee, Precious Jesus,
  I need a friend like thee,
A friend to soothe and pity,
  A friend to care for me:
I need the Heart of Jesus
  To feel each anxious care,
To tell my every trial,
  And all my sorrows share.

3 I need thee, Precious Jesus,
  And hope to see thee soon
Encircled with the rainbow,
  And seated on thy throne;
There, with thy blood-bought children,
  My joy shall ever be,
To sing thy praises, Jesus,
  To gaze, my Lord, on thee.

F. WHITFIELD.

967

7s.

1 CHILDREN of the heavenly King,
  As ye journey, sweetly sing;
Sing your Saviour's worthy praise,
Glorious in his works and ways.

2 Ye are traveling home to God
In the way the fathers trod;
They are happy now, and ye
Soon their happiness shall see.

3 Shout, ye little flock, and blest!
You on Jesus' throne shall rest;
There your seat is now preparèd;
There your kingdom and reward.

4 Fear not, brethren; joyful stand
On the borders of your land;
Jesus Christ, your Father's Son,
Bids you undismayed go on.

5 Lord, submissive make us go,
Gladly leaving all below;
Only thou our Leader be,
And we still will follow thee.

CENNICK.

Chorus.

Victory, victory,
When we've gained the victory;
Oh, how happy we shall be,
When we've gained the victory.

968

7s.

1 CHRISTIAN, let your heart be glad!
March, in heavenly armor clad;
Fight! nor think the battle long:
Victory soon will tune your song.

2 Let not sorrow dim your eye;
Soon shall every tear be dry:
Let not fears your course impede;
Great your strength, if great your need.

MAITLAND.

969

7s.

1 MUCH in sorrow, oft in woe,
Onward, Christians, onward go;
Fight the fight; and worn with strife,
Steep with tears the bread of life.

2 Onward, Christians, onward go;
Join the war, and face the foe;
Faint not: much doth yet remain;
Dreary is the long campaign.

3 Shrink not, Christians, will ye yield?
Will ye quit the battle-field?
Fight till all the conflict's o'er,
Nor your foes shall rally more.

4 But, when loud the trumpet blown,
Speaks their forces overthrown,
Christ, your Captain, shall bestow
Crowns to grace the Conqueror's brow.

H. K. WHITE.

970

7s.

1 FAINT not, Christian! though the road,
Leading to thy blest abode,
Darksome be, and dangerous too,
Christ, thy Guide, will bring thee through.

2 Faint not, Christian! though in rage
Satan would thy soul engage,
Gird on faith's anointed shield,—
Bear it to the battle-field.

3 Faint not, Christian! though the world
Has its hostile flag unfurled;
Hold the cross of Jesus fast,
Thou shalt overcome at last.

4 Faint not, Christian! though within
There's a heart so prone to sin;
Christ, the Lord, is over all;
He'll not suffer thee to fall.

5 Faint not, Christian! look on high;
See the harpers in the sky:
Patient, wait, and thou wilt join—
Chant with them of love divine.

971 7s.

1 SLEEP not, soldier of the cross!
Foes are lurking all around;
Look not here to find repose:
This is but thy battle-ground.

2 Up! and take thy shield and sword;
Up! it is the call of heaven:
Shrink not faithless from thy Lord;
Nobly strive as he hath striven.

3 Break through all the force of ill;
Tread the might of passion down,—
Struggling onward, onward still,
To the conq'ring Saviour's crown!

4 Through the midst of toil and pain,
Let this thought ne'er leave thy breast:
Every triumph thou dost gain
Makes more sweet thy coming rest.

972 7s.

1 LORD! I cannot let thee go,
Till a blessing thou bestow;
Do not turn away thy face,
Mine 's an urgent, pressing case.

2 Once, a sinner, near despair,
Sought thy mercy-seat by prayer;
Mercy heard and set him free—
Lord! that mercy came to me.

3 Many days have passed since then,
Many changes I have seen;
Yet have been upheld till now;
Who could hold me up but thou?

4 Thou hast helped in every need—
This emboldens me to plead:
After so much mercy past,
Canst thou let me sink at last?

5 No—I must maintain my hold;
'Tis thy goodness makes me bold;
I can no denial take,
Since I plead for Jesus' sake.

NEWTON.

973 7s. D.

1 BRETHREN, while we sojourn here,
Fight we must, but should not fear;
Foes we have, but we've a Friend,
One that loves us to the end:
Forward, then, with courage go;
Long we shall not dwell below;
Soon the joyful news will come,
"Child, your Father calls—come home!"

2 In the way a thousand snares
Lie, to take us unawares;
Satan, with malicious art,
Watches each unguarded part:
But, from Satan's malice free,
Saints shall soon victorious be;
Soon the joyful news will come,
"Child, your Father calls—come home!"

3 But of all the foes we meet,
None so oft mislead our feet,
None betray us into sin
Like the foes that dwell within;
Yet let nothing spoil our peace,
Christ shall also conquer these;
Soon the joyful news will come,
"Child, your Father calls—come home!"

SWAIN.

974

7s.

1 HEAVENLY Father, to whose eye
Future things unfolded lie
Through the desert, where I stray,
Let thy counsels guide my way.

2 Lead me not, for flesh is frail,
Where fierce trials would assail;
Leave me not, in darkened hour,
To withstand the tempter's power.

3 Help thy servant to maintain
A profession free from stain;
That my sole reproach may be
Following Christ and fearing thee.

4 Should thy wisdom, Lord, decree
Trials long and sharp for me,
Pain or sorrow, care or shame,
Father, glorify thy name.

5 Let me neither faint nor fear,
Feeling still that thou art near,
In the course my Saviour trod,
Tending still to thee my God.

CONDOR.

975

7s.

1 CHRIST, of all my hopes the ground,
Christ, the spring of all my joy,
Still in thee let me be found,
Still for thee my powers employ.

2 Fountain of o'erflowing grace!
Freely from thy fullness give;
Till I close my earthly race,
Be it "Christ for me to live!"

3 Firmly trusting in thy blood,
Nothing shall my heart confound;
Safely I shall pass the flood,
Safely reach Immanuel's ground.

4 When I touch the blessed shore,
Back the closing waves shall roll!
Death's dark stream shall nevermore
Part from thee my ravished soul.

5 Thus,—oh, thus an entrance give
To the land of cloudless sky;
Having known it "Christ to live,"
Let me know it "gain to die."

WINDHAM.

976

7s.

1 CAST thy burden on the Lord,
Only lean upon his word;
Thou wilt soon have cause to bless
His unchanging faithfulness.

2 He sustains thee by his hand,
He enables thee to stand;
Those, whom Jesus once hath loved,
From his grace are never moved.

3 Heaven and earth may pass away,
His free grace shall not decay;
He hath promised to fulfill
All the pleasure of his will.

977

7s.

1 LORD, forever at thy side
Let my place and portion be;
Strip me of the robe of pride,
Clothe me with humility.

2 Meekly may my soul receive
All thy Spirit hath revealed;
Thou hast spoken, I believe
Though the prophecy were sealed.

3 Quiet as a weanèd child,
Weanèd from the mother's breast,

By no subtlety beguiled,
On thy faithful word I rest.

4 Saints, rejoicing evermore,
In the Lord Jehovah trust;
Him in all his ways adore,
Wise, and wonderful, and just.

MONTGOMERY.

978 7s.

1 TO thy pastures fair and large,
Heavenly Shepherd, lead thy charge,
And my couch, with tenderest care,
'Mid the springing grass prepare.

2 When I faint with summer's heat,
Thou shalt guide my weary feet
To the streams that, still and slow,
Through the verdant meadows flow.

3 Safe the dreary vale I tread,
By the shades of death o'erspread,
With thy rod and staff supplied,
This my guard—and that my guide.

MERRICK.

979 8s & 7s.

1 ONWARD, Christian, though the region
Where thou art be drear and lone;
God has set a guardian legion
Very near thee; press thou on.

2 Listen, Christian; their hosanna
Rolleth o'er thee: "God is love,"
Write upon thy red-cross banner,
"Upward ever; heaven 's above."

3 By the thorn-road, and none other,
Is the mount of vision won;
Tread it without shrinking, brother;
Jesus trod it; press thou on.

4 Be this world the wiser, stronger,
For thy life of pain and peace,
While it needs thee; oh! no longer
Pray thou for thy quick release.

5 Pray thou, Christian, daily rather,
That thou be a faithful son;
By the prayer of Jesus, "Father,
Not my will, but thine, be done."

JOHNSON.

980 8s & 7s.

1 JESUS calls us, o'er the tumult
Of our life's wild restless sea,
Day by day his sweet voice soundeth,
Saying, "Christian, follow me."

2 Jesus calls us—from the worship
Of the vain world's golden store,
From each idol that would keep us—
Saying, "Christian, love me more."

3 In our joys and in our sorrows,
Days of toil, and hours of ease,
Still he calls, in cares and pleasures,
"Christian, love me more than these."

981 8s & 7s.

1 PILGRIMS in this vale of sorrow,
Pressing onward to the prize,
Strength and comfort here we borrow
From the Hand that rules the skies.

2 'Mid these scenes of self-denial,
We are called the race to run;
We must meet full many a trial
Ere the victor's crown is won.

3 Love shall every conflict lighten,
Hope shall urge us swifter on,
Faith shall every prospect brighten,
Till the morn of heaven shall dawn.

HASTINGS.

982 8s & 7s.

1 JESUS only, when the morning
Beams upon the path I tread;
Jesus only, when the darkness
Gathers round my weary head.

2 Jesus only, when the billows
Cold and sullen o'er me roll;
Jesus only, when the trumpet
Rends the tomb and wakes the soul.

3 Jesus only, when in judgment
Boding fears my heart appall;
Jesus only, when the wretched
On the rocks and mountains call.

4 Jesus only, when, adoring,
Saints their crowns before him bring;
Jesus only, I will, joyous,
Through eternal ages sing.

NASON.

983 L. M. 6 l.

1 WHEN gathering clouds around I view,
And days are dark, and friends are few,
On him I lean, who not in vain,
Experienced every human pain;
He sees my wants, allays my fears,
And counts and treasures up my tears.

2 If aught should tempt my soul to stray
From heavenly wisdom's narrow way,
To fly the good I would pursue,
Or do the ill I would not do;
Still, he who felt temptation's power,
Will guard me in that dangerous hour.

3 If wounded love my bosom swell,
Deceived by those I prized too well;
He shall his pitying aid bestow,
Who felt on earth severer woe;
At once betrayed, denied, or fled,
By those who shared his daily bread.

4 When sorrowing o'er some stone I bend,
Which covers what was once a friend,
And from his voice, his hand, his smile,
Divides me for a little while;
Thou, Saviour, mark'st the tears I shed,
For thou didst weep o'er Lazarus dead!

5 And oh! when I have safely past
Through every conflict but the last;
Still, still unchanging, watch beside
My painful bed, for thou hast died!
Then point to realms of cloudless day,
And wipe the latest tear away!

ROBERT GRANT.

984 L. M. 6 l.

1 AS oft, with worn and weary feet,
We tread earth's rugged valley o'er,
The thought—how comforting and sweet!
Christ trod this very path before!
Our wants and weaknesses he knows,
From life's first dawning to its close.

2 Do sickness, feebleness, or pain,
Or sorrow in our path appear,
The recollection will remain,
More deeply did he suffer here!
His life, how truly sad and brief,
Filled up with suff'ring and with grief!

3 If Satan tempt our hearts to stray,
And whisper evil things within,
So did he, in the desert way,
Assail our Lord with thoughts of sin;

When worn, and in a feeble hour,
The tempter came with all his power.

4 Just such as I, this earth he trod,
With every human ill but sin;
And, though indeed the very God,
As I am now, so he has been.
My God, my Saviour, look on me
With pity, love, and sympathy.

WILBERFORCE.

985 L. M.

1 WITH tearful eyes I look around;
Life seems a dark and stormy sea;
Yet midst the gloom I hear a sound,
A heavenly whisper, Come to me!

2 It tells me of a place of rest;
It tells me where my soul may flee:
Oh! to the weary, faint, opprest,
How sweet the bidding, Come to me!

3 When the poor heart with anguish learns
That earthly props resigned must be,
And from each broken cistern turns,
It hears the accents, Come to me!

4 When nature shudders, loth to part
From all I love, enjoy, and see;
When a faint chill steals o'er my heart,
A sweet voice utters, Come to me!

5 Come, for all else must fail and die;
Earth is no resting-place for thee;
Heavenward direct thy weeping eye;
I am thy Portion; Come to me!

6 O voice of mercy, voice of love!
In conflict, grief, and agony,
Support me, cheer me from above,
And gently whisper, Come to me!

HUGH WHITE.

986 L. M.

1 MY God, my Father, while I stray
Far from my home, on life's rough way,
Oh, teach me from my heart to say,
"Thy will be done, thy will be done!"

2 What though in lonely grief I sigh
For friends beloved no longer nigh;
Submissive still would I reply,
"Thy will be done, thy will be done!"

3 If thou shouldst call me to resign
What most I prize, — it ne'er was mine;
I only yield thee what was thine:
"Thy will be done, thy will be done!"

4 If but my fainting heart be blest
With thy sweet Spirit for its guest,
My God, to thee I leave the rest;
"Thy will be done, thy will be done!"

C. ELLIOTT.

987 L. M.

1 THE billows swell, the winds are high,
Clouds overcast my wintry sky;
Out of the depths to thee I call;
My fears are great, my strength is small.

2 Amidst the roaring of the sea,
My soul still hangs her hopes on thee;
Thy constant love, thy faithful care,
Is all that saves me from despair.

3 Though tempest-tost, and half a wreck,
My Saviour through the floods I seek:
Let neither winds nor stormy main
Force back my shattered bark again!

4 O Lord, the pilot's part perform,
And guide and guard me through the storm;
Defend me from each threatening ill;
Control the waves; say, "Peace! be still."

COWPER.

988 L. M.

1 OH, deem not they are blest alone,
Whose lives a peaceful tenor keep:
For God, who pities man, hath shown
A blessing for the eyes that weep.

2 The light of smiles shall fill again
The lids that overflow with tears;
And weary hours of woe and pain
Are promises of happier years.

3 There is a day of sunny rest
For every dark and troubled night;
And grief may bide an evening guest,
But joy shall come with early light.

4 Nor let the good man's trust depart,
Though life its common gifts deny;
Tho' with a pierced and broken heart,
And spurned of men, he goes to die.

5 For God has marked each sorrowing day,
And numbered every secret tear,
And heaven's long age of bliss shall pay
For all his children suffer here.

BRYANT.

989 L. M.

1 I BLESS thee, Lord, for sorrows sent
To break the dream of human power,
For now, my shallow cistern spent,
I find thy fount, and thirst no more.

2 I take thy hand, and fears are still;
Behold thy face, and doubts remove;
Who would not yield his wavering will
To perfect truth and boundless love!

3 That truth gives promise of a dawn,
Beneath whose light I am to see,
When all these blinding vails are drawn,
This was the wisest path for me.

990 L. M.

1 THY will be done! I will not fear
The fate provided by thy love;
Though clouds and darkness shroud me here,
I know that all is bright above.

2 The stars of heaven are shining on,
Though these frail eyes are dimmed with tears;
The hopes of earth indeed are gone,
But are not ours the immortal years?

3 Father! forgive the heart that clings,
Thus trembling, to the things of time;
And bid my soul, on angel wings,
Ascend into a purer clime.

J. ROSCOE.

991 C. M.

1 O LORD! my best desires fulfill,
And help me to resign
Life, health, and comfort to thy will,
And make thy pleasure mine.

2 Why should I shrink at thy command,
Whose love forbids my fears?
Or tremble at the gracious hand
That wipes away my tears?

3 No! rather let me freely yield
What most I prize, to thee
Who never hast a good withheld,
Or wilt withhold, from me.

4 Thy favor, all my journey through,
Thou art engaged to grant:
What else I want, or think I do,
'Tis better still to want.

COWPER.

992 C. M.

1 O LORD! I would delight in thee,
And on thy care depend;
To thee in every trouble flee,
My best, my only Friend.

2 When all created streams are dried,
Thy fullness is the same;
May I with this be satisfied,
And glory in thy name!

3 No good in creatures can be found,
But may be found in thee;
I must have all things, and abound,
While God is God to me.

4 He that has made my heaven secure,
Will here all good provide;
While Christ is rich, can I be poor?
What can I want beside?

5 O Lord! I cast my care on thee;
I triumph and adore;
Henceforth my great concern shall be
To love and please thee more.

RYLAND.

993 C. M.

1 O THOU, who driest the mourner's tear,
How dark this world would be,
If, when deceived and wounded here,
We could not fly to thee!

2 The friends, who in our sunshine live,
When winter comes are flown;
And he who has but tears to give,
Must weep those tears alone.

3 But thou wilt heal the broken heart,
Which, like the plants that throw
Their fragrance from the wounded part,
Breathes sweetness out of woe.

4 When joy no longer soothes or cheers,
And e'en the hope that threw
A moment's sparkle o'er our tears
Is dimmed and vanished too;

5 Oh, who could bear life's stormy doom,
Did not thy wing of love
Come, brightly wafting thro' the gloom
Our peace-branch from above:

6 Then sorrow, touched by thee, grows bright,
With more than rapture's ray;
As darkness shows us worlds of light
We never saw by day.

MOORE.

994 C. M.

1 O THOU, from whom all goodness flows,
I lift my heart to thee;
In all my sorrows, conflicts, woes,
Dear Lord, remember me!

2 When groaning on my burdened heart
My sins lie heavily,
My pardon speak, new peace impart,
In love remember me!

3 Temptations sore obstruct my way;
And ills I cannot flee:
Oh, give me strength, Lord, as my day;
For good remember me!

4 Distrest in pain, disease, and grief,
This feeble body see!
Grant patience, rest, and kind relief;
Hear, and remember me!

5 If on my face, for thy dear Name,
Shame and reproaches be;
All hail reproach, and welcome shame,
If thou remember me!

6 The hour is near; consigned to death
I own the just decree:
"Saviour!" with my last parting breath,
I'll cry, "Remember me!"

THOMAS HAWEIS.

995 C. M.

1 ONE prayer I have—all prayers in one—
When I am wholly thine;
Thy will, my God, thy will be done,
And let that will be mine.

2 All-wise, almighty, and all-good,
In thee I firmly trust;
Thy ways, unknown or understood,
Are merciful and just.

3 May I remember that to thee
Whate'er I have I owe;
And back, in gratitude, from me
May all thy bounties flow.

4 And though thy wisdom takes away,
Shall I arraign thy will?
No, let me bless thy name, and say,
"The Lord is gracious still."

5 A pilgrim through the earth I roam,
Of nothing long possessed;
And all must fail when I go home,
For this is not my rest.

MONTGOMERY.

996 C. M.

1 IN trouble and in grief, O God,
Thy smile hath cheered my way;
And joy hath budded from each thorn
That round my footsteps lay.

2 The hours of pain have yielded good,
Which prosperous days refused;
As herbs, though scentless when entire,
Spread fragrance when they 're bruised.

3 The oak strikes deeper, as its boughs
By furious blasts are driven;
So life's tempestuous storms the more
Have fixed my heart in heaven.

4 All-gracious Lord, whate'er my lot
In other times may be,
I'll welcome still the heaviest grief
That brings me near to thee.

997 C. M.

1 FATHER! whate'er of earthly bliss
Thy sovereign will denies,
Accepted at thy throne of grace,
Let this petition rise:—

2 "Give me a calm, a thankful heart,
From every murmur free!
The blessings of thy grace impart,
And make me live to thee.

3 "Let the sweet hope that thou art mine
My life and death attend;
Thy presence thro' my journey shine,
And crown my journey's end."

STEELE.

998 C. M.

1 "REMEMBER me," my Saviour God,
Whilst here on earth I stay;
Give strength to bear affliction's rod,
And faith to watch and pray.

2 "Remember me," when fortune smiles,
And scenes are bright and fair,
Lest I should fall, through Satan's wiles,
Beneath his baneful snare.

3 "Remember me;" thy voice I'll greet
In all thy dealings here;
Oh, let thy Spirit guide my feet,
And I shall never fear.

4 "Remember me;" stand near my side,
Where'er my lot may be;
And when by Jordan's swelling tide,
O Lord, "remember me."

999 C. M.

1 WHEN musing sorrow weeps the past,
And mourns the present pain,
'Tis sweet to think of peace at last,
And feel that death is gain.

2 'Tis not that murmuring thoughts arise,
And dread a Father's will;
'Tis not that meek submission flies,
And would not suffer still.

3 It is that heaven-born faith surveys
The path that leads to light,
And longs her eagle plumes to raise,
And lose herself in sight.

4 Oh, let me wing my hallowed flight
From earth-born woe and care,
And soar above these clouds of night,
My Saviour's bliss to share.

B. W. NOEL.

1000 C. M.

1 OH, help us, Lord! each hour of need
Thy heavenly succor give;
Help us in thought, and word, and deed,
Each hour on earth we live.

2 Oh, help us, when our spirits bleed
With contrite anguish sore!
And when our hearts are cold and dead,
Oh, help us, Lord, the more!

3 Oh, help us, Father, from on high,—
We know no help but thee!
Oh, help us, Lord, to live and die,
And thine in heaven to be!

MILMAN.

1001 C. M.

1 WHEN languor and disease invade
This trembling house of clay,
'Tis sweet to look beyond the cage,
And long to fly away.

2 Sweet to look inward, and attend
The whispers of his love;
Sweet to look upward to the place
Where Jesus pleads above.

3 Sweet to look back, and see my name
In Life's fair book set down;
Sweet to look forward, and behold
Eternal joys my own.

4 Sweet to reflect, how Grace Divine
My sins on Jesus laid;
Sweet to remember that his blood
My debt of sufferings paid.

5 Sweet in the confidence of faith,
To trust his firm decrees;

Sweet to lie passive in his hand,
And know no will but his.

6 If such the sweetness of the stream,
What must the Fountain be,
Where saints and angels draw their bliss
Immediately from thee!

TOPLADY.

1002 C. M.

1 HOW vain are all things here below!
How false, and yet how fair!
Each pleasure hath its poison, too,
And every sweet a snare.

2 The brightest things below the sky
Give but a flattering light;
We should suspect some danger nigh,
Where we possess delight.

3 Our dearest joys, and nearest friends,—
The partners of our blood,
How they divide our wavering minds,
And leave but half for God!

4 The fondness of a creature's love,
How strong it strikes the sense!
Thither the warm affections move,
Nor can we call them thence.

5 Dear Saviour! let thy beauties be
My soul's eternal food;
And grace command my heart away
From all created good.

WATTS.

1003 C. M.

1 WHEN waves of trouble round me swell,
My soul is not dismay'd;
I hear a voice I know full well,—
"'Tis I; be not afraid."

2 When black the threatening skies appear
And storms my path invade,
Those accents tranquillize each fear,—
"'Tis I; be not afraid."

3 There is a gulf that must be cross'd;
Saviour, be near to aid!
Whisper, when my frail bark is toss'd,
"'Tis I; be not afraid."

4 There is a dark and fearful vale,
Death hides within its shade;
Oh say, when flesh and heart shall fail,—
"'Tis I; be not afraid."

1004 C. M.

1 CHILDREN of God, who, faint and slow,
Your pilgrim path pursue,
In strength and weakness, joy and woe,
To God's high calling true!—

2 Why move ye thus, with lingering tread,
A doubting, mournful band?
Why faintly hangs the drooping head?
Why fails the feeble hand?

3 Oh! weak to know a Saviour's power,
To feel a Father's care;
A moment's toil, a passing shower,
Is all the grief ye share.

4 The orb of light, though clouds awhile
May hide his noon-tide ray,
Shall soon in lovelier beauty smile
To gild the closing day,—

5 And, bursting through the dusky shroud
That dared his power invest,
Ride throned in light o'er every cloud,
Triumphant to his rest.

6 Then, Christian, dry the falling tear,
The faithless doubt remove;
Redeemed at last from guilt and fear,
Oh wake thy heart to love.

BOWDLER.

1005 C. M.

1 JESUS, my sorrow lies too deep
For human ministry;
It knows not how to tell itself
To any but to thee.

2 Thou dost remember still, amid
The glories of God's throne,
The sorrows of mortality,—
For they were once thine own.

3 Jesus! my fainting spirit brings
Its fearfulness to thee!
Thine eye, at least, can penetrate
The clouded mystery.

4 It is enough, my precious Lord,
Thy tender sympathy!
My every sin and sorrow can
Devolve itself on thee.

BONAR.

1006 C. M.

1 LORD, it belongs not to my care
Whether I die or live;
To love and serve thee is my share,
And this thy grace must give.

2 If life be long, I will be glad
That I may long obey;
If short, yet why should I be sad
To soar to endless day?

3 Christ leads me through no darker rooms
Than he went through before;
He that into God's kingdom comes
Must enter by this door.

4 Come, Lord, when grace hath made me meet
Thy blessèd face to see;
For, if thy work on earth be sweet,
What will thy glory be?

BAXTER.

1007 C. M.

1 IF God is mine, then present things,
And things to come, are mine;
Yea, Christ, his word and Spirit too,
And glory all divine.

2 If he is mine, then from his love,
He every trouble sends;
All things are working for my good,
And bliss his rod attends.

3 If he is mine, I need not fear
The rage of earth and hell;
He will support my feeble frame,
Their utmost force repel.

4 If he is mine, let friends forsake—
Let wealth and honors flee—
Sure he, who giveth me himself,
Is more than these to me.

5 If he is mine, I'll boldly pass
Through death's tremendous vale;
He is a solid comfort, when
All other comforts fail.

6 Oh, tell me, Lord! that thou art mine;
What can I wish beside?
My soul shall at the fountain live,
When all the streams are dried.

BEDDOME. *Alt.*

1008 C. M.

1 YE trembling souls, dismiss your fears;
Be mercy all your theme;
Mercy, which like a river flows
In one continued stream.

2 Fear not the powers of earth and hell:
God will these powers restrain;
His mighty arm their rage repel,
And make their efforts vain.

3 Fear not that he will e'er forsake,
Or leave his work undone:
He's faithful to his promises,
And faithful to his Son.

4 Fear not the terrors of the grave,
Or death's tremendous sting;
He will from endless wrath preserve,
To endless glory bring.

BEDDOME.

1009 C. M.

1 SING, ye redeeméd of the Lord,
Your great Deliverer sing:
Pilgrims for Zion's city bound,
Be joyful in your King.

2 A hand divine shall lead you on
Through all the blissful road;
Till to the sacred mount you rise,
And see your gracious God.

3 There garlands of immortal joy
Shall bloom on every head;
While sorrow, sighing, and distress,
Like shadows all are fled.

4 March on in your Redeemer's strength;
Pursue his footsteps still;
And let the prospect cheer your eye
While laboring up the hill.

DODDRIDGE.

1010 S. M.

1 GIVE to the winds thy fears;
Hope, and be undismay'd;
God hears thy sighs, and counts thy tears,
God shall lift up thy head.

2 Through waves, through clouds and storms,
He gently clears thy way;
Wait thou his time; so shall this night
Soon end in joyous day.

3 Still heavy is thy heart?
Still sink thy spirits down?
Cast off the weight, let fear depart,
Bid every care be gone.

4 What though thou rulest not!
Yet heaven, and earth, and hell
Proclaim, God sitteth on the throne,
And ruleth all things well.

GERHARD.

1011 S. M.

1 IF, through unruffled seas,
Toward heaven we calmly sail;
With grateful hearts, O God, to thee,
We'll own the favoring gale.

2 But should the surges rise,
And rest delay to come,
Blest be the sorrow—kind the storm,
Which drives us nearer home.

3 Soon shall our doubts and fears
All yield to thy control:
Thy tender mercies shall illume
The midnight of the soul.

4 Teach us, in every state,
To make thy will our own;
And when the joys of sense depart,
To live by faith alone.

1012 S. M.

1 WHERE wilt thou put thy trust?
In a frail form of clay,
That to its element of dust
Must soon resolve away?

2 Where wilt thou cast thy care?
Upon an erring heart,
Which hath its own sore ills to bear,
And shrinks from sorrow's dart?

3 No! place thy trust above
This shadowy realm of night,
In him, whose boundless power and love
Thy confidence invite.

4 His mercies still endure
When skies and stars grow dim,
His changeless promise standeth sure,
Go,—cast thy care on him.

Mrs. Sigourney.

1013 S. M.

1 THE Lord himself will keep
His people safe from harm;
Will hold the helm, and guide the ship,
With his almighty arm.

2 Then let the tempest roar,
The billows heave and swell;
We hope to reach the peaceful shore
Where all the ransomed dwell.

3 And when we gain the land,
How happy shall we be!
How shall we bless the mighty hand
That led us through the sea!

1014 S. M.

1 YOUR harps, ye trembling saints,
Down from the willows take:
Loud to the praise of Love divine
Bid every string awake.

2 Though in a foreign land,
We are not far from home,
And nearer to our house above
We every moment come.

3 His grace will to the end
Stronger and brighter shine,
Nor present things, nor things to come,
Shall quench the spark divine.

4 When we in darkness walk,
Nor feel the heavenly flame,
Then is the time to trust our God,
And rest upon his name.

5 Blest is the man, O God,
That stays himself on thee!
Who waits for thy salvation, Lord,
Shall thy salvation see.

Toplady.

1015 S. M.

1 FAR from my heavenly home,
Far from my Father's breast,
Fainting I cry, "Blest Spirit, come,
And speed me to thy rest!"

2 Upon the willows long
My harp had silent hung:
How should I sing a cheerful song
Till thou inspire my tongue?

3 My spirit homeward turns,
And fain would thither flee;
My heart, O Zion, droops and yearns,
When I remember thee.

4 To thee, to thee I press,
A dark and toilsome road:
When shall I pass the wilderness
And reach the saints' abode?

5 God of my life, be near!
On thee my hopes I cast;
Oh guide me through the desert here,
And bring me home at last.

Lyte.

1016 S. M.

1 MY soul, with joy attend,
While Jesus silence breaks;
No angel's harp such music yields,
As what my Shepherd speaks.

2 "I know my sheep," he cries;
"My soul approves them well:
Vain is the world's delusive guise,
And vain the rage of hell.

3 "I freely feed them now
With tokens of my love;
But richer pastures I prepare,
And sweeter streams, above.

4 "Unnumbered years of bliss
I to my people give;
And while my throne unshaken stands
Shall all my chosen live.

5 "This tried, almighty hand
Is raised for their defence;
Where is the power shall reach them there,
Or what shall force them thence?"

DODDRIDGE.

1017 6s & 4s.

1 MY faith looks up to thee,
Thou Lamb of Calvary,
Saviour divine!
Now hear me while I pray,
Take all my guilt away,
Oh, let me from this day
Be wholly thine.

2 May thy rich grace impart
Strength to my fainting heart;
My zeal inspire;
As thou hast died for me,
Oh, may my love to thee
Pure, warm, and changeless be,
A living fire.

3 While life's dark maze I tread,
And griefs around me spread,
Be thou my guide;
Bid darkness turn to day,
Wipe sorrow's tears away,
Nor let me ever stray
From thee aside.

4 When ends life's transient dream,
When death's cold, sullen stream
Shall o'er me roll,
Blest Saviour! then, in love,
Fear and distrust remove;
Oh, bear me safe above,
A ransomed soul!

RAY PALMER.

1018 6s & 4s.

1 SAVIOUR, I look to thee,
Be not thou far from me,
'Mid storms that lower:
On me thy care bestow,
Thy loving-kindness show,
Thine arms around me throw,
This trying hour.

2 Saviour, I look to thee,
Feeble as infancy,
Gird up my heart:
Author of life and light,
Thou hast an arm of might,
Thine is the sovereign right,
Thy strength impart.

3 Saviour, I look to thee,
Let me thy fullness see,
Save me from fear;

While at thy cross I kneel,
All my backslidings heal,
And a free pardon seal,
My soul to cheer.

4 Saviour, I look to thee,
Thine shall the glory be,
Hearer of prayer:
Thou art my only aid,
On thee my soul is stayed,
Naught can my heart invade,
While thou art near.

HASTINGS.

1019 7s. D.

1 WHEN, along life's thorny road,
Faints the soul beneath the load,
By its cares and sins oppressed,
Finds on earth no peace or rest;
When the wily tempter 's near,
Filling us with doubts and fear,—
Jesus, to thy feet we flee,
Jesus, we will look to thee.

2 Thou, our Saviour, from the throne
List'nest to thy people's moan;
Thou, the living Head, dost share
Ev'ry pang thy members bear:
Full of tenderness thou art,
Thou wilt heal the broken heart;
Full of pow'r, thine arm shall quell
All the rage and might of hell.

3 Mighty to redeem and save,
Thou hast overcome the grave;
Thou the bars of death hast riv'n,
Open'd wide the gate of heav'n:
Soon in glory thou shalt come,
Taking thy poor pilgrims home;
Jesus, then we all shall be
Ever, ever, Lord, with thee.

1020 7s. D.

1 WHEN our heads are bowed with woe,
When our bitter tears o'erflow,
When we mourn the lost, the dear,
Gracious Son of Mary, hear!
Thou our throbbing flesh hast worn,
Thou our mortal griefs hast borne,
Thou hast shed the human tear:
Gracious Son of Mary, hear!

2 When the solemn death-bell tolls
For our own departing souls,
When our final doom is near,
Gracious Son of Mary, hear!
Thou hast bowed the dying head,
Thou the blood of life hast shed,
Thou hast filled a mortal bier:
Gracious Son of Mary, hear!

3 When the heart is sad within
With the thought of all its sin,
When the spirit shrinks with fear,
Gracious Son of Mary, hear!
Thou, the shame, the grief hast known;
Though the sins were not thine own,
Thou hast deigned their load to bear:
Gracious Son of Mary, hear!

HEBER.

1021 7s. D.

1 JESUS, grant me this I pray,
Ever in thy heart to stay;
Let me evermore abide
Hidden in thy wounded side.
If the evil one prepare,
Or the world, a tempting snare,
I am safe when I abide
In thy heart and wounded side.

2 If the flesh, more dangerous still,
Tempt my soul to deeds of ill,
Naught I fear when I abide
In thy heart and wounded side.
Death will come one day to me;
Jesus, cast me not from thee:
Dying let me still abide
In thy heart and wounded side.

1022 8s & 7s. D.

1 ALL is dying; hearts are breaking
Which to ours were closely bound;
And the lips have ceased from speaking
Which once uttered such sweet sound;
And the arms are powerless lying,
Which were our support and stay;
And the eyes are dim and dying,
Which once watched us night and day.

2 Everything we love and cherish
Hastens onward to the grave;
Earthly joys and pleasures perish,
And whate'er the world e'er gave:
All is fading, all is fleeing;
Earthly flames must cease to glow,
Earthly beings cease from being,
Earthly blossoms cease to blow.

3 Yet unchanged while all decayeth,
Jesus stands upon the dust;
Lean on me alone, he sayeth;
Hope and love, and firmly trust!
Oh, abide, abide with Jesus,
Who himself forever lives,
Who from death eternal frees us,
Yea, who life eternal gives!

1023 8s & 7s. D.

1 GENTLY, Lord, oh, gently lead us
Through this gloomy vale of tears;
Through the changes thou 'st decreed us,
Till our last great change appears.
When temptation's darts assail us,
When in devious paths we stray,
Let thy goodness never fail us,
Lead us in thy perfect way.

2 In the hour of pain and anguish,
In the hour when death draws near,
Suffer not our hearts to languish,
Suffer not our souls to fear.
When this mortal life is ended,
Bid us in thine arms to rest,
Till, by angel-bands attended,
We awake among the blest.

HASTINGS.

1024 8s, 7s & 4s.

1 JESUS, I am never weary,
When upon the bed of pain;
If thy presence only cheer me,
All my loss I count but gain:
Ever near me—
Ever near me, Lord, remain!

2 Dear ones come with fruit and flowers,
Thus to cheer my heart the while
In the deeply anxious hours;—
But it is not Jesus' smile!
Only Jesus
Can my trembling fears beguile.

3 Dearest Saviour! go not from me;
Let thy presence still abide:

Look in tenderest love upon me—
 As I'm nestling in thy side:
  Dearest Saviour!—
 Who for suffering sinners died.

4 Both mine arms I'll clasp around thee,
 And my head upon thy breast;
For my weary soul has found thee
 Such a perfect, perfect rest.
  Dearest Saviour,
 Now I know that I am blest!

1025 8s, 7s, & 4s.

1 O MY soul, what means this sadness?
 Wherefore art thou thus cast down?
Let thy grief be turned to gladness;
 Bid thy restless fears be gone;
  Look to Jesus,
 And rejoice in his dear Name.

2 What though Satan's strong temptations
 Vex and grieve thee day by day;
And thy sinful inclinations
 Often fill thee with dismay;
  Thou shalt conquer
Through the Lamb's redeeming blood.

3 Though ten thousand ills beset thee
 From without and from within;
Jesus saith he'll ne'er forget thee,
 But will save from hell and sin;
  He is faithful
To perform his gracious word.

4 Though distresses now attend thee,
 And thou tread'st the thorny road,
His right hand shall still defend thee;
 Soon he'll bring thee home to God;
  Therefore praise him,
Praise the great Redeemer's name.

FAWCETT.

1026 7s.

1 IN the hour of my distress,
 When temptations me oppress,
And when I my sins confess—
 Then, sweet Spirit, comfort me.

2 When I lie within my bed,
Sick in heart, and sick in head,
And with doubts disquieted—
 Then, sweet Spirit, comfort me.

3 When the house doth sigh and weep,
And the world is drowned in sleep,
Yet mine eyes the watch do keep—
 Then, sweet Spirit, comfort me.

4 When the tempter me pursueth,
With the sins of all my youth,
And condemns me with untruth—
 Then, sweet Spirit, comfort me.

5 When the judgment is reveal'd,
And that opened which was seal'd,
When to thee I have appeal'd—
 Then, sweet Spirit, comfort me.

VAUGHN.

1027 7s & 5s. P.

1 IN the dark and cloudy day,
 When earth's riches flee away,
And the last hope will not stay,
 Saviour, comfort me!

2 When the secret idol's gone
That my poor heart yearned upon,—
Desolate, bereft, alone,
 Saviour, comfort me!

3 Thou, who wast so sorely tried,
In the darkness crucified,
Bid me in thy love confide;
 Saviour, comfort me!

4 Comfort me; I am cast down
By my heavenly Father's frown;
I deserve it all, I own:
Saviour, comfort me!

5 So it shall be good for me
Much afflicted now to be,
If thou wilt but tenderly,
Saviour, comfort me!

1028 8s, 7s & 4s.

1 SAVIOUR, like a shepherd lead us,
Much we need thy tend'rest care;
In thy pleasant pastures feed us,
For our use thy folds prepare.
Blessèd Jesus,
Thou hast bought us, thine we are.

2 We are thine, do thou befriend us,
Be the Guardian of our way;
Keep thy flock, from sin defend us,
Seek us when we go astray.
Blessèd Jesus,
Hear, oh hear us, when we pray.

3 Thou hast promised to receive us,
Poor and sinful though we be;
Thou hast mercy to relieve us,
Grace to cleanse, and power to free.
Blessèd Jesus,
We will early turn to thee.

4 Early let us seek thy favor,
Early let us do thy will;
Blessèd Lord and only Saviour,
With thy love our bosoms fill.
Blessèd Jesus,
Thou hast loved us, love us still.

1029 8s, 7s & 4s.

1 GUIDE me, O thou great Jehovah,
Pilgrim through this barren land:
I am weak, but thou art mighty,
Hold me with thy powerful hand;
Bread of heaven,
Feed me till I want no more.

2 Open thou the crystal fountain
Whence the healing waters flow;
Let the fiery, cloudy pillar,
Lead me all my journey through;
Strong Deliverer,
Be thou still my strength and shield.

3 When I tread the verge of Jordan,
Bid the swelling stream divide;
Death of death, and hell's Destruction,
Land me safe on Canaan's side;
Songs of praises
I will ever give to thee.

WM. WILLIAMS.

1030 8s & 7s. D.

1 HOLY Father, thou hast taught me
I should live to thee alone;
Year by year thy hand hath brought me
On through dangers oft unknown.
When I wandered, thou hast found me;
When I doubted, sent me light,
Still thine arm has been around me,
All my paths were in thy sight.

2 In the world will foes assail me,
Craftier, stronger far than I;
And the strife may never fail me,
Well I know, before I die.

Therefore, Lord, I come, believing
Thou canst give the power I need;
Through the prayer of faith receiving
Strength—the Spirit's strength, indeed.

3 I would trust in the protecting,
Wholly rest upon thine arm;
Follow wholly thy directing,
Thou, mine only guard from harm!
Keep me from mine own undoing,
Help me turn to thee when tried,
Still my footsteps, Father, viewing,
Keep me ever at thy side.

1031 10s & 11s.

1 BEGONE, unbelief! my Saviour is near,
And for my relief will surely appear;
By prayer let me wrestle, and he will perform;
With Christ in the vessel, I smile at the storm.

2 Though dark be my way, since he is my Guide,
'Tis mine to obey, 'tis his to provide;
Though cisterns be broken, and creatures all fail,
The word he has spoken shall surely prevail.

3 Determined to save, he watched o'er my path,
When, Satan's blind slave, I sported with death;
And can he have taught me to trust in his name,
And thus far have brought me to put me to shame?

4 Since all that I meet shall work for my good,
The bitter is sweet, the medicine, food;
Though painful at present, 'twill cease before long,
And then, oh how pleasant the conqueror's song! NEWTON.

1032 10s & 11s.

1 THOUGH faint, yet pursuing, we go on our way;
The Lord is our Leader, his word is our stay;
Though suffering, and sorrow, and trial be near,
The Lord is our Refuge, and whom can we fear?

2 He raiseth the fallen, he cheereth the faint;
The weak and oppressed, he will hear their complaint;
The way may be weary, and thorny the road,
But how can we falter? our help is in God.

3 And to his green pastures our footsteps he leads;
His flock in the desert how kindly he feeds!
The lambs in his bosom he tenderly bears,
And brings back the wanderers all safe from the snares.

4 Though clouds may surround us, our God is our Light;
Though storms rage around us, our God is our Might;

So faint, yet pursuing, still onward we come;
The Lord is our Leader, and heaven is our home.

1033 11s.

1 HOW firm a foundation, ye saints of the Lord,
Is laid for your faith in his excellent word;
What more can he say than to you he hath said,—
To you who for refuge to Jesus have fled?

2 "Fear not, I am with thee, oh, be not dismayed,
For I am thy God, I will still give thee aid:
I will strengthen thee, help thee, and cause thee to stand,
Upheld by my righteous, omnipotent hand.

3 "When through the deep waters I call thee to go,
The rivers of sorrow shall not overflow;
For I will be with thee thy trials to bless,
And sanctify to thee thy deepest distress.

4 "When through fiery trials thy pathway shall lie,
My grace, all-sufficient, shall be thy supply,
The flame shall not hurt thee; I only design
Thy dross to consume, and thy gold to refine.

5 "E'en down to old age my people shall prove
My sovereign, eternal, unchangeable love;
And then, when gray hairs shall their temples adorn,
Like lambs they shall still in my bosom be borne.

6 "The soul that on Jesus hath leaned for repose,
I will not—I will not desert to his foes;
That soul—though all hell should endeavor to shake,
I'll never—no never—no never forsake!"

KIRKHAM.

1034 11s.

1 THE Lord is my shepherd, no want shall I know,
I feed in green pastures, safe-folded I rest;
He leadeth my soul where the still waters flow,
Restores me when wand'ring, redeems when oppressed.

2 Through the valley and shadow of death, though I stray,
Since thou art my guardian, no evil I fear;
Thy rod shall defend me, thy staff be my stay;
No harm can befall, with my Comforter near.

3 In the midst of affliction my table is spread;
With blessings unmeasured my cup runneth o'er;

With perfume and oil thou anointest my head;
Oh! what shall I ask of thy providence more?

MONTGOMERY.

1035 11s.

1 I ONCE was a stranger to grace and to God;
I knew not my danger, and felt not my load;
Though friends spoke in rapture of Christ on the tree;
Jehovah, my Saviour, seemed nothing to me.

2 When free grace awoke me by light from on high,
Then legal fears shook me; I trembled to die:
No refuge, no safety, in self could I see:
Jehovah, thou only my Saviour must be!

3 My terrors all vanished before his sweet name;
My guilty fears banished, with boldness I came
To drink at the fountain, so copious and free:
Jehovah, my Saviour, is all things to me.

4 Jehovah, the Lord, is my treasure and boast;
Jehovah my Saviour, I ne'er can be lost:
In thee I shall conquer, by flood and by field,
Jehovah my anchor, Jehovah my shield!

MCCHEYNE.

1036 11s.

1 THOUGH troubles assail, and dangers affright,
Though friends should all fail, and foes all unite,
Yet one thing secures us, whatever betide,
The Scripture assures us the Lord will provide.

2 No strength of our own, no goodness we claim,
Yet since we have known the Redeemer's great name,
In this our strong tower for safety we hide,—
The Lord is our power, the Lord will provide.

1037 7s & 6s.

1 RISE, my soul, and stretch thy wings,
Thy better portion trace;
Rise from transitory things
Towards heaven, thy native place:
Sun, and moon, and stars decay;
Time shall soon this earth remove;
Rise, my soul, and haste away
To seats prepared above.

2 Rivers to the ocean run,
Nor stay in all their course;
Fire, ascending, seeks the sun;
Both speed them to their source:
So a soul that's born of God,
Pants to view his glorious face,
Upward tends to his abode,
To rest in his embrace.

3 Fly me, riches, fly me, cares,
Whilst I that coast explore;
Flattering world, with all thy snares,
Solicit me no more!
Pilgrims fix not here their home;
Strangers tarry but a night;
When the last dear morn is come,
They'll rise to joyful light.

4 Cease, ye pilgrims, cease to mourn,
Press onward to the prize;
Soon our Saviour will return
Triumphant in the skies:
Yet a season, and you know
Happy entrance will be given,
All our sorrows left below,
And earth exchanged for heaven.

SEAGRAVE.

1038 8s. D.

1 YE angels, who stand round the throne,
And view my Immanuel's face,—
In rapturous songs make him known,
Oh, tune your soft harps to his praise:
He formed you the spirits you are,
So happy, so noble, so good;
When others sank down in despair,
Confirmed by his power, ye stood.

2 Ye saints! who stand nearer than they,
And cast your bright crowns at his feet,
His grace and his glory display,
And all his rich mercy repeat;
He snatch'd you from hell and the grave,
He ransomed from death and despair:
For you he was mighty to save,
Almighty to bring you safe there.

3 Oh! when will the period appear
When I shall unite in your song?
I'm weary of lingering here,
And I to your Saviour belong!
I want—oh! I want to be there,
To sorrow and sin bid adieu—
Your joy and your friendship to share—
To wonder, and worship with you!

DE FLEURY.

1039 8s. D.

1 MY Saviour, whom absent I love,
Whom, not having seen, I adore,
Whose name is exalted above
All glory, dominion, and power,—
Dissolve thou those bands that detain
My soul from her portion in thee;
Ah! strike off this adamant chain,
And make me eternally free!

2 When that happy era begins,
When arrayed in thy glories I shine,
Nor grieve any more, by my sins,
The bosom on which I recline,
Oh! then shall the vail be removed,
And round me thy brightness be poured!
I shall meet him, whom absent I loved,
I shall see, whom unseen I adored.

3 And then, nevermore shall the fears,
The trials, temptations, and woes,
Which darken this valley of tears,
Intrude on my blissful repose:
To Jesus, the crown of my hope,
My soul is in haste to be gone;
Oh! bear me, ye cherubim, up,
And waft me away to his throne!

COWPER.

1040 11s.

1 MY home is in heaven, my rest is not here,
Then why should I murmur when trials appear?
Be hushed, my dark spirit, the worst that can come
But shortens thy journey, and hastens thee home.

2 It is not for thee to be seeking thy bliss,
And building thy hopes in a region like this;
I look for a city which hands have not piled;
I pant for a country by sin undefiled.

3 The thorn and the thistle around me may grow,
I would not recline upon roses below;
I ask not my portion, I seek not my rest,
Till I find them forever on Jesus' breast.

4 Afflictions may press me, they cannot destroy—
One glimpse of his love turns them all into joy;
And the bitterest tears, if he smile but on them,
Like dew in the sunshine, grow diamond and gem.

Chorus.

Then the angels will come, with their music will come,
With music, sweet music, to welcome me home;
In the bright gates of crystal the shining ones will stand,
And sing me a welcome to their own native land!

1041 8s.

1 I LONG to behold him arrayed,
With glory and light from above;
The King in his beauty displayed—
His beauty of holiest love.

2 I languish and sigh to be there,
Where Jesus hath fixed his abode;
Oh, when shall we meet in the air,
And fly to the mountain of God?

3 With him I on Zion shall stand,
For Jesus hath spoken the word;
The breadth of Immanuel's land
Survey by the light of my Lord.

4 But when, on thy bosom reclined,
Thy face I am strengthened to see,
My fullness of rapture I find—
My heaven of heavens in thee!

5 How happy the people that dwell
Secure in the city above!
No pain the inhabitants feel,
No sickness or sorrow shall prove.

6 Physician of souls! unto me
Forgiveness and holiness give;
And when from the body set free,
Oh then to that city receive!

C. WESLEY.

1042 8s.

1 AWAY with our sorrow and fear,
We soon shall recover our home;
The city of saints shall appear,
The day of eternity come.

2 From earth we shall quickly remove,
And mount to our native abode;
The house of our Father above—
The palace of angels and God.

3 Our mourning is all at an end,
When, raised by the life-giving word,
We see the new city descend,
Adorned as a bride for her Lord:

4 The city so holy and clean,
No sorrow can breathe in the air:
No gloom of affliction or sin;
No shadow of evil is there.

5 By faith we already behold
That lovely Jerusalem here:
Her walls are of jasper and gold;
As crystal her buildings are clear.

6 Immovably founded in grace,
She stands as she ever hath stood,
And brightly her Builder displays,
And flames with the glory of God.

C. WESLEY.

1043 8s & 7s.

1 MY days are gliding swiftly by,
And I, a pilgrim stranger,
Would not detain them as they fly
Those hours of toil and danger.

2 We'll gird our loins, my brethren dear,
Our heavenly home discerning;
Our absent Lord has left us word,
Let every lamp be burning.

3 Should coming days be cold and dark,
We need not cease our singing;
That perfect rest nought can molest,
Where golden harps are ringing.

4 Let sorrow's rudest tempest blow,
Each cord on earth to sever;
Our King says, Come, and there's our home,
Forever, oh forever!

D. NELSON.

Chorus.

For oh, we stand on Jordan's strand,
Our friends are passing over;
And just before, the shining shore
We may almost discover.

1044

1 I'M a pilgrim, and I'm a stranger;
I can tarry, I can tarry but a night!
Do not detain me, for I am going
To where the fountains are ever flowing:
I'm a pilgrim, etc.

2 There the glory is ever shining!
Oh, my longing heart, my longing heart is there!
Here in this country so dark and dreary,
I long have wandered forlorn and weary:
I'm a pilgrim, etc.

3 There's the city to which I journey;
My Redeemer, my Redeemer is its light!
There is no sorrow, nor any sighing,
Nor any tears there, nor any dying!
I'm a pilgrim, etc.

1045

1 SHALL we gather at the river,
Where bright angel-feet have trod;
With its crystal tide forever
Flowing by the throne of God?

2 On the margin of the river,
Washing up its silver spray,
We will walk and worship ever,
All the happy golden day.

3 On the bosom of the river,
Where the Saviour-King we own,
We shall meet, and sorrow never
'Neath the glory of the throne.

4 Ere we reach the shining river,
Lay we every burden down;
Grace our spirits will deliver,
And provide a robe and crown.

5 At the smiling of the river,
Rippling with the Saviour's face,
Saints, whom death will never sever,
Lift their songs of saving grace.

6 Soon we'll reach the shining river,
Soon our pilgrimage shall cease,
Soon our happy hearts will quiver,
With the melody of Peace.

Chorus.

Yes, we'll gather at the river,
The beautiful, the beautiful river—
Gather with the saints at the river
That flows by the throne of God.

1046

6s & 4s.

1 I'M but a stranger here;
Heaven is my home!
Earth is a desert drear;
Heaven is my home!
Danger and sorrow stand,
Round me on every hand,
Heaven is my fatherland,
Heaven is my home!

2 What though the tempest rage!
Heaven is my home!
Short is my pilgrimage;
Heaven is my home!
Time's cold and wintry blast
Soon will be overpast;
I shall reach home at last;
Heaven is my home!

3 There, at my Saviour's side,
Heaven is my home!
I shall be glorified;
Heaven is my home!
There are the good and blest,
Those I love most and best,
And there I, too, shall rest;
Heaven is my home!

T. R. TAYLOR.

1047

1 SHALL we meet be- | yond the | river,
Where the surges | cease to | roll—
Where the blessèd | sing for- | ever,
Songs that fill the | raptured | soul?
Shall we meet? Yes! beyond the river.

2 Shall we meet in | that blest | harbor,
When our stormy | voyage is | o'er?
Shall we meet and | cast the | anchor,
By the fair ce- | lestial | shore!
Shall we meet, etc.

3 Shall we meet in | yonder | city,
Where the towers of | crystal | shine,
Where the walls are | all of | jasper,
Built by | workmanship | divine?
Shall we meet, etc.

4 Where the music | of the | ransomed
Rolls its | harmony | around,

And creation | swells the | chorus,
With its sweet me- | lodious | sound?
Shall we meet, etc.

5 Shall we meet with | many a | loved one,
That was torn from | our em- | brace?
Shall we listen | to their | voices,
And behold them | face to | face?
Shall we meet, etc.

6 Shall we meet with | Christ our | Saviour,
When he comes to | claim his | own?
Shall we know his | blessèd | favor,
And sit down up- | on his | throne?
Shall we meet, etc.

1048 P. M.

1 AH! this heart is void and chill,
'Mid earth's noisy thronging;
For my Father's mansions still
Earnestly is longing;
Looking home! Looking home!
Toward the heavenly mansions
Jesus hath prepared for me
In his Father's kingdom!

2 Soon the glorious day will dawn,
Heavenly pleasures bringing;
Night will be exchanged for morn,
Sighs give place to singing.
Looking home! looking home!
Toward the heavenly mansions
Jesus hath prepared for me
In his Father's kingdom!

3 With this load of sin and care,
Then no longer bending,
But with waiting angels there
On our soul attending:—
Blessèd home! blessèd home!
All for which we're sighing;
Soon our Lord will bid us come
To our Father's kingdom!

1049 10s.

1 JOYFULLY, joyfully onward I move,
Bound to the land of bright spirits above;
Angelic choristers sing as I come,
Joyfully, joyfully haste to thy home!
Soon with my pilgrimage ended below,
Home to the land of bright spirits I go;
Pilgrim and stranger no more shall I roam,
Joyfully, joyfully resting at home.

2 Friends, fondly cherished, have passed on before;
Waiting, they watch me approaching the shore;
Singing to cheer me through death's chilling gloom:
Joyfully, joyfully haste to thy home.
Sounds of sweet melody fall on my ear;
Harps of the blessèd, your voices I hear!
Rings with the harmony heaven's high dome—
Joyfully, joyfully haste to thy home.

3 Death, with thy weapons of war lay me low,
Strike, king of terrors! I fear not the blow;

Jesus hath broken the bars of the tomb!
Joyfully, joyfully will I go home.
Bright will the morn of eternity dawn,
Death shall be banished, his sceptre be gone;
Joyfully, then, shall I witness his doom,
Joyfully, joyfully, safely at home.

W. HUNTER.

1050 S. M.

1 I LOVE to sing of heaven,
Where white-robed angels are;
Where many a friend is gathered safe
From fear, and toil, and care.

2 I love to think of heaven,
Where my Redeemer reigns;
Where rapturous songs of triumph rise,
In endless, joyous strains.

Chorus.

There 'll be no sorrow there,
There 'll be no sorrow there;
In heaven above, where all is love,
There 'll be no sorrow there.

1051 6s & 4s.

1 A CROWN of glory bright,
By faith's clear eyes I see,
In yonder realms of light
Prepared for me.

2 Oh may I faithful prove,
And keep the crown in view,
And through the storms of life
My way pursue.

3 Jesus, be thou my guide,
And all my steps attend,
Oh keep me near thy side,
Be thou my friend.

4 Be thou my shield and sun,
My Saviour and my guard,
And when my work is done,
My great reward.

Chorus.

I'm nearer my home, nearer my home,
Nearer my home to-day;
Yes, nearer my home in heaven to-day,
Than ever I've been before.

1052 11s.

1 'MID scenes of confusion and creature complaints,
How sweet to my soul is communion with saints;
To find at the banquet of mercy there's room,
And feel in the presence of Jesus at home.
Home! home! sweet, sweet home!
Prepare me, dear Saviour, for glory, my home.

2 Sweet bonds that unite all the children of peace!
And thrice precious Jesus, whose love cannot cease!
Though oft from thy presence in sadness I roam,
I long to behold thee in glory, at home.
Home! home! etc.

3 I sigh from this body of sin to be free,
Which hinders my joy and communion with thee;
Though now my temptation like billows may foam,
All, all will be peace, when I'm with thee at home.
Home! home! etc.

4 While here in the valley of conflict I stay,
Oh give me submission, and strength as my day;
In all my afflictions to thee would I come,
Rejoicing in hope of my glorious home.
Home! home! etc.

5 Whate'er thou deniest, oh give me thy grace,
The Spirit's sure witness, and smiles of thy face;
Endue me with patience to wait at thy throne,
And find, even now, a sweet foretaste of home.
Home! home! etc.

6 I long, dearest Lord, in thy beauties to shine;
No more as an exile in sorrow to pine;
And in thy dear image arise from the tomb,
With glorified millions to praise thee at home.
Home! home! etc.

DENHAM.

1053 L. M.

1 WHAT sinners value I resign;
Lord, 'tis enough that thou art mine;
I shall behold thy blissful face,
And stand complete in righteousness.

2 This life's a dream, an empty show,
But the bright world to which I go
Hath joys substantial and sincere;
When shall I wake and find me there!

3 Oh, glorious hour! oh, blest abode!
I shall be near and like my God;
And flesh and sin no more control
The sacred pleasures of the soul.

4 My flesh shall slumber in the ground
Till the last trumpet's joyful sound;
Then burst the chains with sweet surprise,
And in my Saviour's image rise!

WATTS.

1054 8s.

1 WE speak of the realms of the blest,
That country so bright and so fair;
And oft are its glories confessed,
But what must it be to be there!

2 We speak of its freedom from sin,
From sorrow, temptation, and care,
From trials without and within—
But what must it be to be there!

3 We speak of its service of love,
The robes which the glorified wear,
The church of the first-born above—
But what must it be to be there!

4 O Lord, in this valley of woe,
Our spirits for heaven prepare,
And shortly we also shall know
And feel what it is to be there!

ELIZABETH MILLS.

1055 7s.

1 WE know not what's before us—
What trials are to come;
But each day passing o'er us
Brings us still nearer home.

2 Though dark our path and lonely,
And clouds our sky o'ercast,

Let us remember only,
That it will soon be past.

3 Whate'er of gloom or anguish
This weary world may bring,
In doubt we will not languish,
But cheerfully we'll sing.

Chorus.

We're nearer, nearer home,
Our blessed, happy home,
Where grief and sin can never come,
We're nearer, nearer home.
Nearer home, nearer home,
Nearer to my happy home,
Nearer home, nearer home,
Our blessed, happy home.

1056

1 "LAND a-head!" its fruits are waving
O'er the hills of fadeless green;
And the living waters laving
Shores where heavenly forms are seen.

2 Onward, bark! the cape I'm rounding,
See, the blessèd wave their hands;
Hear the harps of God resounding
From the bright immortal bands.

3 There, let go the anchor, riding
On this calm and silv'ry bay;
Seaward fast the tide is gliding,
Shores in sunlight stretch away.

4 Now we're safe from all temptation,
All the storms of life are past;
Praise the Rock of our Salvation,
We are safe at home at last!

Chorus.

Rocks and storms I'll fear no more,
When on that eternal shore:
Drop the anchor! furl the sail!
I am safe within the vail!

1057 P. M.

1 THERE is a happy land,
Far, far away,
Where saints in glory stand,
Bright, bright as day.
Oh, how they sweetly sing,
Worthy is our Saviour-King,
Loud let his praises ring,
Praise, praise for aye.

2 Come to that happy land,
Come, come away;
Why will ye doubting stand,
Why still delay?
Oh, we shall happy be,
When from sin and sorrow free!
Lord, we shall live with thee,
Blest, blest for aye.

3 Bright, in that happy land,
Beams every eye;
Kept by a Father's hand,
Love cannot die.
Oh, then, to glory run;
Be a crown and kingdom won;
And bright, above the sun,
We reign for aye.

1058 P. M.

1 HERE we meet to part again,
Here we meet to part again;
But when we meet on Canaan's plain,
There'll be no parting there,

In that bright world above,
In that bright world above,
Shout, shout, the vict'ry,
We're on our journey home.

2 Here we meet to part again,
But there we shall with Jesus reign,
There 'll be, etc.

3 Here we meet to part again,
But when we join the heavenly train,
There 'll be, etc.

1059

1 IN the Christian's home in glory,
There remains a land of rest,
There my Saviour's gone before me,
To fulfill my soul's request.

2 He is fitting up my mansion,
Which eternally shall stand,
For my stay shall not be transient,
In that holy, happy land.

3 Pain or sickness ne'er shall enter,
Grief nor woe my lot shall share;
But in that celestial centre,
I a crown of life shall wear.

4 Death itself shall then be vanquished,
And his sting shall be withdrawn;
Shout for gladness, oh, ye ransomed,
Hail with joy the rising morn!

5 Sing, oh, sing, ye heirs of glory!
Shout your triumph as you go;
Zion's gate will open for you,
You shall find an entrance through.

Chorus.

There is rest for the weary,
There is rest for the weary,
There is rest for the weary,
There is rest for you.
On the other side of Jordan,
In the sweet fields of Eden,
Where the tree of life is blooming,
There is rest for you.

1060 L. M.

1 NOW let our souls, on wings sublime,
Rise from the vanities of time,
Draw back the parting veil, and see
The glories of eternity.

2 Born by a new celestial birth,
Why should we grovel here on earth?
Why grasp at transitory toys,
So near to heaven's eternal joys?

3 Shall aught beguile us on the road,
When we are walking back to God?
For strangers into life we come,
And dying is but going home.

4 To dwell with God, to feel his love,
Is the full heaven enjoy'd above;
And the sweet expectation now
Is the young dawn of heaven below.

GIBBONS.

1061 L. M.

1 AND may I hope, that when no more
My pulse shall beat with life below,
I shall the God of grace adore,
And all the bliss of glory know?

2 I, who deserve no place but hell,
No portion but devouring fire,
Shall I with Christ my Saviour dwell,
Possessed of all I now desire?

3 Will Jesus own a wretch like me?
And tell to saints and angels round,
That when he suffered on the tree,
My sins augmented every wound?

4 Will he from life's eternal book
To earth and heaven proclaim my name;
On me, as on his chosen, look,
And make my lot with theirs the same?

5 He will! I read it in his word,
And in my heart the witness feel:
I shall be with, and like my Lord,
Though sin oppose in league with hell!

1062 L. M.

1 DESCEND from heaven, immortal Dove;
Stoop down and take us on thy wings;
And mount, and bear us far above
The reach of these inferior things;

2 Beyond, beyond this lower sky,
Up where eternal ages roll,
Where solid pleasures never die,
And fruits immortal feast the soul.

3 Oh, for a sight, a pleasing sight
Of our Almighty Father's throne!
There sits our Saviour, crowned with light,
Clothed in a body like our own.

4 Adoring saints around him stand,
And thrones and powers before him fall:
The God shines gracious through the Man,
And sheds sweet glories on them all.

5 Oh, what amazing joys they feel,
While to their golden harps they sing,
And sit on every heavenly hill,
And spread the triumph of their King!

6 When shall the day, dear Lord, appear,
That I shall mount, to dwell above;
And stand, and bow, among them there,
And view thy face, and sing, and love!

WATTS.

1063 L. M.

1 O HAPPY saints, who dwell in light,
And walk with Jesus, clothed in white;
Safe landed on that peaceful shore,
Where pilgrims meet to part no more.

2 Released from sin, and toil, and grief,
Death was their gate to endless life;
An opened cage, to let them fly
And build their happy nest on high.

3 And now they range the heavenly plains,
And sing their hymns in melting strains;
And now their souls begin to prove
The heights and depths of Jesus' love.

4 He cheers them with eternal smile;
They sing hosannas all the while;
Or, overwhelmed with rapture sweet,
Sink down adoring at his feet.

5 Ah! Lord! with tardy steps I creep,
And sometimes sing, and sometimes weep;
Yet strip me of this house of clay,
And I will sing as loud as they.

JOHN BERRIDGE.

1064 L. M.

1 AS when the weary traveller gains
The sight of some o'erlooking hill,
His heart revives, if 'cross the plains
He eyes his home, though distant still.

2 While he surveys the much-loved spot
He slights the space that lies between;
His past fatigues are now forgot,
Because his journey's end is seen.

3 Thus when the Christian pilgrim views
By faith his mansion in the skies,
The sight his fainting strength renews,
And wings his speed to reach the prize.

4 The thought of home his spirit cheers;
No more he grieves for troubles past,
Nor any future trial fears
So he may safe arrive at last.

5 'Tis there, he says, I am to dwell
With Jesus in the realms of day;
Then I shall bid my cares farewell,
And he shall wipe my tears away.

NEWTON.

1065 L. M.

1 THERE is a land mine eye hath seen,
In visions of enraptured thought,
So bright, that all which spreads between
Is with its radiant glories fraught.

2 A land, upon whose blissful shore
There rests no shadow, falls no stain;
There those who meet shall part no more,
And those long parted meet again.

3 Its skies are not like earthly skies,
With varying hues of shade and light;
It hath no need of suns to rise
To dissipate the gloom of night.

4 There sweeps no desolating wind
Across that calm, serene abode;
The wanderer there a home may find
Within the paradise of God.

G. ROBINS.

1066 C. M.

1 THERE is a land of pure delight,
Where saints immortal reign;
Infinite day excludes the night,
And pleasures banish pain.

2 There everlasting spring abides,
And never-withering flowers;
Death, like a narrow sea, divides
This heavenly land from ours.

3 Sweet fields beyond the swelling flood
Stand dressed in living green;
So to the Jews old Canaan stood,
While Jordan rolled between.

4 But timorous mortals start and shrink
To cross this narrow sea,
And linger, shivering, on the brink,
And fear to launch away.

5 Oh, could we make our doubts remove,
Those gloomy doubts that rise,
And see the Canaan that we love
With unbeclouded eyes!—

6 Could we but climb where Moses stood,
And view the landscape o'er,
Not Jordan's stream nor death's cold flood
Should fright us from the shore.

WATTS.

1067 C. M.

1 ON Jordan's stormy banks I stand,
And cast a wishful eye
To Canaan's fair and happy land,
Where my possessions lie.

2 Oh the transporting, rapturous scene
That rises to my sight!
Sweet fields arrayed in living green,
And rivers of delight.

3 All o'er those wide-extended plains
Shines one eternal day;
There God the Son forever reigns,
And scatters night away.

4 No chilling winds, nor poisonous breath,
Can reach that healthful shore;
Sickness and sorrow, pain and death,
Are felt and feared no more.

5 When shall I reach that happy place,
And be forever blest?
When shall I see my Father's face,
And in his bosom rest?

6 Filled with delight, my raptured soul
Would here no longer stay;
Though Jordan's waves around me roll,
Fearless I'd launch away.

STENNETT.

1068 C. M.

1 HOPE of our hearts, O Lord, appear,
Thou glorious Star of day!
Shine forth, and chase the dreary night,
With all our tears, away.

2 No resting-place we seek on earth,
No loveliness we see;
Our eye is on the royal crown,
Prepared for us and thee.

3 But, dearest Lord, however bright
That crown of joy above,
What is it to the brighter hope
Of dwelling in thy love?

4 What to the joy, the deeper joy,
Unmingled, pure, and free,
Of union with our living Head,
Of fellowship with thee?

5 This joy e'en now on earth is ours;
But only, Lord, above,
Our hearts, without a pang, shall know
The fullness of thy love.

6 There, near thy heart, upon the throne,
Thy ransomed bride shall see
What grace was in the bleeding Lamb,
Who died to make her free.

DENNY.

1069 C. M.

1 WHEN I can read my title clear
To mansions in the skies,
I bid farewell to every fear,
And wipe my weeping eyes.

2 Should earth against my soul engage,
And fiery darts be hurled,
Then I can smile at Satan's rage,
And face a frowning world.

3 Let cares, like a wild deluge, come,
And storms of sorrow fall!
May I but safely reach my home,
My God, my heaven, my all.

4 There shall I bathe my weary soul
In seas of heavenly rest,
And not a wave of trouble roll
Across my peaceful breast.

WATTS.

1070 C. M.

1 LO! what a glorious sight appears
To our believing eyes!
The earth and seas are passed away,
And the old rolling skies.

2 From the third heaven, where God resides,
That holy, happy place,
The new Jerusalem comes down,
Adorned with shining grace.

3 Attending angels shout for joy,
And the bright armies sing—
"Mortals, behold the sacred seat
Of your descending King.

4 "The God of glory down to men
Removes his blest abode!
Men, the dear objects of his grace,
And he the loving God.

5 "His own kind hand shall wipe the tears
From every weeping eye;
And pains, and groans, and griefs, and fears,
And death itself, shall die."

6 How long, dear Saviour, oh, how long
Shall this bright hour delay?
Fly swifter round, ye wheels of time,
And bring the welcome day.

WATTS.

1071 C. M.

1 FATHER! I long, I faint to see
The place of thine abode;
I'd leave thine earthly courts, and flee
Up to thy seat, my God!

2 Here I behold thy distant face,
And 'tis a pleasing sight;
But, to abide in thine embrace
Is infinite delight.

3 I'd part with all the joys of sense,
To gaze upon thy throne;
Pleasure springs fresh forever thence,
Unspeakable, unknown.

4 There all the heavenly hosts are seen;
In shining ranks they move;
And drink immortal vigor in,
With wonder and with love.

5 Then at thy feet, with awful fear,
Th' adoring armies fall;
With joy they shrink to nothing there,
Before th' eternal All.

6 The more thy glories strike my eyes,
The humbler I shall lie;
Thus while I sink, my joys shall rise
Immeasurably high.

WATTS.

1072 C. M.

1 THERE is a world of perfect bliss
Above the starry skies;
Oppressed with sorrows and with sins,
I thither lift my eyes.

2 'Tis there the weary are at rest,
And all is peace within;
The mind, with guilt no more oppressed,
Is tranquil and serene.

3 Discord and strife are banished thence,
Distrust and slavish fear;
No more we hear the pensive sigh,
Or see the falling tear.

4 Farewell to earth and earthly things:
In vain they tempt my stay:
Come, angels, spread your joyful wings,
And bear my soul away.

BEDDOME.

1073 C. M.

1 JESUS, to thy dear wounds we flee,
We seek thy bleeding side,
Assured that all who trust in thee
Shall evermore abide.

2 Then let the thundering trumpet sound,
The latest lightning glare;
The mountains melt; the solid ground
Dissolve as liquid air;

3 The huge, celestial bodies roll,
Amidst that general fire;
And shrivel as a parchment scroll,
And all in smoke expire!

4 Sublime upon his azure throne,
He speaks—the Almighty Word;
His fiat is obeyed!—'tis done;
And Paradise restored!

5 So be it! let this system end,
This ruined earth and skies;
The New Jerusalem descend,
The New Creation rise.

C. Wesley.

1074 C. M.

1 ARISE, my soul! fly up, and run
Through every heavenly street;
And say there's nought below the sun
That's worthy of thy feet.

2 There, on a high, majestic throne,
Th' Almighty Father reigns,
And sheds his glorious goodness down
On all the blissful plains.

3 Bright, like a sun, the Saviour sits,
And spreads eternal noon;
No evenings there, nor gloomy nights,
To want the feeble moon.

4 Amidst those ever-shining skies
Behold the sacred Dove;
While banished sin and sorrow flies
From all the realms of love.

5 But oh, what beams of heavenly grace
Transport them all the while!
Ten thousand smiles from Jesus' face,
And love in every smile!

6 Jesus, and when shall that dear day,
That joyful hour appear,
When I shall leave this house of clay,
To dwell among them there?

Watts.

1075 C. M.

1 WHEN wild confusion wrecks the air,
And tempests rend the skies;
Whilst blended ruin, clouds and fire
In harsh disorder rise;—

2 Safe in my Saviour's love I'll stand,
And strike a tuneful song;
My harp all trembling in my hand,
And all inspired my tongue.

3 I'll shout aloud, "Ye thunders, roll,
And shake the sullen sky;
Your sounding voice, from pole to pole,
In angry murmurs try.

4 "Let the earth totter on her base,
And clouds the heavens deform;
Blow, all ye winds, from every place,
And rush the final storm!"

5 Come quickly, blessèd Lord, appear—
Bid the swift chariot fly;
Let angels tell thy coming near,
And snatch me to the sky.

6 Around thy wheels, in the glad throng,
I'd bear a joyful part;
All hallelujah on my tongue—
All rapture in my heart.

Byles.

1076 C. M.

1 THERE'S nothing round these painted skies,
Or round this dusty clod,
Nothing, my soul, that's worth thy joys,
Or lovely as thy God.

2 'Tis heaven on earth to taste his love,
To feel his quickening grace;
And all the heaven I hope above
Is but to see his face.

3 Why move my years in slow delay?
O God of ages why?
Let the spheres cleave, and mark my way
To the superior sky.

WATTS.

1077 C. M.

1 YE golden lamps of heaven, farewell,
With all your feeble light:
Farewell, thou ever-changing moon,
Pale empress of the night.

2 And thou, refulgent orb of day,
In brighter flames arrayed;
My soul, that springs beyond thy sphere,
No more demands thine aid.

3 Ye stars are but the shining dust
Of my divine abode,
The pavement of those heavenly courts
Where I shall reign with God.

4 The Father of eternal light
Shall there his beams display,
Nor shall one moment's darkness mix
With that unvaried day.

5 No more the drops of piercing grief
Shall swell into mine eyes;
Nor the meridian sun decline
Amid those brighter skies.

6 There all the millions of his saints
Shall in one song unite,
And each the bliss of all shall view
With infinite delight.

DODDRIDGE.

1078 C. M.

1 FAR from these narrow scenes of night
Unbounded glories rise,
And realms of infinite delight,
Unknown to mortal eyes.

2 Fair distant land; could mortal eyes
But half its joys explore,
How would our spirits long to rise,
And dwell on earth no more!

3 There pain and sickness never come,
And grief no more complains:
Health triumphs in immortal bloom,
And endless pleasure reigns.

4 No cloud those blissful regions know,
Forever bright and fair;
For sin, the source of mortal woe,
Can never enter there.

5 Oh may the heavenly prospect fire
Our hearts with ardent love,
Till wings of faith and strong desire
Bear every thought above!

STEELE.

1079 C. M.

1 OUR country is Immanuel's ground—
We seek that promised soil;
The songs of Zion cheer our hearts,
While strangers here we toil.

2 Oft do our eyes with joy o'erflow,
And oft are bathed in tears;
Yet naught but heaven our hopes can raise,
And naught but sin our fears.

3 The flowers that spring along the road
We scarcely stoop to pluck;
We walk o'er beds of shining ore,
Nor waste one wishful look.

4 We tread the path our Master trod;
We bear the cross he bore;
And every thorn that wounds our feet
His temples pierced before.

BARBAULD.

1080

C. M.

1 MY soul, amid this stormy world,
Is like some fluttered dove,
And fain would be as swift of wing,
To flee to him I love.

2 May not an exile, Lord, desire,
His own sweet land to see?
May not a captive seek release,
A prisoner, to be free?

3 A child, when far away, may long
For home and kindred dear;
And she that waits her absent lord
May sigh till he appear.

4 I fain would strike my harp divine,
Before the Father's throne,
There cast my crown of Righteousness,
And sing what grace has done!

5 Ah! leave me not in this base world,
A stranger still to roam;
Come, Lord, and take me to thyself;
Come, Jesus, quickly come!

ROBERT C. CHAPMAN.

1081

C. M.

1 OH, for the pearly gates of heaven!
Oh, for the golden floor!
Oh, for the Sun of Righteousness,
That setteth nevermore!

2 The highest hopes we cherish here,
How soon they tire and faint!
How many a spot defiles the robe
That wraps an earthly saint!

3 Oh, for a heart that never sins!
Oh, for a soul washed white!
Oh, for a voice to praise our King,
Nor weary day nor night!

4 Here faith is ours, and heavenly hope,
And grace to lead us higher!
But there are perfectness and peace,
Beyond our best desire.

5 Oh, by thy love and anguish, Lord,
And by thy life laid down,
Grant that we fail not of thy grace,
Nor fail to reach our crown!

C. F. ALEXANDER.

1082

C. M.

1 THERE is a fold whence none can stray;
And pastures ever green,
Where sultry sun, or stormy day,
Or night is never seen.

2 Far up the everlasting hills
In God's own light it lies;
His smile its vast dimension fills
With joy that never dies.

3 One narrow vale, one darksome wave,
Divides that land from this:
I have a Shepherd pledged to save
And bear me home to bliss.

4 'Soon at his feet my soul will lie
In life's last struggling breath;
But I shall only seem to die,
I shall not taste of death.

5 Far from this guilty world to be
Exempt from toil and strife—
To spend eternity with thee—
My Saviour, this is life!

EAST.

1083 C. M.

1 THERE is an hour of peaceful rest,
To mourning wanderers given;
There is a joy for souls distressed,
A balm for every wounded breast:
'Tis found above—in heaven.

2 There is a home for weary souls,
By sin and sorrow driven,—
When tossed on life's tempestuous shoals,
Where storms arise, and ocean rolls,
And all is drear—but heaven.

3 There faith lifts up her cheerful eye
To brighter prospects given;
And views the tempest passing by,
The evening shadows quickly fly,
And all serene—in heaven.

4 There fragrant flowers immortal bloom,
And joys supreme are given;
Their rays divine disperse the gloom;
Beyond the confines of the tomb
Appears the dawn of heaven!

W. B. TAPPAN.

1084 7s. D.

1 WHO are these in bright array,
This innumerable throng,
Round the altar, night and day,
Hymning one triumphant song?

"Worthy is the Lamb, once slain,
Blessing, honor, glory, power,
Wisdom, riches, to obtain,
New dominion every hour."

2 These through fiery trials trod;
These from great affliction came:
Now, before the throne of God,
Sealed with his almighty name,
Clad in raiment pure and white,
Victor-palms in every hand,
Through their dear Redeemer's might,
More than conquerors they stand.

3 Hunger, thirst, disease unknown,
On immortal fruits they feed;
Them the Lamb, amid the throne,
Shall to living fountains lead:
Joy and gladness banish sighs;
Perfect love dispel all fears;
And forever from their eyes
God shall wipe away the tears.

MONTGOMERY.

1085 7s. D.

1 HIGH in yonder realms of light,
Dwell the raptured saints above;
Far beyond our feeble sight,
Happy in Immanuel's love:
Pilgrims in this vale of tears,
Once they knew, like us below,
Gloomy doubts, distressing fears,
Torturing pain and heavy woe.

2 But these days of weeping o'er,
Passed this scene of toil and pain,
They shall feel distress no more—
Never, never weep again:

'Mid the chorus of the skies,
'Mid the angelic lyres above,
Hark, their songs melodious rise,
Songs of praise to Jesus' love!

3 All is tranquil and serene,
Calm and undisturbed repose:
There no cloud can intervene,
There no angry tempest blows:
Every tear is wiped away,
Sighs no more shall heave the breast,
Night is lost in endless day,
Sorrow, in eternal rest.

RAFFLES.

1086

1 BEAUTIFUL Zion, built above,
Beautiful city, that I love,
Beautiful gates of pearly white,
Beautiful temple,—God its light!
He who was slain on Calvary,
Opens those pearly gates to me.
Zion, Zion, lovely Zion,
Beautiful Zion, city of our God.

2 Beautiful heaven, where all is light,
Beautiful angels, clothed in white;
Beautiful strains that never tire,
Beautiful harps through all the choir.
There shall I join the chorus sweet,
Worshiping at the Saviour's feet.
Zion, Zion, etc.

3 Beautiful crowns on every brow,
Beautiful palms the conquerors show;
Beautiful robes the ransomed wear,
Beautiful all who enter there:
Thither I press with eager feet,
There shall my rest be long and sweet.
Zion, Zion, etc.

4. Beautiful throne for Christ our King,
Beautiful songs the angels sing;
Beautiful rest—all wanderings cease—
Beautiful home of perfect peace:
There shall my eyes the Saviour see,
Haste to his heavenly home with me.
Zion, Zion, etc.

1087

7s & 6s.

1 JERUSALEM the golden,
With milk and honey blest!
Beneath thy contemplation
Sink heart and voice oppressed:
I know not, oh, I know not
What social joys are there;
What radiancy of glory,
What light beyond compare.

2 They stand, those halls of Zion,
Conjubilant with song,
And bright with many an angel,
And all the martyr throng.
The Prince is ever in them;
The daylight is serene;
The pastures of the blesséd
Are decked in glorious sheen.

3 There is the throne of David;
And there, from care released,
The song of them that triumph,
The shout of them that feast;
And they who with their Leader
Have conquered in the fight,
Forever and forever
Are clad in robes of white.

4 O sweet and blesséd country,
Shall I e'er see thy face?
O sweet and blesséd country,
Shall I e'er win thy grace?

Exult, O dust and ashes!
The Lord shall be thy part,
His only, his forever
Thou shalt be, and thou art!

BERNARD.

1088 L. M.

1 MY heavenly home is bright and fair;
No pain nor death can enter there:
Its glittering tow'rs the sun outshine;
That heavenly mansion shall be mine.

2 My Father's house is built on high,
Far, far above the starry sky:
When from this earthly prison free,
That heavenly mansion mine shall be.

3 Let others seek a home below,
Which flames devour, or waves o'erflow;
Be mine a happier lot to own
A heavenly mansion near the throne.

Chorus.

I'm going home, I'm going home,
I'm going home to die no more;
To die no more, to die no more,
I'm going home to die no more.

1089 8s & 4s.

1 I KNOW not whether dark or bright
Shall be my lot;
If that wherein my hopes delight
Be best or not.

2 My bark is wafted on the strand
By breath divine,
And on the helm there rests a Hand
Other than mine.

3 One who has known in storms to sail
I have on board;—
Above the ravings of the gale
I have my Lord.

4 He holds me when the billows smite:
I shall not fall;
If sharp, 'tis short; if long, 'tis light:
He tempers all.

5 Safe to the land!—safe to the land!
The end is this;
And then with him go hand in hand
Far into bliss.

1090 C. M.

1 JERUSALEM, my happy home,
Name ever dear to me!
When shall my labors have an end
In joy and peace, in thee?

2 When shall these eyes thy heaven-built walls
And pearly gates behold?
Thy bulwarks with salvation strong,
And streets of shining gold?

3 Oh when, thou city of my God,
Shall I thy courts ascend,
Where congregations ne'er break up,
And Sabbaths have no end?

4 There happier bowers than Eden's bloom,
Nor sin nor sorrow know:
Blest seats! through rude and stormy scenes,
I onward press to you.

5 Why should I shrink at pain and woe,
Or feel at death dismay?
I've Canaan's goodly land in view,
And realms of endless day.

6 Apostles, martyrs, prophets, there
Around my Saviour stand;
And soon my friends in Christ below
Will join the glorious band.

7 Jerusalem, my happy home!
My soul still pants for thee;
Then shall my labors have an end,
When I thy joys shall see.

LATIN HYMN OF EIGHTH CENTURY.

1091 C. M.

1 FAIR vision! how thy distant gleam
Brightens time's saddest hue!
Far fairer than the fairest dream,
And yet how strangely true!

2 With thee in view, how poor appear
The world's most winning smiles!
Vain is the tempter's subtlest snare,
And vain hell's varied wiles.

3 Then welcome toil, and care, and pain,
And welcome sorrow too;
All toil is rest, all grief is gain,
With such a prize in view.

BONAR.

1092 P. M.

1 WE dwell this side of Jordan's stream,
Yet oft there comes a shining beam
Across from yonder shore;
While visions of a holy throng,
And sound of harp and seraph song,
Seem gently wafted o'er.

2 The other side! oh, happy place,
Where saints in joy past times retrace,
And think of trials gone,
The veil withdrawn, they clearly see,
That all on earth had need to be,
To bring them safely home.

3 The other side! oh charming side!
Along its banks still waters glide,
And many a loved one waits;
Across the stream they call to me,
"Fear not—we stay to welcome thee
Beside the pearly gates."

4 The other side! the other side!
Who would not brave the swelling tide
Of earthly toil and care,
To wake one day, when life is past,
Over the stream, at home at last,
With all the bless'd ones there?

Chorus.

O Zion, city fair!
O Zion, city fair!
The other side, the other side,
When shall we meet our loved ones there?

1093 P. M.

1 JERUSALEM, forever bright,
Chorus—Beautiful land of rest!
No winter there, nor chill of night,
Chorus—Beautiful land of rest!
The dripping cloud is chased away,
The sun shines forth in endless day.

2 Jerusalem, forever free. *Cho.*
The soul's sweet home of liberty! *Cho.*
The gyves of sin, the chains of woe,
The ransomed there will never know. *Cho.*

3 Jerusalem, forever dear, *Cho.*
Thy pearly gates almost appear. *Cho.*

And when we tread thy lovely shore,
We'll sing the song we've sung before. *Cho.*

Chorus.

Jerusalem, the beautiful land of rest,
Beautiful land! beautiful land!
We wait impatient to behold
The gates of pearl, the streets of gold,
And rest secure in Jesus' fold,
In the beautiful land of rest.

1094 C. M.

1 AROUND the throne of God in heaven
Thousands of children stand;
Children whose sins are all forgiven,
A holy, happy band.

2 In flowing robes of spotless white
See every one arrayed;
Dwelling in everlasting light,
And joys that never fade.

3 What brought them to that world above,
That heav'n so bright and fair,
Where all is peace, and joy, and love;
How came those children there?

4 Because the Saviour shed his blood,
To wash away their sin;
Bathed in that pure and precious flood,
Behold them white and clean!

5 On earth they sought the Saviour's grace,
On earth they loved his name;
So now they see his blessèd face,
And stand before the Lamb.

Chorus.

Singing glory, glory,
Glory be to God on high.

ANNA SHEPHERD.

1095 C. M.

1 ONE sweetly solemn thought
Comes to me o'er and o'er:
I am nearer home to-day
Than I ever have been before.
Nearer my Father's house,
Where the many mansions be;
Nearer the great white throne,
Nearer the crystal sea.

2 Nearer the bound of life
Where we lay our burdens down;
Nearer leaving the cross;
Nearer gaining the crown;
But lying darkly between,
Winding down through the night,
Is the deep and unknown stream,
That leads at last to the light.

3 Father, perfect my trust!
Strengthen the might of my faith;
Let me feel as I would
When I stand on the rock of the shore of death—
Feel as I would when my feet
Are slipping over the brink;
For it may be, I'm nearer home,
Nearer now than I think.

1096 6s.

1 ONE sweetly solemn thought
Comes to me o'er and o'er:
I'm nearer home to-day
Than I have been before;
Nearer my Father's house,
Where many mansions be,
Nearer the great white throne,
Nearer the crystal sea.

2 Nearer the bound of life,
Where burdens are laid down,
Nearer to leave the cross,
And nearer to the crown;
But lying dark between,
And winding through the night,
The deep and unknown stream
Crossed ere we reach the light.

3 Jesus, confirm my trust;
Strengthen the hand of faith
To feel thee, when I stand
Upon the shore of death.
Be near me when my feet
Are slipping o'er the brink;
For I am nearer home,
Perhaps, than now I think.

PHŒBE CARY.

1097 P. M.

1 AFTER the Christian's tears,
After his | fights and | fears,
After his weary cross,
"All things be- | low but | loss."
What— | then? what | then?

2 Oh, then, a holy calm,
Resting on | Jesus' | arm;
Oh, then, a | deeper | love
For the pure | home a- | bove.

3 After this holy calm,
This rest on | Jesus' | arm;
After this deepened love
For the pure | home a- | bove,
What— | then? what | then?

4 Oh, then, a work for him,
Perishing | souls to | win;
Then | Jesus' | presence | near,
Death's | darkest hour to | cheer.

5 And when the work is done,
When the last | soul is | won,
When Jesus' love and power
Have cheered the | dying | hour,
What— | then? what | then?

1098 11s.

1 IN the far better land of glory and light
The ransomed are singing in garments of white,
The harpers are harping, and all the bright train
Sing the song of redemption—"The Lamb that was slain."

2 Like the sound of the sea swells their chorus of praise
Round the star-circled crown of the Ancient of Days;
And thrones and dominions re-echo the strain
Of glory eternal to him that was slain.

3 Dear Saviour, may we, with our voices so faint,
Sing the chorus celestial with angel and saint?
Yes, yes, we will sing, and thine ear we will gain
With the song of redemption—"The Lamb that was slain."

4 Now let our hearts and our voices unite
In loud hallelujahs with angels in light;
To Jesus we'll sing that melodious strain,
The song of redemption—"The Lamb that was slain."

Chorus.

Hallelujah to the Lamb,
Hallelujah, Amen.

E. S. PORTER.

1099 6s & 5s.

1 FAR, far o'er hill and dell, on the winds stealing,
List to the tolling bell, mournfully pealing;
Hark, hark, it seems to say, as melt those sounds away,
So earthly joys decay, whilst new their feeling!

2 Now through the charméd air, on the winds stealing,
List to the mourner's prayer, solemnly bending;
Hark, hark, it seems to say, turn from those joys away,
To those which ne'er decay, for life is ending.

3 So when our mortal ties death shall dissever,
Lord, may we reach the skies where care comes never,
And in eternal day, joining the angels' lay,
To our Creator pay homage forever.

4 When in their lonely bed loved ones are lying;
When joyful wings are spread to heaven flying;
Would we to sin and pain call back their souls again,
Weave round their hearts the chain severed in dying?

5 No, dearest Jesus, no; to thee, their Saviour,
Let their free spirits go, ransomed forever:
Heirs of unending joy, theirs is the victory;
Thine let the glory be, now and forever.

1100 L. M.

1 ASLEEP in Jesus! blesséd sleep!
From which none ever wake to weep;
A calm and undisturbed repose,
Unbroken by the last of foes.

2 Asleep in Jesus! oh, how sweet
To be for such a slumber meet!
With holy confidence to sing
That death hath lost its venomed sting.

3 Asleep in Jesus! peaceful rest!
Whose waking is supremely blest;
No fear—no woe—shall dim the hour
That manifests the Saviour's power.

4 Asleep in Jesus! oh, for me
May such a blissful refuge be:
Securely shall my ashes lie,
And wait the summons from on high.

5 Asleep in Jesus! far from thee
Thy kindred and their graves may be:
But thine is still a blesséd sleep
From which none ever wake to weep.

MRS. MACKAY.

1101 L. M.

1 DEAR is the spot where Christians sleep,
And sweet the strains their spirits pour;
Oh, why should we in anguish weep?—
They are not lost, but gone before.

2 Secure from every mortal care,
By sin and sorrow vexed no more,
Eternal happiness they share
Who are not lost, but gone before.

3 To Zion's peaceful courts above
In faith triumphant may we soar,
Embracing in the arms of love,
The friends not lost, but gone before.

4 To Jordan's bank whene'er we come,
And hear the swelling waters roar,
Jesus, convey us safely home,
To friends not lost, but gone before.

1102 L. M.

1 HOW blest the righteous when he dies!
When sinks a weary soul to rest!
How mildly beam the closing eyes!
How gently heaves the expiring breast!

2 So fades a summer cloud away;
So sinks the gale when storms are o'er;
So gently shuts the eye of day;
So dies a wave along the shore.

3 A holy quiet reigns around,
A calm which life nor death destroys;
And naught disturbs that peace profound
Which the unfettered soul enjoys.

4 Farewell, conflicting hopes and fears,
Where lights and shades alternate dwell;
How bright the unchanging morn appears!
Farewell, inconstant world, farewell!

5 Life's labor done, as sinks the clay,
Light from its load the spirit flies,
While heaven and earth combine to say,
"How blest the righteous when he dies!"

BARBAULD.

1103 L. M.

1 WHY should we start, and fear to die!
What timorous worms we mortals are!
Death is the gate of endless joy,
And yet we dread to enter there.

2 The pains, the groans, the dying strife
Fright our approaching souls away;
We still shrink back again to life,
Fond of our prison and our clay.

3 Oh, if my Lord would come and meet,
My soul would stretch her wings in haste,
Fly fearless through death's iron gate,
Nor feel the terrors as she passed!

4 Jesus can make a dying bed
Feel soft as downy pillows are,
While on his breast I lean my head,
And breathe my life out sweetly there!

WATTS.

1104 L. M.

1 HOW sweet the hour of closing day,
When all is peaceful and serene,
And when the sun, with cloudless ray,
Sheds mellow lustre o'er the scene!

2 Such is the Christian's parting hour;
So peacefully he sinks to rest;

When faith, endued from heaven with power,
Sustains and cheers his languid breast.

3 Mark but that radiance of his eye,
That smile upon his wasted cheek:
They tell us of his glory nigh,
In language that no tongue can speak.

4 Who would not wish to die like those
Whom God's own Spirit deigns to bless?
To sink into that soft repose,
Then wake to perfect happiness?

BATHURST.

1105 L. M.

1 SAY why should friendship grieve for those
Who safe arrive on Canaan's shore?
Released from all their hurtful foes,
They are not lost—but gone before.

2 How many painful days on earth
Their fainting spirits numbered o'er!
Now they enjoy a heavenly birth;
They are not lost—but gone before.

3 Dear is the spot where Christians sleep,
And sweet the strain which angels pour;
Oh, why should we in anguish weep?
They are not lost—but gone before.

1106 L. M.

1 GO, spirit of the sainted dead,
Go to thy longed for, happy home!
The tears of man are o'er thee shed;
The voice of angels bids thee come.

2 If life be not in length of days,
In silvered locks and furrowed brow,
But living to the Saviour's praise,
How few have lived so long as thou!

3 Though earth may boast one gem the less,
May not e'en heaven the richer be?
And myriads on thy footsteps press,
To share thy blest eternity.

J. N. BROWN.

1107 L. M.

1 AS the sweet flower that scents the morn,
But withers in the rising day,
Thus lovely was this infant's dawn,
Thus swiftly fled its life away.

2 It died ere its expanding soul
Had ever burnt with wrong desires,
Had ever spurned at heaven's control,
Or ever quenched its sacred fires.

3 Yet the sad hour that took the boy
Perhaps has spared a heavier doom;
Snatched him from scenes of guilty joy,
Or from the pangs of ills to come.

4 He died to sin; he died to care;
But for a moment felt the rod;
Then, rising on the viewless air,
Spread his light wings, and soared to God.

CUNNINGHAM.

1108 L. M.

1 OH, stay thy tears; for they are blest,
Whose days are past, whose toil is done;
Here midnight care disturbs our rest;
Here sorrow dims the noonday sun.

2 How blest are they whose transient years
Pass like an evening meteor's flight!
Not dark with guilt, nor dim with tears;
Whose course is short, unclouded, bright.

3 Oh, cheerless were our lengthened way;
But heaven's own light dispels the gloom,
Streams downward from eternal day,
And casts a glory round the tomb.

4 Oh, stay thy tears; the blest above
Have hailed a spirit's heavenly birth
And sung a song of joy and love;
Then why should anguish reign on earth?

NORTON.

1109 L. M.

1 O GOD, thy grace and blessing give
To us, who on thy name attend,
That we this mortal life may live
Regardful of our journey's end.

2 Teach us to know that Jesus died,
And rose again, our souls to save;
Teach us to take him as our guide,
Our help from childhood to the grave.

3 Then shall not death with terror come,
But welcome as a bidden guest,
The herald of a better home,
The messenger of peace and rest.

1110 L. M.

1 HOW vain is all beneath the skies!
How transient every earthly bliss!
How slender all the fondest ties,
That bind us to a world like this!

2 The evening cloud, the morning dew,
The withering grass, the fading flower,
Of earthly hopes are emblems true—
The glory of a passing hour!

3 But though earth's fairest blossoms die,
And all beneath the skies is vain,
There is a land, whose confines lie
Beyond the reach of care and pain.

1111 L. M.

1 SO fades the lovely blooming flower,
Frail, smiling solace of an hour!
So soon our transient comforts fly,
And pleasure only blooms to die.

2 Is there no kind, no lenient art
To heal the anguish of the heart?
Divine Redeemer, be thou nigh:
Thy comforts were not made to die!

3 Then gentle Patience smiles on Pain,
And dying Hope revives again;
Hope wipes the tear from Sorrow's eye,
And Faith points upward to the sky.

STEELE.

1112 C. M.

1 SWEET thought, my God! that on the palms
Of thy most holy hands
Are graven all thy people's names,
Though countless as the sands.

2 Not one too mean to have his place
Amid that record blest,
And if but there our names are found,
We'll share the heavenly rest.

3 How can we then yield to distrust,
Or think we are forgot,
While sharing thus the care of One
Who loves and changes not?

1113 11s.

1 I WOULD not live alway: I ask not to stay
Where storm after storm rises dark o'er the way;
The few lurid mornings that dawn on us here
Are enough for life's woes, full enough for its cheer.

2 I would not live alway, thus fettered by sin,
Temptation without and corruption within:
E'en the rapture of pardon is mingled with fears,
And the cup of thanksgiving with penitent tears.

3 I would not live alway; no, welcome the tomb;
Since Jesus hath lain there, I dread not its gloom;
There sweet be my rest, till he bid me arise
To hail him in triumph descending the skies.

4 Who, who would live alway, away from his God!
Away from yon heavén, that blissful abode,
Where the rivers of pleasure flow o'er the bright plains,
And the noontide of glory eternally reigns:

5 Where the saints of all ages in harmony meet,
Their Saviour and brethren transported to greet,
While the anthems of rapture unceasingly roll,
And the smile of the Lord is the feast of the soul.

MUHLENBERG.

1114 L. M.

1 UNVEIL thy bosom, faithful tomb,
Take this new treasure to thy trust;
And give these sacred relics room,
To seek a slumber in the dust.

2 Nor pain, nor grief, nor anxious fear
Invade thy bounds: no mortal woes
Can reach the peaceful sleeper here,
While angels watch the soft repose.

3 So Jesus slept;—God's dying Son
Passed through the grave and blessed the bed;
Rest here, blest saint, till from his throne
The morning break, and pierce the shade.

4 Break from his throne, illustrious morn!
Attend, O earth, his sovereign word;
Restore thy trust, a glorious form,
Called to ascend and meet the Lord.

WATTS.

1115 C. M.

1 WHY do we mourn departing friends,
Or shake at death's alarms?
'Tis but the voice that Jesus sends,
To call them to his arms.

2 Are we not tending upward, too,
As fast as time can move?
Nor would we wish the hours more slow,
To keep us from our love.

3 Why should we tremble to convey
Their bodies to the tomb?
There the dear flesh of Jesus lay,
And scattered all the gloom.

4 The graves of all the saints he blessed,
And softened every bed;
Where should the dying members rest,
But with the dying Head?

5 Thence he arose, ascending high,
And showed our feet the way;
Up to the Lord we, too, shall fly,
At the great rising day.

6 Then let the last loud trumpet sound,
And bid our kindred rise;
Awake! ye nations under ground;
Ye saints! ascend the skies.

WATTS.

1116 C. M.

1 WHY should our tears in sorrow flow,
When God recalls his own;
And bids them leave a world of woe
For an immortal crown?

2 Is not e'en death a gain to those
Whose life to God was given?
Gladly to earth their eyes they close,
To open them in heaven.

3 Their toils are past, their work is done,
And they are fully blest:
They fought the fight, the victory won,
And entered into rest.

4 Then let our sorrows cease to flow,—
God has recalled his own;
And let our hearts in every woe,
Still say,—"Thy will be done!"

1117 C. M.

1 THERE is an hour when I must part
With all I hold most dear;
And life, with its best hopes, will then
As nothingness appear.

2 There is an hour when I must sink
Beneath the stroke of death;
And yield to him who gave it first,
My struggling vital breath.

3 There is an hour when I must stand
Before the judgment-seat;
And all my sins, and all my foes,
In awful vision meet.

4 There is an hour when I must look
On vast eternity;
And nameless woe, or blissful life,
My endless portion be.

5 O Saviour, then, in all my need
Be near, be near to me;
And let my soul, by steadfast faith,
Find life and heaven in thee.

1118 C. M.

1 HARK! from the tombs a warning sound;
My ears, attend the cry—
"Ye living men, come view the ground
Where you must shortly lie.

2 "Princes, this clay must be your bed,
In spite of all your towers;
The tall, the wise, the reverend head,
Must lie as low as ours."

3 Great God, is this our certain doom?
And are we still secure?—
Still walking downward to the tomb,
And yet prepare no more?

4 Grant us the power of quickening grace,
To fit our souls to fly;
Then, when we drop this dying flesh,
We'll rise above the sky.

WATTS.

1119 C. M.

1 HEAR what the voice from heaven proclaims
For all the pious dead;
Sweet is the savor of their names,
And soft their sleeping bed.

2 They die in Jesus, and are blest;
How calm their slumbers are!
From sufferings and from sin released,
And freed from every snare.

3 Far from this world of toil and strife,
They're present with the Lord;
The labors of their mortal life
End in a large reward.

WATTS.

1120 C. M.

1 THE once-loved form, now cold and dead,
Each mournful thought employs;
And nature weeps her comforts fled,
And withered all her joys.

2 Hope looks beyond the bounds of time,
When what we now deplore
Shall rise in full, immortal prime,
And bloom to fade no more.

3 Cease, then, fond nature, cease thy tears;
Thy Saviour dwells on high;
There everlasting spring appears;
There joys shall never die.

STEELE.

1121 C. M.

1 'TIS Jesus speaks: I fold, says he,
These lambs within my breast;
Protection they shall find in me,
In me be ever blest.

2 Death may the bands of life unloose,
But can't dissolve my love;
Millions of infant souls compose
The family above.

3 Their feeble frames my power shall raise
And mould with heavenly skill;
I'll give them tongues to sing my praise,
And hands to do my will.

4 His words the happy parents hear,
And shout with joy divine,
O Saviour, all we have and are
Shall be forever thine!

STENNETT.

1122 C. M.

1 YE mourning saints, whose streaming tears
Flow o'er your children dead,
Say not in transports of despair
That all your hopes are fled.

2 If, cleaving to that darling dust,
In fond distress ye lie,
Rise, and with joy and reverence view
A heavenly Parent nigh.

3 Tho' your young branches torn away,
Like withered trunks ye stand,
With fairer verdure shall ye bloom,
Touched by the Almighty's hand.

4 I'll give the mourner, saith the Lord,
In my own house a place;
No names of daughters nor of sons
Could yield so high a grace.

5 We welcome, Lord, those rising tears,
Through which thy face we see;
And bless those wounds which through our hearts
Prepare a way for thee.

DODDRIDGE.

1123 C. M.

1 O THOU, whose filmed and failing eye,
Ere yet it closed in death,
Beheld thy mother's agony
The shameful cross beneath!

2 Remember them, like her, through whom
The sword of grief is driven,
And oh, to cheer their cheerless gloom,
Be thy dear mercy given!

3 Let thine own word of tenderness
Drop on them from above;
Its music shall the lone heart bless,
Its touch shall heal with love!

4 O Son of Mary! Son of God!
The way of mortal ill
By thy blest feet in triumph trod,
Our feet are treading still!

5 But not with strength like thine we go
This dark and dreadful way;
As thou wert strengthened in thy woe,
So strengthen us, we pray!

A. R. THOMPSON.

1124 C. M.

1 OH, for an overcoming faith,
To cheer my dying hours;
To triumph o'er approaching death,
And all his frightful powers!

2 Joyful, with all the strength I have,
My quivering lips should sing,—
"Where is thy boasted victory, grave;
And where, O death, thy sting?"

3 Now to the God of victory
Immortal thanks be paid;—
Who makes us conquerors, while we die,
Through Christ, our living Head!

WATTS.

1125 C. M.

1 THROUGH sorrow's night, and danger's path,
Amid the deepening gloom,
We, followers of our suffering Lord,
Are marching to the tomb.

2 There, when the turmoil is no more,
And all our powers decay,
Our cold remains in solitude
Shall sleep the years away.

3 Our labors done, securely laid
In this our last retreat,
Unheeded o'er our silent dust
The storms of earth shall beat.

4 Yet not thus buried or extinct,
The vital spark shall lie:
For o'er life's wreck that spark shall rise
To seek its kindred sky.

5 These ashes, too, this little dust,
Our Father's care shall keep,
Till the last angel rise and break
The long and dreary sleep.

6 Then love's soft dew o'er every eye
Shall shed its mildest rays,
And the long-silent voice awake
With shouts of endless praise.

H. K. WHITE.

1126 C. M.

1 WHEN downward to the darksome tomb
I thoughtful turn my eyes,
Frail nature trembles at the gloom,
And anxious fears arise.

2 Why shrinks my soul?— in death's embrace
Once Jesus captive slept;
And angels, hovering o'er the place,
His lowly pillow kept.

3 Thus shall they guard my sleeping dust,
And, as the Saviour rose,
The grave again shall yield her trust,
And end my deep repose.

4 My Lord, before to glory gone,
Shall bid me come away;
And calm and bright shall break the dawn
Of heaven's eternal day.

5 Then let my faith each fear dispel,
And gild with light the grave;
To him my loftiest praises swell,
Who died from death to save.

RAY PALMER.

1127 C. M.

1 ANOTHER hand is beckoning us,
Another call is given;
And glows once more with angel steps
The path that leads to heaven.

2 Unto our Father's will alone
One thought hath reconciled;
That he whose love exceedeth ours
Hath taken home his child.

3 Fold her, O Father, in thine arms,
And let her henceforth be
A new and lasting tie between
Our human hearts and thee.

4 Still let her mild rebukings stand
Between us and the wrong,
And her dear memory serve to make
Our faith in goodness strong.

WHITTIER.

1128 C. M.

1 AS, bowed by sudden storms, the rose
Sinks on the garden's breast,
Down to the grave our brother goes,
In silence there to rest.

2 No more with us his tuneful voice
The hymn of praise shall swell,
No more his cheerful heart rejoice
When peals the Sabbath bell.

3 Yet, if, in yonder cloudless sphere,
Amid a sinless throng,
He utters in his Saviour's ear
The everlasting song,—

4 No more we'll mourn the absent friend,
But lift our earnest prayer,
And daily every effort bend
To rise and join him there.

L. H. SIGOURNEY.

1129 C. M.

1 BEHOLD the western evening light!
It melts in deepening gloom:
So calmly Christians sink away,
Descending to the tomb.

2 The winds breathe low, the withering leaf
Scarce whispers from the tree:
So gently flows the parting breath,
When good men cease to be.

3 How beautiful on all the hills
The crimson light is shed!
'Tis like the peace the Christian gives
To mourners round his bed.

4 How mildly on the wandering cloud
The sunset beam is cast!
'Tis like the memory left behind
When loved ones breathe their last.

5 And now above the dews of night
The rising star appears:
So faith springs in the heart of those
Whose eyes are bathed in tears.

6 But soon the morning's happier light
Its glory shall restore,
And eyelids that are sealed in death
Shall wake to close no more.

PEABODY.

1130 S. M.

1 IT is not death to die—
To leave this weary road,
And, 'mid the brotherhood on high,
To be at home with God.

2 It is not death to close
The eye long dimmed by tears,
And wake, in glorious repose
To spend eternal years.

3 It is not death to bear
The wrench that sets us free
From dungeon chain,—to breathe the air
Of boundless liberty.

4 It is not death to fling
Aside this sinful dust,
And rise, on strong exulting wing,
To live among the just.

5 Jesus, thou Prince of life!
Thy chosen cannot die;
Like thee, they conquer in the strife,
To reign with thee on high.

BETHUNE.

1131 S. M.

1 A FEW more years shall roll,
A few more seasons come;
And we shall be with those that rest,
Asleep within the tomb;—

2 A few more storms shall beat
On this wild rocky shore;
And we shall be where tempests cease,
And surges swell no more:—

3 A few more struggles here,
A few more partings o'er,
A few more toils, a few more tears,
And we shall weep no more:—

4 Then, O my Lord, prepare
My soul for that blest day;
Oh, wash me in thy precious blood,
And take my sins away!

BONAR.

1132 S. M.

1 REST for the toiling hand,
Rest for the anxious brow,
Rest for the weary, way-worn feet,
Rest from all labor now;—

2 Rest for the fevered brain,
Rest for the throbbing eye;
Through these parched lips of thine no more
Shall pass the moan or sigh.

3 Soon shall the trump of God
Give out the welcome sound,
That shakes thy silent chamber-walls,
And breaks the sealéd ground.

4 Ye dwellers in the dust
Awake! come forth and sing;
Sharp has your frost of winter been,
But bright shall be your spring.

5 'Twas sown in weakness here:
'Twill then be raised in power;
That which was sown an earthly seed,
Shall rise a heavenly flower!

BONAR.

1133 S. M.

1 "FOREVER with the Lord!"
So, Jesus, let it be;
Life from the dead is in that word;
'Tis immortality.

2 Here, in the body pent,
Absent from thee I roam:
Yet nightly pitch my moving tent
A day's march nearer home.

3 My Father's house on high,
Home of my soul! how near,
At times, to faith's aspiring eye,
Thy golden gates appear!

4 "Forever with the Lord!"
Father, if 'tis thy will,
The promise of thy gracious word
Ev'n here to me fulfill.

MONTGOMERY.

1134 S. M.

1 OH, for the death of those
Who slumber in the Lord!
Oh, be like theirs my last repose,
Like theirs my last reward!

2 Their bodies in the ground,
In silent hope may lie,
Till the last trumpet's joyful sound
Shall call them to the sky.

3 Their ransomed spirits soar
On wings of faith and love,
To meet the Saviour they adore,
And reign with him above.

4 With us their names shall live
Through long succeeding years,
Embalmed with all our hearts can give,
Our praises and our tears.

LYTE.

1135 S. M.

1 "SERVANT of God, well done,
Rest from thy loved employ;
The battle fought, the vict'ry won,
Enter thy Master's joy."

2 The voice at midnight came,
He started up to hear;
A mortal arrow pierced his frame,
He fell—but felt no fear.

3 Tranquil amidst alarms,
It found him on the field,
A veteran slumbering on his arms,
Beneath his red-cross shield.

4 The pains of death are past,
Labor and sorrow cease;
And, life's long warfare closed at last,
His soul is found in peace.

5 Soldier of Christ, well done!
Praise be thy new employ;
And while eternal ages run,
Rest in thy Saviour's joy.

MONTGOMERY.

1136 S. M.

1 AND is there, Lord, a rest
For weary souls designed,
Where not a care shall stir the breast,
Or sorrow entrance find?

2 Is there a blissful home
Where kindred minds shall meet,
And live, and love, nor ever roam
From that serene retreat?

3 Are there bright, happy fields
Where nought that blooms shall die,
Where each new scene fresh pleasure yields,
And healthful breezes sigh?

4 Forever blessèd they
Whose joyful feet shall stand,
While endless ages waste away,
Amid that glorious land!

RAY PALMER.

1137 S. M.

1 AND must this body die,
This mortal frame decay,
And must these active limbs of mine
Lie mouldering in the clay?

2 God, my Redemer, lives,
And ever from the skies
Looks down and watches all my dust,
Till he shall bid it rise.

3 Arrayed in glorious grace,
Shall these vile bodies shine,
And every shape and every face
Look heavenly and divine.

4 These lively hopes we owe
To Jesus' dying love;
We would adore his grace below,
And sing his power above.

WATTS.

1138 8s & 7s.

1 PASTOR, thou art from us taken
In the glory of thy years,
As the oak, by tempests shaken,
Falls ere time its verdure sears.

2 Here, where oft thy lip hath taught us
Of the Lamb who died to save,—
Where thy guiding hand hath brought us
To the deep, baptismal wave,—

3 Pale and cold we see thee lying
In God's temple, once so dear,
And the mourners' bitter sighing
Falls unheeded on thine ear.

4 All thy love and zeal, to lead us
Where immortal fountains flow,
And on living bread to feed us,
In our fond remembrance glow.

5 May the conquering faith that cheered thee
When thy foot on Jordan pressed,
Guide our spirits while we leave thee
In the tomb that Jesus blessed.

L. H. SIGOURNEY.

1139 8s & 7s.

1 BROTHER, rest from sin and sorrow;
Death is o'er, and life is won;
On thy slumber dawns no morrow:
Rest; thine earthly race is run.

2 Brother, wake; the night is waning;
Endless day is round thee poured;
Enter thou the rest remaining
For the people of the Lord.

3 Brother, wake; for he who loved thee,
He who died that thou mightst live,

He who graciously approved thee,
Waits thy crown of joy to give.

4 Fare thee well; though woe is blending
With the tones of earthly love,
Triumph high and joy unending
Wait thee in the realms above.

BAP. MEMORIAL.

1140 8s & 7s.

1 CEASE, ye mourners, cease to languish
O'er the grave of those you love;
Pain, and death, and night, and anguish,
Enter not the world above.

2 While our silent steps are straying,
Lonely, through night's deepening shade,
Glory's brightest beams are playing
Round the happy Christian's head.

3 Light and peace at once deriving
From the hand of God most high,
In his glorious presence living,
They shall never, never die.

4 Endless pleasure, pain excluding,
Sickness, there, no more can come;
There, no fear of woe, intruding,
Sheds o'er heaven a moment's gloom.

COLLYER.

1141 8s & 7s.

1 SISTER, thou wast mild and lovely,
Gentle as the summer breeze,
Pleasant as the air of evening,
When it floats among the trees.

2 Peaceful be thy silent slumber—
Peaceful in the grave so low:
Thou no more wilt join our number;
Thou no more our songs shalt know.

3 Dearest sister, thou hast left us,
Here thy loss we deeply feel;
But 'tis God that hath bereft us,
He can all our sorrows heal.

4 Yet again we hope to meet thee,
When the day of life is fled;
Then in heaven with joy to greet thee,
Where no farewell tear is shed.

S. F. SMITH.

1142 8s & 7s.

1 WHAT is life? 'tis but a vapor,
Soon it vanishes away,
Life is but a dying taper—
O my soul, why wish to stay?
Why not spread thy wings and fly
Straight to yonder world of joy?

2 See that glory, how resplendent!
Brighter far than fancy paints;
There, in majesty transcendent,
Jesus reigns the King of saints.
Why not spread, etc.

3 Go, and share His people's glory,
'Midst the ransomed crowd appear;
Thine a joyful, wondrous story,
One that angels love to hear.
Why not spread, etc.

1143 S. H. M.

1 FRIEND after friend departs,
Who has not lost a friend?
There is no union here of hearts
That finds not here an end:
Were this frail world our only rest,
Living or dying, none were blest.

2 Beyond the flight of time,
Beyond this vale of death,
There surely is some blessèd clime
Where life is not a breath.

Nor life's affections transient fire,
Whose sparks fly upward and expire.

3 There is a world above
Where parting is unknown;
A whole eternity of love
Formed for the good alone;
And faith beholds the dying here
Translated to that happier sphere.

4 Thus star by star declines
Till all are passed away,
As morning high and higher shines
To pure and perfect day;
Nor sink those stars in empty night;
They hide themselves in heaven's own light.

MONTGOMERY.

1144 7,6,7,7,6.

1 NO, no, it is not dying
To go unto our God,
This gloomy earth forsaking,
Our journey homeward taking
Along the starry road.

2 No, no, it is not dying
Heaven's citizen to be;
A crown immortal wearing,
And rest unbroken sharing,
From care and conflict free.

3 No, no, it is not dying
To hear this gracious word,
"Receive a Father's blessing,
Forevermore possessing
The favor of thy Lord."

4 No, no, it is not dying
The Shepherd's voice to know;
His sheep he ever leadeth,
His peaceful flock he feedeth,
Where living pastures grow.

5 No, no, it is not dying
To wear a lordly crown;
Among God's people dwelling,
The glorious triumph swelling
Of him whose sway we own.

6 Oh, no, this is not dying,
Thou Saviour of mankind!
There, streams of love are flowing,
No hindrance ever knowing;
Here, drops alone we find.

MALAN.

1145 7s & 8s.

1 TENDER Shepherd, thou hast stilled
Now thy little lamb's brief weeping;
Ah, how peaceful, pale and mild,
In its narrow bed 'tis sleeping,
And no sign of anguish sore
Heaves that little bosom more.

2 In this world of care and pain,
Lord, thou wouldst no longer leave it;
To the sunny, heavenly plain
Thou dost now with joy receive it;
Clothed in robes of spotless white,
Now it dwells with thee in light.

3 Ah, Lord Jesus, grant that we
Where it lives may soon be living,
And the lovely pastures see
That its heavenly food are giving;
Then the gain of death we prove,
Though thou take what most we love.

MEINHOLD.

1146 P. M.

1 BEYOND the smiling and the weeping, |
I shall be soon; ||

Beyond the waking and the sleeping, |
Beyond the sowing and the reaping, |
I shall be soon. ||
Love, rest, and home! Sweet home!
Lord, tarry not, but come.

2 Beyond the blooming and the fading, |
I shall be soon; ||
Beyond the shining and the shading, |
Beyond the hoping and the dreading, |
I shall be soon. ||
Love, rest, and home! Sweet home!
Lord, tarry not, but come.

3 Beyond the rising and the setting, |
I shall be soon; ||
Beyond the calming and the fretting, |
Beyond remembering and forgetting, |
I shall be soon. ||
Love, rest, and home! Sweet home!
Lord, tarry not, but come.

4 Beyond the parting and the meeting, |
I shall be soon. ||
Beyond the farewell and the greeting, |
Beyond the pulse's fever beating, |
I shall be soon. ||
Love, rest, and home! Sweet home!
Lord, tarry not, but come.

5 Beyond the frost-chain and the fever, |
I shall be soon; ||
Beyond the rock-waste and the river, |
Beyond the ever and the never, |
I shall be soon. ||
Love, rest, and home! Sweet home!
Lord, tarry not, but come.

BONAR.

1147

1 OH, for the peace which floweth like a river,
Making life's desert places bloom and smile!
Oh, for the faith to grasp heaven's bright "forever,"
Amid the shadows of earth's "little while!"

2 A little while for patient vigil-keeping,
To face the storm, to battle with the strong;
A little while to sow the seed with weeping,
Then bind the sheaves and sing the harvest home!

3 A little while the earthen pitcher taking
To wayside brooks from far-off fountains fed;
Then the cool lip its thirst forever slaking
Beside the fullness of the fountain head!

4 A little while to keep the oil from failing,
A little while faith's flickering lamp to trim;
And then the Bridegroom's coming footsteps hailing,
To haste to meet him with the bridal hymn!

5 And he who is himself the Gift and Giver,—
The future glory and the present smile,—

With the bright promise of the glad forever
Will light the shadows of the "little while!"
JANE CREWDSON.

1148 10s & 6s. P.

1 'MID the pastures green of the blessed isles,
Where never is heat or cold,
Where the light of life is the Shepherd's smile,
Are the lambs of the Upper Fold.
Where the lilies blossom in fadeless spring,
And never a heart grows old,
Where the glad new song is the song they sing,
Are the lambs of the Upper Fold.

2 There are tiny mounds where the hopes of earth,
Were laid 'neath the tear-wet mold,
But the light that paled at the stricken hearth,
Was joy to the Upper Fold:
Oh, the white stone beareth a new name now,
That never on earth was told,
And the tender Shepherd doth guard with care
The lambs of the Upper Fold.

OCCASIONAL.

1149 L. M.

1 THE heavens declare thy glory, Lord,
In every star thy wisdom shines;
But when our eyes behold thy word,
We read thy name in fairer lines.

2 The rolling sun, the changing light,
And nights and days thy power confess;
But the blest volume thou hast writ,
Reveals thy justice and thy grace.

3 Sun, moon, and stars convey thy praise
Round the whole earth, and never stand;
So when thy truth began its race,
It touched and glanced on every land.

4 Nor shall thy spreading gospel rest,
Till through the world thy truth has run;
Till Christ has all the nations blest,
That see the light, or feel the sun.

5 Great Sun of Righteousness, arise;
Bless the dark world with heavenly light;
Thy gospel makes the simple wise;
Thy laws are pure, thy judgments right.

WATTS.

1150 L. M.

1 GOD, in the gospel of his Son,
Makes his eternal counsels known,
Where love in all its glory shines,
And truth is drawn in fairest lines.

2 Here sinners of a humble frame
May taste his grace, and learn his name;
May read, in characters of blood,
The wisdom, power, and grace of God.

3 Here faith reveals to mortal eyes
A brighter world beyond the skies;
Here shines the light which guides our way
From earth to realms of endless day.

4 Oh grant us grace, Almighty Lord,
To read and mark thy holy word,
Its truths with meekness to receive,
And by its holy precepts live.

BEDDOME.

1151 L. M.

1 NOW let my soul, Eternal King,
To thee its grateful tribute bring;
My knee, with humble homage, bow;
My tongue perform its solemn vow.

2 All nature sings thy boundless love,
In worlds below and worlds above;
But in thy blessèd word I trace
Diviner wonders of thy grace.

3 There Jesus bids my sorrows cease,
And gives my lab'ring conscience peace;
Raises my grateful passions high,
And points to mansions in the sky.

4 For love like this, oh, let my song,
Through endless years, thy praise prolong:
Let distant climes thy name adore,
Till time and nature are no more.

HIGINBOTHEM.

1152 L. M.

1 I LOVE the sacred Book of God!
No other can its place supply;
It points me to his own abode;
It gives me wings, and bids me fly.

2 Sweet Book! in thee my eyes discern
The very image of my Lord;
From thine instructive page I learn
The joys his presence will afford.

3 In thee I read my title clear
To mansions that will ne'er decay;—
Dear Lord, oh, when wilt thou appear,
And bear thy prisoner away?

4 While I am here, these leaves supply
His place, and tell me of his love;
I read with faith's discerning eye,
And gain a glimpse of joys above.

5 I know in them the Spirit breathes
To animate his people here;
Oh, may these truths prove life to all,
Till in his presence we appear.

KELLY.

1153 L. M.

1 THE starry firmament on high,
And all the glories of the sky,
Yet shine not to thy praise, O Lord,
So brightly as thy written word.

2 The hopes that holy word supplies,
Its truths divine and precepts wise,

In each a heavenly beam I see,
And every beam conducts to thee.

3 Almighty Lord, the sun shall fail,
And moon forget her nightly tale,
The deepest silence hush on high
The radiant chorus of the sky;—

4 But fixed for everlasting years,
Unmoved, amid the wreck of spheres,
Thy word shall shine in cloudless day,
When heaven and earth have passed away.

GRANT.

1154. L. M.

1 UPON the Gospel's sacred page
The gathered beams of ages shine;
And, as it hastens, every age
But makes its brightness more divine.

2 On mightier wing, in loftier flight,
From year to year does knowledge soar;
And, as it soars, the Gospel light
Becomes effulgent more and more.

3 More glorious still, as centuries roll,
New regions blest, new powers unfurled,
Expanding with the expanding soul,
Its radiance shall o'erflow the world,—

4 Flow to restore, but not destroy;
As when the cloudless lamp of day
Pours out its floods of light and joy,
And sweeps the lingering mists away.

BOWRING.

1155 C. M.

1 WHAT glory gilds the sacred page,
Majestic, like the sun;
It gives a light to every age;
It gives, but borrows none.

2 The hand that gave it still supplies
The gracious light and heat;
Its truth upon the nations rise—
They rise, but never set.

3 Let everlasting thanks be thine
For such a bright display,
As makes a world of darkness shine
With beams of heavenly day.

COWPER.

1156 C. M.

1 FATHER of mercies, in thy word
What endless glory shines!
Forever be thy name adored
For these celestial lines!

2 Here the Redeemer's welcome voice
Spreads heavenly peace around;
And life and everlasting joys
Attend the blissful sound.

3 Here springs of consolation rise,
To cheer the fainting mind;
And thirsty souls receive supplies,
And sweet refreshment find.

STEELE.

1157 C. M.

1 LAMP of our feet! whereby we trace
Our path, when wont to stray;
Stream from the fount of heavenly grace!
Brook by the traveler's way!

2 Bread of our souls! whereon we feed;
True manna from on high!
Our guide! our chart! wherein we read
Of realms beyond the sky.

3 Pillar of fire, through watches dark!
Or radiant cloud by day!
When waves would whelm our tossing bark,
Our anchor and our stay!

4 Childhood's preceptor! manhood's trust!
Old age's firm ally!
Our hope, when we go down to dust,
Of immortality!

BARTON.

1158 C. M.

1 LADEN with guilt, and full of fears,
I fly to thee, my Lord;
And not a ray of hope appears,
But in thy written word.

2 The volume of my Father's grace
Does all my grief assuage;
Here I behold my Saviour's face
In almost ev'ry page.

3 This is the field where hidden lies
The pearl of price unknown;
That merchant is divinely wise
Who makes the pearl his own.

4 This is the judge that ends the strife
Where wit and reason fail;
My guide to everlasting life
Through all this gloomy vale.

WATTS.

1159 C. M.

1 HOW precious is the book divine,
By inspiration given!
Bright as a lamp its doctrines shine
To lead our souls to heaven.

2 O'er all the strait and narrow way
Its radiant beams are cast;
A light whose never weary ray
Grows brightest at the last.

3 It sweetly cheers our fainting hearts
In this dark vale of tears;
Life, light, and comfort it imparts,
And calms our anxious fears.

4 This lamp through all the dreary night
Of life shall guide our way,
Till we behold the clearer light
Of an eternal day.

RIPPON'S COLL.

1160 C. M.

1 THOU lovely Source of true delight,
Whom I unseen adore!
Unvail thy beauties to my sight,
That I may love thee more.

2 Thy glory o'er creation shines;
But in thy sacred word,
I read in fairer, brighter lines,
My bleeding, dying Lord.

3 'Tis here, whene'er my comforts droop,
And sins and sorrows rise,
Thy love with cheerful beams of hope,
My fainting heart supplies.

4 Jesus, my Lord, my life, my light,
Oh! come with blissful ray;
Break radiant thro' the shades of night,
And chase my fears away.

STEELE.

1161 C. M.

1 HOW shall the young secure their hearts,
And guard their lives from sin?
Thy word the choicest rules imparts
To keep the conscience clean.

2 When once it enters to the mind,
It spreads such light abroad;
The meanest souls instruction find,
And raise their thoughts to God.

3 'Tis like the sun, a heavenly light,
That guides us all the day;
And, through the dangers of the night,
A lamp to lead our way.

WATTS.

1162 C. M.

1 HAIL, sacred truth! whose piercing rays
Dispel the shades of night;
Diffusing o'er a ruined world
The healing beams of light.

2 Thy word, O Lord, with friendly aid,
Restores our wand'ring feet;
Converts the sorrows of the mind
To joys divinely sweet.

3 Oh send thy light and truth abroad,
In all their radiant blaze;
And bid th' admiring world adore
The glories of thy grace.

1163 S. M.

1 HOW beauteous are their feet
Who stand on Zion's hill!
Who bring salvation on their tongues,
And words of peace reveal.

2 How charming is their voice!
How sweet the tidings are!—
"Zion, behold thy Saviour-King!
He reigns and triumphs here."

3 How happy are our ears
That hear this joyful sound,—
Which kings and prophets waited for,
And sought, but never found!

4 How blessèd are our eyes
That see this heavenly light!
Prophets and kings desired it long,
But died without the sight.

5 The watchmen join their voice,
And tuneful notes employ;
Jerusalem breaks forth in songs,
And deserts learn the joy.

6 The Lord makes bare his arm
Through all the earth abroad:
Let every nation now behold
Their Saviour and their Lord.

WATTS.

1164 S. M.

1 YE messengers of Christ,
His sovereign voice obey!
Arise, and follow where he leads,
And peace attend your way.

2 The Master, whom you serve,
Will needful strength bestow;
Depending on his promised aid,
With sacred courage go.

3 Mountains shall sink to plains,
And hell in vain oppose;
The cause is God's—and will prevail,
In spite of all his foes.

VOKE.

1165 S. M.

1 LORD of the harvest! hear
Thy needy servants cry;
Answer our faith's effectual prayer,
And all our wants supply.

2 On thee we humbly wait;
Our wants are in thy view;
The harvest truly, Lord! is great,
The laborers are few.

3 Convert and send forth more
Into thy Church abroad;
And let them speak thy word of power,
As workers with their God.

4 Oh, let them spread thy name;
Their mission fully prove;
Thy universal grace proclaim—
Thy all-redeeming love.

C. WESLEY.

1166 6s. & 4s.

1 O HOLY Lord, our God,
By heavenly hosts adored,
Hear us, we pray:
To thee the cherubim,
Angels and seraphim,
Unceasing praises bring,
Their homage pay.

2 Here give thy word success,
And this thy servant bless;
His labors own;
And while the sinner's Friend
His life and words commend,
Thy holy Spirit send,
And make him known.

3 May every passing year
More happy still appear
Than this glad day;
With numbers fill the place,
Adorn thy saints with grace,
Thy truth may all embrace,
O Lord, we pray.

I. YOUNG.

1167 L. M.

1 "GO, preach my gospel," saith the Lord,
"Bid the whole earth my grace receive;
He shall be saved that trusts my word;
And he condemned that won't believe.

2 "I'll make your great commission known,
And ye shall prove my gospel true,
By all the works that I have done,
By all the wonders ye shall do.

3 "Teach all the nations my commands;
I'm with you till the world shall end;
All power is trusted in my hands;
I can destroy, and I defend."

4 He spake, and light shone round his head,
On a bright cloud to heaven he rode;
They to the farthest nations spread
The grace of their ascended God!

WATTS.

1168 L. M.

1 FATHER of mercies, bow thine ear,
Attentive to our earnest prayer:
We plead for those who plead for thee;
Successful pleaders may they be.

2 How great their work! how vast their charge!
Do thou their anxious souls enlarge:

Their best endowments are our gain;
We share the blessings they obtain.

3 Let thronging multitudes around
Hear from their lips the joyful sound,
In humble strains thy grace implore,
And feel thy Spirit's living power.

BEDDOME.

1169 L. M.

1 LORD of the harvest, bend thine ear,
In Zion's heritage appear;
Oh! send forth laborers filled with zeal,
Swift to obey their Master's will.

2 Our lifted eyes, O Lord, behold
The ripening harvest tinged with gold;
Wide fields are opening to our view,
The work is great, the laborers few.

3 Led by thine own almighty hand,
Let Zion's sons, in many a band,
Arise to bless the dying race,
As heralds of redeeming grace.

HASTINGS.

1170 L. M.

1 FATHER of mercies, in thy house
We pay our homage and our vows,
While with a grateful heart we share
These pledges of our Saviour's care.

2 The Saviour, when to heaven he rose
In splendid triumph o'er his foes,
Conferred his gifts on men below;
And wide his royal bounties flow.

3 Hence sprung th' apostle's honored name,
Sacred beyond all earthly fame;
In lowlier forms to bless our eyes,
Our pastors hence and teachers rise.

DODDRIDGE.

1171 L. M.

1 WE bid thee welcome in the name
Of Jesus, our exalted Head;
Come as a servant, so he came,
And we receive thee in his stead.

2 Come as a shepherd; guard and keep
This fold from hell, and earth, and sin;
Nourish the lambs, and feed the sheep,
The wounded heal, the lost bring in.

3 Come as a teacher sent from God,
Charged his whole counsel to declare;
Lift o'er our ranks the prophet's rod,
While we uphold thy hands with prayer.

4 Come as a messenger of peace,
Filled with the Spirit, fired with love;
Live to behold our large increase,
And die to meet us all above.

MONTGOMERY.

1172 L. M.

1 POUR out thy Spirit from on high;
Lord, thine ordainéd servants bless;
Graces and gifts to each supply,
And clothe them all with righteousness.

2 Within thy temple, as they stand
To teach the truth as taught by thee,
Saviour, like stars in thy right hand
Let all thy chosen pastors be.

3 Wisdom and zeal and love impart,—
Firmness with meekness from above,

To bear thy people in their heart,
And love the souls whom thou dost love.

4 Then, when their work is finished here,
May they in hope their charge resign;
When the Chief Shepherd shall appear,
May they, O God, in glory shine.

MONTGOMERY.

1173 L. M.

1 'TIS done—th' important act is done—
Heaven, earth, its solemn purport know;
Its fruits, when time its race has run,
Shall through eternal ages flow.

2 The covenants of this sacred hour,
Great Shepherd of thy people, seal;
Spirit of grace, diffuse thy power,
Our vows accept, thy might reveal.

3 Behold our guide, and deign to crown
His toils, O Lamb of God, with love;
His lips inspire; each effort own;
Breathe, dwell within him, heavenly Dove.

4 Behold his charge; what wealth shall dare
With its most priceless worth to vie?
Suns, systems, worlds, how mean they are,
Compared with souls, that cannot die!

5 Oh, when, before the judgment-seat,
The wicked quake in dread despair,
May we, all reverent at thy feet,
Pastor and flock, find mercy there.

S. F. SMITH.

1174 C. M.

1 LET Zion's watchmen all awake,
And take th' alarm they give;
Now let them from the mouth of God
Their solemn charge receive.

2 'Tis not a cause of small import
The pastor's care demands,
But what might fill an angel's heart,
And filled a Saviour's hands.

3 They watch for souls, for which the Lord
Did heavenly bliss forego,—
For souls, which must for ever live,
In rapture or in woe.

4 May they that Jesus whom they preach,
Their own Redeemer, see;
And watch thou daily o'er their souls,
That they may watch for thee.

DODDRIDGE.

1175 C. M.

1 OH, still in accents sweet and strong
Sounds forth the ancient word,—
"More reapers for white harvest fields,
More laborers for the Lord."

2 We hear the call; in dreams no more
In selfish ease we lie,
But girded for our Father's work,
Go forth beneath his sky.

3 Where prophets' word, and martyrs' blood,
And prayers of saints were sown,
We, to their labors entering in,
Would reap where they have strown.

1176 C. M.

1 WE thank thee, Lord, for sending here
The publishers of peace:
Speak by them now, and everywhere
By them declare thy grace.

2 So when the harvest-day shall come,
Sowers, and reapers too,
Shall, shouting, enter endless home,
And thee eternal view.

3 That happy morning we desire—
Oh let it hasten on!—
When all shall join the angelic choir
In singing round thy throne.

4 The pastors and the people there
Shall thee in glory see;
Shall keep the long Sabbatic year—
The feast of Jubilee.

1177 C. M.

1 THE earth, O Lord, is one wide field
Of all thy chosen seed;
The crop prepared its fruit to yield;
The laborers few indeed.

2 Therefore we come before thee now
With words of humble prayer,
Beseeching of thy love that thou
Would'st send more laborers there.

3 Not for our land alone we pray,
Though that above the rest,
The realms and islands far away,
Oh, let them all be blest!

1178 C. M.

1 O JESUS, in this solemn hour,
Be with thy people here;
Let thine authority and power
To rule thy church appear.

2 Oh, may the choice which we have made
By thee be ratified;
Thy servants' fitness be displayed,
As they are further tried.

3 With faithfulness may they fulfil
The office in their hands,
And seek to know and do thy will
In all that will demands.

COLLYER.

1179 7s.

1 SON of God, our glorious Head!
On us now thy blessing shed;
From thy throne let mercy flow
To thy waiting flock below.

2 Taught by thee, with prayer sincere,
We have called thy servants here,
For thy needy ones to care,
And thy Holy Feast to bear.

3 May the Spirit from above
Fill their hearts with faith and love;
Make them humble, zealous, wise,
Strife to shun, and good devise.

4 When their earthly work is done,
When the crown of life is won,
Ever in thy house on high,
May they serve beneath thine eye.

G. B. IDE.

1180 L. M.

1 O LORD of hosts, whose glory fills
The bounds of the eternal hills,
And yet vouchsafes, in Christian lands,
To dwell in temples made with hands;

2 Endue the creatures with thy grace
That shall adorn thy dwelling-place;

The beauty of the oak and pine,
The gold and silver, make them thine.

3 The heads that guide endue with skill;
The hands that work preserve from ill;
That we, who these foundations lay,
May raise the topstone in its day.

4 Both now and ever, Lord, protect
The temple of thine own elect;
Be thou in them, and they in thee,
Oh ever-blessèd Trinity! J. M. NEALE.

1181 L. M.

1 THE perfect world, by Adam trod,
Was the first temple built to God;
His fiat laid the corner-stone,
And heaved its pillars one by one.

2 He hung its starry roof on high—
The broad, illimitable sky;
He spread its pavement, green and bright,
And curtained it with morning light.

3 The mountains in their places stood,
The sea—the sky—and "all was good;"
And when its first few praises rang,
The "morning stars together sang."

4 Lord, 'tis not ours to make the sea,
And earth, and sky, a house for thee;
But in thy sight our off'ring stands—
An humbler temple, "made with hands."

5 We cannot bid the morning star
To sing how bright thy glories are;
But, Lord, if thou wilt meet us here,
Thy praise shall be the Christian's tear.
N. P. WILLIS.

1182 L. M.

1 O GOD the Father, Christ the Son,
And Holy Spirit, three in one,
Accept this gift our hearts have sought,
Our hands in Christian love have wrought.

2 Here may the light of gospel truth
Illumine age, enlighten youth:
In many hearts that grace begin,
Which saves from sorrow and from sin.

3 May Jesus here that power display
Which changes darkness into day,
And open wide those gates of love
That lead to blessedness above.

4 O Jesus Christ, our sovereign Lord,
By angels and by saints adored,
Accept this tribute of our praise,
And with thy glory fill this place.

1183 L. M.

1 MAKER of land and rolling sea,
We dedicate this house to thee;
And what our willing hands have done,
We give to God, and to the Son.

2 Come, fill this house with heavenly grace,
While sinners throng the sacred place,
And saints below with saints above,
Unite to sing redeeming love.

3 Here let the cross be lifted high
Before a world condemned to die:
Here flow the blood of sacrifice,
To hush the Law's avenging cries.

4 Here let the mourning soul find rest
Upon the Saviour's loving breast;
And with the sense of sins forgiven,
Each heart aspire to God and heaven.

5 Long may this sacred temple be
A monument of praise to thee;
And when to this no more we come,
Be heaven our high, eternal home.

D. C. EDDY.

1184 L. M.

1 AND wilt thou, O Eternal God,
On earth establish thine abode?
Then look propitious from thy throne,
And take this temple for thine own.

2 These walls we to thine honor raise,
Long may they echo in thy praise;
And thou, descending, fill the place
With the rich tokens of thy grace.

3 Here may the great Redeemer reign,
With all the graces of his train;
While power divine his word attends,
To conquer foes and cheer his friends.

4 And in the last decisive day,
When God the nations shall survey,
May it before the world appear,
Thousands were born for glory here.

DODDRIDGE.

1185 L. M.

1 WHEN Israel's priest the lamb did choose,
He chose of all the flock the best;
No poor, no maim'd, no sickly thing
Upon Jehovah's shrine could rest.

2 When David's son a Temple built,
No common wood or stone was sought,
But rarest wood, and gold, and gems,
A house of wondrous beauty wrought.

3 When Mary would her love display,
A costly gift did she bestow;
And Mary's act the lesson leaves
That precious things to God should go.

4 O Lord, this day we bring our gift,
Not rich, but best we could, and free;
This desk, this cup, this pool, this house,
We dedicate them, Lord, to thee.

5 Accept, O God, this proffered gift;
Here let thy Spirit's power be given;
To many souls let this place be
The House of God—the Gate of Heav'n.

1186 C. M.

1 BUILDER of mighty worlds on worlds,
How poor the house must be,
That with our human, sinful hands,
We may erect for thee.

2 O Christ, thou art our Corner-stone,
On thee our hopes are built;
Thou art our Lord, our light, our life,
Our sacrifice for guilt.

3 In thy blest name we gather here,
And set apart the ground;
The walls that on this rock shall rise,
Thy praises shall resound.

4 May many a soul, from death redeemed,
In heavenly regions fair,
With joy exclaim, "I learned the path
To God and glory there."

1187 C. M.

1 TO thee this temple we devote,
Our Father and our God;
Accept it thine, and seal it now
Thy Spirit's blest abode.

2 Here may the prayer of faith ascend,
The voice of praise arise;
Oh, may each lowly service prove
Accepted sacrifice.

3 Here may the sinner learn his guilt,
And weep before his Lord;
Here, pardoned, sing a Saviour's love,
And here his vows record.

4 Here may affliction dry the tear,
And learn to trust in God,
Convinced it is a Father smites,
And love that guides the rod.

5 Peace be within these sacred walls;
Prosperity be here;
Long smile upon thy people, Lord,
And evermore be near.

J. R. Scott.

1188 C. M.

1 O THOU, whose own vast temple stands,
Built over earth and sea,
Accept the walls that human hands
Have raised to worship thee!

2 Lord, from thine inmost glory send,
Within these courts to bide,
The peace that dwelleth without end,
Serenely by thy side!

3 May erring minds that worship here
Be taught the better way;
And they who mourn, and they who fear,
Be strengthened as they pray.

4 May faith grow firm, and love grow warm,
And pure devotion rise,
While round these hallowed walls the storm
Of earth-born passion dies.

Bryant.

1189 H. M.

1 IN loud exalted strains,
The King of Glory praise;
O'er heaven and earth he reigns,
Through everlasting days;
But Zion with his presence blest,
Is his delight, his chosen rest.

2 Great King of glory, come,
And with thy favor crown
This temple as thy dome,
This people as thy own;
Beneath this roof, oh deign to show
How God can dwell with men below!

3 Here may thine ears attend
Our interceding cries,
And grateful praise ascend,
All fragrant, to the skies.
Here may the word melodious sound,
And spread celestial joys around!

4 Here may our unborn sons
And daughters sound thy praise,
And shine, like polished stones,
Through long-succeeding days;
Here, Lord, display thy saving power,
While temples stand, and men adore.

B. Francis.

1190 H. M.

1 BEFORE the Lord we bow,
The God who reigns above,
And rules the world below,
Boundless in power and love.
In joy and praise our thanks we bring,
Our hearts we raise to heaven's high King.

2 The nation thou hast blest
May well thy love declare,
From foes and fears at rest,
Protected by thy care:
For this fair house and this bright land,
Our thanks we pay, gifts of thy hand.

3 May every mountain height,
Each vale and forest green,
Shine in thy word's pure light,
And its rich fruits be seen!
With rapturous praise may every tongue
Now join to raise a grateful song.

4 And when in power he comes,
Oh, may our native land,
From all its rending tombs,
Send forth a glorious band;
A countless throng ever to sing,
Salvation's song to heaven's high King!

1191 L. M.

1 LOOK from thy sphere of endless day,
O God of mercy and of might!
In pity look on those who stray,
Benighted, in this land of light.

2 In peopled vale, in lonely glen,
In crowded mart, by stream or sea,
How many of the sons of men
Hear not the message sent from thee!

3 Send forth thy heralds, Lord, to call
The thoughtless young, the hardened old,
A scattered, homeless flock, till all
Be gathered to thy peaceful fold.

4 Then all these wastes, a dreary scene,
That make us sadden as we gaze,
Shall grow with living waters green,
And lift to heaven the voice of praise.

BRYANT.

1192 8s & 7s.

1 SONS of day! Arise from slumbers,
For the sluggish night is gone;
Swell the Saviour's marshaled numbers,
Marching where he leadeth on.

2 Soldiers of the cross, appointed,
Girded for the glorious war,
In the name of God's Anointed,
Spread your victories afar.

3 Bid the trumpet of redemption
Greet our country's farthest shore;
Boldly claim our Lord's pre-emption,
For the agonies he bore.

4 On the prairie and the mountain,
In the valley rich and fair,
By the river and the fountain,
Plant the sacred standard there.

5 Where the infant city's founded,
Where the hamlet dots the plain;
Let the Gospel-call be sounded,
Let the church a foothold gain.

6 So shall Error be supplanted,
So shall Truth her vanguard keep,
So shall temple-homes be granted,
To the Shepherd's wandering sheep.

S. D. PHELPS.

1193 7s & 6s.

1 OUR country's voice is pleading,
Ye men of God, arise!
His providence is leading,
The land before you lies;
Day-gleams are o'er it brightening,
And promise clothes the soil;
Wide fields for harvest whitening,
Invite the reaper's toil.

2 Go where the waves are breaking
On California's shore,
Christ's precious gospel taking,
More rich than golden ore;
On Alleghany's mountains,
Through all the western vale,
Beside Missouri's fountains,
Rehearse the wondrous tale.

3 The love of Christ unfolding,
Speed on from east to west,
Till all, his cross beholding,
In him are fully blest.
Great Author of salvation,
Haste, haste the glorious day,
When we, a ransomed nation,
Thy sceptre shall obey.

MRS. G. W. ANDERSON.

1194 7s & 6s.

1 GO preach the blest salvation
To every sinful race,
And bid each guilty nation
Accept the Saviour's grace;
But bear, oh, quickly bear it
Where thronging millions roam,
And bid them freely share it,
Who dwell with us at home.

2 Where blooms the broad savanna,
Where mighty waters roll,
There let the gospel banner
Beam hope on every soul;
Go where the west is teeming,
And yet behold they come!
The fields all ripe are gleaming
For those who reap at home!

3 Our children there are dwelling,
Neglected and astray,
Whose hearts are often swelling
To learn of Zion's way.
Bear, bear to them the treasure,
And bid the exiles come;
There is no sweeter pleasure
Than preaching Christ at home.

SIDNEY DYER.

1195 C. P. M.

1 WHEN, Lord, to this our western land,
Led by thy providential hand,
Our wandering fathers came,
Their ancient homes, their friends in youth,
Sent forth the heralds of thy truth,
To keep them in thy Name.

2 Then, through our solitary coast,
The desert features soon were lost;
Thy temples there arose;
Our shores, as culture made them fair,
Were hallow'd by thy rites, by prayer,
And blossom'd as the rose.

3 And oh, may we repay this debt
To regions solitary yet,
Within our spreading land:
There, brethren, from our common home,
Still westward, like our fathers, roam;
Still guided by thy hand.

4 Saviour, we own this debt of love:
Oh shed thy Spirit from above,
To move each Christian breast;
Till heralds shall thy truth proclaim.
And temples rise to fix thy Name,
Through all our desert west.

1196 C. P. M.

1 FROM yonder Rocky Mountains,
With summits white and cold,
From California's fountains,
That pour down virgin gold;
From every western prairie,
From every mystic mound,
They call on us to carry
The gospel's joyful sound.

2 Oh! shall we close our bosoms,
While every breath 's a cry?
While brothers drop like blossoms,
And there forever die?
Oh! Christian, rest not, sleep not,
But pray, and toil, and fight,
Till those who 're weeping, weep not,
And darkness turns to light.

3 Then, when enthroned in glory,
With Jesus' ransomed fold,
We tell Love's wondrous story,
Upon our harps of gold;
Each effort that we 're making
Will sweeten heaven's employ,
And every cross we 're taking,
Add rapture to its joy.

C. THURBER.

1197

1 MY soul is not at rest. There comes a strange and secret whisper to my | spirit, || like a dream of | night, || that tells me I am on en- | chanted | ground.

Chorus.

The voice of my departed Lord, "Go, teach all nations," comes on the night-air, and awakes mine ear.

2 Why live I here? The vows of God are | on me || and I may not stop to play with shadows or pluck earthly | flowers, || till I my work have done, and | rendered up ac- | count.
The voice of my departed Lord, etc.

3 And I will | go! || I may no longer doubt to give up friends and idle | hopes, || and every tie that binds my heart to | thee, my | country!
The voice of my departed Lord, etc.

4 Henceforth, then, it matters not if storm or sunshine be my | earthly lot, || bitter or sweet my | cup, || I only pray, "God make me holy, and my spirit nerve for the stern | hour of | strife!"
The voice of my departed Lord, etc.

5 And when I come to stretch me for the | last, || in unattended agony, beneath the cocoa's | shade, || it will be sweet that I have toiled for | other worlds than | this.
The voice of my departed Lord, etc.

6 And if one, for whom Satan hath struggled as he hath for | me, || should ever reach that blessed | shore— || Oh, how this heart will glow with | gratitude and | love.

Chorus.

Through ages of eternal years, my spirit never shall repent that toil and suffering once were mine below.

1198 L. M.

1 FROM all that dwell below the skies,
Let the Creator's praise arise;
Let the Redeemer's name be sung,
Through every land, by every tongue.

2 Eternal are thy mercies, Lord;
Eternal truth attends thy word:
Thy praise shall sound from shore to shore,
Till suns shall rise and set no more.

WATTS.

1199 L. M.

1 SOVEREIGN of worlds, display thy power;
Be this thy Zion's favored hour:
Oh, bid the morning star arise!
Oh, point the heathen to the skies!

2 Set up thy throne where Satan reigns,
In western wilds and eastern plains;
Far let the gospel's sound be known;
Make thou the universe thine own.

3 Speak, and the world shall hear thy voice;
Speak, and the desert shall rejoice;
Dispel the gloom of heathen night;
Bid every nation hail the light.

1200 L. M.

1 OH, hallowed is the land and blessed,
Where Christ, the Ruler, is confessed!
Oh, happy hearts and happy homes,
To whom the great Redeemer comes!

2 Lift up your heads, ye mighty gates,
Behold, the King of glory waits!
The King of kings is drawing near;
The Saviour of the world is here.

3 Fling wide the portals of your heart:
Make it a temple set apart
From earthly use for heaven's employ,
Adorned with prayer and love and joy.

WIESZEL.

1201 L. M.

1 JESUS shall reign where'er the sun
Does his successive journeys run;
His kingdom stretch from shore to shore
Till moons shall wax and wane no more.

2 For him shall endless prayer be made,
And endless praises crown his head;
His name, like sweet perfume, shall rise
With every morning sacrifice.

3 People and realms of every tongue
Dwell on his love with sweetest song;
And infant voices shall proclaim
Their early blessings on his name.

4 Blessings abound where'er he reigns;
The joyful prisoner bursts his chains;
The weary find eternal rest,
And all the sons of want are blest.

5 Let every creature rise and bring
Peculiar honors to our King;
Angels descend with songs again,
And earth repeat the loud Amen.

WATTS.

1202 L. M.

1 YE Christian heroes, go proclaim
Salvation through Immanuel's name;
To distant climes the tidings bear,
And plant the Rose of Sharon there.

2 He'll shield you with a wall of fire,
With flaming zeal your breasts inspire;
Bid raging winds their fury cease,
And hush the tempest into peace.

3 And when your labors all are o'er,
Then we shall meet to part no more;
Meet, with the blood-bought throng to fall—
And crown our Jesus Lord of all.

PRATT'S COLL.

1203 L. M.

1 SOON may the last glad song arise
Through all the millions of the skies—
That song of triumph which records
That all the earth is now the Lord's!

2 Let thrones and powers and kingdoms be
Obedient, mighty God, to thee!
And, over land and stream and main,
Wave thou the sceptre of thy reign!

3 Oh, let that glorious anthem swell,
Let host to host the triumph tell,
That not one rebel heart remains,
But over all the Saviour reigns!

1204 L. M.

1 ARISE! arise! with joy survey
The glory of the latter day,
Already is the dawn begun,
That marks at hand the rising sun.

2 The friends of truth assembled stand,
A chosen, consecrated band,
The emblem of the cross display,
And cry aloud—"Behold the way!"

3 Behold the way to Zion's hill,
Where Israel's God delights to dwell;
He fixes there his lofty throne,
And calls the sacred place his own.

4 "Behold the way!" ye heralds! cry,
Spare not, but lift your voices high;
Convey the sound from shore to shore,
And bid the captive sigh no more.

KELLY.

1205 L. M.

1 O SPIRIT of the living God,
In all thy plenitude of grace,
Where'er the foot of man hath trod,
Descend on our apostate race.

2 Give tongues of fire, and hearts of love,
To preach the reconciling word;
Give power and unction from above,
Where'er the joyful sound is heard.

3 Be darkness, at thy coming, light;
Confusion—order, in thy path;
Souls without strength, inspire with might,
Bid mercy triumph over wrath.

4 Baptize the nations; far and nigh,
The triumphs of the cross record;
The name of Jesus glorify,
Till every kindred call him Lord.

MONTGOMERY.

1206 L. M.

1 FLING out the banner! let it float
Skyward and seaward, high and wide;
The sun that lights its shining folds,
The cross on which the Saviour died.

2 Fling out the banner! angels bend
In anxious silence o'er the sign,
And vainly seek to comprehend
The wonder of the Love Divine.

3 Fling out the banner! heathen lands
Shall see from far the glorious sight;
And nations, crowding to be born,
Baptize their spirits in its light.

4 Fling out the banner! sin-sick souls,
That sink and perish in the strife,
Shall touch in faith its radiant hem,
And spring immortal into life.

5 Fling out the banner! let it float
Skyward and seaward, high and wide;
Our glory, only in the Cross,
Our only hope, the Crucified.

6 Fling out the banner! wide and high,
Seaward and skyward let it shine;
Nor skill, nor might, nor merit, ours;
We conquer only in that sign.

DOANE.

1207 L. M.

1 ARM of the Lord, awake, awake!
Put on thy strength, the nations shake,
And let the world adoring see
Triumphs of mercy wrought by thee.

2 Say to the heathen, from thy throne,
"I am Jehovah, God alone:"
Thy voice their idols shall confound,
And cast their altars to the ground.

3 Almighty God, thy grace proclaim
In every land, of every name;
Let adverse powers before thee fall,
And crown the Saviour, Lord of all!

SHRUBSOLE.

1208 L. M.

1 ASSEMBLED at thy great command,
Before thy face, dread King, we stand;
The voice that marshaled every star,
Has called thy people from afar.

2 We meet, thro' distant lands to spread
The truth for which the martyrs bled;
Along the line, to either pole,
The thunder of thy praise to roll.

3 Our prayers assist, accept our praise,
Our hopes revive, our courage raise;
Our counsels aid, to each impart
The single eye, the faithful heart.

4 Forth with thy chosen heralds come,
Recall the wandering spirits home;
From Zion's mount send forth the sound,
To spread the spacious earth around.

COLLYER.

1209 L. M.

1 EXERT thy power, thy rights maintain,
Almighty, everlasting King!
The influence of thy crown increase,
And strangers to thy footstool bring.

2 In one vast symphony of praise,
Gentile and Jew shall then unite,
And unbelief no longer reign,
But sink in shades of endless night.

3 Then Afric's liberated sons
Shall chant to Asia's rapturous song,
Europe resound her Saviour's fame,
And western climes the notes prolong.

4 To every land beneath the sun
Immanuel's kingdom shall extend;
And every man in every clime
Shall meet a brother and a friend.

VOKE.

1210 L. M.

1 ETERNAL Father, thou hast said,
That Christ all glory shall obtain;
That he who once a sufferer bled,
Shall o'er the world, a conqueror, reign.

2 We wait thy triumph, Saviour-King!
Long ages have prepared thy way;
Now all abroad thy banner fling,
Set Time's great battle in array.

3 Thy hosts are mustered to the field;
"The Cross! The Cross!" the battle-call;
The old grim towers of darkness yield,
And soon shall totter to their fall.

4 On mountain tops the watch-fires glow,
Where scattered wide the watchmen stand;
Voice echoes voice, and onward flow
The joyous shouts, from land to land.

5 Oh, fill thy church with faith and power;
Bid her long night of weeping cease;
To groaning nations haste the hour,
Of life and freedom, light and peace.

6 Come, Spirit, make thy wonders known!
Fulfill the Father's high decree;
Then earth, the might of hell o'erthrown,
Shall keep her last great jubilee.

RAY PALMER.

1211 L. M.

1 THOUGH now the nations sit beneath
The darkness of o'erspreading death;
God will arise with light divine,
On Zion's holy towers to shine.

2 That light shall shine on distant lands,
And wandering tribes, in joyful bands,
Shall come, thy glory, Lord, to see,
And in thy courts to worship thee.

3 O light of Zion, now arise!
Let the glad morning bless our eyes!
Ye nations, catch the kindling ray,
And hail the splendors of the day.

L. BACON.

1212 L. M.

1 CHRISTIANS, the glorious hope ye know,
Which soothes the heart in every wo;
While heathen, helpless, hopeless, lie;
No ray of glory meets their eye.

2 Christians, ye taste the heavenly grace
Which cheers believers in their race;
Uncheered by grace, through heathen gloom,
See millions hastening to the tomb.

3 Christians, ye prize the Saviour's blood,
In which the soul is cleansed for God;
Millions of souls in darkness dwell,
Uncleansed from sin—exposed to hell.

4 To distant lands that grace convey,
Which trains the soul for endless day;
Oh strive that pagans soon may view
That precious blood which cleanseth you.

CAWOOD.

1213 L. M.

1 BEHOLD, the heathen waits to know
The joy the gospel will bestow;—
The exiled captive to receive
The freedom Jesus has to give.

2 Come, let us, with a grateful heart,
In this blest labor share a part;
Our prayers and offerings gladly bring
To aid the triumphs of our King.

3 Our hearts exult in songs of praise,
That we have seen these latter days,
When our Redeemer shall be known
Where Satan long hath held his throne.

4 Where'er his hand hath spread the skies,
Sweet incense to his name shall rise,
And slave and freeman, Greek and Jew,
By sovereign grace be formed anew.

VOKE.

1214 L. M.

1 THE heathen perish; day by day,
Thousands on thousands pass away!
O Christians, to their rescue fly,
Preach Jesus to them ere they die!

2 Wealth, labor, talents, freely give,
Yea, life itself, that they may live;
What hath your Saviour done for you?
And what for him will ye not do?

3 Oh, Spirit of the Lord! go forth,
Call in the south, wake up the north;
From every clime, from sun to sun,
Gather God's children into one!

MONTGOMERY.

1215 L. M.

1 DISOWNED of heaven, by man oppress'd,
Outcasts from Zion's hallowed ground,
Oh, why should Israel's sons, once blessed,
Still roam the scorning world around?

2 Lord, visit thy forsaken race,
Back to thy fold the wanderers bring;
Teach them to seek thy slighted grace,
And hail in Christ their promised King.

3 The veil of darkness rend in twain,
Which hides their Shiloh's glorious light,
The severed olive-branch again
Firm to its parent stock unite.

1216 C. M.

1 LIGHT of the lonely pilgrim's heart,
Star of the coming day!
Arise, and with thy morning beams
Chase all our griefs away!

2 Come, blessèd Lord, let every shore
And answering island sing
The praises of thy royal name,
And own thee as their King.

3 Bid the whole earth, responsive now
To the bright world above,
Break forth in sweetest strains of joy,
In memory of thy love.

4 Jesus, thy fair creation groans,
The air, the earth, the sea,
In unison with all our hearts,
And calls aloud for thee.

5 Thine was the cross, with all its fruits
Of grace and peace divine:
Be thine the crown of glory now,
The palm of victory thine!

E. DENNY.

1217 C. M.

1 WE come, O Lord, before thy throne,
And, with united plea,
We meet and pray for those who roam
Far off upon the sea.

2 Oh, may the Holy Spirit bow
The sailor's heart to thee,
Till tears of deep repentance flow,
Like rain-drops in the sea!

3 Then may a Saviour's dying love
Pour peace into his breast,
And waft him to the port above
Of everlasting rest.

1218 C. M.

1 GREAT God, the nations of the earth
Are by creation thine;
And in thy works, by all beheld,
Thy radiant glories shine.

2 But, Lord, thy greater love has sent
Thy gospel to mankind,
Unveiling what rich stores of grace
Are treasured in thy mind.

3 Lord, when shall these glad tidings spread
The spacious earth around,
Till every tribe and every soul
Shall hear the joyful sound?

4 Smile, Lord, on each divine attempt
To spread the gospel's rays,
And build on sin's demolished throne
The temples of thy praise.

GIBBONS.

1219 C. M.

1 JESUS, immortal King, arise;
Assert thy rightful sway;
Till earth, subdued, its tribute brings,
And distant lands obey.

2 Ride forth, victorious Conqueror, ride,
Till all thy foes submit,
And all the powers of hell resign
Their trophies at thy feet.

3 Send forth thy word, and let it fly
This spacious earth around,
Till every soul beneath the sun
Shall hear the joyful sound.

1220 8s, 7s & 4s.

1 O'ER the gloomy hills of darkness,
Cheer'd by no celestial ray,
Sun of righteousness! arising,
Bring the bright, the glorious day;
Send the gospel
To the earth's remotest bound.

2 Kingdoms wide that sit in darkness,—
Grant them, Lord, the glorious light;
And, from eastern coast to western,
May the morning chase the night;
And redemption,
Freely purchased, win the day.

3 Fly abroad, thou mighty gospel!
Win and conquer, never cease;
May thy lasting, wide dominions,
Multiply and still increase;
Sway thy sceptre,
Saviour, all the world around!

WILLIAMS.

1221 8s, 7s & 4s.

1 LOOK, ye saints! the day is breaking;
Joyful times are near at hand;
God, the mighty God, is speaking
By his word in every land:
Day advances—
Darkness flies at his command.

2 Oh, 'tis pleasant, 'tis reviving
To our hearts, to hear, each day,
Joyful news, from far arriving,
How the gospel wins its way,
Those enlightening
Who in death and darkness lay!

3 God of Jacob, high and glorious,
Let thy people see thy hand!
Let the gospel be victorious,
Through the world, in every land;
Then shall idols
Perish, Lord, at thy command.

KELLY.

1222 8s, 7s & 4s.

1 MEN of God, go take your stations,
Darkness reigns o'er all the earth—
Go, proclaim among the nations
Joyful news of heavenly birth—
Bear the tidings,
Tell the Saviour's matchless worth!

2 Go—and when exposed to dangers,
Jesus will your souls defend!
Go, and when 'mid foes and strangers,
He will still appear your Friend—
His kind presence
Shall be with you to the end!

KELLY.

1223 8s, 7s & 4s.

1 SOULS in heathen darkness lying,
Where no light has broken through—
Souls that Jesus bought by dying,
Whom his soul in travail knew—
Thousand voices
Call us, o'er the waters blue.

2 Christians, hearken! None has taught them
Of his love so deep and dear;
Of the precious price that bought them;
Of the nail, the thorn, the spear;
Ye who know him,
Guide them from their darkness drear.

3 Haste, oh haste, and spread the tidings
Wide to earth's remotest strand;
Let no brother's bitter chidings
Rise against us—when we stand
In the judgment—
From some far, forgotten land.

4 Lo! the hills for harvest whiten,
All along each distant shore;
Seaward far the islands brighten,—
Light of nations! lead us o'er:
When we seek them,
Let thy Spirit go before!

1224 8s, 7s & 4s.

1 YES—my native land! I love thee;
All thy scenes I love them well;
Friends, connections, happy country,
Can I bid you all farewell?
Can I leave you,
Far in heathen lands to dwell?

2 Home!—thy joys are passing lovely—
Joys no stranger-heart can tell;
Happy home!—'tis sure I love thee!
Can I—can I say—Farewell?
Can I leave thee,
Far in heathen lands to dwell?

3 Scenes of sacred peace and pleasure,
Holy days and Sabbath-bell,
Richest, brightest, sweetest treasure!
Can I say a last farewell?
Can I leave you,
Far in heathen lands to dwell?

4 Yes! I hasten from you gladly,
From the scenes I love so well;
Far away, ye billows! bear me;
Lovely native land!—farewell!
Pleased I leave thee,
Far in heathen lands to dwell.

5 In the deserts let me labor,
On the mountains let me tell
How he died—the blessed Saviour—
To redeem a world from hell!
Let me hasten,
Far in heathen lands to dwell.

S. F. SMITH.

1225 8s & 7s.

1 WE are living, we are dwelling,
In a grand and awful time,
In an age on ages telling,
To be living is sublime.
Hark! the waking up of nations,
Gog and Magog to the fray.
Hark! what soundeth? is creation
Groaning for its latter day.

2 Will ye play, then, will ye dally,
With your music and your wine?
Up! it is Jehovah's rally!
God's own arm hath need of thine.
Hark! the onset! will ye fold your
Faith-clad arms in lazy lock?
Up, oh up, thou drowsy soldier!
Worlds are charging to the shock.

3 Worlds are charging—heaven beholding;
Thou hast but an hour to fight;
Now the blazoned cross unfolding,
On—right onward, for the right.
On! let all the soul within you
For the truth's sake go abroad!
Strike! let every nerve and sinew
Tell on ages—tell for God!

A. C. COXE.

1226 8s & 7s.

1 ONWARD, onward, men of heaven!
Bear the Gospel's banner high;
Rest not till its light is given,
Star of every pagan sky.
Send it where the pilgrim-stranger
Faints 'neath Asia's scorching ray;
Bid the red-browed forest ranger
Hail it, ere he fades away.

2 Where the Arctic ocean thunders,
Where the tropics fiercely glow,
Broadly spread its page of wonders,
Brightly bid its radiance flow.
India marks its lustre stealing,
Shiv'ring Greenland loves its rays,
Afric, 'mid her deserts kneeling,
Lifts the untaught strain of praise.

3 Rude in speech, or grim in feature,
Dark in spirit though they be,

Show that light to every creature,
  Prince or vassal—bond or free.
Lo! they haste to every nation,
  Host on host the ranks supply;
Onward!—Christ is your salvation,
  And your death is victory.

SIGOURNEY.

1227 S. M.

1 O THOU whom we adore!
  To bless our earth again,
Assume thine own almighty power,
  And o'er the nations reign.

2 The world's Desire and Hope,
  All power to thee is given;
Now set the last great empire up,
  Eternal Lord of heaven!

3 A gracious Saviour, thou
  Wilt all thy creatures bless;
And every knee to thee shall bow,
  And every tongue confess.

4 According to thy word,
  Now be thy grace revealed;
And with the knowledge of the Lord,
  Let all the earth be filled.

C. WESLEY.

1228 S. M.

1 O LORD our God! arise;
  The cause of truth maintain;
And wide o'er all the peopled world
  Extend her blessèd reign.

2 Thou Prince of life! arise;
  Nor let thy glory cease;
Far spread the conquests of thy grace,
  And bless the earth with peace.

3 Thou Holy Ghost! arise;
  Extend thy healing wing,
And, o'er a dark and ruined world,
  Let light and order spring.

4 All on the earth! arise;
  To God the Saviour sing;
From shore to shore, from earth to heaven,
  Let echoing anthems ring.

1229 S. M.

1 O GOD of sovereign grace,
  We bow before thy throne,
And plead, for all the human race,
  The merits of thy Son.

2 Spread through the earth, O Lord,
  The knowledge of thy ways;
And let all lands with joy record
  The great Redeemer's praise.

1230 S. M.

1 COME, kingdom of our God,
  Sweet reign of light and love!
Shed peace, and hope, and joy abroad,
  And wisdom from above.

2 Over our spirits first
  Extend thy healing reign;
There raise and quench the sacred thirst,
  That never pains again.

3 Come, kingdom of our God!
  And make the broad earth thine;
Stretch o'er her lands and isles the rod
  That flowers with grace divine.

4 Soon may all tribes be blest
  With fruit from life's glad tree;
And in its shade like brothers rest,
  Sons of one family.

JOHNS.

1231 7s & 6s.

1 THE morning light is breaking,
The darkness disappears;
The sons of earth are waking
To penitential tears.
Each breeze that sweeps the ocean
Brings tidings from afar,
Of nations in commotion,
Prepared for Zion's war.

2 Rich dews of grace come o'er us
In many a gentle shower;
And brighter scenes before us
Are opening every hour:
Each cry to heaven going
Abundant answer brings;
And heavenly gales are blowing,
With peace upon their wings.

3 See heathen nations bending
Before the God we love,
And thousand hearts ascending
In gratitude above;
While sinners, now confessing,
The gospel call obey,
And seek the Saviour's blessing,—
A nation in a day.

4 Blest river of salvation,
Pursue thine onward way;
Flow thou to every nation,
Nor in thy richness stay:
Stay not till all the lowly
Triumphant reach their home;
Stay not till all the holy
Proclaim—"The Lord is come."

S. F. SMITH.

1232 7s & 6s.

1 ROLL on, thou mighty ocean;
And, as thy billows flow,
Bear messengers of mercy
To every land below.
Arise, ye gales, and waft them
Safe to the destined shore;
That man may sit in darkness
And death's black shade no more.

2 O thou eternal Ruler,
Who holdest in thine arm
The tempests of the ocean,
Protect them from all harm!
Thy presence, Lord, be with them,
Wherever they may be;
Though far from us, who love them,
Still let them be with thee.

PRATT'S COLL.

1233 7s & 6s.

1 FROM Greenland's icy mountains,
From India's coral strand,
Where Afric's sunny fountains
Roll down their golden sand,
From many an ancient river,
From many a palmy plain,
They call us to deliver
Their land from error's chain.

2 What though the spicy breezes
Blow soft o'er Ceylon's isle;
Though every prospect pleases,
And only man is vile;
In vain with lavish kindness
The gifts of God are strown;
The heathen, in his blindness,
Bows down to wood and stone.

3 Can we, whose souls are lighted
With wisdom from on high,

Can we, to men benighted,
The lamp of life deny?
Salvation, oh, salvation!
The joyful sound proclaim,
Till each remotest nation
Has learned Messiah's name.

4 Waft, waft, ye winds, his story,
And you, ye waters, roll,
Till, like a sea of glory,
It spreads from pole to pole;
Till o'er our ransomed nature,
The Lamb for sinners slain,
Redeemer, King, Creator,
In bliss returns to reign! HEBER.

1234 7s & 6s.

1 OH that the Lord's salvation
Were out of Zion come,
To heal his ancient nation,
To lead his outcasts home!
How long the holy city
Shall heathen feet profane?
Return, O Lord, in pity;
Rebuild her walls again.

2 Let fall thy rod of terror:
Thy saving grace impart;
Roll back the veil of error:
Release the fetter'd heart.
Let Israel, home returning,
Her lost Messiah see;
Give oil of joy for mourning,
And bind thy Church to thee. LYTE.

1235 7s.

1 WATCHMAN! tell us of the night,
What its signs of promise are.—
Traveler! o'er yon mountain's height,
See that glory-beaming star!—
Watchman! does its beauteous ray
Aught of hope or joy foretell?—
Traveler! yes; it brings the day—
Promised day of Israel.

2 Watchman! tell us of the night,
Higher yet that star ascends.—
Traveler! blessedness and light,
Peace and truth its course portends!
Watchman! will its beams alone
Gild the spot that gave them birth?—
Traveler! ages are its own,
See, it bursts o'er all the earth.

3 Watchman! tell us of the night,
For the morning seems to dawn.—
Traveler! darkness takes its flight,
Doubt and terror are withdrawn.—
Watchman! let thy wanderings cease;
Hie thee to thy quiet home.—
Traveler! lo! the Prince of Peace,
Lo! the Son of God is come.

BOWRING.

1236 7s.

1 WAKE the song of jubilee,
Let it echo o'er the sea!
Now is come the promised hour;
Jesus reigns with glorious power!

2 All ye nations, join and sing,
Praise your Saviour, praise your King;
Let it sound from shore to shore,
"Jesus reigns for evermore!"

3 Hark! the desert lands rejoice,
And the islands join their voice;
Joy! the whole creation sings,
"Jesus is the King of kings!"

BACON.

1237 7s. D.

1 SONS of men, behold from far,
Hail the long-expected star!
Star of truth that gilds the night,
And guides bewildered men aright.
Mild it shines on all beneath,
Piercing through the shades of death;
Scattering error's wide-spread night;
Kindling darkness into light.

2 Nations all, remote and near,
Haste to see your Lord appear;
Haste, for him your hearts prepare,
Meet him manifested there!
There behold the day-spring rise,
Pouring light on mortal eyes;
See it chase the shades away,
Shining to the perfect day.

LYTE.

1238 7s. D.

1 HARK! the song of Jubilee,
Loud as mighty thunders roar,
Or the fullness of the sea,
When it breaks upon the shore!
Hallelujah! for the Lord
God Omnipotent shall reign:
Hallelujah! let the word
Echo round the earth and main.

2 Hallelujah! hark! the sound,
From the centre to the skies,
Wakes above, beneath, around,
All creation's harmonies.
See Jehovah's banner furled,
Sheathed his sword, he speaks—'tis done;
And the kingdoms of this world
Are the kingdoms of his Son.

3 "He shall reign from pole to pole
With illimitable sway;
He shall reign when, like a scroll,
Yonder heavens have passed away;
Then the end:—beneath his rod
Man's last enemy shall fall:
Hallelujah! Christ in God,
God in Christ is all in all."

MONTGOMERY.

1239 7s. D.

1 SEE the ransomed millions stand—
Palms of conquest in their hands!
This before the throne their strain—
"Hell is vanquished—death is slain!
Blessing, honor, glory, might,
Are the Conqueror's native right;
Thrones and powers before him fall—
Lamb of God, and Lord of all!"

2 Hasten, Lord! the promised hour;
Come in glory and in power;
Still thy foes are unsubdued—
Nature sighs to be renewed.
Time has nearly reached its sum;
All things with the bride say, "Come!"
Jesus! whom all worlds adore,
Come—and reign for evermore.

CONDER.

1240 7s. D.

1 SEE how great a flame aspires,
Kindled by a spark of grace!
Jesus' love the nations fires—
Sets the kingdoms on a blaze.
To bring fire on earth he came;
Kindled in some heart it is:
Oh, that all might catch the flame,
All partake the glorious bliss!

2 When he first the work begun,
Small and feeble was his day:
Now the word doth swiftly run;
Now it wins its widening way.
More and more it spreads and grows,
Ever mighty to prevail;
Sin's strongholds it now o'erthrows—
Shakes the trembling gates of hell.

3 Saw ye not the cloud arise,
Little as a human hand?
Now it spreads along the skies—
Hangs o'er all the thirsty land.
Lo! the promise of a shower
Drops already from above;
But the Lord will shortly pour
All the Spirit of his love.

C. Wesley.

1241 7s. D.

1 COME, Desire of nations, come;
Hasten, Lord, the general doom;
Hear the Spirit and the Bride;
Come, and take us to thy side.
Thou who hast our place prepared,
Make us meet for our reward;
Then with all thy saints descend;
Then our earthly trials end.

2 Mindful of thy chosen race,
Shorten these vindictive days,
Hear us now, and save thine own,
Who for full redemption groan.
Now destroy the Man of Sin,
Now thine ancient flock bring in,
Filled with righteousness divine;
Claim a ransomed world for thine!

3 Plant thy heavenly kingdom here;
Glorious in thy saints appear;
Speak the sacred number sealed,
Speak the mystery revealed:
Take to thee thy royal power;
Reign, when sin shall be no more!
Reign, when death no more shall be!
Reign to all eternity!

1242 8s & 7s.

1 "LIFT your heads" with faith; the morrow
Dawneth brighter than to-day;
Angel hands will lift the shadows,
Chase the gathering gloom away.

2 Does the night seem long and weary—
Dangers threatening 'long the way?
Joy will soon return to bless thee,
Soon will dawn a brighter day.

3 What though wars and earth's commotions
Try your faith, and cause dismay;
God, your Father, rules the nations,
He will send a brighter day.

Chorus.

"Lift your heads," the day is breaking,
Soon the morning will appear;
See the earth from slumber waking;
"Lift your heads," the day draws near.

1243 8s & 4s.

1 HARK! how the gospel trumpet sounds!
Through all the world the echo bounds!
And Jesus, by redeeming blood,
Is bringing sinners back to God,
And guides them safely by his word
To endless day.

2 Hail, Jesus! all victorious Lord!
Be thou by all mankind adored!
For us didst thou the fight maintain,
And o'er our foes the victory gain,
That we, with thee, might ever reign
In endless day.

3 There we shall in full chorus join,
With saints and angels, all combine
To sing of his redeeming love,
When rolling years shall cease to move,
And this shall be our theme above,
In endless day.

MEDLEY.

1244 8s.

1 HEAR the royal proclamation,
The glad tidings of salvation,
Publishing to every creature,
To the ruined sons of nature:

2 See the royal banner flying,
Hear the heralds loudly crying,
"Rebel sinners, royal favor
Now is offered by the Saviour."

3 Shout, ye tongues of every nation,
To the bounds of the creation;
Shout the praise of Judah's Lion,
The Almighty Prince of Zion.

4 Shout, ye saints, make joyful mention,
Christ hath purchased our redemption;
Angels, shout the pleasing story,
Through the brighter worlds of glory.

Chorus.

Jesus reigns, Jesus reigns, Jesus reigns,
Jesus reigns, he reigns victorious,
Over heaven and earth most glorious,
Jesus reigns, Jesus reigns, Jesus reigns.

1245 8s & 7s.

1 SHOUT the tidings of salvation
To the aged and the young,
Till the precious invitation
Waken every heart and tongue.

2 Shout the tidings of salvation,
O'er the prairies of the West;
Till each gath'ring congregation
With the gospel sound is blest.

3 Shout the tidings of salvation,
Mingling with the ocean's roar;
Till the ships of every nation,
Bear the news from shore to shore.

4 Shout the tidings of salvation
O'er the islands of the sea;
Till, in humble adoration,
All to Christ shall bow the knee.

Chorus.

Send the sound the earth around,
From the rising to the setting of the sun,
Till each gath'ring crowd shall proclaim aloud,
"The glorious work is done!"

1246 7s.

1 HASTEN, Lord, the glorious time,
When, beneath Messiah's sway,
Every nation, every clime,
Shall the gospel call obey.

2 Mightiest kings his power shall own;
Heathen tribes his name adore;
Satan and his host, o'erthrown,
Bound in chains, shall hurt no more.

3 Then shall wars and tumults cease,
Then be banished grief and pain;

Righteousness and joy and peace,
Undisturbed, shall ever reign,

4 Bless we then our gracious Lord;
Ever praise his glorious name;
All his mighty acts record;
All his wondrous love proclaim.

LYTE.

1247 P. M.

1 IF I were a voice, a persuasive voice,
That could travel the wide world through,
I would fly on the beams of the morning light,
And speak to men with a gentle might,
And tell them to be true.
I would fly, I would fly over land and sea,
Wherever a human heart might be,
Telling a tale or singing a song
In praise of the right—in blame of the wrong,
I would fly, I would fly,
I would fly over land and sea.

2 If I were a voice, a consoling voice,
I'd fly on the wings of the air;
The homes of sorrow and guilt I'd seek,
And calm and truthful words I'd speak,
To save them from despair.
I would fly, I would fly o'er the crowded town,
And drop, like the happy sunlight, down
Into the hearts of suffering men,
And teach them to look up again:
I would fly, I would fly,
I would fly o'er the crowded town.

3 If I were a voice, a convincing voice,
I'd travel with the wind,
And wherever I saw the nations torn,
By warfare, jealousy, spite or scorn,
Or hatred of their kind,
I would fly, I would fly on the thunder crash,
And into their blinded bosoms flash;
Then, with their evil thoughts subdued,
I'd teach them Christian brotherhood;
I would fly, I would fly,
I would fly on the thunder crash.

4 If I were a voice, an immortal voice,
I would fly the earth around:
And wherever man to his idols bowed,
I'd publish in notes both long and loud
The Gospel's joyful sound.
I would fly, I would fly on the wings of day,
Proclaiming peace on my world-wide way,
Bidding the saddened earth rejoice—
If I were a voice, an immortal voice,
I would fly, I would fly,
I would fly on the wings of day.

1248 8s & 7s.

1 LET us gather up the sunbeams
Lying all around our path;
Let us keep the wheat and roses,
Casting out the thorns and chaff;
Let us find our sweetest comfort
In the blessings of to-day,
With a patient hand removing
All the briars from the way.

2 Strange, we never prize the music
Till the sweet-voiced bird has flown!

Strange, that we should slight the violets
Till the lovely flowers are gone!
Strange, the summer skies and sunshine
Never seem one half so fair,
As when winter's snowy pinions
Shake the white down in the air.

3 If we knew the baby fingers,
Pressed against the window-pane,
Would be cold and stiff to-morrow—
Never trouble us again—
Would the bright eyes of our darling
Catch the frown upon our brow?
Would the print of rosy fingers
Vex us then as they do now?

4 Ah! those little ice-cold fingers,
How they point our memories back
To the hasty words and actions
Strewn along our backward track!
How those little hands remind us,
As in snowy grace they lie,
Not to scatter thorns—but roses—
For our reaping by and by.

MARY RILEY SMITH.

Chorus.

Then scatter seeds of kindness,
For our reaping by and by.

1249 P. M.

1 "NOTHING to do!" in this world of ours,
Where weeds spring up with fairest flowers,
Where smiles have only a fitful play,
Where hearts are breaking every day!
"Nothing to do! nothing to do!"

2 "Nothing to do!" O thou Christian soul,
Wrapping thee round in thy selfish [stole;
Off with the garments of sloth and sin,
Christ, the Lord, hath a kingdom to win.
"Nothing to do! nothing to do!"

3 "Nothing to do!" there are prayers to lay
On the altar of incense day by day;
There are foes to meet thee within and without;
There is error to conquer strong and stout.
"Nothing to do! nothing to do!"

4 "Nothing to do!" there are minds to teach
The simplest forms of Christian speech;
There are hearts to lure thee with loving wile;
From grimmest haunts of sin's defile.
"Nothing to do! nothing to do!"

5 "Nothing to do!" and thy Saviour said,
"Follow thou me in the paths I tread;"
Lord, lend thy help all the journey thro',
Lest faint we cry, "*So much to do!*"
Lest faint we cry, "*So much to do!*"

1250

1 SAY, is your lamp burning, my brother?
I pray you look quickly, and see,
For if it were burning, then surely
Some beams would fall bright upon me.
Straight, straight is the road, but I falter,
And oft I fall out by the way;
Then lift your lamp higher, my brother,
Lest I should make fatal delay.

2 Oh, see! there are many around you
Who follow wherever you go;

And thought you they walked in the shadow
Your lamp would burn brighter, I know:
Upon the dark mountains they stumble,
They're bruised on the rocks, and they lie
With white pleading faces turned upward
To the clouds and the pitiful sky.

3 How many a lamp that is flick'ring
Behold we anear and afar:
Not many among them, my brother,
Shine steadily on like a star:
I think were they trimmed night and morning,
They never'd burn down or go out,
Though from the four quarters of heaven
The winds were all blowing about.

4 If once all the lamps that are lighted
Should steadily blaze in a line,—
Wide over the land and the ocean,—
What a girdle of glory would shine,
How all the dark places would brighten,
How mists would roll up and away!
How earth would laugh out in her gladness
To hail the millennial day!

1251 8s & 7s.

1 THERE are lonely hearts to cherish,
While the days are going by;
There are weary souls who perish,
While the days are going by;
If a smile we can renew,
As our journey we pursue,
Oh, the good we all may do,
While the days are going by.

2 There's no time for idle scorning
While the days are going by;
Let our face be like the morning
While the days are going by.
Oh! the world is full of sighs,
Full of sad and weeping eyes.
Help your fallen brothers rise
While the days are going by.

3 All the loving links that bind us
While the days are going by,
One by one we leave behind us
While the days are going by;
But the seeds of good we sow,
Both in shade and shine will grow,
And will keep our hearts aglow
While the days are going by.

Chorus.

Up! then, trusty hearts and true,
Tho' the day comes, night comes too;
Oh, the good we all may do,
While the days are going by.

1252 C. M.

1 GO forth on wings of faith and prayer,
Ye pages, bright with love;
Though mute, the joyful tidings bear,
Salvation from above.

2 Go, tell the sinful, careless soul
The warning God has given;
Go, make the wounded spirit whole,
With healing balm from heaven.

3 Go to the rude, the dark, the poor,
That live estranged from God;—
Bid them the pearl of price secure,
Bought with a Saviour's blood.

4 O Jesus, Friend of dying men,
Thy presence we implore;
Without thy blessing all is vain;
Be with us evermore.

HASTINGS.

1253 C. M.

1 WEEP for the lost! Thy Saviour wept
O'er Salem's hapless doom;
He wept, to think their day was past,
And come their night of gloom.

2 Weep for the lost! Apostles wept,
That men should error choose;
That dying men should Christ reject,
And endless life refuse.

3 Weep for the lost! The lost will weep,
In that long night of woe,
On which no star of hope will rise,
And tears in vain will flow.

4 Weep for the lost! Lord, make us weep,
And toil, with ceaseless care,
To save our friends, ere yet they pass
That point of deep despair.

COLVER.

1254 6s & 4s.

1 OUR land, with mercies crowned,
This wide, enchanted ground,
O God, is thine:
Our fathers knew thy name;
The trophies of their fame—
Our heritage—proclaim,
A Power divine.

2 Far in the purple west,
Thy hand with beauty drest
These fertile plains,
These rivers dark and deep,
These torrents down the steep,
These mighty woods that sweep
From mountain chains.

3 Dear Native Land, rejoice!
Raise thou thy virgin voice
To God on high;
From all thy hills and bays,
From all thy homes and ways,
Let symphonies and praise
Ascend the sky.

4 And thou, Almighty One,
At whose eternal throne
She bows the knee;
In all the coming time,
Bless thou this favored clime,
And may her deeds sublime
Be hymns to thee!

E. T. WINKLER.

1255 6s & 4s.

1 MY country, 'tis of thee,
Sweet land of liberty,
Of thee I sing:
Land where my fathers died,
Land of the pilgrims' pride,
From every mountain side
Let freedom ring!

2 My native country, thee,
Land of the noble free,
Thy name I love:
I love thy rocks and rills,
Thy woods and templed hills;
My heart with rapture thrills
Like that above.

3 Let music swell the breeze,
And ring from all the trees
Sweet freedom's song;
Let mortal tongues awake,
Let all that breathe partake,
Let rocks their silence break,
The sound prolong.

4 Our fathers' God, to thee,
Author of liberty,
To thee we sing;
Long may our land be bright
With freedom's holy light,
Protect us by thy might,
Great God, our King!

S. F. SMITH.

1256 6s & 4s.

1 GOD bless our native land!
Firm may she ever stand,
Through storm and night:
When the wild tempests rave,
Ruler of wind and wave,
Do thou our country save
By thy great might!

2 For her our prayer shall rise
To God, above the skies;
On him we wait:
Thou who art ever nigh,
Guarding with watchful eye,
To thee aloud we cry,
God save the State!

J. S. DWIGHT.

1257 6s & 4s.

1 LORD, from thy blessèd throne,
Sorrow look down upon!
God save the poor!
Teach them true liberty,
Make them from tyrants free,
Let their homes happy be!
God save the poor!

2 The arms of wicked men
Do thou with might restrain—
God save the poor!
Raise thou their lowliness,
Succor thou their distress,
Thou whom the meanest bless;
God save the poor!

3 Give them stanch honesty,
Let their pride manly be—
God save the poor!
Help them to hold the right,
Give them both truth and might,
Lord of all life and light!
God save the poor!

NICOLL.

1258 8s, 7s & 4s.

1 VISIT, Lord, this land in mercy,
Bid its storms and terrors cease;
Rise in beauteous radiance o'er us,
Sun of Righteousness and Peace:
God of Nations,
Grant from woes a long release.

2 Throw thy shield of strong protection
All thy favored land around:
Under thy benign direction,
Let its ruling minds be found;
Peace diffusing
To the nation's utmost bound.

3 Let not such a land of beauty
Lie beneath the clouds of sin;
Onward urge its glorious duty,
Moral victories to win;
Now in mercy,
Let its brightest days begin.

4 Oh, let smiling peace bend o'er it,
Oh, let constant plenty crown;

Let contention flee before it,
Let it tread all evil down;
While dark discord
Sinks beneath a nation's frown.

5 Let the bright regeneration
Of a noble people come;
And their moral renovation
Bless the States and make them one;
Bidding temperance
Flourish round their hearth and home.

6 Bless the Rulers, bless the nation,
Bless its intellectual sway;
Bless its rising generation,
Be their guide, and be their stay;
Watching o'er them,
To their history's latest day.

1259 8s, 7s & 4s.

1 "EBENEZER! God is with us!"
Sang our fathers long ago:
"Ebenezer? God is with us,"
Sing their grateful children now:
Ebenezer!
Every knee in worship bow.

2 Blessing now and adoration
Young and old in concert sing;
Sing in lofty jubilation
To our great Redeemer, King;
Grace and mercy
His right arm alone did bring.

3 "Ebenezer! God is with us!"
Echo down the stream of time,
"Ebenezer!" till the story
From the hills of glory chime,
And the angels
Swell the glorious song sublime.

1260 7s.

1 WHY, O God! thy people spurn?
Why permit thy wrath to burn?
God of mercy! turn once more,
All our broken hearts restore.

2 Thou hast made our land to quake,
Heal the sorrows thou dost make;
Bitter is the cup we drink,
Suffer not our souls to sink.

3 Be thy banner now unfurled,
Show thy truth to all the world;
Save us, Lord, we cry to thee,
Lift thine arm—thy chosen free.

4 Give us now relief from pain,—
Human aid is all in vain:
We, through God, shall yet prevail,
He will help, when foes assail.

HATFIELD.

1261 6s & 4s.

1 THE God of harvest praise;
In loud thanksgiving raise
Hand, heart, and voice;
The valleys smile and sing,
Forests and mountains ring,
The plains their tribute bring,
The streams rejoice.

2 Yea, bless his holy name,
And purest thanks proclaim
Through all the earth;
To glory in your lot
Is duty,—but be not
God's benefits forgot
Amidst your mirth.

3 The God of harvest praise;
Hands, hearts, and voices raise,
With sweet accord;

From field to garner throng,
Bearing your sheaves along,
And in your harvest song
Bless ye the Lord.

MONTGOMERY.

1262 C. M.

1 LORD, while for all mankind we pray,
Of every clime and coast,
Oh, hear us for our native land—
The land we love the most.

2 Oh, guard our shore from every foe,
With peace our borders bless,
With prosperous times our cities crown,
Our fields with plenteousness.

3 Unite us in the sacred love
Of knowledge, truth, and thee;
And let our hills and valleys shout
The songs of liberty.

4 Here may religion, pure and mild,
Smile on our Sabbath hours;
And piety and virtue bless
The home of us and ours.

5 Lord of the nations, thus to thee
Our country we commend;
Be thou her refuge and her trust,
Her everlasting friend.

WREFORD.

1263 C. M.

1 SEE, gracious God, before thy throne,
Thy mourning people bend!
'Tis on thy sovereign grace alone,
Our humble hopes depend.

2 Alarming judgments from thy hand,
Thy dreadful power display;
Yet mercy spares this guilty land,
And yet we live to pray.

3 Oh, bid us turn, Almighty Lord,
By thy resistless grace;
Then shall our hearts obey thy word,
And humbly seek thy face.

STEELE.

1264 C. M.

1 LORD, thou hast scourged our guilty land;
Behold, thy people mourn;
Shall vengeance ever guide thy hand,
And mercy ne'er return?

2 Our Zion trembles at thy stroke,
And dreads thy lifted hand;
Oh, heal the people thou hast broke,
And spare our guilty land.

3 Then shall our loud and grateful voice
Proclaim our guardian God,
The nations round the earth rejoice,
And sound thy praise abroad.

WATTS.

1265 L. M.

1 GREAT God of nations! now to thee
Our hymn of gratitude we raise;
With humble heart, and bending knee,
We offer thee our song of praise.

2 Thy name we bless, Almighty God!
For all the kindness thou hast shown,
To this fair land the Pilgrims trod,—
This land we fondly call our own.

3 Here, freedom spreads her banner wide,
And casts her soft and hallowed ray:—

Here, thou our fathers' steps didst guide
In safety, through their dangerous way.

4 We praise thee, that the gospel's light,
Through all our land, its radiance sheds;
Dispels the shades of error's night,
And heavenly blessings round us spreads.

1266 L. M.

1 WHEN driven by oppression's rod,
Our fathers fled beyond the sea,
Their care was first to honor God,
And next to leave their children free.

2 Above the forest's gloomy shade,
The altar and the school appeared:
On that the gifts of faith were laid,
On this their precious hopes were reared.

3 The altar and the school still stand,
The sacred pillars of our trust;
And freedom's sons shall fill the land,
While we are sleeping in the dust.

4 Before thine altar, Lord, we bend,
With grateful song and fervent prayer;
For thou, who wast our fathers' Friend,
Wilt make their offspring still thy care.

1267 L. M.

1 LORD, let thy goodness lead our land,
Still sav'd by thine almighty hand,
The tribute of its love to bring
To thee, our Saviour and our King.

2 Let every public temple raise
Triumphant songs of holy praise,
Let every peaceful, private home
A temple, Lord, to thee become.

3 Still be it our supreme delight
To walk as in thy glorious sight;
Still in thy precepts and thy fear,
Till life's last hour, to persevere.

1268 8s & 7s.

1 SWELL the anthem, raise the song;
Praises to our God belong;
Saints and angels, join to sing
Praises to the heavenly King.

2 Blessings from his liberal hand
Flow around this happy land;
Kept by him, no foes annoy;
Peace and freedom we enjoy.

3 Here beneath a virtuous sway
May we cheerfully obey;
Never feel oppression's rod;
Ever own and worship God.

4 Hark! the voice of nature sings
Praises to the King of kings;
Let us join the choral song,
And the grateful notes prolong.

1269 8s & 7s.

1 THANK and praise Jehovah's name!
For his mercies, firm and sure,
From eternity the same,
To eternity endure.

2 Let the ransomed thus rejoice,
Gathered out of every land,

As the people of his choice,
  Plucked from the destroyer's hand.

3 To a pleasant land he brings,
  Where the vine and olive grow,
Where, from flowery hills, the springs
  Through luxuriant valleys flow.

4 Oh, that men would praise the Lord
  For his goodness to their race;
For the wonders of his word,
  And the riches of his grace!

MONTGOMERY.

1270 8s & 7s.

1 PRAISE, oh praise our God and King,
Hymns of adoration sing;
For his mercies still endure,
Ever faithful, ever sure.

2 Praise him that he made the sun
Day by day his course to run;
And the silver moon by night,
Shining with her gentle light.

3 Praise him that he gave the rain
To mature the swelling grain;
And had bid the fruitful field
Crops of precious increase yield.

4 Praise him for our harvest-store,—
He hath filled the garner-floor,—
And for richer food than this,
Pledge of everlasting bliss.

5 Glory to our bounteous King!
Glory let Creation sing!
Glory to the Father, Son,
And blest Spirit, Three in One.

H. W. BAKER.

1271 8s, 7s. & 4s.

1 STAR of peace to wanderers weary!
  Bright the beams that smile on me;
Cheer the pilot's vision dreary,
  Far, far at sea.

2 Star of hope! gleam on the billow;
  Bless the soul that sighs for thee,
Bless the sailor's lonely pillow,
  Far, far at sea.

3 Star of faith! when winds are mocking
  All his toil, he flies to thee;
Save him on the billows rocking,
  Far, far at sea.

4 Star Divine! oh, safely guide him,
  Bring the wanderer home to thee;
Sore temptations long have tried him,
  Far, far at sea.

1272 7s. 6 lines.

1 JESUS, Saviour, pilot me
  Over life's tempestuous sea;
Unknown waves before me roll,
Hiding rock, and treacherous shoal;
Chart and compass came from thee:
Jesus, Saviour, pilot me.

2 When the Apostles' fragile bark
Struggled with the billows dark,
On the stormy Galilee,
Thou didst walk upon the sea;
And when they beheld thy form,
Safe they glided through the storm.

3 As a mother stills her child
Thou canst hush the ocean wild;
Boisterous waves obey thy will
When thou sayest to them "Be still!"

Wondrous Sovereign of the sea,
Jesus, Saviour, pilot me.

4 When at last I near the shore,
And the fearful breakers roar
'Twixt me and the peaceful rest,
Then, while leaning on thy breast,
May I hear thee say to me,
"Fear not, I will pilot thee!"

1273 L. M.

1 ROCKED in the cradle of the deep,
I lay me down in peace to sleep;
Secure I rest upon the wave,
For thou, O Lord, hast power to save.

2 I know thou wilt not slight my call!
For thou dost mark the sparrow's fall!
And calm and peaceful is my sleep,
Rocked in the cradle of the deep.

3 And such the trust that still were mine,
Though stormy winds swept o'er the brine,
Or though the tempest's fiery breath
Roused me from sleep to wreck and death!

4 In ocean cave still safe with thee,
The germ of immortality;
And calm and peaceful is my sleep,
Rocked in the cradle of the deep.

MRS. WILLARD.

1274 7s & 6s.

1 THE sea is wildly tossing,
And often clothed with gloom,
On which we're swiftly crossing
To our eternal home.

2 Though nature in commotion
Defy our power and skill,
Our Jesus rules the ocean,
And bids the winds be still.

3 Sail on then, comrades, boldly,
And make God's word your chart;
Do every duty nobly,
With joyful, trustful heart.

4 We'll float the gospel banner,
And guard it with our life,
And shout at last, "Hosanna,"
Victorious in the strife."

Chorus.

Over the sea, over the sea,
Gracious Saviour, pilot me;
Over the sea, over the sea,
Spirit kind, my guardian be;
Over the sea, wherever I roam,
Father above, oh, bring me home
Under the bright celestial dome.

1275 S. M.

1 THE Saviour kindly calls
Our children to his breast;
He folds them in his gracious arms;
Himself declares them blest.

2 "Let them approach," he cries,
"Nor scorn their humble claim;
The heirs of heaven are such as these;
For such as these I came."

3 With joy we bring them, Lord,
Devoting them to thee,
Imploring that, as we are thine,
Thine may our offspring be.

1276 S. M.

1 OUR children thou dost claim,
O Lord our God, as thine:
Ten thousand blessings to thy name
For goodness so divine!

2 Thee let the fathers own,
Thee let the sons adore;
Joined to the Lord in solemn vows,
To be forgot no more.

3 How great thy mercies, Lord!
How plenteous is thy grace!
Which, in the promise of thy love,
Includes our rising race.

4 Our offspring, still thy care,
Shall own their fathers' God!
To latest times thy blessing share,
And sound thy praise abroad.

1277 S. M.

1 THOU God of sovereign grace,
In mercy now appear;
We long to see thy smiling face,
And feel that thou art near.

2 Receive these lambs to-day,
O Shepherd of the flock,
And wash the stains of guilt away
Beside the smitten Rock.

3 To-day in love descend;
Oh, come, this precious hour;
In mercy now their spirits bend
By thy resistless power.

4 Low bending at thy feet,
Our offspring we resign:
Thine arm is strong, thy love is great,
And high thy glories shine.

1278 S. M.

1 GREAT God, now condescend
To bless our rising race;
Soon may their willing spirits bend,
The subjects of thy grace.

2 Oh, what a pure delight
Their happiness to see;
Our warmest wishes all unite,
To lead their souls to thee.

3 Now bless, thou God of love,
The word of truth divine;
Send thy good Spirit from above,
And make these children thine.

1279 C. M.

1 O LORD, behold us at thy feet,
A needy, sinful band;
As suppliants round thy mercy-seat,
We come at thy command.

2 'Tis for our children we would plead,
The offspring thou hast given;
Where shall we go, in time of need,
But to the God of heaven?

3 We ask not for them wealth or fame,
Amid the worldly strife;
But, in the all-prevailing Name,
We ask eternal life.

4 We seek the Spirit's quickening grace,
To make them pure in heart,
That they may stand before thy face,
And see thee as thou art.

1280 C. M.

1 BE ours the bliss in wisdom's way
To guide untutored youth,
And lead the mind that went astray
To virtue and to truth.

2 Delightful work, young souls to win,
And turn the rising race
From the deceitful paths of sin
To seek redeeming grace!

3 Almighty God, thine influence shed
To aid this good design;
The honors of thy name be spread,
And all the glory thine.

1281 C. M.

1 ON, through Judea's palmy plain,
By Jordan's silv'ry shore,
The Saviour leads the thronging train,
Who follow to adore.

2 'Midst youth, and sire, and blooming maid,
He marked the listening child;
His hand upon its head he laid,
And blest in accents mild.

3 Lord, though no more thy hallowed form
Can greet our children's sight,
Grant that, whilst life their breasts shall warm,
Thy word may guide them right.

4 They may not feel thine earthly touch;
But be thy Spirit given,
To make them holy; "for of such
The kingdom is of heaven."

1282 8s & 7s. D.

1 WE have met in peace together
In this house of God again;
Constant friends have led us hither,
Here to chant the solemn strain;
Here to breathe our adoration,
Here the Saviour's praise to sing;
May the Spirit of salvation
Come with healing in his wing.

2 We have met, and time is flying;
We shall part, and still his wing,
Sweeping o'er the dead and dying,
Will the changeful seasons bring:
Let us, while our hearts are lightest,
In our fresh and early years,
Turn to him whose smile is brightest,
And whose grace will calm our fears.

3 Then he'll aid us, should existence
With its sorrows sting the breast;
Gleaming in the onward distance,
Faith will mark the land of rest:
There, 'midst day-beams round him playing,
We our Father's face shall see,
And shall hear him gently saying,
"Little children, come to me."

1283 8s & 7s. D.

1 SAVIOUR, who thy flock art feeding
With the Shepherd's kindest care,
And the feeble gently leading,
While the lambs thy bosom share,
Now, these little ones receiving,
Fold them in thy gracious arm;
There we know, thy word believing,
Only there, secure from harm.

2 Never, from thy pasture roving,
Let them be the lions' prey;
Let thy tenderness so loving
Keep them all life's dangerous way.
Then, within thy fold eternal,
Let them find a resting-place,
Feed in pastures ever vernal,
Drink the rivers of thy grace.

1284 L. M.

1 BONDAGE and death the cup contains;
Dash to the earth the poisoned bowl!
Softer than silk are iron chains,
Compared with those that chafe the soul.

2 Hosannas, Lord, to thee we sing,
Whose power the giant fiend obeys!
What countless thousands tribute bring,
For happier homes and brighter days!

3 Thou wilt not break the bruisèd reed,
Nor leave the broken heart unbound;
The wife regains a husband freed!
The orphan clasps a father found!

4 Spare, Lord, the thoughtless! guide the blind!
Till man no more shall deem it just
To live, by forging chains to bind
His weaker brother in the dust.

SARGENT.

1285 L. M.

1 WE praise thee, Lord, if but one soul,
While the past year prolonged its flight,
Turned shudd'ring from the pois'nous bowl,
To health, and liberty, and light!

2 We praise thee—if one clouded home,
Where broken hearts despairing pined,
Beheld the sire and husband come,
Erect, and in his perfect mind.

3 No more a weeping wife to mock,
Till all her hopes in anguish end—
No more the trembling mind to shock,
And sink the father in the fiend.

4 Still give us grace, Almighty King,
Unwavering at our posts to stand;
Till grateful at thy shrine we bring
The tribute of a ransomed land.

1286 L. M.

1 GREAT God, whose hand outpours the rills
And springs that burst from all the hills,
At whose command the rock was riven,
Who send'st on all, thy rain from heaven;

2 We bless thee for the crystal draught
By sinless man in Eden quaffed;
Type of that fount whose streams above,
Flood endless worlds with life and love!

3 If there the drunkard may not dwell,
But woes crowd thick his paths to hell,
Oh, wake and help us, Lord, to save
Their souls from thirst beyond the grave!

4 Help them to heed thy word divine,
And look not on the crimson wine,
To fear and flee th' accursed thing
As serpent's bite or adder's sting.

5 Stay thou, O Lord, the tide of death!
Rebuke the demon's blasting breath!
And speed, oh, speed, on every shore,
The day when strong drink slays no more!

1287 C. M.

1 LIFE from the dead, Almighty God,
'Tis thine alone to give;
To lift the poor inebriate up,
And bid the helpless live.

2 Life from the dead! For those we plead,
Fast bound in passion's chain,
That, from their iron fetters freed,
They wake to life again.

3 Life from the dead! Quickened by thee,
Be all their powers inclined
To temperance, truth, and piety,
And pleasures pure, refined.

4 And may they by thy help abide,
The tempter's power withstand;
By grace restored and purified,
In Christ accepted stand.

1288 S. M.

1 MOURN for the thousands slain,
The youthful and the strong;
Mourn for the wine-cup's fearful reign,
And the deluded throng.

2 Mourn for the tarnished gem—
For reason's light divine,
Quenched from the soul's bright diadem,
Where God had bid it shine.

3 Mourn for the ruined soul—
Eternal life and light
Lost by the fiery, maddening bowl,
And turned to hopeless night.

4 Mourn for the lost—but call,
Call to the strong, the free;
Rouse them to shun that dreadful fall,
And to the refuge flee.

5 Mourn for the lost—but pray,
Pray to our God above,
To break the fell destroyer's sway,
And show his saving love.

1289 L. M.

1 ETERNAL Source of every joy,
Well may thy praise our lips employ,
While in thy temple we appear,
To hail thee, Sovereign of the year!

2 Wide as the wheels of nature roll,
Thy hand supports and guides the whole,
The sun is taught by thee to rise,
And darkness when to vail the skies.

3 The flowery spring at thy command,
Perfumes the air, adorns the land;
The summer rays with vigor shine,
To raise the corn, to cheer the vine.

4 Thy hand, in autumn, richly pours,
Through all our coasts, redundant stores:
And winters, softened, by thy care,
No more the face of horror wear.

5 Seasons and months, and weeks and days,
Demand successive songs of praise;
And be the grateful homage paid,
With morning light and evening shade.

6 Here in thy house let incense rise,
And circling Sabbaths bless our eyes,
Till to those lofty heights we soar,
Where days and years revolve no more.

DODDRIDGE.

1290 L. M.

1 GREAT God, we sing that mighty hand
By which supported still we stand;
The opening year thy mercy shows;
Let mercy crown it till it close.

2 By day, by night, at home, abroad,
Still we are guarded by our God;
By his incessant bounty fed,
By his unerring counsel led.

3 With grateful hearts the past we own;
The future, all to us unknown,
We to thy guardian care commit,
And peaceful leave before thy feet.

4 In scenes exalted or deprest,
Be thou our joy, and thou our rest;
Thy goodness all our hopes shall raise,
Adored through all our changing days.

DODDRIDGE.

1291 L. M.

1 OUR helper, God, we bless thy name,
Whose love forever is the same;
The tokens of whose gracious care
Begin and crown and close the year.

2 Amid ten thousand snares we stand,
Supported by thy guardian hand;
And see, when we review our ways,
Ten thousand monuments of praise.

3 Thus far thine arm has led us on;
Thus far we make thy mercy known;
And while we tread this desert land,
New mercies shall new songs demand.

4 Our grateful souls on Jordan's shore
Shall raise one sacred pillar more,
Then bear, in thy bright courts above,
Inscriptions of immortal love.

DODDRIDGE.

1292 6s, 8s, & 4s.

1 THE God of Abrah'm praise,
Who reigns enthroned above;
Ancient of everlasting days,
And God of love:
JEHOVAH, GREAT I AM!
By earth and heaven confessed;
I bow and bless the sacred Name,
Forever blest.

2 The God of Abrah'm praise,
At whose supreme command
From earth I rise, and seek the joys
At his right hand:
I all on earth forsake,
Its wisdom, fame, and power;
And him my only portion make,
My shield and tower.

3 The God of Abrah'm praise,
Whose all-sufficient grace
Shall guide me all my happy days
In all his ways;
He calls a worm his friend:
He calls himself my God!
And he shall save me to the end,
Through Jesus' blood.

4 He by himself hath sworn:
I on his oath depend;
I shall, on eagles' wings upborne,
To heaven ascend;
I shall behold his face;
I shall his power adore,
And sing the wonders of his grace
For evermore.

OLIVERS.

3 The Lord is thy Keeper: the Lord is thy shade upon | thy right | hand:
The sun shall not smite thee by day, | nor the | moon by | night.
4 The Lord shall preserve thee from all evil: he shall pre- | serve thy | soul.
The Lord shall preserve thy going out and thy coming in from this time forth and | even · for | ever- | more.
5 Glory be to the Father, and | to the Son, | and | to the | Holy | Ghost;
6 As it was in the beginning, is now, and | ever · shall | be, || world | without | end. A- | men.

LÆTATUS SUM.

1 I WAS glad when they said | unto | me, || let us go into the | house — | of the | Lord.
2 Our feet shall stand with- | in thy | gates, || O Je- | ru- — | sa- — | lem.
3 Pray for the peace of Je- | rusa- | lem: || they shall | prosper · that | love — | thee.
4 Peace be with- | in thy | walls, || and prosperity with- | in thy | pala- | ces.
5 For my brethren and com- | panions' | sakes, || I will now say, | Peace— | be with- — | in thee.
6 Because of the house of the | Lord our | God, || I will | seek — | thy — | good.

Glory be to the Father, etc.

ALLELUIA. Double.

1 PRAISE | ye the | Lord. || Praise God in his sanctuary; praise him in the | firma-ment | of his | power.
2 Praise him for his | mighty | acts; || praise him according | to his | excel-lent | greatness.
3 Praise him with the | sound · of the | trumpet: || praise him | with the | psal-tery · and | harp.
4 Praise him with the | timbrel · and | dance: || praise him with stringed | in-stru- | ments and | organs.
5 Praise him upon the | loud — | cymbals: || praise him upon the | high- — | sounding | cymbals.
6 Let every thing that hath breath | praise the | Lord: || praise | ye — | the — | Lord.
7 Glory be to the Father, and | to the | Son, || and | to the | Holy | Ghost;
8 As it was in the beginning, is now, and | ever | shall be, || world | without | end. A- | men.

1296 C. M.

1 STERN winter throws his icy chains,
Encircling nature round;
How bleak, how comfortless the plains,
Of late with verdure crowned!

2 The sun withdraws his vital beams,
And light and warmth depart;
And drooping, lifeless nature seems
An emblem of my heart,—

3 My heart, where mental winter reigns,
In night's dark mantle clad,
Confined in cold, inactive chains;
How desolate and sad!

4 Return, O blissful sun, and bring
Thy soul-reviving ray;
This mental winter shall be spring,
This darkness cheerful day.

5 Oh, happy state, divine abode!
Where spring eternal reigns,
And perfect day, the smile of God,
Fills all the heavenly plains.

6 Great Source of light, thy beams display,
My drooping joys restore,
And guide me to the seats of day,
Where winter frowns no more.

STEELE.

1297 C. M.

1 REMARK, my soul, the narrow bound
Of each revolving year;
How swift the weeks complete their round!
How short the months appear!

2 So fast eternity comes on,
And that important day
When all that mortal life hath done
God's judgment shall survey.

3 Yet like an idle tale we pass
The swift-revolving year,
And study artful ways t' increase
The speed of its career.

4 Awake, O God, my careless heart
Its great concerns to see,
That I may act the Christian part,
And give the year to thee.

5 So shall their course more grateful roll,
If future years arise;
Or this shall bear my waiting soul
To joy beyond the skies.

DODDRIDGE.

1298 C. M.

1 THEE we adore, Eternal Name,
And humbly own to thee
How feeble is our mortal frame,
What dying worms are we.

2 The year rolls round, and steals away
The breath that first it gave;
Whate'er we do, where'er we be,
We're traveling to the grave.

3 Great God, on what a slender thread
Hang everlasting things!—
The final state of all the dead
Upon life's feeble strings!

4 Eternal joy, or endless woe,
Attends on every breath;
And yet how unconcerned we go
Upon the brink of death!

5 Awake, O Lord, our drowsy sense,
To walk this dangerous road;
And if our souls are hurried hence,
May they be found with God.

WATTS.

1299 C. M.

1 AND now, my soul, another year
Of thy short life is past;
I cannot long continue here,
And this may be my last.

2 Much of my hasty life is gone,
Nor will return again;
And swift my passing moments run,—
The few that yet remain.

3 Awake, my soul; with utmost care
Thy true condition learn:
What are thy hopes? how sure? how fair?
What is thy great concern?

4 Behold, another year begins;
Set out afresh for heaven;
Seek pardon for thy former sins,
In Christ so freely given.

5 Devoutly yield thyself to God,
And on his grace depend;
With zeal pursue the heavenly road,
Nor doubt a happy end.

1300 C. M.

1 NOW, gracious Lord, thine arm reveal,
And make thy glory known;
Now let us all thy presence feel,
And soften hearts of stone.

2 From all the guilt of former sin
May mercy set us free;
And let the year we now begin,
Begin and end with thee.

3 Send down thy Spirit from above,
That saints may love thee more,
And sinners now may learn to love,
Who never loved before.

4 And when before thee we appear,
In our eternal home,
May growing numbers worship here,
And praise thee in our room.

NEWTON.

1301 C. M.

1 GOD of our lives, thy various praise
Our voices shall resound:
Thy hand directs our fleeting days,
And brings the seasons round.

2 To thee shall grateful songs arise,
Our Father and our Friend,
Whose constant mercies from the skies,
In genial streams descend.

3 In every scene of life, thy care,
In every age, we see;
And constant as thy favors are,
So let our praises be.

4 Still may thy love, in every scene,
In every age, appear;
And let the same compassion deign
To bless the opening year.

5 If mercy smile, let mercy bring
Our wandering souls to God:
In our affliction we shall sing,
If thou wilt bless the rod.

HEGINBOTHAM.

1302 C. M.

1 THE time is short! sinners, beware,
Nor trifle time away;
The word of great salvation hear,
While it is called to-day.

2 The time is short! O sinners, now
To Christ, the Lord, submit;
To mercy's golden sceptre bow,
And fall at Jesus' feet.

3 The time is short! ye saints, rejoice—
The Lord will quickly come;
Soon shall you hear the Bridegroom's voice,
To call you to your home.

4 The time is short! the moment near,
When we shall dwell above,
And be for ever happy there,
With Jesus, whom we love. HOSKINS.

1303 8s, 6s & 11s.

1 COME, let us anew
Our journey pursue,
Roll round with the year,
And never stand still till the Master appear;
His adorable will
Let us gladly fulfill,
And our talents improve,
By the patience of hope, and the labor of love.

2 Our life is a dream;
Our time, as a stream,
Glides swiftly away,
And the fugitive moment refuses to stay;
The arrow is flown;
The moment is gone;
The millennial year
Rushes on to our view; and eternity's near.

3 Oh, that each, in the day
Of his coming, may say,
"I have fought my way through;
I have finished the work thou didst give me to do;"
Oh, that each from his Lord
May receive the glad word,
"Well and faithfully done;
Enter into my joy, and sit down on my throne." C. WESLEY.

1304 7s.

1 THOU who roll'st the year around,
Crowned with mercies large and free,
Rich thy gifts to us abound,
Warm our praise shall rise to thee.

2 Kindly to our worship bow,
While our grateful thanks we tell,
That, sustained by thee, we now
Bid the parting year—farewell!

3 All its numbered days are sped,
All its busy scenes are o'er,
All its joys forever fled,
All its sorrows felt no more.

4 Mingled with the eternal past,
Its remembrance shall decay;
Yet to be revived at last
At the solemn judgment day.

5 All our follies, Lord, forgive!
Cleanse us from each guilty stain;
Let thy grace within us live,
That we spend not years in vain.

6 Then, when life's last eve shall come,
Happy spirits, may we fly
To our everlasting home,
To our Father's house on high!

1305 7s.

1 FOR thy mercy and thy grace
Constant through another year,
Hear our song of thankfulness;
Jesus, our Redeemer, hear.

2 In our weakness and distress,
Rock of Strength, be thou our Stay,
In the pathless wilderness
Be our true and living Way.

3 Who of us death's awful road
In the coming year shall tread,
With thy rod and staff, O God,
Comfort thou his dying bed.

4 Make us faithful, make us pure,
Keep us evermore thine own,
Help thy servants to endure,
Fit us for the promised crown.

5 So within thy palace gate
We shall praise, on golden strings,
Thee the only Potentate,
Lord of lords, and King of kings.

1306 7s & 6s.

1 O SOUL, soul, thou art passing,
Just now, the border lands;
Soul, soul, thy God is calling
Thee, from the border lands.
Soul, soul, what wilt thou answer,
When thou shalt stand alone,
Before thy God and Saviour,
'Midst th' glories of the throne?

2 How hast thou passed the border?
What course pursued below?
Of all I gave thee, warder,
Hast conquered every foe?
Soul, soul, hear Jesus calling!
He waits for thee above,
Oh! answer now, responding
In faith, and hope, and love.

Henry C. Graves.

1307 7s & 6s.

1 TIME is winging us away
To our eternal home;
Life is but a winter's day,
A journey to the tomb;
Youth and vigor soon will flee,
Blooming beauty lose its charms;
All that's mortal soon shall be
Enclosed in death's cold arms.

2 Time is winging us away
To our eternal home;
Life is but a winter's day,
A journey to the tomb;
But the Christian shall enjoy
Health and beauty, soon, above,
Far beyond the world's alloy,
Secure in Jesus' love.

1308 7s & 6s.

1 AS flows the rapid river,
With channel broad and free,
Its waters rippling ever,
And hasting to the sea,
So life is onward flowing,
And days of offered peace,
And man is swiftly going
Where calls of mercy cease.

2 As moons are ever waning,
As hastes the sun away,
As stormy winds, complaining,
Bring on the wintry day,
So fast the night comes o'er us—
The darkness of the grave;
And death is just before us:
God takes the life he gave.

3. Say, hath thy heart its treasure,
Laid up in worlds above?
And is it all thy pleasure
Thy God to praise and love?
Beware, lest death's dark river
Its billows o'er thee roll,
And thou lament forever
The ruin of thy soul. S. F. SMITH.

1309 7s & 6s.

1 THE leaves, around me falling,
Are preaching of decay,
The hollow winds are calling,
"Come, pilgrim, come away!"
The day, in night declining,
Says I must, too, decline;
The year, its life resigning—
Its lot foreshadows mine.

2 The light my path surrounding,
The loves, to which I cling,
The hopes within me bounding,
The joys that round me wing—
All melt, like stars of even,
Before the morning's ray—
Pass upward unto heaven,
And chide at my delay.

3 The friends, gone there before me,
Are calling from on high;
And joyous angels o'er me,
Tempt sweetly to the sky.
"Why wait," they say, "and wither
'Mid scenes of death and sin?
Oh, rise to glory, hither,
And find true life begin."

4 I hear the invitation,
And fain would rise and come—
A sinner to salvation;
An exile to his home:
But, while I here must linger,
Thus, thus let all I see
Point on, with faithful finger,
To heaven, O Lord, and Thee.

1310 8s & 7s.

1 ONE by one the sands are flowing,
One by one the moments fall;
Some are coming, some are going;
Do not strive to grasp them all.

2 One by one thy griefs shall meet thee;
Do not fear an armèd band;
One will fade while others greet thee,
Shadows passing through the land.

3 Hours are golden links, God's token,
Reaching heaven, but one by one;
Take them lest the chain be broken,
Ere thy pilgrimage be done.

1311 8s & 7s.

1 MY times are in thy hand,
O God, I | wish them | there ;||
My life, my friends, my soul I leave
Entirely to thy | care. ||

2 My times are in thy hand,
Whatever | they may | be,
Pleasing or painful, dark or bright,
As best may | seem to | thee.

3 My times are in thy hand,
Why should I | doubt or | fear?
A Father's hand will never cause
His child a | needless | tear.

4 My times are in thy hand,
Jesus, the | cruci- | fied;
The hand my many sins have pierced
Is now my | guard and | guide.

DOXOLOGIES.

L. M.

PRAISE God, from whom all blessings flow;
Praise him, all creatures here below;
Praise him above, ye heavenly host;
Praise Father, Son, and Holy Ghost.

C. M.

LET God the Father, and the Son,
And Spirit, be adored,
Where there are works to make him known,
Or saints to love the Lord.

C. M. Double.

THE God of mercy be adored,
Who calls our souls from death,
Who saves by his redeeming word
And new-creating breath:
To praise the Father and the Son
And Spirit All-Divine,
The One in Three, and Three in One,
Let saints and angels join.

S. M.

TO God, the Father, Son,
And Spirit, glory be,
As was, and is, and shall remain
Through all eternity.

C. P. M.

TO Father, Son, and Holy Ghost,
The God whom heaven's triumphant host
And saints on earth adore;
Be glory as in ages past,
As now it is, and so shall last,
When time shall be no more.

C. L. M.

O FATHER of unbounded might,
O Son, and Holy Ghost,
Adored by all the saints in light,
And by the angel host,—
Our humble praise we bring to thee,
And will, throughout eternity.

H. M.

TO God the Father's throne
Your highest honors raise;
Glory to God the Son;
To God the Spirit, praise;
With all our powers, Eternal King,
Thy name we sing, while faith adores.

7s.

SING we to our God above
Praise eternal as his love;
Praise him, all ye heavenly host,
Father, Son, and Holy Ghost.

7s. 6 lines.

PRAISE the name of God most high,
Praise him, all below the sky,
Praise him, all ye heavenly host,
Father, Son, and Holy Ghost:
As through countless ages past,
Evermore his praise shall last.

7s. Double.

PRAISE our glorious King and Lord,
Angels waiting on his word,
Saints that walk with him in white,
Pilgrims walking in his light:
Glory to the Eternal One,
Glory to his only Son,
Glory to the Spirit be
Now, and through eternity.

8s & 7s.

PRAISE the God of our salvation,
Praise the Father's boundless love,
Praise the Lamb, our expiation,
Praise the Spirit from above.

8s & 7s. Double.

PRAISE the God of all creation;
Praise the Father's boundless love;
Praise the Lamb, our expiation,
Priest and King enthroned above:
Praise the Fountain of salvation,
Him by whom our spirits live:
Undivided adoration
To the one Jehovah give.

8s, 7s & 4s.

GLORY be to God the Father!
Glory be to God the Son!
Glory be to God the Spirit!
Great Jehovah, Three in One:
Glory, glory,
While eternal ages run.

8s, 7s & 4s.

GREAT Jehovah! we adore thee,
God the Father, God the Son,
God the Spirit, joined in glory
On the same eternal throne;
Endless praises
To Jehovah, Three in One.

7s & 6s. Iambic.

TO thee be praise forever,
Thou glorious King of kings!
Thy wondrous love and favor
Each ransomed spirit sings:
We'll celebrate thy glory
With all thy saints above,
And shout the joyful story
Of thy redeeming love.

6s & 4s.

TO God—the Father, Son,
And Spirit—Three in One,
All praise be given!
Crown him in every song;
To him your hearts belong;
Let all his praise prolong—
On earth, in heaven.

11s.

O FATHER Almighty, to thee be addrest,
With Christ and the Spirit, One God ever blest,
All glory and worship, from earth and from heaven,
As was, and is now, and shall ever be given.

CHANTS AND ANTHEMS.

GLORIA IN EXCELSIS.

1 GLORY be to | God on | high, || and on earth | peace, good- | will toward | men.

2 We praise thee, we bless thee, we | worship | thee, || we glorify thee, we give thanks to | thee for | thy great | glory,

3 O Lord God, | heavenly | King, || God the | Father | Al- | mighty.

4 O Lord, the only begotten Son, | Jesus | Christ; || O Lord God, Lamb of | God, Son | of the | Father,

5 That takest away the | sins · of the | world, || have mercy | upon | us.

6 Thou that takest away the | sins · of the | world, || have mercy | upon | us.

7 Thou that takest away the | sins · of the | world, || re- | ceive our | prayer.

8 Thou that sittest at the right hand of | God the | Father, || have mercy | upon | us.

9 For thou | only · art | holy; || thou | only | art the | Lord;

10 Thou only, O Christ, with the | Holy | Ghost, || art most high in the | glory of | God the | Father. || A- | men.

TE DEUM LAUDAMUS.

1 WE praise | thee, O | God; || we acknowledge | thee to | be the | Lord.

2 All the earth doth | worship | thee, || the | Father | ever- | lasting.

3 To thee all angels | cry a- | loud; || the Heavens, and | all the | Powers there- | in.

4 To thee Cherubim and | Sera- | phim || con- | tinual- | ly do | cry.

5 Holy, | Holy, | Holy, || Lord | God of | Saba- | oth.

6 Heaven and | earth are | full || of the | Majesty | of thy | Glory.

7 The glorious company of the Apostles | praise — | thee. || The goodly fellowship of the | Prophets | praise — | thee.

8 The noble army of Martyrs | praise — | thee. || The Holy Church throughout all the world | doth ac- | knowledge | thee;

9 The Father of an | Infi-nite | Majesty; || Thine adorable, | true, and | only | Son;

10 Also the | Holy | Ghost, || the | Com- — | — fort- | er.

11 Thou | art the | King || of | Glory, | O — | Christ,
12 Thou art the ever- | lasting | Son || of | — the | Fa- — | ther.
13 When thou tookest upon thee to de- | liver | Man, || thou didst humble thyself to be | born — | of a | Virgin.
14 When thou hadst overcome the | sharpness of | death, || thou didst open the Kingdom of | Heaven to | all be- | lievers.
15 Thou sittest at the right | hand of | God, || in the | Glory | of the | Father.
16 We believe that | thou shalt | come || to | be — | our — | Judge.
17 We therefore pray thee | help thy | servants, || whom thou hast redeemed | with thy | precious | blood.
18 Make them to be numbered | with thy | Saints, || in | glory | ever- | lasting.
19 O Lord, | save thy | people, || and | bless — | — thine | heritage.
20 Gov- | — ern | them, || and | lift them | up for | ever.
21 Day | — by | day || we | magni- | fy — | thee.
22 And we | worship thy | Name, || ever | world — | without | end.
23 Vouch- | safe, O | Lord, || to keep us | this day | without | sin.
24 O Lord, have | mercy up- | on us, || have | mercy | upon | us.
25 O Lord, let thy mercy | be up- | on us, || as our | trust — | is in | thee.
26 O Lord, in thee | have I | trusted, || let me | never | be con- | founded.

TE DEUM LAUDAMUS.

1 WE praise thee, O God; we acknowledge thee to | be the | Lord. || All the earth doth worship thee, the | Father | ever- | lasting.
2 To thee all Angels | cry a- | loud; || the Heavens, and | all the | Powers there- | in.
3 To thee Cherubim and | Sera- | phim || con- | tinual- | ly do | cry.
4 Holy, Holy, Holy, Lord God of | Saba- | oth. || Heaven and earth are full of the Majesty | of thy | Glo- — | ry.
5 The glorious company of the Apostles | praise — | thee.
6 The goodly fellowship of the Prophets | praise — | thee.
7 The noble army of Martyrs | praise — | thee.
8 The Holy Church throughout all the world | doth acknowledge | thee; || The Father of an | infinite | Majes- | ty; || thine adorable, true, and | only | Son; || also the Holy | Ghost, the | Comfort- | er.
9 Thou art the King of Glory, | O — | Christ. || Thou art the everlasting Son | of the | Fa- — | ther.
10 When thou tookest upon thee to de- | liver | Man, || thou didst humble thyself to be born | of a | Vir- — | gin.

11 When thou hadst overcome the | sharpness of | death, || thou didst open the Kingdom of Heaven to | all be- | liev- — | ers.
12 Thou sittest at the right | hand of | God, || in the glory | of the | Fa- — | ther.
13 We believe that thou shalt come to | be our | Judge. || We therefore pray thee help thy servants, whom thou hast redeemed | with thy | precious | blood.
14 Make them to be numbered | with thy | saints, || in | glory | ever- | lasting.
15 O Lord, save thy people, and bless thine | heri- | tage. || Govern them, and lift them | up for | ev- — | er.
16 Day by day we | magnify | thee. || And we worship thy name | ever, | world without | end.
17 Vouchsafe, O Lord, to keep us this day, with- | out — | sin. || O Lord, have mercy upon us, have | mercy up- | on — | us.
18 O Lord, let thy mercy be upon us, as our trust is | in — | thee. || O Lord, in thee have I trusted, let me | never | be con- | founded.

GLORIA IN EXCELSIS.

1 GLORY be to | God on | high, || and on earth | peace, good | will · towards | men.
2 We praise thee, we bless thee, we | worship | thee, || we glorify thee, we give thanks to | thee for | thy great | glory.
3 O Lord God, | heav'nly | King, || God the | Father | Al- | mighty.
4 O Lord, the only-begotten Son | Jesus | Christ; || O Lord God, Lamb of | God, Son | of the | Father,
5 That takest away the | sins · of the | world, || have | mercy | upon | us.
6 Thou that takest away the | sins · of the | world, || have | mercy | upon | us.
7 Thou that takest away the | sins · of the | world, || re- | ceive — | our — | prayer.
8 Thou that sittest at the right hand of | God the | Father, || have | mercy | upon | us.
9 For thou | only · art | holy, || Thou | only | art the | Lord.
10 Thou only, O Christ, with the | Holy | Ghost, || art most high in the | glory · of | God the | Father. || A- | men.

CANTATE DOMINO.

1 O SING unto the | Lord a new | song; || for he hath | done — | marvel-lous | things.
2 With his own right hand, and with his | holy | arm, || hath he | gotten · him- | self the | victory.

3 The Lord declared | his sal- | vation, ‖ his righteousness hath he openly | showed in the | sight of the | heathen.
4 He hath remembered his mercy and truth toward the | house of | Israel; ‖ and all the ends of the world have seen the sal- | vation | of our | God.
5 Show yourselves joyful unto the Lord | all ye | lands; ‖ sing, re- | joice, — | and give | thanks.
6 Praise the Lord up- | on the | harp; ‖ sing to the harp with a | psalm — | of thanks- | giving.
7 With trumpets | also and | shawms, ‖ O show yourselves joyful be- | fore the | Lord the | King.
8 Let the sea make a noise, and all that | therein | is, ‖ the round world, and | they that | dwell there- | in.
9 Let the floods clap their hands, and let the hills be joyful together be- | fore the | Lord; ‖ for he | cometh · to | judge the | earth.
10 With righteousness shall he | judge the | world, ‖ and the | people | with equi- | ty.
11 Glory be to the Father, and | to the | Son, ‖ and | to the | Holy | Ghost.
12 As it was in the beginning, is now, and | ever · shall | be, ‖ world | without | end. A- | men.

BONUM EST CONFITERI.

1 IT is a good thing to give thanks un- | to the | Lord, ‖ and to sing praises unto thy | name, — | O Most | Highest;
2 To tell of thy loving-kindness early | in the | morning, ‖ and of thy truth | in the | night — | season;
3 Upon an instrument of ten strings, and up- | on the | lute; ‖ upon a loud instrument, | and up- | on the | harp.
4 For thou, Lord, hast made me glad | through thy | works; ‖ and I will rejoice in giving praise for the ope- | rations | of thy | hands.
5 Glory be to the Father, and | to the | Son, | and | to the | Holy | Ghost;
6 As it was in the beginning, is now, and | ever · shall | be, ‖ world | without | end. A- | men.

DEUS MISEREATUR.

1 GOD be merciful unto | us, and | bless us, ‖ and show us the light of his countenance, and be | merciful | unto | us.
2 That thy way may be | known upon | earth, ‖ thy saving | health a- | mong all | nations.

3 Let the people | praise thee, O | God; || yea, let all the | people | praise — | thee.
4 Oh let the nations re- | joice and be | glad; || for thou shalt·judge the folk righteously, and govern the | nations | upon | earth.
5 Let the people | praise thee, O | God; || yea, let all the | people | praise — | thee.
6 Then shall the earth bring | forth her | increase; || and God, even our own | God, shall | give · us his | blessing.
7 God | shall — | bless us; || and all the ends of the | world shall | fear — | him.
8 Glory be to the Father, and | to the | Son, || and | to the | Holy | Ghost;
9 As it was in the beginning, is now, and | ever · shall | be, || world | without | end. A- | men.

BENEDIC, ANIMA MEA.

1 PRAISE the Lord, | O my | soul; || and all that is within me | praise his | holy | name.
2 Praise the Lord, | O my | soul, || and forget not | all his | bene- | fits;
3 Who forgiveth | all thy | sin, || and healeth | all · thine in- | firmi- | ties.
4 Who saveth thy life | from de- | struction, || and crowneth thee with | mercy · and | loving- | kindness.
5 Oh praise the Lord, ye Angels of his, ye that ex- | cel in | strength, || ye that fulfil his commandment, and hearken un- | to the | voice · of his | word.
6 O praise the Lord, all | ye his | hosts; || ye servants of | his that | do his | pleasure.
7 O speak good of the Lord, all ye works of his, in all places of | his do- | minion. || Praise thou the | Lord, — | O my | soul.
8 Glory be to the Father, and | to the | Son, || and | to the | Holy | Ghost;
9 As it was in the beginning, is now, and | ever · shall | be, || world | without | end. A- | men.

LEVAVI OCULUS.

1 I WILL lift up mine eyes unto the hills, from whence | cometh · my | help. My help cometh from the Lord, | which made | heaven · and | earth.
2 He will not suffer thy foot to be moved: he that keepeth thee | will not | slumber.
Behold, he that keepeth Israel shall | neither | slumber · nor | sleep.

3 The Lord is thy Keeper: the Lord is thy shade upon | thy right | hand:
The sun shall not smite thee by day, | nor the | moon by | night.
4 The Lord shall preserve thee from all evil: he shall pre- | serve thy | soul.
The Lord shall preserve thy going out and thy coming in from this time forth and | even · for | ever- | more.
5 Glory be to the Father, and | to the Son, | and | to the | Holy | Ghost;
6 As it was in the beginning, is now, and | ever · shall | be, ‖ world | without | end. A- | men.

LÆTATUS SUM.

1 I WAS glad when they said | unto | me, ‖ let us go into the | house — | of the | Lord.
2 Our feet shall stand with- | in thy | gates, ‖ O Je- | ru- — | sa- — | lem.
3 Pray for the peace of Je- | rusa- | lem: ‖ they shall | prosper · that | love — | thee.
4 Peace be with- | in thy | walls, ‖ and prosperity with- | in thy | pala- | ces.
5 For my brethren and com- | panions' | sakes, ‖ I will now say, | Peace— | be with- — | in thee.
6 Because of the house of the | Lord our | God, ‖ I will | seek — | thy — | good.

Glory be to the Father, etc.

ALLELUIA. Double.

1 PRAISE | ye the | Lord. ‖ Praise God in his sanctuary; praise him in the | firma-ment | of his | power.
2 Praise him for his | mighty | acts; ‖ praise him according | to his | excel-lent | greatness.
3 Praise him with the | sound · of the | trumpet: ‖ praise him | with the | psal-tery · and | harp.
4 Praise him with the | timbrel · and | dance: ‖ praise him with stringed | in-stru- | ments and | organs.
5 Praise him upon the | loud — | cymbals: ‖ praise him upon the | high- — | sounding | cymbals.
6 Let every thing that hath breath | praise the | Lord: ‖ praise | ye — | the — | Lord.
7 Glory be to the Father, and | to the | Son, ‖ and | to the | Holy | Ghost;
8 As it was in the beginning, is now, and | ever | shall be, ‖ world | without | end. A- | men.

BENEDICITE, OMNIA OPERA DOMINI.

1 O ALL ye Works of the Lord, | bless · ye the | Lord, || praise him, and | magnify | him for | ever.
2 O ye Angels of the Lord, | bless · ye the | Lord, || praise him, and | magnify | him for | ever.
3 O ye Heavens, | bless · ye the | Lord, || praise him, and | magnify | him for | ever.
4 O ye Waters that be above the Firmament, | bless · ye the | Lord, || praise him, and | magnify | him for | ever.
5 O all ye Powers of the Lord, | bless · ye the | Lord, || praise him, and | magnify | him for | ever.
6 O ye Sun and Moon, | bless · ye the | Lord, || praise him, and | magnify | him for | ever.
7 O ye Stars of Heaven, | bless · ye the | Lord, || praise him, and | magnify | him for | ever.
8 O ye Showers and Dew, | bless · ye the | Lord, || praise him, and | magnify | him for | ever.
9 O ye Winds of God, | bless · ye the | Lord, || praise him, and | magnify | him for | ever.
10 O ye Fire and Heat | bless · ye the | Lord, || praise him, and | magnify | him for | ever.
11 O ye Winter and Summer, | bless · ye the | Lord, || praise him, and | magnify | him for | ever.
12 O ye Dews and Frosts, | bless · ye the | Lord, || praise him, and | magnify | him for | ever.
13 O ye Frost and Cold, | bless . ye the | Lord, || praise him, and | magnify | him for | ever.
14 O ye Ice and Snow, | bless · ye the | Lord, || praise him, and | magnify | him for | ever.
15 O ye Nights and Days, | bless · ye the | Lord, || praise him, and | magnify | him for | ever.
16 O ye Light and Darkness, | bless · ye the | Lord, || praise him, and | magnify | him for | ever.
17 O ye Lightnings and Clouds, | bless · ye the | Lord, || praise him, and | magnify | him for | ever.
18 O let the Earth | bless · the | Lord, || praise him, and | magnify | him for | ever.
19 O ye Mountains and Hills, | bless . ye the | Lord, || praise him, and | magnify | him for | ever.

20 O all ye Green Things upon the Earth, | bless · ye the | Lord, || praise him, and | magnify | him for | ever.
21 O ye Wells, | bless · ye the | Lord, || praise him, and | magnify | him for | ever.
22 O ye Seas and Floods, | bless · ye the | Lord, || praise him, and | magnify | him for | ever.
23 O ye Whales, and all that move in the Waters, | bless · ye the | Lord, || praise him, and | magnify | him for | ever.
24 O all ye Fowls of the Air, | bless · ye the | Lord, || praise him, and | magnify | him for | ever.
25 O all ye Beasts and Cattle, | bless · ye the | Lord, || praise him, and | magnify | him for | ever.
26 O ye Children of Men, | bless · ye the | Lord, || praise him, and | magnify | him for | ever.
27 O let Israel, | bless · the | Lord, || praise him, and | magnify | him for | ever.
28 O ye Priests of the Lord, | bless · ye the | Lord, || praise him, and | magnify | him for | ever.
29 O ye Servants of the Lord, | bless · ye the | Lord, || praise him, and | magnify | him for | ever.
30 O ye Spirits and Souls of the Righteous, || bless · ye the | Lord, || praise him, and | magnify | him for | ever.
31 O ye Holy and humble Men of heart, | bless · ye the | Lord, || praise him, and | magnify | him for | ever.
32 Glory be to the Father, and | to the | Son, || and | to the | Holy | Ghost;
33 As it was in the beginning, is now, and | ever · shall | be, || world | without | end. A- | men.

JUBILATE DEO.

1 O BE joyful in the Lord, | all ye | lands; || serve the Lord with gladness, and come before his | presence | with a | song.
2 Be ye sure that the Lord | he is | God: || it is he that hath made us, and not we ourselves; we are his | people, · and the | sheep · of his | pasture.
3 O go your way into his gates with thanksgiving, and into his | courts with | praise; || be thankful unto him, and | speak good | of his | name. ||
4 For the Lord is gracious, his mercy is | ever- | lasting; || and his truth endureth from gene- | ration · to | gene- | ration.
5 Glory be to the Father, and | to the | Son; || and | to the | Holy | Ghost;
6 As it was in the beginning, is now, and | ever · shall | be, || world | without | end. A- | men.

STABAT MATER.

1 JEWS were wrought to cruel madness,
Christians fled with fear and sadness,
Mary stood the cross beside;
At its foot her foot she planted,
By the dreadful scene undaunted,
Till the gentle sufferer died.

2 Poets oft have sung her story,
Painters decked her brow with glory,
Priests her name have deified;
But no worship, song, or glory,
Touches like the simple story,
"Mary stood the cross beside!"

3 So when under fierce oppression,
Goodness suffers like transgression,
Christ again is crucified:
But if love be there true-hearted,—
By no grief or terror parted,—
We may stand the cross beside.

SOLID ROCK. L. M. 6 lines.

1 MY hope is built on nothing less
Than Jesus' blood and righteousness;
I dare not trust the sweetest frame,
But wholly lean on Jesus' name.
On Christ, the solid rock, I stand;
All other ground is sinking sand.

2 When darkness seems to vail his face,
I rest on his unchanging grace;
In every high and stormy gale,
My anchor holds within the vail:
On Christ, the solid rock, I stand;
All other ground is sinking sand.

3 His oath, his covenant, and blood,
Support me in the whelming flood:
When all around my soul gives way,
He then is all my hope and stay:
On Christ, the solid rock, I stand;
All other ground is sinking sand.

THE BEATITUDES.

AND he opened his mouth and taught them, saying, Blessed are the | poor in | spirit, || For | theirs · is the | kingdom of | heaven.

2 Blessed are | they that | mourn, || For | they · shall be | com- — | forted.

3 Blessed | are the | meek : || For | they · shall in- | herit · the | earth.

4 Blessed are they which do hunger and | thirst · after | righteousness : ‖ For | they shall | be — | filled.

5 Blessed | are the | merciful ; ‖ For | they · shall ob- | tain — | mercy.

6 Blessed are the | pure in | heart : ‖ For | they shall | see — | God.

7 Blessed are they which are persecuted for | righteousness' | sake : ‖ For | theirs · is the | kingdom · of | heaven.

8 Blessed are ye when men shall revile you, and persecute you, and shall say all manner of evil against you falsely, | for my | sake. ‖ Rejoice, rejoice, and be exceeding glad, ‖ for great is your reward in heaven.

CHRISTUS VICTOR.

1 PRAISE him, praise the conqu'ring King!
Christ our Lord is Lord of all;
Nations! joyful tribute bring;
Princes! low before him fall.
See unfurled his royal banner!
On he cometh to subdue;
Earth's long wail becomes—Hosanna!
Lo! he maketh all things new;
Hallelujah!
Reign, O Christ, thou just and true.

2 Praise him! Praise the Prince of Peace!
Angels! wake your strain again;
Chant his triumphs, ne'er to cease
Till our God shall dwell with men.
Christ hath heard the ages sighing;
Christ hath pitied mortal grief;
At his coming tears are drying,
Millions hail the glad relief;
Hallelujah!
Hell! thy reign shall now be brief.

3 Praise him! Praise the Lord of Life!
Him that liveth and was dead!
Past the Cross and dying strife,
Vanquished Death he captive led,
Ever-living! Life-bestowing!
In thee all the holy live;
Fount exhaustless, overflowing!
Health and gladness thou dost give;
Hallelujah!
Earth and heaven from thee receive.

4 Praise him! Praise the Lamb enthroned!
Radiant at his Father's side;
Him who by his blood atoned;
Him who names the church his Bride!
Thou, O Lamb of God, forever,
Where eternal noontide glows,
Thine own flock wilt feed, and never
Cease to guard their sweet repose;
Hallelujah!
Thou hast crushed their mighty foes!

5 Praise him! Praise Incarnate Love!
Ranks seraphic, legions bright,
Souls redeemed, who fixed above,
Glow in his eternal light;
All on earth who upward gazing,
See his beauty and adore,
One far-sounding chorus raising,
Speak that Name forevermore;
Hallelujah!
Crown him! Once the Cross he bore!

RAY PALMER.

NO TIME TO PRAY.

1 NO time to pray!
Oh, who so fraught with earthly care,
As not to give to humble prayer
Some part of day?

2 No time to pray!
What heart so clean, so pure within,
That needeth not some check from sin—
Needs not to pray?

3 No time to pray!
'Mid each day's dangers, what retreat
More needful than the mercy-seat?
Who must not pray?

4 No time to pray!
Must care or business urgent call,
So press us as to take it all,
Each passing day?

5 No time to pray!
Then sure your record falleth short;
Excuse will fail you as resort
On reckoning day.

6 What thought more drear,
Than that our God his face should hide,
And say through all life's swelling tide,
No time to hear!

7 Cease not to pray;
On Jesus as your all rely.
Would you live happy—happy die?
Take time to pray.

CONSIDER THE LILIES.

1 CONSIDER, consider The | lilies of the field, whose | bloom is | brief,
We are as they, Like them we | fade a- | way, As | doth a | leaf.

2 Consider, consider The | sparrows of the air, of | small ac- | count,
Our God doth view, Whether they | fall or | mount, He | guards us | too.

3 Consider, consider The | lilies that do neither | spin nor | toil,
Yet are most fair; What profits | all this | care, And | all this | toil?

4 Consider, consider The | birds that have no barn, nor | harvest | weeks,
God gives them food; Much more our | Father | seeks To | do us | good.

HOW PLEASANT, HOW DIVINELY FAIR.

1 HOW pleasant, how di- | vinely | fair, ‖
O Lord of | hosts, thy | dwellings | are;
With long desire my | spirit | faints ‖
To meet th' as- | semblies | of thy | saints.

2 My flesh would rest in | thine a- | bode;
My panting | heart cries | out for | God;
My God, my King, why | should I | be
So far from | all my | joys and | thee.

3 Blest are the saints who | sit on | high,
Around thy | throne a- | bove the | sky;
Thy brightest glories | shine a- | bove,
And all their | work is | praise and | love.

4 Blest are the souls who | find a | place
Within the | temple | of thy | grace;
There they behold thy | gentler | rays,
And seek thy | face, and | learn thy | praise.

OUR HABITATION.

1 LORD, thou hast been our dwelling-place, in | all · gene- | rations.

2 Before the mountains were brought forth, or ever thou hadst formed the earth and the world, even from everlasting to ever- | lasting, | thou art | God.

3 Thou turnest man to destruction; and sayest, Return, ye | children of | men.

4 For a thousand years in thy sight are but as yesterday when it is past, and | as a | watch · in the | night.

5 Thou carriest them away as with a flood; they are as a sleep; in the morning they are like grass which | groweth | up.

6 In the morning it flourisheth, and groweth up; in the evening it is cut | down, *cut* | *down,* and | withereth.

7 Who knoweth the power of thine anger? Even according to thy fear; | so is thy | wrath.

8 So teach us to number our days, that we may ap- | ply our | hearts · unto | wisdom.

RESPONSE TO THE COMMANDMENTS. No. 1.

LORD, have mercy upon us, and write all these thy laws in our hearts, we beseech thee.

No. 2.

1 THE law of the Lord is perfect, con- | verting · the | soul ;
The testimony of the Lord is sure, making | wise the | simple.

2 The statutes of the Lord are right, re- | joicing · the | heart :
The commandment of the Lord is pure, en- | lightening · the | eyes.

3 The fear of the Lord is clean, en- | during · for- | ever:
The judgments of the Lord are true and righteous | alto- | gether.

4 More to be desired are they than gold, yea, than | much fine | gold:
Sweeter also than honey and the | honey- | comb.

5 Moreover by them is thy | servant | warned :
And in keeping of them there is | great re- | ward.

No. 3.

LORD, have | mercy up- | on us,
And write all these thy laws in our hearts, we be- | seech — | thee.

THE DYING CHRISTIAN.

1 VITAL spark of heavenly flame,
Quit, O quit this mortal frame ;
Trembling, hoping, lingering, flying,
O, the pain, the bliss of dying !
Cease, fond nature, cease thy strife,
And let me languish into life.

2 Hark, they whisper, angels say,
Sister spirit, come away !
What is this absorbs me quite?
Steals my senses, shuts my sight,
Drowns my spirit, draws my breath ?
Tell me, my soul, can this be death ?

3 The world recedes, it disappears :
Heaven opens on my eyes ; my ears
With sounds seraphic ring:
Lend, lend your wings ; I mount, I fly:
O grave, where is thy victory,
O death, where is thy sting?

OLD EASTER ANTHEM.

THE Lord is risen indeed, Hallelujah!
Now is Christ risen from the dead, and become the first-fruits of them that slept, Hallelujah!
And did he rise? Hear, O ye nations; hear it, O ye dead!
He rose! he burst the bars of death, and triumphed o'er the grave!
Then, then, I rose! then first humanity, triumphant, passed the crystal ports of light, and seized eternal youth,
Man, all immortal, hail!
Heaven, all lavish of strange gifts to man, thine all the glory, man's the boundless bliss.

STRIKE THE CYMBAL.

1 STRIKE the cymbal,
Roll the tymbal,
Let the trump of triumph sound.
Powerful slinging,
Headlong bringing
Proud Goliath to the ground.

2 From the river,
Rejecting quiver,
Judah's hero takes the stone.
Spread your banners!
Shout hosannas!
Battle is the Lord's alone.

3 See advances,
With songs and dances,
All the band of Israel's daughters;
Catch the sound, ye hills and waters.
Spread your banners!
Shout hosannas!
Battle is the Lord's alone.

4 God of thunder,
Rend asunder
All the power Philistia boasts.
What are nations?
What their stations?
Israel's God is Lord of hosts.

5 What are haughty monarchs now?
Low before Jehovah bow.
Pride of princes, strength of kings,
To the dust Jehovah brings:
Praise him, praise him, exulting nations, praise.
Hosanna! Hosanna! Hosanna!

CHIME ON.

1 WE leave the world of care,
To greet one day in seven;
To join in praise and prayer,
And learn the way to heaven.
The Sabbath bells invite us all,—
Faint emblem of God's holy call.
Chime on, sweet bells, your cheerful ring
Shall tune our lips God's praise to sing.

2 We leave our books and play,
To read that "Book Divine;"
There we are taught the way
To joys that ne'er decline;
The music of those Sabbath bells,
How sweetly on the ear it swells!
Chime on, loved bells, your welcome ring
Shall tune our hearts God's praise to sing.

3 We leave our earthly home,
To seek that blest abode,
Where loved companions come
To lift their hearts to God;
List to the joyous sound that tells
The music of those Sabbath bells;
Chime on, sweet bells, long may your ring
Inspire our hearts God's praise to sing.

GENNESARET. 11s.

1 SEE, daylight is fading o'er earth and o'er ocean,
The sun has gone down on the far-distant sea;
Oh, now, in the hush of the fitful commotion,
We lift our tired spirits, blest Saviour, to thee.

2 Full oft wast thou found afar on the mountain,
As eventide spread her dark wing o'er the wave:
The Son of the Highest, and life's endless fountain,
Be with us, we pray thee, to bless and to save.

3 And oft as the tumult of life's heaving billow
Shall toss our frail bark, driving wild o'er night's deep,
Let thy healing wing be stretched over our pillow,
And guard us from evil, though death watch our sleep.

4 To God our great Father, whose throne is in heaven,
Who dwells with the lowly and humble in heart,
To the Son and the Spirit all glory be given;
One God, ever blessèd and praisèd, thou art. HEBER.

---

1 THOU sweet gliding Kedron, by thy silver streams,
Our Saviour, at midnight, when moonlight's pale beams
Shone bright on thy waters, would frequently stray,
And lose, in thy murmurs, the toils of the day.

2 How damp were the vapors that fell on his head!
How hard was his pillow, how humble his bed!
The angels, astonished, grew sad at the sight,
And followed their Master with solemn delight.

3 O garden of Olivet, thou dear honored spot,
The fame of thy wonders shall ne'er be forgot;
The theme most transporting to seraphs above;
The triumph of sorrow,—the triumph of love!

4 Come, saints, and adore him: come, bow at his feet;
Oh, give him the glory, the praise that is meet;
Let joyful hosannas unceasing arise,
And join the full chorus that gladdens the skies. MARIE DE FLEURY.

WHY THUS REPINING?

1 WHY thus repining, sad heart of mine?
Ever entwining round things of time;
Cease thy complaining, 'tis all in love,
Thou need'st refining for joys above;
Rise above sorrow, welcome the cross,
Pleasures we borrow may cloy like dross.

2 Murmur no longer, sad heart of mine,
Ever grow stronger thro' powers divine;
Earth is thy dwelling but for a time,
Heaven's tones are swelling—hark! to their chime.
Turn, then, thou weary one, to thy bright home;
Yearning till life be done, for joys to come.

BAPTISMAL RESPONSES.

MINISTER.—Then cometh Jesus from Galilee to Jordan unto John, to be baptized of him.

1. CHOIR.—But John forbade him, saying, I have need to be baptized of thee, and comest | thou to | me?

MINISTER.—And Jesus answering said unto him, Suffer it to be so now: for thus it becometh us to fulfill all righteousness.

2. CHOIR.—And Jesus, when he was baptized, went up straightway out of the water; and, lo, the heavens were opened unto him, and he saw the Spirit of God descending like a | dove, and | lighting · up- | on him.

MINISTER.—And lo, a voice from heaven, saying, This is my beloved Son, in whom I am well pleased.

1. CHOIR.—Ye are my friends if ye do whatso- | ever · I com- | mand you.

MINISTER.—Go ye therefore, and teach all nations, baptizing them in the name of the Father, and of the Son, and of the Holy Ghost.

2. CHOIR.—Teaching them to observe all things whatsoever I have commanded you, and lo, I am with you alway, even unto the | end · of the | world. A- | men.

MINISTER.—Know ye not, that so many of us as were baptized into Jesus Christ were baptized into his death?

2. CHOIR.—Therefore we are buried with him by baptism into death, that like as Christ was raised up from the dead by the glory of the Father, even so we also should | walk in | newness of | life.

MINISTER.—For if we have been planted together in the likeness of his death, we shall be also *in the likeness* of *his* resurrection.

1. CHOIR.—Buried with him in baptism, whence also ye are risen with him through the faith of the operation of God, who hath | raised him · from the | dead.

MINISTER.—If ye then be risen with Christ, seek those things which are above, where Christ sitteth on the right hand of God. Set your affections on things above, not on things on the earth.

2. CHOIR.—For ye are dead, and your life is hid with Christ in God. When Christ who is our life shall appear, then shall ye also ap- | pear with | him in | glory.

MINISTER.—Whosoever therefore shall break one of these least commandments, and shall teach men so, he shall be called the least in the kingdom of heaven: but whosoever shall do and teach them, the same shall be called great in the kingdom of heaven.

SENTENCE.

CHOIR.—Lord, have mercy up- | on — | us, ‖ and write all these thy laws in our | hearts, — | we be- | seech thee.

GLORIA PATRI.

CHOIR.—Glory be to the Father, and to the Son, and to the | Holy | Ghost; ‖ As it was in the beginning, is now, and ever shall be, world without | end. A- | men! A- | men!

WILT THOU NOT VISIT ME?

1 WILT thou not visit me?
The plant beside me feels thy | gentle | dew;
Each blade of grace I see,
From thy deep earth its quickening | moisture | drew,
Wilt thou not visit me?

2 Wilt thou not visit me?
Thy morning calls on me with | cheering | tone;
And every hill and tree
Lend but one voice, the voice of | thee a- | lone.
Wilt thou not visit me?

3 Come, for I need thy love,
More than the flow'r the dew, or | grass the | rain:
Come like thy holy dove,
And let me in thy sight rejoice to | live a- | gain.
Wilt thou not visit me?

4 Yes! thou wilt visit me!
Nor plant, nor tree, thine eye de- | lights so | well,
As when from sin set free,
Man's spirit comes with thine in | peace to | dwell,
Yes, thou wilt visit me.

JONES VERY.

PAULINA. 11s.

1 O EYES that are weary, and hearts that are sore!
Look off unto Jesus, now sorrow no more!
The light of his countenance shineth so bright,
That here as in heaven there need be no night.

2 While looking to Jesus, my heart cannot fear;
I tremble no more when I see Jesus near;
I know that his presence my safeguard will be,
For, "Why are ye troubled?" he saith unto me.

3 Still looking to Jesus, O may I be found,
When Jordan's dark waters encompass me round:
They bear me away in his presence to be,
I see him still nearer whom always I see.

4 Then, then shall I know the full beauty and grace
Of Jesus, my Lord, when I stand face to face;
Shall know how his love went before me each day,
And wonder that ever my eyes turned away.

HALLELUJAH CHORUS.

HALLELUJAH! Hallelujah!
For the Lord God Omnipotent reigneth!
Hallelujah! Hallelujah!
The kingdom of this world is become the kingdom of our Lord, and of his Christ,

And he shall reign forever and ever, King of kings and Lord of lords.
Hallelujah! Hallelujah!
Hallelujah! Hallelujah! King of kings, and Lord of lords!
And he shall reign forever and ever, King of kings, and Lord of lords!
Hallelujah! Hallelujah!

OH, THERE WILL BE MOURNING.

OH, there will be mourning, mourning, mourning, mourning,
Oh, there will be mourning at the Judgment-seat of Christ.
Parents and children there will part, parents and children there will part,
Parents and children there will part, will part to meet no more.

BURIED WITH CHRIST.

1 BURIED with Christ by | baptism · unto | death,—
We rise in the | likeness of his | resur- | rection.

2 If ye then be | risen with | Christ,
Seek those things which are above, where Christ sitteth at the | right — | hand of | God.

3 For as many as have been baptized into Christ, have | put on | Christ.
Therefore glorify God in your body, and in your | spirit, | which are | God's.

4 Reckon ye yourselves to be dead in- | deed · unto | sin,—
But alive unto God through | Jesus | Christ our | Lord.

5 If we be dead with him, we shall also | live with | him;
If we suffer with him, we shall | also | reign with | him.

6 Blessèd is he whose transgression is forgiven, whose | sin is | covered.
Blessèd is the man to whom the Lord im- | puteth | not in- | iquity.

INDEX OF SUBJECTS.

The figures refer to the numbers of the Hymns.

A.

ABBA FATHER, 209, 427, 808.
Abiding, Christ, with believers, 89, 159, 939, 1021, 1024.
Accepted time, 599, 601, 602.
Activity, 863, 877, 901, 913, 914, 915, 921, 922, 923. 924, 925, 926, 927, 929, 931-934, 954, 957, 959, 961, 965. See also *Benevolence.*
Adoption, 675, 808, 878.
Afflictions and Encouragements, 980-1036, 1040. See also *Conflict* and *Triumph.*
Age of Gold, 287.
All in All, 377, 378, 441, 890.
All is yours, 1007.
All working for good, 1010.
Angels, 271, 285, 321, 365, 367, 453, 1038.
Ashamed of Jesus, 709, 710, 712, 716, 722.
Asleep in Jesus, 1100.
Aspiration, 1037, 1059.
Assurance, 427, 458, 527, 808, 967.
Atonement, 850-900. See *Christ's Sufferings and Death.*
Autumn, 155. See *Year.*

B.

BACKSLIDING, 507, 508, 509, 666. See also *Revival.*
Baptism, 729-764.
Bartimeus, 725.
Beauties of Christ, 714.
Benevolence, 904-934, 1247-1253.
Bible, 334, 1149-1162.
Bridegroom's Voice, 643.
Broken heart, 646, 647.
Brotherly Love, 37, 317. See *Fellowship.*
Burden cast on God, 854, 976, 1018. See *Afflictions.*
Burial—See *Death* and *Heaven.*
A Brother, 1139.
A Child, 1094, 1107, 1108, 1122, 1123, 1127, 1143, 1148.
A Sister, 1141.
A Pastor, 1135, 1138.
A Youth, 1106.

C.

CALMNESS, 918, 919, 987, 997. See *Afflictions.*
Calvary, 324, 326, 355, 357, 358, 570, 812.
Cares cast on God, 976. See *Burdens.*
Cheerfulness, 1004, 1006. See *Joy.*
Children, 10, 295, 303, 305, 306, 307, 490, 491, 518-520, 1028.
Child-Spirit, 303, 427.
Christ:—
Advent at Birth, 269-300, 464.
Advocate and Mediator, 427, 443, 460, 473, 590, 616, 664, 856.
All and in All, 378, 441, 890.
Ark, 590, 616, 695.
Captain, 429.
Childhood, 301-307.
Compassion—See *Pity.*
Conqueror—See *King.*
Crowned—See *King.*
Corner-stone, 1180, 1186.
Crucifixion. See *Christ's Sufferings and Death.* Also *Lord's Supper.*
Day Star, 292, 298.
Desire of Nations, 271, 272, 273, 408.
Divinity, 273, 410, 420, 421.
Ebenezer, 849, 1259.
Example, 304, 314, 315, 317, 335, 342, 343, 345, 368.
Friend, 422, 861, 862, 984.
Hiding-place, 675, 685, 713, 894.
Humanity, 312, 983, 984, 1005. See *Advent and Life of Christ.*
Knocking at Heart, 641.
King, 359, 363, 365, 411, 412, 415, 424, 438, 439, 440, 441, 445.
Lamb, 414, 416, 431, 432, 453, 479, 978.
Life, Incidents of, 309-324.
Lion of Judah, 712.
Love of, 304, 340, 341, 343, 351, 409, 467, 700, 850-900.
Loveliness of, 419, 425, 462, 463, 465, 468, 470, 471, 489.
Loving-kindness, 850.
Morning Star, 280.
Ocean, 410.
Pilot, 987, 1013.
Praise to, 409-492.
Priest, 429, 475, 460.
Prince of Peace, 274, 284, 289, 439.
Physician, 890, 853, 854.
Prophet, 429, 475.
Ransom, 425, 673.
Refuge, 713, 894.
Christ:—
Resurrection and Glory, 9, 360-395.
Rock, 156, 160, 436, 692, 888.
Shepherd, 6, 144, 217, 218, 226, 237, 480, 690, 723, 852, 885, 1016.
Second Coming, 394-408.
Sufferings and Death, 326-359. See *Lord's Supper.*
Transfiguration, 322.
Way, Truth, and Life, 319, 708.
Wisdom, 896.
Wonderful, 300.
Word, 290.
Christians:—
Afflictions and Conflicts, 153, 154, 223, 224, 225, 980-1040.
Duties, 903-937.
Encouragements, 153, 857. See *Afflictions.*
Fellowship, 765-782.
Graces, 903-937.
Security, 141, 145, 147, 152, 153, 159, 204.
Church:—
Beloved of Saints, 13, 45. See *Worship.*
Depression and Success, 815-848.
Missions and Progress of. See *Missions.*
Recognition of, 817.
Communion of Christians:—
With each other—See *Fellowship.*
Communion of Saints—See *Fellowship.*
Completeness in Christ, 426, 879.
Conflict with Sin—See *Fight.*
Conformity to Christ and Consecration, 254-287, 903-937.
Consecration, 644-748, 755, 858.
Consolations—See *Afflictions.*
Corner-stone, laying of, 1180, 1186. See *Dedication.*
Courage, 870.
Creation—See *God's Works of Creation.*
Cross of Christ, Efficacy and Glorying in, 320, 329, 337, 340, 343, 349, 356, 357, 371, 418, 442, 486, 487, 665, 889.
Cross-bearing—See *Self-denial.*

D.

DEACONS, 1179.
Death, 1100-1148. See *Burial.*

Debt of love, 859, 860.
Dedication of Sanctuary, 824, 845, 847, 1180-1190.
Delay, 610, 629, 634.
Delight in Christ, 851, 852.
Denying Christ, 899.
Depravity—See *Invitations and Warnings*, and *Penitence*.
Despondency—See *Conflict* and *Encouragement*.
Devotion—See *Consecration* and *Prayer*.
Diligence—See *Activity*.
Doubt—See *Afflictions and Encouragement*.
Doxologies, *pp.* 410, 411.

E.

EARNESTNESS—See *Activity*.
Education, 1258, 1266.
Energy—See *Activity*.
Eternity—See *Life and Immortality*.
Evening, 23, 25, 31, 33, 34, 35, 36, 38, 56, 57, 63, 66, 78-85, 89-93, 108, 116.
Example of Christians, 903.

F.

FAITH, POWER OF, 128, 999, 912, 915, 917, 928, 1124.
Family, 1248.
Fasting, Day of, 173, 176, 183, 184, 185, 186, 266, 1259, 1260, 1263, 1264.
Fellowship, 765-784. See *Brotherly Love*.
Fight, the Christian, 956, 958, 960, 962, 964, 969, 971, 973, 1030. See *Self-denial*.
Fig-tree, 581.
Forgiveness:—
Of Sin, 98, 165, 665. See *Warning and Invitation*, and *Penitence and Consecration*.
Forever with the Lord, 1133.
Fountain of Cleansing, 473, 672.

G.

GETHSEMANE, 306, 308, 325, 348, 362, 363.
Glory of God—See *God*.
Glorying in the Cross—See *Cross of Christ*.
Go and tell Jesus, 702.
God, 109-559.
Attributes together, 163, 165, 168, 178, 262.
Being, 132.
Benevolence and Love, 135, 139, 182, 188, 189, 197, 205, 214, 231.
Compassion, 208, 239.
Condescension, 262.
Faithfulness, 141, 142, 196, 215, 216.
God:—
Glory, 124, 143, 146, 166, 167.
Goodness—See *Benevolence of God*.
Grace, 120, 130, 187, 191.
Holiness, 174.
Infinity, 119, 158-173, 181.
Justice, 235.
Love, 208, 211, 214, 219, 240, 252, 900.
Majesty, 141, 184, 185, 186.
Mercy—See *Benevolence of God*.
Mystery, 193.
Omnipotence, 122, 125, 127, 141.
Omnipresence, 133, 138, 148, 182.
Omniscience, 181.
Providence and Protection, 159, 161, 162, 183, 197, 228.
Sovereignty, 131, 141.
Spirituality, 194.
Trinity, 109-116.
Truth, 121, 136.
Unchangeableness, 194, 1022.
Wisdom, 122, 252.
Works of Creation, 122, 132, 135, 145, 146, 149, 151, 175, 176, 177, 179, 180, 192, 207, 210, 230, 245, 247, 261, 263-266.
Gospel—See *Bible*.
Gratitude, 847-897, 1341.
Grave of Jesus, 730. See *Baptism*.
Grieving the Holy Spirit—See *Holy Spirit*.

H.

HAPPINESS AT CONVERSION, 892.
Happiness of Christian, 963. See *Joy and Cheerfulness*.
Hard Heart, 658, 691.
Harvest—See *Thanksgiving, Day of*.
Harvest Past, 633.
Hearing the Word—See *Worship*.
Heart-broken by Love, 704.
Heaven, 387, 448, 632, 1040-1099.
Hell—See *Christ's Second Advent*.
Heirship with Christ, 894, 918, 919.
Hiding-place—See *Christ*.
Holiness:—
Of Christians—See *Graces and Duties*.
Holy Scriptures—See *Bible*.
Holy Spirit, 469, 493-559, 1015, 1026.
Hope:—
Under Affliction and Despondency, 870, 1004, 1011, 1014, 1020, 1031, 1032, 1033.
Humiliation—See *Day of Fasting*.
Humility, 977. See *Penitence*.

I.

IMMANUEL.—See *Christ*.
Immortality—See *Death and Immortality*.
Incarnation—See *Advent*.
Infants—See *Children*.
Ingratitude, 571, 679.
Inspiration—See *Bible*.
Intercession of Christ—See *Advocacy of Christ*.
Invitations and Warnings, 550-643.
It is finished, 333, 346, 358.
It is I, be not afraid, 313, 1003.

J.

JESUS only, 697, 982.
Jews, 1215, 1234.
Joy, 850, 851, 871, 967, 968, 1009.
Jubilee, 623, 625.
Judgment-day, 396, 397, 562, 588, 589, 600, 603, 606, 615, 618, 621, 622, 676. See *Second Advent of Christ*.
Justice—See *God*.
Justification—See *Atonement*.

K.

KINDNESS, HUMAN, 504, 920.
Knocking, at Heart, Christ, 571, 578, 641.

L.

LABOR—See *Activity*.
Lamb of God—See *Christ*.
Liberality—See *Benevolence, Christian Graces*, and *Duties*.
Life:—
Brevity and Frailty, 161. Also see *Death and Immortality* and *Year*.
Light of World, 857.
Likeness to Christ—See *Conformity*.
Looking to Christ, 1018, *page* 429.
Lord's Day—See *Sabbath*.
Lord's Prayer—See *Prayer*.
Lord's Supper, 783-814.
Love:—
Of God, 850-900.
Of Christ, 850-900.
Of Holy Spirit, 850-900.
For the Saviour, 859, 860-896, 980.
For the Church—See *Church*.
Lovest thou me, 728.
Lukewarmness—See *Backsliding*.

M.

MEDIATOR—See *Christ*.
Meekness, 315, 317.
Meeting and Parting—See *Parting and Meeting*.
Mercy—See *God*.
Ministry, 356, 1163-1179.
Missions, 1191-1246.
Morning, 24, 30, 32.
Mortality—See *Death* and *Life*.

N.

NAME ABOVE EVERY NAME, 436, 450, 462, 890.

National, 1254-1270.
Nature—See *God, Works of.*
Nearness to Christ, 939, 941, 946, 947, 949, 950.
Nearness to Heaven—See *Heaven Anticipated.*
Needful, One Thing—See *One Thing Needful.*
New Year—See *Year.*
Night—See *Evening.*

O.

ONE Thing Needful, 893, 966.
Ordination—See *Ministry.*

P.

PARTING and Meeting, 54, 448, 780, 782, 793, 1047, 1057. See also *Christian Fellowship.*
Pastor—See *Ministry.*
Patience, 637.
Peace, National, 287. See *Our Country.*
Pearl of Great Price, 449, 475.
Penitence and Consecration, 327-361, 644-728.
Pilate's Hall, 671.
Pity of God and Christ, 338, 350, 354. See *Sympathy.*
Poor—See *Benevolence.*
Praise, 109-268. See also *Worship.*
Prayer, 27, 28, 29, 64, 65, 66, 67, 76, 95, 897.
Prayer, Lord's, 104, 258, 986, 990, 995. *Page* xii.
Preachers—See *Ministry.*
Presence of Christ Unfailing, 930, 945.
Promises, 663.
Providence—See *God.*

R.

REDEMPTION—See *Atonement.*
Refuge—See *Christ* and *God.*
Regeneration:—
Necessary, 703. See also *Warnings and Invitations* and *Penitence and Consecration.*
Remember me, 644, 994, 998.
Resignation, 59, 153, 159, 164, 211, 224, 225, 238. See *Afflictions.*
Rest to Soul, 572, 674, 695, 870.
Resurrection—See *Christ's Resurrection and Second Advent* and *Death and Immortality.*
Revival, 521, 522, 523, 524, 527, 534, 535, 536, 538, 541, 543, 652, 819, 828, 830, 835, 837, 838, 839, 848, 936, 937, 938, 940, 942. See also *Backsliding* and *Penitence, and Consecration.*
Riches of the Christian, 882, 883, 935.

S.

SABBATH, 1-108.
Sabbath School—See *Children.*
Safety of Christians, 354, 1008, 1016, 1018, 1035.
Sailors, 1271-1274.
Salvation—See *Atonement.*
Sanctuary:—
Corner-stone—See *Dedication.*
Dedication, 1180-1190.
Love for, 1-108.
Satan—See *Temptation* and *Fight.*
Scriptures—See *Bible.*
Seamen—See *Sailors.*
Seasons, 192, 247, 249. See also *Year* and *God's Works of Creation.*
Seed, the word, 403, 559.
Self-denial, 717, 720, 874, 884, 979, 981, 1030.
Shadow of the Rock, 888.
Shepherd—See *Christ.*
Sickness—994, 1001. See *Afflictions* and *Encouragements.*
Sight of Christ Subdues, 671, 673, 674.
Sins:—
Brought to Christ, 854, 855.
Forsaken, 344, 347, 711.
Indwelling—See *Penitence* and *Consecration.*
Sins laid on Jesus, 854, 855.
Soldier, Christian—See *Fight* and *Self-denial.*
Soul of Man, 551, 591, 677. See *Immortality.*
Souls, Love for—See *Activity.*
Spirit striving, 568, 596. See *Holy Spirit.*
Spring, 247, 249. See *Year*, and *Thanksgiving, Day of;* also, *God's Works of Creation.*
Standing up for Jesus, 709, 965.
Sting of Death, 334, 364, 366.
Story of Cross told, 863.
Strength Equal to Day, 949.
Submission, 911, 983. See *Afflictions* and *Encouragements.*
Suffering of Christ—See *Christ.*
Summer, 155. See *Year* and *Creation.*
Supper, Gospel, 575, 576, 582.
Sympathy—See *Brotherly Love.*
Sympathy of Christ, 312, 320, 385, 386, 464, 983, 984, 1005, 1020, 1024.

T.

TELLING JESUS, 702.
Temperance, 1258, 1284-1288.
Temptation, 318. See *Conflict;* also *Afflictions* and *Encouragements.*
Thanksgiving, Day of, 155, 198, 199, 200, 210, 249, 253, 254, 255, 256, 257, 1261, 1265.
Time—See *Year.*
Too late, 643.
Tract Distribution, 1252.
Transfiguration of Christ, 322.
Trials—See *Afflictions.*
Trinity—See *God.*
Trust—See *Afflictions.*

U.

UNBELIEF—See *Faith* and *Graces and Duties.*
Union of Saints:—
To Christ, 426, 724, 810, 879, 1021.

V.

VANITY OF WORLD, 758.
Visit of Christ, 892.
Vows of God, 721. See *Baptism.*

W.

WANDERING—See *Backsliding.*
War—See *Our Country.*
Warfare, Christian—See *Soldier.*
Watchfulness—See *Self-denial* and *Fight.*
Watching with Christ, 361.
Weeping over Sinners, 681, 684.
Welcome of Christ to Heart, 726, 757.
Why die, 605, 611, 628.
Winter, 192. See *Year* and *Spring.*
Witness—See *Holy Spirit.*
Works of Christ pleaded, 853.
Word of God—See *Bible.*
Works of God in Creation—See *God.*
World waxing Evil, 406, 408.
World not Satisfying, 565, 605, 609.
World Forsaken, 573, 591, 698, 705, 706, 708, 711, 716, 1065.
Worship, 1-108. See *Family.*
Wounds of Sin, 665.

Y.

YEAR, Opening and Closing, 155, 581, 1289-1311. See also *Seasons* and *God's Works of Creation.*
Yoke of Christ, 572, 649, 728.
Yoke of Sin, 569, 572, 651.
Youth, 566, 567, 569, 583, 585, 586, 587, 595, 640, 1061. See also *Children.*

Z.

ZEAL—See *Activity.*
Zion—See *Church.*

INDEX OF TEXTS.

The figures refer to the numbers of the Hymns.

GENESIS.

1 : 1-3........115, 145, 529
1 : 9-25-31.....122, 146, 175, 1181
2 : 3..........1, 12, 22
3..........672
5 : 24..........942
6 : 3..........568, 601
7 : 1..........590
8 : 21, 22..........192, 1289
12 : 1-4..........900
15 : 12..........326
16 : 13..........138, 181
17 : 18......1276, 1278, 1279
19 : 15-22......601, 610, 619
24 : 31..........773, 776
24 : 56..........743
24 : 63..........57
28 : 10..........946
28 : 16, 17..........133
28 : 20-22..........198
31 : 13..........198
32 : 26..........972

EXODUS.

13 : 21..........1029, 1202
15 : 1..........257, 260
15 : 11..........174, 178
25 : 22..........27, 64, 72
28 : 29.........385, 386, 460
33 : 18..........434, 471

LEVITICUS.

25 : 9, 10.......597, 623, 625

NUMBERS.

10 : 29..........632, 639
23 : 10.......1102, 1104, 1134

DEUTERONOMY.

4 : 35..........157, 173
6 : 7..........198, 215
8 : 2..........205, 206
32 : 4..........153, 156, 160
33 : 25..........949
33 : 27..........685
31 : 1..........1064, 1068

RUTH.

1 : 16, 17..........727

I. SAMUEL.

3 : 1-10..........10
3 : 18..........153
7 : 12..........849
16 : 7..........181, 194, 207
22 : 23..........89

II. SAMUEL.

1 : 1-27..........1140
12 : 15-23...1107, 1108, 1111, 1127, 1143, 1145
22 : 3..........126, 160, 216
22 : 6, 7..........203

I. KINGS.

8 : 27..........1184
18 : 44..........1240

II. KINGS.

2 : 11, 12..........1037, 1077
4 : 26..........1111, 1145

I. CHRONICLES.

16 : 8....71, 96, 123, 136, 210
29 : 11, 12, 15..........161

II. CHRONICLES.

2 : 5..........125
6 : 18..........1184
6 : 20..........1180
7 : 5..........1185

NEHEMIAH.

2 : 5.......1262, 1263, 1258
4..........1260, 1264
9 : 5..........96, 246

ESTHER.

4 : 16..........669
7 : 2..........897

JOB.

1 : 21..........1116
3 : 17, 18..........1131, 1132
5 : 17-19......985, 989, 996
7 : 6..........1294
7 : 16..........1113
9 : 12..........185
13 : 15..........992, 1310
14 : 1, 2..........161, 1110
23 : 3, 4..........667
29 : 2..........666, 667
38 : 11..........127, 147

PSALMS.

1..........97
2..........1210
3 : 5..........30, 31, 34
4..........42, 56, 97
4 : 5..........1012
4 : 8..........35, 56, 108
5..........42, 18
8.....146, 179, 230, 257, 261
9..........136, 163
10 : 16..........141
12 : 6..........1149-1162
14 : 1..........132
16 : 9-12..1065, 1120, 1125, 1137
17 : 15..........1065, 1137
18 : 1-6..........142, 160, 213
19...122, 124, 175, 265, 1149, 1153, 1155, 1160
20..........160, 877
22..........951, 953
22..6, 107, 217, 218, 226, 228, 237, 306, 480, 723, 1028, 1029, 1034
24 : 7-10..........368, 372
26 : 8..14, 21, 47, 49, 69, 72, 73
27 : 1..........103, 202
27 : 4..........49, 72
27 : 5..........1073
27 : 8-14..97, 191, 202, 204, 212
29..........125, 163, 184
30..........204, 213, 996
31 : 15..........1311
32..........857, 871, 880
34..200, 202, 203, 205, 206, 213
36..........168
36 : 7..........850
37 : 5..........1010, 1013
39..........593, 622, 1298
40..........203, 876, 891
41 : 1-3..........905, 913
42..........223, 224, 1025
44..........206, 215
45..........419, 468, 474
45 : 17....436, 453, 462, 1238, 1239
46..........131, 147, 945
47..........140, 141, 206
48 : 1, 2..........833, 836
48 : 14..........1029
50 : 1-5..........12, 43, 1244
51.........644, 646, 647, 661
55 : 16, 17..........206, 213
55 : 22..........97, 976
57 : 5-7..........121
61 : 1-4..........692
63..........42, 48, 213, 224
65.....155, 189, 192, 247, 249, 250, 251
68 : 5..........136
68 : 18..........375, 381
71 : 17, 18..........222
72..........1201, 1228
73 : 23-26.......212, 220, 236
84.......7, 16, 37, 47, 53, 72
85 : 6..........819, 835
87..........47, 815, 818, 824
90.......161, 172, 173, 1294
95......15, 118, 127, 144, 229
97..........163, 184
100..........117, 118, 255
102..........825
103.........98, 130, 231, 259
103 : 13..........239
104..........162
106..........123
107.........1269, 1266, 1260
111........213, 259, 261, 268
116..........106, 203, 205
119.........1155, 1157, 1160
119 : 10..........116
121..........160, 204
122..........13, 14, 45, 47
126..........825, 830
127..........93
131..........977
132..........43
133..........37, 770, 777, 779
136........139, 145, 246, 249
137..........830, 1014, 1015
137 : 5..........832
138..........142
139....138, 181, 182, 186, 194
144..........161, 257
145....129, 136, 139, 140, 169, 215
146..........140, 162, 170
147..........825
147 : 16-18..........192, 1296
148....229, 241, 245, 261, 264
149..........259
150..........241, 242

PROVERBS.

2 : 8..........56
3 : 5, 6, 7..........896, 951
11 : 24..........905, 922
15 : 1..........290
20 : 1..........1286, 1288
23 : 29-32..-1284, 1286, 1288

ECCLESIASTES.

2 : 3-11..........569, 648
11 : 1, 2........909, 913, 932
11 : 6..........923, 932
11 : 9..........567, 591, 605
12.........585, 586, 587, 640

CANTICLES.

1 : 2..........468
1 : 3..459, 463, 465, 466, 470
1 : 7..........852, 885
5 : 9..........714

ISAIAH.

1 : 18..........220
2 : 2..........824

2 : 4 ....831, 846
6.........109, 111, 134, 174
9 : 6 ....273, 274, 300
11.......................831
12.............415, 435, 441
21 : 11..................1235
25 : 8.......1114, 1130, 1132
26 : 3, 4........204, 880, 918
32 : 15..............522, 524
33 : 17......1059, 1061, 1071, 1078
35................1199, 1201
35 : 8, 9, 10..1014, 1042, 1079
40 : 1-5....842, 844, 846, 847 1204
40 : 6-8......161, 1110, 1111, 1307, 1309
40 : 9......823, 829, 841, 844
40 : 11......6, 217, 218, 1034
40 : 27-31.....971, 852, 1009 1032
42 : 1-4.........284, 292, 294
42 : 16..............164, 193
43 : 1, 2..................1033
46 : 4..............222, 1033
48 : 10....................842
49 : 10............1042, 1085
49 : 15..............827, 842
50 : 10...................1014
51 : 11..967, 1004, 1009, 1087
52 : 1, 2........823, 829, 846
52 : 7-10.................1163
53..............353, 620, 855
55.........574, 575, 576, 577
60.....1204, 1211, 1221, 1231
62 ....1163, 1164, 1174
63 : 1-3...................359
65 : 17..............407, 1070
66 : 1.............1184, 1188

JEREMIAH.

2 : 2, 3.............649, 652
3 : 4......................587
3 : 22........563, 654, 670
8 : 20,....561, 602, 606, 633
13 : 23....................672
23 : 6...........450, 475, 881
31 : 3...............850, 876

EZEKIEL.

18 : 20, 21................564
33..................611, 1174
37..............507, 522, 535

DANIEL.

2..............820, 836, 847
7 : 14.. ......294, 393, 439
12 : 2....................1137

HOSEA.

6 : 1, 2.... ....670, 679
11 : 4......................876
14...................645, 677

JOEL.

2 : 28, 29.......522, 524, 529

AMOS.

4 : 12..554, 558, 588, 591, 608

JONAH.

2.......142, 203, 1011, 1013

MICAH.

2 : 10............1040, 1046

NAHUM.

1 : 3...........184, 188, 203
1 : 15...................1163

HABAKKUK.

2 : 14..............1201, 1245
2 : 15..............1284, 1288

ZEPHANIAH.

3 : 14-18......823, 831, 840 842

HAGGAI.

2.............46, 1204, 1241

ZECHARIAH.

9 : 9 321
13 : 1...............473, 642

MALACHI.

3 : 1................271, 277
3 : 2......................615
3 : 10 ....922, 925, 929

MATTHEW.

1 : 21 ...436, 450, 452, 462, 465, 489
2 : 9-11...270, 271, 278, 280 298, 299
3 : 1, 2....................277
3 : 13-17..729, 736, 739, 744 747, 751, 761
5 : 3-13.............903, 911
6 : 11-34..104, 317, 945, 977
7 : 7-11................. 897
8 : 1-17....................312
8 : 23 27............309, 310
10 : 32, 38..709, 710, 712, 720 722
11 : 28-30..533, 569, 572, 614
13 : 1-30....................60
13 : 45, 46.................475
14 : 23-33..309, 310, 987, 1003
17 : 1-9....................322
18 : 1-5....................977
21 : 1-9....307, 308, 321, 343
21 : 42...............818, 845
22 : 1-10..570, 577, 582, 613, 626
24 : 30.....396, 397, 398, 399 400, 401, 404
25 : 1-13............405, 407
25 : 10-12..................643
26 : 11.....................913
26 : 26, 27, 29...783, 784, 786
26 : 36-46..324, 325, 348, 362 363
26 : 64.....................433
27 : 26-53..323, 326, 327, 330 331, 332, 333
27 : 59-66........ 39, 41, 361
28 : 1-9....360, 364, 366, 367 368, 374, 376
28 : 18-20..........964, 1167

MARK.

2 : 17...............626, 627
4 : 3-8......................60
4 : 36-39.......309, 310, 313
6 : 45-51..309, 310, 313, 685
9 : 2-10....................322
9 : 36, 37 591
10 : 13-16.....305, 306, 1281
11 : 1-10...................321
13 : 1-37............400, 405
14 : 22-26..783, 786, 789, 799 804, 805
14 : 32-41..324, 325, 348, 362 363
14 : 66-72..................697
15 : 16-39..326, 327, 330, 331 332, 333, 334, 357
16.........360, 361, 365, 366

LUKE.

1 : 31.........436, 446, 450
2 : 1-20....269, 270, 271, 272 273, 277, 281, 285, 287
2 : 21-35 ....44, 302
2 : 39-52............301, 303
3 : 21, 22...........447, 751
4 : 18-20...................311
5 : 12-20......312, 660, 672
5 : 31, 32...........626, 627
6 : 20-38..905, 908, 913, 922 929
7 : 34......................422
7 : 47......................869
8 : 22-25......309, 310, 313
9 : 23..........716, 717, 720
9 : 28-37...................322
9 : 51......................343
10 : 2...............1169, 1177
19 : 29-37.....920, 921, 925
10 : 38-42..................550
11 : 1-4....................104
11 : 9......................897
12 : 8, 9........712, 720, 722
12 : 28-34.....992, 995, 1006 1008, 1012
12 : 35-40..277, 400, 927, 956
13 : 24-29..588, 591, 610, 619
14 : 16-23...........575, 582
15 : 11-24......645, 649, 653
16 : 5...............859, 860
17 : 5......................687
18 : 10-14..................647
18 : 35-43..660, 689, 699, 725
21 : 25-36..395, 396, 397, 400 401, 404
22 : 14-20. 783, 784, 786, 787
22 : 39-46..324, 325, 327, 348 355, 362, 363, 856
22 : 42 .... 986, 990, 995
23 : 33-48..323, 326, 327, 329 330, 331, 332, 333, 334 335, 338, 339, 340, 344 346, 347, 351, 352, 354 357, 358
23 : 42..............473, 998
24 : 1-12...39, 40, 41, 50, 360 361, 364, 365, 366, 367 368, 369, 370, 372, 374 376, 379
24 : 29.............89, 91, 93

JOHN.

1 : 12......................808
1 : 13...............520, 531
1 : 14......................290
1 : 29...............473, 479
3 : 3................672, 703
3 : 16...............467, 552
3 : 30...............294, 300
4 : 13, 14...........574, 577
5 : 2-15.............473, 642
5 : 39.............1060, 1158
6 : 17-21..309, 310, 313, 987
6 : 53.....784, 785, 789, 791 805
6 : 68...............894, 899
7 : 37...............574, 577
8 : 12.................25, 299
10.......472, 480, 1028, 1034
10 : 27, 28................1016
11 : 35, 36..........320, 304
12 : 8...........877, 887, 925
12 : 15..............307, 321
12 : 32..............329, 339
13 : 9......................674
14 : 2.......1040, 1042, 1052 1054, 1069
14 : 6 319
14 : 16..............497, 526
14 : 27.......861, 1024, 1027
15 : 1-6.............975, 1022
15 : 12, 13..765, 774, 775, 777
16 : 16-23..................897
17 : 23..........771, 774, 775
18 : 1......324, 325, 362, 363
19 : 17-37..326, 327, 329, 330 331, 332, 333, 334
19 : 34.....................692
19 : 38-42......357, 361, 367
20 : 1-18...360, 361, 365, 366 367, 368, 374, 376

ACTS.

1 : 9-11...368, 369, 372, 373 381, 389
2 : 1-13...493, 495, 516, 518
4 : 12......................436
4 : 31...............516, 541
9 : 6................898, 904
14 : 22......1022, 1030, 1031
16 : 9.......1212, 1223, 1233

ROMANS.

1 : 16.........710, 712, 722
6 : 3, 4.........734, 742, 749
7 : 9................873, 891
8 : 14, 15...........808, 857
8 : 31, 32...1007, 1008, 1075
9 : 33...........818, 845, 847
10 : 14, 15................1063
11 : 33-36...........175, 186
12 : 4, 5........769, 771, 775
15 : 30............1108, 1172

I. CORINTHIANS.

1 : 26......................822
1 : 30.....425, 426, 441, 456
2 : 2................330, 337
6 : 19.....858, 859, 898, 904
9 : 24-27........948, 952, 955
10 : 16, 17..........783, 786
11 : 23-25......784, 787, 804
12 : 28....................1170
13...............902, 907, 925
14 : 20..............855, 977
15 : 10.....849, 850, 860, 869 890
15 : 20-57......364, 369, 388 1100, 1114

II. CORINTHIANS.

1 : 3, 4 ... 525, 539, 541, 1001
1 : 20 ... 196, 216
1 : 21, 22 ... 494, 513
2 : 11 ... 958, 962, 964
3 : 14 ... 441
4 : 6 ... 189, 221
4 : 16-18 ... 872, 960, 992
5 : 1-4 ... 1009, 1015, 1037, 1040, 1042, 1071
5 : 7 ... 900, 912, 917
5 : 8 ... 886, 1103, 1113, 1125
5 : 9 ... 1113, 1117, 1126
5 : 17 ... 531
6 : 10 ... 871, 880, 882
6 : 16 ... 511, 513, 527, 530
7 : 1 ... 674, 680, 889
8 : 9 .. 278, 298, 301, 302, 318
10 : 1 ... 315, 317
12 : 9, 10 ... 949, 986, 1008, 1009

GALATIANS.

1 : 4, 5 ... 455, 460, 492
2 : 20 ... 418, 698
5 : 16 ... 530, 533, 538
6 : 14 ... 486, 487

EPHESIANS.

1 : 4 ... 860, 887
1 : 13 ... 511, 849
2 : 11 ...
2 : 20 ... 818, 845, 847
3 : 17-21 ... 415, 420, 433
3 : 15 ... 769, 771
4 : 4 ... 774, 779
4 : 8 ... 1170
4 : 30 ... 508, 530, 568
5 : 27 ... 874
6 : 10-17 .. 962, 965, 968, 971

PHILIPPIANS.

1 : 6 ... 891, 1008, 1009, 1013
1 : 21 ... 904, 975
1 : 23 ... 1038, 1041, 1071, 1113
2 : 2 ... 37, 765, 770, 776, 777, 779
2 : 5 ... 911
2 : 10 ... 436, 446, 450
3 : 1 ... 967, 1009
3 : 3-9 ... 330
4 : 4 ... 849, 869, 967

COLOSSIANS.

1 : 10 ... 910
1 : 12 ... 1006, 1008, 1049
1 : 15-19 ... 420, 426, 433
2 : 12 ... 733, 754
3 : 1-3 ... 880, 895, 1037
3 : 4 ... 397, 398, 399
3 : 12-14 ... 908, 913, 925
3 : 15 ... 918, 919
3 : 16 ... 1150, 1152
4 : 2 ... 958, 964
4 : 3 ... 1168, 1172, 1174

I. THESSALONIANS.

4 : 13, 14 ... 1100, 1101, 1114
4 : 16 ... 1115, 1137
4 : 17 ... 1133
5 : 1-10 .. 926, 927, 933, 953, 956, 959
5 : 16 ... 960, 967, 989, 992
5 : 17 ... 27, 28, 66, 76, 95
5 : 19 ... 509, 525, 530

II. THESSALONIANS.

1 : 7-10 ... 396, 398, 399, 401, 404, 405
3 : 1 ... 1168, 1174

I. TIMOTHY.

1 : 15 ... 552, 626, 627, 638
1 : 17 ... 256, 257
1 : 18 ... 948, 956, 958
3 : 16 ... 273, 278, 420
6 : 6-8 .. 976, 977, 1002, 1008

II. TIMOTHY.

1 : 8 ... 709, 710, 712, 714, 716, 722
2 : 3 ... 948, 958, 962, 965
2 : 19 ... 1030, 1031, 1033
3 : 16 ... 1150, 1152, 1154
4 : 6-8 ... 1130, 1135

TITUS.

2 : 10 ... 903
2 : 13 ... 400, 403, 405, 406

HEBREWS.

1 : 2 ... 1150
1 : 3 ... 165, 420, 434
1 : 8, 9 ... 440
2 : 3 ... 550, 561, 573
2 : 9 ... 439
2 : 11 ... 422
2 : 17, 18 ... 375, 386
4 : 9 ... 22, 1058, 1136
4 : 13 ... 138
4 : 14-16 ... 385, 386
7 : 23-28 ... 429, 463
9 : 12-14 ... 479
9 : 24 ... 385, 386
10 : 19 ... 162, 375, 708
10 : 24, 25 ... 37
11 ... 900, 912, 928
11 : 16 ... 1040, 1046, 1063, 1071
11 : 25 ... 706, 710, 717, 727
12 : 1 ... 953, 955, 959, 979
12 : 6 ... 988, 989, 996
12 : 22-25 ... 769, 826
13 : 14 ... 1040, 1042, 1044

JAMES.

1 : 27 ... 913, 929
2 : 14-26 ... 900, 912
4 : 6-10 ... 977, 1021
4 : 14 ... 1310
5 : 8 ... 400, 405, 406
5 : 16 ... 64, 66, 67

I. PETER.

1 : 3, 4 ... 369, 374, 376, 387, 397
1 : 8 ... 236, 451, 457, 462, 465, 466
1 : 13 ... 927
1 : 19 ... 479, 1017
1 : 25 ... 1153
2 : 6 ... 818, 845
2 : 7 ... 425, 470, 452
2 : 21 ... 314, 317, 345
2 : 24 ... 344, 349, 351, 354
2 : 24, 25 ... 353, 723, 724
4 : 12 ... 758
5 : 4 ... 1051

II. PETER.

1 : 19 ... 1157, 1159
3 : 10 ... 404, 1302
3 : 12 ... 398, 399, 400, 401, 405

I. JOHN.

1 : 7 ... 473, 665, 680, 685, 692
2 : 1 ... 373, 377, 380
2 : 2 ... 881
3 : 1, 2 ... 808, 857
4 : 10 ... 240, 252, 434, 467
5 : 4 ... 864, 935, 953

JUDE.

1 : 14, 15 ... 397, 399, 404
1 : 24, 25 ... 234

REVELATION.

1 : 5, 6 ... 392, 433
1 : 7 ... 396, 398, 399
1 : 18 ... 439
3 : 20 ... 571, 579, 641
5 : 9-13 ... 431, 432, 433, 435, 448, 453
6 : 16 ... 562, 606
7 : 9-12 ... 446, 448, 453, 455, 492, 1098, 1239
7 : 13-17 ... 1084, 1085
11 : 15 ... 484, 1236, 1238
19 : 6 ... 141, 424, 439, 484
19 : 16 ... 390
21 : 1-15 ... 1070, 1086, 1087, 1093
22 : 17 ... 574, 577, 596

INDEX OF FIRST LINES.

	HYMN
A BEAUTIFUL land by faith I see........	632
Abide with me! fast fall the eventide...	89
A broken heart, my God, my King.....	646
A charge to keep I have...............	926
A crown of glory bright..............	1051
A few more years shall roll............	1131
After the Christian's tears..............	1097
Again the Lord of life and light........	39
Ah! this heart is void and chill........	1048
Alas! and did my Saviour bleed.......	347
All-glorious God, what hymns of praise	437
All hail the pow'r of Jesus' name.......	446
All is dying; hearts are breaking......	1022
All that I was, my sin and guilt........	873
All ye nations, praise the Lord........	244
Almighty Father of mankind..........	201
Almighty God, thy word is cast........	60
Almighty God, we praise and own.....	134
Almighty Maker, God..................	233
Almighty Saviour, here we stand.......	752
Although the vine its fruit deny........	266
Always with us, always with us........	930
Amazing grace! how sweet the sound..	891
Amazing sight! the Saviour stands.....	578
Am I a soldier of the cross............	720
Amidst us our Beloved stands.........	790
A mother may forgetful be.............	827
And are we wretches yet alive.........	671
And are we yet alive..................	780
And can I yet delay...................	682
And canst thou, sinner, slight..........	601
And did the Holy and the Just........	349
And dost thou say, "Ask what thou....	897
And is there, Lord, a rest..............	1136
And may I hope, that when no more....	1060
And must this body die.............	1137
And now another week begins.........	40
And now, my soul, another year.......	1299
And will the Judge descend...........	603
And will the Lord thus condescend....	579
And wilt thou, O Eternal God.........	1184
Angels from the realms of glory........	271
Angels rejoiced and sweetly sung......	285
Angels! roll the rock away............	365
Another hand is beckoning us.........	1127
Another six days' work is done........	22
A parting hymn we sing..............	809
A pilgrim through this lonely world....	345
Approach, my soul, the mercy-seat.....	663
Arise! arise! with joy survey..........	1204
Arise, my soul, arise..................	427
Arise, my soul, fly up and run.........	1074
Arise, O King of grace, arise.........	828
Arise, ye people, and adore............	383
Arm of the Lord, awake, awake........	1207
Around the Saviour's lofty throne......	438
Around the throne of God in heaven....	1094
Around thy grave, Lord Jesus.........	730
Around thy table, holy Lord...........	795
As bowed by sudden storms, the rose..	1128
As flows the rapid river...............	1308
Ashamed to be a Christian............	710
Ask ye what great thing I know.......	418
Asleep in Jesus! blessed sleep........	1100
As now the sun's declining rays.......	52
As oft, with worn and weary feet.......	984
As pants the hart for cooling streams...	223
Assembled at thy great command......	1208
As the sweet flower that scents the morn	1107
As when in silence, vernal showers....	503
As when the weary traveler gains......	1064
At anchor laid, remote from home......	504

	HYMN
At even ere the sun was set	312
A throne of grace! then let us go	64
At thy command, our dearest Lord	786
Awake, and sing the song	483
Awake, awake, each drowsy soul	558
Awake, awake, the sacred song	290
Awaked by Sinai's awful sound	703
Awake, my soul, and with the sun	30
Awake, my soul, in joyful lays	850
Awake, my soul, lift up thine eyes	953
Awake, my soul! stretch every nerve	955
Awake, my tongue! thy tribute bring	120
Awake, our souls! away, our fears	952
Awake, ye saints! awake	9
Away with our sorrow and fear	1042
BEAUTIFUL Zion, built above	1086
Before Jehovah's awful throne	117
Before the Lord we bow	1190
Begin, my soul, th' exalted lay	263
Begin, my tongue, some heavenly theme	196
Begone, unbelief! my Saviour is near	1031
Behold a Stranger at the door	571
Behold! behold! the Lamb of God	356
Behold the amazing sight	351
Behold, the day is come	600
Behold the glories of the Lamb	447
Behold, the heathen waits to know	1213
Behold the mountain of the Lord	824
Behold the path that mortals tread	560
Behold the Saviour of mankind	346
Behold the sure foundation stone	818
Behold the western evening light	1129
Behold! what wondrous grace	808
Behold, where, in a mortal form	342
Be joyful in God, all ye lands of the	255
Beneath the shadow of the cross	776
Beneath thy cross I lay me down	340
Be ours the bliss in wisdom's way	1280
Beset with snares on every hand	951
Be thou exalted, O my God	121
Beyond the smiling and the weeping	1146
Blessed angels, high in heaven	931
Blessed are the sons of God	857
Blessed be the dear, uniting love	775
Bless, O my soul, the living God	130
Blest be the tie that binds	779
Blest Comforter Divine	539
Blest feast of love divine	805
Blest is the man whose softening heart	913
Blest morning, whose young dawning	41
Blest Saviour, we thy will obey	741
Blood is the price of heaven	355
Blow ye the trumpet, blow	625
Bondage and death the cup contains	1284
Bound upon th' accursed tree	357
Bread of heaven, on thee we feed	784
Bread of the world in mercy broken	813
Brethren, while we sojourn here	973
Brightest and best of the sons of the	298
Bright was the guiding star that led	299
Broad is the road that leads to death	556
Brother, rest from sin and sorrow	1139
Builder of mighty worlds on worlds	1186
Buried beneath the yielding wave	744
Buried with Christ by baptism unto. *Page*	430
By cool Siloam's shady rill	585
CALM me, my God, and keep me calm	919
Cast thy burden on the Lord	976
Cease, ye mourners, cease to languish	1140
Children of God, who, faint and slow	1004
Children of the heavenly king	967
Choose ye his cross to bear	762
Chosen not for good in me	860
Christ, above all glory seated	423
Christian, let your heart be glad	968
Christians, the glorious hope ye know	1212
Christ is coming! let creation	397
Christ is our Corner-stone	845
Christ, of all my hopes the Ground	975
Christ the Lord is risen again	367
Christ the Lord is risen to-day, Sons of.	364
Christ, who came my soul to save	732
Church of the ever-living God	822
Come, all ye saints of God	416
Come at the morning hour	76
Come, blessed Spirit! source of light	499
Come, dearest Lord, and feed thy sheep	51
Come, dearest Lord, descend and dwell	505

	HYMN
Come, Desire of nations, come	1241
Come, every pious heart	428
Come, gracious Spirit, heavenly Dove	501
Come, happy souls, adore the Lamb	736
Come hither, all ye weary souls	572
Come, Holy Ghost, Creator, come	515
Come, Holy Ghost, who ever one	512
Come, Holy Spirit, calm my mind	502
Come, Holy Spirit, come, Let thy bright	538
Come, Holy Spirit, come, With energy	543
Come, Holy Spirit, Dove divine	737
Come, Holy Spirit, Heavenly Dove	521
Come in, thou blessed of our God	766
Come in, thou blessed of the Lord	773
Come join, ye saints, with heart and voice	426
Come, kingdom of our God	1230
Come, let our voices join to raise	144
Come, let us anew our journey pursue	1303
Come, let us gladly sing	254
Come, let us join our cheerful songs	453
Come, let us join our friends above	769
Come, let us join our songs of praise	460
Come, let us lift our joyful eyes	443
Come, let us sing of Jesus	490
Come, let us sing the song of songs	432
Come, let us strike our harps afresh	54
Come, Lord, and tarry not	407
Come, Lord, in mercy come again	819
Come, my soul, thy suit prepare	6
Come, O Creator Spirit blest	497
Come, O my soul, in sacred lays	124
Come, O my soul, to Calvary	814
Come, sacred Spirit, from above	507
Come, said Jesus' sacred voice	614
Come, shout aloud the Father's grace	191
Come, sinner, to the gospel feast	582
Come, sound his praise abroad	229
Come, Spirit, source of light	542
Come, take my yoke, the Saviour said	569
Come, thou Almighty King	114
Come, thou celestial Spirit, come	510
Come, thou Desire of all thy saints	46
Come, thou eternal Spirit, come	511
Come, thou Fount of every blessing	849
Come to Jesus	638
Come to the ark, come to the ark	590
Come to the house of prayer	75
Come to the land of peace	598
Come, trembling sinner, in whose breast	670
Come, weary souls, with sins distressed	553
Come, we that love the Lord	68
Come, ye disconsolate, where'er ye	630
Come ye lofty, come ye lowly	278
Come, ye sinners, heavy laden	627
Come, ye sinners, poor and needy	626
Come, ye that know and fear the Lord	208
Come, ye that love the Saviour's name	451
Complete in thee! no work of mine	879
Constrained by love, we follow where	753
Crown his head with endless blessing	421
DARK was the night, and cold the	348
Daughter of Zion, from the dust	823
Day of judgment, day of wonders	615
Dearest of all the names above	471
Dear is the hallowed morn to me	19
Dear is the spot where Christians sleep	1101
Dear Lord, and will thy pardoning love	746
Dear Saviour! we are thine	810
Dear Saviour, when my thoughts recall	662
Dear Shepherd of thy people, here	55
Delay not, delay not, O sinner, draw	629
Deny thee? what! deny the way	899
Depth of mercy! can there be	700
Descend, celestial Dove	731
Descend from Heaven, immortal Dove	1062
Descend, immortal Dove	535
Did Christ o'er sinners weep	681
Did Jesus weep for me	684
Disowned of heaven, by man oppress'd	1215
Does the Gospel word proclaim	695
Do not I love thee, O my Lord	875
Down to the sacred wave	761
Draw near, O Holy Dove, draw near	789
EARLY, my God, without delay	48
Earth has nothing sweet or fair	419
Ebenezer! God is with us	1259
Enthroned is Jesus now	484
Enthroned on high, Almighty Lord	528

	HYMN
Ere another Sabbath's close	83
Eternal Father, thou hast said	1210
Eternal Source of every joy	1289
Eternal Spirit, God of truth	517
Eternal Spirit, we confess	496
Eternal Wisdom! thee we praise	187
Eternity! Eternity	559
Eternity is just at hand	557
Exert thy power, thy rights maintain	1209
FADE, fade, each earthly joy	862
Fading, still fading, the last beam is	94
Faint not, Christian! though the road	970
Fair shines the morning star	623
Fair vision! how thy distant gleam	1091
Faith adds new charms to earthly bliss	912
Faithful, O Lord, thy mercies are	216
Faith is a precious grace	928
Far as thy name is known	833
Far, far o'er hill and dell	1099
Far from my heavenly home	1015
Far from these narrow scenes of night	1078
Far from the world, O Lord, I flee	62
Father! beneath thy shelt'ring wing	945
Father! how wide thy glory shines	179
Father! I long, I faint to see	1071
Father! I stretch my hands to thee	687
Father of heaven! whose love profound	110
Father of love and power	116
Father of mercies, bow thine ear	1168
Father of mercies, in thy house	1170
Father of mercies, in thy word	1156
Father, whate'er of earthly bliss	997
Fiercely came the tempest sweeping	309
Fling out the banner! let it float	1206
Flow fast, my tears! the cause is great	323
For a season called to part	84
Forever here my rest shall be	675
Forever with the Lord	1133
For thy mercy and thy grace	1305
Friend after friend departs	1143
From all that dwell below the skies	1198
From Calvary a cry was heard	326
From every stormy wind that blows	27
From Greenland's icy mountains	1233

	HYMN
From the cross, uplifted high	613
From thee, my God, my joys shall rise	457
From whence does this union arise	777
From whence these direful omens	344
From yonder Rocky Mountains	1196
GENTLY, gently, lay the rod	696
Gently, Lord, oh, gently lead us	1023
Give to the winds thy fears	1010
Give thanks to God, he reigns above	139
Glorious things of thee are spoken	815
Glory to God on high	414
Glory to thee, my God, this night	33
Go and tell Jesus	702
God bless our native land	1256
God calling yet! shall I not hear	573
God, in the gospel of his Son	1150
God, in the high and holy place	207
God is a Spirit, just and wise	194
God is love; his mercy brightens	252
God is the refuge of his saints	147
God moves in a mysterious way	193
God, my supporter and my hope	212
God of eternity, from thee	555
God of mercy! God of love	694
God of my life, through all my days	162
God of our lives, thy various praise	1301
God of our salvation, hear us	87
God of the morning, at whose voice	32
God of the world! thy glories shine	167
God's glory is a wondrous thing	916
God with us! oh, wondrous name	275
Go forth on wings of faith and prayer	1252
Go, labor on; spend and be spent	906
Go, labor thou, while it is day	901
"Go, preach my gospel," saith the Lord	1167
Go, preach the blest salvation	1194
Go, spirit of the sainted dead	1106
Go thou in life's fair morning	640
Go to dark Gethsemane	362
Go, tune thy voice to sacred song	449
Grace, 'tis a charming sound	477
Gracious Spirit! love divine	544
Great Father of our feeble race	522
Great Former of this various frame	152

	HYMN
Great God! how infinite art thou.......	173
Great God! indulge my humble claim..	150
Great God! now condescend..........	1278
Great God of nations! now to thee.....	1265
Great God! the nations of the earth....	1218
Great God! to thee my evening song...	35
Great God! we in thy courts appear....	738
Great God! we sing that mighty hand..	1290
Great God! whose hand outpours the..	1286
Great is the Lord our God.............	836
Great is the Lord! What tongue.......	143
Great Ruler of all nature's frame.......	188
Great Spirit! by whose mighty power..	494
Guide me, O thou great Jehovah.......	1029
HAD I the tongues of Greeks and Jews.	902
Hail! morning known among the blest.	374
Hail, my ever-blessed Jesus...........	869
Hail, sacred truth! whose piercing rays	1162
Hail, sov'reign love! that form'd the...	713
Hail, sweetest, dearest tie, that binds...	772
Hail the day that sees him rise.........	368
Hail, thou happy morn so glorious.....	395
Hail, thou long-expected Jesus.........	276
Hail, thou once despised Jesus.........	393
Hail to the brightness of Zion's glad....	846
Hail to thee, our risen King...........	369
Hail to the Lord's anointed.............	294
Hail to the Prince of life and peace.....	439
Hail, tranquil hour of closing day......	63
Happy the heart where graces reign....	907
Happy the souls to Jesus joined.......	771
Hark! a thrilling voice is sounding....	277
Hark! from the tombs a warning sound	1118
Hark! hark! the notes of joy.........	297
Hark! how the gospel trumpet sounds.	1243
Hark, my soul, how every thing........	247
Hark! my soul, it is the Lord.........	728
Hark! ten thousand harps and voices..	392
Hark, the glad sound! the Saviour.....	284
Hark! the herald angels sing.......272,	273
Hark! the song of jubilee.............	1238
Hark! the sound of holy voices........	488
Hark! the voice of love and mercy.....	358
Hark! what celestial sounds..........	296
Hark! what mean those holy voices....	269
Hasten, Lord, the glorious time........	1246
Hasten, sinner, to be wise.............	610
Haste, traveler, haste! the night comes.	634
Hast thou within a care so deep........	31
Hear, O sinner! mercy hails you.......	619
Hear the heralds of the gospel.........	620
Hear the royal proclamation...........	1244
Heart of stone, relent, relent..........	691
Hear what the voice from heaven.	1119
Heavenly Father, to whose eye........	974
Heavenly Shepherd, guide us, feed us..	107
He dies! the Friend of sinners dies....	335
He has come, the Christ of God........	274
He lives, my kind, wise, heavenly......	380
He lives! the great Redeemer lives....	377
Heralds of creation! cry..............	245
Here at thy table, Lord, we meet.......	801
Here, Saviour, we do come............	763
Here we meet to part again............	1058
He's come! let every knee be bent.....	493
He that goeth forth with weeping......	932
High in the heavens, Eternal God......	168
High in yonder realms of light.........	1085
Holy and reverend is the name........	174
Holy Father! thou hast taught me.....	1030
Holy Ghost! dispel our sadness.......	514
Holy Ghost! with light divine.........	546
Holy, holy, holy is the Lord............	267
Holy Spirit! from on high.............	548
Holy Spirit! in my breast.............	547
Holy Spirit! Lord of light.............	545
Holy Spirit! source of light...........	549
Hope of our hearts, O Lord, appear....	1068
Hosanna be our cheerful song.........	445
Hosanna! raise the pealing hymn......	482
Hosanna to the Prince of Light........	381
How beauteous are their feet..........	1163
How beauteous were the marks divine.	315
How blest the hour when first we gave.	742
How blest the righteous when he dies..	1102
How blest the sacred tie that binds.....	765
How calmly wakes the hallowed morn..	750
How can I sink with such a prop......	877
How charming is the place............	72

	HYMN
How condescending and how kind.....	350
How did my heart rejoice to hear......	45
How dread are thine eternal years......	197
How firm a foundation, ye saints of the.	1033
How gentle God's commands..........	238
How happy every child of grace........	871
How helpless guilty nature lies........	533
How long, sometimes, a day appears...	225
How pleasant! how divinely fair.......	16
How pleased and blest was I..........	13
How precious is the book divine.......	1159
How sad our state by nature is.........	673
How shall the young secure their hearts	1161
How short and hasty is our life........	593
How sweet and awful is the place......	796
How sweet! how heavenly is the sight..	770
How sweetly flowed the gospel sound..	311
How sweet the hour of closing day.....	1104
How sweet the name of Jesus sounds...	470
How sweet to bless the Lord	73
How sweet to leave the world awhile...	17
How sweet, upon this sacred day	102
How tedious and tasteless the hours ...	938
How vain are all things here below	1002
How vain is all beneath the skies......	1110
How vast the treasure we possess......	882
How wondrous was the burning zeal...	343
I AM coming to the cross.............	680
I bless thee, Lord, for sorrow sent......	989
I bring my sins to thee................	854
I feed by faith on Christ; my bread	792
If God is mine, then present things.....	1007
If human kindness meets return.......	800
If I were a voice, a persuasive voice....	1247
If thou dost truly seek to live..........	566
If, through unruffled seas..............	1011
I hear a voice that comes from far......	570
I heard the voice of Jesus say.........	870
I know not whether dark or bright.....	1089
I know that my Redeemer lives, And...	458
I know that my Redeemer lives; He...	461
I know that my Redeemer lives; What.	378
I lay my sins on Jesus...............	855
I left the God of truth and light........	649

	HYMN
I'll praise my Maker with my breath ...	170
I long to behold him arrayed..........	1041
I love, I love thee, Lord most high.....	887
I love thee, O my God, and still........	476
I love the sacred Book of God.........	1152
I love thy kingdom, Lord	832
I love to see the Lord below...........	49
I love to sing of heaven...............	1050
I love to steal awhile away............	57
I love to tell the story.................	863
I'm a pilgrim, and I'm a stranger.......	1044
I'm but a stranger here................	1046
I'm not ashamed to own my Lord......	722
In all my Lord's appointed ways.......	743
In all my vast concerns with thee......	181
Incarnate Word! by every grief........	318
In Christ I've all my soul's desire......	441
I need thee, precious Jesus............	966
In evil long I took delight.............	674
In God's own house pronounce his.....	61
In loud exalted strains...............	1189
Inquire, ye pilgrims! for the way......	580
In stature grows the heavenly Child....	301
In the bright morn of life..............	587
In the Christian's home in glory	1059
In the cross of Christ I glory..........	486
In the dark and cloudy day............	1027
In the far better land of glory and light.	1098
In the hour of my distress.............	1026
In trouble and in grief, O God.........	996
I once was a stranger to grace and to...	1035
I saw, beyond the tomb................	606
I say to all men, far and near..........	387
I see the crowd in Pilate's hall.........	671
I send the joys of earth away	706
I sing th' almighty power of God.......	175
Is this the kind return................	679
It came upon the midnight clear.......	287
I think, when I read the sweet story of..	305
I thirst, but not as once I did..........	864
I thirst, thou wounded Lamb of God....	654
It is not death to die..................	1130
I've found the pearl of greatest price ..	475
I was a foe to God...	724
I was a wandering sheep..............	723

	HYMN
I worship thee, sweet Will of God......	914
I would love thee, God and Father.....	868
I would not live alway: I ask not to stay	1113
Jehovah God! thy gracious power....	182
Jehovah reigns, his throne is high......	163
Jerusalem, forever bright..............	1093
Jerusalem, my happy home............	1090
Jerusalem the golden.................	1087
Jesus a child his course begun.........	303
Jesus, and didst thou condescend......	660
Jesus! and shall it ever be............	712
Jesus calls us, o'er the tumult.........	980
Jesus comes, his conflict over..........	424
Jesus comes to souls rejoicing.........	401
Jesus! delightful, charming name......	459
Jesus, engrave it on my heart.........	893
Jesus, grant me this, I pray............	1021
Jesus, I am never weary..............	1024
Jesus, I come, I come to-night.........	689
Jesus, I love thy charming name.......	465
Jesus, immortal King, arise............	1219
Jesus, I my cross have taken..........	705
Jesus invites his saints................	806
Jesus is gone above the skies..........	787
Jesus, let thy pitying eye..............	697
Jesus, lover of my soul................	685
Jesus, mighty King in Zion............	734
Jesus, my all, to heaven is gone........	708
Jesus, my sorrow lies too deep.........	1005
Jesus only, when the morning.........	982
Jesus, our Lord, ascend thy throne.....	382
Jesus, Saviour, pilot me...............	1272
Jesus shall reign where'er the sun......	1201
Jesus—the name high over all.........	450
Jesus, the sinner's Friend, to thee......	657
Jesus, the very thought of thee.........	468
Jesus! thou art the sinner's Friend.....	664
Jesus, thou everlasting King..........	435
Jesus, thy boundless love to me........	865
Jesus! thy love shall we forget........	799
Jesus! thy name I love...............	890
Jesus! thy robe of righteousness.......	881
Jesus, to thy dear wounds we flee......	1073
Jesus, we look to thee................	74
Jesus wept! those tears are over.......	320
Jesus, we thus obey..................	807
Jesus, while this rough desert soil......	950
Join all the glorious names of wisdom..	429
Joyfully, joyfully onward I move.......	1049
Joy to the world, the Lord is come.....	281
Just are thy ways and true thy word....	156
Just as I am, without one plea.........	656
Keep silence, all created things	186
Keep us, Lord! oh keep us ever.......	88
Kindred in Christ! for his dear sake...	767
Kingdoms and thrones to God belong..	125
Laborers of Christ, arise..............	924
Laden with guilt, and full of fears......	1158
Lamp of our feet! whereby we trace....	1157
"Land ahead!" its fruits are waving....	1056
Late, late, so late! and dark the night..	643
Let all the earth their voices raise......	171
Let children hear the mighty deeds.....	215
Let every mortal ear attend............	576
Let me but hear my Saviour say........	949
Let sinners take their course..........	97
Let songs of praise fill the sky.........	526
Let us awake our joys	411
Let us gather up the sunbeams	1248
Let vain pursuits and vain desires......	804
Let Zion and her sons rejoice..........	825
Let Zion in her King rejoice...........	131
Let Zion's watchmen all awake........	1174
Life from the dead, Almighty God......	1287
Life is the time to serve the Lord......	554
"Lift your heads" with faith...........	1242
Light of life, seraphic fire..............	8
Light of the lonely pilgrim's heart......	1216
Like sheep we went astray.............	353
Lo, God is here!—let us adore.........	133
Lo, he comes! let all adore him........	816
Lo! he comes, with clouds descending! Hark! the trump...................	399
Lo! he comes, with clouds descending! Once for favored.....................	396
Lo! he cometh,—countless trumpets...	398
Look from thy sphere of endless day...	1191

	HYMN
Look, ye saints! the day is breaking....	1221
Look, ye saints! the sight is glorious...	394
Long as I live I'll bless thy name......	206
Long have I sat beneath the sound	940
Lo! on a narrow neck of land.........	622
Lord, as to thy dear cross we flee.......	908
Lord, at this closing hour	81
Lord, at thy table we behold...........	803
Lord, at thy temple we appear.........	44
Lord, dismiss us with thy blessing	86
Lord, forever at thy side...............	977
Lord, from thy blessed throne	1257
Lord, from thy unexhausted store......	154
Lord God of hosts, by all adored.......	169
Lord God the Holy Ghost.............	534
Lord, how delightful 'tis to see.........	21
Lord, how mysterious are thy ways.....	164
Lord, how secure and blest are they....	880
Lord, I am thine, and in thy aid........	756
Lord, I am thine, entirely thine........	655
Lord, I cannot let thee go.............	972
Lord, I hear of showers of blessing.....	686
Lord, I know thy grace is nigh me.....	699
Lord, in humble, sweet submission.....	735
Lord, in the morning thou shalt hear...	42
Lord, in thy garden agony.............	325
Lord, it belongs not to my care........	1006
Lord Jesus, when we stand afar........	339
Lord, let thy goodness lead our land ...	1267
Lord, may the spirit of this feast.......	798
Lord of all being! throned afar........	166
Lord of earth! thy forming hand.......	248
Lord of hosts! how bright, how fair....	53
Lord of the harvest, bend thine ear.....	1169
Lord of the harvest! hear..............	1165
Lord, shall we part with gold for dross.	935
Lord, thou hast scourged our guilty....	1264
Lord, thou hast searched and seen me..	138
Lord, thou hast won—at length I yield.	704
Lord, thou on earth didst love thine....	774
Lord, thou wilt hear me when I pray...	56
Lord, 'tis an infinite delight...........	219
Lord, we come before thee now........	5
Lord, when my raptured thought.......	177
Lord, when we bow before thy throne...	659
Lord, while for all mankind we pray....	1262
Lord, with glowing heart I'd praise.....	106
Lo! the day of rest declineth..........	93
Loud hallelujahs to the Lord..........	129
Love divine, all love excelling.........	513
Love is the fountain whence...........	925
Lo! what a glorious sight appears.....	1070
MAGNIFY Jehovah's name.............	246
Majestic sweetness sits enthroned......	474
Make channels for the streams of love..	922
Maker of land and rolling sea.........	1183
Man has a soul of vast desires.........	551
Mary to the Saviour's tomb............	360
Meekly in Jordan's holy stream........	751
Men of God, go take your stations.....	1222
"Mercy, O thou Son of David"........	725
Messiah! at thy glad approach	289
'Mid scenes of confusion and creature..	1052
'Mid the pastures green of the blessed..	1148
Mighty God! while angels bless thee...	420
Millions within thy courts have met....	24
Morning breaks upon the tomb........	366
Mortals, awake! with angels join......	283
Mourn for the thousands slain.........	1288
Much in sorrow, oft in woe............	969
Must Jesus bear the cross alone.......	717
My country, 'tis of thee................	1255
My days are gliding swiftly by.........	1043
My dear Redeemer, and my Lord......	314
My drowsy powers, why sleep ye so....	957
My faith looks up to thee..............	1017
My God, and is thy table spread.......	791
My God, accept my heart this day......	719
My God, I love and I adore...........	148
My God, is any hour so sweet..........	28
My God, my Father, while I stray......	986
My God, my King, thy various praise..	140
My God, my Life, my Love.............	236
My God, my portion, and my love......	220
My God, permit me not to be..........	895
My God, the spring of all my joys......	221
My God, thy boundless love I praise...	265
My God, what silken cords are thine...	876
My gracious Lord, I own thy right.....	904

	HYMN
My heavenly home is bright and fair....	1088
My home is in heaven..................	1040
My only Saviour, when I feel..........	943
My opening eyes with rapture see......	18
My precious Lord, for thy dear name...	884
My Saviour! my almighty Friend......	444
My Saviour, whom absent I love.......	1039
My Shepherd will supply my need.....	218
My soul, amid this stormy world.......	1080
My soul, be on thy guard..............	958
My soul doth magnify the Lord........	469
My soul, how lovely is the place.......	47
My soul is not at rest.................	1197
My soul, it is thy God.................	959
My soul, repeat his praise.............	98
My soul, weigh not thy life............	964
My soul, what hast thou done for God..	954
My soul, with joy attend	1016
My sufferings all to thee are known....	648
My times are in thy hand..............	1311
NATURE with open volume stands......	334
Nearer, my God, to thee...............	946
No change of time shall ever shock	160
No more, my God, I boast no more.....	707
No more, ye wise, your wisdom boast ..	883
No, no, it is not dying................	1144
No room for mirth or trifling here......	677
Not all the blood of beasts.............	479
Not all the nobles of the earth.........	878
Not all the outward forms on earth.....	531
Nothing but leaves! the Spirit grieves..	701
Nothing either great or small..........	635
"Nothing to do!" in this world of ours.	1249
No track is on the sunny sky..........	495
Not to condemn the sons of men.......	552
Not to the terrors of the Lord..........	826
Now be my heart inspired to sing......	440
Now for a tune of lofty praise..........	373
Now, gracious Lord, thine arm reveal..	1300
Now I have found a Friend............	861
Now, in the heat of youthful blood......	567
Now is th' accepted time..............	599
Now let my soul, Eternal King	1151
Now let our cheerful eyes survey.......	385
Now let our souls, on wings sublime...	1060
Now, O God, thine own I am..........	858
Now that the sun is beaming bright.....	105
Now to the Lord a noble song.........	434
Now to the Lord, who makes us know.	433
Now to thy sacred house..............	11
O BLESSED feet of Jesus.....	856
O blessed God, to thee I raise...... ...	100
O Christ! our King, Creator, Lord.....	329
O Christ, what gracious words.........	485
O day of rest and gladness............	1
O dearest Lamb, take thou my heart....	874
O'er the distant mountains breaking....	400
O'er the gloomy hills of darkness......	1220
O'erwhelmed in depths of woe..........	352
Of all the joys we mortals know	886
O Father, Lord of earth and heaven....	740
O God of Bethel! by whose hand......	198
O God of Sovereign grace.............	1229
O God, our help in ages past..........	172
O God the Father, Christ the Son......	1182
O God, thy grace and blessings give....	1109
O God, unseen, yet ever near..........	794
O happy saints, who dwell in light.....	1063
Oh, bless the Lord, my soul...........	231
Oh, come, and mourn with me awhile ..	336
Oh, come, loud anthems let us sing.....	127
Oh, could I find, from day to day.......	939
Oh, could I lose myself in thee.........	669
Oh, could I speak the matchless worth.	425
Oh, deem not they are blest alone......	988
Oh, do not let the word depart.........	565
Oh, for a closer walk with God.........	942
Oh, for a faith that will not shrink......	917
Oh, for a glance of heavenly day.......	658
Oh, for a heart to praise my God........	911
Oh, for an overcoming faith............	1124
Oh, for a shout of sacred joy...........	389
Oh, for a thousand tongues to sing.....	452
Oh, for the death of those..............	1134
Oh, for the happy hour................	837
Oh, for the peace which floweth like a..	1147
Oh, for the pearly gates of heaven......	1081
Oh, gift of gifts! oh, grace of faith......	872

	HYMN
Oh, hallowed is the land and blest.....	1200
Oh, happy day that fixed my choice on..	715
Oh, help us, Lord! each hour of need..	1000
Oh! how happy are they..............	851
Oh, how the hearts of those revive......	821
Oh, it is hard to work for God.........	915
Oh, not my own these verdant hills.....	898
O Holy Ghost, the Comforter..........	525
O holy, holy, holy Lord..............	109
O holy Lord, our God.................	1166
O Holy Spirit, Fount of Love..........	532
Oh, not to fill the mouth of fame.......	936
Oh, render thanks to God above.......	123
Oh, sing to him who loved and bled....	455
Oh, stay thy tears! for they are blest...	1108
Oh, still in accents sweet and strong...	1175
Oh that I knew the secret place........	667
Oh that my load of sin were gone......	651
Oh that the Lord's salvation...........	1134
Oh, there will be mourning.........*Page*	429
Oh, turn ye, oh, turn ye, for why will ye	628
Oh, what amazing words of grace......	574
Oh what, if we are Christ's..............	758
Oh, where are kings and empires now..	820
Oh! where is now that glowing love...	652
Oh, where shall rest be found..........	605
Oh, who'll stand up for Jesus..........	709
Oh, worship the King, all glorious.....	257
O Israel, to thy tents repair............	956
O Jesus, bruis'd and wounded more....	785
O Jesus, in this solemn hour..........	1178
O Jesus, Lord of heavenly grace.......	101
O Jesus, thou art standing.............	641
O Jesus, thou the beauty art...........	466
O Jesus, when I think of thee..........	464
O Lord, and shall our fainting souls....	509
O Lord, behold us at thy feet..........	1279
O Lord, how joyful 'tis to see..........	37
O Lord, I would delight in thee........	992
O Lord! my best desires fulfill........	991
O Lord of hosts, whose glory fills......	1180
O Lord our God! arise...............	1228
O Lord, our heavenly King............	230
O Lord, thy heavenly grace impart.....	711
O Lord, thy work revive..............	835
O Lord, we in thy footsteps tread......	749
O Love Divine! that stooped to share..	944
O Love! who gav'st thy life for me.....	867
O my soul, what means this sadness....	1025
Once more, before we part............	781
Once, O Lord, thy garden flourished...	839
Once upon the heaving ocean..........	309
One by one the sands are flowing......	1310
One prayer I have—all prayers in one..	995
One sweetly solemn thought......1095,	1096
One there is, above all others..........	422
One thing alone, dear Lord! I dread...	937
On Jordan's stormy banks I stand......	1067
On the mountain's top appearing.......	841
On, through Judea's palmy plain.......	1281
Onward, Christian, though the region..	979
Onward, onward, men of heaven.......	1226
Opprest with noon-day's scorching heat	797
O praise the Lord in that blest place...	126
O praise ye the Lord! prepare your....	259
O sacred Head, now wounded.........	354
O Saviour, is thy promise fled..........	403
O Spirit of the living God.............	1205
O soul, soul, thou art passing..........	1306
O thou, by long experience tried.......	159
O thou, from whom all goodness flows..	994
O thou, in whose presence.............	852
O thou, my soul, forget no more.......	788
O thou that hear'st the prayer of faith....	676
O thou, who driest the mourner's tear..	993
O thou, who in Jordan didst bow thy..	729
O thou, whom we adore...............	1227
O thou, whose filmed and failing eye..	1123
O thou, whose own vast temple stands..	1188
O thou, whose tender mercy hears......	661
Our children thou dost claim..........	1276
Our country is Immanuel's ground.....	1079
Our country's voice is pleading.......	1193
Our Father, God, who art in heaven....	104
Our Father in heaven, we hallow thy...	258
Our Father, through the coming year...	1295
Our helper, God, we bless thy name....	1291
Our land, with mercies crowned.......	1254
Our Lord is risen from the dead........	372
Our Saviour bowed beneath the wave..	739

	HYMN
Our souls, by love together knit	768
Our spirits join t'adore the Lamb	338
O wondrous type! O vision fair	322
O Zion! tune thy voice	844
PASTOR, thou art from us taken	1138
Peace, troubled soul, whose plaintive	636
People of the living God	727
Pilgrim, burdened with thy sin	607
Pilgrims in this vale of sorrow	981
Pity, Lord, the child of clay	690
Planted in Christ, the living vine	817
Pleasant are thy courts above	7
Plunged in a gulf of dark despair	467
Pour out thy Spirit from on high	1172
Praise, everlasting praise, be paid	128
Praise, Lord, for thee in Zion waits	155
Praise, oh praise our God and King	1270
Praise the Lord! his glories show	241
Praise the Lord! his power confess	242
Praise the Lord! oh, praise him	268
Praise the Lord! ye heavens, adore him	250
Praise to God, immortal praise	249
Praise to thee, thou great Creator	251
Praise to the Lord on high	430
Praise ye the Lord, his servants, raise	99
Praise ye the Lord, immortal choir	190
Praise ye the Lord! my heart shall join	136
Prayer is the breath of God in man	67
Prayer is the soul's sincere desire	65
Prostrate, dear Jesus, at thy feet	668
RAISE your triumphant songs	478
Rejoice, all ye believers	405
Remark, my soul, the narrow bound	1297
Remember me, my Saviour God	998
Remember thy Creator now	586
Repent! the voice celestial cries	584
Rest for the toiling hand	1132
Resting from his work to-day	361
Return, O wanderer, return	563
Return, O wanderer, to thy home	594
Rich are the joys which cannot die	910
Ride on, ride on in majesty	321
Rise, glorious Conqueror, rise	412
Rise, my soul, and stretch thy wings	1037
Rocked in the cradle of the deep	1273
Rock of ages, cleft for me	692
Roll on, thou mighty ocean	1232
SAFELY through another week	2
Saints in glory! we together	410
Salvation! oh, the joyful sound	481
Saviour, breathe an evening blessing	108
Saviour, I look to thee	1018
Saviour, I think upon that hour	337
Saviour, like a shepherd lead us	1028
Saviour, thy gentle voice	947
Saviour, thy law we love	764
Saviour, visit thy plantation	838
Saviour, when, in dust, to thee	688
Saviour, who this day didst break	3
Saviour, who thy flock art feeding	1283
Saw you never in the twilight	280
Say, brothers, will you meet us	778
Say, is your lamp burning, my brother	1250
Say, sinner, hath a voice within	568
Say, why should friendship grieve for	1105
Scorn not the slightest word or deed	909
See, from Zion's sacred mountain	843
See, gracious God, before thy throne	1263
See how great a flame aspires	1240
See how he loved! exclaimed the	304
See, in the vineyard of the Lord	581
See the kind Shepherd, Jesus, stands	306
See the ransomed millions stand	1239
See th' eternal Judge descending	618
Servant of God, well done	1135
Shall we gather at the river	1045
Shall we meet beyond the river	1047
Shepherds, hail the wondrous stranger	270
Shout the glad tidings, exultingly sing	279
Shout the tidings of salvation	1245
Show pity, Lord! O Lord, forgive	644
Silently the shades of evening	90
Since all the varying scenes of time	211
Sing of Jesus, sing forever	409
Sing, my soul, his wondrous love	240
Sing, sing, his lofty praise	415
Sing to the Lord Jehovah's name	210

	HYMN
Sing to the Lord most high	253
Sing to the Lord our might	71
Sing to the Lord that built the skies	145
Sing to the Lord, ye distant lands	282
Sing we the song of those who stand	448
Sing, ye redeemed of the Lord	1009
Sinner, hear the melting story	617
Sinner, oh, why so thoughtless grown	564
Sinner, rouse thee from thy sleep	612
Sinners, turn ; why will ye die	611
Sinner, the voice of God regard	592
Sinner, what has earth to show	609
Sister, thou wast mild and lovely	1141
Sleep not, soldier of the Cross	971
So fades the lovely blooming flower	1111
Soft be the gently-breathing notes	328
Softly fades the twilight ray	82
Softly now the light of day	85
Soldiers of Christ, arise	962
So let our lips and lives express	903
Some seraph, lend your heavenly	178
Songs of praise the angels sang	243
Son of God, our glorious Head	1179
Sons of day ! Arise from slumber	1192
Sons of men, behold from far	1237
Soon may the last glad song arise	1203
Souls in heathen darkness lying	1223
Sound, sound the truth abroad	413
Sovereign of all the worlds on high	209
Sovereign of worlds, display thy power	1199
Sow in the morn thy seed	923
Speak gently—it is better far	920
Spirit Divine ! attend our prayer	519
Spirit of faith come down	537
Spirit of holiness, descend	524
Spirit of holiness, look down	523
Spirit of mercy, truth, and love	506
Spirit of power and might, behold	529
Spirit of truth ! on this thy day	518
Stand up, and bless the Lord	96
Stand up, my soul, shake off thy fears	948
Stand up, stand up for Jesus	965
Star of peace to wanderers weary	1271
Stay, thou insulted Spirit, stay	508
Stern winter throws his icy chains	1296
Still one in life and one in death	793
Stretched on the cross, the Saviour dies	331
Sun of my soul, thou Saviour dear	36
Sure the blest Comforter is nigh	500
Sweet hour of prayer	95
Sweet is the light of Sabbath eve	23
Sweet is the memory of thy grace	200
Sweet is the work, my God, my King	15
Sweet is the work, O Lord	69
Sweet Saviour, bless us ere we go	25
Sweet the moments, rich in blessing	487
Sweet thought, my God ! that on the	1112
Sweet was the time when first I felt	666
Swell the anthem, raise the song	1268
TARRY with me, O my Saviour	91
Tender Shepherd, thou hast stilled	1145
Thank and praise Jehovah's name	1269
That awful day will surely come	588
That day of wrath, that dreadful day	562
The billows swell, the winds are high	987
The bird let loose in eastern skies	941
The blessed Spirit, like the wind	520
The Church has waited long	408
The Church's one foundation	847
The Comforter has come	541
The cross ! the cross ! the blood-stained	889
The day approacheth, O my soul	589
The day is past and gone	79
The day of praise is done	80
The day, O Lord, is spent	78
The earth, O Lord, is one wide field	1177
Thee we adore, Eternal Lord	111
Thee we adore, Eternal Name	1298
The God of Abrah'm praise	1292
The God of grace will never leave	530
The God of harvest praise	1261
The goodly land I see	1293
The harvest dawn is near	961
The head that once was crowned with	390
The heathen perish ; day by day	1214
The heavens declare thy glory, Lord	1149
The Holy Ghost is here	536
The King of heaven his table spreads	575
The leaves, around me falling	1309

	HYMN
The Lord himself, the mighty Lord.....	226
The Lord himself will keep............	1013
The Lord, how fearful is his name......	185
The Lord! how wondrous are his ways!	165
The Lord into his garden comes.......	848
The Lord is great! ye hosts of heaven..	256
The Lord is King! lift up thy voice....	141
The Lord is my shepherd, no want shall	1034
The Lord Jehovah reigns, His throne...	262
The Lord Jehovah reigns; Let all the..	232
The Lord my Shepherd is.............	237
The Lord of glory is my light..........	103
The Lord, our God, is full of might.....	184
The Lord our God is Lord of all.......	176
The Lord will come! the earth shall....	404
The mercies of my God and King......	222
The mind was formed, to mount sublime	678
The morning dawns upon the place....	327
The morning kindles all the sky.......	379
The morning light is breaking.........	1231
The morning purples all the sky.......	388
The once-loved form, now cold and dead	1120
The people of the Lord................	960
The perfect world, by Adam trod.......	1181
The pity of the Lord..................	239
There are lonely hearts to cherish......	1251
There is a fold whence none can stray..	1082
There is a fountain filled with blood....	473
There is a God!—all nature speaks....	132
There is a happy land.................	1057
There is a land mine eye hath seen.....	1065
There is a land of pure delight.........	1066
There is a little lonely fold............	217
There is a name I love to hear..........	462
There is an eye that never sleeps.......	66
There is an hour of peaceful rest.......	1083
There is an hour when I must part	1117
There is a safe and secret place........	228
There is a world of perfect bliss........	1072
There is no name so sweet on earth....	489
There is none other name than thine ...	436
There's not a star whose twinkling light	180
There's nothing bright, above, below...	149
There's nothing round these painted....	1076
The Saviour, by whose name I'm called.	718
The Saviour calls; let every ear........	577
The Saviour kindly calls...............	1275
The Saviour! oh, what endless charms.	456
The Saviour smiles! upon my soul.....	653
The Saviour, what a noble flame.......	341
The sea is wildly tossing..............	1274
The Shadow of the Rock..............	888
The spacious firmament on high.......	122
The Spirit, in our hearts...............	596
The Spirit, like a peaceful dove........	498
The starry firmament on high..........	1153
The swift declining day...............	604
The time is short! sinners, beware.....	1302
The voice of free grace cries, Escape to.	642
The wondering world inquires to know.	714
The Word, with God the Father One...	302
The world is very evil.................	406
Thine earthly Sabbaths, Lord, we love..	20
This is the day of light................	77
This is the day the Lord hath made.....	50
Thou art the Way; to thee alone.......	319
Thou dear Redeemer, dying Lamb.....	463
Though faint, yet pursuing, we go on...	1032
Though now the nations sit beneath....	1211
Though troubles assail, and dangers....	1036
Thou God of sovereign grace..........	1277
Thou hast said, exalted Jesus..........	733
Thou lovely Source of true delight.....	1160
Thou, Lord, who rear'st the mountain's.	151
Thou only Sovereign of my heart	894
Thou, whom my soul admires above....	885
Thou who roll'st the year around.......	1304
Thou, whose almighty word...........	115
Through all the changing scenes of life.	202
Through endless years thou art the same	195
Through every age, eternal God........	161
Through sorrow's night, and danger's ..	1125
Thus far the Lord hath led me on......	34
Thy goodness, Lord, our souls confess..	189
Thy way, O Lord, is in the sea.........	183
Thy will be done! I will not fear.......	990
Thy works, not mine, O Christ	853
Thy works proclaim thy glory, Lord....	146
Till he come! oh let the words........	810
Time is winging us away..............	1307

HYMN
'Tis by the faith of joys to come........ 900
'Tis done—th' important act is done.... 1173
'Tis finished !—so the Saviour cried.... 333
'Tis God the Father we adore.......... 748
'Tis God, the Spirit, leads 540
'Tis heaven begun below.............. 14
'Tis Jesus speaks ! I fold, says he...... 1121
'Tis midnight ; and on Olive's brow.... 324
'Tis not the skill of human art......... 866
To-day, if you will hear his voice....... 595
To-day the Saviour calls............... 631
To God the only wise................. 234
To heaven I lift my waiting eyes....... 204
To him that chose us first............. 113
To Jordan's stream the Saviour goes ... 747
To our Redeemer's glorious name 454
To praise our Shepherd's care 480
To sit at Jesus' feet.................. 759
To the ark away ! or perish............ 616
To thee be glory, honor, praise......... 308
To thee, my righteous King and Lord.. 199
To thee, my Shepherd, and my Lord.... 472
To thee this temple we devote......... 1187
To thy pastures fair and large.......... 978
To thy temple I repair 4
To us a Child of hope is born.......... 300
To weary hearts, to mourning homes... 637
Triumphant Zion ! lift thy head 829
'Twas on that dark, that doleful night .. 783

UNTO thine altar, Lord................. 683
Unveil thy bosom, faithful tomb........ 1114
Upon the Gospel's sacred page........ 1154
Up to the fields, where angels lie....... 137

VAIN, delusive world, adieu........... 698
Vainly through night's weary hours.... 92
Vain man, thy fond pursuits forbear.... 591
Visit, Lord, this land in mercy......... 1258

WAIT, O my soul ! thy Maker's will.... 153
Wake, O my soul, and hail the morn... 293
Wake the song of jubilee.............. 1236
Watchman ! tell us of the night........ 1235
We are living, we are dwelling........ 1225
Weary of wandering from my God 645

HYMN
We bid thee welcome in the name...... 1171
We bless thee for thy peace, O God.... 918
We come, O Lord, before thy throne ... 1217
We dwell this side of Jordan's stream.. 1092
Weep for the lost ! thy Saviour wept.... 1253
Weeping soul, no longer mourn....... 693
We give immortal praise.............. 112
We give thee but thine own........... 929
We have met in peace together........ 1282
We know not what's before us......... 1055
Welcome, delightful morn.............. 12
Welcome, O Saviour ! to my heart..... 757
Welcome, sweet day of rest............ 70
Welcome, thou Victor in the strife...... 391
Welcome, welcome, dear Redeemer.... 726
We long to move and breathe in thee... 755
We praise thee Lord, if but one soul ... 1285
We 're traveling home to heaven above. 639
We sing the praise of him who died.... 442
We speak of the realms of the blest.... 1054
We thank thee, Lord, for sending here.. 1176
What are those soul-reviving strains.... 307
What cheering words are these......... 963
What equal honors shall we bring...... 431
What finite power, with ceaseless toil... 158
What glory gilds the sacred page....... 1155
What grace, O Lord, and beauty shone. 317
What is life ? 'tis but a vapor.......... 1142
What shall I render to my God........ 203
What sinners value I resign........... 1053
What various hindrances we meet...... 29
When all thy mercies, O my God....... 205
When, along life's thorny road......... 1019
When at thy footstool, Lord, I bend.... 650
When Christ came down on earth of old 402
When downward to the darksome tomb 1126
When driven by oppression's rod 1266
When faint and weary, toiling 934
When gathering clouds around I view.. 983
When God descends with men to dwell. 831
When God of old came down from..... 516
When God revealed his precious name.. 892
When his salvation bringing........... 295
When I can read my title clear......... 1069
When Israel's priest the Lamb did choose 1185
When I survey the wondrous cross..... 330

	HYMN
When I the holy grave survey	376
When Jesus dwelt in mortal clay	905
When Jordan hushed his waters still	292
When languor and disease invade	1001
When like a stranger on our sphere	316
When little Samuel woke	10
When, Lord, to this our western land	1195
When man grows bold in sin	235
When marshall'd on the nightly plain	291
When morning gilds the skies	417
When morning's first and hallowed ray	227
When musing sorrow weeps the past	999
When on Sinai's top I see	812
When our heads are bowed with woe	1020
When power divine, in mortal form	313
When shall we meet again	782
When, streaming from the eastern skies	26
When the harvest is past, and the	633
When the worn spirit wants repose	58
When this passing world is done	859
When thou, my righteous Judge	621
When thy mortal life is fled	608
When waves of trouble round me swell	1003
When wild confusion wrecks the air	1075
When wounded sore, the stricken soul	665
Where high the heavenly temple stands	375
Where wilt thou put thy trust	1012
While angels thus, O Lord, rejoice	286
While in this sacred rite of thine	745
While life prolongs its precious light	561
While now upon this Sabbath eve	38
While shepherds watched their flocks	288
While thee I seek, protecting Power	59
While to its grief my soul gave way	830
While with ceaseless course the sun	1294
Whither, oh, whither should I fly	896
Who are these in bright array	1084
Who can forbear to sing	834
Who is this that comes from Edom	359
Who is thy neighbor? he whom thou	921
Who shall sing, if not the children	491
Why do we mourn departing friends	1115
Why, O God! thy people spurn	1260
Why should our tears in sorrow flow	1116
Why should the children of a King	527
Why should we start, and fear to die	1103
Why will ye waste on trifling cares	550
With all my powers of heart and tongue	142
With broken heart and contrite sigh	647
With Christ we share a mystic grave	754
With deepest reverence at thy throne	119
With earnest longings of the mind	224
With glory clad, with strength arrayed	157
With humble faith, and thankful heart	802
Within thy house, O Lord, our God	43
With joy we meditate the grace	386
With songs and honors sounding loud	192
With tearful eyes I look around	985
With willing hearts we tread	760
Witness, ye men and angels now	721
Work, for the night is coming	933
Worthy, worthy is the Lamb	492
Wouldst thou learn the depth of sin	363
YE angels, who stand around the throne	1038
Ye boundless realms of joy	261
Ye Christian heroes, go proclaim,	1202
Ye dying sons of men	624
Ye fields of light; celestial plains	264
Ye golden lamps of heaven, farewell	1077
Ye hearts with youthful vigor warm	583
Ye humble souls, approach your God	214
Ye humble souls, that seek the Lord	384
Ye messengers of Christ	1164
Ye mourning saints, whose streaming	1122
Ye nations round the earth, rejoice	118
Ye saints! your music bring	371
Ye servants of God, your Master	260
Ye servants of the Lord	927
Yes, God is good; in earth and sky	135
Ye sinners, fear the Lord	602
Yes, I will bless thee, O my God	213
Yes—my native land! I love thee	1224
Yes, the Redeemer rose	370
Ye that pass by, behold the Man	332
Ye trembling captives! hear	597
Ye trembling souls, dismiss your fears	1008
Ye valiant soldiers of the cross	716
Your harps, ye trembling saints	1014
ZION, dreary and in anguish	840
Zion stands with hills surrounded	842

INDEX OF CHANTS AND ANTHEMS.

	PAGE
AND he opened his mouth	420
Buried with Christ	430
Consider, consider the lilies	422
Glory be to God on high	412
Glory be to the Father	428
God be merciful unto us	415
How pleasant, how divinely fair	423
Hallelujah, hallelujah	429
It is a good thing to give thanks	415
I was glad when they said unto me	417
I will lift up mine eyes unto the hills	416
Jews were wrought to cruel madness	420
Lord, have mercy upon us	423
Lord, have mercy upon us	424
Lord, thou hast been our dwelling-place	423
My hope is built on nothing less	420
No time to pray	422
O all ye works of the Lord	418
O be joyful in the Lord	419
O eyes that are weary, and hearts that	429
O sing unto the Lord	414
Oh, there will be mourning	429
Praise him, praise the conquering King	420
Praise the Lord, O my soul	416
Praise ye the Lord	417
See, daylight is fading o'er earth	426
Strike the cymbal, roll the tymbal	425
The law of the Lord is perfect	424
The Lord is risen indeed	425
Then cometh Jesus from Galilee	427
Thou sweet gliding Kedron, by thy	426
Vital spark of heavenly flame	424
We leave the world of care	425
We praise thee, O God	412, 413
Why thus repining, sad heart of mine	427
Wilt thou not visit me	428

www.ingramcontent.com/pod-product-compliance
Lightning Source LLC
LaVergne TN
LVHW020938110826
845150LV00004B/895
* 9 7 8 1 4 2 5 5 5 1 9 1 9 *